SAGE
Premium
Video

BOOST COMPREHENSION. BOLSTER ANALYSIS.

- SAGE Premium Video **EXCLUSIVELY CURATED FOR THIS TEXT**
- **BRIDGES BOOK CONTENT** with application and critical thinking
- Premium content is **ADA COMPLIANT WITH TRANSCRIPTS**
- Comprehensive media guide to help you **QUICKLY SELECT MEANINGFUL VIDEO** tied to your course objectives

SAGE Publishing:
Our Story

Founded in 1965 by 24-year-old entrepreneur Sara Miller McCune, SAGE continues its legacy of making research accessible and fostering **CREATIVITY** and **INNOVATION**. We believe in creating fresh, cutting-edge content to help you prepare your students to thrive in the modern world and be **TOMORROW'S LEADING COMMUNICATORS.**

- By partnering with **TOP COMMUNICATION AUTHORS** with just the right balance of research, teaching, and industry experience, we bring you the most current and applied content.

- As a **STUDENT-FRIENDLY PUBLISHER**, we keep our prices affordable and provide multiple formats of our textbooks so your students can choose the option that works best for them.

- Being permanently **INDEPENDENT** means we are fiercely committed to publishing the highest-quality resources for you and your students.

INTRODUCTION TO
STRATEGIC PUBLIC RELATIONS

Sara Miller McCune founded SAGE Publishing in 1965 to support the dissemination of usable knowledge and educate a global community. SAGE publishes more than 1000 journals and over 800 new books each year, spanning a wide range of subject areas. Our growing selection of library products includes archives, data, case studies and video. SAGE remains majority owned by our founder and after her lifetime will become owned by a charitable trust that secures the company's continued independence.

Los Angeles | London | New Delhi | Singapore | Washington DC | Melbourne

INTRODUCTION TO
STRATEGIC PUBLIC RELATIONS

Digital, Global, and Socially Responsible Communication

JANIS TERUGGI PAGE

George Washington University

LAWRENCE J. PARNELL

George Washington University

Los Angeles | London | New Delhi
Singapore | Washington DC | Melbourne

FOR INFORMATION:

SAGE Publications, Inc.
2455 Teller Road
Thousand Oaks, California 91320
E-mail: order@sagepub.com

SAGE Publications Ltd.
1 Oliver's Yard
55 City Road
London EC1Y 1SP
United Kingdom

SAGE Publications India Pvt. Ltd.
B 1/I 1 Mohan Cooperative Industrial Area
Mathura Road, New Delhi 110 044
India

SAGE Publications Asia-Pacific Pte. Ltd.
3 Church Street
#10-04 Samsung Hub
Singapore 049483

Acquisitions Editor: Terri Accomazzo
Content Development Editor: Anna Villarruel
Editorial Assistant: Erik Helton
Production Editor: Jane Haenel
Copy Editor: Pam Schroeder
Typesetter: C&M Digitals (P) Ltd.
Proofreader: Eleni-Maria Georgiou
Indexer: Nancy Fulton
Cover and Interior Designer: Gail Buschman
Marketing Manager: Jenna Retana

Printed in Canada

Library of Congress Cataloging-in-Publication Data

Names: Page, Janis Teruggi, author. | Parnell, Lawrence J., author.

Title: Introduction to strategic public relations : digital, global, and socially responsible communication / Janis Teruggi Page, George Washington University, Washington D.C., USA, Lawrence Parnell, George Washington University, Washington D.C., USA.

Description: First Edition. | Thousand Oaks : SAGE Publications, [2018] | Includes bibliographical references and index.

Identifiers: LCCN 2017039375 | ISBN 9781506358031 (pbk. : alk. paper)

Subjects: LCSH: Public relations.

Classification: LCC HM1221 .P34 2018 | DDC 659.2—dc23
LC record available at https://lccn.loc.gov/2017039375

This book is printed on acid-free paper.

18 19 20 21 22 10 9 8 7 6 5 4 3 2 1

BRIEF CONTENTS

DETAILED CONTENTS

iStock.com/PeopleImages

THE BOSTO

SECTION TWO: PRACTICING PUBLIC RELATIONS IN A SOCIALLY RESPONSIBLE WORLD

UNIT TWO: Public Relations Tactics

Right: iStock.com/Yuri_Arcurs
Left: Reza/Getty Images

CHAPTER 12: Issues Management and Crisis Communication

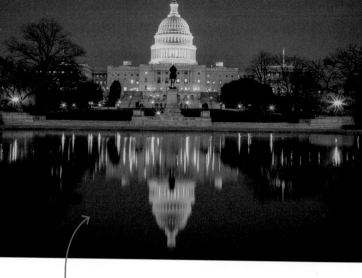

Right: iStock.com/TommL
Left: Carol T. Powers/Bloomberg/Getty Images

PREFACE

What is it about the field of public relations (PR) that makes it so hard to define, detail, or document? How does the growing field of social responsibility (SR) intersect with PR in today's global and digital world?

This book answers these questions from a unique and contemporary perspective, explaining the process and purpose of PR by connecting it to business, social, and environmental trends and values. At the same time this perspective is designed to augment—not replace—the traditional approach of an introductory text in PR and includes all the key elements of history, theory, skills, and strategy that you would expect.

The authors believe that SR is a global movement that businesspeople, public officials, and students at all levels understand, and as such, it will draw the reader into the text. Regardless of industry or position, most stakeholders appreciate the benefit of SR to companies, the public sector, and society. Corporations take a visible role in SR, thus we use the term CSR (corporate social responsibility) and SR interchangeably in this text.

For example, a corporation decreasing its carbon footprint, promoting more women into management, bringing fresh produce to urban food deserts, or improving water quality for distressed communities improves the quality of life for citizens and can benefit business outcomes as well.

In its review of the trends and best practices of SR and strategic public relations (SPR), the connection of these key activities to the concept of organizational purpose will be explored as well.

Our goal in this text is to define and teach PR as a *strategic* activity, put it into a business context using SR as a connecting point, and provide readers with the essential theoretical and practical foundations. Ultimately this approach, we believe, will increase awareness of the vital role of PR in organizational success and launch the next generation of PR professionals toward effective and ethical leadership.

ORGANIZATION OF THIS TEXT

This book is specifically designed and structured in a user-friendly format for Introductory Public Relations classes at both the undergraduate and graduate levels. It provides solid ground on which students can build their knowledge of the profession within a PR major or apply it to communications, business, law, or political science courses.

The book is organized into two progressive sections separating the essentials from the specifics:

Understanding Public Relations (Chapters 1–5): The first five chapters of this text cover an introduction to the profession, its history, ethical and legal considerations, and the PR process: research, theory, strategy, programming, evaluation, and stewardship.

Practicing Strategic Public Relations in a Socially Responsible World (Chapters 6–16): The remaining chapters cover the major skills, functions, and practice areas in the field of PR.

FEATURES AND PEDAGOGY

Each chapter of *Introduction to Strategic Public Relations* includes several learning tools to help students engage with the field of PR and connect the lessons in this book with present-day practice.

▶ **Learning Objectives.** Learning objectives help prepare students to focus on concepts they will learn throughout the chapter.

▶ **Scenario.** We start off each chapter with a contemporary issue that ties directly to the concepts discussed in the chapter. The opening scenario presents a problem—students are provided with an overview of the situation and some guiding questions they can use to reflect on these issues as they progress through their reading. We revisit the scenario at the end of each chapter, where we outline the solution and provide students with some major takeaways.

▶ **Insights** are special-topic boxes that add depth or expose practices that make PR such a fascinating field.

▶ **PR Personality** boxes feature current practitioners or subject matter experts describing challenges they have faced in their own careers. These veterans and rising stars share their combined experience and backgrounds to help the next generation of leaders of the PR profession. These profiles will inform, entertain, and educate readers and students using this text.

▶ **Social Responsibility in Action** boxes feature short, specific cases highlighting best practices and effective tactics, showing the link between sound public relations strategy and meaningful social responsibility programs.

▶ **Social Responsibility** callouts use symbols to identify where focused social responsibility examples appear throughout each chapter.

▶ **Wrap Up.** The Wrap Up section provides the reader with a chapter summary to reinforce students' understanding of the content.

▶ **Key Terms.** Key terms in each chapter are listed, with a glossary at the end of the book.

▶ **Think About It.** These exercises encourage students to apply what they have learned through focused individual and group discussion prompts.

▶ **Write Like a Pro.** These exercises provide students with a specific writing assignment to practice in the context of PR.

▶ **Social Responsibility Case Studies**. The book includes dozens of current case studies from well-known companies, agencies, NGOs, and governmental organizations such as Google, Nike, NBC Universal, the UN Foundation, GlobalGiving, and the Department of Defense. These chapter case studies illustrate the key responsibilities of a modern PR professional—such as media relations, crisis communications, employee communications, applied communications research, corporate- and government-specific communications. The cases encourage student discussion through ***Engage*** and ***Discuss*** prompts and problem-solving questions.

We hope you find this text an insightful and valuable introduction to the field of PR through the unique lens of SR and how they can blend together to provide strategic communications leadership for an organization. Our intent is to build students' knowledge and confidence in pursuing successful careers in this dynamic and exciting profession.

DIGITAL RESOURCES

http://edge.sagepub.com/page

$SAGE coursepacks

SAGE COURSEPACKS FOR INSTRUCTORS makes it easy to import our quality content into your school's learning management system (LMS)*. Intuitive and simple to use, it allows you to

Say NO to...

▸ required access codes

▸ learning a new system

Say YES to...

▸ using only the content you want and need

▸ high-quality assessment and multimedia exercises

Don't use an LMS platform? No problem, you can still access many of the online resources for your text via SAGE edge.

SAGE coursepacks include:

▸ Our content delivered **directly into your LMS**

▸ **Intuitive, simple format** that makes it easy to integrate the material into your course with minimal effort

▸ **Assignable SAGE Premium Video** (available via the interactive eBook version, linked through SAGE coursepacks) that is tied to learning objectives, and curated exclusively for this text to bring concepts to life and appeal to diverse learner, featuring:

  o **Video Case Studies** breathe life into concepts with stories drawn from important contemporary public relations cases. Every case is designed to test student application of the theories and concepts discussed in the text.

▸ Comprehensive, downloadable, easy-to-use ***Media Guide in the Coursepack*** for every video resource, listing the chapter to which the video content is tied, matching learning objective(s), a helpful description of the video content, and assessment questions

---

*For use in: Blackboard, Canvas, Brightspace by Desire2Learn (D2L), and Moodle

- **Assessment tools** that foster review, practice, and critical thinking, and offer a more complete way to measure student engagement, including:
  - o Diagnostic chapter **pre tests and post tests** that identify opportunities for improvement, track student progress, and ensure mastery of key learning objectives
  - o **Test banks** built on Bloom's Taxonomy that provide a diverse range of test items with ExamView test generation
  - o **Activity and quiz options** that allow you to choose only the assignments and tests you want
  - o **Instructions** on how to use and integrate the comprehensive assessments and resources provided
- EXCLUSIVE, influential **SAGE journal content**, built into course materials and assessment tools, that ties important research and scholarship to chapter concepts to strengthen learning
- Editable, chapter-specific **PowerPoint® slides** that offer flexibility when creating multimedia lectures so you don't have to start from scratch but you can customize to your exact needs
- **Sample course syllabi** with suggested models for structuring your course that give you options to customize your course in a way that is perfect for you
- **Integrated links to the interactive eBook** that make it easy for your students to maximize their study time with this "anywhere, anytime" mobile-friendly version of the text. It also offers access to more digital tools and resources, including SAGE Premium Video
- **All tables and figures** from the textbook

$SAGE edge™ for students

http://edge.sagepub.com/page

SAGE edge for students enhances learning, it's easy to use, and offers:

- **eFlashcards** that strengthen understanding of key terms and concepts, and make it easy to maximize student study time, anywhere, anytime
- **eQuizzes** that allow students to assess how much they've learned and where they need to focus their attention
- **Video and multimedia links** that allow students to engage with the material
- **Exclusive access to influential SAGE journal content** that ties important research and scholarship to chapter concepts to strengthen learning

ACKNOWLEDGMENTS

The authors would like to thank their students and alumni for inspiring and challenging us to create this book and extend our practical, applied approach to PR education to the broader market. We also want to acknowledge our colleagues and administrators at The George Washington University, the Graduate School of Political Management, and the College of Professional Studies for their support during the research and writing of this book.

Specifically the authors want to note the contributions of William S. Page and Jeanine D. Guidry, PhD, and April Delacruz Rongero, MPS, for their assistance in the research, referencing, and editing stages of the project.

We also deeply appreciate the contributions from the professionals and academics who shared cases, insights, and profiles in our chapters. We would also like to extend thanks to the reviewers for their expertise and their insightful suggestions throughout the development of this book:

Charles F. Byers, Santa Clara University

Tori Martin Cliff, The University of Memphis

Colleen Fitzpatrick, Saint Mary's College

S. Catherine Foster, Canisius College

Maxine Gesualdi, West Chester University of Pennsylvania

Kirk Hazlett, Curry College

Carolyn J. Higgins, Purdue University Northwest

John Kerezy, Cuyahoga Community College

Lucyann S. Kerry, Middlesex University Dubai

Kate S. Kurtin, California State University, Los Angeles

Anne Marie Males, Humber College

Christopher J. McCollough, Columbus State University

Dana Alexander Nolfe, Bryant University

Peggy O'Keefe, New York University

Maxey Parrish, Baylor University

Pam Parry, Eastern Kentucky University

Claire M. Regan, Wagner College

Ann Strahle, University of Illinois

We are especially grateful for the clear guidance from the editors at SAGE, particularly Anna Villarruel, who continuously provided essential critique, advice, and assurance throughout the long process of this project.

Janis is grateful to her doctoral alma mater, Missouri School of Journalism, and her constant mentor and collaborator, Margaret Duffy. She also pays tribute to her past colleagues, employers, and clients who inspired her with worthy projects and challenges that increased her knowledge and professionalism. Janis dedicates her work on this book to her older brother Frank Teruggi, Jr., whose life of pursuing social justice drives her commitment to build a better world through communication. She also salutes her family, who supported her with inspiration and feedback throughout the process, including her daughters, Johanna and Marguerite, and sons, Ben and Nick.

Larry would like to dedicate this book to his parents—Pat and Bill Parnell—lifelong educators who taught him at an early age that teachers don't just teach; they care. Over the years he has had mentors, colleagues, and friends in both business and academia too numerous to mention here. Collectively they have contributed to his professional growth and development, and he is indebted to them for their advice and continuing friendship. Larry is also dedicating his work on this book to his four children—Sara, Matthew, Erin, and Jessica—and three wonderful grandchildren—Maya, Isaac, and Kyla.

Finally the authors would like to thank their spouses, William Page and Janice Parnell, for their constant encouragement over the years and patience with our preoccupation to get this book "right." This project took many nights and weekends from family time, and we hope you are as proud of the final product as we are.

Janis Teruggi Page, PhD
Lawrence J. Parnell, MBA

ABOUT THE AUTHORS

Our combined professional backgrounds—representing deep experience as PR practitioners, academic researchers, and classroom instructors at leading universities—informs the text and underscores the conclusions and recommendations within.

Janis Teruggi Page draws from 20 years of executive experience managing strategic communications for regional and national media companies. She managed corporate, consumer, and media relations, creating programming partnerships with major TV networks, directing PR for national industry trade show events, and supervising new product launches. She is a member of PRSA and IABC and continues to serve clients through her consultancy, MediawerksPR.

Since earning a Ph.D. from Missouri School of Journalism in 2005, her faculty appointments have included the University of Florida, American University, and The George Washington University, where she is on the Strategic Public Relations faculty in the Graduate School of Political Management. In 2016 she was named Professor of the Year in GW's College of Professional Studies. She has developed and taught both undergraduate and graduate-level PR courses such as principles, writing, cases, campaigns, corporate advocacy, issues management, sustainability, theory, and visual communication.

An active and award-winning scholar, she has produced more than 50 conference papers, book chapters, and refereed articles. Her work appears in the *Journal of Political Management*, the *Handbook of Strategic Communication*, and in edited volumes on PR and visual persuasion ethics. She has presented research at many national and global conferences.

Lawrence J. Parnell is an award-winning practitioner and educator. In 2003 he was selected the PR Professional of the Year by *PRWeek*; in 2009 he was named to the PR News Hall of Fame, and in 2015, the George Washington University Master's in Strategic Public Relations, which he leads, was named Best PR Education program by *PRWeek*. He is an active member of PRSA, NIRI, and the Arthur W. Page Society.

He offers the practical experience of more than 30 years of communications work in government, corporate, and agency settings and 10 years in academia as an associate professor and program director at The George Washington University. He has advised elected officials, government leaders, and corporate executives at the national and global levels on major business and communications issues. He continues to provide high-level communications consulting and training to corporations, nonprofits, and government organizations through his firm Parnell Communications.

His research in CSR, PR, and public diplomacy has been presented at national and global conferences and published in *Shaping International Public Opinion: A Model for Nation Branding and Public Diplomacy*.

1

Strategic Public Relations
A Constantly Evolving Discipline

Learning Objectives

1.1 Understand the perception and realities of PR

1.2 Define PR

1.3 Define corporate social responsibility

1.4 Explore the growth of the PR industry in the United States and abroad

1.5 Review roles and functions in the field of PR

1.6 Review career options in the field of PR

IBM Employees Celebrate 100 Years of Service

On June 16, 2011, IBM marked its 100-year anniversary as a corporation. While this is a rare milestone for any company, it is almost unheard of in the fast-paced, boom-and-bust technology industry. In setting out to mark the occasion, the company challenged itself to answer the key question: What would be the most meaningful way to celebrate the milestone? The answer was not commissioning a coffee-table book or commemorative video or presenting a large check to a charity.

Instead it was a giant, hands-on global Celebration of Service—a year-long employee initiative designed to support local community organizations worldwide. The event was to be a combination of strategic communications planning, global and local social responsibility initiatives, employee engagement, and a worldwide exhibition of IBM's corporate character—all in one package.

IBM commemorated its centenary with a global Celebration of Service intended to support local community organizations worldwide.

Sean Gallup/Getty Images

Listening to 15,000 voices. In October 2010, IBM held a massive online brainstorm in which 15,000 executives, innovators, philanthropists, volunteers, and students from 119 countries shared ideas on volunteerism and service to create positive change in their local communities. The ideas and suggestions for the "Service Jam" were catalogued, researched, and where possible, matched with a local organization in or near an area of the world where IBM people (called "IBMers") lived and worked.

Serving communities. The insights from the brainstorm and the follow-up research led to the overarching plan: Design the Celebration of Service to enable IBM and its clients and business partners to engage with local communities on volunteer projects locally while expressing IBM's brand and corporate values to the world. That meant encouraging IBM's broad base of employees to donate approximately 1 million hours of service to improving conditions in their communities—in most of the 170 countries in which IBM operates.

Spreading the word. The plan also created awareness of the IBM brand in the broadcast and print media, and online, by garnering coverage and visibility both inside and outside the United States. Media coverage featured the volunteer events along with key messages about IBM's commitment to service. The Celebration of Service involved nongovernmental organizations (NGOs) and non-profit organizations, clients and potential clients, former employees, and the 400,000+ IBM current employees worldwide—more than half of whom had been with the company less than five years and were unfamiliar with the company's history.

This celebration leveraged the 100-year anniversary as an opportunity to communicate IBM's brand and values to the world and celebrate its employees' long-standing commitment to community service. Instead of a one-off project, the Celebration of Service included thousands of local volunteer projects *throughout the year* to engage current and former employees, business partners, clients, NGOs and nonprofit organizations. Each volunteer activity was designed to leverage the experience and brainpower of the IBM volunteers (such as legal, computer, and marketing skills).

After reading this chapter, you should be able to answer the following questions:

1. How did IBM take a major milestone celebration— a common public relations (PR) tactic—and expand it into a comprehensive company-wide event?

2. How did IBM make sure that they included all facets of communications— marketing, corporate, and employee communications?

3. How did they measure success of the communications activities?

4. How did they work in a social responsibility initiative? Was it successful in your view, and if so why?

The goal of this introductory chapter is to provide you with a foundation and understanding of the field of PR, its development into a strategic management function, and how you can pursue a career in this dynamic global industry.

The chapter will also connect PR to the growing field of corporate social responsibility (CSR)—referred to as sustainability or corporate philanthropy—and illustrate how one discipline informs and enriches the other. Later in the chapter you will read the first of a series of "Personality Profiles." In this section, you will be introduced to a successful, young PR professional who will share her advice for starting out and building a career in PR.

In subsequent chapters, the profiles will feature other professionals and experts with experience and advice to share on the material covered in the chapter, such as media relations, crisis management, or CSR.

THE IMAGE OF PUBLIC RELATIONS IN POPULAR CULTURE

≫ LO 1.1   Understand the perception and realities of PR

In this chapter, you will read about the public perception—accurate and not so accurate—of PR and how it contributes to an organization or cause. This issue has been discussed and debated since the early days of the profession. Historically, PR was focused primarily on generating publicity or "hype" versus today, when the goal has shifted to impacting public opinion, influencing behavior and driving business results (see Chapter 2 on the history of PR). The historical image of the **publicist** or "flack" is a common one of PR people driven, in part, by how the profession has been depicted in movies and on television.

$SAGE edge™

Master the content
edge.sagepub.com/page

According to Joe Saltzman, director of The Image of the Journalist in Popular Culture project at the Norman Lear Center at the University of Southern California (USC), "Many public relations practitioners believe that the image of the publicist and the public relations professional (in the media) is one of the most negative in history." In Saltzman's USC research, he studied more than 300 films and TV programs from 1901 to 2011. The negative images of PR range from press agents (men and women) who will do anything, including "charm" clients or lie, cheat, and steal—even commit murder—to save their reputations and protect clients. For example, the character Don Draper is immortalized as a powerful and unethical executive on the popular A&E Network show *Mad Men*.

Olivia Pope, on the hit ABC TV show *Scandal*, is involved in high-stakes crisis communications work each week. The show is based on the life and career of Judy Smith, a Washington, DC-based crisis manager. Smith serves as a consultant to the show providing suggestions and guidance on how PR and crisis management in Washington, DC works. However, she insists her work, while demanding, is nowhere near as dramatic as the life and career of Olivia Pope.

In her pioneering study, "Public Relations in Film and Fiction, 1930 to 1995," Karen Miller wrote that today's "fictitious characters . . . display very little understanding of PR or what practitioners do" (1999, p. 24). Miller explained, "Sometimes (in the movies) PR is magic," and other times, "it is almost embarrassingly easy." Nowhere in these shows or movies do you see PR people like the ones working at IBM on making the 100th anniversary something more than just a celebration. Perhaps that is because while the work ultimately benefited thousands of people around the world, it is not as entertaining as watching high stakes intrigue or satire and parody.

These stereotypes should not be taken lightly and must be countered, as with any profession or group of people. The best way to do that is by engaging with people and clients and showing them the value that PR brings to the management table and market. At the end of this chapter is an exercise for you to engage in and explore this challenge.

> "Moving dead bodies from crime scenes—that doesn't happen in my office in Washington DC."
>
> —Judy Smith (Burton, 2014)

DEFINING PUBLIC RELATIONS: WHAT'S IN A NAME?

>> LO 1.2   Define PR

Moving beyond the perception of public relations, let's examine the various definitions of PR and see if there is a consensus. Defining PR has been a goal for much of the profession's history. Often people have relied on saying what PR was not—for example, *advertising*, which traditionally relies on paid media "ads" or *sales*, which is an in-person transactional exercise. At its best, PR involves an information exchange between two or more people or "publics" with a goal of sharing information and influencing the behavior of the recipient.

Other key elements of PR that distinguish it from advertising include the need to master skills

Judy Smith, a Washington, DC–based crisis manager (*right*), was the inspiration for the character Olivia Pope, played by Kerry Washington (*left*), on the television show *Scandal*.

Frederick M. Brown/Getty Images

such as issues and crisis management, internal communications, and providing strategic communications advice. These and other related elements are unique to PR and are not found in advertising, sales, or marketing activity.

While the strategies, tactics, and vehicles may differ over time, PR professionals are engaged in delivering messages and attempting to influence behavior or public opinion. Whether it is buying a certain brand or product, voting for a candidate, donating to a cause or charity, or investing in a **public company**, in PR you are in the business of building reputation and creating trust. This must be done in an ethical and transparent manner to best serve your client or company's interests.

A CROWD-SOURCED DEFINITION FROM THE PUBLIC RELATIONS SOCIETY OF AMERICA

In response to the lack of an agreed-upon definition, the Public Relations Society of America (PRSA), the leading professional organization for public relations professionals, launched an effort in 2011 to develop a more "current and accurate definition of public relations." The project took the form of a "crowd-sourced" effort involving PRSA members, top academics, and industry leaders to solicit their input for an "official" definition of PR to be used going forward. That months-long process produced the following definition which was published in 2012:

> Public relations is a strategic communication process that builds mutually beneficial relationships between organizations and their publics.
>
> (Public Relations Society of America, n.d.)

Chartered in 1947, the PRSA is the world's largest and foremost organization of PR professionals with more than 22,000 PR and communications professionals in addition to more than 10,000 university and college students through the Public Relations Student Society of America (PRSSA).

PRSA provides professional development, sets standards of excellence, and upholds principles of ethics for its members. It also advocates for greater understanding and adoption of public relations services and acts as one of the industry's leading voices on pivotal business and professional issues (Public Relations Society of America, n.d.).

PUBLIC RELATIONS SCHOLARS WEIGH IN

Academics and authors have developed their own definitions over the years that share many elements with the PRSA's. Scott Cutlip, Allen Center, and Glen Broom, in the seminal text *Effective Public Relations* (first published in 2000) defined PR as the "management function that identifies, establishes and maintains mutually beneficial relationships between an organizations and the various publics on whom its success or failure depends" (Cutlip, Center, & Broom, 2000). This definition has echoes both in the PRSA version as well as the one put forth by leading PR scholars James E. Grunig and Todd Hunt (1984), which suggested that "public relations is the management of communication between an organization and its publics."

What Is Public Relations?

If you Google "public relations" you get this: "the professional maintenance of a favorable public image by a company or other organization or a famous person" or "the state of the relationship between a company or other organization or a famous person and the public."

Despite its varied definitions, Paul Holmes, founder and chair of The Holmes Group, likes the term "public relations." He has been writing about public relations for more than 25 years. To reduce the term down to its component parts, the words "public" and "relations" are in common usage and appear to be well understood: "public" (of or concerning the people as a whole; done, perceived, or existing in open view; or ordinary people in general; the community) and "relations" (the way in which two or more people or things are connected or the way in which two or more people or groups regard and behave towards each other).

Holmes offers his own definition, rooted in the meaning of these two words: "Public relations is the discipline of managing the relationship between an organization and the people upon whom it depends for success and with whom it interacts, and ensuring that those relationships facilitate the organization's strategic objectives."

There are significant reasons why he likes this definition. First, it makes it clear that the end product of public relations—and therefore the main focus of every campaign—is a relationship, hopefully, a stronger, more rewarding relationship with employees, consumers, shareholders, regulators, or the communities in which organizations operate.

Second, if you think about how relationships are formed, one thing should be clear: Communication is important, but it is far from the most important factor. Ad agencies, digital firms, and even management consultancies can all claim to be in the communications business. PR is unique in looking beyond the transactional and focusing on the long-term, mutually beneficial value of relationships. To remove that key element would be to surrender the critical differentiator between what PR pros bring to the table and what others offer.

Holmes says that despite some current angst around the term "public relations," it's the result of a particular moment in time, of changes in the relationship between marketing and corporate communications, and of increased competition among advertising agencies, digital firms, management consultancies, and others.

At a time when public relations people are anxious to define themselves more broadly than ever before, when senior in-house people are needed at the policy-making table more urgently than ever before, and when public relations firms have embraced integrated campaigns that use paid, shared, and owned channels, Holmes suggests that PR professionals need to double down on the term "public relations." In possibly jettisoning the term "public relations," practitioners might be turning their backs on the one thing that differentiates PR from all of those other disciplines: the focus on relationships. ●

Source: Holmes (2017b).

Regardless of which definition you find most relevant, each of them has elements and concepts in common. Note the use of the terms "mutually beneficial," "management function," "strategic," and "publics." At its heart, PR is, in fact, a business process that keeps the interests of all parties in mind. It is strategic, not tactical. It is a relationship—not a one-way street where pronouncements of policies are taken verbatim. It is a process that occurs over time, not a transaction or isolated event or activity.

These distinctions convey a give-and-take relationship in which the interests of all parties are addressed and communications goals are achieved within the context of that relationship.

PUBLIC RELATIONS VERSUS ADVERTISING: UNDERSTANDING THE DIFFERENCE

While the lines between PR and advertising/marketing are increasingly blurred, there are some distinct differences, even though both disciplines work through the media to convey a message. To begin with, as noted earlier, PR involves persuasion, not purchasing. The result the PR pro is seeking (obtaining news coverage, influencing public opinion, enhancing a reputation or rebuilding one, etc.) comes through interaction between the PR professional and a gatekeeper (e.g., a journalist, **blogger,** or **influencer**). This process of outreach to and persuasion of a reporter to write or film a story is referred to as "earned" media.

On the contrary, advertising is a transaction, thus the term "paid" media. A company that wishes to get public attention for a product or a cause pays for the ad

Public Relations or Advertisement?

Comparing the cost and benefit of an advertisement versus a PR program can be a useful exercise in communications planning. Advertising might seem to be the easiest way to go, and for some purposes it probably is. But advertising can be very expensive—it requires research, creative input, shooting, and editing the commercial or producing copy and artwork for a print ad. These costs can range in the millions of dollars to produce an ad campaign. Plus, once it is developed, there is the additional cost of purchasing the space or airtime. For example, a full-page ad in a major daily newspaper, like *The New York Times*, could cost more than $100,000, and a 30-second network TV spot costs hundreds of thousands of dollars (*millions* if you advertise during the Super Bowl). For example, commercials aired during the 2017 Super Bowl game averaged $5 million for a 30-second ad (Dorfman, 2017).

By any measure, PR is less expensive. The costs for PR typically consist of the time or salary of the PR professional and his/her out-of-pocket costs for travel, entertainment, and events (e.g., a news conference

or product launch). In their recent book, *The Fall of Advertising and the Rise of Public Relations*, Al Ries and coauthor Laura Ries (2002), commented:

> We are beginning to see research that supports the superiority of PR over advertising to launch a brand.

The authors suggest that with PR, audiences believe what they read or see on the news because they assume the journalist has done the work to make sure the story is accurate and balanced. Further, while an ad covers most of the key variables, the critical one—audience attention—is not guaranteed. Current technology provides the viewer the option to skip ads or switch the channel, and the ad's impact becomes limited.

As a result, the tide is turning in PR's favor due to these relative costs and benefits. Time will tell how the advertising community reacts, but for now the analysis seems to increasingly favor PR as the less expensive and more impactful option (Table 1.1). ●

TABLE 1.1

Media Exposure: Advertisements Versus Public Relations

ADVERTISEMENTS	PUBLIC RELATIONS
Expensive	Less Expensive
Based on Research	Based on Research
Creative Team Needed	PR Professionals' salary and expenses
Production Time & Costs Space or airtime Costs	Limited production cost, if any. No cost for placement in print or broadcast
Seen as a paid ad and likely to be skipped	Credible: filtered through journalist gatekeeper; more likely to get attention and get read or heard

space or air time, then develops their print ad or radio/TV commercial, and it is run as is with no interpretation. This distinction—between earned and paid media—has been captured in a short but accurate quote (Wynne, 2014):

PR is what you *pray* for. Advertising is what you *pay* for.

DEFINING CORPORATE SOCIAL RESPONSIBILITY AND SUSTAINABILITY COMMUNICATIONS: DOING WELL BY DOING GOOD, OR IS IT MORE COMPLEX?

>> LO 1.3 **Define corporate social responsibility**

Many PR campaigns incorporate CSR, and it's important now to examine the various definitions and lay the groundwork for a more robust discussion in a later chapter. CSR has been defined as the "economic, legal, ethical, and *discretionary* expectations that society has of organizations" (Carroll & Buchholtz 2014, p. 36) to give back or contribute to society. In 2007 a peer-reviewed study of the top 50 global business schools, defined CSR as "the sum of the *voluntary* actions taken by a company to address the economic, social and environmental impacts of its business operations and the concerns of its principal **stakeholders**" (Christensen Peirce, Hartman, Hoffman, & Carrier, 2007, pp. 347–368). The use of the word voluntary is key here—no one is making these companies do this activity.

Ideally CSR should function as a built-in, self-regulating mechanism whereby a business monitors and ensures its support of the law, ethical standards, and international norms. Consequently, businesses would embrace responsibility for the impact of its activities on the environment, consumers, employees, communities, stakeholders, and all other members of the public sphere. Essentially, CSR is the deliberate inclusion of public interest into corporate decision-making, and honors a triple bottom line: people, planet, and profit.

EVOLUTION OF CORPORATE PHILANTHROPY INTO CORPORATE SOCIAL RESPONSIBILITY

Carol Cone, generally regarded as the pioneer of CSR as a business and communications strategy, described the evolution of CSR in a 2010 study published by Edelman (2010):

Nearly two-thirds of consumers feel that it is not adequate for corporations to simply give money away to charity or good causes, they need to integrate them into their day-to-day business," she notes. "It is no longer enough to slap a 'green' ribbon on a product and call it CSR. Americans seek deeper involvement in social issues and expect brands and companies to pro- vide various means of engagement . . . we call this the rise of the "citizen consumer."

Arguments in Favor of Corporate Social Responsibility

In 2004, CVS pharmacies across the United States stopped selling cigarettes after the company decided that doing so was incompatible with its goal of promoting health.

Andrew Burton/Getty Images

Business professors David Chandler and William B. Werther, Jr. (2014), identify the arguments for CSR:

A Moral Argument for CSR

CSR broadly represents the relationship between a company and the principles expected by the wider society within which it operates. It assumes businesses recognize that for-profit entities do not exist in a vacuum and that a large part of their success comes as much from actions that are congruent with societal values as from factors internal to the company. For example, while not all its stakeholders may care or think about CSR in the short term, Walmart has aggressively promoted sustainability with its ambitious Sustainability Index—winning the support of firms, activists, and government agencies.

A Rational Argument for CSR

CSR is an opportunity for businesses seeking to maximize their performance by minimizing restrictions on operations. In today's globalizing world, where individuals and activist organizations feel empowered to enact change, CSR represents a means of anticipating and reflecting societal concerns to minimize operational and financial constraints on business. For example, the alcoholic beverage industry has responded to concerns about alcoholism and underage drinking with its well-known "Drink Responsibly" campaign.

An Economic Argument for CSR

There are two economic arguments in favor of CSR.

Economic Self-Interest

CSR is an argument of economic self-interest for business. CSR adds value because it allows companies to reflect the needs and concerns of their various stakeholder groups. By doing so, a company is more likely to retain its societal legitimacy and maximize its financial viability over the medium to long term. Simply put, CSR is a way of matching corporate operations with societal values and expectations that are constantly evolving. For example, think in terms of a manufacturer or utility that improves its energy and water management process. Not only does it respond to public concerns, but it also can reduce operating expenses and increase profits.

Responsibility Beyond What Is Required

Regardless of your specific definition, the concept of CSR generally focuses on the idea that organizations have moral, ethical, and philanthropic responsibilities in addition to the responsibility to earn a fair return for investors and comply with the law. This is an evolution of the early thinking that the only purpose of business was to be profitable and reward investors. For example, this trend is exemplified by offering generous family leave programs. The result is often a happy and motivated workforce (therefore more productive) as well as enhanced standing as a good place to work for future hires.

When CSR is done well, for example, at CSR leaders like Timberland, IBM, Intel, Cisco, GE, and Starbucks, the organization adopts a broader view of its responsibility to society. That view includes many other constituencies beyond just the company—including employees, suppliers, and customers; the local community; local, state, and federal governments; environmental groups; and other special interest groups. ●

What Cone is talking about is the difference between allocating a share of the proceeds from product sales to a charity, for example, Lord & Taylor donating to St. Jude's Hospital during a "special sale" versus integrating **sustainable business practices** into the company's operations as companies like Starbucks, Nike, CVS, and other CSR leaders do. In short, one company is making a charitable donation—no doubt welcomed by the charity—while the other is fundamentally changing the way it does business and how it treats its suppliers and employees. Where would you rather work or do business?

SOCIAL
RESPONSIBILITY

VALUE OF CORPORATE SOCIAL RESPONSIBILITY TO CORPORATE REPUTATION

There is abundant research that demonstrates the value of successful CSR activity in building corporate reputation. It should be no surprise then that most of the companies on the *Fortune*'s Most Admired list—a coveted form of recognition for corporate leaders—are also CSR leaders and pioneers. This is because, according to *Fortune* and the Korn Ferry Hay Group, social responsibility is one of the key factors considered in selecting a company for this list and helping determine its place on it (Fortune, 2017). The Most Admired process begins with a universe of 1,500 companies—made up of the 1,000 largest U.S. companies ranked by revenue and the members of the *Fortune* Global 500 database (non-U.S. companies that have revenues of $10 billion or more).

Once the list has been reduced to the best regarded companies in each of the industry categories, *Fortune* and the Korn Ferry Hay Group polls a select group of "executives, directors, and analysts to rate companies in their own industry on nine criteria—from investment value and quality of management and products to social responsibility and ability to attract talent" (Fortune, 2017). Beside the recognition of leading publications like *Fortune*, companies are learning that well-planned and implemented sustainability initiatives can make a difference in recruitment and retention, customer acceptance, and reputation enhancement.

In 2006, Andrew Winston and Daniel Esty wrote that building **corporate reputation** and trusted brands is one of the ways smart companies can profit from sustainability: "The better a company does at protecting its reputation and building brand trust, the more successful it will be at gaining and maintaining competitive differentiation" (Esty & Winston, 2006).

Looking ahead, Chapter 9 will profile companies and organizations doing a good job of communicating their CSR progress and activities and examine the elements of effective CSR communications strategy.

GROWTH OF PUBLIC RELATIONS INTO A GLOBAL INDUSTRY

>> **LO 1.4** Explore the growth of the PR industry in the United States and abroad

Looking ahead to Chapter 2, the PR industry has its roots in U.S. history, business, and politics. But there can be no doubt that it has now become a global

Gap Year Leads to Global Stage for Nongovernmental Organizations

After her senior year of high school, Nicole Mortimer decided to take a gap year before beginning her freshman year at George Washington University. She traveled to Russia, China, Cambodia, Israel, Jordan, South Africa, and Tanzania. In each country, she spent time volunteering at schools, hospitals, and orphanages. During her travels, she came across many small NGOs and charities doing amazing work in their local communities. In a small coastal town in Tanzania, she worked with a school that taught street children vocational skills so they could escape poverty. In Cambodia she assisted an organization that repaired broken water pumps in rural villages so people could have access to clean drinking water.

Scarce Resources and Funds Limit Impact— After gaining hands-on experience with several organizations, she realized that the impact of these organizations on their community was limited because they lacked resources and funds. Because these NGOs were small and located in remote areas, many of them did not have the know-how or the technology to use the Internet to promote their missions or to reach out to potential donors. After beginning college and becoming a Compass Fellow (see www .compassfellows.org), she kept these foreign NGOs in mind. I wanted to find a way to help these organizations, and others like them, achieve their missions and be as effective as possible.

Donated Video Equipment Used to Extend Impact and Awareness— Give Impact Films provides an outlet for small NGOs to express their mission statements and accept donations on a global stage, so they can maximize their influence. Give Impact Films mails NGOs video cameras. The NGO then records what they do and explains the social issue they are trying to address.

Short Amateur Videos Improve Fund-Raising— Give Impact Films edits the footage into a mini-documentary and posts it on their website, along with a biography of the NGO. Through this process people can learn more about the issues discussed and donate to the NGOs featured. ●

Source: CSRlive Commentary (2011).

business and that several countries in Europe—such as Great Britain—have long traditions of PR as well. Within the United States, PR remains an attractive career choice with steady growth in employment opportunities and salaries driven by increasing spending by clients and companies on PR-related activity. The U.S. Department of Labor, Bureau of Labor Statistics (BLS) estimates job growth in the PR field at 6% per year from 2014 to 2024 with a median income of $58,000 per year (Bureau of Labor Statistics, 2014b). The BLS's most recent report indicates that as of the end of 2014, there were 240,700 people nationwide employed in the PR industry as public relations specialists. The BLS projected about 14,000 new jobs in PR will be added each year until 2024 (Bureau of Labor Statistics, 2014b).

DIGITAL AND SOCIAL MEDIA KEY TO GROWTH

A lot of this growth is attributable to the impact of digital communications on the industry and the growing demand for skilled communicators who can leverage social media for their employers. For those of you with these skills, the career upside is almost unlimited. The BLS concurs, noting in its most recent report that the growth of the PR industry "will be driven by the need for organizations to maintain their public image, especially with the growth of social media" (Bureau of Labor Statistics, 2014a).

While much of the increase in PR spending in the United States is attributable to an improving economy, the growing recognition of PR as an effective platform for supporting both business and **sustainability communications** activity is a factor as well.

There is no doubt that social media has accelerated this trend, moving rapidly from a platform for leisure time use to a powerful marketing and communications platform for organizations all over the globe.

GLOBAL PUBLIC RELATIONS SPENDING TRENDS

On a worldwide basis, the Global Alliance estimates that in 2015, the top 10 global PR firms generated a fee income of close to $4.9 billion (Global Alliance PR, 2016). Overall global spending on PR is hard to track as there are often different terms or activities included in the category (e.g., advertising, marketing, and special events) in different countries, and the documentation is not as reliable as it is in the United States. Estimates range from $13.5 billion in income for small, medium, and large global firms as reported by The Holmes Report (2015a) and $14 billion according to the Council of PR Firms (see http://prcouncil.net), a New York City-based PR agency trade group[1] (Sudhaman, 2016). Particularly strong markets worldwide, besides the United States, include China (now the second largest in the world) and the Middle East.

EMERGING AND DEVELOPING NATIONS

In developing countries where there is not as much traditional media or a traditional free press, PR's growth is driven by social media platforms like Facebook, Twitter, Instagram, and others. In these economies, private citizens and advocacy groups use social media to spread their message(s), build followers, and conduct business without ever dealing with a newspaper or broadcast media outlet for a news story or a paid ad.

Pew Research noted in its 2016 *Online Media Report* (Poushter, 2016):

Once online, people in emerging and developing nations are hungry for social interaction. The majority of adult Internet users in developing nations surveyed say that they use social networking sites, such as Facebook and Twitter for news and information, as well as to keep in touch.

The report adds: "Unlike overall internet access, online adults in emerging and developing nations are more likely to use these forms of social media compared with their rich-country counterparts" (Poushter, 2016).

---

[1] http://prcouncil.net

Smartphones in developing nations, such as India, Mexico, and Vietnam (*left to right*), can be essential tools for the spread of information, given the lack of traditional press.

iStock.com/boggy22; Jeffrey Greenberg/UIG via Getty Images; Hoang Dinh Nam/Getty Images

ROLES AND FUNCTIONS FOR PUBLIC RELATIONS PROS

>> LO 1.5 **Review roles and functions in the field of PR**

As noted earlier, some organizations rely on PR professionals solely to "play defense" in media relations and offset the impact of bad stories or help manage a crisis or major issue facing the organization. However, many enlightened organizations see the benefit of using the PR staff and professionals to "play offense" as well and build or enhance the reputation of the company, cause, or candidate.

What are the key roles PR professionals play in an organization? What are the key strategies and tactics they use? How do you get started and build a career in PR? Let's examine these questions now and set the stage for a more in-depth discussion of strategies and tactics in subsequent chapters.

ROLES

WRITER

First and foremost, to be effective as a PR professional, you *must* be an accomplished writer. Your role will be to take complex or controversial subject matter and prepare press releases, statements, opinion pieces, and occasionally, speeches and white papers for your clients or senior management team. In addition, your writing must not only be succinct and complete, but it will also need to be persuasive. After all, your goal is to influence the reader's or listener's thinking and stimulate behavior—e.g., making a purchase, supporting a cause or political candidate, or raising funds for a charity—so being persuasive as well as accurate and honest is key.

STRATEGIC ADVISOR

Good PR advisers are a strategic resource to their company or client. They keep them abreast of current issues, trends in public opinion, and on marketplace developments. No communications plan occurs in a vacuum. Knowing what competitors are doing, how the public is feeling, and what government officials might do or say that impacts your organization is critical to developing strategic plans and selecting tactics that will work. To do this well, you will need to be current on your company and industry and on overall business trends. You will also need to be comfortable with PR strategies and tactics to advise your company on the best path to follow given the situation.

MARKETING COMMUNICATIONS EXPERT

Occasionally the role of PR is to support product introductions or ongoing sales and marketing programs. While this is most often the case with consumer product companies—sometimes referred to as **business-to-consumer (B-to-C) communications**—increasingly PR is being leveraged to boost sales and launch new products across many types of industries, including **business-to-business (B-to-B)** and **business-to-government (B-to-G)** situations. (*Note: see the case study at the end of the chapter on the Nature Conservancy's efforts to reach utility companies and local governments with a message about water management. This is an example of B-to-G communic*ations.)

This can take the form of news conferences or events to introduce new products, testimonials, and case studies and posting content on social media platforms (e.g., Facebook, Instagram, Twitter, and Snapchat) to create interest and conversation about the product or service. This has evolved to a practice referred to as **integrated marketing communications (IMC)**.

CRISIS MANAGER

This is one of the most well-known and glamorized roles for PR (e.g., *Scandal*) and is one that most PR pros see as the ultimate test of their abilities. In a crisis something *big* has gone wrong: The industry has changed dramatically; a natural disaster has occurred; negligence or discrimination has been discovered; a product is being recalled; or internal financial wrongdoing is uncovered. Your company is in the spotlight. The so-called court of public opinion is in session, and its judgments can be harsh and swift—especially in a 24/7 digital media world. However, be aware that this kind of work is very stressful and the stakes are high—so it is not for the inexperienced or timid.

Also, keep in mind that what is usually remembered the most about a crisis is not the details but how well the company (and the PR team) handled the situation and responded to the issues it created. One need only look at the Deepwater Horizon explosion and oil spill in April 2010 to see what happens when a crisis is poorly managed. More people recall the dramatic underwater footage of oil pouring into the Gulf of Mexico, the damaged coastline, and stricken wildlife than remember what happened to cause the damage. But they have not forgotten the company responsible.

While many have forgotten the details of what happened on the Deepwater Horizon rig, they probably recall that BP was responsible. Images like this one, of a pelican slicked with oil after the Deepwater Horizon disaster, stick with people, as does the company responsible, in this case BP.

THE PUBLIC RELATIONS TOOL KIT

As a PR professional, you will learn to deploy various tools and tactics to accomplish your communications goals. While there are many skills you will utilize in your career, there are some basic ones you must master to be successful. Later in this text, in the practice areas chapters, there will be a more in-depth discussion of each of these items. For now, let's summarize them as follows: media relations, employee communications, research and strategic planning, and social media (see Figure 1.1).

Let's take each one separately.

MEDIA RELATIONS

Media relations and PR are terms that are often used interchangeably, especially by non-practitioners. However, while they are related, they are not the same thing. Generally media relations strategies are designed to accomplish one specific goal, for example, publicity, while PR is a category with various goals and specific elements.

Media relations can be described as a company's interactions (directly or through intermediaries) with editors, reporters, and journalists at national, local, specialty, and trade publications and broadcast outlets. The goal is to communicate a client's message, story, or information by convincing the journalist(s) that it is newsworthy and deserves mention or focus in their publication, online, or broadcast outlet.

On occasion media relations can mean working with the media to avoid a "bad" story or "balance" it to minimize the damage. For example, a reporter may approach you with a story idea or tip that is based on a rumor or misleading information.

FIGURE 1.1

The Public Relations Tool Kit

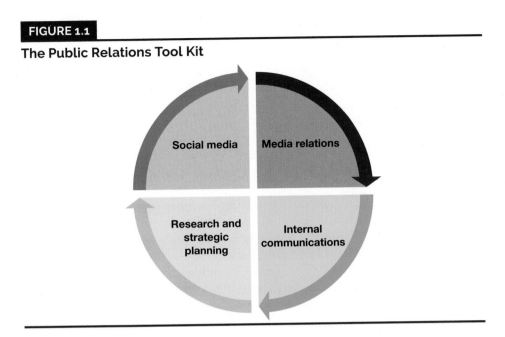

Your role is to provide sufficient data and details to convince them that the story idea is flawed or incomplete and provide them with the information to support that conclusion.

Another component to media relations that can be critical to your long-term success as PR professional is to be an intermediary or liaison between the company and the media. Dana Perino, who served as press secretary to President George W. Bush (from September 2007 to January 2009) and is now a commentator on Fox News, explains it by saying; "Your job is to represent the president to the media, as most people expect, but it also to represent the media to the president—both roles are crucial to your success in the job" (D. Perino, personal communication, 2017).

EMPLOYEE COMMUNICATIONS

Those of you whose career path leads you to work for a company or inside a large organization may find yourselves asked to manage communications to your fellow employees. This can concern routine matters such as employee benefits and updates to company policy or involve more complex matters like communicating before, during, and after a merger or similar major corporate event. Generally employee communications can involve creating newsletters, websites, videos, intranets, or frequently asked questions (FAQs) and preparing remarks for senior management to convey their vision for the company to employees.

However, communications can be a crucial factor in whether the benefits of a major organizational change (e.g., a merger) are achieved or not, research shows. Depending on which research source you use, it is estimated that anywhere between 50% and 85% of mergers fail to deliver on the promises made the day the deal was announced. Often one of the reasons cited for the failure is poor communication to the employees impacted by the transaction and lack of clarity on the vision and goals going forward.

RESEARCH AND STRATEGIC PLANNING

In a time when documenting results matters more and more, PR professionals need to develop and utilize their strategic planning and research capabilities. As such, a full chapter will be spent reviewing this topic in detail later in the book (see Chapter 4). Whether you conduct the research yourself or delegate it to a colleague or an outside firm, your plans will be much more likely to succeed if they are based on solid research. This can take the form of **secondary research** (reviewing already available materials) or **primary research** (e.g., conducting new surveys and/or focus groups). In an ideal situation, your communications plan will benefit from both these forms of research.

You research plan should include testing your message(s), identifying your target audience, and measuring progress toward the goals you have set. The upfront investment of time and resources on research will provide a strong foundation and greatly enhance the outcome of your plan (Stacks & Michaelson, 2010). The importance of the research and planning element was also outlined well in the IBM Centennial of Service case presented at the beginning of the chapter. Their efforts included preliminary research on what the employees felt were key issue or opportunities to address and post campaign research to document the hours of volunteer time, projects undertaken, and the news coverage obtained for the campaign's activities around the world. As noted there will be a more in-depth discussion of research and strategic planning in Chapter 4.

SOCIAL MEDIA

The explosive growth in digital media as an alternative media and information source—particularly in the developing world—has dramatically increased the need for social media skills as a prerequisite for a career in public relations in addition to the more traditional ones (Elliott, 2011; Perrin, 2015). Deirdre Breakenridge, a noted author and social media expert, suggests that "people in the PR industry need to

The explosive growth in social media has required companies to combine traditional PR and cutting-edge social media skills. PR crises can quickly go viral online, as United learned after several incidents in which passengers were mistreated and, in one instance, injured by their employees.

Joshua Lott/Stringer/Getty Images

become hybrid professionals" (Cision Bloggers, 2012), combining traditional PR and cutting-edge social media skills.

Breakenridge recommended the following skills development goals:

▸ Integrate traditional PR practices with digital and social communications while moving the best of both practices forward.

▸ Work outside of the PR "silo" and cross-functionally with marketing, including learning and applying marketing tactics.

▸ Collaborate with other departments, such as web/IT, sales, customer service, human resources, and so on.

▸ Be flexible and adaptable in an ever-changing global communications environment.

Given this trend, employers will be looking for professionals who are comfortable in this space and competent in leveraging this evolving resource to accomplish their business and communications goals. It is no longer sufficient to know how to use Facebook, Instagram, Twitter, or Snapchat for personal outreach. Employers are looking for staff that know how to work with social media to reach new customers, engage with them, and drive sales and marketing programs.

In the corporate arena, this can include managing a company's social media profile, monitoring online conversations, and developing content that enhances the company's reputation and supports its business objectives.

In the nonprofit arena, an effective social media strategy is a cost-efficient way to build followers, raise money for operations and charitable activities, as well as activate and engage people to support a cause or issue.

Finally in government and in politics—social media represents a direct route to reach citizens and voters to inform and educate them about government services, policy, candidates, and in the case of an election, can be a highly effective get-out-the-vote weapon.

CAREER PATHS FOR PUBLIC RELATIONS PROFESSIONALS: WHICH WAY IS RIGHT FOR YOU?

>> LO 1.6   **Review career options in the field of PR**

While there are many variables and options, there are generally four paths or concentrations your PR career might take. These are agency (such as a PR or consulting firm); corporate, in a communications staff role; government (e.g., local, state, or federal), or working for a nonprofit organization (like the United Way) or an association (such as National Restaurant Association; see Figure 1.2).

Let's review each one individually and put them into perspective.

AGENCY

The path of working in an agency setting is one many PR professionals take—especially early in their careers when they are learning their craft. As a young PR

How I Started and Built My Career in Public Relations and Corporate Social Responsibility

Erin Munley DeWaters, MetLife

Research shows Millennials will change jobs four times before the age of 32. I beat the average. I've held six roles with titles from assistant to strategist to vice president but not in that order. I've done many types of communications—from digital to crisis—and even helped launch an award-winning CSR program. I have had an interesting, challenging, and rewarding career so far. I joke that I have good career karma, but I also fueled my success by leveraging two things: education and opportunities.

Careers start with decisions about education. When you select a college, you begin to create your network. Professors, counselors, and peers will be avenues to career opportunities. People you know from childhood, like friends of your parents, are also your initial network. That's how my career started.

My mom had a friend whose daughter worked on Capitol Hill. Through that connection, I got an internship in a congressional office. When I graduated, I wanted to go back to D.C., so I scoured the job boards and applied to entry-level roles. I was open to all opportunities, and I encourage you to be too.

My first job was in a nonprofit membership organization. It wasn't a PR agency or well-known company; yet, today, I do PR for a global corporation. When you're evaluating roles, know there is no "typical" career path.

Another major influence on my career was graduate school. Two years after college, I got my master's in PR. I learned a ton, broadened my network, and built confidence. Through that confidence, I've raised my hand many times to take on new responsibilities at work so I could learn and gain experience.

It was by raising my hand that I was asked to help launch a new CSR program for regional grocer Food Lion. There was a vacant position, and I stepped into a lead role on the project. Food Lion was looking to integrate PR and CSR, and that's exactly what we did through Food Lion Feeds. It was the most rewarding experience of my career. After that, I joined MetLife, where I now do PR for two of its U.S. divisions. MetLife's reputation as a good corporate citizen is one of the things that drew me to the company.

CSR isn't a nice-to-do; it's a must-do, and smart companies get that. An integrated PR/CSR strategy creates opportunities to tell stories, reach consumers, and much more. If you're entering PR today, you'll be at an advantage by understanding the intersection.

As you think about the road ahead, lean into your education, and value the relationships it helps you create. Be open to opportunities. Raise your hand and learn. You'll build competency and credibility, and that will be the foundation for your career path—whatever that may be. ●

Erin DeWaters is an "Older Millennial," working wife, mom, and graduate of the University of North Carolina at Chapel Hill and The George Washington University. She serves as lead communications strategist for global insurance company MetLife.

Source: E. DeWaters (personal communication, 2017).

professional, joining an agency has many advantages. First and foremost is that the focus and business is on public relations—that is what they do for clients every day. As such you would be in an environment where nearly everyone you work with is a PR professional. The opportunity to learn new tactics and strategies, benefit from a colleague's industry experience, or bounce an idea off someone with more experience is actively encouraged. Some people make an entire career of working for an agency, rising to become practice leaders, office managing partners, or even senior management of a firm.

Barri Rafferty, worldwide president of Ketchum Public Relations, got her start in the industry working at Cone Communications while in graduate school in

FIGURE 1.2

PR Career Paths

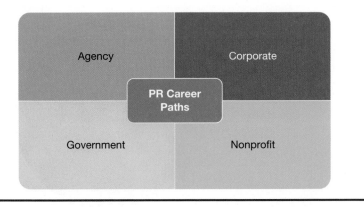

Boston. She then moved to New York and experimented with a big agency (Burson-Marsteller), on the corporate side (SlimFast), and at a small beauty boutique (Lippe Taylor). Rafferty decided that a big agency would provide a supportive environment as she started her family, so she joined Ketchum as a vice president and account supervisor in New York.

Working her way up to her present position at Ketchum, Rafferty has held several key roles, including group manager for the New York Brand Practice, associate director of the New York office, and director of the Global Brand Marketing Practice. She relocated to Atlanta to be director of the office and later became director of the Ketchum's South region. She came back to New York to serve as office director. In 2012, Rafferty became CEO of North America, and in 2016 she was named worldwide president.

After working in an agency for a few years, you might decide to move to an internal (or client-side) position in a government, corporate, or nonprofit setting. Others decide to start their own firms or set up shop as independent counselors to leverage the skills and contacts gained while working for a larger firm.

Barri Rafferty is now worldwide president of Ketchum Public Relations.

© Barri Rafferty

CORPORATE

For those PR professionals who pursue a career working in a corporate environment, there are challenges and opportunities to develop skills not found in other work settings. As a corporate PR professional, you would generally work in the communications department, although it may have many different names depending on the nomenclature and culture of the company. Some companies refer to the department as public relations; others will use variations of corporate communications, external affairs, corporate affairs, public affairs, and/or just communications or marketing.

This is also dependent on the corporate structure and reporting relationship of the function. According to a recent study by USC Annenberg Center (Holmes, 2017a), in most

FIGURE 1.3

In-House Reporting Lines

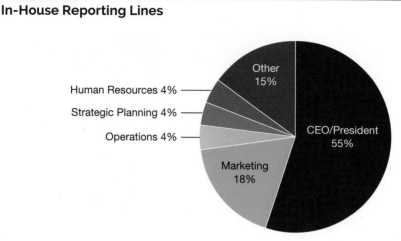

Regardless of the reporting relationship, staff members in a corporate communications department are usually responsible for media relations, executive, internal (sometime shared with HR), and financial communications if the company has public shareholders and is listed on a stock exchange, for example, the New York Stock Exchange or NASDAQ.

Source: Holmes (2017a).

companies, PR reports to marketing or the CEO, but in some cases, it reports to others including legal or human resources (HR). Reporting to the CEO is viewed as desirable because it positions the function as a key corporate department with direct access and interaction with top management (see Figure 1.3).

For these individuals, there is often the added responsibility of writing the company's annual report to stockholders, news releases on quarterly financial results, announcement on mergers and acquisitions, and senior management changes. These are known as **material events**, and publicly traded companies are required to produce them in a timely manner.

A career in corporate PR can be challenging and rewarding, and the compensation and benefits are often quite good. As well, corporate PR positions can be somewhat more stable and less susceptible to economic downturns or client-mandated changes that can directly impact agency work and staffing.

Recent research suggests that succeeding in a corporate role requires communications executives "to be knowledgeable about the business—from strategy to operations—so they are able to provide strategic input on issues that span business functions" (Arthur W. Page Society, 2017). The Page report quotes one CEO as suggesting, "I don't think a healthy organization can do much without (communications) being involved in every part of the strategy and every part of the operation."

One cautionary note about this path—unlike the agency world, it is likely you will be one of only a handful of people who work on PR for your company. This can limit your internal network and be challenging because your fellow employees may not understand what you do and how it adds value to the company's business objectives. As a result, many PR pros wait to pursue corporate opportunities until later in their careers when they have more general PR experience.

GOVERNMENT

Many PR professionals have long careers in a government communication role working at the federal or state level. In the federal government, the function is more commonly referred to as **public affairs**. Most every cabinet department—from the U.S. Department of Agriculture (USDA) to Health and Human Services (HHS) and the Department of Homeland Security (DHS)—has a public affairs office. In larger departments with a national or international focus (like the U.S. State Department), there are often regional offices where communications professionals interact with the regional media around the world and serve constituents (e.g., US citizens and companies) locally instead of referring them to headquarters in Washington, D.C. Generally, the focus of this work is more reactive and service oriented as opposed to proactive or lobbying/advocating for the reasons already noted.

Similarly, at the state, county, or city level, public information and public service is the driving force and primary focus. Most elected officials, for example, a governor, county commissioner, or mayor, often have a dedicated press secretary, who is a political appointee, serving at the pleasure of the elected official. In each major city or state department, there is usually also a public information office, and its focus is on responding to the media and the public, providing information about essential services and responding in crisis or disaster situations. As with the other career paths noted here, the PR professional (or public affairs officer) is usually part of a small group. As such, there are few others in the office who understand your role and can offer suggestions or advice.

NONPROFIT AND/OR ASSOCIATION PUBLIC RELATIONS

Nonprofit and association work is an increasingly popular path for young PR professionals, especially in the Washington, D.C., area and in metro New York, where many of these organizations are headquartered. However, the measure of success in this setting is more often measured in awareness, membership growth, and fund-raising success. Non-profits, like the United Way, the Red Cross, and the World Wildlife Federation are focused on a key cause or issue, such as community service, disaster relief, or protecting endangered species. The PR professionals in this environment will have responsibility for traditional PR activities like media relations and executive counsel as well as supporting the ongoing fund-raising efforts and membership communications.

The membership looks to their association to monitor events and activity of the local, state, and federal government as well as advance the profession through research, training, and overall visibility. Often these organizations take on the additional role of managing industry-wide issues and crises on behalf of their members or assist member companies as they work their way through the situation.

Jeff Joseph is senior vice president of communications and strategic relationships at the Consumer Technology Association (CTA), based in Northern Virginia. According to its website, The CTA "advocates for the entrepreneurs, technologists and innovators who mold the future of the consumer technology industry" (J. Joseph, personal communication, 2017). The CET (formerly the CEA) is perhaps best known as the host of the huge Consumer Electronics Show (CES) each year in Las Vegas, which draws thousands of tech suppliers and customers to see what's new and cool

The Red Cross PR team is actively involved in community outreach and fundraising support, as well as community and media relations activity when the organization responds to disaster situations across the United States and around the world.

Joe Burbank/Orlando Sentinel/Getty Images

in high technology and popular entertainment from the biggest names in technology. "Association PR allows me to engage in a variety of PR disciplines. One moment I'm focused on public affairs. The next, media relations, or crisis communications. All while supporting our singular mission—to help grow our industry," he concludes.

SCENARIO OUTCOME

At the beginning of this chapter, you read about IBM's strategy to turn its 100th anniversary into a celebration of service for its thousands of employees worldwide. The goal was to celebrate the event in a way that emphasized the company's commitment and tradition of community service and social responsibility and highlighted the many contributions of its employees and business partners.

You were asked to consider how IBM turned this milestone celebration into a comprehensive, year-long, company-wide event; how employee, corporate, and marketing communications were addressed; how success was measured; and how social responsibility was included.

Here is what the company did: IBM created a comprehensive, company-wide event with its Celebration of Service by driving engagement in multiple ways. It established a highly visible Service Pledge on the IBM Centennial website that constantly updated total hours pledged. Activity kits in seven languages offered grab-and-go volunteer ideas. It also provided detailed service leader training modules and grants to support IBMers' volunteer activities.

A Global Communications Guidebook was created to support the local IBM communications teams, and an NGO Communications Guidebook was provided as well to enable NGOs to amplify their partnerships with IBM through numerous global communications channels and on social media.

To communicate with employees, as well as corporate and marketing management, IBM visually represented the sheer volume of the volunteer work through a Volunteerism by the Numbers infographic. It featured key stats on the global progress of the thousands of volunteer projects underway all year long. This infographic was kept current and made available to media and bloggers, and a photo slideshow of global volunteer efforts was kept current and made available as well on the Celebration of Service site.

The IBM Celebration of Service was a huge success, with many socially responsible activities. Some of the volunteer projects included IBM's CEO teaching math and science to a middle school class in Baltimore; volunteers in California installing solar panels on low-income houses; IBM employees in Uruguay helping young people in impoverished neighborhoods get their first jobs; and IBM technicians in New Zealand teaching senior citizens how to text and use their smartphones.

HIGHLIGHTS

▸ Three million hours of service were donated by IBM employees worldwide.

▸ Ten thousand clients, business partners, and others participated.

▸ Projects were completed in 120 countries.

▸ More than a 1,000 news articles were generated, most in major target media outlets—many of which were outside the United States.

▸ IBM brand awareness was enhanced globally, and the Centennial Celebration of Service was cited as a proof point in independent research.

Source: Eckels (2012).

WRAP UP

This initial chapter discussed the definitions of PR throughout history and the "official" one by the PRSA, developed in 2012. The chapter also examined the differences between PR and advertising, noting the credibility gap between what people read and see on the news and in paid advertisements. The impact of social media was addressed, with a focus on "sponsored" and "owned" content used to bridge the gap between "paid" and "earned" media.

In addition the skills that PR professionals utilize in their work—including media relations, employee communications, research, and strategic planning—were reviewed. Finally the chapter looked at the career paths a PR professional might follow.

As you move through the remainder of the text, there will be detailed chapters on these concepts as well as the areas of specialization for a career in this dynamic and exciting industry.

KEY TERMS

Blogger: An individual who writes and posts his or her thoughts about news, issues, or trends on a blog that is then shared, liked, or re-posted by others on social media, **6**

Business-to-Business (B-to-B): Communications efforts focused on a business audience or customer, **13**

Business-to-Consumer (B-to-C): Traditional PR focused on promoting a product or service to consumers, **13**

Business-to-Government (B-to-G): Outreach designed to support the purchase of goods and services by government agencies, **13**

Corporate Reputation: How a company (or organization) is perceived by its key stakeholders, **9**

Influencer: An individual who develops a following and becomes a trendsetter or opinion leader and can influence the success or failure of a communications campaign, **6**

Integrated Marketing Communications (IMC): A strategic communications activity combining the activities of advertising, promotion, and PR to plan, develop, and implement brand-focused communications programs to generate sales or attract customers to a product or service, **13**

Material Events: News or developments that the Securities and Exchange Commission views as potentially having an impact on the stock price of a public company, including a new product or a product recall, a change in senior management, the announcement of a merger or major transaction, a major news or economic event, or annual and quarterly earnings announcements, **20**

Public Affairs: (1) Communications activity engaged in by companies directed at impacting government policy or legislation; (2) Communications outreach and public information activities by government employees to the public in place of the term PR, **21**

Public Company (Publicly Traded Company): A company that sells stock (shares) to the public to raise money (capital) to fund its growth and expansion, **4**

Publicist: Most common in the entertainment, fashion, and celebrity arenas, this professional focuses on keeping the client visible and in the news to boost popularity and promote projects (e.g., movies and television shows), **2**

Primary Research: New research activity undertaken to prepare a communications plan or activity (e.g., a survey, focus group, or other form of research), **16**

Secondary Research: Reviewing existing research for new insights or trends, including reviewing a recent public opinion survey; scanning news coverage on a topic, issue, or individual; or reading scholarly research for insights on communications theory and its application to a current issue or opportunity, **16**

Stakeholders: People or organizations who have a "stake" in a company/organization, including employees, voters, government agencies and elected officials, customers, prospective employees, as well as customers and other similar individuals, **7**

Sustainable Business Practices (Sustainability Communications): Activities that improve an organization's reputation that can also have positive economic and social aspects, **9, 11**

THINK ABOUT IT

Early in the chapter, you read about the perception of PR and PR people based on the research from USC and others on how popular culture (movies, television, etc.) have portrayed PR over the years. As part of that research, they produced a YouTube video with a compilation of scenes from movies and television over the past 50+ years. For this activity, it is suggested that you form small work groups. The link to the video follows: https://www.youtube.com/watch?v=hqGCgg68Wt4.

Your task:

▸ View the YouTube video from USC.
▸ Discuss your thoughts and reactions to how it portrays PR.
▸ Capture your notes on the discussion, and share them with the class.
▸ Brainstorm ideas to change the perception (if necessary).
▸ Determine if you can (or feel you need to) improve the public's understanding of PR.

WRITE LIKE A PRO

After reading about the IBM Centennial Celebration of Service, assume you are on the PR team for a regional bank nearing its 150th anniversary. The bank serves both its economically challenged headquarters city and an affluent state in the Northeast United States. As such the bank's customers have a variety of challenges, including home affordability, paying for college and healthcare, reducing unemployment, and caring for senior citizens. Remember, as a bank, your company's expertise lends itself more to some challenges than others. How do you decide which ones to take on and which to leave for others? How do you leverage and engage your employees and customers?

1. Develop an outline of a plan (250 words) to celebrate the bank's anniversary, based on these suggestions.

2. Make sure to include tactics from PR (media relations and community events) and social responsibility initiatives (employee volunteers, contributions, or fund-raising) into one comprehensive outline.

SOCIAL RESPONSIBILITY CASE STUDY

Allstate Purple Purse: Raising Awareness and Funds for Victims

The issue of domestic violence has become a national phenomenon in recent years. Research indicates that one in four women will be a victim of domestic violence in her lifetime and that financial abuse occurs in 98% of those cases. Financial abuse (withholding funds, destroying credit, and jeopardizing jobs) provides abusers with another way to control and punish their victims.

The Allstate Foundation created Purple Purse in 2010 to ignite a national conversation about domestic violence and financial abuse. The Allstate Foundation committed to an expanded Purple Purse program in 2014, including a fashion statement around the Purple Purse imagery, a social statement on a serious issue, and increased financial support for the local organizations that victims depend on to rebuild their lives.

Research and Strategy

The Allstate Foundation commissioned a national survey "Silent Weapon: Domestic Violence and Financial Abuse," which showed that two-thirds of Americans believe domestic violence is a serious problem, while revealing that just over one in three has ever talked about it. Further, nearly eight in 10 said they were not familiar with financial abuse and considered it the least likely form of abuse to be recognized by others. In fact 65% believed their own family or friends would not know if they were in a financially abusive relationship, and 70 percent said family or friends would not know how to help them. Strategies included media relations, social media, celebrity involvement, and fund-raising challenges.

Execution

The centerpiece of the program was a launch event held in New York City, timed to coincide with Fashion Week, and featuring a purple purse designed by celebrity campaign ambassador Kerry Washington, star of the hit TV show *Scandal*. An Associated Press exclusive interview was placed to break the story the morning of the event, creating a cascade of media coverage. Washington also appeared in a public service announcement (PSA) on the program, conducted interviews with national media, engaged fans through her social media feeds, and introduced new audiences to the cause by showcasing her personally designed purple purse at numerous high-profile events during Fashion Week.

At the local level, the Allstate Foundation issued the Purple Purse Challenge to 140 nonprofits across the country. The goal was to raise money for domestic violence survivors and the organizations that serve them. The challenge was launched through the PurplePurse.com program site, with $650,000 in incentives from the Allstate Foundation. Each program partner company received a package of purple purses, purple purse charms, and other collateral to generate awareness and promote fund-raising.

The Allstate Foundation delivered program kits internally to help company employees and allied Allstate agents involve their local communities in the campaign, thereby expanding the program's impact.

To engage the Hispanic audience fully, the Allstate Foundation placed an exclusive on the Hispanic survey statistics with the international news agency Agencia EFE. A Spanish-language satellite media tour, audio news release, and a new Spanish-language site—BolsoMorado.com (PurplePurse.com)—completed this outreach initiative and provided key information to an essential program audience.

Evaluation

In only one month, the Purple Purse Challenge raised nearly $2.5 million to benefit financial empowerment services for survivors, a 614% increase from the revenues raised in 2013. More than half of all donations were at $25 and under, demonstrating that this was truly a successful grassroots fund-raising campaign. The program resulted in more than 23,000 media placements through earned media and social platforms as well as paid amplification, a 447% increase in program media results from 2013.

Earned broadcast placements included ABC's *Good Morning America*, MSNBC's *Morning Joe*, CNN, and E! *Extra* and *Access Hollywood*. Top print and online placements included stories in the Associated Press, WSJ.com, Huffington Post, CBSNews.com, Yahoo! Celebrity, TIME.com, and many more. Other print placements appeared in *People*, *Living*, *Ebony*, *ESPN The Magazine*, *Money*, *Martha Stewart Living*, *TIME*, and *Working Mother*.

Online, Allstate Foundation Purple Purse became a continuing topic of conversation, with more than 13,500 #PurplePurse social posts across Twitter, Facebook and Instagram. On September 17, a few days after the program launch, Kerry Washington was trending on Facebook due to her involvement in the Purple Purse campaign.

Source: Adapted from PRSA Silver Anvil Case Study—Winners, 2015.

ENGAGE

1. Explore the National Network to End Domestic Violence website to see how it communicates with its various stakeholders.

2. Search for "controversial celebrity endorsements," and learn what can go wrong and what can be done.

DISCUSS

1. The Purple Purse campaign deals with a very sensitive and controversial topic. Do you think it is wise for the Allstate Company to connect itself so visibly? What are the downsides of this approach for customers, employees, and the public?

2. How do the issues of domestic violence and financial abuse connect or relate to the business of the Allstate Company?

3. Is there a risk of tying your CSR campaign to a celebrity so closely? What if he/she gets into difficulty or has his/her own crisis? How does Allstate protect itself from any backlash?

4. The case mentions special outreach to the Hispanic community. Why do you think this is a key part of the program?

SOCIAL RESPONSIBILITY CASE STUDY

The Nature Conservancy: Connecting City Water Supplies With Nature

We all know that cities need clean water to thrive, but public drinking water supplies in the United States and globally are threatened by overuse, pollution, and climate change. The Nature Conservancy released the "Urban Water Blueprint" report in 2014 to educate city leaders and utility managers worldwide on nature's ability to improve water quality.

To support that launch, the Nature Conservancy implemented an international communications campaign to promote the blueprint's findings to government decision makers and build support for investing in nature instead of infrastructure (treatment plants, pipes, and storage reservoirs). A secondary goal was to position the Nature Conservancy as a credible partner and authority in watershed management.

Research and Strategy

The blueprint concluded that for many cities, protecting water at its source can be cheaper and more efficient than treating it after it is already polluted and also provides recreational value and job growth for area residents. Based on the research, there were three primary objectives for the campaign: a business objective (increase municipal and utility investment in natural infrastructure and watersheds) and two communications objectives (increase awareness and understanding among city and utility leaders of non-infrastructure options to improve urban drinking water quality and position the Nature Conservancy as a resource for information and advisor on watershed protection). It was important to make the report data more easily understood by using existing media channels to reach the target audience(s) for blueprint information distribution. The campaign aimed to connect the report with topics trending in the news cycle and launched the report by leveraging the Global Water Summit to engage a captive audience.

Execution

Several key steps were taken:

1. Messaging—Messages were developed to connect findings to concerns of audience(s).
2. Urban Water Blueprint Microsite—A dedicated microsite was created and promoted.
3. Infographics—Two sharable infographics were created to present data from the report.
4. Stakeholder Engagement—The organization reached out to key groups to participate on launch day.
5. Trade Publication Outreach—The PR team submitted feature stories to utility and water industry trade publications.
6. International Media Outreach—The PR team pitched top-tier global media outlets on the findings.
7. Launch Event—The organization launched its report at the Global Water Summit to reach decision makers and key media already there.

Evaluation

To increase awareness among key audiences of nature-based solutions to water treatment, 11 stakeholder groups published the Nature Conservancy's prepackaged media materials. Media pitching efforts resulted in earned coverage in more than 20 outlets, including Reuters and *Bloomberg Businessweek*. Feature stories appeared in three key trade publications—*American City and County*, *Journal of the American Water Works Association*, and *Water World*. In addition to the 400 people at the Global Water Summit, nearly 300 people attended the session virtually. Viewership was recorded in the United States, Canada, United Kingdom, Italy, Mexico, Peru, Ecuador, and Venezuela.

To position the Nature Conservancy as a resource on watershed protection and management, three op-eds and two blog posts were published in top-tier publications, including the *Chicago Sun-Times*, *The Guardian*, GreenBiz, Project Syndicate, and TreeHugger. The Nature Conservancy's promotion of the report and microsite resulted in 18,000 people from 143 countries visiting the website.

Source: Adapted from PRSA Silver Anvil Cases—Winners, 2015.

ENGAGE

1 Visit the Nature Conservatory at www.nature.org to discover how it's communicating about natural solutions for water management.
2. Visit the website's newsroom and explore the various press releases, newsfeeds, expert testimonials, and blogs.

DISCUSS

1. What is the connection between the Nature Conservancy and the issue of water resource management, and how does that involve local government?
2. Advocating for natural solutions for water management and purification is admirable, but is it realistic that cities and towns are going to shift their plans and policies to emphasize that approach versus traditional means—sewage treatment plants, filtration, and other forms of infrastructure?
3. While generating news coverage and awareness of the report, which the Nature Conservancy clearly achieved in this case, how will they know if the government audiences adapt and change their approaches?
4. After a successful launch event and rollout of the report, what should the Nature Conservancy do next to advance their agenda for natural solutions to water management?

Starbucks: Corporate Social Responsibility

Since the company's founding, Starbucks' coffee operations have been accompanied by various efforts at social responsibility, from fair trade coffee to covering tuition for its employees at Arizona State University. CEO Howard Schultz has been the face of Starbucks for more than 30 years.

In the following clip, Schultz speaks on the occasion of Starbucks' entry into the Italian market and discusses his view of the company's philanthropic efforts.

VIDEO

1. How did "responsibility beyond what is required" help Starbucks build its business?

2. How did Howard Schultz use the opening of Starbucks stores in Italy as a PR opportunity?

3. Make an argument for corporate social responsibility at Starbucks from a moral, a rational, and an economic viewpoint.

PRACTICE AND APPLY WHAT YOU'VE LEARNED

edge.sagepub.com/page

CHECK YOUR COMPREHENSION
ON THE STUDY SITE WITH:

- eFlashcards to strengthen your understanding of key terms

- Practice quizzes to test your comprehension of key concepts

- Videos and multimedia content to enhance your exploration of key topics

Popperfoto/Getty Images

2

The History of Modern Public Relations

From Barnum to Lee, Bernays to Page, and Other Public Relations Pioneers

Learning Objectives

2.1   Identify key developments in the modern history of PR

2.2   Explain the growth of the PR agency business model and the contributions of women and minority professionals

2.3   Understand how social and environmental responsibility have become an integral part of PR

2.4   Summarize the challenges PR will face in the years to come

Scenario

Breaking Ground in Crisis Management—Ivy Lee and the Pennsylvania Railroad

It is in the fall of 1904, and Ivy Lee has just opened a new PR firm with his partner, George Parker, in New York City. Lee was a former business journalist in New York City, and his focus was on telling the story of American business. Parker was a former journalist as well, having worked in Buffalo, New York. He and Lee met when Parker was working for the Democratic National Committee, and Lee was hired as his assistant.

Vision for PR's Future. In launching the firm, they had a vision for the future of PR. Their goal was to serve as the PR counsel to their clients—much like attorneys, accountants, and bankers counsel their clients.

Ivy Lee was enlisted by the Pennsylvania Railroad to assist in managing media interest in accidents.

© Corbis/Getty Images

"This is not a secret press bureau," Lee wrote when they started the business. "All our work is done in the open. We aim to supply news. . . . In brief, our plan is, frankly and openly, on behalf of the business concerns and public institutions, to supply to the press and public of the United States prompt and accurate information concerning subjects which it is of value and interest to the public to know about" (Turney, n.d.).

First Case of Crisis Management. In one of the first examples of crisis management, Lee was engaged to assist the Pennsylvania Railroad in managing media interest in covering accidents that occurred as the railroad increased its services nationally. Previously the company had followed a no-comment approach during and after an accident, viewing it as a company matter.

However, as their profile grew, they recognized they had an obligation to respond to the media about accidents, especially as they needed government permission to expand their operations and regulatory approval to increase rates for passengers and freight. Moving forward, they knew their reputation and the public's perception would be a factor in these decisions. Simply put, they could not afford to be viewed as indifferent or unaccountable to accidents and injuries if they expected to get permission to expand their operation.

After reading this chapter, put yourself in Lee's place, and suggest some tactics for the company to improve its crisis communications procedures. You should be able to answer the following questions (remember the time-period is in the early 20th century):

1. How would you convince the company to be more open and responsive?

2. What tactics would you use to manage the crisis?

3. What role should media relations play?

4. How would you minimize the reputation damage to the railroad?

5. How would this case be different today versus the early 1900s?

This chapter will take the reader through a brief history of the public relations industry—with an emphasis on the "modern era" as it is most relevant to the PR business today. In the pages that follow, you will learn about some well-known industry pioneers like Ivy Lee, Edward Bernays, and Arthur W. Page and some of the colorful figures in history—such as P. T. Barnum—who practiced early forms of PR and advertising to generate awareness for their businesses.

You will also read about unsung industry pioneers—notably women and minorities—whose contributions to PR are not as well-known but are no less significant. This is an area of industry history that is essential to provide you with a more complete heritage of the PR profession.

Later in the chapter you will also learn about the growth of the PR agency business and how it has become a force in the industry and a rewarding career path for many practitioners. Much of the innovation and creative strategies now commonly deployed by PR professionals (e.g., media tours, thought leadership, and competitive intelligence) originated in agencies and their client work. Further, the agency business is an excellent training ground for young professionals regardless of their ultimate career path.

Finally this chapter looks at the trends that impact the future of the PR industry and assesses how you can prepare for and respond effectively.

A HISTORY OF PUBLIC RELATIONS IN THE MODERN ERA

>> LO 2.1 Identify key developments in the modern history of PR

The biggest challenge in writing a history of PR is where to start.

Do you begin with Plato and the ancient Greeks? Or examine how communication tactics were used by the Catholic Church in the 1500s to spread Christianity and by kings and emperors in the Middle Ages and Renaissance to expand empires, build followers, and stabilize their leadership positions?

After all when viewed through the lens of influencing public opinion or driving change, one can see public relations elements at work in the Norman Conquest, the Crusades, and both the French and American Revolutions (Bates, 2006). When America was a British colony in the late 1700s, PR tactics like the Boston Tea Party "event" led by Sam Adams (called by some historians the "father of press agentry") built support for the American Revolution by encouraging dissent and disagreement with British rules and regulations. Thomas Paine's *Common Sense*, an influential pamphlet on American Independence, may have been the first political

communications campaign and an early example of PR as activism. The *Federalist Papers*, authored by Alexander Hamilton, John Jay, and James Madison were written to support ratification of the U.S. Constitution, similar to today's opinion pieces written and published to influence public opinion.

PUBLIC RELATIONS AND PRESS AGENTRY: THE ERA OF THE 1800s

In the 18th century, as America expanded, PR moved from its noble heritage of building support for American Independence to a more commercially focused enterprise. Driven by the dramatic expansion of newspapers nationally that needed copy and by entrepreneurs launching new businesses and looking to promote them, PR moved into what is often referred to as the "Golden Age of Press Agentry."

The period saw the rise of the press agent, whose job it was to "hype" companies, products, entertainment and/or "celebrities"—by almost any means necessary. Tactics deployed during this era were noticeably short on ethics and focused on achieving publicity. Exaggeration, lies, and outright fabrication became common practice among many of these "publicists" along with free tickets, gifts, or other means to get reporters to write positive stories about their clients. Characters like Davy Crockett, Daniel Boone, Annie Oakley, or Buffalo Bill were created or their exploits exaggerated to sell tickets, win votes, or get coverage. Unfortunately, for many people today, this image remains as their principal perception of PR professionals.

One of the best-known figures from these freewheeling times was P. T. Barnum—considered the Great American Showman—whose namesake circus and museum continued to operate long after his death. Many believe Barnum, who was reportedly the second millionaire in the United States, might have been the originator of the **press event** or **publicity stunt**—which is an event or activity created and executed solely to get news coverage. Former Librarian of Congress Daniel Boorstin described these as "pseudo-events" and suggested Barnum was the acknowledged master of his time at this tactic.

Examples of Barnum's work include Joyce Heth—whom he promoted as the 161-year-old former nursemaid to George Washington and the Feejee Mermaid—a stuffed half-monkey and half-fish creature, both of which he exhibited at his American Museum in New York. Barnum knew that controversy sells and used it to draw people to his museum to see what was fact and what was fiction. Once they were in the door, other exhibits and shows were there to entertain and educate.

P. T. Barnum is credited by some as the originator of the "press event" or "publicity stunt."

Hulton Archive/Getty Images

"Whatever your occupation, whatever your purpose, if you need the support of the public then take the steps necessary to let them know about it."

—P. T. Barnum

SOCIAL
RESPONSIBILITY

Kathleen Maher, curator of the Barnum Museum in Bridgeport, Connecticut (Barnum's adopted hometown for which he served one term as mayor in 1875), has studied his legacy and suggests that Barnum's contributions go beyond eccentric exhibits and bombast. His worldwide tours for General Tom Thumb, a midget who could sing, dance, and act, and his promotion of Jenny Lind, the "Swedish Nightingale," may be considered precursors to today's reality television and musical contest shows. P. T. Barnum would often donate a portion of the proceeds of his shows to a local charity to boost sales and generate positive publicity—an early example of SR and strategic philanthropy.

"Whether fact or fiction, the conclusion was less relevant than the experience or opportunity," Maher continues. "Barnum was ingenious in presenting speculation within a world of curiosity. He offered a chance to explore the irrational, examine imaginative possibilities, and derive opinions and truths. His pioneering spirit of promotion and his acumen for business transformed popular conceptions of the era, in turn molding and defining many ideals of today," she concludes (K. Maher, personal communication, 2017). A colorful character to be sure, Barnum deserves further study and, perhaps, reevaluation for his contributions to the growth and development of promotional PR and strategic philanthropy.

RAILROADS DRIVE PUBLIC RELATIONS' DEVELOPMENT

As you read at the outset of this chapter, the railroad industry was a major factor in the growth and development of PR. In the latter stages of the 18th century, the railroad industry initiated and utilized many PR tactics now seen as commonplace. These tactics include: distribution of pamphlets and materials to the press and public promoting migration to the western United States; creating publicity and information offices in target recruiting areas; and staging promotional "road shows" that traveled the country on railroad cars (naturally) and featured murals, artwork, and artifacts promoting the quality of life in the western United States.

By all accounts these and other tactics worked well, and westward migration swelled—with 5 million people resettling in the Midwest and more than 2 million farms being established. Commenting on this achievement, Andy Piasecki (2000), a lecturer at Queen Margaret College in Edinburgh, Scotland, and a PR historian, suggests that "none of this could have been achieved without complex communications strategies closely linked to business objectives." Clearly, as the 1800s wound down, PR had begun yet another transformation, moving away from publicity for publicity's sake to implementing communications strategies designed to achieve specific business objectives.

PUBLIC RELATIONS' TRANSFORMATION

Building on the work of late 19th century activists like Ida Wells and John Muir, PR began to take on more substantive social issues as the 20th century approached. These two activists, and others like them, made significant contributions that paved the way for the **modern era of PR**. Ida Wells was born a slave and rose to fight discrimination as a speaker, editor and founder of an anti-segregation newspaper in Memphis. She was also a cofounder and early leader of the National Association for the Advancement of Colored People (NAACP). Lesser known is that in 1884, at the age of 22, Wells refused to move to the "colored section" when ordered to do so by a

The movement of public relations into social issues in the 20th century built upon the work of 19th-century activists like Ida B. Wells (*left*) and John Muir (*right*).

Chicago History Museum/Getty Images; Bettmann/Getty Images

railroad conductor, many years before Rosa Parks became famous for a similar act on a bus in Alabama in 1955 (Museum of PR, n.d.b).

Like Wells, John Muir was an activist, although his focus was on preserving and protecting nature. John Muir was active in the 1860s, wrote books and magazine articles, and gave speeches to engage U.S. citizens in conservation and the creation of parks across the country (National Park Service, n.d.). Muir founded the Sierra Club and his environmental activism helped preserve the Yosemite Valley, Sequoia National Park, and other wilderness areas for future generations. In many ways he was an early proponent of sustainability due to his efforts to encourage the government and business to exercise restraint in dealing with natural resources.

> **SOCIAL RESPONSIBILITY**

PIONEERS OF MODERN PUBLIC RELATIONS

Most scholars agree that the three pioneers of the new, modern style of PR were: Ivy Lee, regarded as the originator of the *public relations counsel* concept; Edward Bernays, often referred to as the *father of modern public relations;* and Arthur Page, revered for his groundbreaking work as the *first corporate PR officer* at AT&T. These leaders took PR into the corporate boardroom, politics, and government. Through the work of these and other trailblazers, PR began to take on major social issues and critical business challenges well beyond the hype and bombast of P. T. Barnum and the generation of publicists.

Ivy Lee, alongside his partner George Parker, in 1904 opened one of the first PR firms in New York. His successful campaign in support of a rate hike for the Pennsylvania Railroad is considered a landmark in the history of PR.

Ullstein bild dtl./Getty Images

IVY LEE

With the opening of one of the first PR firms, Parker and Lee, in 1904 in New York, Ivy Lee and his partner George Parker raised the bar for the industry by declaring themselves as "public relations counselors." Their major clients were the Pennsylvania Railroad, the Rockefeller family, the American Tobacco Company, as well as some Hollywood studios and the New York subway system.

One of the firm's first clients, the Pennsylvania Railroad Company, hired them to build support for the approval of a 5% rate hike. Ivy Lee developed a comprehensive PR campaign, reaching out to all the company's key stakeholders—for example, the media, railroad employees, passengers, customers, state and federal elected officials, as well as college presidents, religious leaders, and other opinion leaders—to help make the company's case and convince the government regulators to approve the increase (St. John, 2006). These efforts paid off. Public opposition declined, multiple outside groups wrote in support of the rate hike, and the federal government approved the 5% rate hike. This campaign is heralded as "a landmark in the history of advocacy public relations" (St. John, 2006, p.225).

However, Ivy Lee was not without his detractors. While he is generally lauded for his pioneering role, he was also accused of not being honest about his more controversial clients. He was heavily criticized for his work for the American Russian Chamber of Commerce during the Stalin era and for promoting the German Dye Organization, which was later discovered to be a Nazi party-owned organization. Notwithstanding these issues, Ivy Lee made major contributions to the practice of modern PR. Commenting on Lee's contributions Fraser P. Seitel concluded that Lee, more than any other, brought the practice of PR into the 21st century (Seitel, 2013).

EDWARD L. BERNAYS

Following in the tradition of Lee, Edward L. Bernays was a pivotal figure in the development of modern PR. He believed that PR was most effective when social science and behavioral psychology were leveraged to develop campaigns to change behavior or shape public opinion (Bernays, 2015b). Reflecting his family heritage as the nephew of Sigmund Freud, his model was based on using scientific persuasion techniques to advocate for a position or product. He was one of the first to emphasize identifying your target audience, conducting research to listen to and understand their views, and then tailoring your message accordingly.

He detailed this and other thoughts on PR in his seminal book *Crystallizing Public Information*, first published in 1923 and still read today by students and scholars of the discipline. Later in his career, Bernays was invited to join the faculty of New York University (NYU) and teach one of the first courses on PR in the United

Edward Bernays was one of the first PR professionals to use social science and behavioral psychology in developing his techniques.

Bettmann/Getty Images

States (Bernays, 2015b). "The three main elements of public relations are practically as old as society: informing people, persuading people and integrating [connecting] people with people. Of course, the means and methods of accomplishing these ends have changed as society has changed," Bernays (2015b) wrote, summing up his views.

As his many innovative campaigns demonstrate, Bernays was an innovator and a creative genius. Whether it was his work for the Ivory Soap brand, when he created a children's soap carving contest that sold millions of bars of soap; the famous "Torches of Freedom" campaign for American Tobacco in 1929, in which he hired fashion models to smoke in public (then considered taboo for women) during New York's Easter parade; or his campaign for a "Hearty American Breakfast," which included eggs and bacon (Hormel was his client), he was all about the "big idea" (The Museum of Public Relations, n.d. a,b).

According to Larry Tye (2002), the author of *Father of Spin: Edward L. Bernays and the Birth of Public Relations*, Bernays was "the first to demonstrate for future generations of PR people how powerful their profession could be in shaping America's economic, political and cultural life."

Lesser known, but well appreciated within the PR industry, was the role his wife Doris E. Fleischman, a writer, feminist, and former editor of the *New York Tribune* played in his work. She was his partner in life and in business and took on many of the responsibilities of a PR executive behind the scenes for their clients as well as writing and editing books and articles on her own (Tye, 2002). Bernays and Fleischman were also active in promoting causes and charities—pioneering the concept of **pro bono work** in PR.

> **SOCIAL RESPONSIBILITY**

ARTHUR W. PAGE

The philosophy and approach of Arthur W. Page, a pioneer in the world of corporate PR and career executive at AT&T, is summed up in his statement: "All business in a democratic country begins with public permission and exists by public approval. If that is true, it follows that business should be cheerfully willing to tell the public what its policies are, what it is doing, and what it hopes to do. This seems practically a duty" (Block, n.d.). AT&T had a long history of pioneering the use of publicity to build its business. As far back as the early 1900s, the company hired the Publicity Bureau of Boston, one of the first PR agencies in the United States, to promote its products and services. One of the staff members on their account was James Ellsworth, whom the company later enticed to join them and create their first PR department at AT&T. Arthur Page was hired in 1927 by the president of AT&T as the company's first vice president of PR and appointed a corporate officer. He remained with the company until his retirement in 1948.

PR PERSONALITY

Paving the Way for Corporate Public Relations—Arthur W. Page and AT&T

Arthur W. Page, who served as vice president of PR at AT&T, is celebrated as the first corporate PR executive to hold a strategic senior management position. Prior to that, he had a long, successful run as the head of the magazine group of Doubleday Page, the publishing house founded by his father. He wrote often in *The World's Work* about the special obligations of corporations in a democratic society.

One day Page received a telephone call from Walter Gifford, the chief executive of AT&T. When the two met a few days later, Gifford asked Page if he would write a book about AT&T. Page declined, explaining that it might be a nice ego trip for management, but it wouldn't do the company any good. Page believed that reputation was earned by actions, not through publicity.

As their conversation drew to a close, Gifford asked Page if he would like to put his ideas into practice at AT&T. Page said yes but only if it would be a policy-making position. He became not only a member of senior management but also was elected to the AT&T board of directors and later served on several other corporate boards and as an advisor to several presidents of the United States.

The founding members of the Arthur W. Page Society, which was established in 1983 following the breakup of the Bell System, named the organization after Page. They extracted the seven Page principles from his lifetime of work and his writings, which have become guidelines

for modern-day PR. The first of these is "Tell the truth," and the second is "Prove it with action." Throughout his career, Page focused not only on what AT&T should *say* but also on what it should *do*. In a 1932 speech to the New York Telephone Company, Page explained his view of PR (Arthur W. Page Center, 1932):

> To begin with, our whole public relations effort depends on our service. If that isn't good, then there is no story we can tell that will do any good and make anybody believe in us, and it is furthest from the minds of the Public Relations Department to try to tell any story except the truth. Therefore, we can't start with anything but good service.

Page also said, "Your public relations are your relations with the public and the relations with the public, you know, occur where our people operating the business come into contact with the public." That was translated into the Page principle that says, "Remember that a company's true character is expressed by its people."

Today, Page Society members—corporate and nonprofit chief communication officers and PR agency CEOs—seek to live up to Page's legacy. They help their enterprises build a strong corporate character by aligning mission, purpose, values, culture, business model, strategy, and brand to create a company's unique, differentiating identity. In today's business environment, which is characterized by transparency and hyper-connectivity, the Page principles are more relevant than they were first articulated. ●

Roger Bolton is president of the Arthur W. Page Society.

Source: R. Bolton (personal communication, 2017).

OTHER INNOVATORS OF MODERN PUBLIC RELATIONS

While Ivy Lee, Edward Bernays, and Arthur Page were towering figures in the development of modern PR practice, others made significant contributions to the profession but are not as well known or celebrated. These innovators include George Creel, Amos Kendall, Leonne Baxter, and Elmer Davis in the political and governmental communications arena.

George Creel's work on behalf of the war effort (World War I) under President Woodrow Wilson was also groundbreaking for several reasons. Among Creel's many accomplishments was the creation of the "Four Minute Men" group, who traveled the country speaking to the public about World War I and supporting the president's positions and views (Creel, 1920). In those days the local movie theater was the gathering spot for communities across the country—especially on the weekends. However, the projectors in these theaters were manually operated, and the films had to be changed mid-movie. During this downtime—usually about four minutes—speakers from the U.S. Committee on Public Information would update moviegoers on current events and the progress of the war, thus the name, Four Minute Men. This effort is regarded as one of the first instances of a *speaking tour* to support a communications objective (Creel, 1920).

Other notable PR pioneers include Warren Cowan, whose firm Rogers and Cowan remains one of the leaders in entertainment PR today with a stable of global celebrities as clients, and Eleanor Lambert, a major figure in fashion PR who first introduced designers like Bill Blass and Calvin Klein and created the "Best Dressed List." Others, like Chester Berger, made major contributions in the planning and implementation of corporate PR. Burger pioneered the use of television news by PR professionals and advised companies, like AT&T, on how to package stories for the new medium—when it debuted in the 1950s (Gregory & Kirschenbaum, 2012).

TABLE 2.1

Notable Early Political Communicators

NAME	PROFESSION	CONTRIBUTION
George Creel	Headed U.S. Committee on Public Information during WWI	Use PR to sell liberty bonds and build the Red Cross
Amos Kendall	First White House press secretary	Worked for President Andrew Jackson in the 1830s
Leone Baxter	Founded the first political consulting firm in United States	Founded in 1933 with partner, Clem Whitaker, developing strategies still used today
Elmer Davis	Conceived and promoted WWII victory gardens	Worked for President Franklin D. Roosevelt to encourage citizens to grow their own vegetables to help the war effort

GROWTH OF THE PUBLIC RELATIONS AGENCY

>> **LO 2.2** **Explain the growth of the PR agency business model and the contributions of women and minority professionals**

No review of the history of modern PR would be complete without a discussion on the role of the PR agency business and the contributions of its early pioneers, including Harold Burson, Daniel J. Edelman, and John W. Hill. While there are many outstanding businesspeople who founded, or now head up, small and large PR firms or agencies, there is almost universal agreement among agency professionals that Burson, Edelman, and Hill are three of the pioneers and builders of the PR agency business.

HAROLD BURSON

Regarded by his peers, clients, and current and former employees as a legend in the agency business, Harold Burson began his PR career in the 1940s as a journalist working for the Armed Forces Radio Network. In this capacity he was assigned to cover the post-World War II International War Crimes Trial in Nuremberg, Germany, of Nazi officers and sympathizers. He founded his firm in 1953 with Bill Marsteller when they began working on the Rockwell manufacturing account. In the early 1960s the partners saw the potential of PR as a worldwide business and opened Burson-Marsteller's first overseas office in Geneva, Switzerland.

PRWeek, citing a recent survey of industry leaders, described Harold Burson as one of "the 21st century's most influential PR figures" (PRWeek, 2016b). Throughout its history, B-M has been viewed a great place to work and a leader in crisis communications and reputation management. Most famous among its work in this arena was the Johnson & Johnson Tylenol poisoning case in 1982 (see case study at end of chapter).

As with many major figures in the industry, B-M and Harold Burson are not without their critics. In the case of B-M, this was due to some controversial clients and assignments. These assignments include representing controversial government leaders in Nigeria, Argentina, and Indonesia; corporate clients facing crises like the Three Mile Island nuclear plant, Union Carbide, and the big tobacco companies; and companies seeking to discredit a competitor with negative media coverage, such as B-M client Facebook allegedly did with Google in 2011 (Benady, 2014).

Commenting on these controversies, Burson noted, "I believe that every institution, every person is entitled to have public relations representation. However, I do not believe I am compelled in any way or manner to be the one who provides that representation" (Benady, 2014). His easygoing manner, years of experience, and extensive global contacts have made Burson a beloved figure in the industry, and as such, his views on client service, staffing, and agency management are closely followed.

DANIEL J. EDELMAN

Dan Edelman founded his PR firm, Daniel J. Edelman, Inc. in 1952 and led its growth to the world's largest independent PR firm as ranked by fee income (PRWeek, 2016d). He began his career as a sports reporter in Poughkeepsie, New York, after World War II and became a news writer for CBS. Later he served as PR director for the Toni Company (hair and beauty products) before founding his firm in Chicago. The initial focus of the firm was on marketing communications or PR to support sales and new production

African American and Women Pioneers in the Agency Field

Moss Kendrix was a pioneer among African American PR professionals.

Bettmann/Getty Images

Although not as well known as Burson, Edelman, or Hill, other key figures in the PR agency field are also recognized as pioneers. These include Joseph V. Baker, Moss Kendrix, Barbara Hunter, Muriel Fox, and Inez Kaiser.

Joseph V. Baker

After working for the *Philadelphia Inquirer* as the first African American journalist (and also its city editor), in 1934 Baker opened the first black-owned PR firm in the United States. He went on to acquire significant accounts from large corporations and became the first black president of the Philadelphia PRSA chapter.

Moss Kendrix

An African American, Kendrix founded his own PR firm in Washington, DC, in 1944 to advise Coca-Cola and other major brands. He was instrumental in advising several large consumer product companies to stop using stereotypical images like Aunt Jemima and Uncle Ben in their advertising (The Museum of Public Relations, n.d.c).

Barbara Hunter

Hunter purchased the PR firm Dudley, Anderson Yutz (known as DAY) in the early 1960s, along with her sister Jeanne Schoonover, becoming the first female owners/proprietors of a major PR firm. Over the years, the sisters made DAY into a force in consumer PR and marketing communications. The firm, now called Hunter PR, is still in operation today.

Muriel Fox

Fox was the first female PR executive at Carl Byoir & Associates and later went on to work as the communications advisor to feminist icon and author Betty Friedan, who cofounded the National Organization for Women (NOW) and was its first president.

Inez Kaiser

Kaiser opened the first PR firm (in 1980) headed by an African American woman in the United States. Her firm, whose clients included Seven Up, Lever Brothers, and Sears Roebuck, was also the first African American–owned business in Kansas City, Missouri. A former home economics teacher who came late to her career in PR, Kaiser gave the following advice to young PR practitioners: "Always be thorough and honest with your clients, and try your best to develop personal relationships with them" (The Museum of Public Relations, 2016). ●

introductions. "He is credited by many as the father of marketing PR; he understood the potential of earned media to enhance the marketing message," Richard Edelman (2014) noted in a memorial speech to the Arthur Page Society in September 2014.

Dan Edelman is credited with creating the idea of a **media tour**, during which company spokespeople travel to meet with local media and promote a product or service through events, interviews, and public appearances. One of the earliest versions of this tactic was for his client Toni, where Edelman had worked before starting the firm. The veteran publicist sent six pairs of identical twins, one with a Toni home permanent and one with a salon permanent, on a tour of 72 cities to publicize the "Which Twin Has the Toni?" ad campaign (Wisner, 2012). The concept was very successful, earning extensive media coverage for the client, and media tours soon became commonplace across the PR industry. It is now a staple tactic used by PR pros to promote products and services as well as companies and issues.

Public Relations' Focus Differs by Organization

For the business community, media relations research, planning, and implementation are crucial in understanding public opinion and identifying market opportunities. As the media has grown and shifted, the need for media relations specialists to accomplish corporate goals has also grown. Whether it is the mainstream business media—like the *New York Times*, *Wall Street Journal*, or *Fortune* magazine; the television networks that grew to include cable news (CNN, MSNBC, etc.); and YouTube and Facebook or the countless trade publications covering every major trade from accounting to zoology—getting a firm's story told or broadcast on the news and defending its reputation are paramount.

For government agencies and elected officials, PR strategies and tactics are now critical tools in delivering information and government services to people more effectively. Plus, for elected officials, mounting election or reelection campaigns requires effective media and community outreach, deep research to understand public opinion, and efficient message delivery to reach voters.

Nonprofit organizations have benefited well with PR. Fund-raising is more successful, and campaigns have more impact through strategic PR. Working with the public and generating awareness via media coverage have become fundamental to a positive outcome. Digital media and social media have "democratized" the process of reaching the public, reduced costs, and increased efficiency. As a result most organizations have an active social media presence and understand it must be constantly updated.

Issue-based activist organizations like Greenpeace or Occupy Wall Street and political causes like Rock the Vote or the Conservative Political Action Conference (CPAC) have made effective use of PR strategies to advance their agendas. These groups have leveraged social media to develop coalitions, attract donations, and put pressure on government leaders.

Most recently, social media drove the Women's March on Washington, DC, held January 21, 2017, the day after President Trump's inauguration. The event drew close to a million protesters to the nation's capital and to cities and towns on all seven continents. The protest movement reportedly began with a Facebook post by a concerned woman in Hawaii and grew through "shares" and "likes" by others who felt similarly about the results of the 2016 election. After the event, all four of the women who led the effort were selected by *Time* magazine as among the 100 most influential people of 2016.

In addition to social media, activist groups have made effective use of traditional PR tactics including media relations, thought leadership, staged events, and original research to promote their causes and create awareness and conversation. These will be explored in greater detail in subsequent chapters. ●

As the firm grew Edelman expanded into all forms and disciplines of PR—corporate, public affairs, sustainability, employee communications, financial communications, social media, and of course, marketing communications. Edelman has encountered criticism for some of its client work as it has grown, much the same as its global competitors. For example, in 2015, the firm faced controversy over advocating for climate change at the same time it represented several so-called "climate change deniers", like the American Petroleum Institute (API). Soon after the firm resigned its work for the API, which was a multimillion-dollar account (Edelman 2015; Goldenberg, 2015). Although he is gone now, Edelman staffers believe that the spirit and philosophy of their founder is evident in their work and interactions with clients every day.

JOHN W. HILL

Hill, who would go on to establish Hill & Knowlton (H&K) in 1933, began his career as a newspaper reporter, editor, and financial columnist. He established his firm in 1927 in Cleveland, Ohio, and developed a clientele of banks, steel companies, and industrial companies operating in the Midwestern United States. The firm became known as Hill & Knowlton in 1933, when Donald Knowlton, a former client, joined the firm as a partner. One year later the partnership moved to New York to serve a major new client (the American Iron and Steel Institute [AISI]), and the beginnings of a major global firm were in place.

H&K was the first American PR firm to establish an office in Europe and, at its high point, was said to have a "hung out its shingle" in hundreds of countries around the world. In building his firm with Knowlton, Hill was known for a simple business philosophy guided by "the essential requirements for PR: integrity and truth; soundness of policies, decisions and acts, viewed in the light of the public interest and use of facts that are understandable, believable and presented to the public with imagination" (PRSA New York, 2016). As with other major firms, there have been controversial clients (e.g., Church of Scientology, the government of Kuwait, and the tobacco industry). However, the firm has also been recognized for its outstanding work for clients, promoting diversity, and being a good place to work by industry publications such as *PRWeek*.

PUBLIC RELATIONS COMES OF AGE

Following the path of these leaders, PR came of age and moved into an era of growth in the 1960s—both in the United States and around the world. Many experts attribute this to the booming economy in the post–World War II era, rapid advances in technology, and growth of the media—particularly television and eventually online—as well as more active and more politically aware citizens.

Another factor was the recognition by leaders in the business, government, and nonprofit communities of the potential for PR to help their businesses or organizations. They had witnessed firsthand the positive impact PR had in building support for the war effort and how Bernays, Lee, Page, and other early leaders had helped businesses build awareness and market share for their corporate clients.

This was also a period of social unrest and change, beginning in the 1960s, including the Civil Rights, the anti-Vietnam War, and women's liberation movements—all of which had high-profile activists adept in working with the media and shaping public opinion.

ORIGINS, DEFINITIONS, AND DRIVING FORCES OF CORPORATE SOCIAL RESPONSIBILITY

>> **LO 2.3** **Understand how social and environmental responsibility has become an integral part of PR**

How CSR became a major PR function can be understood best by looking at public calls for social responsibility and efforts to influence organizational behavior throughout history. In the United States, early movements for the rights of workers, shareholders, and customers versus corporate rights all help explain the history and evolution of CSR. David Chandler (2017) begins with the 18th century in a timeline of key CSR events, presented in the infographic (see Figure 2.1). It shows an early convergence of public concerns about the impact of business on society that grew exponentially until the present day.

SOCIAL RESPONSIBILITY

FIGURE 2.1

The History and Evolution of CSR

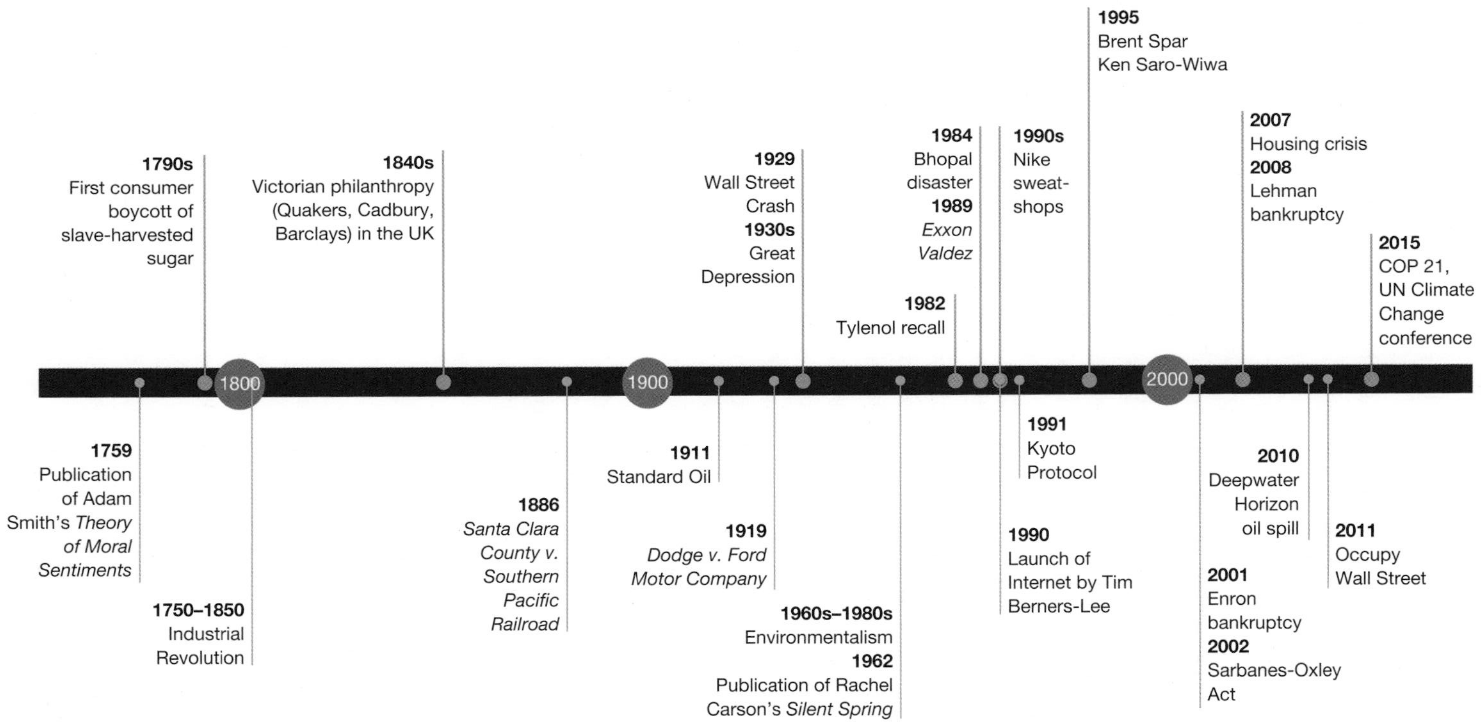

1759
Publication of Adam Smith's *Theory of Moral Sentiments*

1790s
First consumer boycott of slave-harvested sugar

1840s
Victorian philanthropy (Quakers, Cadbury, Barclays) in the UK

1750–1850
Industrial Revolution

1886
Santa Clara County v. Southern Pacific Railroad

1911
Standard Oil

1919
Dodge v. Ford Motor Company

1929
Wall Street Crash
1930s
Great Depression

1960s–1980s
Environmentalism
1962
Publication of Rachel Carson's *Silent Spring*

1982
Tylenol recall

1984
Bhopal disaster
1989
Exxon Valdez

1990s
Nike sweat-shops

1990
Launch of Internet by Tim Berners-Lee

1991
Kyoto Protocol

1995
Brent Spar
Ken Saro-Wiwa

2001
Enron bankruptcy
2002
Sarbanes-Oxley Act

2007
Housing crisis
2008
Lehman bankruptcy

2010
Deepwater Horizon oil spill

2011
Occupy Wall Street

2015
COP 21, UN Climate Change conference

1800   1900   2000

Source: Chandler (2017).

TABLE 2.2

Modern Evolution of Corporate Social Responsibility in the United States

TIME PERIOD	EVENT
1900 to 1950s	Corporate Power Questioned
1960s and 1970s	Business Addresses Social Issues
1980s and 1990s	Call for Business Ethics and Corporate Citizenship
21st Century	Standards and Best Practices Established

In the early 20th century, a backlash against business began to arise. Large, powerful corporations were accused of lacking concern for employees, community, or society. In 1914 Henry Ford doubled the wages of his Model T assembly line workers—however, he did it specifically to secure his business. In 1929 Eastman Kodak Company offered profit sharing, retirement bonuses, a pension plan, and sickness benefits to its workers.

Philanthropy was another early form of CSR, and from 1930 onwards, corporations began to be seen as institutions that had social obligations. Howard Bowen was one of the first to define social responsibility (SR), citing the obligations of business to pursue policies, make decisions, and follow actions that are desirable for society. He has been called the father of corporate social responsibility.

CSR grew significantly in the 1960s and accelerated in the 1970s. The Civil Rights Movement, consumerism, and environmentalism affected society's expectations of business. People called for the business world to be more proactive in ceasing to cause societal problems and starting to participate in solving societal problems. Legal mandates required equal employment opportunity, product safety, and worker safety. Business philanthropy increased, as did employee improvements, customer relations, and stockholder relations. Businesses also addressed minority hiring and training, environmental concerns, support of education and the arts, urban renewal, and community affairs (Eilbirt & Parket, 1973; Holmes, 1976). Companies began to plan for and organize CSR, assessing their social performance and adopting corporate social policy and strategy.

In the 1980s and 1990s many issues rose to the surface. These issues grew to include businesses' impact on environmental pollution, employment discrimination, consumer abuses, employee health and safety, quality of work life, deterioration of urban life, and questionable or abusiveness practices of multinational corporations. Concerns for **business ethics** arose due to notorious instances of corporate wrongdoing, for example, Union Carbide's 1984 disaster in Bhopal and the *Exxon Valdez* oil spill in 1989. CSR then evolved into subfields of corporate social performance, sustainability, corporate citizenship, and the concept of stakeholder theory. Philanthropy expanded considerably, and CSR became part of business practice. Many early adopters of significant CSR programs include The Body Shop, Ben & Jerry's, Patagonia, Johnson & Johnson, Nike, IBM, and McDonald's.

The 21st century established SR standards and best practices. In 2000, 44 businesses signed the United Nation's Global Compact that set standards on human rights, workers' rights, environmental stewardship, and anti-corruption policies. By 2016 more than 9,100 had signed. Well into the first few decades of the 2000s, CSR was moving toward full integration with strategic management and corporate governance (Carroll, 2008).

PR News Award for Best Corporate Social Responsibility Annual Report

Each year *PR News*, one of the leading publications covering the PR industry and the sponsor of numerous workshops and recognition events, sponsors the CSR Awards competition. The awards, which culminate in a major event at the National Press Club in Washington, DC, have more than 20 categories where companies and agencies submit their CSR work for review by a panel of distinguished judges.

Best Annual Report on CSR Activity

One of the key categories, and an area where PR professionals are often called in to assist, is the annual report on sustainability or CSR. In some cases this can be part of the corporate annual report (a yearly document required of publicly traded companies), or it can be a separate document. In any case it is a key document in which organizations and companies report on their CSR activities to the community and employees.

Raising Voices: Viacom 2015 Social Impact Review Viacom Wins 2016 Award

At the 2016 awards ceremony, the winner in this category was Viacom. A major global entertainment company, Viacom's media networks, including Nickelodeon, Comedy Central, MTV, VH1, Spike, BET, CMT, TV Land, Nick at Nite, Nick Jr., Channel 5 (UK), Logo, Nicktoons, TeenNick, and Paramount Channel, together reach a cumulative 3.4 billion television subscribers worldwide.

Viewers, Employees, and Management Involved

In selecting it as the winner, the judges noted that Viacom's report reflects "its deep commitment to telling viewers' stories, amplifying their voices to educate and empower people to make a difference. Through Viacom's on-the-ground efforts, volunteers' time and skills, its employees feel valued and heard, and the company operates its business in ethical and sustainable ways."

"Viacommunity" Celebrated

Viacom's CSR efforts are detailed in a 100-page report that covers its "Viacommunity" initiatives and achievements for the year ending December 31, 2014. President and CEO Philippe Dauman explained that similar to its global business, Viacom's social initiatives are constantly accelerating. "To ensure our efforts are at their strongest and push further forward, we have laid out a series of social responsibility goals for the company," he said.

Opportunities for Women, Young People, and Minorities

A few highlights, he explained, include partnering with external organizations to support increased opportunities for women, young people, and underrepresented minorities in tech; expanding employee volunteerism to 100,000 hours; and increasing and expanding social change moments across Viacom's networks. ●

Source: PR News (2016).

THE FUTURE OF PUBLIC RELATIONS

>> **LO 2.4** **Summarize the challenges PR will face in the years to come**

Looking ahead, what are the key trends to watch and understand to become valued as a strategic advisor to your clients, companies, and candidates? For the PR industry specifically, there are a few key issues worth examining: the growth and impact of digital media, the increased emphasis on measurement and return on investment (ROI), the integration of PR and marketing, the integration of PR and CSR, the need to improve diversity and inclusion, and globalization.

GROWTH AND IMPACT OF DIGITAL MEDIA

Without question, digital media is changing the way traditional PR is performed and, in the process, raising the expectations of management and clients for results. Recent research indicates that this is not an easy challenge. More people are online more often and consuming news and information, and fewer are getting their news from

With the growth in social media, many companies, including Procter & Gamble, have established social media command centers like this one.

Richard Levine/Corbis/Getty Images

the traditional newspapers and cable and broadcast news stations. This will require a whole new set of skills for tomorrow's PR professionals.

According to the Pew Research's Social Media Usage 2005–2015 study, nearly two-thirds of American adults (65%) use social networking sites, up from 7% when Pew Research Center began systematically tracking social media in 2005. This is a tenfold increase in usage in the past 10 years (Perrin, 2015). Key statistics from Pew's research on media and news consumption, show the following: A majority of U.S. adults—62%—get their news on social media, and 18% do so often, compared to 49% of U.S. adults in 2012, who reported seeing news on social media (Gottfried & Shearer, 2016).

INCREASED EMPHASIS ON MEASUREMENT AND RETURN ON INVESTMENT (ROI)

With the advent of social media and more sophisticated measurement techniques now available for PR activity, measurement of PR campaigns has become more commonplace. For years, the PR industry relied on unscientific and barely defensible measurement tools such as advertising value equivalency (AVE; e.g., what purchasing the airtime or space in the publication would have cost) and/or tracking media impressions (calculations based on the circulation or viewership ratings of a media outlet). Management and clients have become sophisticated and are demanding measurement of specific outcomes (vs. outputs) and evidence of ROI for company resources allocated to PR activity.

"The single most important thing people need to remember when measuring the impact of a communications program is their definition of impact, which should come from the initial, measurable objectives of the program. Often, clients want to dive in and measure before we are all clear what we are measuring and why…. And, this is why, I believe many PR efforts fail—they don't have objectives to guide the strategies and tactics," Forrest Anderson (2014), a leading PR research expert and founding member of the Institute for PR's Measurement Commission.

INTEGRATION OF PUBLIC RELATIONS AND MARKETING

One of the more significant trends in recent years is the integration of marketing and product-related publicity into a field that is being called integrated marketing communications (IMC). In this concept, PR, advertising, product development, and research professionals all work together to identify a need for a product, assess competitive activity or presence, identify and understand the target audience, and reach out to them via traditional and social media platforms.

The concept of integrated marketing communications, as described by Phillip Kotler, a noted professor and author of several foundational books on marketing, involves coordinating the promotion elements to deliver a "clear, consistent, and compelling message about the organization and its products" (Kotler & Gertner, 2002). It calls for more than just developing a product, pricing it, and making it available to customers, he notes. "Companies must also communicate with current and prospective customers, and what they communicate should not be left to chance. All their communications efforts must be blended into a consistent and coordinated communications program. Just as good communication is important in building and maintaining any kind of relationship, it is a crucial element in a company's efforts to build profitable customer relationships."

INTERSECTION OF PUBLIC RELATIONS AND CORPORATE SOCIAL RESPONSIBILITY

While the practice of CSR has come a long way since its inception in the 1970s, some companies are just now beginning to capitalize on the bottom-line benefits and reputation enhancement potential that strategic CSR can produce. John Browne, former CEO of BP, and Robin Nutall of McKinsey, suggest in an article published by McKinsey in March of 2013, that companies may be failing to deliver on their CSR efforts due to poorly "integrated external engagement" (Browne & Nuttall, 2013).

SOCIAL RESPONSIBILITY

"In practice, most companies have relied on three tools for external engagement: a full-time CSR team in the head office, some high-profile (but relatively cheap) initiatives, and a glossy annual review of progress" write Browne and Nuttall (2013). In their view, more effort and resources are merited, given the positive returns of strategic CSR.

This is an area for focus and emphasis in the coming years. Many if not all company or client stakeholders are expecting leadership in CSR activities and initiatives as they seek to identify the winners and losers in this critical corporate activity. The expectations have grown along with the CSR field, and the role of the PR profession going forward in this will be paramount.

U.S. Secretary of State's Award for Corporate Excellence

In 1999 the secretary of state of the United States, Madeline Albright, established the ACE Awards program to "recognize the important role U.S. businesses play abroad as good corporate citizens" (U.S. Department of State, n.d., para 1).

Global CSR Activity of U.S. Companies Highlighted

In making the announcement of the new program, Secretary Albright said in a statement, "The [ACE] award sends a strong signal of the [State] Department's commitment to further corporate social responsibility, innovation, exemplary practices and democratic values worldwide. The ACE awards help define America as a positive force in the world. It highlights our increasing outreach to the business community, our public private partnerships and our public diplomacy efforts."

Awards Process

The awards winners are chosen from companies nominated by the local heads of U.S. diplomatic missions worldwide. Following extensive research, evaluation, and feedback from the local citizens, business, and local government officials, the award winners are chosen in two categories—multinational companies and small to medium enterprises. The CSR engagement of U.S. companies in countries around the world that are recognized by the ACE Award illustrate the range and impact of SR and sustainability being conducted globally by U.S. companies internationally.

35 Companies Recognized Since 1999

Since the launch of the awards, more than 35 companies have been recognized, including CSR leaders like P&G (2011) for its work in Nigeria and Pakistan and Plantronics (2013) for its work in Mexico (U.S. Department of State, n.d.). Some examples include the following:

P&G worked to improve the water supply in Nigeria through community education and providing water purification technology. In Pakistan, P&G was recognized for the humanitarian assistance it provided (drinking water, hygiene products, medical care, and laundry services) after extreme flooding devastated the country.

Plantronics built a major lab in Mexico and set up agreements with local colleges and trade schools to provide work-school collaboration and training as well as create health and wellness initiatives for the workers and their families.

CSR Activity Promotes U.S. Values Worldwide

Former Secretary of State Hillary Clinton summed up the importance of the awards and of CSR by U.S. companies abroad, saying, "for many people around the world, the most direct contact they will have with the United States is through American businesses. . . . That's how they learn what we stand for, who we are and what aspirations we share. So, this is really very important, not just to the bottom line but to our national security, our interests and values and the future of our global leadership" (Clinton, 2012, para 7). ●

For more information on the program, visit the State Department site: www.state.gov/e/eb/ace/

IMPROVE DIVERSITY AND INCLUSION

In a multicultural society the expectation is that PR professionals will understand and respect diverse racial, religious, and sexual orientation differences and reflect that in the strategies and tactics. For employers the industry is well past the point where there is an excuse for a lack of diversity. Whereas in the past the contributions of female and minority professionals might have been overlooked, today companies and PR firms are actively seeking diversity in their employee base to more accurately reflect the marketplace they are trying to serve. While that is a positive step, clearly more work needs to be done.

According to the Bureau of Labor Statistics (n.d.), the demographics of advertising, marketing, and PR jobs in the United States indicate that 8.7% are African Americans/Blacks and 15.3% are Hispanics/Latinos. This compares to the demographics of the U.S. population that is 14% black and 17% Hispanic for the same period. The situation in the United Kingdom (England, Scotland, Wales, and Northern Ireland) is equally low. According to the UK Office of National Statistics, 14% of the British population have minority or ethnic backgrounds, but only 8% of UK PR practitioners identify themselves as being from these groups, according to research from the Public Relations Consultants Association (PRCA) (Stimson, 2013).

Many industry groups—including PRSA, the International Association of Business Communicators (IABC), the Arthur W. Page Society, and the Council of PR firms—recognize that the industry must have employees who reflect the backgrounds and experiences of the people they are trying to reach if they are to be successful.

Clearly, to be effective at delivering messages, motivating behavior, and influencing public opinion, PR professionals (and companies) need to be representative of the audiences they are trying to reach. Simply translating copy or messages into different languages or using different models or celebrities to endorse products is not sufficient.

GLOBALIZATION

Given the rate of change in the world and the ever-present nature of social media, the world is now a very small, interconnected place. Events—good or bad—in one part of the world become known, discussed, and debated throughout the rest of the world in a matter of minutes. Each day brings another example of this new reality. There are no unique, "local" markets anymore, and PR professionals must be aware and capable of managing this reality. Cision, a media monitoring service and source of periodic thought leadership, said in a recent post, "PR is facing challenges. But they're NOT insurmountable," and suggests that "glocalization—thinking globally and acting locally—is the new normal" (Mireles, 2014).

Stakeholders all over the world, and especially in key markets, are expecting a meaningful relationship with companies with whom they do business or who operate in their country. The media in these areas expects a responsive and culturally aware attitude and a level of transparency and accountability that was not the case a few years ago. The penalty for not meeting these requirements can be harsh—both in terms of sales and profits as well as reputation, government support, or market acceptance. Strategic CSR, as we will learn later, is a key tool to meet this new global reality.

SCENARIO OUTCOME

At the beginning of this chapter, you were presented with a scenario and a challenge: put yourself in the place of Ivy Lee in 1904 and make recommendations to the senior management of the Pennsylvania Railroad to improve its media response to rail accidents. Specifically you were asked to think in terms of how the company would be perceived if it continued to be unresponsive and standoffish to the media and the public in the event of an accident. Several questions are suggested to guide your thinking as you read through the chapter:

▸ How would you convince the company to be more open and responsive to the public?

▸ What tactics would you use to manage the crisis?

▸ What role should media relations play?

▶ How would you minimize the reputation damage to the railroad?

▶ How would this case be different today versus in the early 1900s?

As you think about your responses and recommendations, and discuss them with your classmates, consider how Ivy Lee and his partner responded.

What did they recommend? In a breakthrough strategy for the time, Lee convinced company management to be more open and responsive to the media and the public when the next incident occurred. Specifically he recommended the company create a plan to set up a press room near the scene of the accident and quickly issue a news release (which was a new concept) with details on what happened and what was being done in response; and he advocated taking select reporters to the site of the accident to see firsthand what had happened and how the railroad was managing the situation (Cutlip, 2013a, b).

The company adopted these and other recommendations, and to the surprise of many except Lee, the company received more balanced press coverage of the next accident, and their reputation was not as damaged as it might have been. This became even more important as the company expanded its operations nationally.

This scenario illustrates how visionary Ivy Lee was in helping business leaders realize the power of strategic communications, including working closely with the media and government officials in a crisis to preserve and protect corporate reputation.

WRAP UP

This chapter covered a lot of territory and many years. You learned how communications has been a part of civilization as long as there have been different groups of people—rulers and subjects, activists and citizens, politicians and voters, and businesses and customers—trying to understand and influence each other.

You read short profiles of some of the well-known leaders of the modern era of PR, including Bernays, Lee, and Page, and you discovered other PR professionals who made major contributions. You then took an in-depth look at the PR agency business and its pioneers as well as lesser known, but equally important, women and African Americans who made significant contributions.

You were also introduced to the concept of SR and traced its evolution into a worldwide movement. The chapter closed with a look at the issues impacting PR in the next five to 10 years and the social issues that will challenge PR professionals throughout the rest of the 21st century.

KEY TERMS

Business Ethics: A process or theory in which companies are expected to conduct their business in an open and honest and way to gain market acceptance and build a solid reputation, **45**

Media Tour: A media relations tactic that involves a multi-city tour, usually with a celebrity or other spokesperson, to promote a new product or service, **41**

Modern Era of PR: The time period beginning in the early 1900s when PR moved beyond the era of the publicists and promoters to the current era of applying the strategies and tactics advanced by Edward Bernays and others to corporations and organizations, **34**

Press Event/Publicity Stunt: An event or activity specifically designed to draw attention to a product, service, or celebrity that creates lots of news coverage or publicity, **33**

Pro Bono Work: Professional work undertaken voluntarily and without expectation of payment, **37**

The issue of diversity and inclusion continues to be a challenge for the PR profession. Since the early 1900s, minorities and women have been underrepresented or underappreciated for their contributions. The problem is evident by the disconnect between the demographics of the U.S. population and the employment trends in the PR industry.

As a reminder, in the section of this chapter outlining key challenges for the future of the PR profession, you read the following statistic: The demographic breakdown of advertising, marketing and public relations jobs in the United States indicates that 8.7% are African Americans/Blacks and 15.3% are Hispanics/Latinos. This compares to a population in the United States that is 14% black and 17% Hispanic.

Your challenge is to break into groups, discuss this issue, and develop one or two proposals on how PR can improve on its diversity and inclusion performance. This might take the form of CSR initiatives between companies catering to minority customers or women and/or affiliations with nonprofits such as the United Negro College Fund, La Raza, or the National Organization for Women.

Prepare a short memo listing your ideas and an outline of a plan of action to begin implementation.

WRITE LIKE A PRO

In this chapter, you read a lot about the history of PR, notably the modern era, and some industry leaders whose contributions helped create the PR practices of today.

You were also introduced to The Museum of Public Relations, a relatively new organization in New York City that highlights the leaders of the early days of PR. There are also artifacts exhibited there from other professionals—many of them people of color or women—who were pioneers as well.

Prepare a short backgrounder that summarizes the work of a featured pioneer—preferably one of the lesser known personalities that appeals to you. The document should be suitable in style and format to be submitted to a reporter seeking coverage or to a potential donor to encourage their interest in the museum and its mission.

Note: A backgrounder is a short overview that provides background information to encourage the reader to learn more about a given topic. In this case, you could describe the purpose and history of the museum, and your chosen personality in detail, and then summarize the information and materials available there to learn more.

You should start by visiting the museum's website at www.prmuseum.org.

SOCIAL RESPONSIBILITY CASE STUDY

Edward Bernays and Light's Golden Jubilee

The late 1920s were an era in which PR was coming under heavy scrutiny and attack as the public still looked upon it as sensationalism and a menace to the integrity of the press. Edward Bernays was looking for an opportunity to prove to the public and his critics that PR was indeed an honorable profession. In May of 1929, General Electric and Westinghouse approached Bernays with the task of handling the 50th anniversary of the first incandescent light, a celebration that would honor both Thomas Edison and his invaluable invention.

Research and Strategy

The campaign, titled Light's Golden Jubilee, began in May, with a massive publicity effort and ended in late October with a massive event. Six months before the dedication ceremony, stories about Edison and the history of the incandescent light were sent out to the managing editors of local and national newspapers. The letterhead included the names of such supporters as President Hoover and Henry Ford. The American press joined in, newspapers and magazines began to run their own stories on the event, and towns across America planned ceremonies in honor of Edison.

After Bernays approached the postmaster general, a commemorative stamp for the anniversary was issued. Bernays planned several smaller events such as the Diamond Jubilee, a light extravaganza, which took place in Atlantic City.

Execution

On October 21, President Hoover dedicated the Edison Institute of Technology in Dearborn, Michigan. The event was attended by notables such as Henry Ford, Orville Wright, John D. Rockefeller, Jr., and Madame Curie. Press representatives included members of the wire services, weekly newsreels, and photographers. Members of 15 of the most important newspapers in the country were invited as well as several leading journalists. Edward Bernays had organized an event that had shown the world the potential of positive PR.

Evaluation

Edward Bernays had organized an event that had shown the world the potential of effective PR. It was one of his greatest triumphs, becoming a landmark in PR history as well as in his own long and distinguished career.

Bernays later said, "Public relations had passed a milestone on the road to public understanding and respect" (Bernays, 2015a). For here was a coordinated, planned effort that demonstrated that the consent of the public to an idea could be engineered if the time for the idea had come.

ENGAGE

▸ Explore GE's CSR website at www.gesustainability.com to discover the breadth of the company's "alignment of business strategy to meet societal needs."

▸ Explore GE's Ecomagination initiative and its numerous innovations. How are employees involved?

DISCUSS

▸ In the case, Bernays is quoted as saying, "Public relations had passed a milestone on the road to public understanding and respect." Do you think this was premature at the time? Is it still true, or does PR need to constantly justify itself?

▸ If you were planning a similar event for GE or another innovative technology company today, how might you factor in a CSR/sustainability angle to a celebration of this nature, for example, the anniversary of a technological breakthrough?

▸ Similarly, how might social media be used today to mark such an occasion?

▸ How would you engage the employees of GE more in the celebration?

SOCIAL RESPONSIBILITY CASE STUDY

Johnson & Johnson's Tylenol Crisis

M-M advised Johnson & Johnson during the now-famous Tylenol crisis—a case regarded as a classic and historical example of managing a crisis.

In the fall of 1982, packages of Tylenol Extra-Strength already on store shelves were opened, and cyanide-laced capsules were randomly placed in them by an unidentified individual or individuals. The containers were resealed and put back on the shelves of several pharmacies and food stores in the Chicago area.

The poison capsules were subsequently purchased, and seven unsuspecting people died. Johnson & Johnson, parent company of McNeil Consumer Products Company, which makes

Tylenol, suddenly, and with no warning, had to explain to the world why its trusted product was suddenly killing people (Ten Berge, 1990).

Research and Strategy

Robert Andrews, assistant director for PR at Johnson & Johnson at the time recalls how the company reacted in the first days of the crisis:

> We got a call from a Chicago news reporter. He told us that the medical examiner there had just given a press conference-people were dying from poisoned Tylenol. He wanted our comment. As it was the first knowledge we had here in this department, we told him we knew nothing about it. In that first call we learned more from the reporter than he did from us. (Ten Berge, 1990)

Johnson & Johnson Chair James Burke reacted to the media coverage by forming a seven-member strategy team and he engaged their PR agency, which was Burson-Marsteller. The strategy guidance to the agency from Burke was, first, "How do we protect the people?" and, second, "How do we save this product?"

Execution

Johnson & Johnson, acting on the advice of its agency and internal team moved ahead—stopping the production and advertising of Tylenol and withdrawing all Tylenol capsules from the store shelves in Chicago and the surrounding area. After finding two more contaminated bottles elsewhere, Johnson & Johnson ordered a national withdrawal of every capsule (Broom, Center, & Cutlip, 1994).

By withdrawing all Tylenol, even though there was little chance of discovering more cyanide laced tablets, Johnson & Johnson showed that they were not willing to risk the public's safety, even if it cost the company millions of dollars. The result was the public viewing Tylenol as the unfortunate victim of a malicious crime (Broom et al., 1994).

Subsequently, Johnson & Johnson announced the creation of new triple safety seal packaging with a press conference at the manufacturer's headquarters. Tylenol became the first product in the industry to use the new tamper-resistant packaging just six months after the crisis occurred (Ten Berge, 1990).

Evaluation

Throughout the crisis more than 100,000 separate news stories ran in U.S. newspapers, and there were hundreds of hours of national and local television coverage. A post-crisis study by Johnson & Johnson said that more than 90% of the American population had heard of the Chicago deaths due to cyanide-laced Tylenol within the first week of the crisis. Two news clipping services found more than 125,000 news clippings on the Tylenol story. One of the services reported this story had been given the widest U.S. news coverage to date since the assassination of President John F. Kennedy (Kaplan, 2005).

Scholars and PR practitioners have come to recognize Johnson & Johnson's handling of the Tylenol crisis as the top example for success when confronted with a threat to an organization's existence. Ten Berge (1990, p. 19) lauds the case in the following manner, "The Tylenol crisis is without a doubt the most exemplary case ever known in the history of crisis communications. Any business executive, who has ever stumbled into a public relations ambush, ought to appreciate the way Johnson & Johnson responded to the Tylenol poisonings. They have effectively demonstrated how major business has to handle a disaster."

ENGAGE

▸ Explore Johnson & Johnson's CSR website at www.jnj.com/caring/citizenship-sustainability to see how it communicates what it's achieved.

▸ Drawing from its website, put together a list of the internal and external stakeholders touched by its CSR. How are employees involved?

DISCUSS

▸ In the Tylenol poisoning case, there is no discussion of how the news and the company's response were communicated to Johnson & Johnson's employees. While this no doubt happened then, how would you recommend a company faced with a similar crisis now manage its internal messaging?

▸ Should the company have considered reworking the packaging and handling of all its over-the-counter medications? Or was this just a random incident?

▸ If you worked for a competitor of Johnson & Johnson, how might you have recommended your company respond? What, if anything, should your company have done to make sure it was not the next victim of this criminal behavior?

Source: Crisis Communications Strategies (n.d.).

VIDEO CASE

Red Bull Sky Dive: Publicity Stunt

In 2012, Red Bull sponsored sky diver Felix Baumgartner's attempt to complete the highest sky dive on record. On October 14, Baumgartner rode a helium balloon into the stratosphere and jumped from a height of 39 kilometers. A video of Baumgartner's jump, in which Red Bull's branding is prominent, has been viewed on YouTube more than 40 million times.

Compare Red Bull's PR efforts in this case to P. T. Barnum's strategies promoting his circus in the 1800s.

VIDEO

1. What is the value of a publicity stunt of the type Red Bull conducted with Baumgartner?

2. If you were working in PR for Red Bull at the time, what strategies would you use to publicize Baumgartner's jump?

iStock.com/DNY59

3

Ethics and Law in Public Relations

Learning Objectives

3.1   Identify ethical issues in PR and explain the three moral guidelines

3.2   Survey professional codes of ethics and describe the responsibilities of the individual practitioner

3.3   Understand key legal issues confronting PR practitioners and identify the links among social responsibility, ethics, and law

Scenario

"Doing Good" in the Face of Cultural Norms

Nicaragua is the poorest country in Central America and second poorest in the Western Hemisphere. It has vast underemployment and poverty, particularly impacting poor, rural, and indigenous people. Widespread deforestation destroyed its rain forest in the 1970s and 1980s—with the goal of converting it to agricultural land. Yet the shallow rain forest soils could not sustain intensive agriculture. The land was finally turned over to pastureland, but in another doomed twist of fate, non-native cattle caused severe compaction of the soils.

Attempts at agriculture in the Central American rain forest left much of the land deforested. EcoPlanet Bamboo saw both a business and ethical opportunity and began growing and harvesting sustainability-certified commercial bamboo in Nicaragua.

De Agostini/Getty Images

EcoPlanet Bamboo stepped in. A U.S.-owned bamboo plantation and processing company, EcoPlanet Bamboo (EPB) began to regenerate the degraded land that was once lush tropical rain forest. Its cofounder and CEO, Troy Wiseman, calls it an example of "conscious capitalism"—approaching business from an ethical standpoint that generates value for all stakeholders, including both people and the environment.

The company dedicates a minimum of 20% of its plantations as a natural habitat that protects remaining standing forest and associated biodiversity. EPB has a strong culture of equal opportunity and focuses on empowering women, placing them in both unskilled and managerial positions. In 2014 it was honored by the U.S. secretary of state with the Award for Corporate Excellence (ACE).

The situation. As the only sustainability certified commercial bamboo company on the planet, it is not only providing a solution that reduces deforestation and restores degraded and marginal land but also provides hundreds of jobs to communities suffering from abject poverty and a lack of opportunity. It is also reversing the effects of global climate change through the sequestration and storage of atmospheric carbon dioxide.

The company employs 300 local workers, of which approximately 27% are women, a stunning statistic for Central America. And the jobs EPB creates are permanent and long term. Although Nicaragua, of all Central American countries, has made the greatest impact in narrowing its gender gap in the formal employment sector, women in Nicaragua remain highly disenfranchised. Statistics from 2015 show that only 18% of Nicaraguan women attended a university, and the gender gap index remained at 78% (with 100% showing gender equality).

As you read this chapter, consider the following:

You have been newly hired as EPB's first public relations manager and have two major tasks:

1. You identify specific needs between the company and its local employees: to educate them in the ethical mission of the company (its eight internal policies and 10 social and environmental sustainability principles), communicate all the positive benefits of its operation to members of the local community, as well as build pride in the company, helping with employee recruitment and retention.

   - How will you approach this communication need considering the employees are from rural communities and are likely undereducated with low literacy?

2. During its first year of operations, while still becoming established into the local culture and context, the company promotes its first female to a managerial field position. About 80% of the male workforce protests by refusing to show up for work and demanding her removal.

   - What type of response and communication should address this situation?

To find guidance in handling sensitive issues like this, you'll need to engage in the following discussion of ethics, ethical issues, and ethical decision-making.

In this chapter you will learn how ethical concerns and legal issues impact the practice of PR. As a practitioner, you'll be confronted with many decisions based not only on rules and expectations but also on the possible outcomes affecting various publics and the resulting degrees of harm versus good. Knowing in advance what might be the negative results of a decision will help guide your actions.

This chapter first reviews the main ethical philosophies relevant to PR and also takes a magnifying glass to the professional codes of ethics. The codes are the standards by which you'll practice and that provide you with guideposts to help with decisions. Case studies help illustrate how companies are striving to operate ethically and PR's role in assisting in that effort. You'll also learn how ethical lapses lead to reputation loss and how PR and CSR help recovery. The chapter also guides you on how to make important ethical decisions when serving your organization or client.

You'll also become familiar with the most common legal concerns that should flash warning signals to any PR practitioner: the First Amendment, defamation, disclosure, privacy, and copyright. The takeaway lesson is to vigilantly respect legal parameters when serving your organization.

ETHICS IN PUBLIC RELATIONS

>> **LO 3.1** **Identify ethical issues in PR and explain the three moral guidelines**

Ethics is the study of what is right and wrong, fair and unfair, and how we should make decisions. PR practitioners have power in both management and communication decisions to shape society—providing information, forming attitudes, and encouraging behaviors. With power comes the obligation to their organization, to their stakeholders, and to themselves—as well as to the public in general—to perform ethically.

$SAGE edge™

Master the content
edge.sagepub.com/page

PR practitioners hold a unique internal and external perspective—knowing and understanding the organization itself as well as the multiple publics it impacts. This broad understanding is developed through constantly nurtured relationships and open, effective communication. They are the strategic link between the organization and key stakeholders, with two broad areas of critical responsibility:

▸ An obligation to function ethically

▸ An opportunity to serve as ethics counsel to the organization

PUBLIC RELATIONS MIX-UPS AND ETHICAL DEFICITS

The profession can be misunderstood as simply a one-way message-pushing service that promotes only the good sides of a product, service, or entity. You've likely heard the phrase "PR spin" to describe persuasive communication or "spin doctor" in reference to a persuasive communicator. This language suggests PR practitioners intend to make ideas, products, events, politicians, and so on seem better than they really are. This misconception of PR as a practice of manipulation can be attributed to the profession's early history; its portrayal in film, television, and news reporting; and also some well-publicized cases of unethical clients and ethically questionable services provided by some PR firms.

Actress Kim Cattrall played Samantha Jones, the owner of a PR firm on the television show *Sex and the City*, which first aired in 1998 and is still in reruns. She was seen as a poster child for the industry, stereotyping the PR professional as self-centered and frivolous, and focused on celebrity management and planning star-studded events and glamorous parties.

Getty Images

For example, after the federal government's multibillion-dollar bailout of multinational insurer AIG in 2008, the following year MSNBC's Rachel Maddow reported some of the money was used to hire PR firm Burson-Marsteller (B-M) to "shine up" AIG's image. Harold Burson, considered one of the founders of the PR industry (as you read in Chapter 2), launched B-M in 1953. It then developed an expertise in the field of reputation and crisis management.

In 1982 B-M was credited with creating the template for crisis management by guiding Johnson & Johnson's response to the Tylenol deaths. As you read in the case study "Johnson & Johnson's Tylenol Poisoning Crisis" in Chapter 2, seven people in metropolitan Chicago died due to ingesting capsules laced with cyanide due to criminal tampering. B-M advised the company to remove all products from the market, stop advertising, and keep communication open and available.

Today B-M is one of the top 10 global public relations and communications firms.

On her MSNBC news broadcast, Maddow described B-M in the following set of questions (MSNBC, 2009):

▸ Who is B-M? Well, let me put it this way. When Blackwater killed those 17 Iraqi civilians in Baghdad, they called B-M. When there was a nuclear meltdown at Three Mile Island, Bobcock and Wilcox, who built that plant, called B-M.

▶ After the Bhopal chemical disaster that killed thousands of people in India, Union Carbide called B-M. Romanian dictator, Nicolae Ceausescu—B-M. The government of Saudi Arabia, three days after 9/11—B-M. The military junta that overthrew the government of Argentina in 1976, the generals dialed B-M.

▶ The government of Indonesia, accused of genocide in East Timor—B-M.

▶ The government of Nigeria accused of genocide in Biafra—B-M. Philip Morris—B-M. Silicone breast implants—B-M. The government of Colombia, trying to make all those dead union organizers not get in the way of a new trade deal—they called B-M.

▶ Do you remember Aqua Dots, little toy beads coated with something that turned into the date-rape drug, when kids put the beads in their mouths and all those kids ended up in comas? Yes, even the date-rape Aqua Dots people called B-M.

Maddow concluded, "When evil needs public relations, evil has Burson-Marsteller on speed dial."

B-M's CEO Mark Penn addressed his employees (Gordon, 2009) in an internal memo, clarifying the work for AIG "has nothing to do with 'burnishing their image' but is all about helping this company handle the massive volume of media, government and employee interest in their situation." What about the other controversial clients? Penn wrote, "Our work for Aqua Dot was to help remove a dangerous product off the shelves as quickly as possible."

Alluding to the Maddow segment, Penn clarified, "Just like lawyers and management consultants, PR firms are often called in to help when companies face difficult problems. Our role is crucial to companies operating in open and transparent business and media environments.... We always counsel our clients to be open and honest."

In a later interview (Benady, 2014), Harold Burson admitted some mistakes, such as following State Department advice to help the Argentine junta (which eventually murdered and disappeared more than 30,000 citizens). He explained other client controversies as mischaracterized: working for Romania before the leader Ceausescu became a tyrant and representing Nigeria as a legitimate country engaged in a civil war (he alleged the Biafrans themselves misused PR by propagating myths).

CONTEMPORARY PUBLIC RELATIONS SERVES THE PUBLIC GOOD

Since its beginning less than 100 years ago, the PR profession in the United States has experienced negative misperceptions of its responsibilities and practices and also suffered some notorious cases of unethical PR. Yet discovery of the truth and open, honest communication are its primary concerns—leading to the dominant practice of issues management. For the benefit of all, PR professionals work to discover and address potential issues, such as customer dissatisfaction with a service, *before* they become a problem or even a crisis. Skills involve asking, listening, and empathizing to function as the ethical conscience in the organization—and then evaluating and recommending to resolve issues, often resulting in customer retention, positive social sharing, and possible economies in legal, lobbying, media relations costs.

Social Movement Organizations and Ethics

Social movement organizations such as PETA use attention-getting and at times controversial communications campaigns to advance their goals.

Justin Sullivan/Getty Images

Activist groups like People for the Ethical Treatment of Animals (PETA) launched a controversial "Holocaust on Your Plate" campaign in 2003. To promote vegetarianism and attack agribusiness, the campaign made striking visual and verbal comparisons between the mistreatment and industrialized mass killings of humans in the Holocaust and of farmed animals in factory farms. The exhibit moved throughout North America and Europe to media attention and strong reactions, including boycotts.

Can Public Relations Ethics Be Applied to Social Movement Organizations?

Published ethical guidelines for PR focus on corporate, nonprofit, government, or otherwise mainstream organizations. Yet social movement organizations (SMOs) often have the unique challenge of using persuasive communication campaigns to redefine accepted social practices into social problems. They may use forceful appeals to gain attention or even purposely cause contention (Freeman, 2009). However, SMOs must communicate about problems perceived as severe and unresolved by authorities, creating a sense of urgency that motivates social intervention. SMOs must walk a line between extremes; if they are too moderate, they risk being assimilated and "blunted" (Gitlin, 2003, p. 290), yet if they are too critical, they risk being marginalized and trivialized.

Visual Spectacles or Strategic Actions?

SMOs have gained leverage through disruptive actions deliberately staged for the media. Greenpeace flotillas, the AIDS Coalition to Unleash Power (Act Up) die-ins, and the unruliest aspects of the anti-globalization World Trade Organization (WTO)—such as sit-ins and street theater—are examples of successful visual communication that was newsworthy. More playfully, protestors have used carnivalesque street performances to highlight contradictions and the absurdity of social, environmental, or economic issues.

Ethical Questions of the Social Movement Organization

▸ To what extent is the organization marginalized (both in terms of lack of power and resources and in terms of posing a challenge to those in power)?

▸ To what extent are its goals socially responsible and in the public interest (such as promoting truth, justice, and minimization of harm)?

▸ To what extent are its primary moral claimants (potentially victimized parties) experiencing harm or disadvantage (this could include the cause's urgency and severity)?

▸ To what extent is it targeting its message at parties directly responsible for causing the problem or who have more control in solving it?

Ethical Questions of Its Communication Means and Messages

▸ To what extent are its goals confrontational and critical of power and social norms?

▸ To what extent does it use persuasion (asymmetry) versus dialogue (symmetry)?

▸ To what extent will it cause audience members to experience dissonance or emotional discomfort?

The more an SMO fits the organizational factors, the more ethically justified it is in using the communication means and messages. ●

Source: Freeman (2009).

WHAT ETHICAL GUIDELINES SHOULD BE USED IN PUBLIC RELATIONS?

Most PR practitioners have done little formal study of ethical philosophies; rather they tend to rely on situational ethics. PR ethics scholar Shannon Bowen finds limited usefulness with this route: "It sees no universal or generally applicable moral norms but looks at each situation independently" (2013, p. 306). There are three major types of **normative ethics** that guide moral actions: **teleological**, **deontological**, and **virtue ethics**. Bowen suggests the first two, the teleology theory of **utilitarianism** (or **consequentialist theory**) and the deontological theory of **absolutism** (or **nonconsequentialist theory**) are the most appropriate ethical guides for PR.

TABLE 3.1

Normative Ethics

CATEGORY	NAME	DESCRIPTION	CRITICISM
Teleological (values)	Utilitarianism	Emphasizes consequences of actions—the greatest good for the greatest number of people.	Is it possible for someone to accurately predict outcomes?
Deontological (rules)	Absolutism	Emphasizes duties or rules. What's morally right applies to everyone.	Should we act as if our own ethical choices were universal law?
Virtue (character)	Agent-Based	Emphasizes individual moral character—guided by one's virtue and practical wisdom.	Different people may have quite different concepts of what constitutes virtue.

HOW TO APPLY UTILITARIANISM

1. Do not be guided by established rules or duties.

2. Predict the possible consequences of decisions and weigh the good and bad of each potential outcome (see Figure 3.1).

3. Draw a conclusion: The ethical choice will be the decision or outcome that has the *most* possible consequences and *least* negative consequences.

4. Another way to view this is to choose to produce the greatest good for the greatest number of people.

HOW TO APPLY ABSOLUTISM

1. Do not use possible outcomes as a decision-making guide.

2. Rather, determine what is morally right, applying equally to all people (see Figure 3.2).

3. Follow moral principles objectively: The ethical choice is doing what's morally right for everyone.

HOW TO APPLY VIRTUE ETHICS

1. Do not weigh the consequences to project best outcomes.

2. Do not be guided by rules or proscribed duties.

3. Individual moral character guides motivation for a decision.

4. Decisions are guided by courage, honesty, benevolence, compassion, justice, and temperance (see Figure 3.3).

FIGURE 3.1

Utilitarianism Challenge

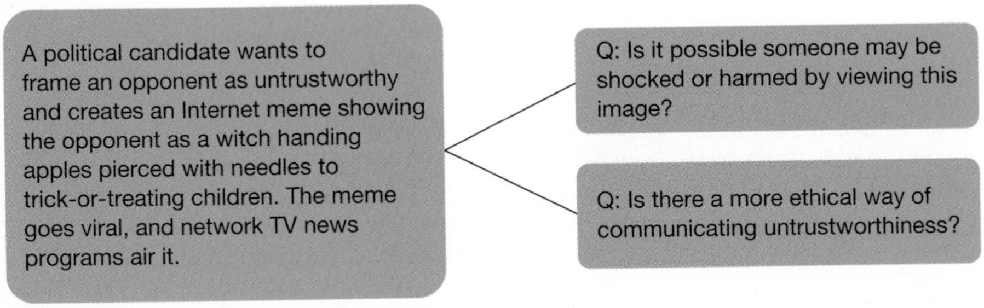

A political candidate wants to frame an opponent as untrustworthy and creates an Internet meme showing the opponent as a witch handing apples pierced with needles to trick-or-treating children. The meme goes viral, and network TV news programs air it.

Q: Is it possible someone may be shocked or harmed by viewing this image?

Q: Is there a more ethical way of communicating untrustworthiness?

FIGURE 3.2

Absolutism Challenge

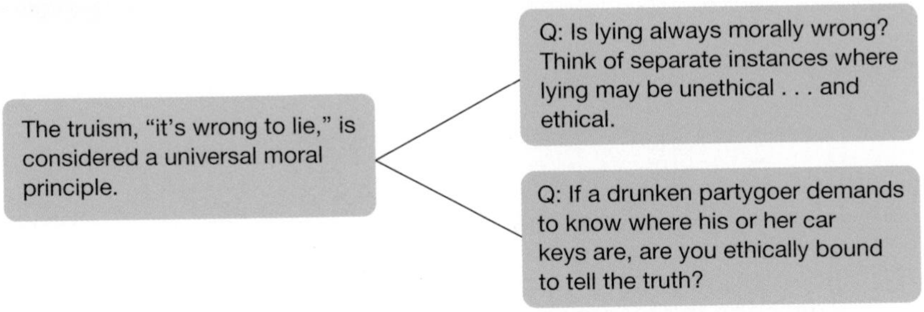

The truism, "it's wrong to lie," is considered a universal moral principle.

Q: Is lying always morally wrong? Think of separate instances where lying may be unethical . . . and ethical.

Q: If a drunken partygoer demands to know where his or her car keys are, are you ethically bound to tell the truth?

FIGURE 3.3

Virtue Ethics Challenge

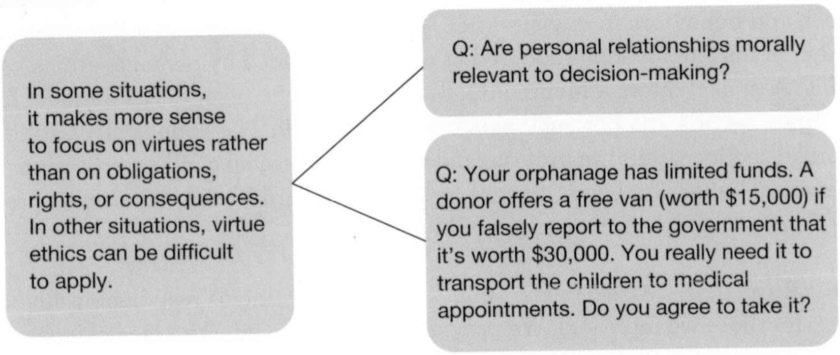

In some situations, it makes more sense to focus on virtues rather than on obligations, rights, or consequences. In other situations, virtue ethics can be difficult to apply.

Q: Are personal relationships morally relevant to decision-making?

Q: Your orphanage has limited funds. A donor offers a free van (worth $15,000) if you falsely report to the government that it's worth $30,000. You really need it to transport the children to medical appointments. Do you agree to take it?

A Personal Framework for Ethical Reasoning in Public Relations

To bridge all three approaches to ethical reasoning—consequences, duty, and virtue—Martin and Wright (2015) propose a personal framework for ethical reasoning in public relations. It has four parts:

1. Define the issue.
   A. Describe the issue in one or two sentences, then list the facts in order of relevance. Include any external pressures you feel: political, economic, interpersonal, or social.

2. Identify stakeholders.
   A. List all people who might be affected and all people to whom you owe a duty. Suggest their current state of mind and heart.

3. Define and evaluate options.
   A. Consider all three ethical approaches, listing best and worst cases for each.
   B. For each of the approaches listed, identify pros and cons (benefits and costs) for each of the stakeholder groups, including the client. Take into account the following:

      i. *Harms/Cares.* How would they benefit? Would anyone be harmed? What costs may have to be paid?
      ii. *Duties.* What are your duties? Do they respect the integrity and freedom of those affected? Are you free of vested interest or ulterior motives? Would you expect others to follow this as a rule?
      iii. *Rights.* What are stakeholders' rights? Might any invalidate any of your options? Does your relationship with stakeholders carry any explicit or implicit rights?

4. Make and justify a decision.
   A. Now choose your course of action, selecting the option that allows you to fulfill your most important duties, in keeping with your own values, and that has best consequences for the affected people. If the choice is among harmful actions, choose the least harmful. Then justify your decision based on ethical reasoning—as if you were addressing the person least likely to agree. ●

STAY INFORMED, BE VIGILANT, DEVELOP PERSONAL ETHICS

>> **LO 3.2** **Survey professional codes of ethics and describe the responsibilities of the individual practitioner**

PR practitioners must actively observe, evaluate, and often respond to the many issues that organizations face—frequently unexpected or at first appearing harmless. Social media posts, comment threads, meme generators, and YouTube videos can amplify criticisms or concerns about an organization's behavior. To guide ethical choices and behaviors in any situation, PR practitioners should follow the ethical code her or his employer has adopted as well as be guided by personal ethics.

PRSA (n.d.c.) offers a Member Code of Ethics, which serves as a model for all U.S. organizations and professionals that practice PR. The code is structured into two broad sections: guiding professional values and ethical conduct provisions. The Professional Values Statement sets the industry standard for the professional practice of PR. These core values include the following:

▶ *Advocacy*—"We serve the public interest by acting as responsible advocates for those we represent. We provide a voice in the marketplace of ideas, facts, and viewpoints to aid informed public debate."

TABLE 3.2

Helpful Third-Party Sources of Communication Ethics Codes

INTERNATIONAL, NATIONAL, AND REGIONAL PROFESSIONAL PUBLIC RELATIONS ASSOCIATIONS	
Global Alliance for Public Relations and Communication Management (GA)	Code of Ethics http://www.globalalliancepr.org/code-of-ethics
International Association of Business Communicators (IABC)	Code of Ethics https://www.iabc.com/about-us/governance/code-of-ethics/
International Public Relations Association (IPRA)	Code of Conduct https://www.ipra.org/member-services/code-of-conduct/
Arthur W. Page Society	Page Principles http://www.awpagesociety.com/site/the-page-principles
Canadian Public Relations Society (CPRS)	Code of Professional Standards http://www.cprs.ca/aboutus/code_ethic.aspx
UK's Chartered Institute of Public Relations (CIPR)	Code of Conduct (with an interactive ethics assessment): https://www.cipr.co.uk/content/our-organisation/professionalism-and-ethics
Public Relations Society of America (PRSA)	Member Code of Ethics https://www.prsa.org/ethics/code-of-ethics

▶ *Honesty*—"We adhere to the highest standards of accuracy and truth in advancing the interests of those we represent and in communicating with the public."

▶ *Expertise*—"We acquire and responsibly use specialized knowledge and experience. We advance the profession through continued professional development, research, and education. We build mutual understanding, credibility, and relationships among a wide array of institutions and audiences."

▶ *Independence*—"We provide objective counsel to those we represent. We are accountable for our actions."

▶ *Loyalty*—"We are faithful to those we represent while honoring our obligation to serve the public interest.

▶ *Fairness*—"We deal fairly with clients, employers, competitors, peers, vendors, the media, and the general public. We respect all opinions and support the right of free expression."

The Code Provisions of Conduct (PRSA, n.d.b) provides detailed recommendations in the following categories, briefly explained here:

▶ *Free Flow of Information*—"Protecting and advancing the free flow of accurate and truthful information," which is "essential to serving the public interest and contributing to informed decision-making in a democratic society"

▶ *Competition*—"Promoting healthy and fair competition among professionals" to "preserve an ethical climate while fostering a robust business environment"

▶ *Disclosure of Information*—"Fostering informed decision-making in a democratic society"

▶ *Safeguarding Confidences*—The "appropriate protection of confidential and private information"

▶ *Conflicts of Interest*—"Avoiding real, potential, or perceived conflicts of interest" to "build the trust of clients, employers, and publics"

▶ *Enhancing the Profession*—Working "to strengthen the public's trust in the profession"

PUBLIC RELATIONS LEADERSHIP ON SOCIAL RESPONSIBILITY ETHICS

SOCIAL RESPONSIBILITY

There is a common direction between both schools of business and communication to encourage students to become leaders that transform not just organizations but the societies that house them. Corporate ethics codes are also drivers of PR ethics. Economic events in the early 21st century, including the 2007–2008 financial crisis and increased globalization, have greatly influenced business behaviors and decision-making, as have activist movements powered by social media. Along with this shift to social responsibility, notable firms are evaluating the companies' codes and compliance and publishing rankings of the world's most reputable or ethical companies. Among them are Ethisphere, GMI Ratings, and the Reputation Institute.

INDIVIDUAL ETHICS

Derina Holtzhausen, professor and past editor of the *International Journal of Strategic Communication*, argues that professional and corporate codes interfere with individual ethical decision-making, making ethical decisions a group responsibility that people "hide behind" (2015, 7, p. 771). This is not an isolated criticism: other critics (Curtin & Boynton, 2000) reason that most professional codes of practice, while good guidelines, are 'vague, unenforceable, or applied inconsistently' and that they cannot account for the diversity of views in a globalized society.

A **moral impulse** should guide individual PR practitioners, steering them to consider perspectives of multiple stakeholders. While admittedly often tempered by binding laws, contracts, financial expediency, or strategic intent, the practitioner has to accept responsibility in ethical decision-making. This ideal application of virtue ethics—one that's individually guided by moral responsibility and selflessness—then yields subsequent actions, words, and images that are manifestations of the ethical choice.

VISUAL COMMUNICATION AND ETHICS

PR continuously adapts to evolving communication technologies as various publics, especially Millennials and Gen Xers, are fast to adopt and embrace them. Today visual media is the dominant mode for creating, sharing, and consuming information, with many platforms including Pinterest, Instagram, Periscope, Snapchat, Facebook Live, Tumblr, YouTube, and Virtual Reality. Brands are quick to interact with consumers in these new spaces, yet for a PR practitioner, there is both power and responsibility in designing visual messages for the public.

Does Public Relations Mean Lying?

Shannon A. Bowen, Arthur W. Page Society

Not too long ago, a study reported that 65% of public relations professionals report telling a lie "occasionally" to keep their jobs (Polls Indicate, 2008). Earlier, a *PRWeek* study indicated that 25% of PR pros said they lied on the job (Kuczynski, 2000).

Fast forward to the 2015 BledCom International Public Relations Research Symposium, where one researcher reported that of more than 20 interviewees, 17 admitted lying to the media on a regular basis; 16 said they would lie again.

The credibility of PR suffers, and communicators have to work daily to conquer these negative impressions. Perhaps worst of all, lies erode trust of the stakeholders and publics we seek to serve.

Recent Edelman Trust Barometer (2014) findings on the top actions that erode perceived ethics include failure to show responsibility during a crisis, using unethical business practices, failing to keep information secure, substandard working conditions, or misrepresenting the organization. PR is involved in most of or all of these practices, so we are part of the trust problem—but we can also help solve it through fostering ethical behavior. Our responsibility to the public necessitates honesty and ethical reflection in the organization's actions as well as how they are communicated to stakeholders and publics.

We need honesty to foster a reputation that can help organizations grow, reach their goals, and meet the needs of stakeholders and publics. Telling the occasional white lie, either out of pressure, fear, or obligation, does not serve our management or clients well, undermines the credibility of the profession, and may harm our own career interests.

A better model for the PR professional is to be a counselor and advocate of honesty—sometimes even when that honesty is damaging to the organization. Refusing to engage in dishonesty, manipulation, or even white lies helps one to become a counselor to management, helping participate in determining the correct course of action for an organization.

When issues or crises emerge, PR practitioners will be called upon to provide counsel in how to handle these uncomfortable situations. Maintaining honesty at all times is the best policy, but having a model, approach, or guideline to really examine the ethics of a situation thoroughly is the best practice.

Consider the Ethical Implications

Considering the ethics of your decision, in addition to using honest communication, helps advance not only the responsibility of the organization but also the value of the PR counsel within it. Issues of ethics are even more crucial when PR is defined as building relationships with publics and stakeholders that are based on credible and accurate communication. Good ethics is good business for everyone involved. Remember:

▸ *Be rational.* Gather data from multiple sides and points of view and analyze it logically. Be as objective as possible and determine which arguments have the most merit.

▸ *Be consistent.* Follow the vision, mission, and ethics statement of your organization. What do your publics and stakeholders expect you to reliably deliver? How can you do that?

▸ *Be principled.* Strive to maintain the principles that can be valued across situations and even cultures. What decision maintains equity, liberty, responsibility, honesty, and so on?

▸ *Respect other views.* Listen to the perspectives of those on the other side of an issue. When it makes sense, incorporate some of their values into your decision-making. Even those who disagree with your decision can likely understand it when they feel heard and it maintains a common value or principle.

▸ *Do the right thing.* Even when things go awry, a good intention can help get matters back on the right footing. Advise your team and your management on what you should be doing, not just what you could be doing. Ethics always prioritizes *should* over *could*. ●

Contributed by Shannon A. Bowen, Ph.D., University of South Carolina; member, Arthur W. Page Society; board member

(Continued)

(Continued)

Note: BledCom research is discussed in more depth in my PRWeek column that can be found at http://www.prweek.com/article/1359922/ we-professional-manipulators-pr-pros-lying-ourselves.

References

Edelman Trust Barometer. (2014). Retrieved from www .edelman.com/insights

Kuczynski, A. (2000, May 8). In public relations, 25% admit lying. *New York Times*, sec. C, p. 20, col. 5.

Polls indicate public relations pros must lie to remain employed. (2008, January/February). *Journal of Employee Communication Management*, p. 8. Retrieved from http://www.lexisnexis.com.pallas2.tcl.sc.edu/hottopics/ lnacademic/?verb=sr&csi=314324 retrieved 8/24/16 via LEXIS-NEXIS

Images spread fast with tech-savvy Gen Xers and Millennials, so PR visual messaging must be based on ethical decision-making. Some practitioners might consider it unethical to use this image to raise awareness and donations for disadvantaged children.

iStock.com/olesiabilkei

The PRSA ethics code doesn't specifically address visual communication, but if pictorial imagery is employed, ethical issues may be raised—especially if they mislead or wrongfully influence viewers negatively. As we now have the vast capacity to create, manipulate, and quickly transmit visual messages, we must be aware of the potential for ethical issues. A familiar issue is with imagery used by nonprofits to raise awareness and donations for disadvantaged children. Sometimes called "poverty porn," the images can be viewed as unethical.

HOW DOES LAW AFFECT PUBLIC RELATIONS?

>> **LO 3.3** Understand key legal issues confronting PR practitioners and identify the links among social responsibility, ethics, and law

Morality and ethics are often confused with a question of legality: Something thought of as unethical may not be illegal, and something considered unethical or immoral may be completely legal. This section deals with PR decision-making based on considerations of *legality*, as public communication in the United States is conditioned by legal rights and legal restrictions. Issues of **free speech**, **defamation**, **disclosure**, **privacy**, and **copyright** in the ever-expanding boundaries of the Internet all concern the PR practitioner. We also cover the field of litigation PR.

FREE SPEECH

The U.S. Constitution's First Amendment reads in part, "Congress shall make no law … abridging the freedom of speech, or of the press." However, there are exclusions, for example, due to national security needs, obscenity laws, and prohibited language that incites hatred or violence. Freedom of speech also permits gathering of information, protected by the federal Freedom of Information Act (FOIA, n.d.), a law giving citizens the right to access information from the federal government. Thanks to FOIA, each state has "sunshine" laws, under various names, granting public access to state records (Ballotpedia, n.d.).

Socially responsible business practices include respecting human rights and fair labor practices. The UN (n.d.) Global Compact is the world's largest corporate sustainability initiative calling companies to follow and advance its universal principles on human rights, labor, environment, and anti-corruption. All members must submit an annual "Communication on Progress," reporting on their progress in meeting the principles. Although not all comply, this reporting is a voluntary effort to provide open access of information to interested publics. Turning from external to internal communication, the U.S. National Labor Relations Board (NLRB) has policies that prohibit restrictions on employee speech. As much of this dialogue flows through social media, often it's the PR practitioner who sets policy and monitors activity. There are many issues to be aware of; for example, a social media policy must be written carefully to avoid restricting public criticism—it's OK to complain, but the policy must protect the company's business interests. And while companies invest time and expense in establishing their names and logos—which are protected under copyright laws against any use for profit—the NLRB allows employees to freely use them to communicate workplace grievances (Myers, 2013).

> **SOCIAL RESPONSIBILITY**

DEFAMATION

Defamation is the act of making a statement that can be proven to be false with the intention of causing harm to another's reputation or livelihood. It has two categories: **Libel** is a written or published defamatory statement, while **slander** is defamation that is spoken (NOLO, n.d.a).

Technology invites the PR professional to explore many ways to engage with key publics. Likewise, customers, employees, investors, and sometimes adversaries may use digital platforms to express dissatisfaction or objections with your organization. The easy access to a public court of opinion can be influential and potentially damaging if the content is defamatory.

The Communications Decency Act of 1996 has significant jurisdiction on Internet and online speech. It protects "interactive" websites and Web hosts from being held liable for content provided by its third-party users. In other words the harmed party can take action only against the actual author of defamatory content, not the websites (Facebook, Twitter, etc.) themselves. Online defamation or "cyberlibel" can appear on

The Ethical Implications of *Citizens United*

Attorney David J. Dale, a former PR practitioner, offers this scenario on the legal and ethical issues raised by the *Citizens United* ruling. Dale is an associate with Staub Anderson, Chicago, Illinois.

You are the PR manager for ABC Inc., a mid-sized for-profit corporation with a strong regional presence that employs around 5,000 workers. It's an election year, and your boss, the founder and current president of the company, is solidly behind the Republican candidate for president. You've heard that he's been considering using his business's goodwill and resources to help get the word out in support of his candidate. Thus it comes as no surprise when he e-mails you to schedule a one-on-one meeting to discuss some of his latest ideas, and ahead of the meeting he asks you to consider the following questions:

▸ Can ABC Inc. use its social media presence to spread the word about the candidate's political platform and even openly endorse this candidate?

▸ Can ABC Inc. offer incentives to its customers in return for promises of support and perhaps even donations to the candidate's campaign?

▸ Can ABC Inc. use its own workforce to get out and support the candidate by attending rallies, canvasing communities, and even soliciting donations?

▸ More important, does ABC Inc. have to reimburse its workers for their time?

▸ What if an employee refuses to take part?

Only five years ago your answer would have been markedly different than it is today, thanks to a single Supreme Court decision most commonly known and referred to as *Citizens United*.

Citizens United v. FEC, 130 S. Ct. 876 (2010), involved a nonprofit, tax-exempt corporation (Citizens United) and its attempts to publicly advertise and promote its documentary film titled *Hillary the Movie*, an unabashed appeal to voters not to vote for Hillary Clinton for president. Under existing federal laws, specifically the Federal Election Campaign Act of 1971 (FECA), corporations (both for- and nonprofit) were barred from making "a contribution or expenditure in connection with any election to any political office."[1] The statute was purposefully written to define "contribution" in the broadest sense, restricting not only monetary contributions but "anything of value," which included funding communications, compensating employees for time contributed to campaign activities, and even uncompensated time if the employees were directed to participate by management.[2] In addition to restricting corporations from using their employees to outwardly support political campaigns, businesses were also restricted from engaging in election-related communications with its employees.[3]

Thus, in a pre-*Citizens United* landscape, and based on the then-existing restrictions, you might have advised your boss to err on the side of caution and steer clear of any ideas or initiatives that purported to use ABC Inc.'s resources or its employees to support a specific candidate. However, in its landmark *Citizens United* decision, the Supreme Court struck down the ban on independent political expenditures, holding that the First Amendment prohibited restrictions on corporations' use of its own money to fund communications advocating for specific candidates or political parties.

As a result, corporations (both for- and nonprofits) now have the authority to "use [their] own resources, including paid work-hour time of its employees, for independent expenditures" in support of a chosen political candidate or party.[4] And while companies are still prohibited from making direct contributions to candidate campaigns or firing an employee for voluntary participation in political efforts, they are no longer prohibited from firing an employee for declining to participate in employer-mandated political activity. In the wake of this decision, company executives now openly urge employees to support specific candidates, solicit donations directly from their workforce, invite political candidates to speak at company meetings, and even disseminate political advertisements via employees' payroll checks. While most companies readily acknowledge the difficulty of forcing its employees to participate in political endeavors in practice, the fact remains that under *Citizens United*, there is no federal restriction prohibiting it.

Having reviewed the state of the corporate/political world post *Citizens United*, and considering both the ethical and practical ramifications of his proposed plans, you tell your boss that the question is not "Can we do it?" but "Should we do it?" You explain that while your company may be legally permitted to issue communications on behalf of a specific candidate, and even direct its employees to participate in campaign-related events, you remind your boss that doing so may alienate not only your customers but also your workers. And given the repeated criticisms of the *Citizen United* decision and calls for its repeal, any perceived gain from forcing ABC Inc. and its workers to campaign for a candidate may be quickly lost in the long run. ●

---

[1] 2 U.S.C. §441b(a).

[2] 2 U.S.C. § 441b(b)(2); see also 11 C.F.R. § 100.54 (2014); FEC MUR 5664, General Counsel's Report #2, supra note 14, at 5.

[3] 11 C.F.R. § 114.2(b)(2)(ii). While employers were permitted to discuss basic policy issues and pending litigation, they were not permitted to advocate for specific candidates or political parties.

[4] FEC MUR 6344, First General Counsel's Report at 7.

blogs, in forums, on websites and within social networking platforms. For example, Reddit, the online news aggregator that brands itself as a source for what's new and popular on the Web rarely removes defamatory content even though it tends to go viral (Gibson, 2014).

Because of the often anonymous and pseudonymous nature of Internet posts, the best strategy for a PR practitioner is watchfulness and quick response as well as maintaining a strong Web presence.

DISCLOSURE

"Bloggers who make endorsements must disclose the material connections they share with the seller of the product/service," stated the Federal Trade Commission (FTC) when it amended its guidelines regarding endorsements and testimonials (FTC, 2009). Even the mere sharing of a link on social media to show you're a fan of a particular business or product requires disclosure *if* you're being rewarded by that entity for your action. This legality supports the PRSA's established advocacy of full disclosure of information.

While bloggers seek access to products to review, they prefer to maintain editorial control over the review process (Walden, Bortree, & DiStaso, 2014; Lahav & Zimand-Sheiner, 2016). Thus it's important for PR professionals who help to place products with bloggers to confirm the issue of transparency with them. Consumers are increasingly consulting blogs for product information, and when PR practitioners encourage trustworthy and open communication with their publics, it has the potential to positively impact attitudes about the product company and translate into bottom-line outcomes.

Celebrities or experts have a duty to disclose their relationships with companies when making endorsements outside the context of traditional ads, such as on talk shows or in social media (FTC, 2009). This applies to their promotional statements on their blogs or websites as well. When in doubt, send questions to endorsements@ftc.gov.

Instagram now requires that users mark posts for which they have been paid. Here, Aimee Song's post has a banner noting that it is a paid partnership with Volvo.

Instagram.com/songofstyle

Nike and Sweatshop Labor

After a lawsuit accused Nike of lying about conditions in its factories, the company vowed to improve conditions and root out child labor.

Peter Charlesworth/Lightrocket/Getty Images

The Suit

Nike was sued for lying about sweatshop labor in 1998 by San Francisco resident Marc Kasky under California's unfair business practices law, which bans false claims and advertising. The suit centered on the company's news releases and other public statements regarding accusations its athletic shoes were made in Asian sweatshops. The lawsuit charged Nike had lied about its reliance on sweatshop labor.

Nike's Defense

Although Nike claimed its comments were protected free speech—aspects of public debate and not commercial speech—opponents counterargued that the First Amendment doesn't extend to false public statements aimed at making products more acceptable to consumers.

Enter the California Supreme Court

The court ruled 4-to-3 against Nike, stating that "when a business enterprise makes factual representations about its own products or its own operations, it must speak truthfully" (Savage, 2002). The company then took its case to the U.S. Supreme Court. Subsequently the high court decided against ruling on it, leaving the earlier ruling to stand.

The Settlement: Nike Embraced CSR

Kasky agreed to drop the suit because Nike had improved factory conditions and had accepted outside scrutiny. Nike's CEO vowed to root out child labor, "The Nike product has become synonymous with slave wages, forced overtime and arbitrary abuse" (Banjo, 2014). Nike's payment of $1.5 million to settle the charges went to the Fair Labor Association for factory monitoring in developing countries worldwide. The association's executive director, Auret Van Heerden, celebrated Nike's agreement that "even though it doesn't own the factories, it will be responsible for conditions in any supplier plant" (Girion, 2003).

Today a Social Responsibility Champion

Not too long after the lawsuit was resolved, in 2005 Nike became the first company in its industry to publish a complete list of its contract factories, along with its first CSR report (Newell, 2015). In 2006 Nike ranked in the top 10 for its social responsibility reporting (Nike, 2006). In 2015 Triplepundit.com published "How Nike Embraced CSR and Went from Villain to Hero," documenting the company's CSR leadership (Newell, 2015). The following year the esteemed Reputation Institute ranked Nike 22nd in the world's top 100 companies with the best CSR reputations (Ranking The Brands, 2016). A visit to www.nikeresponsibility.com reveals its Supply Chain Disclosure and its Code of Conduct. ●

COPYRIGHT AND FAIR USE

Social media affords PR practitioners vast potential to engage stakeholders, yet it also presents legal challenges when it comes to copyright law. A copyright provides legal protection for any creative work that is published, broadcast, or presented or displayed publicly, including video, audio, imagery, or written work on the Web (Conway, 2012). However, the Internet legal site Nolo.com states that in some situations, under the **fair use** rule, you may make limited use of another's copyrighted work without asking permission or infringing on the original copyright (NOLO, n.d.b).

What determines fair use can be complex, but factors include the purpose of its use, nature of copyrighted work itself, amount of use, and effect of use on the work itself. The media monitoring firm BurrellesLuce provides a helpful source on fair use for PR practitioners, found at http://www.burrellesluce.com/newsletter/2013/january_2013.

Dawn Conway (2012) advises the PR professional on what *not* to do:

▸ Don't copy an entire article and e-mail it to a distribution list or place it on a network where others can access it.

▸ Don't make reprints of an article to distribute without formal, written permission from the copyright holder—and pay for the rights if need be.

▸ Don't quote even short excerpts from copyrighted material without fully identifying the source, and don't quote extensively from any copyrighted content without permission.

▸ Only post an excerpt from another source on your blog or website if you are using it to illustrate an original point you are making; always identify the source and link to it.

Negotiating the issue of copyright is complex. Erin Feldman (2015) offers some tips:

▸ *Attribution.* Citing sources is the golden rule of copyright compliance.

▸ *Education.* Don't violate another person's copyright due to lack of knowledge. Feldman recommends creating an internal copyright wiki that houses up-to-date information and resources.

▸ *Monitor.* Keep track of your own content with alerts and social listening software to learn where and how your content is being used.

PRSA offers a question-and-answer section on copyright found at http://www.prsa.org/network/communities/technology/programming/secure/2012_di_trade-marklaw.pdf, as does the PR Council, found at http://prcouncil.net/resources/how-to-copy-right-and-how-not-to-copy-wrong.

PRIVACY

The right of privacy protects citizens from harm caused by the public dissemination of truthful but private information about them (Heath, 2001). Invasion of privacy is divided into four legal actions: **intrusion**, disclosure, **false light**, and **appropriation**. Most states include a fifth **right of publicity**, meaning a citizen may control the commercial use of his or her identity (p. 252). See Table 3.3 for a more detailed look into a citizen's right to privacy.

TABLE 3.3

Privacy Legal Actions

Intrusion	It's important for a PR professional to secure permission from a private or secluded individual to protect against intrusion—the intentional disturbance, physically or otherwise, upon the solitude or seclusion of another that causes offense, mental anguish, or suffering (praccreditation.org, n.d.).
Disclosure	It's equally important to know, regarding disclosure, that photos taken publicly and facts already publicly known (either released by the person or on public record) are not seen as private information, and publishing them is not an invasion of privacy (Heath, 2001).
False Light	False light requires that the information be either untrue or suggestive of false impressions and be widely publicized.
Appropriation	Appropriation involves using some aspect of a person's identity that causes mental or physical distress.
Right of Publicity	Heath (2001) advises that it belongs to those whose celebrity gives their names, images, or identities financial value.

WORKING FOR THE LAW: LITIGATION PUBLIC RELATIONS

A media strategy is particularly important during high-profile litigation. When PR firms represent law firms as clients, under U.S. law they are granted legal protection to confidential information—an extension of attorney-client privilege to nonlawyers—although this is a complex issue that may be contested.

For firms practicing PR litigation and claiming attorney-client privilege, Cayce (2015) recommends it is important to be hired by the client's lawyers, not by the client; that PR is involved with actual litigation strategy or preparation; and that PR is involved with the immediate effects of litigation and not the aftermath; these are easier to prove for in-house PR counsel than for outside consultants.

Using PR methods—without a professional—to support litigation strategy can be controversial. In a civil lawsuit against professional basketball player Kobe Bryant for sexual assault, the judge said his lawyers engaged in "public relations litigation" by using pleadings to attract media attention. Rather, a better approach would have been for a PR professional to responsibly use court documents to communicate with the public (Terilli, Splichal, & Driscol, 2007).

SCENARIO OUTCOME

At the beginning of this chapter, we provided a real-life scenario of EcoPlanet Bamboo's (EPB's) needs to communicate with employees. To review, the Nicaraguan subsidiary of a U.S. company was faced with two communication challenges: the first was one of awareness—to educate its rural employees of its ethical mission and practices; the second was a more sensitive issue—to address an internal revolt by its male employees over the promotion of a woman to upper management. As the company's first, newly hired PR manager, we asked you the following:

1. How will you approach the communication need to educate employees in the company's ethical mission—considering the employees from rural communities are likely undereducated and have low literacy?

2. What types of responses and communication should address the work stoppage in response to promoting women?

We applied the personal framework for ethical reasoning in PR in both cases.

1. **Define the issues** (facts in order of relevance and noting any external political, economic, interpersonal or social pressures):
    A. The first situation is that most employees have a very personal understanding of the company's benefits: It provides them with a fair income and supplements their health-care and nutritional needs.
    B. The second situation is that while in line with the company's culture, the promotion of a woman to management challenges a cultural norm of gender inequality in Central America.

2. **Identify the stakeholders** (those affected and those to whom you owe a duty, noting their current state of mind and heart):

    A. This includes all employees, taking into account different ages and levels of literacy and education, ranging from unskilled, illiterate workers through to university graduates and managerial positions. Indirect stakeholders include local community leadership and regional and national government.

    B. Primary stakeholders affected are the male employees who are resistant to the promotion of women; secondary stakeholders are all employees, particularly females and the newly promoted female manager.

3. **After considering benefits and harms, duties to stakeholders, and rights of stakeholders, make and justify a decision:**

    A. *Action taken:* Management needed to communicate essential messages of benefit to all parties in a clear way for employees to easily understand and share them with family and community members. The solution was to use visual communication in a format to be readily accessed, understood, and shared: a magazine with sequential illustrations and very simple prose—essentially, a basic comic book.

    Justification: Respecting employee literacy limitations allows employees to understand the bigger picture and feel a part of something good rather than just having a job.

    B. *Action taken:* Members of management and worker leaders used face-to-face dialogue with resistant male workers to communicate that the equal opportunity policy of the company is of benefit to all employees and part of the company ethos that's improving local conditions.

    Justification: All people should be treated equally and provided with the same rights. Promotions and employment positions are given to the most qualified and suitable individual, regardless of gender, belief systems, and so on.

WRAP UP

In this chapter, you learned ethical guidelines, drawing from both professional codes of ethics and a personal framework for ethical decision making in PR. You considered examples of ethical challenges facing corporations and how they were addressed. You learned how some decisions created bigger issues for a corporation while others correctly addressed a problem. The key legal issues facing PR practitioners were introduced with examples of the issues and how they continue to add complexities to the practice. You also studied the ethics and legal considerations of social responsibility and practiced making ethical and legal decisions in the role of a PR professional.

KEY TERMS

Absolutism: A deontological theory (also called nonconsequentialism) that emphasizes duties or rules; what's morally right applies to everyone, **62**

Appropriation: Involves using some aspect of a person's identity that causes mental or physical distress, **73**

Consequentialist Theory: Utilitarianism (see definition), **62**

Copyright: Legal protection for any creative work that is published, broadcast, presented, or displayed publicly, including video, audio, imagery, or written work on the Web, **69**

Defamation: The act of making a statement that can be proven to be false, with the intention of causing harm to another's reputation or livelihood (see definitions for libel and slander), **69**

Deontological Ethics: Ethics that are rules based, **62**

Disclosure: Release of information, for example, the FTC mandates that bloggers or celebrities who make endorsements must disclose the material connections they share with the seller of the product/service; disclosure also establishes that publishing information already publicly disclosed is not an invasion of privacy, **69**

Fair Use: In some situations, under this rule limited use of another's copyrighted work may be allowed without asking permission or infringing on the original copyright, **72**

False Light: Refers to information either untrue or suggestive of false impressions that is widely publicized, **73**

Free Speech: Legally protected right to public speech defined by the U.S. Constitution's First Amendment, **69**

Intrusion: The intentional disturbance, physically or otherwise, upon the solitude or seclusion of another that causes offense, mental anguish, or suffering, **73**

Libel: A written or published statement of defamation, **69**

Moral Impulse: The human instinct to behave morally, **66**

Nonconsequentialist Theory: Absolutism, **62**

Normative Ethics: Ethical frameworks or theories that present moral standards guiding right or wrong conduct, **62**

Privacy: A right that protects citizens from harm caused by the public dissemination of truthful but private information about them; it is divided into four legal actions: intrusion, disclosure, false light, and appropriation (see definitions) and in most states also right of privacy, **69**

Right of Publicity: Most states allow a citizen to control the commercial use of his or her identity, **73**

Slander: Defamation (see definition) that is spoken, **69**

Teleological Ethics: Ethics that are values based, **62**

Utilitarianism: A teleological theory (also called consequentialism) that emphasizes consequences of actions, weighing the greatest good for the greatest number of people, **62**

Virtue Ethics: Ethics that emphasize individual moral character, guided by one's virtue and practical wisdom, **62**

THINK ABOUT IT

Some business practices that are considered normal in many parts of the world are frowned upon here and are even illegal by U.S. standards. Assume you work for a U.S.-based company, So-Chai, which owns tealeaf plantations in the West African country of Burkina Faso. You travel there twice a year to manage PR for its sustainability programs—supporting relationships with in-country managers, supply-chain partners, and government officials. You've developed positive relationships and established that both the company and its leadership are honest and trustworthy. On a recent trip, several newly appointed government officials asked for "gifts" and money to give the necessary approvals for So-Chai. What do you do? (Hint: first, investigate the Foreign Corrupt Practices Act https://www.justice.gov/criminal-fraud/foreign-corrupt-practices-act ; then, consider cultural norms for Burkina Faso https://geert-hofstede.com/Burkina_Faso .html.)

WRITE LIKE A PRO

You're the PR manager for Swift Airlines. During a recent heatwave, one of its planes was stranded on the runway for four hours due to a baggage handlers' strike. More than 175 passengers and crew were kept on board with limited food and beverages and backed-up toilets. Many tweeted about the situation, and their photos went viral, prompting the media (and late-night comics) to cover the incident. Draft an e-mail to be sent to all Swift Airlines employees under the CEO's name. Acknowledge the situation, reveal the airline's position, and emphasize its concern for both the passengers and employees. Choose an ethical perspective or a professional code to guide your response (and identify it as a note at the bottom of your draft). Separately, draft a cover memo to the CEO explaining your rationale for the content of the e-mail.

SOCIAL RESPONSIBILITY CASE STUDY

Coca-Cola's Fight Against Obesity

Situation

Two-thirds of adults and one-third of children in the United States are either overweight or obese (IHME, 2014). Obesity has risen to the forefront of American health concerns, leading medical professionals and policy makers to focus on finding ways to reduce these alarming statistics.

Research and Strategy

Soft drink consumption is considered a leading cause by influential leaders such as former New York City mayor Michael Bloomberg, despite other contributing factors. According to Professor Barry Popkin, one of the nation's top nutrition experts, "The biggest single source contributor to child and adult obesity in the USA is sugar-sweetened beverages" (Hellmich, 2013).

With sugary drinks frequently attacked as a leading contributor to the problem, soft drink sellers face intense scrutiny. Industry leader Coca-Cola Company knew it had to join the fight against obesity or risk being labeled an apathetic contributor to one of America's top health concerns.

Execution

In January 2013 the Coca-Cola Company jumped on the anti-obesity bandwagon when it launched its "Coming Together" communications campaign. It was a call for the public to join the company in its efforts to fight obesity and an attempt to inform the public about Coca-Cola's efforts in CSR.

The campaign's message was summed up in a two-minute introductory video (https://www.youtube.com/watch?v=SKi2A76YJlc), which announced, "Beating obesity will take action by all of us based on one simple, commonsense fact: All calories matter, no matter where they come from, including Coca-Cola and everything else with calories." Two days later, a video titled "Be OK" launched (https://www.youtube.com/watch?v=yfh0BeNMxGY), this time announcing that a can of Coca-Cola provides "140 happy calories to spend on extra happy activities."

Many in the media, and numerous health professionals, spoke out against the campaign, dismissing it as an insincere attempt for Coca-Cola to position itself as a solution to the problem it played a large role in creating. The Center for Science in the Public Interest (CSPI) led the charge against "Coming Together" with the release of a negative translation of the two-minute "Coming Together" video (https://www.youtube.com/watch?v=RyeImvWtnr4) and social media posts attacking the campaign.

In spite of Coca-Cola's efforts to steer the conversation toward uniting to fight obesity, most critics have been unable to look past the notion that the campaign is simply a PR ploy at damage control. Furthermore, some critics say "Coming Together" is largely an attempt for Coca-Cola to recover from declining soft drink sales, as consumers turn to alternative beverages such as tea and water.

Evaluation

Despite links between soft drinks and obesity, Coca-Cola stands by its statement that evidence is lacking to prove its products are connected to the obesity problem. The company's efforts to fight obesity include low-and no-calorie options in every market, nutrition information on the front of all packages, support of physical activity programs, and responsible marketing. Coca-Cola has also addressed concerns about artificial sweeteners, claiming aspartame's safety has been "supported by more than 200 studies over the last 40 years" (Horovitz, 2013).

The Coca-Cola Company faces PR challenges, similar to those cigarette companies have faced for years. With declining soft drink sales and increased criticism from opinion leaders and consumers, how can a long-established soft drink manufacturer stay relevant without giving up traditions such as the secret formula for one of the world's favorite beverages? As the "Coming Together" campaign continues on a global scale, Coca-Cola struggles to find ways to keep selling its most popular brands, Coke and Diet Coke, while also showing concern for the public's well-being.

ENGAGE

▸ Search for recent news on Coca-Cola's obesity research and anti-obesity efforts.

▸ Search to learn how Coca-Cola is talking about the obesity issue now.

▸ Explore http://www.coca-colacompany.com/sustainability.

DISCUSS

▸ Is Coca-Cola's stance that its products do not contribute to obesity unethical? Does Coca-Cola mislead consumers by refusing to acknowledge the validity of studies suggesting soft drinks contribute to obesity?

▸ As a responsible PR professional, how would you recommend soft drink companies educate consumers about living healthy lifestyles while also encouraging them to purchase a company's products? Is there evidence of recent progress?

Note: "Are All Calories Created Equal?" was the grand prize winner of the Arthur W. Page Society's 2014 Case Study Competition in Corporate Communications. Find the complete study at http://www.awpagesociety.com/study_competitions/2014-case-study-competition.

SOCIAL RESPONSIBILITY CASE STUDY

Burson-Marsteller's "Whisper Campaign"

Situation

In 2011 *USA Today* ran an exposé on an alleged whisper campaign waged by B-M on behalf of an unnamed client (Acohido & Swartz, 2011). The article noted that B-M is one of the top international PR firms.

Strategy and Tactics

B-M staff members, led by CNBC ex-anchor Jim Goldman and former political columnist John Mercurio, apparently engaged reporters and bloggers about the Google Gmail feature Social Circle and how it was a huge privacy breach to Google users. They also claimed a variety of privacy concerns about Google products and services that the company wasn't disclosing to users. In an e-mail, Mercurio solicited a former FTC researcher and influential blogger to write an op-ed about Google's dangerous products, which Mercurio even offered to ghost write. At the same time, Goldman was pitching the story to *USA Today*. Seemingly unbeknownst to Goldman and Mercurio, however, the blogger posted online the full text of his e-mail exchange with Mercurio—including the question he asked, "Who's paying for this [campaign]," and Mercurio's response that he "can't disclose my client yet."

Execution

After journalists saw the blogger's post and fact-checked Goldman's pitch about Google's products (finding large portions of it factually incorrect), the PR firm became the story—and an unflattering one. The article in USA Today and another in PRNewser (Garcia, 2011) portrayed B-M as trying to shield the identity of its client and as circulating misleading, if not false, information.

Facebook later confirmed it had hired B-M to plant negative stories about Google in the U.S. media (Lyons, 2011). The exposé of this clandestine effort was embarrassing for Facebook at the time, due to its struggle to brand itself as trustworthy.

Evaluation

For B-M, it was a bigger failure. B-M was ridiculed: "Here were two guys from one of the biggest PR agencies in the world, blustering around Silicon Valley like a pair of Keystone Kops" (Lyons, 2011). In its long history, this respected PR firm has represented scores of elite corporate clients, and this story could have ended much differently. Rosanna M. Fiske, past PRSA chair and CEO, asked, "As a profession, don't we learn from our mistakes?" (Fiske, 2011).

There have been a variety of high-profile unethical practices by PR firms and their clients. For example, looking back to 2005, PR was implicated in "fake news" when it was revealed that the U.S. Department of Education paid the PR firm Ketchum for a video that promoted a new education law strongly supported by President Bush. The video was then placed with a leading black conservative media commentator and appeared as a news story—without making clear the reporter was hired as part of the deal (Collins, 2005).

In 2006 a pro-Walmart blog called Wal-Marting Across America—ostensibly launched by a pair of average Americans chronicling their cross-country RV travels and overnighting in Walmart parking lots—was really a promotional tactic engineered by "Working Families for Walmart," an organization launched by Walmart's PR firm, Edelman (Schofield, 2006). In these instances, some of the world's most respected and successful public relations firms engaged in unethical practices.

ENGAGE

▸ Review the PRSA Code of Ethics.

▸ Review ethics expert Shannon Bowen's advice in this chapter, "Does PR Mean Lying?"

▸ Review this chapter's disclosure, privacy, and defamation sections.

DISCUSS

▸ What parts of the PRSA Code of Ethics, and/or Bowen's ethics considerations, did the PR agency staff members fail to adhere to? Did they cross any legal lines?

▸ In the Google situation, what do you think about the blogger's decision to post online an assumed-to-be private e-mail exchange? How would you judge this ethically? Legally?

▸ What, if any, effect do these instances of PR agency unethical behavior have on your beliefs about the PR profession and how you might conduct yourself professionally?

▸ Imagine an example of an ethical gray area you might need to navigate in your future PR career. How do you propose to do this?

VIDEO CASE

Lisa Bloom and Harvey Weinstein: Ethics in Crisis Management

On October 5, 2017, after years of rumors, the *New York Times* published a lengthy investigative article in which several women accused Hollywood mogul Harvey Weinstein of sexual harassment. His attorney, Lisa Bloom, quickly emerged as his defender and representative, attempting to help him navigate the storm of criticism and salvage his reputation, in part by questioning the veracity of the report and reliability of the women who had come forward.

VIDEO

1. How effective do you think Bloom's efforts to support Weinstein in this video are?

2. Was it ethical for Bloom to accept Weinstein as a client? Were her tactics ethical? Why or why not?

3. Would you be willing to represent someone in a similar circumstance? Explain your reasoning.

4

Foundations of Public Relations
Research and Theory

Learning Objectives

4.1   Understand the ROPES planning process in PR

4.2   Identify the common research methods used in PR to plan a research strategy

4.3   Recognize the role theory plays in PR

The "Biggest Healthy Snacking Brand in the World"?

Graze is a health-conscious online weekly subscription snack service started in the UK. It was launched in 2008 by seven friends who grew tired of conventional and generally unhealthy snacks. They also had backgrounds in technology development and foods. The company initially offered more than 100 snack options to appeal to a variety of different consumers, using around 200 ingredients from 70 countries around the world (Pendrous, 2016). Personalization is key: People can select foods they prefer and exclude others. Graze's website is informational and promotes its promise to never use artificial ingredients. To encourage subscriptions, promotions like "first box free" and "first box half price" are offered to new customers. For CSR engagement in line with its products, Graze founded a school of farming in Kabbubu, Uganda, that's primarily funded through donations when friends of Graze subscribers place orders.

When Graze, a British snack subscription service, decided to penetrate the U.S. market, it made strategic moves to gain visibility and tailor its products to American tastes.

urbanbuzz/Alamy Stock Photo

After much success in the UK, when Graze expanded into the United States in 2013, it initially had trouble establishing a foothold. It found stiff competition with other mail-order snack companies in the "healthy" or "gourmet" categories as well as with retailers such as Trader Joe's, Natural Grocers, and even Starbucks. It was priced competitively and earned some positive press coverage in specialty and business magazine websites. Its primary publics were health-conscious women ages 20 to 40 years old, and its main communication vehicles were Twitter, Facebook, Instagram, and Pinterest. Its social media activity was strong and mostly positive; however, some platforms carried negative comments about Graze's lack of customer service and communication.

Expansion to stores. In 2016 following its launch into UK retailers, Graze created a new line of prepackaged snacks sold through Walgreens stores and select regional retailers in the United States. *Retail Week* tied the retail move into a "strategy to become the biggest healthy snacking brand in the world" (Tugby, 2016). One food couponing blogger explained, "If you have been wanting to try them, but don't want to sign up for a subscription (even though the first box is free), now is your chance!" (Hewitt, 2016). With this strategic move, Graze intended to generate more acceptance in the U.S. market, and new products included snack mixes named Sweet Memphis BBQ and New York Everything Bagel (Ruddick, 2016).

U.S. visibility and preference. Despite its on-shelf presence in select retail stores, Graze's lack of visibility in the United States requires a PR plan to help boost awareness and preference, stimulate both online and in-store sales, and create customer loyalty. As the firm's newly hired PR consultant, consider the following:

1. What questions would you need to answer through secondary research?

2. What primary research would you suggest to inform your PR recommendations? Graze's key publics are "health obsessed-consumers" with busy lifestyles. Consider the niche market of women 20 to 40 years old—recognizing they not only shop for themselves but for their families. Be sure to explore the Graze.com website.

3. For the online component of your plan, what communication strategies would you recommend—guided by which theories?

To begin to answer this challenge and make meaningful recommendations to your client, you'll need to get a foundational understanding of how to begin the PR process.

In this chapter you will be introduced to the PR process guided by the **ROPES** model: research, objectives, programming, evaluation, and **stewardship**. The first step, research, is explained as foundational in PR for solving any problem or addressing any situation. Asking and answering key questions are critical: What is the situation? What is the organization's goal? Who is the target audience? How can they be reached? What is the essential message?

After you're armed with good and vital information, you'll then need to use it strategically—and that's another focus of this chapter: how to draw on communication theory to guide your strategy. A primer on communication theory explains its role in predicting and analyzing outcomes of PR efforts. You'll understand *why* the media have the power to influence public opinion, *how* to best approach certain people you absolutely need to reach, and *when* to advise your client to say, "I'm sorry."

Of course, the PR challenge of solving a client's problem with a PR campaign involves more than research and guiding theory. It requires that you use theory to determine a communication strategy (objectives), what you'll specifically do (tactics), how you'll know if they're working (evaluation), and how to maintain the good relationships gained (stewardship). But those steps are for another chapter; now let's start at the beginning.

HOW TO BEGIN

>> LO 4.1   Understand the ROPES planning process in PR

Having vital information is essential to making life's big decisions. How did you decide which college to attend? What laptop to buy next? What guides your path to good health and fitness? Which car, or which job, do you *really* want? You may first be thinking of **word-of-mouth (WOM)** advice and recommendations from close friends and family members. But you're also likely to be considering the numbers: how popular *is* that new laptop, what are its ratings, and how much does it cost? If possible, you'll want to get a closer look at these critical choices ... visit the college campus, interview a current employee, test drive some cars. The more

Researching products and services online, particularly reading reviews written by past customers, has become an essential part of the decision-making process for many Americans.

iStock.com/ilkercelik

you look, it's likely the more questions you'll have. Eventually, the *big* questions will be asked and answered to your satisfaction, and you'll be confident about making a decision.

This is research, and you've been doing some form of it all your life. So as we turn to the important first step in the practice of PR—research—you can understand it's a vital key to knowledge that leads to smart decisions. Nearly all PR practitioners and educators agree that PR should begin with research, leading to a clearer understanding of a situation and how to address it with a PR plan. Successful PR entails careful research that not only guides initial activities but also evaluates programs when they are ongoing as well as once they are completed. With good research, PR practitioners can plan strategically and produce effective tactics and various components that will ultimately lead to the achievement of end goals. In Chapter 5 you will learn about the evaluation stage of the PR Process: using research to measure the results of a campaign. The focus of this research discussion is how to begin.

RESEARCH: FIRST STEP IN THE PUBLIC RELATIONS PROCESS

There are various acronyms for the PR planning process, and all are essentially in agreement: RACE (research, action, communication, evaluation), RPAE (research, planning, action/communication, and evaluation), and RPIE (research, planning, implementation, and evaluation). This book follows Kathleen Kelly's ROPES schema (see Figure 4.1), which stands for research, objectives, programming, evaluation, and stewardship. Kelly, a fund-raising scholar, identified stewardship as an essential step in cultivating and retaining donors. We find that it is also an essential step with other key publics to ensure the positive relationships built through a PR program are then nurtured and maintained.

FIGURE 4.1

ROPES Process

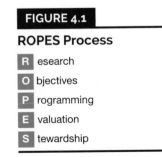

R esearch
O bjectives
P rogramming
E valuation
S tewardship

Research plays a critical role throughout the PR campaign process. Consider the important tool of social media where timing is critical. Research (Fontein, 2016) from Kissmetric tells us that the best time to post on Twitter is on weekdays at 5 p.m., and the best time to post on Facebook is Thursdays and Fridays from 1 p.m. to 3 p.m. PR practitioners use both secondary and primary research to guide planning decisions. Secondary research is gathering essential information that already exists—the research findings of others (e.g., published reports), whereas primary research is gathering essential information through research that you conduct—or contract out for (e.g., surveys). You will need to research your client organization, its business environment, the PR problem or opportunity, and the affected public.

ORGANIZATIONAL BACKGROUND

If you are handling internal PR for your own organization, likely you already have good knowledge of its business, the publics it serves, its competition, and the current state of your industry—perhaps both nationally and locally. What shapes the environment in which it does business? Research the competition, the organization's share of the market, and its position in the market. In a client situation, you'll need to have an adequate understanding of the organization and all the factors that affect it. It's important to consider the implications of this information and how it might apply to the planning of a PR campaign.

COMMUNICATIONS ANALYSIS

This involves the collection and evaluation of relevant external public messaging about the organization (including from mainstream and specialized sources and social media content) as well as that produced by the organization itself (internal messaging, such as press releases, newsletters, websites, etc.). Externally, what are the organization's image and reputation? Internally, what PR initiatives have been engaged in recently? What communication channels have been and are currently being used? Look at what is being said *about* the organization both externally and internally. Once answered, you must consider how this information might impact your PR plan.

ISSUE ANALYSIS

Consider the organization's history to help you understand its current situation. Also evaluate the organization's relationship with its publics and communities and how it may be unique in any way. Be sure to identify the *key* opportunity or challenge that faces the organization. Ancillary issues are important to note. With all this knowledge, you should now be able to concisely state the central issue the PR campaign will address, determine the goal for the client, and PR's role in achieving it. It's important now to also anticipate problems that may be encountered. A complete issue analysis should reveal some pathways for your PR campaign.

TARGET PUBLICS AND PUBLIC OPINION

Issues usually affect more than one public, but a single public may be evident as a primary focus for a PR campaign. Consider both internal (e.g., employees) and external (e.g., customers) publics, identify and describe the primary public, and then those publics of secondary and tertiary importance. These are the targets your PR campaign should consider when planning. Know what their relationships are with the organization and what their knowledge, attitudes, and behaviors are concerning

Learning as much as you can about your client's organization, history, and past PR efforts is essential to planning your campaign.

iStock.com/ferrantraite

the organization and/or the issue at hand. Publics can be classified into three types: latent (they do not recognize the problem or opportunity); aware (they develop from **latent publics** after they recognize the problem or opportunity); and **active publics** (they develop from **aware publics** after they begin to *do something* about the problem or opportunity) (Dozier & Grunig, 1992, p. 400). A careful evaluation of the target publics will help you strategically develop your plan.

PRIMARY RESEARCH METHODS

>> **LO 4.2 Identify the common primary research methods used in PR to plan a research strategy**

Once you've thoroughly conducted secondary research, you have a clearer understanding of what you still *need to know*. Depending on the need, decide which types of primary research to conduct and specifically with whom and for what purposes. Formulate research questions for each method. PR challenges very often require multiple research methods, and there are important considerations when choosing which ones to use and in what order.

TABLE 4.1

Common Public Relations Research Methods

TYPE	METHODS
Quantitative	Survey Content Analysis Digital Analytics
Qualitative	Focus Group Depth Interview Participant Observation

Dos and Don'ts: Research Ethics

A practical list of dos and don'ts when conducting professional research is found on the Institute for Public Relations's (IPR's) website (PR Measurement Standards, n.d.). This summary reveals the importance of correct research procedures and behaviors.

Before doing research *do* the following:

▸ Accurately and honestly communicate to your colleagues and clients the precise way you plan to report the results.

▸ Establish a baseline for measurement, and track results against the baseline.

When reporting research results *don't* do the following:

▸ Use terminology loosely; for example, don't use ROI (return on investment) unless it involves financial investment and return.

▸ Measure something against an "industry standard" unless indeed it is that—and not just a collective opinion.

▸ Claim that PR results, such as media hits or impressions (numerical evidence), suggest changes in attitudes or behaviors.

▸ Compare PR value to advertising value—the fields have distinctly different characteristics.

Another good source for best practices in research methods and findings is found in *A Practitioner's Guide to Public Relations Research, Measurement and Evaluation* (Michaelson & Wright, n.d.):

Methods should have the following characteristics:

▸ Clear and specific research objectives

▸ Well-defined and well-selected sample of respondents

▸ Well-designed research instruments that are appropriate, unbiased, and accurate

▸ Rigorous execution to generate reliable results

▸ Detailed supporting documentation with full transparency

Findings should accomplish the following:

▸ Demonstrate effectiveness of the PR campaign

▸ Link outputs (what you did) to outcomes (what resulted)

▸ Aid in development of better communications programs

▸ Include data to demonstrate impact on business

▸ Apply to a broad range of business activities, for example, marketing, product development, and corporate reputation

In an academic setting, any research involving people as subjects must first be approved by the university's institutional review board (IRB). Check with your institution's IRB (or ask your instructor) to see if a classroom research project must undergo IRB evaluation and approval. The reason for this procedure is to ensure your subjects will be treated ethically: with decency and dignity; without coercion; with full awareness of what will be asked of them; with full knowledge of the purpose for the research; with knowledge of who is conducting the research and who, whether a person or organization, is sponsoring it; and who will have access to the results (Smith, 2013). ●

QUANTITATIVE METHODS

Quantitative methods observe effects, test relationships, and generate numerical data that is considered objective. Results can be obtained through computerized statistical analysis and can be projected to a larger population than just those studied.

SURVEY

Surveys are one of the most common methods used in PR research for various reasons: their capacity to reach a large sample of a desired group of people, their low cost, their wide geographic distribution, the analytical data they generate, and the

Surveys are a key form of primary research in planning a PR campaign.

iStock.com/kasayizgi

ease of execution via software solutions on the Internet or via mobile apps or e-mail. Phone or in-person surveys allow for immediate results. In all surveys, you can ask both closed questions (multiple choice, yes or no, and true or false) and open-ended questions that allow for individual statements. The facility of survey data to make correlations can help better define publics. For example, questions about attitudes or behaviors can be measured against questions about demographics or social or economic characteristics, providing a clearer understanding of active and passive publics. The anonymity and structure of surveys help encourage participation. The disadvantages of the survey method are that the people who choose to respond only represent a sample of your public, and you will omit hard-to-reach respondents. Likewise, responses may not be entirely truthful, and the survey itself may be flawed if not properly designed and worded.

CONTENT ANALYSIS

Content analysis is a method of examining and categorizing existing communication and involves a structured coding system. It can be helpful for communication audits to get a good idea of *what's* being said and *how*—perhaps to compare across media, or over time, or to contrast against an opponent's messaging. It has the benefit of being relatively low cost, but one must be very careful to design the coding system to note all essential information and how it should be counted. It also *does not* consider characteristics of storytelling, metaphoric constructions, and other forms of rhetoric—which a qualitative rhetorical analysis would do.

DIGITAL ANALYTICS

Digital analytics tools allow you to collect, organize, and analyze online data, for example, from websites and social media platforms about customer and user conversations, activities, trends, and patterns. This allows you to get insights fast and accurately from multiple sources. As with other measurement and analytical methods, you may not be responsible for this process, but you should be aware of its value and application in listening to publics, guiding decision-making, and informing content changes.

QUALITATIVE METHODS

Qualitative methods are useful to explore attitudes, perceptions, values, and opinions. They are useful to confirm or refute your hunches and overall can help guide direction. Your research questions typically ask, "How do participants feel about X, and why," "How do participants interpret X," and so on or very simply, "What is going on here?" Some reasons PR professionals use qualitative methods are to build understanding of an issue by getting some preliminary information, to gather immediate information needed to address a pressing issue, and to inform the development of further research tools. Qualitative research is descriptive and interpretive, and results cannot be generalized to a larger group.

DEPTH INTERVIEW

A **depth interview** is a probing, one-on-one conversation that helps answer questions that ask how and why. It's also appropriate for engaging response on sensitive topics or with anyone who may have difficulty completing a questionnaire. A researcher typically uses a semi-structured list of questions and can adapt questioning to follow important threads in content that may be revealed. Thus the intimacy helps establish comfort and trust, and one can get a lot of detail and discover unexpected information. There are some disadvantages to be aware of: availability of time is a factor, as you will have *a lot* of material to transcribe and interpret; and there is no preliminary guarantee that your interviewee will be as cooperative as you wish.

Focus groups allow you to conduct essentially multiple depth interviews simultaneously.

Ammentorp Photography/
Alamy Stock Photo

Ask, Answer, Recommend—Using Research to Understand Business Goals and Develop Innovative Public Relations Strategies

Forrest Anderson, Forrest W. Anderson Consulting

My career has been built on these two simple premises:

1. Asking and answering the right questions

2. Making the leap from information to recommendations

I began my communications career as technical writer at a research institute and moved into their PR department. While the salary was low, the institute reimbursed education, so I got my MBA in marketing and management policy from The Kellogg School of Management at Northwestern University.

My studies taught me to develop strategies for organizations by understanding their business goals, strengths, weaknesses, stakeholder wants and needs, and trends and issues in the business environment. When I joined a major PR agency, I was assigned to write strategies for the PR programs we proposed to prospective clients because my MBA enabled me to link communications strategies to prospective business goals.

But I encountered a problem. The agency had very little information to guide the strategy. It did, however, have a research department, which I soon joined. In my research role, I would gather information about potential clients, their target audiences, and their business environments—everything necessary to build communications strategies that would support meeting goals, such as increasing sales or reducing employee turnover.

Then another problem arose. Many of the client contact staff were unable to translate this information into logical communications recommendations. So I advised them to tell the client: Based on this information, the communications program to help you achieve your business goals needs to:

Target this audience (clearly defined and drawn from demographic and psychographic research) . . .

With this message (developed and tested through secondary research, qualitative and quantitative primary research, and assessment of external trends and issues) . . .

Via these media (identified through researching the targets' media choices for similar information)

PR practitioners can also use stakeholder insights gained through research to reinforce the value of their seat at the "management table."

A Favorite Project

At one agency I worked with a major bank that had grown after acquisition and wanted to position itself as very customer oriented. Their own customer research and new employee research indicated the bank was *not* customer oriented. For example, a customer in one state could not cash a check at the bank's kiosk in another state. The issue was technology. While this is hard to imagine now, not too long ago, many technology platforms did not talk to each other.

We recommended against the customer-oriented positioning because it wasn't true. Moreover, customers and employees would not have believed it. Instead we suggested the bank explain how it was working *to become* more customer oriented. To reach this goal, we observed, they needed to fix their technology issues.

This is an example of communications professionals recognizing a business problem that couldn't be solved by communications, advising management of the issues needing attention, and recommending an alternative path. ●

Before starting his own research firm, Forrest W. Anderson Consulting, Anderson led research at Golin, Applied Communications, and Text 100.

Source: F. Anderson (personal communication, 2017).

FOCUS GROUP

Focus group research is a very common method for PR as well as advertising. It is relatively inexpensive and allows for recruiting and assembling participants rather quickly, yielding immediate findings. It is essentially a collective depth interview ideally conducted with between six and 12 participants. Thus it allows for the flexibility of follow-up questions, and the group situation stimulates discussion. It's typically video recorded for later analysis of both spoken and visual expressions. However, there are some disadvantages. Depending on circumstances, it may be hard to get a group of suitable participants all together at the same time in the same place. It's also unpredictable: Some participants may be inhibited by public speaking or being recorded. And the moderator's skill is crucial in establishing rapport, posing questions, probing for insight, and managing any participants who might tend to control the conversation. As with any qualitative methods, results cannot be generalized to a larger population.

PARTICIPANT OBSERVATION

Participant observation involves the researcher participating in an activity to observe and better understand those involved in that activity and their perspectives. For example, if a client needs an internal communication plan, observing office dynamics in the workplace could lead to conclusions your client may be unaware of. Or, if your client has physical venues for events or products, engaging in the attendee experience may give you a clearer understanding of what the publics encounter and how they behave. A researcher should be aware of several considerations:

▸ Maintain objectivity; don't "go native."

▸ Be unobtrusive; don't change group dynamics.

▸ It can be difficult to record observations.

▸ It's easy to confuse recollections with interpretations.

THE BIG IDEAS BEHIND PUBLIC RELATIONS STRATEGIES

>> LO 4.3 Recognize the role theory plays in PR

How do the findings from *formative* research, undertaken to help understand and solve a problem, translate into a PR campaign? By guiding your strategy and tactics. Research clarifies what your campaign needs to achieve and how to get there. It allows you to confidently confirm the end goal you first identified—or were assigned—and also helps reveal any modifications needed in that goal. Research also helps guide your strategy to achieve that goal through specific objectives. Theory enters the space between research and strategy. You'll see the relationship in 10 theories illustrated with application examples from the classroom and the world beyond.

There are many theories relevant to the practice of PR. Ten are listed and described in Table 4.2 to provide a baseline in your understanding of how theory connects to practice. These selected theories of media and mass communication, persuasion, and management include examples to illustrate how theory can be both predictive and explanatory.

TABLE 4.2

Ten Theories for Public Relations

Media and Mass Communication Models	Agenda Setting/Framing Two-Step Flow Spiral of Silence Diffusion of Innovations Uses & Gratifications
Persuasion Models	Elaboration Likelihood Model Cialdini's Principles of Influence ▸ Reciprocation ▸ Commitment and Consistency ▸ Social Proof ▸ Liking ▸ Authority ▸ Scarcity Inoculation
Management Models	Excellence Image Restoration Theory

MEDIA AND MASS COMMUNICATION

These theories concern the sender, the message, and the audience via various forms including traditional television, radio, newspapers, and more recently, film, music, and all the new communication technologies. We'll briefly introduce five theories here: agenda setting (including framing), two-step flow, spiral of silence, diffusion of innovations, and uses and gratifications. Once we look at examples, you should recognize them in your own media experiences.

AGENDA-SETTING THEORY

Agenda-setting theory was first developed by Maxwell McCombs and Donald Shaw and states that the media have a large influence on audiences by choosing which stories to make prominent (influencing what to think about—known as first-level agenda setting) and by using selective attributes to shape the stories (influencing how to think about them—known as second-level agenda setting). Thus the theory says the media determine for the public what's important and why. Consider, however, are the news media always influencers of public opinion? Actually alternative media, advertising, film, entertainment TV, and music may have a greater effect than news. But no matter the conduit, when the content is no longer user created, there is always a gatekeeper author that you turn your story over to, who then controls the story, which that sets the agenda for your audience.

▸ *A Student's Example:* In a campaign plan for the U.S. Secret Service, students applied agenda-setting theory to their strategy to change the tone of media coverage by driving specific messages that media relay to the public.

▸ *Agenda Setting in Action:* Superfoods is a term applied to a wide range of foods with potential health benefits. An analysis of a sample of news articles reporting on superfoods revealed how influential press releases are in shaping news content. Interviews confirmed the role of PR in promoting research (Weikamp & Torill, 2014).

The How and the Why of Theory

Research guides your PR strategy, but theory helps explain how and why things should work the way you intend them to. There are three types of theory (see Figure 4.2). Typically one of the first ways we try to understand a problem is to draw from anecdotal information—our past experiences, stories we've heard, and situations we've observed. That's called **commonsense theory,** and it's a good start but only as a warm-up.

Certain job-related generalizations are called **working theory**—agreed-upon ways of doing things, such as shooting a film with specific camera shots to evoke specific emotions. In higher education, where we are preparing for leadership positions in the communication field, we need to think in a more structured way by drawing on **scholarly theory**.

Systematic research to understand human behavior and events has provided more thorough and accurate explanations behind why things did—or didn't—work. These scholarly explanations are what we call "capital T" theories. For example, the widely tested theory of agenda setting might support an aggressive media campaign to help launch a new business. Why agenda setting? Because different levels of the theory explain that the news media set the agenda with the public on both *what* to think about and *how* to think about it.

Thus it's important to develop some perspective, based on theory, on how PR can address and solve a problem or turn an opportunity into a success. There are many different scholarly theories on why things work the way they do, drawn from the study of communication but also

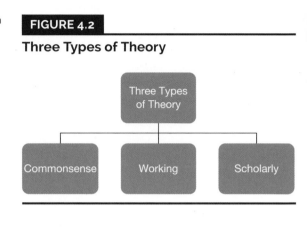

FIGURE 4.2

Three Types of Theory

from psychology, sociology, cultural studies, and even art history (such as telling us why certain symbols can evoke cultural meanings).

Theory goes beyond description to prediction. When studying the PR approach to a past situation, theory is explanatory: why *did* something succeed or fail? When preparing a PR recommendation, theory is visionary, telling us what *should* guide our strategies to succeed. Theories provide an understanding of the relationships between actions and events. As a PR practitioner, you'll need to explain why and how your plans will work. Knowing and being able to explain the science behind your proposals bolsters both your confidence and credibility. ●

Framing theory is a concept first put forth by Erving Goffman and similar to second-level agenda setting. It suggests that how something is presented to the audience (called "the frame") influences the choices people make about how to process that information. You may be familiar with the word mastery of Frank Luntz, the Republican strategist who skillfully renamed "global warming" as the much more benign "climate change." And in the attack mode, why was his phrase "death taxes" more effective than "estate taxes" in persuading Americans and eventually Congress to reduce estate taxes? Framing is the careful choice of words, imagery, sound, motion, or any rhetorical device to influence a certain meaning. And that makes it also a persuasion theory as well.

▸ *A Student's Example:* A campaign plan for Sprint applied framing theory to support a strategy of portraying the offer of their competitor, Verizon, not as a "deal" but really as "quite an expense" for consumers and businesses.

▸ *Framing in Action:* (Note: this example illustrates both framing and **two-step flow theory**.) The United States is one of the few places in the world that allows direct-to-consumer advertising (DTCA) of prescription drugs. In most countries it is banned, and the pharmaceutical industry relies primarily on PR activities to promote its products. An analysis of press releases used by pharma companies in Israel, where DTCA is banned, found their content predominantly used third-party influencers such as leading experts and physicians to frame the message as credible and the drugs as heroes. Conversely the messages also villainized the diseases and used negative framing of patients as "ticking time bombs" (Shir-Raz & Avraham, 2017, p. 387).

TOMS "One Day Without Shoes"

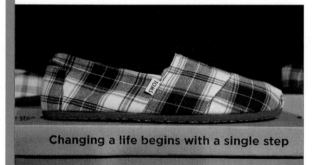

Changing a life begins with a single step

In 2007, TOMS Shoes launched a PR campaign to raise awareness about the many serious problems that can arise for children who lack shoes while simultaneously promoting the company's charitable efforts.

Noel Vasquez/Getty Images

Mission

TOMS Shoes was founded on the premise of donating a pair of shoes to a child in need for every pair purchased. Millions of children live without shoes. Many are not allowed to attend school. They are exposed to injury and disease every day, and shoes are a critical resource for health, education, and fulfilling their potential.

TOMS Annual "One Day Without Shoes" (ODWS)

The campaign was created in 2007 to spread awareness that a simple pair of shoes can prevent disease and infection and allow access to education for millions of children. In the spring of 2011, Ketchum and TOMS PR were charged with turning this day into a true global movement. With a goal to engage more than 500,000 people and double traffic to TOMS.com, PR became the leading marketing tactic to drive the company toward its most successful campaign yet.

Key Research Insights/Target Audience Analysis

To influence the media strategy, TOMS shared key learnings from the first three ODWS campaigns. The leading insight was a need for more news pre-event as people needed time to learn about the project and plan how they would participate. Ketchum turned to secondary data and a media audit around the TOMS consumers and their media consumption habits. While the movement was global, research revealed that local anchors, bloggers, and writers would have a big impact in moving their communities to make a difference. Ketchum then implemented a targeted effort to captivate local media to cover the cause.

Strategy

The TOMS community (primary: men and women 18–32; secondary: mothers) who were most influenced by WOM (digital included) and Twitter (fast becoming a top source for news) together guided a social media plan toward driving participation.

Results

PR's social media strategy sparked a global Twitter trending topic and exceeded desired engagement results—1 million people globally went barefoot (four times more participants than the year prior), and there was a 300% spike in traffic to TOMS.com. The campaign generated thousands of "likes" and comments in response to ODWS posts on TOMS Facebook page; on April 5 it was the fourth-most searched term on Google and AOL's Hot Search of the Day. More than 1,400 companies joined the TOMS Barefoot Challenge, more than 25 countries participated, and more than 500 schools got involved to show their support. ●

Source: PRSA (2012).

Note: The ODWS campaign was the 2012 Silver Anvil Award of Excellence Winner—Events and Observances—Seven or Fewer Days—Business Products.

TWO-STEP FLOW

Two-step flow theory was conceived by Paul Lazarsfeld and Elihu Katz. It says the media can also influence key spokespeople, experts, and leaders—early adopters of new ideas—who then influence certain groups of publics. These opinion leaders receive mass media messages and then pass on the content filtered through their own interpretations. Individuals with this "personal influence" can significantly aid in getting people to change their attitudes and behaviors. The concept of **upward flow theory** reverses direction, for example, employees advising management on existing or potential issues; a grassroots movement organized to sway political leaders; and generally, any opinion study with the goal of discovering public interests and concerns.

> ▸ *A Student's Example:* A class team applied two-step flow to a campaign plan to "recover, reclaim, sustain" a failing college by influencing community opinion leaders to then influence other publics about positive steps taken by the college.

> ▸ *Two-Step Flow in Action:* A study on the flow of information in Twitter-based discussion groups found opinion leaders emerged during the information flow. While not creators of the content, these opinion leaders had an influential function. This finding is important as it suggests beyond the purposeful incorporation of opinion leaders in a PR Plan, leaders may emerge independently and with opinions not necessarily aligned with the plan's goals.

SPIRAL OF SILENCE

Ideas and opinions expressed in mass media can discourage expressions by people who hold dissenting opinions due to their sensitivity of feeling isolated or rejected. Elisabeth Noelle-Neumann's **spiral of silence theory** helps explain the power of public opinion, especially regarding topics that have moral arguments. PR professionals wanting to encourage expression from those in the "minority" should publicize some minority opinion to draw out the silent voices; also, surveys and questionnaires should carry carefully worded questions to encourage response on controversial topics.

> ▸ *A Student's Example:* A campaign plan to build awareness of child abuse in the Southwestern United States held intimate focus groups with similar participants to encourage open discussion on a topic that's culturally sensitive.

> ▸ *Spiral of Silence in Action:* How do people differ in their willingness to express their opinions in hostile social situations? A survey of college students exploring this raised two controversial topics (gun possession and climate change). The survey found that (1) fear of isolation suppresses people's willingness to express their opinions in public; and (2) active publics (who are more aware of and active about their beliefs) are more likely than other types of publics to express their opinions (Lee, Oshita, Oh, & Hove, 2014). Here, spiral of silence theory explains the reticence in expressing opinions when public dissent is perceived. Acknowledging the effect of the spiral of silence helps PR practitioners to predict which types of publics would be more or less likely to express their opinion and, knowing so, to find ways to encourage those less likely.

How Merck Communicated With AIDS Activists

In 1996, Merck introduced its first protease inhibitor, part of the first wave of drugs to treat HIV/AIDS, and conducted a campaign to engage with the activist community.

Peter Probst/Alamy Stock Photo

The AIDS crisis gained status as a critical issue in the mid-1980s, by which time AIDS activist groups, formed at the beginning of the decade when the disease was first identified, had become extremely vocal, aggressive, and sometimes violent. The war against AIDS was being fought on two fronts: a search for a vaccine and treatments for those already infected.

Increasing Frustration

In the 1980s, there were several basic research breakthroughs that held promise for people suffering from HIV and AIDS, but there were few medicines on the market. A diagnosis of HIV was a virtual death sentence. Many pharmaceutical companies were working on medicines and vaccines. This dependence on the pharmaceutical industry frustrated many activists.

Mock Funerals and Demonstrations

Organizations such as ACT UP used a strategy of confrontation in the hope of bringing treatments at the earliest possible date to the marketplace. ACT

UP tactics intended to pressure pharmaceutical companies included mock funerals, demonstrations, and disrupting trading at the New York Stock Exchange. Other organizations such as the Treatment Action Group used a strategy of accommodation to ensure reliability in the research associated with AIDS drugs. This group recognized that confrontational strategies may actually delay the real objective of all AIDS activists—safe, effective treatments.

The Breakthrough

Government funding for research was also spurring new developments for future disease treatments, and by decade's end, university and industry researchers were working aggressively to discover and develop treatments. By the mid-1990s, two companies, Hoffmann-LaRoche Inc. and Abbott Laboratories, had begun to market new therapies called protease inhibitors. In March 1996, after 10 years of research, Merck introduced the third protease inhibitor, CRIXIVAN.

Engagement Approach Brings Opponents Together

Merck enacted a series of relationship-building tactics to engage its activist publics. These changes were both internal and external to the organization and showed the dynamics of an engagement approach. The PR team at Merck researched the AIDS activist groups, finding they were diverse. Interviews with activists were placed in employee newsletters and magazines. Merck organized tours of research facilities and multiple meetings among researchers and activists. The company made changes after listening. Through multiple strategies, Merck created an internal AIDS communication program that helped members communicate and build relationships with the activist publics (Taylor, Vasquez, & Doorley, 2003). ●

DIFFUSION OF INNOVATIONS

Diffusion of innovations theory draws from the fields of both marketing and psychology, stating that a new idea or a product must pass through a sequential process with a public to ultimately be adopted. Everett Rogers's theory has a six-step process: awareness—knowledge—evaluation—trial—adoption—reinforcement. Research shows that a public's response to a certain persuasive appeal that calls for behavior change depends on where it lies in the diffusion process. Note the steps that must be accomplished before you reach "trial." Also consider how other theories may fit in; for example, early adopters can wield personal influence to spread awareness.

▸ *A Student's Example:* A campaign plan for rebranding the Chevy Volt was guided by principles of diffusion of innovations because a reorientation process was needed to build understanding and acceptance for an electric vehicle with new technology components.

▸ ***Diffusion in Action:*** Lu Zheng (2013) studied car manufacturer Audi's press releases from 1999 to 2007 and interviewed with Audi PR professionals. She found that diffusion of innovations theory helped explain Audi's strategy of cultivating relations with leading media professionals to help influence Chinese consumers. While traditionally adhering to Confucian values of thrift and simplicity, they moved from awareness to adoption.

USES AND GRATIFICATIONS THEORY

Uses and gratifications theory was developed by Elihu Katz and says that users of media take an active role by choosing and using certain media. They're goal oriented. A person selects a source that best meets his or her needs. Uses and gratifications theory assumes that the user has alternate choices to satisfy a need. When it was first developed, the theory defined four types of need (Note: due to changes in technologies and consumer use, recent research expands on these):

▸ *Diversion:* Media fills the need to escape from everyday life, to relax.

▸ *Personal Relationships:* We use media to fulfill needs for companionship and to form relationships with others (e.g., interest groups).

▸ *Personal Identity:* We tend to use media to find out about ourselves; people profiled may reflect our desires, needs, fantasies, or secrets.

▸ *Surveillance:* We use media to find out what is going on around us.

So, for a strategic campaign planner, the application is clear: Determine the needs of your target public, and then address them using appropriate media channels and tactics.

▸ ***A Student's Example:*** A campaign plan recognized that Millennials shared music preferences in social media platforms to both express identity and support relationships, so YouTube and Facebook were chosen as channels to communicate the client's message.

▸ ***Uses and Gratifications in Action:*** A survey targeting individual investors addressed the types, qualities, and sources of information they seek and value. In keeping with uses and gratifications theory, results identified specific conditions associated with investors seeking and selecting sources of information. Significantly they sought PR communication, revealing this content has as much or more value than information from the news media or other sources (Penning, 2011).

PERSUASION

Persuasion is typically defined as human communication that is designed to influence others by modifying their beliefs, values, attitudes, or behaviors. Now we'll introduce three persuasion theories: Elaboration Likelihood Model (ELM), Cialdini's Influence Principles, and Inoculation Theory.

ELABORATION LIKELIHOOD MODEL

Elaboration Likelihood Model (ELM) is a major persuasion theory developed by Richard Petty and John Cacippio. It states that persuasive messages are received by people through two different routes: either the central route or the peripheral route.

▸ Via the central route, one's mental processing is based on thought, analysis, and reflection. Active thinking internalizes the message, and attitudes formed are more persistent and resistant to change. Some publics *are* central processors by nature, so when addressing them it's extremely important that your argument has cognitive strength.

▸ Via the peripheral route, one's processing is based on mental shortcuts with little effort, thus attitudes formed are more short-lived. With the crescendo of chatter in our world, most messages are processed this way. Although the listener may immediately change an attitude, it's not long-lasting.

As PR strategists, because we know the central route to mental processing is more likely to stick and affect attitude and behavior change, we need to know how to motivate the central route! Here's how:

▸ Increase motivation to engage: Explain why your message is relevant and how it affects the receiver personally.

▸ Increase ability to engage: Adapt to the receiver's level of understanding and experience. Eliminate distractions.

As a result of this, receivers will actively think about your message and are more likely to change attitude.

▸ ***A Student's Example:*** A campaign plan for Military OneSource used ELM to guide its detailed and compelling strategies and tactics, with the goal of changing attitudes on posttraumatic stress disorder (PTSD) in service members and their families.

▸ ***ELM in Action:*** The Sesame Street Talk, Listen, Connect (TLC) initiative is a multimedia example of entertainment education that leveraged the popular Sesame Street platform to deliver key information to military families about how to communicate with children about feelings related to deployment, homecomings, and other tough issues related to military life. A case study compared the TLC initiative against the ELM model, as well as other communication models, finding it to be an exemplar in entertainment education (Desens & Hughes, 2013).

> **SOCIAL RESPONSIBILITY**

PRINCIPLES OF INFLUENCE

Social psychologist Robert Cialdini identified six different cues (see Figure 4.3) that trigger peripheral route processing (as explained with ELM, peripheral equals the use of mental shortcuts). Here are **Cialdini's Influence Principles**:

FIGURE 4.3

Influence Principles

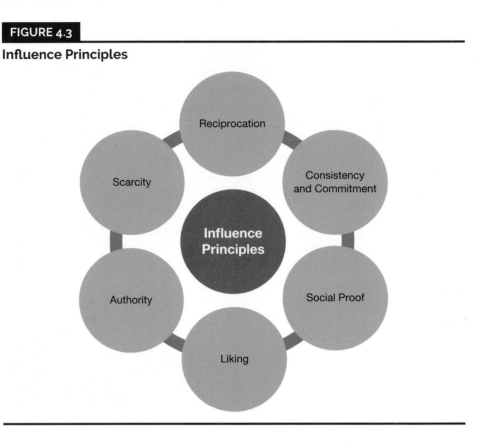

▸ *Reciprocation* refers to the drive to respond to another's positive action with your own positive action. It also can be used persuasively and is a principle behind negotiating with concessions.

▸ *Consistency and commitment* are the desire to be (and to appear to be) *in agreement, in harmony, and compatible* . . . with who we think we are or what we have already done. Once we make a choice or take a stand, we encounter personal and interpersonal pressures to behave consistently with that commitment. A strategist seeking influence might consider the power of the highly valued consistency principle.

▸ *Social proof* is Cialdini's term for behavior influenced by the fact that "everyone's doing it." There are various explanations for group conformity, and it can be a very powerful weapon of influence.

▸ *Liking*—Cialdini's studies showed that people tend to say yes to those they like. There are multiple components of liking: repeated contact, similarity, flattery, and physical attractiveness.

▸ *Authority*—most cultures have a sense of duty to it. Our obedience to authority often takes place with little deliberation and makes so much "sense" to us that we comply when it does not make sense. It's automatic. This principle can explain the persuasive power of visual "trappings" of authority (clothing, status symbols, titles, etc.).

▸ *Scarcity* accounts for people's behavior when confronted with limited numbers, time, opportunities, and loss in general. We want something more when there's less of it. And we are more motivated by the prospect of losing

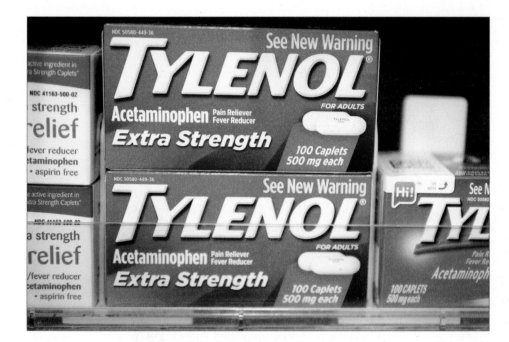

Despite knowledge of the dangers of overdose, the maker of Tylenol, Johnson & Johnson, failed to conduct an inoculation campaign to forestall both reputational damage and actual harm to consumers. Only in 2004 did the company make changes, including new warning labels.

Scott Olson/Getty Images

something than we are by the prospect of gaining something of equal value. In fact, known as psychological reactance, we react against any interference by wanting and trying to possess the item more than we did before.

▸ **A Student's Example:** A campaign plan to help the National Football League (NFL) manage its crisis with chronic traumatic encephalopathy (CTE) applied all Cialdini's influence principles.

▸ **Reciprocity in Action:** In a study on stewardship (the "s" in ROPES) in nonprofit fund-raising, Richard Waters found that donors favor the strategy of reciprocity and that it has significant impact on how donors evaluate their relationships with the organization (Waters, 2009).

INOCULATION

Here's a theory that we call a "weapon" of influence as it was developed and tested in competitive situations. **Inoculation theory** by William J. McGuire, a social psychologist, states that inoculation builds resistance to persuasive messages. Based on the metaphor of a medical inoculation or vaccination, the theory says that if you give your audience a small dose of your opponent's argument, and then you immediately provide a counterargument, it triggers a process of counterarguing by the audience members themselves—on their own—which eventually makes them resistant to later, stronger persuasive messages from your opponent. For example, often used in litigation and political campaigns, the inoculation strategy might begin: "My opponent (or defense counsel) will tell you . . ."

▸ **A Student's Example:** A campaign plan for a political candidate proposed a series of videos telling her story and touching on negative aspects of her opponent's story.

▸ **Inoculation not in Action:** In this situation, a company failed to implement an inoculation campaign resulting in consumer harm. Maker of Tylenol, Johnson & Johnson, long known for excellence in CSR, launched a responsible dosing campaign in 2004 only after overdoses of its acetaminophen drug resulted in 56,000 emergency room visits annually, resulting in 100 deaths, according to the Food and Drug Administration (FDA), and a wrongful death suit had been filed. Company research revealed that decades earlier, it had been aware of overdose risks. An earlier inoculation campaign to change attitudes and behaviors, and protect consumers, could have prevented the unknowing drug abuse and deaths (Veil & Kent, 2008).

MANAGEMENT MODELS

Management theories consider input from and relationships with various stakeholders in an organization. Next we describe Excellence Theory, which supports PRSA's principle of mutuality, and **Benoit's Image Restoration Theory**, which guides response to, and evaluation of, issues that negatively impact reputation.

EXCELLENCE THEORY

Excellence theory is a major PR theory developed by James Grunig and others. An organization's good relationships with its stakeholders (publics) helps it develop and achieve goals desired by both the organization and its publics; reduce costs of negative publicity; and increase revenue by providing needed products and services. To maximize the value of PR, a campaign must identify strategic publics and build long-term relationships with them through two-way symmetrical communication programs. This means the organization and its publics both talk and listen to each other with mutual respect and willingness to adapt. Organizations that embrace this theory place PR professionals in a critical management function.

 ▸ *A Student's Example:* In this campaign plan, the Port of Houston Authority confronted alleged misconduct, negative media attention, and a state investigation. The students chose Excellence Theory to create public-organization relationships through social media.

 ▸ *Excellence in Action:* A case study examined a state health department's relationships with its employees, finding it did not make optimal use of its interactions with them. By the adoption of recommendations based on the Excellence Theory, the study proposed the organization could increase its organizational effectiveness (Wise, 2003).

IMAGE RESTORATION THEORY

Image restoration theory, developed by William Benoit, helps evaluate—or recommend—a response to a harmful situation. It suggests five strategies that depend on the contexts: denial, evading responsibility, reducing offensiveness, corrective action, and mortification. Many case studies have applied Benoit's theory to analyze damaging situations involving celebrities, politicians, and corporations.

 ▸ *A Student's Example:* A campaign plan applied Benoit's theory to recommend how Carnival Cruise Lines should rebuild its image and reputation.

 ▸ *Image Restoration in Action:* Two researchers studied how image repair work is carried out in face-to-face communication with members of the media, specifically politicians' press conferences (Eriksson & Eriksson, 2012).

They found that image repair strategies like apologizing and mortification during the speech section of a press conference tend to be more effective as they give the accused greater opportunities to take control of the interaction.

Note: Em Griffin's *A First Look at Theory* helped inform some of these descriptions (Griffin, 2017).

SCENARIO OUTCOME

At the beginning of this chapter you read about the healthy snack company Graze and its need for a PR plan to help increase visibility, sales, and customer loyalty in the United States. Putting yourself in the role of the company's newly hired PR consultant, we ask you the following:

What questions would you need to answer through secondary research?

Secondary research would focus on giving you a clear understanding of the organization's marketing goals in the United States. Are they firm or fluid? Who are their target publics now, who is competing against Graze for this public, and what is Graze's position with this public? Backing up, what *is* the state of the healthy snack industry in the United States?

You will also ask how the company has been communicating to this public, through both controlled means (company website, social media platforms, blogs, etc.) and uncontrolled means (media coverage). Review this communication to determine what messages are being sent or reported. What image and reputation does Graze have now?

Finally you will try to learn more about the targeted public. Some questions might be: What are their communication preferences? Who or what influences them? How do current customers feel about Graze? What are their needs and desires regarding healthy snacking?

How will these answers affect your PR plan and guide your primary research?

What primary research would you suggest to inform your PR plan?

In your next step you'll conduct some primary research with members of a segment of the target public, 20- to 40-year-old women who have children under age 18. You begin with a focus group, asking questions like, "Is healthy snacking important to you? To your family members? What are healthy snacks? What does organic mean to you? What are your family's snacking habits? What roles does convenience play in your healthy snack purchases? How would you feel about a healthy snack company that funds a giving-back social responsibility program?"

Drawing on your focus group results, you will design an online survey to reach a much larger population within the same target public, asking, "Where do you find information about healthy eating? Where do you look for organic healthy snacks? How important is it for a healthy snack company to source from local U.S. food growers? Are you aware of Graze?"

For the online component of your plan, what communication strategies would you recommend—guided by which theories?

Your online PR strategy might look like this:

▸ Use social media for customer-company dialogue and interactivity (Excellence Theory).

▸ Use consistent messaging (consistency and commitment, tying the public's valuing of healthy, quality snacks to Graze).

▸ Increase media relations efforts with food bloggers (agenda setting).

▸ Encourage WOM from influencers (two-step flow).

▸ Encourage visits to website and social media platforms (uses and gratifications).

WRAP UP

In this chapter, you were introduced to the ROPES planning process in PR—research, objectives, programming, evaluation, and stewardship—and gained a specific understanding of the research stage. You also explored the common research methods in PR, both quantitative and qualitative: content analysis, survey, data analytics, focus group, depth interview, and participant observation. And you explored the relationship between theory and PR strategy, seeing how mass communication, persuasion, and management theories help guide strategic planning. Beyond guidance, you discovered theory is also useful to diagnose what *might* have been done to achieve a better outcome and to explain why something did work well or missed the mark.

KEY TERMS

Active Publics: PR term for people who do something about their beliefs, problems, or opportunities, **85**

Agenda-Setting Theory: Explains that media have a large influence on audiences by choosing which stories to make prominent, **91**

Aware Publics: PR term for people who recognize a problem or opportunity, **85**

Benoit's Image Restoration Theory: Explains how to evaluate, or recommend, a response to a harmful situation, **100**

Cialdini's Influence Principles: Six different cues that trigger mental shortcuts, **97**

Commonsense Theory: Using anecdotal information to guide understanding, **92**

Content Analysis: Research method of examining and categorizing existing communication, **87**

Depth Interview: Research method that searches to answer how and why through a one-on-one conversation, **88**

Diffusion of Innovations Theory: Theory explaining that a new idea or a product must pass through a sequential process with a public to ultimately be adopted, **95**

Digital Analytics: Tools that allow collection, organization, and analysis of online data, **87**

Elaboration Likelihood Model (ELM): A major persuasion theory explaining that persuasive messages are received by people through two different routes: central and peripheral, **97**

Excellence Theory: General theory of PR that explains characteristics of excellent communications, **100**

Focus Group: Research method that involves a collective depth interview, **90**

Framing Theory: Suggests that how something is presented to the audience (called "the frame") influences the choices people make about how to process that information, **92**

Inoculation Theory: Explains that inoculation (giving audiences a small dose of an opposing argument and then refuting it) builds their resistance to future opposing messages, **99**

Latent Publics: People who are not aware of a problem or opportunity, **85**

Participant Observation: Research method in which the researcher participates in an activity to observe and better understand the people involved and their perspectives, **90**

Qualitative Methods: Types of research useful to explore attitudes, perceptions, values, and opinions, **88**

Quantitative Methods: Types of research to observe effects, test relationships, and generate numerical data that is considered objective, **86**

ROPES: Acronym for the PR process, standing for research, objectives, programming, evaluation, and stewardship, **82**

Scholarly Theory: Widely tested explanations of human behavior and events generated through systematic research, **92**

Spiral of Silence Theory: Explains that ideas and opinions expressed in mass media can discourage expressions by people who hold dissenting opinions due to a sensitivity of feeling isolated or rejected, **94**

Stewardship: Tactics to maintain relationships with publics after a communication campaign has been executed, **82**

Surveys: Research method that asks both closed questions (multiple choice, yes or no, true or false) and open-ended questions, **86**

Two-Step Flow Theory: Explains that media can also influence early adopters of new ideas (called "opinion leaders") who filter the content through their own interpretations and then pass it on to influence certain groups of publics, **92**

Upward Flow Theory: Explains how grassroots or general public opinions can influence an organization or political leaders, **94**

Uses and Gratifications Theory: Explains that users of media take an active role by choosing and using certain media to meet various needs, **96**

WOM: Word of mouth, **82**

Working Theory: Agreed-upon ways of doing things; a hypothesis that has not been tested or proven through structured research, **92**

THINK ABOUT IT

Simulate a focus group in class. First use your university or college to identify an issue that the administration should monitor. It may be the level of satisfaction of commuter students, or safety on campus, or the experience of international students—issues like this. Ideally choose an issue that impacts students in your class. Then choose a moderator (it's OK if several students moderate together) and develop a script with questions to ask focus group members). About eight students should be the focus group participants. Remaining students will serve as the "client" (members of the administration) who will quietly observe the focus group, noting facial expressions, body language, and making general observations. After the focus group is conducted, critique and debrief with each student, sharing how they experienced the process.

WRITE LIKE A PRO

As a newly hired PR assistant at the West Coast agency, JDG-PR, you are expected to be an expert in social media. One of your first assignments is to support the social media team for their client, Tee-Shirt Winery. The client's nearest competitor is Barefoot Wines, and their wines are quite comparable in price point and quality. Tee-Shirt's brand positioning is fun, quirky, carefree, and organic. Your assignment is to conceive of a Snapchat video that tells part of the brand's story and then prepare a storyboard for it. The goal of the video is to send fans to the client's YouTube channel. Cialdini's influence principles are good sources to guide your narrative strategy as they explain how influence transfers in momentary experiences. (Identify how Cialdini's principles guided you at the end of your submission).

SOCIAL RESPONSIBILITY CASE STUDY

Allstate Reality Rides® Combats Distractions With a Virtual Driving Simulator

Situation

More than 3,000 deaths occurred in the United States in 2010 and 2011 due to distracted driving, and drivers who text are 23 times more likely to crash. For nearly a decade, Allstate Insurance Company's media relations team engaged multiple stakeholders in efforts to end distracted driving. In April 2013, Allstate launched Reality Rides to combat distracted driving. Between 2013 and 2014, Reality Rides visited 70 metropolitan areas, using a real—but stationary—car equipped with virtual reality technology to simulate the dangers of distracted driving.

Research and Strategy

Because distracted driving persists as the number one cause of collisions, Allstate proactively researched studies to ensure the focus of its campaigns met the needs of the communities and stakeholders it serves.

According to the National Highway Traffic Safety Administration (NHTSA), Allstate found that car crashes are the primary cause of death for Americans ages 1 to 34, with teens crashing four times more than any other age group. NHTSA also reported that in 2010 and 2011, more than 3,000 people died each year in crashes involving a distracted driver, and more than 400,000 were injured.

Research also revealed that texting and driving can increase the risk of crashing by 23 times. A Virginia Tech Transportation study found that texting takes a driver's eyes off the road for an average of 5 seconds. Texting while driving at 55 miles per hour is like driving the length of a football field blind or driving impaired after four beers.

Graduated Driver Licensing (GDL) laws have been shown to reduce traffic fatalities by as much as 40 percent. The Allstate Foundation conducted research on the outcomes of these laws. Allstate's subsequent License to Save report found GDL laws have been shown to reduce traffic fatalities by as much as 40 percent and could save an estimated 2,000 lives and $13.6 billion annually.

Allstate measures its own reputation through annual surveys, and safety programs were identified among 83 percent of customers and 78 percent of consumers as important to highlight.

These findings directed further research, concluding that Allstate could make a positive influence on local communities through an event-based distracted driving campaign focused on anti-texting.

Execution

Target audiences included drivers with a focus on young adults, teens, and their families. Allstate allocated $1.7 million over two years to Reality Rides and identified 70 metropolitan areas to implement the program. Community impact was maximized by including a variety of event venues: young adult policy conventions, community fairs, shopping malls, sporting events, and colleges and high schools.

Allstate appealed to the target market with a tech-focused and accessible experience by partnering with Unite, a driving simulation and experiential marketing firm. Reality Rides launched nationwide with integrated media, using a wire press release, targeted pitches, and resources on AllstateNewsroom.com.

Turnkey resources for local implementation were created. Allstate developed a tool kit equipped with internal messages for employee and agency engagement in addition to a full suite of press materials, event activation guides, and GDL advocacy materials.

Evaluation

Measurable outcomes and lasting impressions were gained. Pre- and post-event surveys measured drivers' perceptions, understanding of driving laws, and awareness of distracted driving. The events were successful at increasing awareness of distracted driving dangers among all stakeholders: its targeted audiences, agency owners and employees. As well, their perception of Allstate's reputation increased since the campaign's inception.

Reality Rides engaged more than 2,000 stakeholders with a positive response. On site, among 4,500 participants surveyed, 85% stated it was a "fun and effective program;" 63% positively answered they will "never text and drive."

ENGAGE

▸ Go to Allstate's site on teen driving: https://www.allstatefoundation.org/teen_safe_driving_driver_license.html. Select the graduated license laws (either Spanish or English version). Find your state and see what rules govern teen drivers. Note the "texting and driving" restrictions for all drivers.

DISCUSSION

▸ Compare and discuss your state's GDLs and texting rules with classmates from different states. What differences do you find? As PR advisor on this issue, how do you think these laws and rules can be best communicated?

Note: This case was winner of a 2015 PRSA Silver Anvil award, © 2015, Public Relations Society of America, Inc.

SOCIAL RESPONSIBILITY CASE STUDY

The Monster-Free Mouths Movement: AAPD Makes a Big Deal About the Importance of Little Teeth

Situation

The American Academy of Pediatric Dentistry (AAPD) is an organization representing 9,300 primary care and specialty providers for millions of children from infancy through adolescence. Its challenge was to raise awareness of children's oral health, the unique expertise of pediatric dentists, and the need for children to have an established home base for their oral health-care needs—much like a pediatrician oversees a child's overall health through the year.

Research and Strategy

A review of the latest research led to development of the AAPD's "State of Little Teeth Report." The issues it examined were who is most likely to suffer from tooth decay and the immediate and long-term health, social, and economic effects and possible solutions for halting the increase of tooth decay in little teeth. The report also explored what should be done to address these issues.

A survey of 1,000 parents and caregivers revealed a gap in knowledge about pediatric oral health. A key insight was that although parents and caregivers wanted to provide their children with the best care possible, they had conflicting information on how to do it. They were unsure when to take children for their first dental visit or to whom to take them. This discovery played a decisive role in the development of campaign strategy.

Based on research, AAPD identified a lack of clarity surrounding pediatric dental care. Its strategy called for an education campaign that would urge parents and caregivers to take prompt action to ensure healthy teeth for their kids. The campaign would also highlight pediatric dental professionals.

The following objectives were established:

▸ Elevate children's oral health as a gateway to their overall health.

▸ Establish pediatric dentists and the AAPD as trusted resources for children's oral health.

▸ Motivate parents to use pediatric dentists.

AAPD developed the "Monster-Free Mouths Movement," an educational campaign to help fight the Mouth Monsters. It created Tooth D.K, Tartar the Terrible, and Ginger Bite-Us, to help bring the campaign to life with imagery and characters to appeal to children and parents.

The organization itself rebranded with a new consumer-friendly logo and tagline, "The Big Authority on Little Teeth," to better connect with parents and caregivers and educate them on the critical need for early checkups and regular oral care.

Execution

On January 28, 2014, the "Monster-Free Mouths Movement" launched with a two-day media tour in New York City featuring parenting advisor Rosie Pope. The consumer awareness campaign included releasing the "State of Little Teeth Report" and introducing the Mouth Monsters characters.

The campaign came alive on AAPD's website, www.mychildrensteeth.org, featuring original Mouth Monster content. Parents and caregivers could download the Mouth Monster Defense Kit with printable materials including a brushing tracker, mirror posters, and reward certificates aimed to drive enthusiasm for taking care of little teeth. Consumer engagement was driven on social media with Facebook posts.

Evaluation

The objective of raising awareness of pediatric dentistry through widespread media coverage was met in the full year of communications activities. The success of the campaign was notable given the significant amount of national consumer media that covered data released in the report, launch of the consumer awareness campaign, or both. Original coverage appeared in *USA Today* print and digital editions and was widely syndicated. Supporting original coverage appeared in The Huffington Post, Kaiser Health (which was picked up by WebMD, *USA Today* and PBS Newshour), *Working Mother, Pregnancy & Newborn*, and SheKnows.com.

Spokesperson Pope was featured in coverage resulting from a media tour and blogger interviews, and her social posts on Facebook and Twitter garnered nearly a half million impressions.

AAPD's Facebook community grew from 6,343 to 36,319 between the launch in late January through June 2014. Its consumer video reached 1.7 million users and was viewed more than 84,000 times. AAPD website traffic increased 61% from the launch of the consumer awareness campaign in late January 2014 through June 2014.

ENGAGE

▸ Go to http://www.mychildrensteeth.org/, click on the Mouth Monsters link, and read several of the articles.

DISCUSSION

▸ Much of the material on the Mouth Monsters link is aimed at parents and caregivers of young children. Using the same materials and with the same awareness goals, create an outline of a PR campaign for organizations that come in contact with children of the same age (Brownies, Cub Scouts, primary grade teachers, youth sports, etc.)

Note: This case was winner of the 2015 Silver Anvil Award (Public Service, Nonprofit Organizations), © 2015, Public Relations Society of America, Inc.

VIDEO CASE

Apple's iPod vs. Microsoft's Zune: ROPES and Research

In 2001, Apple launched the iPod as a portable music player. Three years later, after Apple made the iPod compatible with Windows PCs, the iPod took off. In 2006, Microsoft brought out a competitor, the Zune. In 2009, both companies debuted updates to their products, going head to head in the marketplace.

VIDEO

1. Use the ROPES method to outline the approach you would have taken to promote the iPod versus the Zune.

2. What obstacles might you have faced in each of these campaigns?

3. What research methods might you have pursued and why?

5 Implementing Your Strategic Communications Plan

Learning Objectives

5.1 Understand the structure of strategic communications plans

5.2 Demonstrate how to formulate objectives to reach a goal

5.3 Demonstrate how to prepare programming to meet objectives

5.4 Explain the roles of evaluation, ongoing research, and stewardship

Scenario

Creating Awareness of Skin Cancer Among African Americans

Sixty-five percent of African Americans say they have never used sunscreen (Skin Cancer Foundation, 2016). The American Association of Dermatologists (AAD) reports that darker skinned people are equally susceptible as Caucasians to many forms of skin cancer, particularly melanoma, which is one of the deadliest forms. For example, Bob Marley, the pioneering reggae musician and Jamaican icon, died from a form of melanoma (ALM) in 1981 (Skin Cancer Foundation, n.d.).

The AAD and SkinCancer.org have worked together and supported Skin Cancer Awareness Month each May for several years. The program has achieved good visibility and awareness in the spring and summer timeframe.

Despite the risk of skin cancer, most African Americans do not use sunscreen.

iStock.com/XiXinXing

Focus on behavior change. However, AAD wants to develop and launch a new program focused on the African American community, encouraging the daily use of sunscreen and regular visits to the dermatologist. The overall goals include an overall increase in dermatological office visits and the sale and use of sunscreen by African Americans. AAD is interested in working on a combined PR/CSR program with a major partner company on this project. It believes this is an excellent vehicle for the right company to engage in corporate philanthropy and/or a cause-related marketing campaign.

Campaign challenge. Your agency has been retained by the AAD to develop and implement this plan to raise awareness about skin cancer prevention and detection as a daily, year-round activity. AAD has corporate partners that market over-the-counter (e.g., sunscreens) and prescription-strength products to prevent and treat severe skin damage. The association is confident that with the right concept and plan, it can get additional corporate sponsors to sign on and support the efforts with product, promotion, and publicity to build awareness and achieve key objectives.

As you read through this chapter, consider the following:

1. How would you get started in developing a plan?
2. What type(s) of research would you undertake?
3. What specific objectives would you propose?
4. What tactic(s) would you propose?
5. How will you measure progress or success?
6. What budget considerations are there to consider?
7. How does your plan reflect current best practices in PR and CSR communications?

In this chapter you will continue to review the ROPES planning process (covering the remaining steps, i.e., Objectives, Planning, Evaluation, and Stewardship). In the prior chapter we reviewed the role of research in developing a strategic communications plan. We also identified the major communications theories that form the foundation for PR planning.

In this chapter, you will consider the process of completing your plan, implementing it, and measuring progress toward achieving the desired objectives. This is critical to understand because strategic planning is central to both strategic public relations (SPR) and Social Responsibility (SR) initiatives.

As you go through this chapter, you will learn the building blocks of strategic planning and the importance of measurement and evaluation before, during, and after the planning stage. Clients or senior managers you encounter during your career will want to be assured that the resources put into SPR and SR programs will demonstrate a return on the investment they are making. This requires a dedication to strategic planning and an understanding of how to build a plan that delivers meaningful results.

FOUNDATIONS OF STRATEGIC PLANNING IN STRATEGIC PUBLIC RELATIONS

>> **LO 5.1**   **Understand the structure of strategic communications plans**

The communications planning process is, by definition, fluid and dynamic, but there is a recommended structure and process to be followed consistent with the ROPES approach. Following the steps and maintaining the planning discipline as you move through the process is key to accomplishing your goals. Dozier and Broom (1995, p. 23) describe this process, noting, "Strategic planning is deciding where you want to be in the future (the goal) and how to get there [the strategy]. It sets the organization's direction proactively—avoiding 'drift' and routine repetition of activities." Each of the components of an SPR plan is critical. Each section has its own purpose and challenges if the plan is to have the desired outcome.

SITUATION ANALYSIS

The situation analysis (developed through research as covered in Chapter 4) is one of the most important parts of the plan, which is why it is the first step. It is designed to set the stage and define the problem or opportunity. A well-written, succinct summary is key to achieving consensus among your management team or from the client. It allows you to explain why the plan is needed and how it reflects the current situation facing the company. If properly drafted it also demonstrates to your management or client that you understand the company or industry and the factors—positive or negative—that are impacting it currently. Finally it sets up the communications plan that follows and introduces the solution (e.g., the *objectives*) you are proposing.

$SAGE edge

Master the content
edge.sagepub.com/page

FIGURE 5.1

ROPES Process

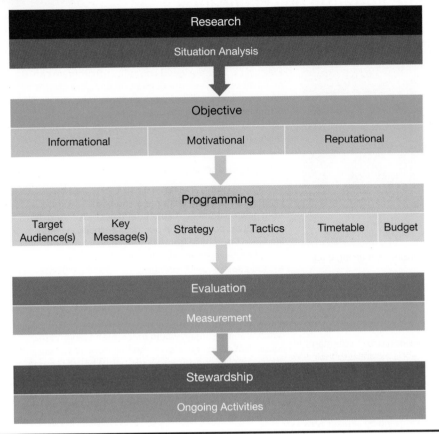

A recent employee-driven project by Food Lion, a $17.3 billion regional supermarket chain based in North Carolina, serves as a good example of how important a situation analysis is in planning. Based on consumer and employee research, the company set its key objective to reinvent its charitable programs into **strategic philanthropy** and make it more closely aligned to the company's core business.

SOCIAL RESPONSIBILITY

The situation analysis the communications team prepared included a summary of their internal and external research and an assessment of customer and employee awareness of the company's current SR efforts and recommended a new way forward. This set up the plan that followed and led management to approve the initiatives they were recommending.

The launch of the Food Lion Feeds program was extremely successful, garnering considerable positive press and increased community goodwill, building employee pride and producing a clear understanding among stakeholders of the company's sustainability programs. The program also won several awards in the communications and SR arenas. In this case, a strong, clearly stated situation analysis was key to convincing management to approve the Food Lion Feeds project and enabled the PR/CSR team to build a successful program to reinvent its charitable activity.

Starting a Corporate Philanthropy Program

More and more companies are realizing that giving back is smart business.

iStock.com/baona

Giving Back Is Essential

Leaders at companies of all shapes and sizes understand that creating a culture of giving back is essential to their own bottom lines. According to America's Charities (2017), workplace giving is one of the most cost-effective ways to support charities, with approximately $4 billion being raised each year. And, recent industry research found that companies that increased total giving by at least 10% between 2013 and 2015 saw increases in revenue and pretax profit, as opposed to all other companies, which saw *decreases* in both metrics.

Employee Engagement Is Key

When employees are involved in corporate giving, companies reap the rewards as well as nonprofits—in the form of increased employee engagement, recruitment, retention, and productivity. According to Project ROI (n.d.), a well-designed corporate SR program can increase employee engagement up to 7.5%, increase employee productivity by 13%, reduce employee turnover by 50%, and increase revenue by as much as 20%. Workplace giving is a central component of these programs.

Building Brand Loyalty

Workplace giving also has a positive effect on brand loyalty from existing customers and brand awareness from new customers. A 2012 Edelman study found that as social purpose's role in purchasing decisions has increased, purchase frequency has also intensified: 47% of global consumers buy brands that support a good cause at least monthly, a 47% increase from a few years past. "Not only are consumers making purchase decisions with purpose top of mind," notes Edelman's Carol Cone (2012), "They are also buying and advocating for purposeful brands. Seventy-two percent of consumers would recommend a brand that supports a good cause over one that doesn't. Seventy-one percent of consumers would help a brand promote their products or services if there is a good cause behind them. Seventy-three percent of consumers would switch brands if a different brand of similar quality supported a good cause."

Make a Difference

Beyond these benefits to the business, there is also the satisfaction of making a true impact in one's community. Companies that follow this model find that infusing social impact into their corporate DNA helps everyone prosper. ●

Source: Plato (2017).

> In any situation there will be those who advocate for business as usual and keeping the status quo. However, the Food Lion Feeds program was based on solid research, it was consistent with the company's core business, and it was creative in its tactics and execution.

OBJECTIVES

>> **LO 5.2** Demonstrate how to formulate objectives to reach a goal

In developing plan objectives, two or three are recommended by most scholars and practitioners. This provides more focus and discipline to the planning process and avoids overwhelming the plan with too many objectives. Further, to be most useful, these objectives need to be specific, measurable, and tied to the corporate strategy and mission. Dozier (1985, p. 21) explained this critical connection in an article in *Public Relations Review*: "The prudent and strategic selection of a few specific public relations goals and objectives linked to organizational survival and growth serves to justify the public relations program as a viable management activity." Dozier's point is that objectives are key to an effective plan. Management buy-in and support for the proposed plan or activity often hinges on the quality of the plan's objectives. While management may not be PR experts, they know their business, and by connecting your plan to the corporate strategy, you are creating a basis for a mutual understanding. As you draft your objectives, keep this vital connection in mind.

Consider also the overall goal and the time frame—for example, short term or long term—and if it is product specific or reputation focused. These factors will impact your approach to developing the objectives—the building blocks to meet your goal. In practice, strategic objectives can be *informational, motivational* or *reputational* (see Table 5.1) depending on the audience and purpose of the plan you are developing (Regester & Larkin, 2008).

TABLE 5.1

The Three Types of Strategic Objectives

TYPE OF OBJECTIVE	FOCUS
Informational Objectives	Creating awareness by sharing information and attributes
Motivational Objectives	Changing the attitude and influencing the behavior of your target audience
Reputational Objectives	Rebuilding or enhancing trust and confidence around a corporate event or crisis

INFORMATIONAL OBJECTIVES

Informational objectives are focused on creating awareness of a product, company, or issue by sharing information and attributes. It is worth noting that these can be harder to measure because awareness and perceptions are difficult to quantify. A recent example of a campaign with informational objectives is one implemented by Johnson & Johnson, one of the world's leading health-care companies and its agency, Cone Communications. The company wanted to address the lack of awareness among health-care providers of the benefit of adopting sustainability initiatives in its workplace.

According to the company's research, the health-care industry generates more than 5.9 million tons of waste each year, contributes 8% of U.S. greenhouse gas emissions, and spends almost $8 billion on energy alone. Yet audience surveys showed there was little to no awareness of these statistics within the industry, and thus participation in Johnson & Johnson-sponsored sustainability initiatives was inconsistent (Sutter, 2012).

In response the company launched the "Measures That Matter, Messages That Motivate: Making the Case for Sustainability in Healthcare" campaign to address this issue. The short-term plan Cone designed for Johnson & Johnson had two clear informational objectives:

SOCIAL RESPONSIBILITY

Johnson & Johnson's "Measures That Matter, Messages That Motivate: Making the Case for Sustainability in Healthcare" campaign successfully raised awareness of the environmental impact of the healthcare industry.

iStock.com/FatCamera

1. Engage and educate health-care professionals about sustainability best practices.

2. Increase dialogue and media coverage on the intersection of sustainability and healthcare.

The overall goal was to develop an awareness program that would "equip health-care professionals with insights on how to advance the organization's (Johnson & Johnson's) commitment to and investment in sustainability" (Cone Communications, 2014). The plan was successful by all accounts. In other cases, where it is necessary to change behavior or offset misperceptions, a different set of objectives is required.

MOTIVATIONAL OBJECTIVES

Motivational objectives are designed to educate and inform your target audience so that the desired behavior or activity is more prevalent. By definition, motivational objectives are more complex because they are designed to share information, change attitudes, and influence behavior. Ironically these objectives can be easier to measure than informational ones. This is because you are trying to drive a specific change in attitude and behavior. With the proper tools you can measure that progress among your target audiences easier than you can gauge awareness created by a media-focused, informational campaign (Stacks, 2010).

A good example of a long-term plan with motivational objectives is one that was organized for the American Academy of Pediatric Dentists (AAPD) by its agency (Weber Shandwick) in 2015 (American Academy of Pediatric Dentistry, 2014). As you read in the complete case study in Chapter 4, the principal concern to be addressed was that the role of the pediatric dentist was not well understood among the target publics such as parents with young children.

The Monster-Free Mouths Movement award-winning plan responded to this concern with a goal of raising awareness about children's oral health and two key motivational objectives:

1. Establish pediatric dentists and the AAPD as trusted sources and champions for children's oral health.

2. Drive parents to take young children to pediatric dentists for preventative care.

The objectives in the plan were specific and measurable. For example, the AAPD could track the increase in first visits by children to its member dentists, monitor inquiries and visits to its dedicated campaign website, and log requests for and use of the campaign materials by member dentists. Media coverage in target publications and on social media were monitored and measured as well. In addition, the objectives were tied directly to the goals of the organization (AAPD), whose purpose includes building awareness of the field of pediatric dentistry and the need for early oral healthcare for children. Finally the objectives were geared toward changing behavior in this case among parents with young children.

REPUTATIONAL OBJECTIVES

Reputational objectives are objectives and plans that are tied to a major corporate event or crisis. The timing can be either short or long term, and they are designed to change perceptions and rebuild or enhance trust and confidence (Stacks, 2010).

A program developed by Carnival Corporation to respond to a series of events that shook the company and the entire cruise line industry is a clear example of a reputational objective. As you may recall the company and its reputation suffered, beginning in 2012, with the sinking of the Costa Concordia ship (a Carnival brand) off the coast of Italy. Later (2013) a Carnival cruise had multiple passengers get sick, and the ship's services and facilities were overwhelmed. These two incidents received worldwide publicity—most of it negative—that damaged the company's reputation and put their brand at severe risk.

The reputation of the Carnival Corporation took a major hit when its ship, the *Costa Concordia*, sank off the coast of Italy.

iStock.com/reeixit

Planning for Growth: How Public Relations Planning and Implementation Can Drive Social Change

Aaron Pickering, Vice President, Cone Communications

I work in PR because I believe it is one of the best drivers of business, political, environmental and social change. As a vice president at Cone Communications, I develop CSR and PR plans to enhance the value of brands that respect people and the planet—and provide reliable, quality products to the marketplace.

I believe it is an exciting time to work at the intersection of PR and CSR because the case for responsible business and sustainability has never been as compelling:

▸ By 2020 a third of all retail sales are expected to come from Millennials—and 87% of them prefer to purchase products with a social or environmental benefit.

▸ Most people prefer to work for socially responsible companies, with 62% of Millennials willing to take a pay cut to do so.

▸ CSR efforts support the bottom line. For example, in 2016, Fortune 500 companies collectively saved nearly $3.7 billion through climate change and energy conservation activities.

Through SPR planning and implementation, we support this work by calling attention to social issues and engaging the key stakeholders in the process.

I began my career as a defense contract analyst in Washington, DC, while pursuing a graduate degree in SPR at George Washington. Soon after graduating, I pivoted to the nonprofit sector to apply my skills to the causes and issues I care about. In my work—whether it was fighting for Proposition 8 in California or for public service loan forgiveness—I began to see that SPR was often the "secret sauce" in driving change. I also recognized that corporations had the most resources and influence to support these efforts and, in many ways, had the largest stake in the outcome.

In 2012 I began managing communications for the Fair Labor Association—the multi-stakeholder initiative formed by President Clinton in response to the sweatshop scandals in the 1990s. I handled PR for the organization through its investigation of Apple's largest supplier, Foxconn, and saw firsthand how CR and PR could be used to impact an entire industry. Soon after, other suppliers and major brands began to address labor challenges in their own supply chains.

After that I joined Ceres, the coalition that issued the world's first code of corporate environmental conduct and helped form the Global Reporting Initiative (GRI). There I developed complex plans to mobilize institutional investors on responsible sourcing and financial disclosure and leveraged PR to encourage global companies to support the Paris Climate Agreement. I am continuing to do this type of work in my role at Cone, a leading PR agency focused on SR.

While the political landscape may have changed, the issues that matter have not. My strong belief is that SPR planning will continue to be critical for advancing CSR initiatives and addressing pressing social issues. I look forward to continuing to contribute to this important work. ●

Aaron Pickering plays a leadership role in one of the leading social responsibility focused PR firms in the country.

Source: A. Pickering (personal communication, 2017).

A major brand renovation and corporate image repair were clearly required. The company developed and launched a reputation-based, long-term communications plan built around the core objective of increasing "Collaboration, Cooperation and Communication"—or the three Cs as it became known inside the company.

By the end of the program, the company's brand and corporate image had improved dramatically; media coverage became more balanced, some positive news articles also appeared, and passenger bookings began to rebound (Marzilli, 2014). This plan succeeded due to its specific, measurable reputational objectives, which included the following:

1. Mitigating negative news with good news about the company and its new CEO

2. A company-wide focus on improving the passenger experience

These objectives were designed to reposition the company's cruise lines as "safe, well-run operations" and restore consumer confidence in the brand. The company's sustained outreach and focus on the plan and its objectives produced the desired improvements, its reputation was rebuilt, and its bottom-line results improved as well.

PROGRAMMING

>> LO 5.3 Demonstrate how to prepare programming to meet objectives

The programming stage involves the execution of the campaign plan. It encompasses defining a target audience, determining strategy, choosing key messages, and tactics (activities).

TARGET AUDIENCE

One of the fundamental rules of effective PR is: Know Your Audience. This is especially true in strategic planning development and program implementation. In most cases you will have a definite target group you are trying to reach with a specific message and a limited time to accomplish that objective. Budgets are a factor as well because resources are not unlimited. Researching and identifying your target audience is a critical step in developing a viable communications plan. Target audience segments, if they are not already known, can be identified through market research—secondary or primary—as outlined in Chapter 4.

For example, in the Monster Free Mouths Movement program, the AAPD knew it wanted to reach three specific groups: parents of young children, childcare workers, and members of the AAPD itself. The AAPD plan's primary audience was parents of

Identifying your target audience is an essential step in planning a successful campaign.

iStock.com/Rawpixel

young children, and the plan was designed with them front and center. However, the children themselves were identified as a secondary audience, and cartoon characters and kid-friendly materials were created to make the dental visit fun.

Strategic communications plans can have more than one audience, and your objectives, program, tactics, and evaluation need to take this into consideration and be tailored accordingly. In this case creating awareness about the need for oral healthcare for young children was a great start. However, providing the AAPD member dentists with collateral material to make that first visit enjoyable for the kids was equally important to delivering on the overall objective.

STRATEGY

When you get to this section of the plan, you have already established the situation, identified your objectives, and segmented your target audience. This is where you develop the strategy that will produce the results you have set out to do in the objectives section of the plan.

Your strategy should be a clear statement of how you will achieve the objectives of your plan and what will guide your tactics (the specific activities you will undertake to meet the objectives). At some point in your career, management may come to you with a tactic in mind that was used previously with good results—for example, hiring a celebrity spokesperson, launching a competition, or holding a press conference—and ask you to execute that tactic before you have done your research or planning. You need to politely resist the urge to do this, noting that tactic, and others, will be fully considered when you get to that stage of your plan.

You will not produce the desired results by jumping ahead to tactics without having done all the foundational work: defining the situation or opportunity, settling on your objective(s), identifying the audience you are trying to reach, and preparing the message(s) you are trying to convey. Plus you will be the one most likely to be held accountable because you are the expert, not the manager who suggested the tactic that didn't work. In this instance the best option is to step back, acknowledge the request, and get all the planning steps done as quickly as possible. After the process is completed, you can identify which tactic or tactics will have the best chance of accomplishing your goals.

KEY MESSAGES

Simply put, a **key message** is what you want your target audience to understand and accept after the program has been implemented. This is not an easy process and should be done thoughtfully. The messages must be clear, have interest or relevance to the recipient, and include a call to action to drive the change or have the impact you are seeking.

**SOCIAL
RESPONSIBILITY** ⟨ An example of a key message from the Johnson & Johnson medical waste case is: *Johnson & Johnson is the leader in sustainability in the health-care industry.* The message was based on research conducted on health-care professionals in Europe, South America, and the United States. The results showed there was a gap between health-care facilities' desire to participate in sustainability initiatives to manage waste and the awareness of how to get started. This central message positions the company to help in both cases.

Social Responsibility Planning: A Competitive Advantage?

Corporate social responsibility can create new revenue streams and give companies a competitive advantage with customers.

iStock.com/HS3RUS

CSR—creating business value while promoting positive social change—is getting a lot of attention today—and for good reason. In her book *Just Good Business*, UC Berkeley business professor Kellie McElhaney (2008, p. 16) cites an IBM Institute for Business Value study finding that more than two-thirds (68%) of business leaders are focusing on CSR to create new revenue streams, and more than half (54%) are convinced that their companies' CSR activities give them a competitive advantage over their top competitors.

Consider the following strategies in developing your CSR plan:

1. Develop a vision.

Socially responsible behavior starts with an awareness of who you are and what you believe as an organization. Ask questions about core beliefs, business strategies, and the model of success. Once you answer these questions, you can search for programs and initiatives that fit with your organization's mission.

2. Don't just talk a good game.

When looking for socially responsible programs, strive to promote your business as well as your business practices. In this transparent age, any hypocrisy, or perception of hypocrisy, can seriously damage your CSR efforts. Companies that launch a plant-a-tree program one week to great fanfare, only to make the news the following week in a toxic waste scandal, clearly don't get what CSR is all about.

3. Launch strong and monitor intensely.

Once you have designed your CSR program you'll want to create awareness and implement your initiatives effectively, but don't forget to create ongoing procedures for monitoring how well these initiatives work.

4. Consider your customers' needs and preferences.

Evaluate CSR programs in the context of meeting your customers' needs. The good news is that most people support ethical business practices. Customers want to buy from and support businesses that are doing good in the world.

5. Use CSR to enhance talent recruitment.

By practicing or implementing programs that promote CSR, your organization will attract enthusiastic, educated, and talented employees who value your initiatives and philosophies. This can create a virtuous circle, as success begets success, powered by people who are committed to and aligned behind your vision. ●

Source: Economy (2017).

TACTICS

SOCIAL RESPONSIBILITY

Tactics are the part of the plan where the rubber meets the road, so to speak. Tactics always follow strategy; they are the how, not the what, of the plan. These are the specific activities you recommend be implemented to convey the message(s) to the target audience. Depending on the objectives, this could entail placing stories in target media, staging an event or activity to convey the messages, conducting

Strategic Public Relations Planning: A GPS for Success

It's such an exciting time for PR. The landscape of the profession is rapidly changing, and new methods and tactics are emerging. It is shedding its past approach from just disseminating information to a focus on promoting engagement, identifying influencers, and developing brand advocates.

Strategic planning is at the heart of the changes in PR. Launching a PR campaign without a strategic plan is like embarking on a trip without a map or GPS. In today's business environment, with limited resources and ramped up accountability, it's not enough to head off in a general, vague direction. A GPS-like strategic plan requires a destination. It keeps PR practitioners on track.

The ability to think and act strategically is the key that enables professionals to advance from tactical PR practitioners to sought-after strategic planners. Today effective communicators not only need to know what to do and why, they also need to know how to evaluate the effectiveness of the chosen approach.

Martha Whiteley's experience in corporate communications and PR consulting has exposed her to many real-world success stories. She's learned that one of the best ways to sharpen strategic thinking is to critically evaluate case studies of PR campaigns. She advises that it's worth the time to analyze campaigns you have worked on and other programs you come across. What worked well, and what was not so effective? See if you can uncover any takeaways or insights that might apply to current or future PR challenges.

Richard Bach once said, "You are all learners, doers and teachers." Isn't that the truth! A big part of life is learning from one another. By critically evaluating real-world case studies of other PR campaigns, Whiteley believes we can enhance our creativity and strategic thinking. Awareness of the mistakes or missed opportunities of others can help us avoid similar scenarios. More importantly, we can benefit immensely from observing, understanding, and emulating best practices. With each successful campaign, PR professionals gain the opportunity to advance the field and elevate the entire profession. ●

Martha Whiteley, former corporate communications manager for Panasonic headquarters, is a corporate communications and PR consultant.

Source: Whiteley (2013).

outreach online or directly to the public, or any number of other ideas in the PR tool box that fit the needs of the plan.

There are good examples of tactics in these cases as well. For example, in the Johnson & Johnson case, to accomplish its objective of "engaging and educating health-care professionals about sustainability best practices," the company used the primary tactic of a major industry conference on that specific topic. Its second objective, "increase dialogue and media coverage," was accomplished through a targeted media relations program focused on key health-care and sustainability publications and influential social media platforms.

TIMETABLE AND BUDGET

As with any strategic plan, the timetable scheduled for the program rollout is a critical element. It provides all parties with a sense of the timing of key elements and when results can be seen in the marketplace.

The timetable allows the company or client to coordinate new product offerings, website updates and enhancements, employee briefings, and so on to coincide with the program rollout and to get maximum benefit. It is also useful as a budget management tool as it indicates when certain expenditures are likely to occur and when resources, such as additional staff, volunteers, experts, or spokespeople, will need to be mobilized or ready. Finally it is a tracking mechanism to monitor the plan's rollout and allows you to know if things are on schedule and progressing as expected.

Similarly the program's budget is a resource-focused document—it provides a plan for expenditures related to the plan. It also helps create a discipline on how resources are utilized as there is a finite budget set aside for the plan, and it is up to the program manager(s) to use these resources carefully and in accordance with the plan. Finally a clearly defined budget will allow you to calculate return on investment (ROI) because the expenditures for each step can be more easily identified and compared.

EVALUATION, ONGOING RESEARCH, AND STEWARDSHIP

>> **LO 5.4** **Explain the roles of evaluation, ongoing research, and stewardship**

Winston Churchill once said, "However beautiful the strategy, you should occasionally look at the results." As the quote suggests, strategic planners should always build measurement and evaluation steps into their plans to improve overall results.

EVALUATION

Every plan should have a built-in **assessment** or **evaluation phase** at the end of implementation. Here is where the specific, measurable objectives you built into the plan are critical. If the objectives are properly crafted and reflect the company's business strategy, the PR professional can demonstrate the impact of the plan against those objectives. This can be very helpful in seeking additional budget and resources to continue the plan (if needed) or in supporting future budget requests for other plans to be developed in the future. A track record of delivering on the stated objectives and meeting your overall program goals can be very helpful in getting management or client support for the next one you develop.

The cases examined in this chapter have several good examples of measurement inclusion in program planning and implementation. In the Food Lion case, the company did extensive, upfront, primary and secondary research on internal and external awareness of its sustainability initiatives. This data served as a benchmark to measure awareness among its key publics after the campaign was completed.

ONGOING RESEARCH

The strategic planning process begins and ends with research. To develop your plan you must make sure it is based on current and accurate information about the company, industry, market, and key audiences. The research in the preliminary phase can draw insights from available materials—secondary research—or can be based on new, specific data—for example, primary research. In most cases, secondary research is the basis for developing PR plans because it is already available and less expensive and time-consuming to produce.

Moving From Charity to Strategic Philanthropy—SAP Leads the Way

Companies worldwide are implementing corporate philanthropy programs. Some encourage or match employee donations. Levi's participated in Back to School programs, donating school supplies and their employees' time.

Tim Mosenfelder/Getty Images

Is strategic philanthropy smart business? More and more companies are developing plans and implementing programs to donate goods, services, or cash for good causes that fit a company's overall strategy. **Corporate philanthropy** often gets a bad rap, but the reality is the largesse of industrialists past and present has helped many around the world.

Business and Social Benefit

Companies worldwide are actively engaging in corporate philanthropy. One company embarking on this agenda is the multinational IT consulting company, SAP. The company recently ramped up donations of its technologies across the world. At first glance they are compassionate, but there is more behind giving out free software than just supporting a good cause. As in the case of many companies, emerging and frontier global markets are the last places where SAP can grow,

and they offer potentially huge rewards and returns. So strategic philanthropy as part of CSR in emerging markets is a wise policy.

Increasing Employee Engagement

In an age where professionals and staff want more than a paycheck and to work at a company they believe has a strong social purpose, philanthropic programs like SAP's are the building blocks for employee engagement and positioning themselves as solid, responsive stakeholders.

Developing Talent for the Future

For SAP, this is not just about keeping smiles on the faces of employees at its headquarters or in regional offices—establishing programs for social good is a way to groom and develop local talent to sustain the company's long-term future.

Boosting Economic Opportunity

With its mantra of providing software products that "make the world better," the company is on a mission to foster a supportive business climate and create opportunity. For many global communities and countries, the work of SAP and other firms helps boost economic opportunities that are much needed where unemployment is a stubborn challenge. And depending on the nature of its software donations, varying results will bear fruit, including a healthier population, a stronger business climate, and a more educated workforce.

It's Good Business

SAP will need both skilled employees and successful customers, entrepreneurs who can develop services that complement the company's suite of products, and of course, healthier and more mobile communities to help SAP maintain and grow its business worldwide. ●

Source: Kaye (2013).

Research also comes into play during the implementation of the plan—to measure your progress and course adjust if needed—and at the end when you are looking to determine the impact of your efforts. Ideally your plan will benefit from all three of these types of research—preplanning, interim, and post implementation. Each of the examples used in the chapter demonstrate the value of upfront and ongoing research to develop and fine-tune a program to maximize your results. In Chapter 4 there is a discussion of research where these concepts are explored in more detail.

STEWARDSHIP TO MAINTAIN MOMENTUM

The final letter in the ROPES model stands for stewardship. Depending on the context of the situation, stewardship is an important consideration; some PR scholars say it's essential. Once a campaign has successfully engaged publics, stewardship considerations help ensure a healthy, ongoing relationship with them. Dr. Kathleen Kelly conceived of it based on her research in fund-raising. She identified stewardship's four dimensions or elements (see Figure 5.2): reciprocity, responsibility, reporting, and relationship nurturing. These elements of stewardship in PR help build goodwill and are closely aligned with SR. Kelly explains them this way:

▸ Reciprocity recognizes stakeholders by showing gratitude and is the essence of SR.

▸ Responsibility refers to the organization keeping its word or fulfilling promises and meeting the key publics' expectations. It means that the organization acts in a socially responsible way.

▸ Reporting requires organizations to keep their publics informed and communicate with them about ongoing changes and developments. It is a basic requirement of accountability.

▸ Relationship nurturing involves going beyond reciprocity, responsibility, and reporting in treating publics well. It demonstrates continued relationship building with a focus on taking care of existing stakeholders and fostering new relationships.

Kelly proposes that without stewardship, the practice of PR is incomplete. PR practitioners "must ensure that expressions of appreciation are provided, recognition activities are planned, responsibility is monitored, a system of reporting is in place, and strategies for relationship nurturing are carried out" (Kelly, 2001, pp. 279–289).

FIGURE 5.2

The Four Dimensions of Stewardship

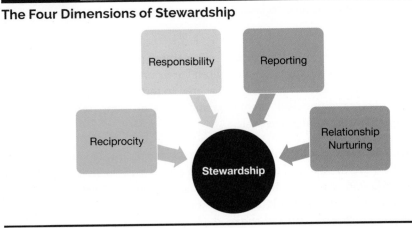

SCENARIO OUTCOME

At the beginning of this chapter you were given a challenge: Develop a plan for a combined PR/CSR program with a partner company and the AAD. Based on the content in this chapter, follow the ROPES process in this manner:

Research is your foundation. First you will want to review the medical research the AAD has on hand to get background information. You should also examine industry marketing data to see if there is a pattern to African Americans purchasing and using sunscreen products. Armed with this secondary research, you might choose to recommend some primary research—for example, focus groups, e-mail surveys, or one-on-one interviews or mall intercepts, where research staff interview people while they are shopping, to quantify your initial findings.

Objectives are critical. You will need to set specific, measurable objectives to help increase sunscreen use and office visits to the dermatologist. The objectives can stress visits to a campaign website by the target audience or requests for information kits and samples by member doctors. They can also be media focused—articles in the target media and/or new postings on social media sites, for example, Twitter, Instagram or Facebook.

Program development follows. First you craft campaign messages that convey key data about skin cancer to the members of the target audience. These objectives connect to the next programming step, tactics. To address the CSR angle or opportunity, you could work with the AAD to identify current partners or new companies to approach about a cause-related marketing program to increase sales and/or use of sunscreen. Think of companies that target the skin care or African American markets.

To increase awareness, a media outreach program could be undertaken targeting general interest magazines, major newspapers, and local television as well as African American-focused media. To drive office visits, the program could include a coupon for an initial appointment with an AAD member dermatologist. The AAD and its partner might also engage a spokesperson with a strong following in the target audience—for example, a sports, entertainment, or public figure—to launch a media tour or a series of community appearances.

Evaluation measures your progress. The remaining pieces of the plan, notably measurement and evaluation, should follow. For example, performance against the CSR goals and objectives can be measured in terms of visits to the dermatologist or community-based screenings and traffic on campaign websites for campaign information and materials.

Stewardship keeps good relationship. The goal is to produce results that show progress toward the goals of the program and a return on the investment made by the AAD and its corporate partner(s). The relationships created with key publics need to be maintained through ongoing communications and outreach to keep all parties informed and engaged.

WRAP UP

Strategic planning and successful PR programs are inextricably linked. Planning is the difference between the PR practitioner who just executes communications tactics and the strategic adviser who designs, develops and implements plans to achieve business objectives. One is usually viewed as a technician, the other as a strategist.

Which would you rather be?

In this chapter, we reviewed the remaining steps after research in the ROPES approach to planning. We also considered the elements of a strategic plan—situation analysis, objectives, target audience(s), key message(s), strategy, tactics, measurement and evaluation, timetable, and budget—and introduced the idea of stewardship to maintain the relationships the plan helped build.

The strategic planning process need not be time-consuming and can flow smoothly and quickly, even in crisis situations. By practicing this discipline routinely in your daily work, you will be able to do so again, even under the most difficult of circumstances.

KEY TERMS

Assessment or Evaluation Phase: The element in a strategic plan (usually at the end) that allows you to measure progress toward the stated goals and objectives, **121**

Corporate Philanthropy: Direct contribution to a charity or cause, **122**

Informational Objectives: Objectives focused on creating awareness of a product, company, or issue by sharing information and attributes, **113**

Key Message: Theme or idea in a strategic plan that is specially designed to communicate an essential point or view

that is critical to accomplishing an overall objective, **118**

Motivational Objectives: Designed to share information, change attitudes, and influence behavior, **114**

Reputational Objectives: Designed to change perceptions and rebuild reputations or trust after a crisis, **115**

Strategic Philanthropy: When the materials donated or the recipient organization has a connection to the core business of the company making the donation, **111**

THINK ABOUT IT

In this chapter you read about several organizations and how they developed communications plans for a market opportunity or to manage an issue they faced. Pick one that is of interest to you and your fellow students.

Assume you all work for a PR firm that has been engaged to continue or sustain (e.g., stewardship) the progress it made with the initial program. What strategy or tactics would you suggest the organization or company implement now, and how would you measure your results to determine if you were on target?

WRITE LIKE A PRO

Identify a company or organization in the news in your area or nationally. Taking into consideration the ROPES approach to communications planning, develop an outline of a plan for the company or organization to manage the newsworthy issue or crisis or take advantage of the opportunity the situation presents.

Consider if this situation is an industry problem—for example, the impact of consuming sugary drinks or soda on the health of young people—or a company-specific problem—for example, a food handling or sourcing problem that creates health concerns for customers.

If it is both a company and an industry concern (e.g., auto safety), what role might a trade group or association play in addressing the problem? For example, would you recommend working with government officials in Washington, DC? If it is solely a company concern, what role might employee relations or CSR initiatives play?

Outline your response to the situation noting each of the ROPES steps.

SOCIAL RESPONSIBILITY CASE STUDY

TuDinero con TD: Empowering the U.S. Hispanic Community Through Financial Education

Hispanics represent 52 million consumers in the United States and are one of the fastest-growing demographics, according to the U.S. Census Bureau (2011). However, they remain in the minority in everyday banking, financial planning, and insurance needs. Recognizing the situation, TD Bank set out to educate and empower the Hispanic community in personal finance. To meet this need, the bank established a media-focused financial education campaign called "TuDinero con TD" to educate Hispanic consumers and provide information and resources to help them achieve financial independence.

Research and Strategy

TD Bank and Pinta, its PR agency for this program, developed a campaign to promote the insights generated by the primary and secondary research conducted in the early stages of the program. The bank also sought to position its executives with Hispanic heritage as experts available to assist customers.

The "TuDinero con TD" campaign's audiences were Hispanic media outlets and consumers ages 18 and older, with an emphasis on the TD Bank Maine-to-Florida footprint. The campaign targeted three groups:

▸ Hispanics already acculturated to the United States

▸ First-, second-, or third-generation U.S. residents of Hispanic origin

▸ Hispanics who were "underbanked"

"Underbanked" is an industry term that the Federal Deposit Insurance Corporation (FDIC), defines as: "those that used non-bank check cashing, nonbank money orders, non-bank remittances, payday lending, pawnshops, rent-to-own agreements, or tax refund anticipation loans (RALs) at least once in the previous 12 months (FDIC, 2013). As such, this program also had a key SR theme, along with its clear business goal. Many of the services noted in the FDIC definition have been the subject of government and law enforcement investigations in recent years amid allegations of predatory lending due to unfairly high interest rates and other terms.

The campaign objectives included the following:

▸ Position TD Bank as the premium bank of choice for the U.S. Hispanic community.

▸ Emphasize checking accounts as the entry point to the overall bank experience.

▸ Understand the financial service needs of this community, and guide them through their banking journey.

Execution

The campaign launched in Miami and then in three other Hispanic markets: New York City, Philadelphia, and Washington, DC. TD Bank created a branded platform for the campaign to connect with Hispanic consumers in the three markets and to link TD Bank to opening and maintaining personal checking accounts. The bank also aimed to introduce its Hispanic executives as thought leaders and experts to educate the Hispanic media, clients, and prospects about the importance of financial literacy for all customers.

Bank executive media tours were conducted to establish relationships with top-tier Hispanic media and promote the bank's thought leadership on retail banking trends, with a special focus on the Hispanic community.

TD used its sponsored national survey to provide data on Hispanic consumers' needs and wants from banks—with a specific focus on personal checking and lending—for example, home mortgages. The national and regional survey data was used to publicize insights on Hispanic consumer concerns and banking experiences in the top-tier, trade, local, and hyper-local media. Via the survey, a yearly information platform was created on Hispanic consumer behavior and placed a range of TD-connected content to extend the reach and impact of the campaign beyond the launch.

Evaluation

The campaign was successful in establishing critical relationships with Hispanic media and educating the growing Hispanic market in the United States. The brand was showcased in top-tier Hispanic publications and outlets including CNN en Español, Univision, EFE, Terra, and *El Diario La Prensa*, *Impacto Latin News* among others.

By leveraging newsworthy consumer insights and highlighting TD's brand position as "America's Most Convenient Bank," the campaign drove both media and bottom-line results. They included extensive coverage in the target market media and led to more than 1.3 million new checking accounts being opened. Through "TuDinero con TD," the bank sent a strong message about the importance of financial education to this fast-growing population segment.

ENGAGE

▸ Visit the TD Bank website to learn more about the bank, its key markets (both geographic and demographic), and its track record on sustainability. Consider other needs—besides financial literacy—that TD Bank has addressed or could address, consistent with their SR philosophy.

DISCUSS

▸ What other needs in their markets should TD consider developing SR programs for?

▸ How does the bank engage its employees in its SR efforts?

▸ How could the bank leverage its community activities and generate more media visibility or customer engagement?

SOCIAL RESPONSIBILITY CASE STUDY

Be the Match: Inspiring the African American Community to Step Up and Save Lives

African Americans have the lowest odds of finding a matching marrow donor compared to all other racial and ethnic groups. For thousands of African Americans, this can be the difference between life and death. Be the Match, the nonprofit that operates a national registry of volunteer marrow donors, partnered with PadillaCRT to raise awareness about this issue during African American Bone Marrow Awareness Month in July 2014.

Research and Strategy

Research had shown African Americans between the ages of 18 and 44 were preferred by transplant doctors more than 90 percent of the time and provide the greatest chance for transplant success due to their relative health. This became the target audience.

The team confirmed that sharing personal stories of patients and donors would drive the most media interest and target audience engagement. African American marrow donors and patients were identified and interviewed to find compelling human-interest stories. National African American publications with the widest reach and engagement were researched.

The previous media coverage was analyzed to determine best methods for media outreach. Ten key markets for media outreach were identified. They included New York, Los Angeles, San Francisco, Philadelphia, Baltimore, Chicago, Miami, Dallas, Houston, and Minneapolis.

An aggressive media outreach campaign was planned, targeting national African American-focused media outlets: local print, broadcast, and online media in the 10 identified markets.

The campaign's objectives were these:

- Increase the number of African American donors joining the registry by 20%.
- Achieve significant media coverage from African American-focused media outlets.
- Land three to four national media stories in African American-focused media outlets to drive awareness beyond local market efforts.
- Drive traffic to campaign landing page (BTMItsOnYou.org).

Execution

The team created and launched "It's on You," a month-long awareness campaign and call to action to the African American community to step up and help save lives. Relationships with donors and patients were leveraged, resulting in them sharing their stories. Blog posts featuring patient and donor stories were written, emphasizing the need for more diverse donors and dispelling the myths of donation. Compelling human-interest story angles beyond the basic awareness month messages were supplied to media outlets. Interviews, live shots, and additional media requests were coordinated.

The campaign delivered key messages that more African American registry members are needed now, and it only takes a few minutes to join the Be the Match registry. An invitation to visit BTMItsOnYou.org and a call to take some action were included in all communications. Local media outreach guidelines were created, along with media lists, media materials and a list of local African American-focused events to assist staff with media outreach in the 10 target markets.

Evaluation

The first objective was to increase the number of African American donors by 20% during the month of July. In fact more than 246 African Americans joined the registry online—26% more than average.

The second objective was to achieve coverage from African American-focused media outlets.

The campaign gained extensive coverage through stories incorporating the key messages from those outlets. One hundred percent of stories included messaging about the need for diverse donors, and 94% included a link to BTMItsOnYou.org or BeTheMatchBlog.org.

The third objective was to land at least three to four national media stories in African American-focused media outlets to drive awareness beyond local market efforts. In reality, nine national media stories were secured, including *Essence Magazine*, *Today's Black Woman*, *Juicy Magazine*, American Urban Radio Networks (AURN), Journey To Wellness, Arise.tv, *Real Health*, *The Tom Joyner Morning Show*, and BlackAmericaWeb.com.

The final objective was to drive traffic to the campaign landing page. There were more than 41,664 unique visits to BTMItsOnYou.org between June 26 and July 31. Of these unique visitors, 8.1% took some action on the landing page.

ENGAGE

- While this was only a month-long event, the problem it was designed to address is national and growing. Visit Be the Match (BTMItsOnYou.org) to get an overview of the issue and the scope of the challenge the group is facing.

DISCUSS

- What ideas do you have to help increase the number of donor volunteers?
- Is there a company or fraternal organization that might be a good partner organization?
- Is there an employee volunteer or fund-raising opportunity for a company with a market focus on African Americans or other ethnic groups with a need for more matching donors?
- How about a celebrity or athlete—with a connection to the issue—as a spokesperson?

ALS Ice Bucket Challenge: Campaign Development

In 2014, the Ice Bucket Challenge swept the Internet, with celebrities and average people dumping buckets of ice water over their heads to raise awareness about ALS and challenging others to do the same and donate to ALS charities. The campaign is credited to the family and friends of Pete Frates, who was diagnosed with ALS in 2013.

VIDEO

1. Using the ROPES method, identify objectives for a campaign to promote the ice bucket challenge and ALS awareness.

2. What programming would you prepare to accomplish those objectives?

3. How would you evaluate the campaign's success?

6 Public Relations Writing
Persuasive and Audience Focused

Learning Objectives

6.1   Understand the style and structure of PR writing and foundational models of communication

6.2   Identify the characteristics of compelling, persuasive, newsworthy, and targeted messaging

6.3   Develop proficiencies in effective writing for essential PR tactics

What Do Taylor Swift, Jason Mraz, and David Mayfield Have in Common?

To put it another way, what special connection do pop rock, folk rock, and bluegrass share? The answer is the rich acoustic tones of a Taylor guitar.

Guitar hero. Cofounded by Bob Taylor in 1974 and based in El Cajon, California, the guitar maker is a global leader in the manufacture of premium acoustic and electric guitars, with a prestigious international reputation and a loyal following in the music industry. Its quality guitars rely on quality materials, and that includes the wood in their fingerboards: the rare high-density black ebony. The best musicians and guitar makers demand it. In fact, beyond manufacturing, Taylor is also a major supplier of black ebony to the industry.

Taylor Guitars, a maker of high-quality instruments, is known for strict attention to ethical sourcing of sustainable materials.

Joby Sessions/Guitarist Magazine/Getty Images

As a fundamental part of its corporate ethos, Taylor Guitars is devoted to best practices throughout its building process, starting with sound forest management, ethical sourcing of tonewoods, and rigorous attention to environmental sustainability. Their green practices extend to the final steps in the process, with repurposing of wood scrap and sawdust and the use of recyclable packing materials.

The West African country of Cameroon has one of the world's last ebony rain forests. However, ebony's journey from a tree in the rain forests of Africa to an instrument in an artist's hands is long, complicated, and fraught with environmental concerns, social issues, and strict regulations.

Over the years a combination of market demands, poor economic conditions in Cameroon, and lack of sufficient forest management has caused stress on the supply of ebony. Such factors have led to problems for suppliers, low worker wages, and an environment of irresponsible procurement. In 2011 Taylor Guitars stepped in to secure its supply of ethically sourced ebony by purchasing Crelicam, the largest ebony mill in Cameroon.

Situation. Once Taylor Guitars learned more about the social and environmental issues impacting the Cameroonian ebony trade, it commenced to make improvements. The company enhanced local incomes by hiring local workers, trained workers to use state-of-the art equipment, and encouraged Cameroonian legal and policy reforms to improve transparency and traceability of logging permits and respect for the rights and needs of other forest users.

Bob Taylor also made a shocking discovery; 90% of the harvested ebony was left lying to decay on the forest floor simply because it was not pure black but variegated in color. Bob then made a decision to change the industry standard by using all of the harvested variegated ebony for guitar fretboards and save the rain forest at the same time.

After reading this chapter, you should be able to answer the following questions:

1. How can Bob Taylor convince the musicians and manufacturers who are diehard fans of black ebony to change their perception of what defined ebony—to abandon their views and accept what was considered "inferior" as the new standard?

2. As the PR manager for Taylor Guitars, how would you advise him to achieve this goal?

3. After brainstorming, what messaging strategies you would recommend to Taylor Guitars?

This scenario is drawn from Page and Page (in press).

In this chapter, you'll first get a basic understanding of various communication models that help explain the communication process—a process you will often lead as a PR writer. Effective communication doesn't just happen; it's the result of careful adherence to established guidelines. Instructions and examples are included to help you understand how to produce the most common writing tactics in contemporary PR for both external and internal publics. Different writing styles are used when addressing the general public, which may be unfamiliar with industry jargon, versus the company workforce that does.

Essential for future PR professionals, emphasis is given to the critical need to improve and maintain quality writing skills. Nothing hurts communication more than poorly written copy; grammatical errors and unnecessary typos will get your release, pitch, or op-ed tossed into a real or virtual trash can. To support this goal, you'll find detailed examples of the written tactics most frequently required in internships, introductory, and mid-level positions.

Although some may seem dated, such as a standard press release designed for a print outlet, the structures are not. An effective communicator is a good writer who knows the proper formats. (Note: social media and new technologies are covered in a separate chapter.)

FOR A PUBLIC RELATIONS CAREER, YOU HAD BETTER BECOME A GOOD WRITER

>> **LO 6.1** **Understand the style and structure of PR writing and foundational models of communication**

Good PR writing starts with research and an understanding of how the process of communication works. Your research should make you a near expert about your topic, your reader, and your PR goal (Inform? Entertain? Influence attitudes?

$SAGE edge™

Master the content
edge.sagepub.com/page

Encourage behavior?). You will know enough about your reader that your words will be interesting, useful, helpful, and so on. Even if you know a lot about your topic at the start, you still should find out what's new. With our 24/7 information cycle, some strategic searches will ensure you've found credible and insightful news and not just hobbyists' blogs.

Understanding your reader allows you to write concisely and effectively. Who are you writing to and for what purpose? What do they know already, and what do they need to know? What are your goals?

In most writing for PR, providing the 5Ws and H—who, what, when, where, why, and how—up front gives readers enough critical information and encourages them to read on. The facts, themes, words you use, and knowledge of your reader will help increase interest and engagement. We talked about framing in Chapter 4, that is, how journalists and PR writers selectively use content that tells a story in a certain way to appeal to readers and clearly make intentional points.

UNDERSTANDING COMMUNICATION

In 1948 political scientist Harold Lasswell wrote, "A convenient way to describe an act of communication is to answer the following questions: 'Who? Says what? In which **channel**? To whom? With what effect?' thereby establishing an early model of communication (McQuail & Windahl, 1993, p. 13). However, notice there is no consideration of interrupted speech, flawed channels, inattentive listening, or varying reactions.

The following year, Shannon and Weaver offered a more exacting communication model that included the concept of **noise** (McQuail & Windahl, 1993, p. 17), meaning unplanned factors that affect the communication process including whether the listener is distracted due to illness, worries, or preoccupations or whether physical noise in the environment sidetracks the listener or nullifies a message. The prospect of a message being interrupted or filtered through internal or external noise is of great concern to PR practitioners, which explains the multipronged tactical approach—the PR campaign that repeats and reinforces messaging—as a standard PR practice. As well, PR recognizes and values two-way symmetrical communication, thus the need for *feedback* is crucial. This concept was first developed by Norbert Wiener (1988), a leading scholar of **cybernetics**, a theory of message transmission. Feedback responds to the PR practitioners' need to talk *with* publics, not *at* them.

SCHRAMM'S MODEL OF MASS COMMUNICATION

Wilbur Schramm then developed a classic model of mass communication (McQuail & Windahl, 1993, p. 19) in 1954 (see Figure 6.1). Schramm's model looks complicated, but it's really very linear. Consider the following example:

1. "Message **encoded** by the transmitter" is the starting point in Schramm's model—I type an e-mail message about coffee beans, selecting words and content (encoding) drawn from my knowledge (transmitter's field of experience).

FIGURE 6.1

Schramm's Model of Mass Communication—1954

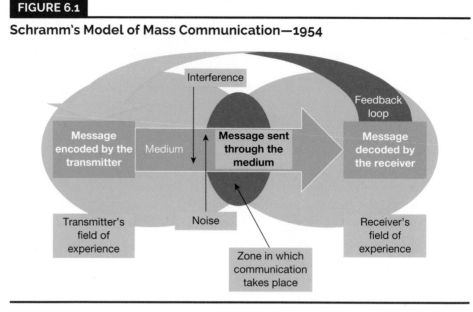

Source: Blythe (n.d.).

2. It travels via the Internet (medium) but ends up in a spam folder (interference).

3. When the intended recipient locates it, she's annoyed and exhausted as it's midnight (noise) and she's still in her office communicating online via her computer (zone).

4. She's familiar with coffee beans as Starbucks is a regular stop (receiver's field of experience), and she understands my message is about some exotic new sources (message decoded by receiver).

5. Yet she's fatigued and not fully processing some information (noise). She shoots back an e-mail (feedback loop) telling me she's not ready to purchase any yet but needs more time to investigate the offer.

PUBLIC RELATIONS WRITING STRATEGY AND STYLE

>> **LO 6.2** **Identify the characteristics of compelling, persuasive, newsworthy, and targeted messaging**

Beginning with an understanding of how the communication process works, PR writers must then proceed strategically. Whatever the tactic, if it requires the written word, you should always ask and answer these basic questions before beginning:

1. Why are you writing?

2. Who are the target readers—and what is most relevant to them?

3. What is the PR's desired objective? What do I want to happen?

4. What is the organization's need and key message?

5. What communication channel will be used?

6. When is the deadline?

7. What are the legal aspects, and who needs to approve it?

The answers to the seven basic questions will help you reach your reader, focus on the core message, and write more easily and quickly, increasing the likelihood of it being approved and released.

ALWAYS APPROACH WRITING STRATEGICALLY

Your strategy can differ, depending on the context, but it generally gives you a framework or path to achieve a goal. You must begin at the end: Know what you want to achieve. What is the big idea or takeaway? This knowledge allows you to proceed with a conscious plan to get there.

The answer to the "How do I want to end up?" question may also guide your writing to support your client's brand positioning—a marketing term that typically guides corporate communication. Being strategic about your writing gives you a course of action to confidently follow. Your writing may seek to inform, impress, influence and/or persuade. These objectives support various goals, for example, publicizing, building relationships, reinforcing a brand, resolving crises, generating votes, attracting investors, and so on.

> "Ask yourself: Have I addressed their interests or only mine?"
>
> —Don Bates

RECIPE FOR SUCCESS

For most purposes, following Chip and Dan Heath's SUCCESs principles will sharpen your writing and increase its effectiveness. In their book *Made to Stick: Why Some Ideas Die and Others Survive* (Heath & Heath, 2007), they introduce the acronym SUCCESs, which stands for simple, unexpected, concrete, credible, emotional, and storytelling (see Table 6.1). While the authors left the last S unattributed, we see it standing for strategic.

TABLE 6.1

SUCCESs Principles

SIMPLE	UNEXPECTED	CONCRETE	CREDIBLE	EMOTIONAL	STORYTELLING
Simplicity asks writers to identify the essential core of their ideas; exclude the nonessentials to get to the heart. Don't just make it short; make it simple yet meaningful.	The unexpectedness principle asks the writer to engage people's curiosity by opening gaps in their knowledge, and then filling them.	Concreteness requires that ideas be clearly understood through the use of selective wording that evokes mental images—do not be ambiguous.	Credibility in writing helps make people believe our ideas; achieve credibility through knowing your readers' interests and needs and speaking to them.	Emotions expressed in writing help people care about our ideas; look for the right emotions to harness.	Storytelling, one philosopher wrote, characterizes all human communication. It's how we judge what's believable and what's not—and what motivates us to accept an idea because it resonates with stories we've heard and know to be true.

AP Style "Cheat Sheet"

Months/Dates/Times

RULE OF THUMB	EXAMPLE
Abbreviate months with six or more letters if they are used with a specific date. Spell out those with five or fewer letters.	Aug. 13, June 6, May 31.
Spell out the month when it is used without a specific date.	In September the football team . . . The class begins in February 2015.
For days of the month, use only numerals. Do not use nd, rd or th.	Aug. 2, Sept. 3, April 4.
Do not abbreviate days of the week. You usually do not need both a day of the week and a date.	Wednesday, Monday The next game is Oct. 13.
Use numerals, a space, lowercase letters, and periods for a.m. and p.m. Do not use extra zeros on times.	7 p.m., 10 a.m., 1:45 p.m.
Use noon or midnight rather than 12 p.m. or 12 a.m.	The club will meet at noon.

Numbers/Money

1. In most usage, spell out numbers under 10. Exceptions beyond dates and times are shown as follows:

   ‣ Addresses: 6 Maple St.

   ‣ Ages, even for inanimate objects: Beth, a 15-year-old; the 2-year-old building

   ‣ Dollars and cents: $5; 5 cents.

   ‣ Measurements (such as dimensions and speed): 6 feet tall, 9-by-12 rug; 7 miles per hour

‣ Temperature: 8 degrees

‣ Millions, billions: 3 million people

‣ Percentages: 4 percent (and spell out "percent")

2. Spell out any number that appears at the beginning of a sentence. The one exception to this rule is a year: 1981 was the last time the high school won a state title.

3. Do not spell out monetary amounts or use extra zeros: $6 or $2.30, but not $6.00 or six dollars.

Punctuation/Abbreviations/Quotes

RULE OF THUMB	EXAMPLE
Apostrophes usually show possession, so usually you shouldn't use them to make acronyms and numbers plural. An exception is with individual letters such as in grading.	1970s; ABCs; she received six 4s; she received six A's.
Not all cities need a state name with them, but those that do should *not* get a postal code but rather AP abbreviations (see stylebook).	Seattle; Bellevue, Wash.; Portland, Ore. (*not* WA or OR).
Place quotation marks around almost all composition titles but not reference, newspaper, or magazine names.	"American Idol"; "Born This Way"; Time magazine.
Capitalize the first letter of a full-sentence quote.	Jones said, "All of us were excited."
When a full-sentence quotation is introduced or followed by attribution, place a comma between them, unless the quote is a question.	"All of us were excited," Jones said. "Were we all excited?" Jones asked.
When using a sentence fragment as a quotation, do not set it off with a comma unless the sentence requires one for proper grammar. Do not capitalize the first letter of a sentence fragment quote.	Jones told the crowd to "get pumped up" about the pep rally.

THE CURSE OF KNOWLEDGE

The "curse of knowledge" is a major writing pitfall says Steven Pinker (Sleek, 2015), a linguist at Harvard University. It's a cognitive bias that many adults must fight to overcome. We assume others understand the words we use, share the same skills we possess, and know the obscure facts that we perceive as common knowledge.

"I think the curse of knowledge is the chief contributor to opaque writing," Pinker explained. "It simply doesn't occur to the writer that readers haven't learned their jargon, don't seem to know the intermediate steps that seem to them to be too obvious to mention, and can't visualize a scene currently in the writer's mind's eye. And so the writer doesn't bother to explain the jargon, or spell out the logic, or supply the concrete details—even when writing for professional peers." To escape this curse, Pinker suggests trying to empathize with your reader, show early drafts to a reader, and use a simple yet visually descriptive and conversational style of writing.

BEYOND STRATEGY: FORM

Good PR writing is concerned with style, grammar, and punctuation. The range of writing styles for PR is wide—using AP style (defined elsewhere) for news releases, persuasive strategies for pitch letters and PSAs, conversational narratives for blogging, informative approaches for newsletters, analytical writing for white papers and reports, and so on. Examples in this chapter reflect some of these styles.

If you need to refresh your knowledge of correct grammar and/or punctuation, ask your instructor to direct you to resources provided by your college or university. There are also good online resources including at the Purdue Online Writing lab (OWL) at https://owl.english.purdue.edu/exercises/.

GENERATING CONTENT: PUBLIC RELATIONS WRITING ESSENTIALS

>> LO 6.3 Develop proficiencies in effective writing for essential PR tactics

The focus of PR writing will range widely due to the varying communication needs of a corporation, nonprofit organization, or government agency.

- ▸ Corporations usually focus on customers or consumers, financial relations, internal relations, and social responsibility or sustainability communications.
- ▸ Not-for-profit organizations typically concentrate on issue advocacy, membership development, service promotion, and fund-raising support.
- ▸ Government agencies stress public information and public awareness.

At times, all these entities may have specific needs, for example, in issue or crisis management, reputation enhancement or repair, general relationship building, media relations, and/or lobbying. The writing tactics that address these situations and goals are multiple, but the most common forms when dealing with the media are news releases, pitch letters, fact sheets, and alerts.

PR writers will often also create newsletters, brochures or presentations and serve many online needs, including content for blogging, websites, wikis, and social media platforms. As with today's journalists, the PR writer also now has moved into writing for video, podcasts, websites, social media platforms, and more. Advanced forms of PR writing include op-eds, speeches, feature articles, briefing reports, white papers, and annual reports. These generally require more background research and careful thinking before they're written. Usually they also require more persuasive or more polished writing owing to their varied purposes and specific audiences.

When you consider these many communications and their importance to the credibility of an organization or individual, it should be clear why they should be written not only strategically but respect legal, societal, and professional norms. Seeing how important content is, it is also clear why PR writers should become experts in their subject areas and support their views with fact, not fiction or exaggeration.

THAT FIRST JOB

A "first job" in PR for the intern or newly graduated student typically requires a lot of writing and technical skills, for example, drafting various media releases, contributing blog entries, providing website content, and even updating Wikipedia pages. The writing styles differ depending on the tactic. Writing in AP style is required for any news item sent to newspapers, whether print or online, because that is their established writing style. Releases that are not in AP style do not get serious consideration, experience shows. When it's your job to write about your organization or client and see it through to media placement, following the "rules" of writing is essential.

Even if you start out on the local level, you should be ready to step into the shoes of the seasoned journalist because times have changed in the news business. Newsrooms were once staffed with dozens of reporters, each with a different specialty or "beat." If you handled PR for a school district, you'd send news about a new superintendent to the education reporter, alert the sports reporter about athletic awards, and announce the drama club's spring musical to the entertainment editor.

PR writers are often tasked with creating video scripts, along with brochures, presentations, website content, and more.

iStock.com/sturti

Nespresso in South Sudan

Nespresso has worked with South Sudanese coffee farmers to improve their welfare and revive the coffee industry harmed in the country's civil war.

Reza/Getty Images

Nespresso works with coffee farmers in war-torn South Sudan to improve their welfare and revive the industry that was all but destroyed during the war that preceded the country's independence from Sudan in 2011. South Sudan's eastern border is one of the only places in the world where the coffee bean is found growing in the wild. The coffee plant is deeply rooted in this area's history, but the conflict and violence saw production brought to a virtual halt. However, despite all obstacles, with the determination of some courageous South Sudanese farmers, coffee is making a comeback.

Partnering With an NGO

Nespresso's work in South Sudan is part of its "The Positive Cup" strategy to improve farmer welfare and drive sustainability in coffee sourcing and consumption. Nespresso began working to revive coffee production in South Sudan with the help of the nonprofit organization TechnoServe, which helped build partnerships with local farmers. TechnoServe provided tools, technical assistance, and training to help farmers grow a crop suitable for export.

Communicating Through Celebrity

Nespresso brand ambassador George Clooney has traveled to South Sudan many times to support efforts to end conflict in the country. He believes coffee is important for the country's future, and his involvement has helped spread the story of Nespresso's efforts.

Around 300 farmers were initially involved in the coffee cooperatives; now that number has grown to 730. Since the program began, 1,270 households have attended at least one of the training sessions that help them build vital agricultural skills and knowledge. The project aims to increase the number of fully trained farmers to 8,000 by 2020.

Communicating Across the Battleground

Although the conflict means that TechnoServe staff are no longer able to work in South Sudan, they are still supporting the farmers. A weekly radio broadcast helps with seasonal advice and provides follow-up training. Produced from neighboring Uganda, the program is broadcast in three different languages on South Sudan's popular radio station, Spirit FM.

Building Peace

The United States Agency for International Development (USAID) has recently joined the Nespresso/TechnoServe partnership and is helping expand the project. It will now assist more farmers in areas where coffee farming is starting up. Just as in existing growing areas, coffee will provide much-needed income and security for these farmers and their families. ●

Unfortunately, at too many newspapers, those beats and the reporters who covered them are long gone. However, the newsworthy stories still need to be shared with the public. Thus your news release must be complete, accurate, and correctly formatted from the beginning as there is a possibility it may be run as you wrote it—with little or no changes by the editors.

THE NEWS RELEASE

Traditionally one of the most important tools used in PR is this tactic requiring precise writing. The news release is used to secure attention and coverage with multiple media outlets: radio, television, newspapers, magazines, and appropriate Internet sites and social media platforms. The news release has been the gold standard vehicle, recognized and respected, to get essential news and information to members of the media. No matter who or what your organization or client is—a corporation, nonprofit, celebrity, politician, government agency, university, and so on, the news release is a common mode of communicating to the media. According to the media database company Cision (2017), its 2017 State of the Media Report confirms that journalists rank news releases as one of their most valuable resources.

A valuable news release will have newsworthy content. You must determine what is of interest to the viewers, readers, or listeners of a news outlet. Gatekeepers at the news outlets are looking for news and information that fits their specific scope of interest (entertainment, sports, lifestyle, features, business, politics, etc.). Thus you must be careful to deliver your specific news to the right media source or news worker. It should be targeted and relevant to their audience. Don't hope for it to be passed along to the right person; with pared-down staffs and tight deadlines, it's unlikely your news will be handed off. So do your research. Watch, read, and listen to the sources you think are right for your client. This is generally the case with mainstream media. Typically trade and specialized business media are more accommodating about moving news to the right department.

INVERTED PYRAMID

When writing a news release, follow the **inverted pyramid** formula (see Figure 6.2), designed for ease of use by the media outlet, leading off with the most important information and continuing in diminishing levels of importance. This format helps news professionals decide if the news is relevant to their audience and gives them a clear structure for editing. The content flow is nearly identical to how a journalist would write a news story but with a significant difference: your choices of what's most important reflects your organizational goals.

For example, when announcing a change in company leadership, your lead paragraph might reference a major accomplishment or received honor of the incoming CEO to frame the organizational shift as positive and noteworthy. A journalist might have the same facts yet place them later in a story. Your role as a PR writer is to respect the inverted pyramid structure that privileges the five Ws and H but to also prioritize the information important to the organization.

THE FORMAT, STEP BY STEP

The main mode of distribution for a news release is via e-mail, which dictates its structure. The e-mail's subject line should carry the release's headline—in about 20 words or less. Note the wording in the subject line is critical to having it opened and

FIGURE 6.2

The Inverted Pyramid

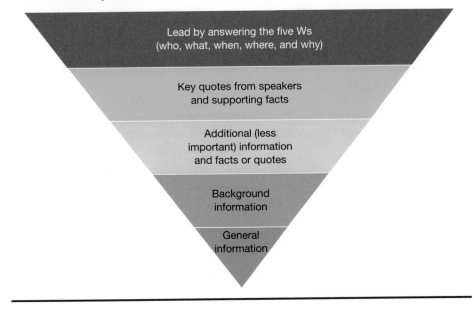

Lead by answering the five Ws
(who, what, when, where, and why)

Key quotes from speakers
and supporting facts

Additional (less
important) information
and facts or quotes

Background
information

General
information

read. In the body of the e-mail (<u>not</u> in an attachment), the release content begins with the name of the organization (or logo) followed by the date of distribution. The third line carries the headline in boldface (and often a subhead).

The body of the release then begins. Its first paragraph (called the **lead**) begins with the city from which the news originates and continues with just one or two sentences on the most important elements of your "news." A second paragraph, also short, provides the *next* most important elements. Often the third paragraph is a quote from the CEO or a person significant to the news—and it should be highlighted by indenting or boxing. The rest of the release concisely provides all the necessary facts that help explain your earlier information or provide necessary background information. End with a brief, summary paragraph on the organization (called the **boilerplate**).

IT'S DIGITAL! AND THAT'S GOOD

Since it's digital, within the release be sure to include *relevant* URL links with further information. The release ends with the PR person's full contact information so a news writer can easily identify how to get any questions answered.

Look at actual, current news releases on the websites of PR Newswire, Business Wire, and CSRwire. These releases are written by in-house or agency PR practitioners, but keep in mind they're all not necessarily good releases. However, all of them are written for the online environment, single-spaced with the news portion ideally about 250 words long. Due to cyberspace considerations—including the spread of viruses, increase in spam, restrictive bandwidth, computer screen constraints, and so on—news releases now are delivered to the media in the body of an e-mail (not in an attachment) or are previewed with a 100- to 200-word summary in an e-mail with a hyperlink to the organization's online newsroom or to another server, where the full text can be read. Figure 6.3 shows an example news release from Yum! Brand's online newsroom.

FIGURE 6.3

Sample News Release

YUM! IN THE NEWS

YUM! BRANDS RECOGNIZED AS A 2016 HEALTHIEST 100 WORKPLACE IN AMERICA®

LOUISVILLE, KY, September 7, 2016 – (BUSINESS WIRE) – Yum! Brands (NYSE: YUM)has been recognized as a 2016 Healthiest 100 Workplace in America, an awards program presented by Springbuk®.

The top one hundred employers will be recognized at the Corporate Wellness Conference® in Washington D.C. The winning organizations are honored for their commitment to employee health and exceptional corporate wellness programming. Over 5,000 employers applied for the Award nationally.

Award applicants were evaluated across six key categories: Vision, Culture/Engagement, Learning, Expertise, Metrics and Technology. Applicants were evaluated with the proprietary Healthiest Employer Index, a 1-100 metric for wellness programming. These organizations have achieved lasting success through a wide array of employee wellness initiatives and corporate wellness programs.

"At Yum! Brands we've created a culture that inspires and supports employees to lead healthy, balanced, energetic lives so that they can achieve breakthrough results at work and at home. We are excited to be publicly recognized for this work," said Tracy Skeans, Chief People Officer, Yum! Brands.

"Year after year, we see strong growth and continued investment in worksite wellness programs," noted Rod Reasen, CEO of Springbuk, the scoring engine behind the national Healthiest Employer® Awards Program. "These 100 organizations are the best of the best. Their efforts are improving the health of their workforce and community."

About Yum! Brands, Inc.
Yum! Brands, Inc., based in Louisville, Kentucky, has nearly 43,000 restaurants in almost 140 countries and territories. Yum! is ranked #218 on the Fortune 500 List with revenues of over $13 billion in 2015 and is one of the Aon Hewitt Top Companies for Leaders in North America. The Company's restaurant brands – KFC, Pizza Hut and Taco Bell – are the global leaders of the chicken, pizza and Mexican-style food categories. Worldwide, the Yum! Brands system opens over six new restaurants per day on average, making it a leader in global retail development.

About Springbuk, Inc.
Springbuk is the leading health intelligence platform for employers. The tool arms employers with a complete view of their population to target engagement, pinpoint spending and measure results. Springbuk is the scoring engine behind the Healthiest Employer® Awards Program that includes over 18,000 employers that represent over 60 million employee lives. Learn more at www.springbuk.com and www.HealthiestEmployers.com.

Contacts
Yum! Brands, Inc.
Laurie Schalow
502-874-8200
Laurie.Schalow@yum.com

Source: Yum! (2016)

The Appeal of Multimedia

"Today's most compelling news articles include a good headline and an interesting and relevant story, augmented by intriguing multimedia," reports businesswire.com (*Business Wire*, 2015). A 2015 survey asked 400 journalists how likely they would be to use a company-issued news release if it included multimedia elements. The results show that 36.3% of responding reporters said they would be likely to use a news release if it included multimedia. The elements most preferred were listed as follows:

- Photograph (82.8%)
- Graphics (48.4%)
- Video files (38.1%)
- Infographics (35.8%)
- Logos (27.4%)

To explain these results, *Business Wire's* CEO (Tamraz, 2015) reported that 63% of people are kinesthetic learners, preferring to actively engage with resources to learn, versus the 37% who prefer passively reading text. *Business Wire's* director of social and evolving media reports, "We see news releases with multimedia assets generating 3x more activity than text-only news releases" (Ehrlich, 2016).

The study also found that the responding journalists suggested PR professionals could do more in support, specifically the following (*Business Wire*, 2015):

- The most requested step asks communication professionals to spend more time researching the journalist's publication or beat before reaching out to them (57.2%).
- Too often releases are sent to journalists who do not cover the subject of the release, resulting in the release being discarded.
- Sharing the journalists' articles via social platforms followed at 39.5%. PR professionals must help those who help them. Sharing helps a journalist reach a wider audience and is a professional courtesy as well as good practice.

Approximately one-third want a PR professional to be more responsive, to provide more story-related assets, and to be available to speak with them. When a journalist needs more details for a story, he or she needs to be able to get that information easily. PR professionals must be accessible for story follow-up and additional materials. ●

MULTIMEDIA NEWS RELEASES

The multimedia news release is delivered digitally and not only offers a written component but has embedded live URL links to relevant material, including social media sites, downloadable JPEGs of posters and logos, and in many cases, accompanying visual elements such as links to photos, videos, and PSAs.

The Ad Council produced a multimedia news release to announce the PSA ad campaign it produced for First Lady Michelle Obama's "Let's Move" initiative to combat childhood obesity. It carries not only a traditionally written news release with embedded hyperlinks but separately offers links to TV and radio spots in English and Spanish, along with full-color screen shots, and also provides JPEGs of print and outdoor ads. View it at http://multivu.prnewswire.com/mnr/adcouncil/48526/. Browse more multimedia news releases at PR Newswire's http://www.multivu.com/ and at Business Wire's http://www.businesswire.com/portal/site/home/news/multimedia/.

> **SOCIAL RESPONSIBILITY**

FACT SHEET

Often a fact sheet is a companion release to the traditional news release, carrying only the five Ws and H in an outline format, with bold heads and short explanatory paragraphs. It may be bulleted, organized by dates, or structured in some other obviously relevant way. It allows the news worker to quickly see the entire scope of the "news" and provides a clear reference tool for specific information. As with the news release, it should end with a summary paragraph on the organization (called the "boilerplate"). It may or may not be labeled "Fact Sheet" at the top and provides a headline and dateline, similar to the news release (see Figure 6.4).

FIGURE 6.4

Sample Fact Sheet

ART ON NEPESSING ST.

A Celebration of the Arts in Downtown Lapeer, Michigan

Art on Nepessing Street 2017

WHAT

A celebration of the arts in historic Downtown Lapeer including an exhibit of high quality original artwork. Pieces are donated by artists, displayed in downtown Lapeer businesses, and then become part of a silent auction during the street festival. There are two ways to participate:

1. Get a free vendor booth when you donate a piece of original artwork for the silent auction – your donated piece will be exhibited in a local business and automatically be entered into our Best of Show competition for a grand prize of $1,500
    OR
2. Pay for a vendor booth and join us for just the street festival.

This event will also include an art walk, pub crawl, chili cook off, and several concerts TBA. Proceeds benefit the Center for the Arts of Greater Lapeer and the Lapeer Downtown Development Association

WHEN

Art Walk Exhibition from **May 9 – June 1**
Art Walk Pub Crawl: **Friday May 19th**
Street Festival: **June 2nd – Noon – 8:00pm**
                    June 3rd – 10:00am – 6:00pm

WHERE

Exhibition throughout downtown Lapeer culminating with a two day Art Festival on Nepessing St. in front of the Center for the Arts of Greater Lapeer

WHO

The Center for the Arts of Greater Lapeer, Inc. which is made up of Gallery 194 and the PIX Theatre
Lapeer Downtown Development Authority
Local and National Artists
Downtown businesses exhibiting art during the art walk
The public who visits each business displaying art and votes for the people's choice award.

PUBLICITY

This event is widely covered by newspapers and electronic media. Print materials: ads, press releases, posters, flyers, signs. Postings, including artists' names, bios, and images of representative artwork, on several websites: (see above organizations) centerfortheartslapeer.org, DowntownLapeer.com, and on social media

HOW TO PARTICIPATE   Please see the "Request to Enter" form for more information on participation

Contact: **Artist Contact:**
Katie Beth Chrismer/Gallery 194
194 West Nepessing St. Downtown Lapeer, Michigan 48446
Email: info@gallery194.com   phone: (810)667-1495 Fax: **(810)667-1502**

Business Contact:
James Alt – DDA Executive Director
Email: james@lapeerdda.com   phone: 810-728-6598

Source: Art on Nepessing St.

BACKGROUNDER

A common component in a media kit is the **backgrounder**. It offers the news worker the "story behind the story." How did this issue arise? Why did this event become so notable? Where did the company come from? It offers some history, some illustrations or vignettes that a journalist might use to appeal to reader interests but also summarizes the current situation. The backgrounder allows a news worker to develop a deeper story beyond the facts in the news release. A "reference" piece must be fact-checked and the content approved by the client before use.

THE ONE-ON-ONE PITCH

The written pitch is a short letter, typically e-mailed to specific people you've identified as gatekeepers at their media outlets. Unlike the news release, it is not a mass distributed one-size-fits-all letter but is personalized to each specific media outlet and contact person. Its goal is to put a spotlight on a news item or a story angle that is distinctive and of interest to the gatekeeper's readers or audience—and to hopefully begin a one-on-one, back-and-forth process that results in coverage. Consider it an exchange relationship: You have some important news, or an attractive news "opportunity," of high interest to a community targeted by your chosen media. Often the pitch parcels out the news with tidbits versus giving it all away in the first contact. If you get a response indicating interest, provide more details, and work to secure the placement.

Depending on the news, you may be offering one media outlet an exclusive, or at least a "first," opportunity in their media category. Again, depending on the news, you may choose one or more newspapers, or a TV news or radio program with a large or devoted audience, or perhaps a specialized magazine with a targeted audience, or even just local media outlets. All likely have online components, but pitching influential bloggers should also be considered.

The written pitch must quickly communicate its value and substance to the recipient. This is not the place for tentative phrases or polite "How are yous?" However, because this is a personal letter, use a professional yet friendly tone. Transmitted in the body of an e-mail, the best pitches have a succinct yet alluring subject line—use your creativity. Once opened, the e-mail begins with a personal salutation and immediately describes the newsworthy item and suggests why she or he should cover it. Knowing your chosen media well is critical here as your goal is for the recipient to react with: "That's a perfect fit for us!"

If you are pitching an event to a TV news editor, be sure to use descriptive language to help the reader visualize the camera shots. If you're pitching a guest for a soft news program, bring the guest to life with suggestions of what he or she would show, do, say, and so on. Or your objective may be to secure an in-depth story, so you would provide enough significant and compelling facts to secure interest to know more. Make it as long as only one screen length, and do include relevant URL links. Always close your pitch with your direct contact information and a promise to follow-up within a day or two. Then do it.

NEWS FEATURES AND OP-EDS

News features and op-eds are similar in that they both require a more sophisticated style of writing and far more ambitious content than news releases and pitch letters.

A PR professional must be prepared to speak on TV, at news conferences, and at media presentations of new products.

iStock.com/wdstock

News features are relatively timeless "soft news" that tell a good story as opposed to the time-limited "hard news" of news releases. They can be published immediately, but they can also be published weeks, even months, later. They may be one page or several pages in length, but they typically provide a behind-the-scenes perspective on the topics addressed. They're also creatively composed, for example, an insider's how-to for gardening in the city or a profile of a person who does magic tricks at your restaurant chain. They "go beyond the facts." Look for material within your organization for feature treatment. This could be an executive's experience in a hands-on CSR initiative or your company's creative solution for day-care alternatives.

Op-eds, alternatively, are opinion pieces that usually concern current issues. They're more analytical and focused than a feature, providing insight rather than information. The best op-eds usually provide a provocative and insightful perspective on topics of great interest to the public.

In writing both features and op-eds, the PR writer controls the content; however, the writing has to be of journalistic quality. Thus you would research carefully, write clearly, and structure tightly. The idea is to mimic the media's approach because your aim is to have the media use what you've written because it conforms to accepted journalistic standards. If you meet these standards, your piece will probably run pretty much as you wrote it or with modest editing.

FEATURES

Writing features begins with generating ideas for stories. This requires a creative and inquisitive mind. An employer expects a PR writer to be an expert in releases and pitches, but the one who generates ideas for stories to be published or covered is a step above the rest and more likely to become a valued and respected member of the management team. These ideas should contribute, first and foremost, to the success of your client or employer. The best ones connect in some way to current events or trends and tie in your company or client. For example, a health-branded nutrition product ties in with the arrival of summer or Heart Awareness month.

Once a topic is approved by your supervisor or client, and once you've researched the topic sufficiently, good storytelling skills are required. It may be light or serious, but it should have the essential elements of narrative: characters, setting, and plot. It requires descriptive writing and often even dialogue. You should strive for engaging and entertaining language with substantive quotes and also provide photos or illustrations. Good endings to features usually deliver some surprise; an aha detail or resolution that satisfies the reader. A PR feature is typically 1,000 to 2,000 words in length and, if accepted, often uses the author's (or client's) byline.

Well-written news features are welcome by the media for several reasons, but the most important is that they need help getting content. No medium today has enough money and/or staff to write about everything interesting or important that goes on in their community or state or region. Outside contributions enhance the media's ability to write about and publish news and information that is beneficial to their readers.

Often the media prefers topics that have a how-to or service angle; that is, features that help improve their readers' lives. You likely can't go wrong if you write about improving physical, emotional, psychological, economic, educational, and social well-being. For examples of good features, browse some of the major life-style or special-interest magazines online, such as *Vanity Fair* or *Men's Health*. While longer than a PR feature, you'll see some top-quality writing by experienced authors.

You may be wondering where you should send your feature, and there are many options: newspapers, both local and national, and particularly the life-style, arts and business sections; general magazines, local, regional, and national life-style titles; specialty and trade magazines, where their special-interest editorial targets a more devoted reader interested in golf, cars, fitness, travel, or specialty business topics; and in-house and internal publications—many large corporations publish magazines where your content might be appropriate.

OP-EDS

The term *op-ed* originated in 1970, when the *New York Times* published the first op-ed page. The name referred to the page's placement opposite the editorial page. Today the term is also thought of as "opinion editorial."

The op-ed is typically submitted to a newspaper by a reader or an outside expert with a view on a timely and relevant topic. The writing may be informational, persuasive, critical, and even satiric. As a PR writer, you would research and write an op-ed to be submitted under the name of your client or CEO—or you would edit and finalize one already drafted. Your topic must be relevant to the news outlet's readers and must be well argued, defended, or articulated.

As well, an op-ed must be carefully proofed and edited before submission; it is then reviewed and, if chosen for publication, carefully edited again. Op-eds are longer than news releases—the *Washington Post* caps them at 800 words; however, other newspapers may draw the limit at 500. They are exclusively offered to one media outlet and not sent to other outlets or posted online.

Placing an op-ed in a prestigious newspaper can lend credibility to your organization, its author, and the issue. For a well-written example, read Warren Buffett's stock market advice in an op-ed that provokes, challenges, and makes clear where he stands. Find it at https://rbcpa.com/warren-e-buffett/ny-times-op-ed-october-17-2008-buy-american-i-am/. Buffett, considered one of the most successful investors of all time, is chief executive of Berkshire Hathaway and the second wealthiest person in the United States (Forbes, 2017).

When Children Benefit, So Does the Entire Community

Sahlman Seafood, which runs shrimp farms like this one, began to develop a CSR initiative as a way to address problems faced by its workforce.

Pulsar Imagens/Alamy Stock Photo

Sahlman Seafood is a family-run, U.S.-based company that owns shrimp farms in Nicaragua, and employs several thousand Nicaraguan citizens. The company operated for a number of years without a structured CSR program but began changing their overall corporate philosophy when they addressed problems faced by its workforce.

The Philosophy of the Owner Became the Guiding Principle

Led by company owner, Jack Sahlman, a commitment was made to help these workers, the majority of whom were women with children who had limited access to healthcare, education, and clean water. This effort to help began at the local elementary school. Sahlman has donated numerous types of infrastructure to the school and installed a well that serves the entire community. The company also remodeled the preschool classrooms and provided uniforms to all the students. Sahlman provides scholarships to elementary school graduates so that they may continue with secondary education that's not available in the nearby community.

Employees Are Engaged, Too

To further promote education and environmental awareness, company biologists routinely make presentations to the school and invite the students to participate in activities such as planting mangrove seedlings in the area. Another project supported by employee efforts is the local health clinic. After rehabilitating the clinic facility, Sahlman company volunteers made possible the installation of electrical power to the building. Internal communication about volunteerism opportunities and other company CSR initiatives are covered in a quarterly employee newsletter.

A Philosophy That Endures

Jack Sahlman believed in being a good corporate citizen, and that advice has been the impetus for employees in Nicaragua to expend time, effort, and energy trying to make a difference in the environment and the communities in which they work. The recently formed Sahlman Foundation continues to provide funds, supplies, and time to the local community. The foundation also solicits donations from other companies and outside sources to help with our outreach programs.

Good Works Recognized

These efforts, which continue to expand, led to Sahlman being awarded the U.S. State Department's Award for Corporate Excellence (ACE) in 2011 and being honored by the Nicaraguan government. The ACE award was a newsworthy event in Nicaragua, and Sahlman's Nicaraguan communications department had the award publicized in the major media outlets by issuing press releases, pitching local and state television, and arranging for a video link of the ceremony. ●

MEDIA KIT

Due to the unfortunate decrease in the size of news organizations' staffs, journalists are left to multitask for both online and print editions. However, a positive outcome is the need for more content supplied by PR practitioners. It is, in fact, easier today than in the past to place a story *if* it is well written and appropriate to the specific outlet. This new dynamic also gives the media kit (also called press kit) more importance now in providing all the elements needed for

PR professionals may be closely involved in the crafting of op-eds, either by determining the information to be conveyed, editing the piece, or writing it on behalf of a client.

Ognian Setchanov/Alamy Stock Photo

the journalist to work with. What should go into a media kit? In many cases, the following are included:

1. A hard news release giving the latest information about your client and the product, event, announcement, or campaign

2. A soft feature release with the same focus

3. A fact sheet with key bullet-point details to accompany the press release (usually this provides the five Ws and H, a quote, and selective ancillary information)

4. A background article about your client and background details about the product, event, or campaign itself

5. A bio sheet with biographical material about a key leader of the organization.

6. A photo opportunity sheet, offering specific occasions for still photos and video shoots, to help the media better illustrate their stories or segments

7. Photographic images, if available and appropriate, of your "newsworthy" item

A physical media kit, with the multiple components placed in a pocketed folder, should be produced for distribution at a press conference. However, most journalists prefer a digital media kit, which should be stored and accessible in your website's online newsroom.

SPEECHWRITING

Writing speeches is a challenging art form—crafting words and selecting visuals to inform, entertain, influence, or inspire. As with all PR writing, it begins with knowing the speech's purpose and audience.

I Love What Public Relations Is All About

**Don Bates, Management Consultant
and PR Writing Instructor**

I began my career at Northeastern University in Boston. As a sophomore I got an after-class gig in the public information office. I wrote "hometown" news releases. These announce the names of students who make the dean's list, receive scholarships, win awards, get elected to student organizations, and otherwise distinguish themselves on campus. Letting their hometown media know about their achievements is a great way to say, "Job well done." It's also a great way to make the students and their families feel proud, to attract local college-bound high schoolers, and to enhance the university's reputation.

I didn't know how to write releases, but my freshman journalism professor told me to try because I had "a knack for words." What he didn't tell me is how difficult it can be to turn that knack into workable copy. In any event, I learned because I had a mentoring boss who gave me wings and student-writer friends who taught me to edit like Ernest Hemingway. Later I got a co-op job as a *Quincy Patriot Ledger* reporter. There I got my first daily newspaper byline. I began to study and practice writing like my pants were on fire. I still feel the heat.

After graduation, I moved to New York City and got my first job in PR, a profession about which I knew zip. A headhunter said it paid twice what journalism paid. I was married. Money was important. I jumped at the chance.

I'm thrilled I did. I love what PR is all about, warts and all. And I love the role writing plays in its delivery.

Methodically, I evolved from wordsmith to what I call "wordworker"—someone who intentionally crafts language to make favorable things happen to those for whom he or she is employed. I went from FYI (for your information) to FYA (for your action) writing. One of my writing rules is everything written for PR purposes must include a concrete call for action. If it's not obvious, make it so. Create something recipients can buy, write for, or take part in. Don't waste people's time with information-only documents. PR is doing, not diddling.

Writing isn't the only skill one needs in PR, but it's one of the essentials because just about everything practitioners do requires something written: plan, program, publication, speech, video and, sooner than we think, virtual reality and human-like robot scripts. It's also the tool we use to think through and solve employer or client problems with commonsense logic built around strategic messages that persuade audiences to purchase, invest, volunteer, donate, organize, vote, create, or otherwise engage the world.

More to the point, I like the influence, however modest, I have as a PR writer, even though I and all PR professionals handle many other responsibilities and challenges in a given week. I like the feeling I get when what I write leads to something tangible, meaningful, and helpful for others. I think everyone else in PR feels the same. ●

Don Bates, New York University PR and business writing instructor, is a PR management consultant for corporate communication executives and PR agencies interested in growing their businesses or merging with another agency.

Source: D. Bates (personal communication, 2017).

Let's assume you are drafting a speech for the company president to give to employees. This fact makes your audience research easier but can also present challenges in writing depending on the purpose (is the company downsizing, merging, relocating, shifting strategic direction, etc.).

Most speeches follow the same formatting guidelines; double- or triple-spaced using large typeface with **serifs** (short lines attached to ends of letter strokes) for ease of reading, indented paragraphs, numbered loose pages, and annotated in the margins (in the text) or with cues for the speaker (such as "pause for emphasis").

Regarding the structure of the speech, the old golden rule of speechwriting applies: (1) Tell your audience what you're going to tell them; (2) tell them; and (3) tell them what you've told them. The language of a speech is unlike other PR writing; it can be elegant, poetic, emotional or persuasive, rational, and plain-spoken. It often incorporates story elements, visual imagery, and a sense of **immediacy**. The purpose and topic of the speech will guide what language is appropriate. A reasonable time length for a speech is 20 minutes or less; anything longer and there's serious risk of losing, if not annoying, the audience. For speech ideas, visit https://ispeeches.com/.

WRITING FOR ORGANIZATIONAL MEDIA AND DIGITAL ENVIRONMENTS

More and more readers and viewers are getting their news online and via social networks. This diverse and fluid field of media consumption represents challenges, opportunities, and dangers for the PR profession. Writers must shift from a more traditional style, structuring content to the social and digital environment.

These environments provide opportunities to deliver content directly to specific publics—employees, clients, special interest bloggers, and so on—without concern for geographical boundaries or the need to place a news item with traditional media for it to be disseminated. However, there are drawbacks; most critically the standards required in the traditional press release can loosen without a gatekeeper to check facts and format. What goes out on the Web and in social networks may not have the rigor, clarity, and veracity of carefully vetted information. Yet, with the evolution of digital and social media, the PR writer benefits from access to forms of distribution that allow for reaching more people, more frequently, and at less cost. It's essential that professional standards are maintained in this cornucopia of media to ensure your organization is well represented: clear, accurate, and concise writing that communicates credibility. Anyone who follows the news can recall more than one incident when an ill-conceived Tweet or Facebook post has destroyed the reputation of the writer and reflected badly on his or her organization.

One of the reasons the PR profession is growing is that while newspapers have suffered from loss of readers and advertising revenue due to free online content, PR's utility has expanded with the ability to directly reach specific publics expeditiously and at less cost. You'll explore writing for social media, digital environments, and emerging technologies in Chapter 8.

SCENARIO OUTCOME

At the beginning of this chapter, we provided a real-life scenario of Taylor Guitars's need to communicate an industry-changing decision with its various stakeholders. To review, due to the diminishing supply of black ebony wood in the world's rain forests, Bob Taylor made a decision to cease using only black ebony in premium acoustic guitars. As a supplier of guitars to celebrity musicians and guitar retailers, and as a supplier of black ebony to other guitar manufacturers, Taylor was faced with the major challenge of convincing everyone that ebony with variegated color is just as "good" as black ebony and to accept it in place of the rare black ebony. As the PR manager for Taylor Guitars, we asked you how you would advise him to achieve this goal—what messaging strategies would be most effective?

To shift the mind-set, Taylor Guitars used the industry stature and influence of its CEO to launch a concerted PR campaign aimed at multiple publics. Bob Taylor began a series of presentations and meetings with other guitar makers who were end users of Crelicam ebony. To these manufacturers, he explained the ebony trade in Cameroon and the threat to the future of the wood. He then set out the new direction the company was taking to provide ethical, legally sourced, and sustainable ebony.

He explained Crelicam's intent to use variegated wood and he shared what he had learned from his cutters. Almost all the manufacturers Taylor spoke with agreed to use the variegated wood. This acceptance of the different coloration by virtually the entire industry spurred a PR effort to encourage consumer acceptance, too.

Taylor Guitars's PR campaign was spearheaded by a company-produced 13-minute online video, featuring Bob Taylor: "The Truth of the Forest: The State of Ebony in the World." Watch it at https://www.youtube.com/watch?v=anCGvfsBoFY and note how the spoken words reflect the components of a well-written speech. In the video Taylor relates the story of the acquisition of Crelicam, explains the threat to the world's supply of ebony, and informs guitar buyers of the inclusion of variegated ebony in new products from Taylor Guitars. Using a guitar with a fretboard made of variegated ebony as an example, Taylor makes the case for the change as being environmentally and ethically sound without compromising the guitar's tone or quality.

The PR efforts also included a series of articles on the subject. The acquisition of Crelicam, the obstacles that Taylor faced, the ethical and social issues, and the case for using variegated ebony were featured in Taylor Guitars's magazine for owners, *Wood&Steel*. In addition, the PR campaign resulted in featured media coverage on the firm's sustainability efforts in Cameroon, which appeared in lifestyle and industry magazines, websites, and major metro U.S. newspapers.

The unique feature of this PR thrust was that it had a very specific audience to address with a very specific message. The real targets of all the efforts were the guitar-buying public and guitar manufacturers and distributors. Bob Taylor's personal presentations, the online video, and the in-depth articles all reached these publics with a consistent message that changed the perception of what is and what is not acceptable ebony.

WRAP UP

In this chapter you honed your PR skills by analyzing how a company should communicate to multiple stakeholders about a significant change in its product. You solved this problem for Taylor Guitars through a journey beginning with a look at the communication process.

As PR is a profession guided by strategy, you learned that when writing, too, you must ask and answer essential questions. Both the quality and structure of PR writing are keys to engaging your reader; while diverse tactics require differing structures, they always must be exceptionally well written. With this chapter, you now have a good understanding of the widely used writing tactics in PR, and you've been challenged to read, review, and practice them.

KEY TERMS

Backgrounder: A written document, usually part of a media kit, that provides additional information on an organization and its situation to help a media worker craft a story, **145**

Boilerplate: A paragraph appearing at the bottom of a news release, summarizing information about the sending organization, **141**

Channel: The medium of communication, such as television, radio, e-mail, and so on, **133**

Cybernetics: A theory of message transmission, **133**

Encoded: The way meaning is produced in a message to ensure comprehension by the receiver, **133**

Immediacy: The quality or experience of something happening now or "being in the moment", **150**

Inverted Pyramid: The traditional structure of news writing and the writing of news releases, **140**

Lead: The first paragraph of a news story or news release, **141**

Noise: Unplanned factors that affect the communication process, **133**

Op-Eds: Opinion pieces that usually concern current issues, **146**

Serifs: On some typefaces, short lines attached to ends of letter strokes, **150**

Brainstorm how you would pitch a client's new product to a news writer or media outlet.

Your client manufactures PeakStrength products aimed at the active athlete and is rolling out a new product, Barknola, an organic energy bar for dogs. Research shows that athletes in the more challenging sports tend to have canine companions who accompany them into remote areas. Feeding these dogs is a problem because it requires "packing in" pouches of food, resulting in extra weight and less backpack storage space for the athlete's own needs. A single Barknola bar is the size of a normal granola bar and provides the average dog with all the nutrition needed for eight hours. In product pretrials, cases of Barknola have been donated to dog owners at climbing competitions and bike races, 12 police departments with K-9 units, and a Wounded Warriors program that provides companion dogs to veterans suffering from PTSD. Determine a news angle or opportunity, and then choose a specific (and real) person at a media outlet to e-mail your pitch to. Most critical is what will the wording in your subject line be?

As the PR director for Taylor Guitars, you are in charge of producing its first sustainability report video.

Considering what you now know about both Taylor Guitars's environmental and social engagement, draft a storyboard for a 60- to 90-second video. Use PowerPoint to create 9 to 12 slides that suggest the visual sequencing and the verbal narrative. Also propose one interview in your video.

Defend your proposed video in a memo to Bob Taylor:

▸ Specify the target audience(s).

▸ Identify some of the SUCCESs principles used: simple, unexpected, concrete, credible, emotional, and/or storytelling (covered earlier in this chapter).

▸ Explain your interview choice.

Note: Before completing this assignment, read How Can Video Storytelling Support Social Responsibility Efforts at the end of this chapter.

SOCIAL RESPONSIBILITY CASE STUDY

Whirlpool: Care Counts™

Situation

The Whirlpool brand is part of Whirlpool Corporation, the world's leading manufacturer and marketer of major home appliances. Whirlpool Corporation is also one of Habitat for Humanity's largest corporate partners for more than 15 years, donating a refrigerator and range to every new Habitat for Humanity home built in North America.

In 2015 an elementary school principal in Fairfield, California, asked Whirlpool to donate a washer and dryer to the school. The reason? Students weren't going to school because they didn't have clean clothes, staying home instead to avoid bullying and mockery.

Research and Strategy

A Whirlpool survey conducted together with its PR firm, Ketchum, discovered that as many as one in five American students struggle with access to clean clothes. In response, Care Counts by Whirlpool was born. Whirlpool brand worked with internationally recognized developmental psychologist and researcher, Dr. Richard Rende, Ph.D., to design this pilot laundry program, exploring the connection between access to clean clothes and attendance rates.

As a part of the program, each school identified students with a need for clean clothes and anonymously tracked their loads of laundry, attendance, and grades throughout the school year. To measure additional behavioral changes, each student's primary teacher also completed a qualitative survey asking if they believe access to clean clothes improved his or her student's ability to do a variety of activities, from participating in class to enjoying school.

Execution

The pilot program began in the 2015–2016 school year with washers and dryers placed in 17 schools in two districts, St. Louis, Missouri, and Fairfield, California. Program leaders equipped with data-tracking tools let students manage the laundry schedule and the machines.

In the first year, the program provided approximately 2,000 loads of clean clothes to students across two school districts. After examining the correlation between student attendance and loads of laundry washed and dried, more than 90% of tracked students in the program improved their attendance, averaging 6.1 more days in school than the previous year. The program impacted the most at-risk participants even more, with an average of nearly two more weeks in school than the previous year.

"When we learned that a child's education could be at risk because they do not have access to clean clothes, we were determined to help," said Chelsey Lindstrom, brand manager, Whirlpool brand. "It's incredible to see how the simple act of laundry can have such a profound impact on students' lives and we are excited to bring this resource to even more schools across the country" (Whirlpool Corporation, 2016).

Evaluation

Students in the pilot program improved more than just attendance rates. Teachers surveyed saw the results listed in Table 6.2:

TABLE 6.2

Pilot Program Results

> ▸ 95% of participants showed increased motivation in class.
>
> ▸ 95% of participants were more likely to participate in extracurricular activities.
>
> ▸ 95% of participants interacted with peers and enjoyed school more.
>
> ▸ 89% of participants got good grades.

"Every single day of school matters. When students miss school, they are missing an opportunity to learn," said Martha Lacy, principal, David Weir K–8 Academy. "Absenteeism strongly impacts a student's academic performance. In fact, students with excessive absence rates are more likely to fall behind, graduate late and even drop out" (Whirlpool Corporation, 2016).

With the success of its inaugural year, the Care Counts program will continue to help students gain access to clean clothes by expanding to additional school districts starting this summer.

A documentary-style video, media materials, microsite, and school officials and brand spokespeople told the story of the program and shared its results with more than 600 earned stories in outlets including *ABC World News Tonight*, Today.com, *Business Insider, U.S. News & World Report*, and NPR. There were 64 broadcast segments across 18 states and more than 700 interested school representatives spanning 48 states.

ENGAGE

▶ Go to https://www.whirlpool.com/. Click on the "Learn More" tab under "Improving Attendance Through Laundry" and watch the video.

▶ Back on the home page, scroll down to "About Whirlpool Corporation," select "Press and Media." Choose the May 15, 2017, story "Whirlpool's Care Counts™ Laundry Program Expands to Provide Additional Students Across the Country With Access to Clean Clothes," and read the update to the program (you may also want to view several of the videos on this page).

DISCUSS

▶ Whirlpool's Care Counts program appears to have a great impact on the students who benefit from having access to clean clothes. Did you know this issue existed? If so, do you think there's enough attention brought to the subject? What tactics would you employ to spread the word about Care Counts?

▶ Whirlpool has now partnered with Teach for America to bring the Care Counts program to other areas of the country. Suggest corporate or product manufacturers they might consider as other partners, and explain why.

Sources: *PRWeek* (2017); Whirlpool Corporation (2016).

SOCIAL RESPONSIBILITY CASE STUDY

How Can Video Storytelling Support Social Responsibility Efforts?

Situation

It's a PR writer's job to help produce an annual sustainability or SR report for companies who choose to issue one. Such reporting is of great interest to investors of publicly held companies as well as to the media, consumers in general, and partners in a company's supply chain. Beyond written reports found on the corporate website, CSR reporting is also communicated through video.

Research and Strategy

A study of 200 CSR videos created and published between 2000 and 2015 found critical insights on both their content and framing (Bortree, 2016). In Chapter 4 you read about framing and its usefulness in suggesting *how* readers or viewers should think about the information they consume. This study suggests that companies are using the legitimacy strategies of competence (quality products that meet society's needs) and concern (socially and environmentally responsible behaviors).

The study found that competence is communicated in CSR videos most often through the presence of numbers and statistics: 77% used them, followed by content on economics and financial information in 71%, and then by content on company activities in 70%. Concern is communicated most often in the videos through the presence of an employee or employees: 77% picture them, followed by content on education in 70%, and then by images of community in 62% (see Table 6.3). The social responsibility videos addressed "community" more often than did the environmental videos.

TABLE 6.3

How CSR Videos Communicate Legitimacy

COMPETENCY CONTENT	CONCERN CONTENT
Numbers, Statistics	Employees
Economics, Financials	Education
Company Activities	Community

Execution

Companies are increasingly using video to communicate their CSR. They are also getting experimental with content presentation to engage Millennials. This influential demographic is keenly interested in socially responsible companies. Creative CSR content distributed via social media is attempting to arrest their attention and get them talking about it.

In 2014 Samsung presented a sustainability rap presented by Korean rapper Mad Clown. In 2015 Heineken promoted its annual sustainability report through a rap video featuring Dutch hip-hop star Blaxter freestyling about Heineken's reduced water consumption (edie.net, 2016a). The company also has used gamification to engage consumers in uncovering the progress that Heineken USA has made in key environmental areas.

The BT Group (British Telecommunications) created a rap video to explain the sustainable design principles in its Home Hub router. Other digital innovations for CSR reporting include Virgin Media, one of the first businesses to stop producing hard-copy versions of its CSR reports in 2010. In 2015 it released the first ever 360-degree sustainability video that provides viewers with an immersive experience (edie.net, 2016b).

Evaluation

Companies today need to drive engagement with CSR and sustainability reports to reach wider audiences. Louise Koch, Dell's corporate sustainability lead, claims that some of the CSR video and social media content is being watched and absorbed at a greater rate than other core business information. This consumption is largely because sustainability enables firms to attach a story to the figures in a way that areas like finance can't (edie.net, 2017). Chris Libre, eBay's senior director of global impact and giving, advises that if an organization wants to engage the growing spectrum of stakeholders interested in sustainability, it must embrace a range of modern communication tactics that foster engagement, and even dialogue, with stakeholders. He sums it up, "I think a more audience-specific approach to sustainability communication is the way of the future" (Bendeler, 2017).

ENGAGE

▸ Stakeholder engagement is becoming a more critical aspect of sustainability and sustainability reporting; thus companies are reaching out to key stakeholders through various communication channels to promote the value and content of their reports.

▸ What are Heineken and Virgin Media doing now? Check them out.

▸ Explore some videos by searching YouTube with the following terms "sustainability report" coupled with any of the following: Daimler, H&M, Samsung, P&G, and Lowe's. You may also simply type "sustainability report videos" in any search engine for results.

DISCUSS

▸ In sustainability report videos, what differences do you notice between videos (scripts and imagery) that address environmental concerns versus social concerns? How can you explain those differences? What do you think the creators' strategies were?

▸ Note some specific legitimacy appeals in these videos (or other sustainability reports you find on YouTube). How are competency and concern communicated, in language and visually? Does everyone in your group agree?

▸ How are elements of storytelling incorporated into the videos and other digital media? Refer to the SUCCESs principles.

▸ Observe if there are diverse and gendered representations of competency and concern. Does the video or media communicate diversity? Why are women featured or omitted? Children? Whose voice in narrating? What is the significance of your findings?

Tesla Powerwall Solar Batteries: News Release

Elon Musk founded Tesla in 2003 to build battery-powered cars. Since then, the company has expanded to related fields, including solar panels and other types of large batteries. In 2015, Musk launched a new product, the Powerwall, a battery intended to store the power generated by a home's solar panels when supply exceeds demand.

VIDEO

1. Imagine you were tasked with writing a news release on the new Tesla Powerwall. Provide answers to some of the basic questions of PR writing: Why are you writing? Who is the target reader and what is most relevant to them? What is the public relations' desired objective? What is the organization's key message? What communication channel will be used?

2. What is the key advantage to consumers that you would emphasize to elicit interest in the product?

3. Following the inverted pyramid structure, write a sample news release for the Powerwall.

iStock.com/Yuri_Arcurs

7

Media Relations in a Digital World

Learning Objectives

7.1   Understand the current state of the news media

7.2   Explore communications theory's application to media relations

7.3   Measure the impact of news coverage in achieving business goals

7.4   Identify global trends and practices in media relations

Scenario

Real Warriors Campaign: You Are Not Alone

Between September 2001 and 2014, 2.5 million service members were deployed (some several times) to support combat missions in Iraq and Afghanistan. The pace and number of deployments have been unprecedented in recent times. Also, independent research has shown that each deployment increases a soldier's risk of experiencing psychological health concerns—both while on deployment and when he or she returns to civilian life. Many suffer from what are referred to as "invisible wounds"—for example, psychological or emotional problems (like posttraumatic stress disorder [PTSD]) that surface periodically, especially when the veteran is in a stressful situation.

The Real Warriors Campaign is designed to raise awareness and reduce stigma regarding mental illness in the military.

Ahmad Al-Rubaye/AFP/Getty Images

A wall of resistance. Past research from the Defense Department (DOD), Veterans Administration, and others indicated that only a minority of those experiencing invisible wounds seek readily available psychological healthcare (Vaughn et al., 2009). Current research revealed significant challenges: Service members are often in denial and don't associate symptoms with psychological health concerns but rather the "cost" of deployment; they perceived the severity of their invisible wounds to be less than physical wounds and not deserving of attention; any psychological health-care treatment has widely been perceived as a sign of weakness and a career ender; and they needed proof that others like themselves could carry out successful military or veteran careers after receiving care.

Fought with evidence-based techniques. The "Real Warriors" campaign (see http://www.realwarriors.net) was developed for the DOD by Booz Allen Hamilton in response to a 2007 federal task force that instructed the DOD to "implement an anti-stigma public education campaign using evidence based techniques to provide facts and information about mental disorders."

The goals were to create the following:

▸ **Awareness about resources available** for psychological healthcare and support among service members, their families, their commanders, and the public at large.

▸ **Knowledge of service members' challenges** that may prevent them from seeking care or support for psychological health concerns.

▸ **Understanding of resilience and early intervention** as well as the roles they play in successful care, recovery, and reintegration for returning service members and overall force readiness.

This was a comprehensive communications campaign with both digital and media relations components that were key to its execution and success. It is an excellent example of a public service/CSR project designed to address a critical social issue.

As you read through this chapter, consider the following:

1. Which strategies would you include in the media relations aspects of this project?

2. Which tactics would you include for media relations?

Note: In 2014, this program was awarded a Silver Anvil by the PRSA. This scenario is adapted from that case.

For most non-PR practitioners, *media relations* and *PR* are viewed as synonymous. This has been the case since the early days of the profession, when PR pros were often referred to as "publicity agents" or "flacks." As discussed in Chapter 2, these publicists worked mostly on behalf of major companies and politicians. But there is a difference between generating publicity and engaging in SPR. In 1942 Baus (1942) described publicity as "the dissemination of information for a motive." But he also noted that "all publicity is public relations, but not all public relations is publicity."

This chapter will lay the foundation to prepare you to generate meaningful publicity as part of an SPR campaign. It begins with an overview of the current state of the news media, specifically the economic and demographic trends impacting both journalists and news organizations.

Then the basics of media relations will be reviewed along with the communications theories that inform it. Finally we will look at how media relations practices differ around the world and explore how U.S.-based PR professionals should interact with the global media to accomplish their global communications goals.

THE STATE OF THE NEWS MEDIA TODAY

⟩⟩ LO 7.1   Understand the current state of the news media

One of the first, and most basic, rules of PR is to *know your audience*. This entails reviewing research data, talking with the target audience to learn what motivates them, and determining the key messages you want to communicate. The practice of modern media relations is no different. To work effectively with reporters, bloggers, or other influential people (i.e., influencers), you need to understand the state of the news media now and the trends that are impacting the industry for the future.

The rationale for this is simple. As Lori Beecher, partner and director of media and content strategy for Ketchum, explained: "The ability to be successful in your media relations efforts is directly proportionate to an understanding of the reporters, editors and producers and the industry in which they work. You will be much more successful if your outreach efforts are consistent with their needs and reflect the realities of today's news media" (L. Beecher, personal communication, 2016).

⑤SAGE edge™

Master the content
edge.sagepub.com/page

RESEARCH ON THE MEDIA

There is no question that the media industry—which includes newspapers, magazines, television, and radio as well as the online media—is vastly different from the media industry just a generation ago (Pew Research Center, 2016b). In most of the major U.S. metropolitan areas today, there are fewer daily papers, more cable television, and three television network affiliates, along with a variety of radio formats including talk, all news, music, sports, and entertainment. In addition, there are new entrants. These range from online news outlets, podcasts, broadcasts on demand and news aggregator sites that collect stories and videos and deliver them directly to your Facebook or Twitter page based on your preferences and search history.

To get a sense of how much things have changed and what is ahead for the U.S. media, let's review some recent research from the Pew Research Center. However, do not assume that these changes in the traditional news media mean that the practice of media relations is less important. The targets may have increased or shifted, but coverage and visibility—in all its forms—is what management and clients still want and expect from PR pros. In fact, a recent study of the PR profession estimates that approximately 80% of PR practitioners practice media relations, in one form or another, during their typical workweek (Darnowski et al., 2013, cited in Supa, 2014).

In its annual "State of the News Media Report" for 2016, the Pew Research Center (2016b) paints a challenging picture for the media industry in the United States and globally. The picture is one that will challenge you as future PR professionals in getting your messages to target audiences. Nonetheless media coverage in all its forms will still be expected of you. For example, the Pew Research Center (2016b) reports that the newspaper sector "had perhaps its worst year in 2015 since the 2008 recession." Some key indicators support this conclusion:

▸ Average weekday circulation (print and digital combined) fell 7% in 2015, the greatest decline since 2010.

▸ Total advertising revenue (for publicly traded media companies) declined 8%.

▸ Newsroom employment (reporters, editors, and photographers) declined 10%, the most since 2009 (right after the 2008 recession). As a result, the workforce in the newspaper industry is 20,000 positions smaller than 20 years ago.

▸ Readership of daily newspapers is on the decline overall (digital and print) as more and more people get their news delivered online or from other sources.

The television industry (network, cable, and local) fared somewhat better according to the report, which noted the following;

▸ Network TV grew ad revenues 6% for evening programming and 14% for the morning shows (e.g., *Today*, *Good Morning America*, and *CBS This Morning*).

▸ Cable television increased ad and subscriber revenue by 10%.

▸ Local TV (network affiliates and independents) showed increases as well—particularly in areas where political advertising is prevalent, reflecting the 2016 election campaign.

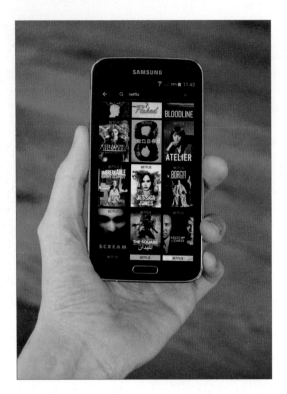

Increasing numbers of Americans have "cut the cord" on traditional cable providers and rely on streaming services like Netflix, Hulu, and Amazon.

JHPhoto/Alamy Stock Photo

However, there are troubling trends for the television industry due to the seasonality of viewing trends (based on the presidential election cycle) and so-called cord cutting, Pew suggests. Cord cutting is a phenomenon in which people discontinue (or "cut") their cable subscriptions and rely on Internet-based providers (Hulu, Roku, etc.) for entertainment and news content. This trend, by most accounts, is expected to accelerate as costs of basic cable increase and patterns of viewing change. In support of this point, Pew reported that as many as one in seven Americans in 2016 had discontinued their cable or satellite TV subscriptions.

Among minority and special interest publications, the media picture is mixed as well. Pew reports that Hispanic weekly papers saw some circulation growth, but the major Hispanic dailies (such as *La Opinión*) posted declines in subscriptions and advertising, and the largest Hispanic-focused television networks (e.g., Univision) lost both audience and revenue as well. The number of African American newspapers remained the same in 2015 versus the prior year (approximately 200), but there is evidence of a decline in the number of subscribers and advertisers.

The rise of the digital news outlets—such as the Huffington Post and Vox Media—has changed the reading and viewing habits of Americans—especially Millennials (defined as those currently between the ages of 18 and 34 at the time of the research). The Pew data indicates an increase in the total audience and in the time spent on these sites—often at the expense of time on the sites of traditional media organizations or reading the actual, physical publications. Specifically, 38% of U.S. adults reported that they "often" get their news first from digital sites, for example, news websites, news apps, or social networking sites. This compares to only 20% of U.S. adults who get their news primarily from a print newspaper.

Pew reports that those under 30 years old are more likely to name social media as a main source of news than a traditional outlet. And, Pew adds, this is increasingly common among *all* adults in the United States, noting that 62% of all U.S. adults now get their news on social media sites (Pew Research Center, 2016b). To be clear though, most of these sites do not generate their own news stories. So working with reporters to obtain coverage in target publications is still critical as the reach of the article you place is likely to be extended by these services.

Another key consideration for media relations professionals is the changing U.S. population **demographics** which are shifting toward more Millennials and away from the baby boomer generation (ages 51–69). This is significant because this latter group has driven the media's business model for the past 20 to 30 years.

With this industry data and demographic trends as a backdrop, let's examine the implications for the practice of media relations and suggest how PR professionals can and should respond.

CURRENT PRACTICE OF MEDIA RELATIONS

Dustin Supa of Boston University suggests that media relations is an integral part of SPR. He offers a definition of media relations that speaks to both its "tactical" and "strategic" importance: "media relations is the systematic, planned, purposeful and mutually beneficial relationship between a public relations practitioner and a mass media journalist." In the current environment, Supa suggests, most PR practitioners would agree that "media relations is an integral part of the strategic plan for any public relations campaign" (Supa, 2009, cited in Supa, 2014, p. 4).

Supa suggests five guiding principles to understand media relations:

1. Media relations should be viewed as a strategic function of PR, not just a tactical.

2. Every organization has different media relations goals; some want or need coverage, some don't, and some only want it in specific publications versus the national media.

3. In media relations, the relationship is key—for example, you need to understand the needs and expectations of both parties (reporters and PR professionals)

4. Media relations is not a means to an end—journalists are a stakeholder group, not a vehicle to reach stakeholders.

5. The tools used in media relations do not define media relations—media relations is defined by the use of the tools to achieve goals, not the tools themselves.

Generating media coverage is what management expects PR people to do and what PR people spend a great deal of their professional lives doing. Yet it is important to note that as a PR professional, you have the responsibility to seek fair and balanced news coverage. The reporters and producers have a responsibility as well—to provide reliable information that informs, entertains, or improves the lives of their audience in a meaningful fashion. No one wins in the long run if a news story is fabricated, incomplete, misleading or "fake."

The issue of **fake news** became a major talking point during the 2016 U.S. presidential elections and surfaced again in national elections across Europe in the

The issue of "fake news" became a major one during the 2016 U.S. presidential campaign.

Jaap Arriens/NurPhoto/Getty Images

spring of 2017. Paul Chadwick (2017), writing in a May 2017 column in the *Guardian* newspaper (U.S. edition), suggests that "fake news is not new, but it is a more serious threat now than ever before to journalism" and thus to the practice of media relations. He suggests this definition of fake news: "Fake news means fictions deliberately fabricated and presented as non-fiction with the intent to mislead recipients into treating fiction as fact or into doubting verifiable fact." PR professionals must reject fake news and expose it when it occurs if the profession is to be regarded as trustworthy and ethical. For more discussion on ethics and PR, see Chapter 3.

To examine how the process of media relations works, the next section focuses on the role of the PR professional and how he or she can get the job done without misleading the public, journalists, or the media. It all comes back to understanding your target audience—in this case, the media and their publics—and learning what motivates them to act.

MONITOR THE MEDIA FOR BEST RESULTS

As a PR professional, you have many roles to play in a successful media relations effort. To begin with you must be a constant reader and observer of the news media—who is covering what topics and what types of stories are of interest to which publications? You also need to know the answers to these questions: How is the media covering your industry, competitors, and company or client? Which reporters are interested in topics that connect with the story you want them to tell?

Once you have determined the answers to these and other preliminary questions, you can begin to develop your approach or **pitch**, as it is referred to in the PR industry. The pitch, to be effective, should include a short summary of the story, and a connection or relevance to the publication and its readers and be accurate, intriguing, and complete.

Given the demands on the media today, you also must summarize the story idea succinctly because they will not read a long, drawn-out note. Think "elevator pitch" and keep it simple and straightforward, so they can tell right away if it is of interest. If they want to know more, give them the tools to do that—for example, links to studies, new research, or access to experts. If they don't, accept that outcome and move on.

PR people and the media share a tenuous working relationship at best and a distrustful, non-communicative relationship at worst (Supa, 2014). This potential disconnect is at the center of strategic media relations: Two parties with different goals and agendas must find common ground where a fair, accurate, and balanced news story can result. Paul Farhi, media reporter for the *Washington Post*, suggests that PR professionals can be "helpful" to a reporter (and help themselves) by identifying stories of interest to a reporter and suggesting them, with some caveats.

A key consideration in a successful pitch is to determine the right reporter to approach. This requires that you do the research to find reporters interested in the topic and leave others out of the pitch altogether. Pitching multiple reporters when only a handful will be interested is counterproductive and annoying to the reporter or producer. This analysis is best accomplished by using a commercial database—such as Meltwater, Cision, or BurrellesLuce—to search the topic, media, and geographic area you are interested in. Some of these services can also scan social media platforms, locate conversations about your client/company or competition, and assess them in terms of the tone and frequency.

Begin by doing your research, developing a tightly focused and current media list, and crafting a simple but persuasive pitch to get targeted reporters interested.

"PR people can be vital to reporters, . . . if they can supply timely and accurate information, if they are responsive to inquiries on deadline, if they are knowledgeable and trustworthy, and if they can be a conduit for reporters to the newsmaker."

—Paul Farhi (personal communication, 2017)

Hyundai Motors Introduces Drivers to the Future

Hyundai's launch of the Tucson Fuel Cell, the first mass-produced fuel cell car, was preceded by a year-long media campaign to prepare the marketplace for the vehicle's arrival.

Ethan Miller/Getty Images

Hyundai Motor Company was ready to bring its new Tucson fuel cell vehicle to market. This was to be the first mass-produced fuel cell vehicle that consumers could purchase and drive right away. Working with their agency (Ketchum) Hyundai launched a year-long media relations-based campaign to educate both the industry and consumers on the benefits of fuel cells and introduce drivers to a different take on the future of the automobile.

Launching First Fuel Cell Car

In supporting the launch of the Tucson fuel cell vehicle, the first of its kind, the agency recognized that changing the minds of a highly skeptical industry and consumer base would not easy. The task was made more difficult by the opposition to fuel cell-powered vehicles from automotive industry leaders like Elon Musk (Tesla) and Bob Lutz (GM).

Focus on Building Consumer Awareness Then Demand

Ketchum mounted a year-long campaign that relied on media relations and events/activities focused on customers, not industry leaders. Through creating a groundswell of publicity and reaching the public directly, the firm was able to help achieve its goals so that the entire allotment of these vehicles was leased *before* they reached the dealer.

Preparation Is Key

This case demonstrates that when seeking to publicize an event, product, person, or activity, you need to put yourself in the reporters' and public's shoes. Your questions should include these:

▸ Is the news I want to share important to the readers, viewers, or listeners of the media outlet?

▸ Is my news current and actual news? Are there elements or details to the story that bring new insights or benefits to the readers or viewers?

▸ Is the reporter or producer I am contacting interested in the topic? Is he or she covering the industry and knowledgeable about it?

▸ Is my information accurate, timely, and truthful?

Set for Success

With these questions answered, you are prepared to pursue a story opportunity. You should also be familiar with the various reporters' points of view and be prepared that they may seek comments and experts to balance the story. In this case, the agency and client had done the work, knew who covered automotive news, and had a sense of what competitors might say when contacted. As a result the launch goals were met, and the coverage was balanced, not critical. ●

Source: Hyundai Motor America With Ketchum (2015).

Note: This case is a PRSA 2015 Silver Anvil case study.

It helps if you have worked with them or interacted before you make the pitch so you are not a total stranger seeking news coverage. This familiarization process can entail sending them new research, the names of experts to meet and talk to for background information, or commenting constructively on relevant stories they have written—whether they involve your company/client or not. Remember, it is called "media relations" for a reason. It is a *relationship*, and both parties have needs and expectations to be fulfilled.

How to Be Pitch Perfect With Corporate Social Responsibility Stories

Advance research is key. If you worked for a regional bank in the Midwest, and you want to publicize the bank's community relations or CSR work, begin by looking up banking or finance reporters in the area as well as trade media and blogs covering banking and finance.

Prepare a target list. Focusing your list before doing any reporter outreach is a key step. If you are seeking to place a CSR-themed story, such as making home ownership more affordable for veterans, you should only approach reporters who cover banking and community relations stories in your area. This is a common mistake of PR practitioners. Expanding the target media list too broadly can create the perception that PR pros are "spammers," and it is damaging to other PR professionals trying to place stories.

Read and review previous stories. The next step after compiling the list would be to review the stories the reporters have written to see if they cover or are interested in the topic. Often you can predict how a reporter might cover your story idea based on a review of their past stories. This preliminary analysis is especially important in a CSR-related media pitch because many reporters are skeptical about such stories and might agree to pursue them but take a negative or critical angle later.

Focus on the cause, not the company. To add credibility to a pitch for coverage of CSR-related activity, focus the story on the organization you are supporting instead of your bank. Often you will find this appeal is stronger due to the human-interest angle, and your bank will still get coverage as the benefactor in the process. If you are pitching local or national television, you must also make sure that there is a visual element to the story—as that is essential to getting the interest of a TV news producer and obtaining coverage.

Extend the impact. Once you have secured a story and it comes out fair and balanced, make sure to post it on your company site and push it out on social media to extend the impact; make sure your target audience sees it. Also, tweet the reporter with a note that the story is being posted and shared with others who may not have seen it. Reporters are tracked by editors to see how often their stories get re-posted and shared to measure engagement of readers and the public. ●

SOCIAL RESPONSIBILITY ⟨ Obtaining coverage of CSR initiatives—new or continuing—can be difficult. A Harvard study (Hamilton, 2003) on the early years of CSR found it was challenging to obtain news coverage for SR activities by companies or other organizations, especially from the national broadcast media. This was due to several factors: Sustainability initiatives take considerable time to show an impact, are often localized, and lack a visual element making it suitable for television coverage. The same research found that the print media, notably those papers serving local markets and business and financial readers, were more receptive to covering CSR. This was attributed to increased interest in the topic generally and because individuals are seeking "good corporate citizen" stocks to invest in.

More recent findings reveal there is growing interest on the part of the news media for reporting CSR, thus there are ample ways for organizations to garner CSR news coverage (Carroll, 2011). A wide range of sources are used for CSR stories than are used in mainstream news topics, suggesting that PR practitioners should engage CSR partners in their media outreach. The research also underscores that an understanding of how news is *produced* will also help with CSR story placements: Knowing the outlet's news values will help PR practitioners translate their stories through those values. However, there remains a lack of clarity on what the term "CSR" means and how it operates, so educating the media may be a necessary aspect of some media relations activities.

Media Relations—It's All About Building Relationships

Michelle Leff Mermelstein, APR
Wireless Device Public Relations, Sprint

Initially, I was laser focused on a career as a journalist. I was fortunate enough to have an inspiring teacher in high school who helped me develop a love of writing and accurately covering the news of the day.

After studying journalism and political science in college, I landed a job as an associate editor for a magazine covering insurance, finance, and tax law. I often had to reach out to financial services companies to get a comment on legislation that impacted their industry. Some of the media relations professionals I reached out to were incredibly helpful and buttoned-up. As a reward for getting me the information or executive quote I needed to complete my story, I would go back to them again and again. But the PR people who weren't particularly helpful, or only focused on what they needed from me, didn't get a lot of coverage in the magazine. It was simple—the relationship needed to work for both of us.

It wasn't long before I "switched sides of the desk." As a new PR professional, I remembered the talented PR pros who helped me get my story done and, in turn, got featured in my coverage.

Good media relations is not complicated—it is all about walking a careful line between serving the media and your employer or client. The best campaigns begin with the premise that the news media and PR staff work on parallel lines and come together when it is mutually beneficial. PR people should aim to be a resource, not a pain or one sided.

In my experience, there are three things that define the best media relations practitioners:

1. They are strong writers and don't view writing as a chore. They can translate a complicated issue into concise messages so reporters can make it relevant to their readers.

2. They are smart and know their subject matter as well—or better—than their management or spokespeople. One of the greatest compliments I have ever received was when a senior executive told me I knew the product better than he did. Also, I have never had a reporter give me grief if tell them I need to get more details before I respond to a question.

3. They respect reporters and treat them as peers. *The Wall Street Journal* has an audience that can be just as important as a tech blog or a fashion magazine.

I am extremely grateful to have a career focused on media relations. This specialty of public relations is right for you if you are passionate about being a storyteller. You will be amazed at how rewarding it can be to build positive, professional relationships with the media. You may even create some lifelong friendships along the way. ●

Source: M. Leff Mermelsten (personal communication, 2017).

MEDIA RELATIONS IN POLITICAL COMMUNICATIONS

The practice of media relations in the political arena has some similarities to traditional media relations for a company or nonprofit. In short the tactics may be similar, but the goals are different. In a political environment your goal is to generate support, raise money, and ultimately, secure voters for your candidate or cause. In a business situation, you are more likely promoting a new product or service or seeking recognition of your company's charitable and sustainability efforts.

Traditionally most candidates for elected office seek coverage in the mainstream and social media and then "echo" it in handouts, Facebook posts, or other materials. Others will generate their own materials—position papers, statements, photo opportunities, and so on—and post them on the campaign site, supplementing or even bypassing the traditional media.

While the goals of public relations in the political arena may be different from the corporate world, the tactics are similar.

Brendan Smialowski/AFP/Getty Images; Dominick Reuter/AFP/Getty Images

A look at the 2016 presidential campaign reveals both strategies were utilized by the two finalists. A recent study by Pew on the media strategy by the two final candidates in the 2016 presidential election—Donald J. Trump and former Secretary of State Hillary Clinton—revealed some interesting insights about media strategy in modern political campaigns.

During the 2016 campaign, the Clinton campaign relied heavily on the owned content it produced and posted on the campaign website. As a reminder, owned content is material a company or, in this case a candidate, produces themselves versus being prepared by the news media. This material, such as studies, position papers, or features on voters and how the candidate plans to respond to issues, is prepared by the campaign staff, posted on the campaign website, and pushed out via

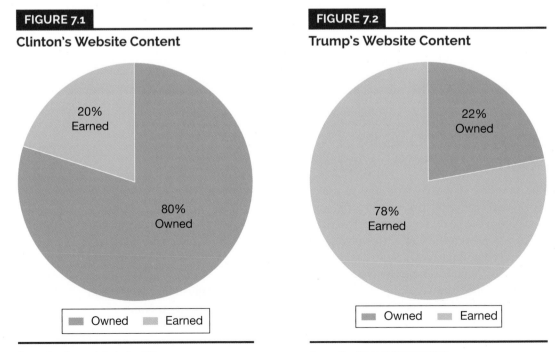

FIGURE 7.1

Clinton's Website Content

20% Earned

80% Owned

Owned   Earned

Source: Pew Research Center (2016b).

FIGURE 7.2

Trump's Website Content

22% Owned

78% Earned

Owned   Earned

Source: Pew Research Center (2016b).

social media to supporters and prospective voters. The candidates are not relying solely on media coverage to get their messages out.

According to Pew, as of the date of the research (July 2016), 80% of the material posted on the Clinton site was content produced by campaign staffers or freelancers working for the campaign (see Figure 7.1). Meanwhile, the Trump campaign did quite the opposite (see Figure 7.2). The same Pew research showed that 78% of the content on the Trump campaign website was re-posting of "earned" media articles and interviews generated by the candidate and/or his campaign staff (Pew Research Center, 2016b). There was very little owned content (self-generated) on the site, Pew found, almost the opposite of the material on the Clinton campaign site.

There may be many reasons for this variation—for example, strategic or fewer resources being allocated to content generation—and clearly there were other issues and considerations that led to the election result. However, as a tactical matter it is interesting to note that the Trump campaign focused on generating media coverage and re-posting it instead of creating its own materials for the campaign as the Clinton campaign chose to do.

MEDIA RELATIONS IN CRISIS SITUATIONS

No discussion of the topic of media relations would be complete without a mention of the critical role it can play in a crisis. While there is a full discussion of crisis and issues management in Chapter 12, it is worth a brief note here. Most PR professionals agree that how well you manage media relations in a crisis is a major factor in the duration and damage done by the crisis. Sometimes the impact of the media coverage on a company's reputation can be as bad as the crisis itself, especially if it is not well handled.

By definition, a crisis—whether it is a natural disaster, a product recall, questionable behavior by management, or any other situation that impacts the company—is a major news story and will generate a lot of inquiries and coverage but not all accurate or flattering.

PR professionals must be prepared to respond in a crisis, such as the revelation that Volkswagen had programmed their diesel cars to cheat on emissions tests, which prompted congressional hearings.

Andrew Harrer/Bloomberg/ Getty Images

Crisis expert and author James Lukaszewski suggests: "Crises are sloppy, random affairs that only slowly reveal the extent of the damage and the actual response requirements." He adds, "those who actually have survived a crisis understand that all crises tend to happen explosively, but resolving them happens incrementally" (J. Lukaszewski, personal communication, 2017).

In other words crises are dynamic and changeable, and the media is both an audience/stakeholder and a vehicle to address the public. And, fair or not, the rules and expectations are different for the company involved than for nearly everybody else, he suggests. Any crisis, or natural disaster, will generate media inquiries and coverage, as noted by Lukaszewski. How well they are handled, and the tone of the response, is a critical consideration in managing and surviving the situation with your personal and corporate reputation intact.

Lukaszewski adds, "In crisis, breaking news is too often 'broken news.'"

According to Tim Coombs, PhD, author and professor, who researches and writes extensively about crisis management, the PR team plays an important role in this process. "Public relations plays a critical role in preparing **spokespersons** for handling questions from the news media. The media relations element of public relations is a highly valued skill in crisis management. The public relations personnel provide training and support because in most cases they are not the spokesperson during the crisis" (Coombs, 2014).

BLOGGERS

There are a variety of media outlets—national, local, trade and online—a PR practitioner should consider to accomplish media relations goals. Historically media relations efforts have been directed primarily at the major business and local papers and broadcast outlets that reach the majority of your target audience. This is logical, but remember that everyone—including your competitors—is also seeking coverage from the same reporters and outlets. In addition you cannot overlook the digital media—for example, bloggers, influencers, and online media—as they can extend your story and reach more of your target audience.

Sony Electronics Imaging Division, based in San Diego, has found including bloggers and influencers in its product launches to be particularly effective: "As the media landscape continues to change, we have learned to be flexible with our media outreach to accomplish our goals. We have made it a priority to include bloggers and influencers at our major events, putting them right alongside the traditional media. So far the results have been better than we ever could have imagined. The 'nontraditional media' brings a level of excitement that simply wouldn't exist at a typical product launch press conference, and the resulting media coverage/social buzz reflects that," commented Matt Parnell (personal communication, 2017), a marketing communications manager at Sony Electronics.

TRADE AND PROFESSIONAL MEDIA

Another area of the media that is often overlooked in media relations is the trade or professional media. Coverage in a key trade publication, which is read by industry members and or enthusiasts, can be very beneficial to generating interest in your product or service.

Coverage in key trade publications is vital when you are promoting CSR initiatives—since these publications cover innovation in their industries in more depth than traditional national or local media due to a more general focus.

An example might be an industrial manufacturing company that has improved its water management process and, in the process, saved money and made better use of a key natural resource. This story may not be interesting to a reporter at a daily paper, but it would be to one who covers that industry in depth and whose readers are interested in this issue. Professional journals and trade papers cover new products and industry trends and developments for more than the traditional media, and they are read closely by industry leaders and insiders.

Equally important, articles in trade journals often spark interest among journalists who cover the industry for the **mainstream media**. Also keep in mind that when the mainstream media are looking to hire a new reporter to cover an industry, they often look to the leading trade and technology industry publications for their top candidates. Thus the advantage in working with trade reporters is that they may someday be the one you will work with at mainstream media outlets. In the meantime coverage in a leading trade journal can be very useful in reaching your short-term communications goals—both generally and in CSR-related activity.

COMMUNICATIONS THEORY AND MEDIA RELATIONS

>> **LO 7.2** **Explore communications theory's application to media relations**

The study of communications theories that support the practice of media relations is a developing area, but most scholars agree that a few traditional theories have application (Supa, 2014). These include *gatekeeping*, *agenda setting*, and *framing* (Entman, 1993).

GATEKEEPING

Kurt Lewin coined the term **gatekeeper** in 1947, describing a process where a person of authority decides what information should move forward to a group or individual and what information should not. Soon afterward, David Manning White (1950) related it to journalism in the first study of its kind, "The 'Gate Keeper': A Case Study in the Selection of News." In a media setting, the editor or producer plays this vital role. They decide which news items will be published, broadcast, or posted on social media and what will not. For PR professionals seeking news coverage or visibility, it is important to identify the gatekeepers and appeal to them specifically and convincingly to get a positive response.

AGENDA SETTING

Maxwell McCombs and Donald Shaw were among the first communication scholars to argue that public opinion is shaped, in part, by media coverage.

Their seminal study, "The Agenda-Setting Function of Mass Media" (McCombs & Shaw, 1972), established agenda-setting theory. It states the news media have an agenda; they tell audiences what news to consider important. Further studies revealed that the media also influence people's perceptions—*how* to think about the news.

FRAMING

Robert Entman (1993) reinforced media's *shaping* of news by explaining it as "framing" that affects how people think about it. He extended Erving Goffman's (1974) scholarship on how people make sense of the world based on frameworks that help them to interpret data. Thus, the *way* the story is told by the media (without any altering of actual facts)—the "frame" surrounding an issue— may influence readers' or viewers' perceptions.

Ron Smith (2011) a professor and author who writes on PR theory and strategic planning, suggests, "Much can be said about the role of the media in influencing the way people perceive public relations messages. . . . [S]ometimes the media influence is intentional, sometimes apparently accidental. Regardless of the motivation, media influence is inevitable. Public relations practitioners [who are] aware of the media's role can consider [the best] ways to deal with it." Media tell us what to think *about* (agenda setting) and also provide a *focus* and *environment* for reporting a story, influencing how audiences will understand or evaluate it (framing; see Figure 7.3).

A more detailed discussion of these and other key communications theories is provided in Chapter 4. These theories are part of the interaction between the journalist and the PR practitioner and the process of placing a story in target media. The good news is that if you are successful with your pitch, and the reporter produces a story that meets his or her needs and yours, the benefits are significant. Richard Branson (2013)—a global entrepreneur, multi-billionaire, and opinion leader—summarized it as follows: "Publicity is absolutely critical. . . . You have to get your brand out and about, particularly if you're a consumer-oriented brand. A good PR story is infinitely more effective than a front page ad."

FIGURE 7.3

Communications Theory and Media Relations

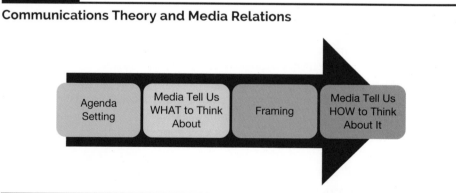

MEASURING NEWS COVERAGE

>> **LO 7.3** **Measure the impact of news coverage in achieving business goals**

There is growing widespread industry agreement that the focus of measuring the impact of media relations and PR in general should be on outcomes—for example, business created or opinions changed—and not on outputs—for example, the total number of articles generated or a dollar figure estimating the benefit of news coverage.

ADVERTISING VALUE EQUIVALENCE

A *Wall Street Journal* reporter, Carl Bialik (2011), looked into the ways that PR people assess the impact of media coverage after some PR "experts" were quoted as estimating that a photo of President Obama drinking a Guinness (while on a trip to Ireland) had "$32 million in publicity value."

While the company that manufactures Guiness, Diageo (see www.diageo.com), was likely pleased to see this photo published all over the world and go viral on social media, they wisely declined to comment on the estimated PR value of the photo. Most likely because the dollar figure—which they did not issue—was not substantiated nor could anyone prepare a verifiable estimate on the value of the coverage. Actually when the "PR expert" who gave the "$32 million in PR value" quote was pressed to provide supportive details, he replied that it was an "estimate" and not an actual, documentable number (Bialik, 2011).

Photographs of President Barack Obama drinking Guinness beer while in Ireland went viral, providing the brand with valuable exposure. The exact value of that exposure, however, is difficult to calculate.

Brendan Smialowski/AFP/Getty Images

MoneyWi$e: A Consumer Action and Capital One Partnership

Capital One and Consumer Action partnered with community-based organizations to teach financial literacy and skills to low- and moderate-income families.

iStock.com/cigdemhizal

In 2001 Capital One and Consumer Action, a consumer education and advocacy group, partnered to create MoneyWi$e—a national personal financial education program offering free, multilingual materials and community-based training opportunities to provide families in low- to moderate-income communities with tools to achieve financial security. The program fused Capital One and Consumer Action's joint strengths in finance and financial education to create educational content and training programs for consumers. To date (2017), 12 modules have been produced on topics such as banking, money management, credit, saving, identity theft, elder fraud, micro-business, and homeownership.

Financial Literacy Content

The main objective of the MoneyWi$e program is to create and deliver content where it is needed and to ensure that people use it effectively. To accomplish this objective, Consumer Action uses its national network of more than 10,000 community-based organizations (CBOs); Capital One brings associate volunteers and a robust communications infrastructure. The combination makes for a powerful outreach engine that has reached more than 3 million consumers via free materials available at managing.money.org.

In 2008 Capital One and Consumer Action partnered to develop an online set of interactive web-based tools, tips, and resources for consumers.

Profound Community Outcomes

"Capital One's approach to working with the community—based on an understanding of the great value they can offer by leveraging the same capabilities that have made them a successful business—is unique among corporations," said Ken McEldowney, executive director of Consumer Action. "By bringing to bear not only their financial resources, but their talented people and business expertise, Capital One has generated profound, positive outcomes for Consumer Action, our community partners, and their clients" (Capital One, n.d.).

Good Works Equals Positive Media Attention

"The principal benchmark of quality CSR performance for banks is how well they meet the needs of low-income communities. MoneyWi$e is one of many programs underway at Capital One designed to achieve this goal," commented Richard Woods (personal communication, 2017), senior vice president of Corporate Affairs. "Strong adoption by community groups of this curriculum has translated into positive media attention in local markets nationwide." ●

You have no doubt heard and seen examples like this where someone will say "that's a million dollars in free publicity," but you know this is not an actual hard number or fact. This practice reflects an older standard of PR measurement known as **advertising value equivalence (AVE),** which seeks to estimate the relative value of a news story generated by PR by comparing it with a paid advertisement.

Over the years, many publicists have tried to translate news coverage into dollar figures, and some have used a simplistic approach: a newspaper article is worth as much as a newspaper ad of the same size. Or 30 seconds of television news coverage is comparable to a 30-second ad on the same television station. Compounding this, some PR specialists, reasoning that news coverage carries greater weight with consumers than paid advertising, have maintained that a news article's value is a multiple—sometimes two or three times more—of an equivalent-size ad. However, there is no scientific documentation for either approach.

David Rockland (2010), global director of research and measurement for Ketchum, says one of the many problems with publicity equivalency calculations is that they assume all news stories are equally effective. Yet, he notes, the coverage you are "measuring" might make only a glancing mention or even be negative, while some other coverage might focus entirely on the client or product. Surely these are not equivalent, he maintains.

To bring more order and clarity to measuring the impact of media relations and PR in general, the industry has been actively debating the issue. In 2010, after a landmark conference in Barcelona, Spain, the PR industry publicly stated that AVE is not a valid measure of PR (Michaelson & Stacks, 2011). The Barcelona Principles of 2010 took a more scientific approach to measuring the impact and value of PR and were updated in 2015 (see Figure 7.4).

FIGURE 7.4

Barcelona Principles

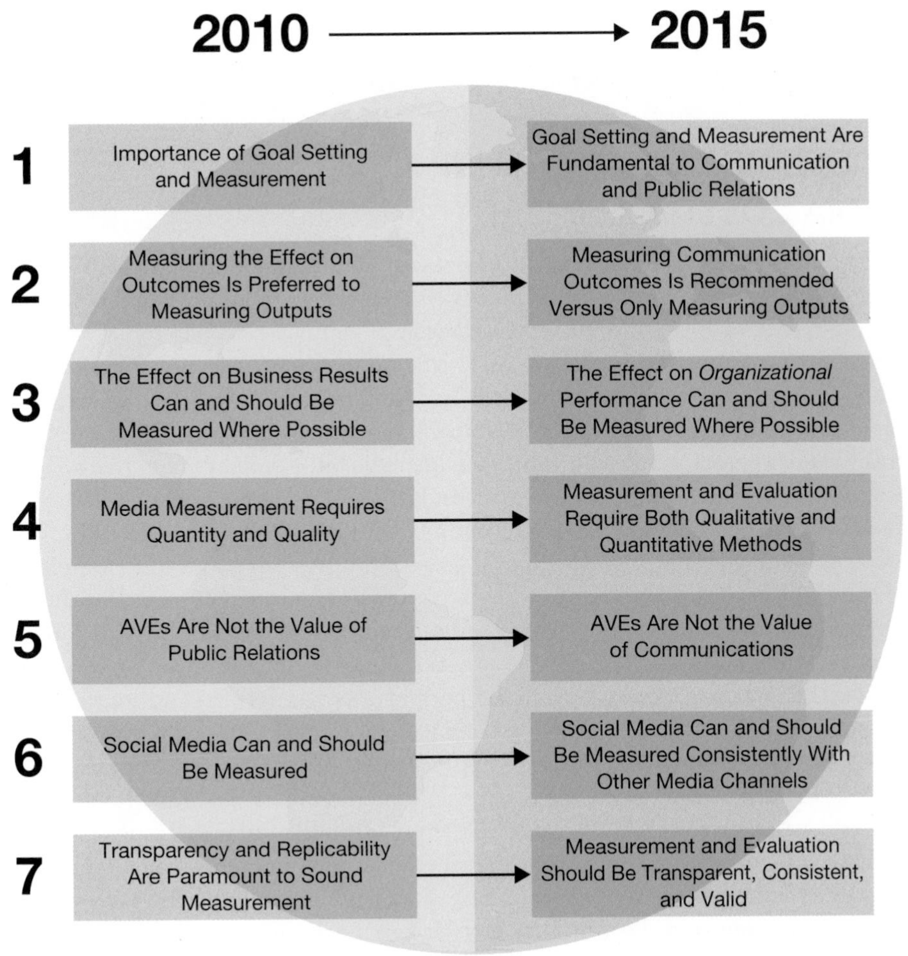

2010 ⟶ 2015

	2010	2015
1	Importance of Goal Setting and Measurement	Goal Setting and Measurement Are Fundamental to Communication and Public Relations
2	Measuring the Effect on Outcomes Is Preferred to Measuring Outputs	Measuring Communication Outcomes Is Recommended Versus Only Measuring Outputs
3	The Effect on Business Results Can and Should Be Measured Where Possible	The Effect on *Organizational* Performance Can and Should Be Measured Where Possible
4	Media Measurement Requires Quantity and Quality	Measurement and Evaluation Require Both Qualitative and Quantitative Methods
5	AVEs Are Not the Value of Public Relations	AVEs Are Not the Value of Communications
6	Social Media Can and Should Be Measured	Social Media Can and Should Be Measured Consistently With Other Media Channels
7	Transparency and Replicability Are Paramount to Sound Measurement	Measurement and Evaluation Should Be Transparent, Consistent, and Valid

Source: Barcelona Principles 2.0 (n.d.).

IMPRESSIONS—BETTER BUT NOT GOOD ENOUGH

Another common means of assessing the impact or value of media relations is a metric referred to as **impressions** to indicate the impact of a story or product mention in the media. Under this approach, the value of the coverage is calculated using the number of readers or viewers who *might* have read the story or seen the broadcast. This is usually done using audited subscription or viewership numbers of a given media outlet. For example, if a story ran in *The New York Times* on a weekday morning, the number of impressions cited under this approach would be based on the number of subscribers to the daily *New York Times*—or 590,000 (Ember, 2016).

Similarly if a news segment is broadcast on local TV in New York during the 6 p.m. local newscast, the number of impressions might be estimated at hundreds of thousands, using WNBC Channel 4 as an example. If the segment made the network news, the number would be 8.6 million, based on the reported viewership of the network newscast NBC's *Nightly News* (Katz, 2016).

While this approach may be a clear improvement over AVE in that it is based on audited subscription and viewership numbers, there are flaws to this approach as well. For example, no one would suggest that all 590,000 readers of *The New York Times* read the story on the given day it ran. As well, no one can guarantee that all the viewers of WNBC in New York or the 8.6 million viewers who watch NBC's *Nightly News* nationally saw the piece and/or remember it.

GUIDELINES FOR MEASURING MEDIA COVERAGE IMPACT

"Impressions are definitely not what they seem," stated Tim Marklein (2016), a well-regarded PR researcher and CEO of Big Valley Marketing, in his post on the Institute for Public Relations website. At first, impressions were used as a foundational unit of measure for publishers and advertisers who built an entire economy negotiating to buy impressions by the thousands. They then evolved into a lingua franca of marketing measurement, providing a comparable way to evaluate reach (impressions) and efficiency across marketing vehicles and media outlets. They were then adapted to digital and social channels as visits and unique visitors were used alongside impressions to compare reach among old and new media.

"The reality is that impressions . . . only count how many people potentially had the opportunity to see your ad, story and/or content," Marklein (2016) explains. Impressions "are typically calculated based on a publication's reach [circulation] or a site's traffic, but unless you own the site [and monitor it constantly], you don't know how many people *actually* saw the individual piece of content."

One of the reasons that AVE and impressions—and other simplistic methods—continue to be used is that no simple, verifiable alternative has emerged for putting a monetary value on the effectiveness of PR work. While research continues to search for these measurements, there are some simple and more reliable ways to measure the impact of media coverage that can help in quantifying the results. They include assessing the tone and the visibility of your key messages in the coverage that is generated.

POSITIVE, NEGATIVE, AND NEUTRAL ANALYSIS AND KEY MESSAGE VISIBILITY

Once a collection of news stories has been generated, it can be collected and analyzed. Once these are in hand, you can conduct a basic analysis to get a sense of the tone of the articles and whether the key messages are coming through to the reader or viewer. This analysis can be very helpful in demonstrating the value of PR efforts, determining if the assessments are fair and objective. Clients and management can understand and trust these more than other measures because they are observable and do not depend on a false formula like AVE or impressions that estimate the potential audience.

The approach to measuring the tone of news coverage is to read the entire article or view or listen to the broadcast and make an independent assessment of the tone of the article. The most common process is to use a scale of "positive, negative, or neutral" and assess the article and its impact accordingly.

Let's return to the example earlier in the chapter, where you are serving as the PR director of a regional bank and you have developed a target media list to place a story about your company's CSR activity. Once your news release has been distributed and covered by some of the key media, you can conduct this analysis.

Measuring your impact can be made easier by a report from an online monitoring service that provides an analysis of the percentage of target media you reached by gathering the news stories that resulted and providing an assessment on the tone of the stories placed. If the tone of the article is overwhelmingly supportive, it can be said to be *positive*. If it has some good and some bad, but is accurate and balanced, it can be categorized as *neutral*. And, of course, if it is highly critical or supports a different product or point of view, it would be scored as *negative*.

MESSAGE TESTING

Another useful tool is to review the coverage obtained and examine it to see if the message(s) you wanted to convey are present. The process is to assess if they are highly visible in the piece, mentioned briefly, or not mentioned at all. While this method is more subjective, it is a useful device to getting a sense of whether your messages are getting through to your target audiences who read, heard, or viewed the story. This allows you to "score" the story from a point of view of message visibility and impact and adjust or enhance the message if necessary.

GLOBAL MEDIA RELATIONS TRENDS AND TACTICS

>> **LO 7.4** Identify global trends and practices in media relations

The practice of global media relations is an undertaking that most PR professionals will face at some point in their careers. In today's rapidly changing, globally connected world, the field is a challenging one. Making sense of emerging markets, keeping tactics local, finding the influencers, and how to be flexible and adapt to widely differing cultures and changing conditions are problems that PR scholars have researched.

Effective Global Public Relations Requires Specific Knowledge and Strategy

In her book, *Pitch, Tweet, or Engage on the Street: How to Practice Global Public Relations*, Kara Alaimo (2016a) suggests that global PR practitioners adapt their strategies and approaches to reflect the customs and culture of each country.

"I conducted interviews with 74 global public relations practitioners from 31 countries. I asked them how they advise global organizations to adapt their strategies for particular cultures and what factors they need to take into account when implementing global public relations strategies in their countries," she noted in a post on the Institute for Public Relations site (Alaimo, 2016c).

First, Alaimo notes, expectations of global companies or organizations differ dramatically throughout the world. In some parts of the world, the local government and citizens may expect companies to provide services outside of that company's area of expertise. For example, she mentions infrastructure projects (roads and schools) and "high expectations for corporate social responsibility" by local citizens of companies operating in their country. Often the local or national government is not viewed as capable of mounting major improvement projects; as such they look to companies

operating—or seeking to operate—in their country to pay for these projects. These companies are asked to build roads, housing, schools, and medical facilities to obtain permits for development projects or market entry. These projects are beneficial to the country while the project is underway, and when the company leaves, the improved infrastructure is left behind.

The second category relates specifically to media relations by large U.S. companies. The standard practice in the United States is for companies to seek news coverage of their CSR activity and then repurpose it on the company's social media platforms (Yu, Asur, & Huberman, 2011).

However, the interviews of experts in the Alaimo study suggest that in many countries, people do not respect the media because it is government controlled and censored. Instead, she found, the citizens rely on so-called influencers for insights and information. These opinion leaders have a reputation for sharing independent and accurate information on social media. As such, the research concludes, global PR practitioners with CSR projects to promote in these countries might be better off targeting these people instead of the state-controlled media. ●

EXCELLENCE THEORY AND GLOBAL APPLICATIONS

The most well-known theory of international PR, put forth by Verčič, Grunig, and Grunig (1996) and Grunig, Grunig, and Verčič (1998), is based on the principles of PR excellence theory. The scholars determined that the core principles of PR are the same worldwide, but specific applications of these principles differ in different settings.

Excellence theory considers PR as strategic and part of upper management's role, and it advocates a two-way symmetrical model of communication. However, specific variables apply depending on the country context. Professionals should keep in mind five different dimensions when practicing international PR and media relations. The five dimensions for global PR and media relations include: (1) the political and economic system, (2) culture(s), (3) levels of activism, (4) level of economic development, and (5) the media system in a given country. Based on her research, Alaimo (2016c) suggested two additional dimensions: social expectations and local influencers.

ETHICAL STANDARDS IN GLOBAL MEDIA RELATIONS

Another key challenge to be faced in global media relations is the ethical challenge of paying for news coverage. It is not at all uncommon for the media in a developing country to expect payment in the form of advertisements—or cash payments to their reporters—to get editorial coverage. In addition, in some markets, it is common for journalists to expect to be paid "expenses" to attend a press event and then write a story or broadcast a news segment afterward. In some cases, PR practitioners even get to review the copy before it is published.

"Pay for play" is an issue researched by Katerina Tsetsura (2011), Ph.D., of the University of Oklahoma, who conducted interviews with both global PR practitioners and locally based journalists. In both group, the notion of paying for coverage was viewed as a "problem" and "inappropriate"—with 84% of the respondents indicating that the practice is *not* acceptable in their view. This does not mean that it doesn't happen—some respondents noted that such arrangements happen at higher levels of the media outlet or broadcast company, for example, editors and publishers and company management, but both the journalists and practitioners interviewed said they are not a party to it.

"I think it can be a fuzzy line. It's hard to know if they do or they don't unless senior management is working with the magazine or newspaper leadership separately to advertise" commented one global PR professional who participated in the study (Tsetsura, 2011).

A journalist who also participated in the study added, "In my experience such things are seldom if ever direct. The publisher and senior editors will of course be acquainted with some of the ad sales folks, who will of course have opinions about whatever industry is being covered and about how major advertisers feel about the work (e.g., coverage) the publication is doing. I've never received specific guidance on such things, but one always knew who the big players were" (Tsetsura, 2011).

This is a rare practice in the United States, especially where there is a clear separation between the editorial and advertising side of most national and local publications and networks. However, this is a consideration for companies that operate on a global scale, especially if they have plants or marketing offices in countries where this is expected. While there are clear industry guidelines on ethics, ultimately it comes down to each company making a policy decision and enforcing it.

SCENARIO OUTCOME

At the beginning of the chapter, the Department of Defense, assisted by Booz Allen Hamilton, developed and implemented a public service and philanthropic program. Its purpose was to assist veterans returning from Iraq and Afghanistan in coping with PTSD and other post-combat mental health issues. You were asked to consider what strategies would guide your media relations and what tactics would you include.

Research guided strategy. Foundational research laid the path to strategy. To review key findings, multiple deployments increased risks of invisible wounds that would then surface in civilian life during stressful situations. Only a minority of vets have sought psychological healthcare. Veterans are in denial or discount the severity of their invisible wounds, and they perceive care as a sign of weakness and a career ender. These findings led to specific communication strategies for all parties involved: Spread awareness about available resources, educate about the challenges preventing service members from seeking care, and build understanding about the need for early intervention. The publics targeted were current service members, veterans, military families, and the health professionals who care for them.

Media relations tactics reached millions. Media outreach included news releases and PSAs carrying the campaign's message to millions of service members, veterans, and military families—in communities across the country and on military bases around the world. The campaign produced 31 radio and television PSAs, arranged for nine bloggers' roundtables, and created 15 audio news releases.

Social media during the campaign made it one of the most mentioned and engaging programs on the topic of military health, reaching 1.1 million unique individuals on Facebook, Twitter, YouTube, and Scribd. An interactive website featured Real Warriors in a live chat on April 7, 2013. Multimedia video and podcast profiles featured personal stories of warriors.

Military reports success. Through the team's targeted efforts, the campaign reached service members and key stakeholders around the world with its messages of strength, resilience, and reintegration, resulting in positive outcomes for an increased number of military members seeking care. The campaign's website garnered 741,008 unique visitors, 974,000 visits, and 5.2 million page views. Online audiences engaged (visits, likes, and reposts) with the campaign 1,101 times *every day* in the first year. The campaign generated almost 68,000 news stories worldwide in target publications, virtually 100% of which were positive in tone and contained key messages prominently. Its PSAs aired more than 430,000 times on television and radio channels.

Note: This scenario demonstrates the power of strategic media relations to advance an important social message. The challenges that veterans face in returning to their civilian lives after a deployment are significant. A communications campaign that enables them to ask for and get help is a vital step in their recovery and reentry to society. The DOD, and its partner firm Booz Allen Hamilton, devised and implemented a program that made a difference for these veterans and their families. Its success is a great model for socially focused communications campaigns.

Source: PRSA (2014a).

WRAP UP

In this chapter, the groundwork was set to help you develop or enhance your strategic media relations skills. As noted, while there are many aspects of PR that you will be asked to execute during your careers, media relations will nearly always be one of them. This chapter included data from the Pew Research Center on the current media environment and looked at the different types of media you might include in your outreach plans. This discussion introduced the concepts of *paid* (advertising) and *earned* (PR/media relations) as well as company/client-*sponsored* and *owned* media. Measuring the impact of media relations results was covered as well—noting what works and what does not—and examples were provided to illustrate the difference. The current state of global media relations as well as media relations in politics and crisis communications were introduced.

Advertising Value Equivalency (AVE): a practice, now largely discredited and abandoned, whereby the impact or value of an article in a publication or a news segment is measured by the relative cost of purchasing that same amount of space or airtime, **174**

Demographics: A term used to categorize or analyze the audience for a media outlet or, more broadly, a segment of the population, **162**

Fake News: The proposed practice of publishing news stories online (initially) or in the traditional media that are not based on acts or proven research, **163**

Gatekeeper: A person who controls access to the media and decides if a story or news item will be published, posted, or put on the air at a TV or radio station, for example, an editor, producer, or reporter, **171**

Impressions: A tactic designed to measure the impact of news coverage that assumes that the number of subscribers to a publication or viewers/listeners to a broadcast is equal to the audience reached with a news item or story they placed, **176**

Mainstream Media: Media that consists of newspapers, magazines, television (network and local), and radio that have existed in one form or another throughout history (also known as traditional media), **171**

Pitch: Outreach from a PR professional to reporters to get them to consider a story idea they are proposing to seek news coverage, **164**

Spokespersons: People or experts associated with a company, organization, or government entity who are authorized to speak to the media, **170**

THINK ABOUT IT

Working with your instructor, form into small groups and choose a current news story, preferably with a CSR or philanthropy focus. Review the story for details, and then develop an outline for a media relations strategy to respond on behalf of the company or organization involved. *Note: CSRwire.com is a great source for recent news releases and studies on CSR.*

Your outline should include an overview of the situation and a summary of the tone and focus of the news coverage to date (using the positive, negative, or neutral scale).

Develop one objective for your media relations plan: one key message you want to convey and one tactic to create media coverage. Finally you should include one example of research you would use to measure the impact of your media relations activity. This can include newsclips (their tone and message prominence), coverage in target media, increased visits to a dedicated website, or donations or sign-ups by volunteers, for example.

This exercise is designed to help you look at a situation and develop a framework for a strategy and an approach to responding. Once the framework is in place, you can fill it in with objectives, messages, target audiences, and goals.

WRITE LIKE A PRO

Assume you work for an agency that has been retained to advise a regional grocery chain on increasing visibility of its CSR activity. Your task is to prepare a media pitch for a new CSR initiative for your company—a food drive to generate donations to a local food bank that is struggling. You also want to include expanded CSR plans of the company.

Your firm has prepared a target media list—including the local papers, television and radio stations, and influential bloggers who cover CSR topics in your area. You also have a good list of influential people in the local nonprofit community who are supportive of the company's decision to expand its local sustainability activity. Remember what you read in this chapter about the need to localize the story and provide a visual element for best results.

Send the pitch to your instructor—remember the premium is on short, succinct requests and targeted story suggestions.

SOCIAL RESPONSIBILITY CASE STUDY

Deepwater Wind: Launching America's First Offshore Wind Farm

American dependence on fossil fuels, and the harmful effects of its emissions, has created a need to explore and employ alternate energy sources. Solar and wind power are two of the most common "clean" energy producers in use, but these generators are located on land, creating aesthetic and environmental concerns.

The summer of 2016 would see that change when Deepwater Wind, America's first offshore wind farm, three miles off the coast of Block Island, Rhode Island, would finally power up and usher in a new era for renewable energy in the United States.

Research and Strategy

"Communicating clearly and effectively about a new technology—in this case, offshore wind energy—can be a challenge," said Jon Duffy, president of Duffy & Shanley (D&S), the wind farm's local PR firm. "We've worked hard to build our own understanding of offshore wind and become trusted resources for news media explaining this new technology to their audiences. Our role was as much about educating the news media as it was publicizing our client's project," he explained.

Garnering prominent national news coverage was a top priority of the campaign. The PR team wanted to position the new wind turbines off the coast of Block Island as symbols of American innovation and Deepwater Wind as leaders of a new American industry.

In preparing to launch the facility, the PR team had developed close media relationships with top national and international energy and environmental journalists. They knew that to tell the story of the Block Island Wind Farm's completion, they needed to demystify a project that people believed might never actually come to fruition.

Execution

To bring media close to the action, D&S chartered a Block Island-based fishing boat for eight separate, successful tours over the course of two weeks. High-impact visuals were another crucial element. Through visual storytelling—web and social media videos, photography, aerial and time-lapse footage—D&S brought this first-ever project to life for all the project stakeholders and the public. The visuals became an important tool to help media outlets that couldn't travel to Block Island.

One of the firm's most important media targets was the *New York Times*. The team spent several hours touring the construction site with the *Times* environmental reporter and photographer, followed by a two-hour sit-down interview with Deepwater Wind's CEO.

The effort generated a cover story in the *Times* "Science" section, which included several stunning photographs of the Block Island Wind Farm. The story received prominent online play at nytimes.com. It also led to a *Times* editorial advocating for growth of the offshore wind industry in the United States—and positioned Deepwater Wind as leading that charge. Finally, then President Obama shared the *Times* story in a tweet that was "liked" more than 7,000 times and re-tweeted nearly 3,000 times.

Evaluation

Overall, PR efforts for this campaign resulted in more than 350 print, online, and broadcast stories—over just a four-month period—and by much of the country's most influential media including *The Wall Street Journal*, Associated Press, Reuters, *Bloomberg BusinessWeek*, *USA Today*, *Washington Post*, *CBS Evening News*, *NBC Nightly News*, CNBC, MSNBC, PBS News Hour, NPR, Yahoo!, Mashable, and more.

D&S's work for Deepwater Wind helped position the company as a leading offshore wind developer. The campaign also won the Bulldog Reporter Award for Media Relations in 2017—the only major PR award competition whose entries are judged by working journalists.

One month after the Block Island Wind Farm began operations, Deepwater Wind received contract approval for its larger South Fork Wind Farm off Long Island, New York, and the company began actively planning additional projects for Massachusetts, Rhode Island, and Maryland. The Block Island Wind Farm had jumpstarted America's offshore wind industry.

ENGAGE

- ▸ Visit the Deepwater Wind website (http://dwwind.com) to learn about this technology and its expected benefits.

- ▸ Review other sites and research to assess if this approach and technology are viewed as effective—what if any criticisms are there that need to be addressed?

- ▸ Read *The New York Times* article (https://nyti.ms/2jGVAzz) and visit the D&S site (http://www.duffyshanley.com) to learn more about the company, technology, and the firm advising support for both.

DISCUSS

- ▸ How did D&S make the story compelling enough to merit media coverage? Note recent research on reluctance of the media to cover CSR initiatives.

- ▸ How might Deepwater Wind utilize social media more to extend their impact and results?

- ▸ What best practices or new ideas should D&S (and the company) consider for future wind farms approved or planned elsewhere in New England and the United States?

- ▸ With a new administration in place in Washington, D.C., what ideas or options should the company consider to build on its momentum from this event?

Source: Carufel (2017).

SOCIAL RESPONSIBILITY CASE STUDY

World Wildlife Fund's Campaign to Stop Wildlife Crime

Media relations can play a significant role in an advocacy or issues-based communication program. Good examples of this work are the World Wildlife Fund (WWF) campaigns. They generated major media coverage in their target media to support the WWF fight to protect endangered animals globally. This is a key initiative for the WWF due to some alarming global trends.

Research and Strategy

Illegal trade in wildlife, including timber and fish, is a serious worldwide issue. It comprises the fourth-largest global illegal trade after narcotics, counterfeiting of products and currency, and human trafficking and is estimated to be worth at least $19 billion per year. It is a lucrative business for criminal syndicates because the risk involved is low compared to other crimes and high profits can be generated. It significantly hinders social and economic development, including potential economic loss for governments, and has direct consequences on rule of law, national and international security, and the environment (WWF, n.d.).

Execution

In response, the WWF put a major focus on this issue in its PR efforts, which included lobbying, features pitched to prominent news outlets, a social media campaign, and newsworthy events. The WWF's success at pitching stories about the tragedy of wildlife crime was a big part of the organization's strategy to boost its agenda in 2013.

Evaluation

In 2013 the WWF accomplished important breakthroughs in the worldwide fight against animal traffickers:

▸ President Obama designated an additional $10 million on July 1, 2013, for training and technical assistance in Africa to stop animal trafficking.

▸ He also created the Presidential Task Force on Wildlife Trafficking to receive advice from an advisory council of independent experts, appointing Carter Roberts, WWF CEO, to serve.

▸ Consequently the WWF was by far the most prominent NGO in traditional and social media coverage of the president's executive order, mentioned in nearly 65% of related content on Twitter.

The campaign resulted in a 50% increase in mainstream global media coverage of the wildlife crisis from July 1, 2013, to June 30, 2014. High-profile pieces on the slaughter of big animals appeared on NBC, in *Time* magazine, and in *The Wall Street Journal*. In November 2013 the U.S. Fish & Wildlife Service destroyed the U.S. stockpile of seized illegal ivory. The WWF helped plan and stage this event that raised awareness. Several other countries followed by destroying their own illegal ivory.

The WWF had two consecutive outstanding years of award-winning media relations achievements. From July 1, 2012, when the WWF first alerted the world to the critical dangers being faced by rhinos, tigers, and elephants from poachers until June 30, 2014, the WWF saw an increase in coverage by the media of these issues of nearly 270%.

The WWF's communications outreach created unprecedented media attention and provoked strong action by the U.S. government on many conservation fronts. This successful and meaningful issues-based advocacy campaign illustrates how important work is done well through media relations.

ENGAGE

▸ Visit www.wwf.org to learn more about the organization and its efforts to preserve and protect endangered species and wildlife globally.

▸ Review its mission and values, and assess its communication strategy and approach.

▸ Review its other campaigns, both advocacy and awareness based, and compare and contrast the others with this campaign.

DISCUSS

▸ How could the WWF have improved their results (if at all) from this campaign?

▸ What best practices from the award-winning anti-trafficking campaign could be repeated in other campaigns? *Note: Examine the details of the campaign statements, media coverage, visibility, and so on, and make your best guess.*

▸ What next steps would you recommend for the WWF to maintain this momentum into new fund-raising, employee-, or current donor-focused communications?

▸ What are other wildlife-oriented NGOs doing (search "wildlife NGO") that WWF might want to emulate?

Source: PR Daily (n.d.e).

Note: This campaign won PR Daily's Grand Prize: Media Relations Campaign of the Year Award 2014.

iClick: Press Coverage

Lon McGowan started his personal electronics company, iClick, with little more than an idea and several credit cards. The company now sells a wide range of phone and camera accessories, including chargers, USB drives, phone mounts, and more.

VIDEO

1. Why was McGowan's outreach to the local media effective?

2. Discuss McGowan's efforts in terms of gatekeeping, agenda-setting, and framing.

3. If you worked for iClick during the period being discussed, how would you have suggested the company measure the effectiveness of the newspaper story?

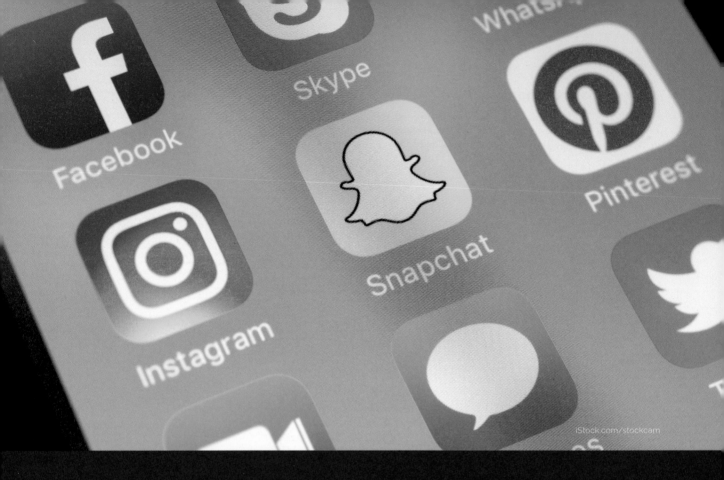

Social Media and Emerging Technologies

Learning Objectives

8.1 Describe social media's historical context and its contemporary place in society

8.2 Understand the purpose and use of various social media tools in the field of PR

8.3 Evaluate best practices for social media use in the field of PR

8.4 Identify how to measure social media effectiveness, and craft a strategy for staying abreast of trends

Scenario

Owning a VW Is Like Being in Love

Or so proclaimed *Popular Mechanics* magazine in 1956— just a few years after the first Beetle shipped to the United States—marking the beginning of a decades-long love affair between Volkswagen (VW) and American car buyers and reviewers.

The iconic "Think Small" campaign by ad agency DDB, which ran from 1959 to the early 1970s, turned the VW Beetle's drawbacks—small, air-cooled engine, rear-wheel drive, and overall size—into virtues (Garfied, 1999).

The Volkswagen Beetle gained popularity in the 1950s and eventually became one of the most influential cars of the century.

Photo by Evan Kirby on Unsplash

Sales of the model exploded in the 1960s, fueled by the innovative ad campaign and the "Bug's" status as something of an antiestablishment vehicle. This was the era of finned, chromed, and high-horsepower automobiles rolling out of Detroit, and the Beetle was the perfect counter to those behemoths. Small, but powered enough to cruise at 72 mph, it was about half the price of base models from the "Big 3."

The popular 1969 Disney movie, *The Love Bug*. This movie featured the Beetle as a starring character, and the VW van or "microbus," was marketed to families as an alternative to station wagons. Embraced by many young people in the 1960s, the vans were painted and modified to create what became known as a "hippie van."

In 1999 the VW Beetle was named one of the most influential cars of the 20th Century (Cobb, 1999). Already VW had greatly expanded its product line to include Rabbit, Passat, and Golf—its first diesel car. By 2014 VW was one of the biggest firms in the world, with factories in 31 countries (Bowler, 2015). In 2015 the Golf MK7 won *the Motor Trend* Car of the Year award (Jurnecka, 2015).

That same year, a monumental scandal broke. On September 18, 2015, the U.S. Environmental Standards Agency (EPA) publicly filed a Notice of Violation of the Clean Air Act to the Volkswagen Group. It accused VW of designing "defeat device" software and installing it in 500,000 diesel vehicles to intentionally trick regulators and deceive the EPA's emissions tests.

▸ Notably, VW had admitted this deception to the EPA 15 days earlier but hadn't publicly disclosed it. Undoubtedly now this publicized situation was critically damaging to the VW brand. Four days after the news broke, on September 22, VW admitted its emissions fraud was much larger, involving up to 11 million vehicles. The CEO announced his resignation the next day. A headline in a German newspaper announced, "'Made in Germany' in the Gutter" (Leveille, 2015).

▶ Social media is an efficient way for organizations to release information and respond quickly during a crisis. Not only are organizations posting on social media sites, but consumers are increasingly turning to social media sites, such as Twitter, during crises to share information and opinions.

▶ During a 10-day period shortly after the news broke, a researcher examined conversation on Twitter about VW's emission crisis (Whytas, 2016). More than 40,000 English-language tweets were examined that included at least one of the following **hashtags**: #VW, #VWGate, #DieselGate, #VWscandal or #Volkswagenscandal. Three main concerns were voiced: loss of trust in VW, sales staffs worried about their livelihoods, and alarm at the implications to health with so many VWs on the road with higher emissions.

As you read this chapter, consider the following:

1. How did VW PR handle this crisis via social media?

2. As their official PR agency or in-house council, what would your advice have been for VW?

3. What publics would be critical to communicate with, through which social channels, and with what messaging?

To answer these questions, you can begin to outline your recommendations as you engage with the lessons in this chapter. At the end, you will find how VW responded.

This chapter explores the dynamic world of social media and emerging technologies and their impact on the PR profession. First it considers the antecedents of social media and how it evolved through innovation after innovation, each expanding the ability of people and organizations to communicate with each other in real time. Peeling back the labels and personalities of social media platforms, the chapter explains how social networking theory, first developed in the mid-20th century, helps us understand the usefulness of social media and why it's spread so fast.

Then the chapter illustrates how organizations effectively use social media tools to reach their communication goals, which include establishing credibility and building relationships. To illustrate you'll find specific explanations and case examples of the major digital platforms used in PR—Facebook, Twitter, LinkedIn, YouTube, Instagram, Pinterest, blogs, Periscope, Facebook Live, and Snapchat.

Cases and tips from PR executives also teach how digital communications strategies interact with more traditional communications methods and how to successfully integrate both. As Linda Descano of Havas PR reveals later in this chapter, "The best PR campaigns today take a surround-sound ecosystem approach, threading stories across paid, earned and owned media channels, and through online social activations, offline marketing experiences and PR stunts" (L. Descano, personal communication, 2017).

Critical to PR today are both a social media strategy and measurement of its results. The chapter provides an overview and examples of campaigns' use of analytics to evaluate success. You'll also find sources to keep abreast of the latest developments in social media.

Master the content
edge.sagepub.com/page

SOCIAL MEDIA

>> **LO 8.1 Describe social media's historical context and its contemporary place in society**

Social media has undoubtedly transformed how PR is practiced. Social media allows PR practitioners to speak directly with target audiences without interference or alteration by a media gatekeeper as in traditional media relations. It's 24/7. It's a world of voices, words, and images converging without restriction. It's ever changing. It demands engagement, dialogue, content, and constant watchfulness.

HISTORICAL CONTEXT

In PR one major goal of social media is to encourage visitor interaction—to like, comment, share, pin, vote, buy, and travel to the client's various other social media sites or to its main website.

We can trace the idea of social media back to the groundbreaking invention of the telegraph that allowed long-distance transmission of messages in real time. It laid the foundation for a revolution in communications that now has our world spinning with innovations. Assuredly, as you read this now, some platforms have disappeared as more innovations have arrived. Let us consider the contemporary state of social media within American society—what many have dubbed "the revolution in communication."

A BIG EMBRACE: SOCIAL AND EMERGING MEDIA USE

Pew Research Center's study of American adults (Pew Research Center, 2015a), "Social Media Usage: 2005-2015," revealed almost two-thirds of all American adults (65%)

FIGURE 8.1

Antecedents and Timeline of Social Media

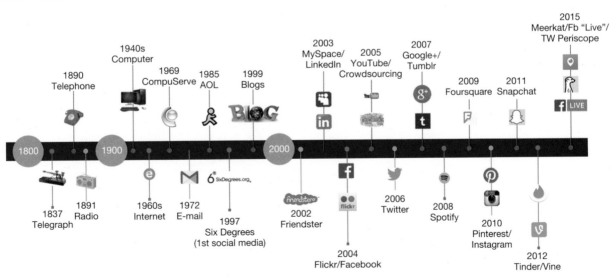

used social networking sites, up from 7% when Pew began tracking usage in 2005. The highest users of social media were young adults 18 to 29, with the 30-to-49 age bracket not far behind. And it reported more than a third of those 65+ are using social media. Pew found no significant differences between usage of men and women or among racial and ethnic groups.

Various sources rank and publish social media site data with some variation; however, Facebook has been and remains most popular. A 2016 Pew Research Center report on platform use by Americans found Facebook the most popular social media site by far (Pew Research Center, 2016a).

Figure 8.2 shows results from Pew's national survey of 1,520 adults conducted March 7 through April 4, 2016. Nearly eight in 10 *online* Americans (79%) now use Facebook, more than double the share that uses Twitter (24%), Pinterest (31%), Instagram (32%) or LinkedIn (29%). On a total population basis (accounting for Americans who do not use the Internet at all), that means that 68% of all U.S. adults are Facebook users, while 28% use Instagram, 26% use Pinterest, 25% use LinkedIn, and 21% use Twitter (Pew Research Center, 2016a).

The Pew data is based on users. However, according to the eBizMBA Rank (n.d.), that accounts for number of visits, as of April 2017, Facebook, and YouTube were virtually tied for the most number of unique monthly U.S. visitors (estimated at 1.5 billion), followed by Twitter with an estimated 400 million, Instagram with an estimated 274 million, and LinkedIn with an estimated 250 million.

How can the explosion of social media be explained? One way to understand its role in our lives is explained by social network theory (SNT), which we'll learn more about in the next section.

FIGURE 8.2

Social Network Dominance, 2016

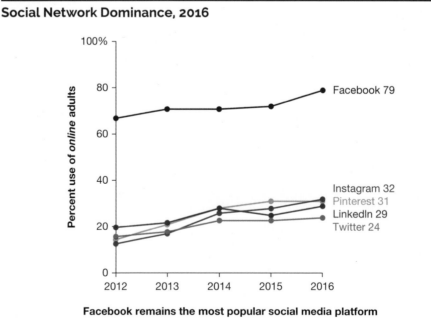

Facebook remains the most popular social media platform

Source: Pew Research Center (2016a).

Note: 86% of Americans are currently Internet users

FIGURE 8.3

Unique Monthly U.S. Visitors, April 2017

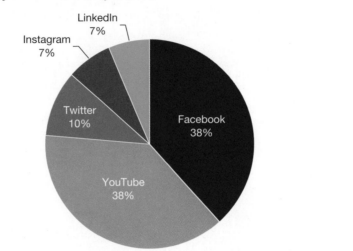

Source: ebizMBA (n.d.).

THE VALUE AND STRATEGIES OF SOCIAL MEDIA

>> **LO 8.2** Understand the purpose and use of various social media tools in the field of PR

SOCIAL NETWORK THEORY

Social media open up a world of networking and relationship-building for PR practitioners. The concepts behind social media can be found in **social network theory (SNT)**, a model researched by sociologists and organizational behavior scholars beginning in the 1950s (Granovetter, 1973).

The theory examines the web of interrelationships among people and organizations. Its concepts of network *size and quality, social distance, network diffusion,* and *complexity* all help explain the usefulness of social media platforms. *Business Communication Quarterly* explains how SNT connects to familiar social media platforms (Sacks & Graves, 2012):

▶ While Facebook only arrived in 2004, it illustrates the SNT concepts of *size* and *quality*: within organizational PR, often larger networks are attractive but require time and energy to maintain high-quality ties and nurture meaningful relationships. Size does not necessarily correspond to network quality.

▶ LinkedIn demonstrates the principle of *social distance*, which states that people are more likely to do favors for others with whom they have close connections. Even second-order and third-order connections have more

Within the wide world of social media networking, PR professionals zero in on the specific platforms used by a client's publics.

Photo by Luc Legay on flickr

power than non-relationships. You can see why PR is in the business of building and nurturing relationships.

▸ Twitter's speed and ease mirror the principles of *network diffusion* (how quickly a positive or negative message spreads) and *complexity* (the simpler the message, the faster and wider it spreads).

Understanding that the dynamics of social media have deep roots in tested theory reinforces the need to be strategic about using the various platforms.

PUBLIC RELATIONS EMBRACES SOCIAL MEDIA

For PR purposes, one needs to analyze target publics and their social media use to identify platforms that work best strategically for a particular client's needs. The dramatic changes the PR practice has experienced in the 21st century are identified in a 2014 research study of PR professionals over a nine-year period, 2006 to 2014, coauthored by Donald K. Wright, fellow PRSA and professor at Boston University (Wright & Hinson, 2014).

Significantly the major finding shows Twitter narrowly replacing Facebook for the first time in 2014 as the most frequently accessed social media site for PR activities. LinkedIn and YouTube ranked as third and fourth most frequently used sites. Inevitably new social and emerging media are also changing the way external PR is practiced as well as influencing traditional mainstream media.

DRIVER OF PUBLIC RELATIONS GROWTH

The Holmes Report (n.d.b) revealed that social media management was the strongest driver of growth in PR agencies worldwide in 2014, and digital/online communications were predicted, by far, to make the strongest gains in all countries in the next few years.

The 2016 Global Communications Report, issued by the USC Annenberg Center for Public Relations and The Holmes Report (2015b), finds that both agency and client-side PR practitioners predicted an increased demand for content creation (81%) and social media (75%).

The variety of social media options offer a special set of challenges and opportunities. PR practitioners agree that communication strategy dictates using different messages for various social media platforms. One must think digitally and strategically on which platforms are the best way to communication to specific target publics.

MEDIA RELATIONS

Reaching journalists through social media is a critical practice in media relations. Cision's (2016) State of the Media Report reveals that Twitter, followed by Facebook, meets journalists' needs (see Figure 8.4). Looking toward the future, they see Twitter growing in value the most.

Social media often blurs the line between the personal and the professional, so a key proficiency for PR practitioners is to master building and managing your organization's online identity and reputation.

FIGURE 8.4

Most Valued Social Network by Journalists

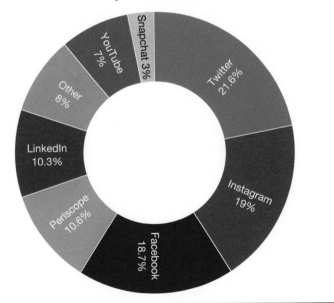

Source: Cision (2016).

THE DARK SIDE

PR professionals must also be prepared to deal with the dark side of social media, negative **memes**, and cyber attacks. Your organization or issue may be targeted with fake news to influence beliefs that support a deliberate agenda. A widely discussed example is the Russian propaganda that infiltrated into the 2016 U.S. presidential election. Clint Watts, former FBI agent and fellow at the Center for Cyber and Homeland Security, advises that a first step to counter a cyber attack is to get a baseline for fact and fiction (MSNBC, 2017).

The ability via social media to communicate directly and interactively should not overshadow the other ways in which digital communication has affected PR. In particular it has made media relations a 24-hour-a-day job with reporters expecting websites to have up-to-the-second information available without them having to go through a PR staffer.

As a result Internet content must be carefully screened and diligently organized so that journalists' investigative efforts will bear fruit. Both academic research and professional surveys suggest that while social media has increased the ability to connect with publics, its 24-hour nature has increased both workload and job-related stress (Argenti, 2016).

USING SOCIAL MEDIA TO BUILD CREDIBILITY

Publics have high expectations for how organizations interact with them, typically expecting communication that is authentic, honest, candid, and two-way. We can sum up these expectations in one word: credibility. Research on social media concludes credibility is an umbrella term that encompasses the dimensions of *personal interaction, expertise, welcoming language,* and *trustworthiness* (Kim & Brown, 2015).

> ▸ *Personal interaction* is the single most significant aspect of credibility. Organizations should interact and relate in a personal way with their publics. This humanizing communication shows a level of transparency and altruism.

> ▸ *Expertise*—long before social media—was identified as a foundational aspect of credibility, and it remains key to the social media space. Both content and appearance—well developed and visually attractive—help communicate expertise.

> ▸ *Welcoming language* (also called "invitational rhetoric") is language that invites others' perspectives and does not try to control or censor conversations. It recognizes the mutuality concept of relationship building and emphasizes the value of listening.

> ▸ *Trustworthiness*, as with expertise, has long been identified in media studies as essential to credibility. With social media it can be considered the sum of the preceding factors: Well-performed personal interactions, well-formed expressions of expertise, and consistent use of welcoming language all contribute to building trust between a public and an organization. Trust is foundational to long-term relationships.

Why a Public Relations Campaign Is Only as Good as Its Social Media Strategy

Linda Descano, Executive Vice President, Havas PR North America

I can't think of a bigger game changer for PR than technology. It's empowered consumers to set the terms for the way brands communicate with them. And as people have increasingly gone to different places to find news and information (places that can often be held in the palm of the hand), traditional media has become only a part of the recipe for engagement.

The best PR campaigns today take a surround-sound ecosystem approach, threading stories across paid, earned, and owned media channels and through online social activations, offline marketing experiences, and PR stunts. Social media is being used to establish brand voices, fuel larger stories, elevate individuals into industry thought leaders and extend the reach of events beyond their attendees.

Best of all the social space is rich with content that, while not organic, is a great way for brands to engage in conversations with an audience and listen to what they have to say. Although pay-to-play is a reality on social media to get a message in front of an audience (e.g., buying ads or promoting posts), the real payoff is getting the audience to interact with your content and especially to share it across their own social networks—basically to cultivate individuals as brand ambassadors. The trick is to craft a message in a way that draws people in, inspiring them to care and to share what you have to say.

Another reason to make social media part of every PR plan is that our raucous multichannel news cycle demands a constant supply of sensational news that it will either find or create. An old-fashioned communication strategy could be compromised by anybody anywhere who has a connection. Although the social space is a place where any cranky comment can grow legs, it's also the only place where messaging and audience targeting can be adjusted in real time to capitalize on fast-moving media opportunities and to head off negative events.

Whatever you do, don't forget the most important part: Output is not the same as outcome, so measure what you do. Start every social media campaign with an understanding of what **ROI** means for a client and its social media efforts. (For some clients, the primary objective of social media is to generate engagement in the form of social shares, while others may want to drive newsletter sign-ups, downloads of an app, or traffic to a destination page.) By extension, determine whether ROI means the total number of social conversations about the company or year-over-year growth in the number of advocates (people sharing its content).

Once you've established clear metrics, track those metrics using social analytics platforms like Google Analytics. Historical performance is one necessary benchmark for tracking performance and optimizing ongoing efforts. Another way of gauging effectiveness: Look holistically at the total reach and engagement through a campaign, and track what percentage is earned versus paid and owned.

As the very definitions of who is making the news and how it's being made are shifting beneath us, social media may just be the best way to get a client's messages into the news. Once you figure out how to blow up the Internet, you've figured out the hard part—at least for now. ●

Before joining Havas, Linda Descano served as managing director and global head of content marketing and social media for Citi.

Source: L. Descano (personal communication, 2017).

A SHOWCASE OF PUBLIC RELATIONS PRACTICES WITH SOCIAL NETWORKS

>> LO 8.3   Evaluate best practices for social media use in the field of PR

Some of the top PR agencies, brands, and nonprofits are using multiple social media platforms aggressively and successfully. The following examples offer instruction and inspiration, but remember—it's an evolving social media world out there, so be

Southern California's Metrolink system combined service updates and customer information with high-quality photographs and video to make its Facebook page a valuable destination for its riders.

Al Seib/Los Angeles Times/ Getty Images

sure to refer to industry blogs and websites to keep current (see five reliable blogs recommended later in this chapter).

FACEBOOK

As the social media leader, Facebook offers great opportunities for PR. Once you identify it's where your target publics are, and you craft the right strategy to move them beyond personal use, the results can be, well, award winning. See how Metrolink used the social media platform expertly to win *PR Daily's* (2015a) Best Use of Facebook award.

Metrolink, Southern California's passenger rail system, created a compelling Facebook strategy to attract a new generation of commuters. While an impressive 50% of current customers were already fans of Metrolink's Facebook page, the rail needed to increase ridership during off-peak hours *and* attract a new, younger demographic. *PR Daily* writes:

> To succeed, communications had to alter existing perceptions of public transit as unsafe, dirty, and uncomfortable. To accomplish these goals, as well as to tap into Facebook's ability to serve as a customer service center, Metrolink balanced service updates and responses to customer inquiries with a content strategy focused on gorgeous photography and video (which included aerial shots captured by a drone Metrolink's communicators had purchased and learned to fly).

Much of the content focused on weekend travel, local vacations (also called "staycations") and day trips. Video in particular proved useful due to Facebook's autoplay feature.

The strategy paid off. The page produced more than 1.3 million organic impressions and attracted more than 7,600 comments, 100,000 likes, and 7,200 shares. More impressively, the number of page likes—which had been holding steady at 27,000—more than doubled as a result of these efforts. So effective was Metrolink's Facebook focus that Facebook awarded it its coveted "verified" status—the only public transit entity to earn the status.

TWITTER

With the immediacy of a tweet's limited characters, first 140 and now 280, Twitter has transformed citizen engagement in politics, popular culture, product experience, customer service, news consumption, issue advocacy, and more as well as the communication practices of organizations, media professionals, and most definitely the field of PR. However, unlike Facebook, Twitter's character limit does restrict the content, encouraging multiple tweets that can bury your messages. Yet with the right strategy, innovative campaigns can use Twitter to effectively promote topics some may consider bland or even "boring."

Transamerica turned some simple questions about its industry—financial services—into a trending topic on Twitter; a campaign that *PR Daily* (2015b) lauded

---

SOCIAL RESPONSIBILITY IN ACTION

Children's Specialized Hospital—#FightFace

Children's Specialized Hospital launched its #FightFace campaign to raise the organization's profile and draw attention to the struggle faced by its patients.

Instagram.com/childrensspecnj

Children's Specialized Hospital is the nation's largest pediatric rehabilitation hospital caring for children from birth to 21 years of age facing special health challenges, from chronic illnesses and complex physical disabilities like brain and spinal cord injuries to developmental and behavioral issues like autism and mental health.

At 13 different New Jersey locations, pediatric specialists partner with families to make the hospital's many innovative therapies and medical treatments more personalized and effective, so children can achieve more of their goals.

The hospital launched a social media campaign in July 2015 with a music video featuring Rachel Platten's "Fight Song" and dozens of its patients and staff. The video showed children "fighting" for their lives in therapy sessions and when learning to walk again—and also celebrating their victories. The video asked people everywhere to take and share a picture of their best #FightFace selfie on Facebook, Twitter, and Instagram to encourage children to keep fighting to get better.

Soon after the video's release, ABC's *The View* featured Rachel Platten performing her hit song and segments of the Children's Specialized Hospital's music video. Two patient families were also invited to be on the show and share their personal stories of being in the video and how the song had helped them. Other major media outlets also covered the campaign including NJ.com/*The Star Ledger* (New Jersey's largest daily newspaper), and TheMighty.com (a national disability advocacy website).

One year later the video had more than 55,000 views, and the hospital had received more than 550 #FightFace selfies. (See the #FightFace selfie wall and watch the music video at www.childrens-specialized.org/fightface.) ●

Source: Children's Specialized Hospital (2016).

Note: This case was winner of PR News 2016 Social Media Award: Facebook Best Use of Video and received honorable mention in the Facebook Public Relations Campaign and Twitter Use of Hashtag categories.

as Best Use of Twitter. Transamerica disrupted the financial advice industry with a microsite called The Finfluencer. It invited people to enter their e-mail addresses and agree to follow Transamerica on Twitter. The Finfluencer algorithm then looked at their tweets, crunching data on 140 characteristics to answer two questions for its users:

1. How "Finfluential" am I in financial services?
2. How "Finfluential" is the financial services expert I'm following on Twitter?

It rated users on points in comparison to others who were rated. Nearly 2,500 people participated, and upon receiving results nearly half took some action such as following a Twitter user who scored high. In a competitive marketplace Transamerica's use of Twitter helped position it as a leader and innovator in the industry.

LINKEDIN

The business networking site LinkedIn offers myriad ways for an organization to use it strategically as an extension of its professional brand. A company page should carry impressive images and content, some ideally written by employees—humanizing it *and* establishing it as a thought leader. It is definitely more time-consuming to set up than are some other social media tools, but here's an example of one company using LinkedIn for PR value.

"Email Security Company Gets Attention by Making LinkedIn the Focus of Its Campaign" is the *PR Daily* (n.d.b) headline announcing Zix Corporation's award for Best LinkedIn Campaign. In an effort to take advantage of popular concern around e-mail security issues, the company's PR firm, The Hoffman Agency, took a four-pronged approach with its LinkedIn page (see Table 8.1). Zix's followers grew from 600 to 2,400, nearly two-thirds of them senior executives, managers, and directors, and LinkedIn began driving more than 85% of the company's social traffic.

TABLE 8.1

LinkedIn Transformation

ISSUE	APPROACH
1. Executive profiles	Updated to be: ▸ More compelling ▸ More discoverable through key words like "e-mail encryption" and "BYOD"
2. Presentation	Polished to: ▸ Humanize ▸ Use a storytelling approach
3. Content	Posts emulated most popular content on the Web: ▸ Customer spotlight features ▸ Thought leadership on industry news ▸ Highlights of consumer surveys ▸ Best-practice Q&As
4. Action strategies	Executive participation: ▸ Used for promotion ▸ Drove engagement

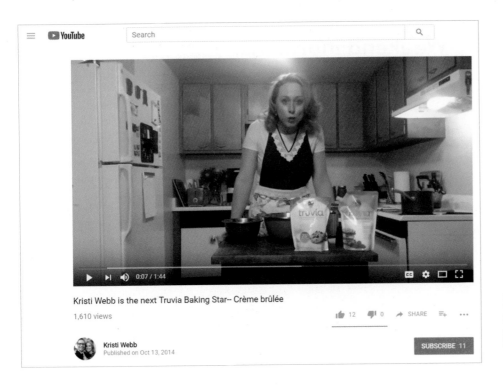

Low-calorie sweetener Truvia launched an online baking contest, which it promoted with the help of influential vloggers.

Kristi Webb via YouTube

YOUTUBE

Far more than a video sharing service among individuals, YouTube is a fluid digital storytelling site for organizations to engage more deeply with publics, grow audiences, and communicate more authentically. Some ways PR professionals are using YouTube include: uploading how-to tutorials about a client's product or experience; providing show-and-tell vignettes on production facilities, user profiles (especially influencers), and so on; or kicking off a campaign (sometimes with a mystery to be solved, a challenge to be met, or funny enough to go **viral**).

Naturally the video should be top quality (requiring a bigger budget than content on other social media platforms), and you enter a fishbowl that includes all sorts of other videos, some poorly done or with negative content. Let's look at an example of one company's use of influencers on YouTube as a fire starter for a campaign:

When the low-calorie sweetener Truvia needed to promote the launch of its newest product, Truvia Brown Sugar Blend, it partnered with PR agency RF|Binder to get food and baking influencer **vloggers** to create recipe videos featuring the product that were subsequently released on YouTube to encourage people to enter their own recipe videos. To spark submissions, a contest promised its three finalists a trip to NYC for a bake-off (PR Daily, n.d.c).

INSTAGRAM

Instagram goes hand in hand with visual storytelling. The mobile platform can be viewed on a laptop as well and lets users share photos and videos. This visual attraction also presents challenges: Organizations need to know what visuals will

Honest Tea's #RefreshinglyHonest campaign asked people to share their unfiltered moments of truth, like the reality of a weekend with kids.

Instagram.com/goodhousekeeping

attract viewers—and which may offend—and make sure the visuals reflect their brand. And high technical quality is essential.

Consider how Honest Tea used Instagram in a PR campaign to reinforce the "honest" in its brand. The company encouraged people to highlight the unfiltered, imperfect "#RefreshinglyHonest" moments in their lives with **tagged** photos on Instagram. Honest Tea then uploaded the photos to its campaign site.

Apparel company Anthropologie won first place in the Best Use of Instagram in PR Daily 2015 Digital PR and Social Media Awards (PR Daily, n.d.a). Much of Anthropologie's Instagram content is generated by customers, sharing photos of themselves in Anthropologie clothing. The company solicits this content through its catalogs, e-mails, store displays, signage, and other social media channels. As a result, the #Anthropologie hashtag not only has a heavy presence on Instagram, but it has resulted in high conversion rates and has led to partnerships with Instagram influencers, casting calls for fashion shows and other themed campaigns (like the #SummerInASnap campaign that encouraged users to share their most inspired Anthropologie moments of the summer).

PINTEREST

This social media platform calls itself "the world's catalog of ideas," and most of that idea sharing takes place on mobile devices. It allows members to share content by pinning visual images to their virtual bulletin board—images that connect back to sites of origin (a website, blog, etc.). Visitors can browse specific categories or follow a board they like. The platform offers a guide for businesses and organizations with advice on how to build relationships with users. Tips include understanding your key public(s), being authentic and listening, and monitoring before jumping in.

Multiple research studies suggest that dialogic features on organizations' websites and social media accounts improve relationship building. Dialogic features include: being easy to use and informative, encouraging staying on the site, generating return visits, and offering a feedback loop (to engage with users). An analysis of the top 10 most-followed organizations' Pinterest profiles (Agozzino, 2015) revealed a significant missing feature—lack of interactive engagement.

How Can a Small Brand Use Google Analytics . . . and a Blog . . . to Grow?

You're a communicator at a tiny company. Almost nobody knows the brand. And you're based in New York City (NYC), a place where bigger often is perceived as being better. The founder of your company, which was started in an apartment, wants you to get the brand to rank high—number one, if possible—on Google search pages. Oh, and you have about $500 in your budget.

Certainly communicators can identify or at least empathize with some elements of this story. This was the situation confronting Fluent City, a language school in NYC, several years ago. The challenge is how to get noticed, going up against large, well-known language schools and online language programs. The solution is a blog.

You may be thinking, "Another blog?" How could that break through the clutter? The short answer is by using key words and Google Analytics smartly. Take what your audience is interested in, and write about it. Equally important is to create compelling content and write for people, not machines (**SEO** and **SEM**). Here are some tips:

Be smart about your potential customers. Fluent City knew its potential customers were people interested in learning foreign languages but also people interested in things *related* to foreign languages—such as foreign food and foreign films. Thus the blog carried compelling articles about the six best Russian restaurants in NYC.

Before writing that article, though, Fluent City searched Google to find out if there were other articles about top Russian restaurants in the city. None were found. Bingo!

Another regular practice Fluent City used was checking Google Analytics to inform its content strategy, finding out what people were searching for that related to foreign languages. In addition, it put key words into Google without clicking, so it showed the history of the word being searched. It also checked Google to avoid repeating articles that already existed.

Classify your content. Fluent City also divided its content into evergreen (Russian cuisine) and seasonal (10 foreign films to see).

Don't lose your momentum. Many small brands fall into the trap of launching a blog and fail to realize that it's a living thing requiring consistent care (meaning fresh content posted regularly). Fluent City held regular events with speakers, not only raising awareness but generating articles and images for the blog.

Remember your goal. It's crucial to not only build your **click-through rate** but to convert clicks into *customers*. Never miss a chance to ask visitors to sign up for more information.

See the results. After using Google Analytics to strategize with the blog, Fluent City's students increased over a period of four years from 2,000 to 23,000—and it had a *very well-read* blog. ●

Source: Arenstein (2016).

The framework of Pinterest allows users to comment and "like" pins as well as to participate in games, contests, and re-pinning activities; therefore, Pinterest itself inherently has dialogic features built in for organizations to connect with publics. However, of all of the 10 organizations analyzed, none took this engagement a step further to respond or comment to users' questions, inquiries, and so on.

BLOGS

Content is certainly key on blogs. Often a personality offers engaging observations about an industry, reviews products, or provides commentary on economic, political, or cultural issues. But blogs are about much more than written posts; they're also about community and conversation, attracting select target publics: the media, customers, investors, volunteers, and so on. While blogs can be time-consuming, requiring thoughtful content and regular updates, today they are solidly established communication tools. McDonald's New York Tri-State (the company's largest U.S. region) created an award-winning blog (PR Daily, n.d.c) to support the redesign

Doritos used social media to give away prizes promoting its new Roulette chips.

Lenscap/Alamy Stock Photo

of its stagnant regional website—and it became the centerpiece of its revival. The key to success: humanized stories about workers' climbs up the company ladder.

Blogs can strategically target specialized publics. For example, the Phase Change Matters blog from Entropy Solutions was the first in its industry to highlight news and research on phase change material and thermal energy storage. Its keys to success included a reliable network of sources, an authoritative voice, an independent perspective, and daily postings (PR Daily, n.d.d).

PERISCOPE

This live-streaming video **app** lets viewers interact with the video and keep the clip for 24 hours after it broadcasts. It's owned by Twitter—another advantage for accessing. PR professionals use it for engaging publics. The platform recently caught the attention of credit and personal finance company Experian. Choosing Periscope as an outlet to build community and foster engagement, Experian expanded its #CreditScope streaming program with daily periscopes sharing best practices in credit and personal finance, and it also archived the conversations on Twitter (Seymour, 2016c). Other brands to use Periscope for PR purposes include Red Bull's live streaming of its music events, Adobe Photoshop's introduction of a new Creative Cloud product, Doritos' #DoritosRoulette contest to promote a new chip, and even heritage auto brands like Lincoln showcasing their vintage designs and modern technology to the younger Periscope audiences (Ruggieri, 2016).

FACEBOOK LIVE

Also a live-streaming video feature, it allows you to stream to a specific group of friends and generate discussion. It lets them replay the video forever as well as comment on it. It also can be downloaded for other use. Airbnb partnered with Disney to promote its "Love This? Live There" travel campaign. Disney's The Jungle Book Facebook page live streamed interviews from the red carpet at the film's 2016 premier, where Airbnb had built a treehouse for the occasion. It helped emphasize the Airbnb brand: Beyond providing a "local" alternative to hotels, it conjures up "fantasy" spaces that are now within easy reach.

SNAPCHAT

This smartphone image messaging and multimedia app, once known for a largely teenage base, has expanded through Gen Zs to Millennials. It sends photos and videos that self-destruct after a few seconds of a person viewing them. That could be a disadvantage, but not for West Virginia University (WVU). The school understood that prospective students wanted to be where their relatives weren't, so WVU made it a priority to have a Snapchat-first mentality. That means planning all their outreach content with Snapchat in mind and winning a string of awards from *PR News*, PRSA, the Association of Marketing & Communication Professionals, and the education association Council for Advancement and Support of Education (CASE). WVU's Snapchat content includes road trips across West Virginia, "takeover" Snapchats run by a student, and an "Ask WVU" Snapchat invitation, **Snapchat stories** and conversing back and forth with multiple snaps (Nelson, 2015).

FOURTH SCREEN TECHNOLOGY

American adults now spend more time on mobile devices (smartphones and tablets) than on any other type of medium except television (Alaimo, 2016b). Kara Alaimo, a PR professor at Hofstra University, offers the following advice for PR practitioners:

▸ *Create tools.* Let publics explore, connect, and order.

▸ *Produce hyper-personalized content.* Differentiate: Offer what publics need or desire.

▸ *Make interactions easy.* Don't ask for too much information, and don't omit needed information. Ask how to serve them better.

▸ *Make content platform relevant.* Adapt to different social media platforms and their users' expectations and behaviors.

▸ *Be fast.* Quickly respond to news relevant to your brand with conversations in real time.

▸ *Use rich media.* Use games, animation, or 360-degree videos (a mobile-friendly 15 seconds and 5 MB or less).

GAMIFICATION

Game on! Smartphones are a popular gaming device, and some of the most engaging PR strategies have elements of a game, both in live events and in campaigns. The Bay Area Rapid Transit (BART) partnered with Foursquare, a local search-and-discovery service mobile app, to bring new riders and reward faithful riders through "badges" to be unlocked by riders checking in at BART stations—thus entering them into a lottery for $25 worth of tickets. Users said it was more "fun" to ride; they liked the interactivity and recommended BART to friends. Rewards programs are a popular illustration of **gamification** elements. Starbucks Rewards uses game mechanics such as progress bars, incentives, and motivation strategies for bigger rewards (Hector, 2015).

Starbucks has gamified its customer loyalty program, awarding stars for every purchase that can be used for free food or drinks and giving consumers opportunities to earn more by participating in challenges and games.

© Starbucks

STARBUCKS REWARDS™   Account

DOUBLE STAR DAY

2x

Double Stars on almost all your purchases means getting to free drinks and food* doubly quick. Grab an extra shot or a bite to eat, and watch the Stars roll in.

Double Star Day is:
Wednesday, October 18

CareFirst used a particularly creative gaming strategy to address significant changes the Affordable Healthcare Act held for a specific under-65 health insurance buyer: the Millennial. First research showed that those born between 1982 and 2002 had a great interest in mobile gaming apps. It developed a health and wellness themed gaming app, FRNZY, that allowed players to test their knowledge, train their brains, earn trophies and badges, and use social media to challenge friends. Done purely as a brand awareness effort, the gaming app was promoted on all CareFirst social media channels (Seymour, 2015).

EVALUATING SOCIAL MEDIA AND LOOKING TO THE FUTURE

>> **LO 8.4**   **Identify how to measure social media effectiveness, and craft a strategy for staying abreast of trends**

Content creation is one of the top services that will drive future growth in the PR industry. For that content, basic written and verbal skills are surely important; however, due to the digital nature of much content now, PR leaders must also be stronger in analytics, better at technology, and more creative.

You read about measurement of PR efforts in Chapter 5—essential to establishing the value of your recommended strategies and tactics. To begin to evaluate your social media PR efforts, consider your audience and determine which social channels—and which messages—drive the most traffic to your website or result in your desired outcomes. It's essential to adjust your PR tactics to each platform based on what you learn about their audience demographics and based on the nature of the platform.

VALUE OF MEASUREMENT IN PUBLIC RELATIONS

Obtaining data analytics is a standard way of measuring social media activity and results: **mentions**, **sentiment**, **reach**, **exposure**, **engagement**. There are various web metrics tools available to evaluate social media channels. Google Analytics is a free tool developed by Google and probably the one that is most widely used. Two resources from Google, one free and the other for a fee, can get you started with Google Analytics. The free resource offers open courses in the Google Analytics Academy. One course, Digital Analytics Fundamentals, has some well-produced video and text lectures. Topics in that course include the following:

▸ An overview of the current digital measurement landscape

▸ Guidance on how to build an effective measurement plan

▸ Best practices for collecting actionable data

▸ Descriptions of key digital measurement concepts, terminology, and analysis techniques

▸ Deep dives into Google Analytics reports with specific examples for evaluating your digital marketing performance

Trending: A Speedway Into the Future

Although social media has been around for just over a dozen years, its near-exponential growth and intensity of experience has permeated society and thrust itself into prominence in PR practice. Digital marketing blogger Jeff Bullas (2016) notes the newest trends that are changing the communication landscape.

Live-Streaming Video

‣ With the mobile phone as a handy broadcast device, we can capture live moments and share raw footage. Twitter, Periscope and Facebook Live make live streaming easy, allowing PR practitioners to tell stories, share real-time events, and educate publics. With the authenticity of live streaming, it also helps build credibility and trust.

Chatbots

‣ **Chatbots** are computer programs, programmed to answer questions, that mimic conversation with people using artificial intelligence. It's the same technology behind Apple's Siri. For PR, consider the usefulness of inviting journalists to subscribe to your client's Chatbot messaging for updates on relevant news. For any public interested in the client's CSR, updates can be channeled and help build reputation at the same time.

24-Hour Content

‣ The appeal of expiring content is that it's creative, exciting, and engaging. Case in point—Snapchat, with a 100% mobile audience, offers a triple wallop of lively brand content, event-based interaction, and video storytelling—with an immediacy of constantly refreshed content. For PR practitioners, it allows you to target the 18- to 24-year-old audience pretty much in isolation, allowing your "snaps" to reflect that and have the urgency of soon-to-be-expiring content.

Social Influencers

‣ Reaching media gatekeepers—usually journalists—has always been a traditional media relations goal in PR. Companies have routinely used celebrity spokespeople, like Nike and Tiger Woods, to elevate brands. Now influencers, those online experts with a ubiquitous presence who've cultivated a recognized and respected personal brand, are the social media gatekeepers. They're using YouTube, Twitter, Instagram, and even Snapchat, offering a level of credibility and trust in supporting your client's PR objective, which likely may get publics talking about your brand. ●

FIGURE 8.5

Industry News

Stay Informed

Get motivated. Be innovative. Keep on top of the ever-changing world of social media with a frequent visit to these respected industry sources:

‣ Edelman, a leading global PR firm established more than 60 years ago, shares insights via its digital blog at http://www.edelman.com/conversations/edelman-digital/.

‣ Ragan's *PR Daily*, more than a blog, is truly a hub for the PR industry with a dedicated social media page: https://www.prdaily.com/SocialMedia/SocialMedia.aspx.

‣ Meltwater, the media monitoring company, offers news on social media at https://www.meltwater.com/blog/.

‣ Shift Communications covers social media marketing and PR at http://www.shiftcomm.com/blog/.

‣ *PR News* maintains an up-to-date list with hyperlinks of PR industry blogs at http://www.prnewsonline.com/resources/blogs.

The American Foundation for Suicide Prevention's Fight to Stop Suicide

The American Foundation for Suicide Prevention is active on social media, particularly behind the hashtag #stopsuicide.

Twitter.com/afspnational

The American Foundation for Suicide Prevention (AFSP) generated momentum for National Suicide Prevention Week in 2015 with the message: "You Can #StopSuicide." As part of its ongoing research efforts, the foundation had recently partnered with the National Action Alliance for Suicide Prevention and the Anxiety and Depression Association of America to conduct a poll, finding some encouraging results on public opinion of mental health and suicide prevention. Nearly all respondents think suicide is sometimes or often preventable (94%) and would do something if someone close to them was thinking about suicide (93%). Those receiving mental health treatment in the past thought it was helpful, whether psychotherapy (82%), medication (78%), or another form. Two-thirds said they'd tell someone if they had suicidal thoughts (Gebbia, 2015).

These poll results drove media outreach: AFSP'S top executive interviewed with journalists and radio and TV stations across the country to not only spread awareness but encourage involvement. A digital and social media effort included a Twitter chat and blog posts in the Huffington Post and WebMD. Partner organizations helped spread the message; National Alliance on Mental Illness (NAMI), Mental Health America, and the Treatment Advocacy Center all posted articles on their websites. The foundation also encouraged a grassroots WOM movement asking key stakeholders to reach out to family, friends, coworkers, and classmates to spread the word that mental health is important and suicide is preventable (Gebbia, 2015).

What resulted? Partnerships with eight mental health organizations helped magnify the message. A #SOSChat cohosted with the Association for Behavioral Health earned more than 1.7 million impressions. Equally successful, a Selfies to #StopSuicide effort generated the same powerful response. Nearly 150,000 Talk Saves Lives brochures were distributed, and merchandise carrying the message #StopSuicide helped spread the word. The campaign even influenced AP style, officially discouraging journalists from using the phrase "committed suicide" (AFSP Annual Report, 2015, p. 12). ●

Note: This case was the winner of PR News 2016 CSR Award: Social Media Campaign.

SOCIAL RESPONSIBILITY

SOCIAL MEDIA AND CRISES

The use of social media in a crisis is essential. A future chapter covers crisis management in depth, so we'll just briefly mention it here. In a crisis, companies know that Twitter is the major link to the media and their customers. It reveals how information about the crisis is spreading and reflects what's across social media. Public comments may favor outrage and punishment over understanding, and this conversation cannot be downplayed or disregarded. Social conversations must be vigilantly monitored and addressed expeditiously, guided by transparency and sincerity. Boston College's Center for Corporate Citizenship conducts research on social media's facility to amplify CSR communication. One strategy they suggest is encouraging employees to engage in the corporate social media content to put a human face to the company. Intel offers three simple guidelines to employees participating in corporate social media: disclose, protect, and use common sense. Also corporations should encourage nonprofit partners and supportive influencers to collaborate on issues and initiatives important to them.

SOCIAL MEDIA AND CORPORATE SOCIAL RESPONSIBILITY

A robust communication strategy is needed for any CSR engagement, and that means social media plays a key role. As seen in examples of award-winning social media campaigns, the authenticity of social media is an important part of their success. Business professor Paul Argenti (2016) notes that transparency and authenticity are particularly important for businesses trying to explain their understanding of and their efforts in sustainability and social responsibility. Social media allows these businesses to connect with target publics in meaningful ways. Examine the following examples:

▶ TOMS "Ticket to Give" contest brought 50 customers each on a Giving Trip throughout 2013 to one of 40 countries where TOMS shoes are donated. First the 100-word essay entries were shared across platforms encouraging votes, and the resulting personal stories from the winners' trips appeared on YouTube, Facebook, Pinterest, and beyond.

▶ Pepsico was one of the first CSR-focused companies to use **crowdsourcing** to build an online CSR campaign, the Pepsi Refresh Project. Its social media campaign was such a success that one month after its January launch, it opted out of traditional advertising in the Super Bowl after a 23-year commitment (Argenti, 2016).

SCENARIO OUTCOME

At this chapter's beginning we provided a real-life scenario requiring VW to respond to a crisis. To review VW was caught intentionally violating the Clean Air Act. The EPA revealed VW had developed software purposefully designed to deceive the EPA's emissions tests. We asked you these questions:

▶ How did VW PR handle this crisis via social media?

▶ As their official PR agency or in-house council, what would your advice have been for VW?

▶ What publics would be critical to communicate with, through which social channels, and with what messaging?

You should have arrived at the judgement that immediate and comprehensive social media monitoring, and then quick and sincere engagement, should have guided U.S. VW's response.

However, what did VW do? U.S. VW stopped posting to Facebook and Twitter on Friday, September 18, the day the news broke in the United States. The social media accounts remained dormant for one full week, with no responses to comments. Later, Michael Horn, the U.S. CEO, posted a statement on the accounts.

Thus, for eight days after the news, U.S. VW's social media accounts provided no information—only an apology video from the CEO. However, Twitter was exploding with consumer outrage. The U.S. financial news website, The Street, noted, "Social media shows how big a blow emissions scandal is" (Stuart, 2015).

On the ninth day, VW posted a frequently asked questions page directing customers to a customer care phone number and e-mail address. Three months after the news, *The Financial Times* (n.d.) revealed, "Volkswagen blunders through communications over emissions scandals: Customers and investors have been left exasperated by carmaker's public statements." Five months later, the *New York Times* headlined a follow-up story, "VW's Crisis Strategy: Forward, Reverse, U-Turn," with the opening line, "Someday, Volkswagen's emissions cheating scandal will be studied in crisis communications textbooks. And not in a good way" (Hakim, 2016). Following the *New York Times* the *Christian Science Monitor's* editorial board stated, "The industry must be as transparent as possible and cooperate with its many stakeholders" (Editorial Board, 2016).

Thus if your suggestions addressed the need to escalate social media engagement across the board with its multiple publics, you were smarter than the execs calling the shots at VW. You may also have identified U.S. VW employees as a significant target public as frustrated staff may turn to company social sites to express concerns, ask questions, and seek advice. And beyond the CEO's apology video, you may have suggested other multimedia visual messaging to deliver a more authentic and emotive response from the company.

WRAP UP

This chapter substantiated the critical relevance of social media in PR today. It traced its historical antecedents and early development through a timeline illustrating social media's exponential growth in the 21st century. This foundational understanding explains why the practice of PR has shifted dramatically in very recent years and must continue to respond and adapt to new platforms and technologies.

To help you recognize and understand how organizations are *best* using social media in PR campaigns, you read about award-winning campaigns in all the major platforms and engaged in detailed case studies. You also got a baseline understanding of the value and need for measuring social media PR efforts.

Looking to the future it introduced trends that may become major social media avenues or may be replaced by another innovation as the culture of social media and digital technology is a fast and fluid one.

KEY TERMS

The rise of social media brings a new vocabulary—a list that seems to be forever growing. Here are some of the most common social media words and phrases a PR practitioner should know:

App: Short for application—software designed to run on a smartphone or other mobile devices, **202**

Chatbots: Computer programs designed to answer questions that mimic conversation with people using artificial intelligence, **205**

Click-Through Rate: A ratio showing how often people who see an online ad end up clicking it, **201**

Crowdsourcing: Obtaining information or input from a large number of people, typically via the Internet, **207**

Engagement: A state of attention, comprehension, interest, attitude formation, and/or participation; in social media, interactions people have with content, for example, likes, comments, shares, and re-tweets, **204**

Exposure: Frequency and timeframe of content's appearance on a media platform, **204**

Gamification: Process of incorporating game-playing elements into marketing or communication campaigns, **203**

Hashtags: Words or phrases, with hash or pound sign appearing before them, for use on social media sites, **188**

Memes: Virally transmitted cultural symbols, often a photograph and often captioned, **194**

Mentions: Direct reference or quotes of an entity by a media outlet, **204**

Reach: Measurement of audience size; the number of people who are exposed to content, **204**

ROI: Return on investment, **195**

SEM: Search engine marketing; promotion of websites by increasing their visibility in search engine results pages primarily through paid advertising, **201**

Sentiment: The analysis of sentiment, also known as opinion mining; identifies the feelings (attitudes, emotions, etc.) expressed through social media communication, **204**

SEO: Search engine optimization; affecting the visibility of a website or a Web page in a search engine's unpaid results—often referred to as "natural," "organic," or "earned" results, **201**

Snapchat Stories: Compilation of Snaps posted over a 24-hour period that become a "story" lasting for 24 hours, **203**

Social Network Theory (SNT): Examines and explains the web of interrelationships among people and organizations, **191**

Tagged: The act of a social media user identifying someone in a post, photo, tweet, or update; the "tag" is a clickable name that notifies the person that they have been identified, **200**

Viral: Describes a piece of information, that is, a story, image or video, that is circulated rapidly and widely from one Internet user to another, **199**

Vloggers: People who produce video blogs (a form of Web television), **199**

You will participate in a form of crowdsourcing with your classmates, working together to write a *social media recommendation report* for an organization or situation of your choice (e.g., your university needs to recruit more out-of-state students). Each student is then responsible for one paragraph of the report.

▸ Use Google Docs or another platform to communicate with one another.

▸ Begin with a paragraph on the hypothetical or real organization and situation.

▸ Each student should contribute a paragraph (write your name at the end of it).

▸ The final social media recommendation report should be five to six pages in length.

▸ When completed, one student will upload to a class online discussion board.

Each student then posts in the discussion thread: Comment on the experience of writing the report, how it relates to crowdsourcing, and what you learned about social media for PR. Next each student responds to the comments of at least one other classmate.

You handle PR for Spaulding Health Research (SHR), headquartered in Flint, Michigan. SHR has just received $1.4 million funding from the All One World Foundation—for creating a global research initiative on risk reductions for childhood lead poisoning. The funds were awarded to support the human and capital investment needed to launch and sustain this initiative. Sylvia Wallander, president of SHR, attributed its selection to Spaulding's breakthrough research in 2015 on preventing HIV in pregnancies.

Your task is to communicate, via Twitter, with one category of Spaulding's many publics <u>except </u>the media (employees, influencers, researchers in the field, donors, activists, victims of lead poisoning, etc.). Once decided, provide the following:

1. Identify the public.

2. Write the best tweet (140 characters or less) to inspire someone to read, react, and re-tweet your message. Create and include at least one hashtag.

3. Provide rationale: What was the thought process you used to create "the perfect tweet"?

SOCIAL RESPONSIBILITY CASE STUDY

M&M'S Red Nose Day Raises Money for Children Living in Poverty

Situation

The first Red Nose Day was started in the U.K. in 1988 by Comic Relief, a British charity, which was responding to famine in Ethiopia. Since then, it has continued as a campaign dedicated to raising money for children and young people living in poverty—by simply having fun and making people laugh. Its proceeds fund charity partners that support children in need around the world. In 2015, it moved across the Atlantic to the United States, and M&M'S launched the movement to raise money and awareness for this first U.S. Red Nose Day.

Research and Strategy

How did M&M'S spread awareness and help spark donations? It started off with a $750,000 donation from M&M'S to the Red Nose Day Fund, and then the company rallied its enormous M&M'S fan base to help make a difference by making someone laugh. When fans made someone laugh, usually by wearing a red rubber clown nose, and made it known with hashtag #MakeMLaugh across social media, a dollar went to Red Nose Day from M&M'S.

The idea was simple and quickly became a fun competition, spread almost exclusively on social media. Successful CSR campaigns don't happen by themselves; they're powered by social media posts and re-posts that reach huge audiences.

People tweeted friends and posted photos of themselves sporting bright red noses on Facebook. The friends in turn posted their own red-nosed photos, fueling the spread of the campaign. Soon photos and videos of sports figures, celebrities, and public officials wearing red noses appeared in posts to their fan bases and followers.

The most obvious benefit of a social media based strategy is the multiplier effect. Social media such as Facebook was king in this campaign as M&M'S partnered with a wide array of influencers to share messaging and #MakeMLaugh. Top-tier YouTubers, bloggers, content creators, and more posted social content and triggered donations.

Execution

A coordinated media push among M&M'S, Comic Relief, and NBC helped unveil the partnership around the first-ever U.S. Red Nose Day, including a stream of social media shares from stars with red noses, including Heidi Klum, Nick Canon, Howie Mandel, Joe Jonas, Chris D'Elia, and even Kermit the Frog.

Comedian and *Saturday Night Live* cast member Jay Pharaoh hosted the "funniest five minutes" at M&M'S World in New York City to help generate laughs—and donations. His five-minute barrage of jokes raised a quick $1,000—and launched the program. Social media influencers were in attendance to share the content across their channels using the dedicated hashtag, and Jay conducted a media tour to continue to spread awareness.

Evaluation

In total, M&M'S made a combined donation to the Red Nose Day Fund of $1.25 million. Media coverage also resulted in 188.8 million media impressions; additionally, the social campaign, influencer participation and celebrity push generated 269.7 million social media impressions, of which 123.1 million were earned. The hashtag was used more than 78,000 times, with 2.9 million engagements on #MakeMLaugh content.

ENGAGE

▸ Explore how M&M'S used PR strategies to promote Red Nose Day in 2017 (a campaign that won the *PR News*'s 2017 CSR Award).

▸ Search and discover which organizations have joined as sponsors since the 2015 U.S. launch.

DISCUSS

▸ CSR engagement should be linked to a corporation's core business. How does Red Nose Day relate to M&M'S business purpose? What about the new partners?

▸ How have efforts changed or evolved since the campaign's beginning?

Sources: Seymour (2016c); Shorty Social Good Awards (n.d.).

Note: This campaign was a Facebook/Social Good campaign winner, *PR News* 2016 Social Media Awards and a finalist in the Food & Beverage, Social Good campaign, 8th Annual Shorty Awards 2016.

SOCIAL RESPONSIBILITY CASE STUDY

Giving Tuesday: The Day the World Gave Back

Situation

The 92nd Street Y in New York City, in partnership with the United Nations Foundation, launched #GivingTuesday (GT) in 2012 in response to the shopping season that begins with Black Friday and Cyber Monday. The one-day event kicked off the holiday giving season as a global day dedicated to charitable giving on the Tuesday after Thanksgiving.

Research and Strategy

Initial research showed that in 2011, Americans gave almost $300 billion to favorite causes, and the assumption was people are willing to give if asked. So, to transform how people participate in the giving season, GT built on the collective power of a unique blend of partners—charities, families, businesses, and individuals.

Goals for the movement included inspiring and celebrating generosity, increasing fans and engagement on social platforms, amplifying GT partner messaging online, providing relevant content for advocates and supporters, and encouraging a diverse community to rally behind GT and connect with its partners' campaigns and initiatives. Almost 27,000 partners globally were mobilized.

The previous year, the #UNselfie, or the selfless selfie, was introduced. It asked people to celebrate generosity by posting photos of themselves sharing why they give and to which organizations. It was so incredibly popular and effective that it remained a key part of the strategy in 2014.

The 2014 campaign also focused on sharing best practices and educating nonprofits and for-profits alike on ideal strategies for giving on GT. Crowdfunding initiatives took on a new level of prominence: Indiegogo offered support and education leading up to the event, and CrowdRise built a holographic Giving Tower that generated a "brick" for every donation.

Execution

The GT team worked closely with these crowdfunding partners and others to share free resources on the GT website for all partners to use. Larger, well-established partners shared their experience in webinars, meet-ups, tool kits and other forums that included sample graphics, posts, and tweets that they could grab to promote their own campaigns and help make the movement viral on all social platforms.

A "comms corps" was activated. This unique alliance of eight top PR agencies included Coyne PR, Edelman, Fenton, FleishmanHillard, Havas PR North America, Sunshine Sachs, Turner 4d, and Weber Shandwick. The team kicked off in early 2014 by targeting a large array of media, then launched a full media rollout in September. No matter the market, local media were also targeted with dedicated press releases, event information, and support. GT grew to have activities in more than 68 countries in 2014 (up from 46 the previous year).

The #GivingTuesday hashtag was used in all references, and on December 2, others were inspired to use the free tools and resources to share stories and photos about people giving back as it happened.

The campaign was a coordinated, shareable conversation that raised support for causes worldwide. On Twitter alone, the hashtag was tweeted 754,000 times, up 180% over last year. During the same period (December 1–3), the hashtag #UNselfie was tweeted 39,700 times (183% more than 2013), and 7,600-plus #UNselfie photos were posted on Instagram.

Tweets ranged from *The Economist* to Calgary United Way, from Bill Gates to Justin Timberlake, among so many others. Events ranged from the United Nations Development Program's first global digital art show and auction, which raised funds and awareness for the continuing Ebola plight to challenge grants and more on Ireland's first #GivingTuesday.

Evaluation

The overall campaign received more than 20 billion total print, online, and broadcast media impressions. On #GivingTuesday nonprofits raised amounts up 63% over 2013 on five major donation-processing platforms. Indiegogo raised more than $9.4 million for 423 organizations (three times the amount raised in 2013), Network for Good reported processing $4.6 million, with the number of donations up 195%, and PayPal saw a year-over-year increase of 66% in payments to Canadian and U.S. charities (with a 101% increase in mobile payments).

ENGAGE

▸ Search and discover which organizations have joined as sponsors since 2015 and their experiences. For example, GlobalGiving is a crowdfunding community that participated as a partner in #Giving Tuesday in 2016.

▸ Search on csrwire.com for "GlobalGiving Breaks Donation Records on #GivingTuesday," and explore how they did this.

DISCUSS

▸ #GivingTuesday is not focused on a single charity but rather on suggesting many ways people may be generous and supportive of whatever cause they choose. How does this approach differ from simply asking for funds to support a specific charity?

Note: This case describes a 2015 PRSA Silver Anvil Award of Excellence Winner, Nonprofit Organizations.

VIDEO CASE

Panera Bread: Social Media Campaign Development

In 2010, Panera Bread, a national chain of bakery-cafés, opened the first of several Panera Cares cafés, where patrons are not charged a fixed amount for menu items but, instead, pay whatever they are able. Some customers get their food for free or very little, while others choose to pay more to subsidize meals for those in need.

VIDEO

1. How could Panera Bread use social media to launch a new Panera Cares location most effectively?

2. What would be the pros and cons of using each of the major social media platforms in this endeavor?

3. How would you measure the effectiveness of the social media campaign?

PRACTICE AND APPLY WHAT YOU'VE LEARNED

edge.sagepub.com/page

CHECK YOUR COMPREHENSION
ON THE STUDY SITE WITH:

- eFlashcards to strengthen your understanding of key terms

- Practice quizzes to test your comprehension of key concepts

- Videos and multimedia content to enhance your exploration of key topics

Corporate Social Responsibility and Community Relations

Learning Objectives

9.1   Understand the connection between PR and CSR

9.2   Examine how successful CSR activity is part of organizational culture and reputation management

9.3   Evaluate the opportunities and challenges in mounting an effective internal and external CSR campaign

9.4   Understand the PR practice of community relations and its connection to CSR

How Do Smaller U.S. Businesses Practice and Communicate Their Corporate Social Responsibility?

Cheerios partners with the American Heart Association and makes that obvious on its packaging with a heart-shaped cereal bowl, but what do the Blue Goose Market or Graham's Chocolates do to be good citizens and let their communities know?

This is the question posed to eight small Illinois businesses by one of this book's authors (Page & Page, 2013). It's an important question because 89.6% of U.S. firms had less than 20 employees in 2012 according to the Small Business and Entrepreneurship Council (SBE, n.d.).

All locally owned, the eight businesses included an insurance company, a coffee shop, a bicycle retailer, an entertainment venue, a sweet shop, a grocery store, a sports club, and a sandwich shop. Half of the businesses were family owned, and employees numbered between 13 and 90.

Small businesses can find that informing the public about their charitable work or efforts at sustainability can be challenging.

iStock.com/4×6

"It's the right thing to do." All owners agreed that "community philanthropy" is their preferred CSR practice, which included donating gift cards, discounted or free products, coupons, rent-free space, and sometimes just cash. A culture of giving flows from employees and family members as well as walk-in requests. Their charitable practices are motivated by personal principles and a sense of community obligation. Some of the owners explained, "It's how I was raised." "It comes from my roots in a small town." In all cases the most common word used when describing their reasons for engaging in CSR was "community." And the biggest beneficiaries of all charitable efforts were children.

"Our acts are seeding more acts." Did they expect anything in return for their good works? A few had no expectations, some placed further philanthropy expectations on the recipients, and others hoped it would build awareness and understanding of who they were. A majority saw their business ethos as playing a key role in building a better community. "We do what we do to bond the community together."

"We do things quietly." When asked if they publicize their charity in any way, however, the response from every participant was not only that they did not, but they felt to do so was somehow distasteful. Indeed most of the respondents appeared slightly offended by the question and often answered in a reproachful tone. Their answers sometimes derided boasting: "I wouldn't polish my own badge." "We don't go around tooting our own horn." Or their answers indicated some distaste with the question: "That would be bragging." These attitudes carried through any of the various ways questions were asked about how they communicated CSR to the public and the media or what their expectations were of their charitable efforts. Nearly all agreed that their CSR involvement is "strategic," yet most of them had no communication strategy and little structure to measure effectiveness.

Use the lessons in this chapter to help you answer these questions:

1. Why should the businesses communicate CSR with their publics?

2. What benefits are these local businesses missing from failing to communicate their good works?

3. What methods should the businesses use to communicate their good works?

At the end of the chapter, you'll find some advice.

This chapter reveals how the CSR movement is influencing firms to perform as good corporate citizens with obligations to society and the environment while, at the same time, nurturing the health of their business. You'll find the wisdom for guiding CSR is understanding an organization's multiple stakeholders, ranging from employees to investors. You'll also learn why choosing CSR programs that match up with a firm's brand identity and organizational culture is essential.

Profiles, insights, and cases demonstrate how CEOs lead CSR through example and activism, how employees become more engaged through volunteering, and how PR plays an integral role. You'll also discover the six major areas of CSR activity: **cause promotions**, **cause-related marketing**, **corporate social marketing**, **corporate philanthropy**, **community volunteering**, and **socially responsible business practices**. How and why certain businesses perform responsibly is explained, covering differences among multinational corporations, benefit corporations, and social entrepreneurships—and the varying roles of PR in each.

Finally the chapter covers the essential elements of effective CSR communications strategy, including research, traditional and social tactics, evaluation, and an important focus on community relations.

SOCIAL RESPONSIBILITY AND THE ESSENTIAL ROLE OF PUBLIC RELATIONS

>> LO 9.1   Understand the connection between PR and CSR

Most definitions of CSR agree that it is the deliberate inclusion of public interest into corporate decision-making. This honoring of a **triple bottom line** (the three Ps) refers to people (social), planet (environmental), and profit (economic), suggesting the three performance areas that a company should serve and measure. As stated in Chapter 1, CSR is widely defined as "the sum of the voluntary actions taken by a company to address the economic, social and environmental impacts of its business operations and the concerns of its principal stakeholders" (Jones-Christensen et al., 2007).

Master the content
edge.sagepub.com/page

The key word in this definition is "voluntary" because the actions or activities are not required of the company or organization by any government or regulatory body. They are done at a company's discretion. This distinction is one key to actually considering something to be CSR versus a legal obligation such as paying taxes, maintaining safe working conditions, paying a minimum wage, and so on. While in many European countries there are national policies and legislation surrounding CSR, in the United States, social, environmental, and economic factors drive the implementation of CSR.

SOCIAL RESPONSIBILITY IS FOUNDATIONAL IN PUBLIC RELATIONS TODAY

Behind the more obvious impetus for a company's socially responsible actions—flood victims in need of shelter or beaches needing a cleanup—it is the business's stakeholders who serve as a driving force for organizational change, encouraging more ethical behavior and transparency. Companies and organizations are transforming the way they do business, resulting in a broad spectrum of socially responsible activities and practices, aligned with stated organizational values.

A critical role of PR professionals today, whether in agencies or in house, is to serve as counselors to executive management. Guided by the business's values and stakeholders, PR shapes relationship-building programs and communication strategies toward positive outcomes, generating multiple SR benefits while at the same time building trust, positive reputation, a competitive market position, and bottom-line rewards.

EVER-CHANGING DEMANDS OF STAKEHOLDERS

To develop an SR strategy, it is necessary to recognize and consider an organization's many stakeholders. PR collaborates with leadership to identify and understand the makeup of an organization's stakeholders and how to prioritize them. This practice has been studied and analyzed through research: Over the past decade, the majority of studies on CSR and PR reveals that stakeholder concerns are the most dominant perspective (Ho Lee, 2017).

Stakeholders are the various individuals or groups who affect or are affected by an organization. Understanding the needs and concerns of stakeholders, for example, by meeting with employees, is one way to develop a social responsibility strategy.

Paul J. Richards/AFP/Getty Images

WHO IS A STAKEHOLDER?

Collectively stakeholders are the various groups or individuals who can affect or are affected by (either voluntarily or involuntarily) the actions of an organization. An accepted way to categorize stakeholders is into three different groups (see Figure 9.1), with connecting relationships among each of them (Chandler, 2017).

A pragmatic consideration is to determine which stakeholders have the capacity to affect a firm's operations and are motivated to act. The answers are often situational; while the organizational and economic stakeholders may at times be more *meaningful* stakeholders, the agents and entities not directly connected to an organization (societal stakeholders) may also become significant. For example, Exxon's stance on climate change is one that a number of stakeholders may feel is relevant, yet it is particularly relevant to groups like Greenpeace, which may act to shape the behavior they want from the corporation.

PRIORITIZING STAKEHOLDERS

One way to prioritize stakeholders is by categorizing them as primary and secondary:

▸ Primary stakeholders have some direct interest or stake in the organization, for example, shareholders or owners, employees, customers, business partners, and often communities.

▸ Secondary stakeholders, in contrast, are those that do not have a direct stake in the organization but are still affected by its operations, for example, public or special interest groups, competitors, and the media.

However, the complexities of the issue at hand and instances of stakeholders' competing interests can make prioritizing a challenge. Issues may range widely, from an institutional crisis that places a firm in a defensive mode to a proactive adoption of environmental practices that can create a leadership platform around an emerging issue.

What's important to realize is that organizations do not define societal values; they reflect them (Chandler, 2017, p. 93). Ultimately, important to CSR as a logical argument, it is in an organization's best interests to recognize and meet needs and desires of the broadest swath of its stakeholders to the best of its ability.

FIGURE 9.1

Who Is a Stakeholder?

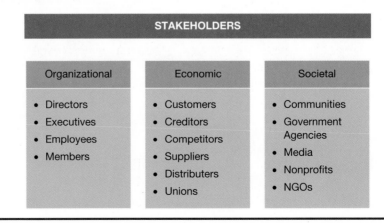

TABLE 9.1

Seven Pillars of Strategic CSR

PILLAR	FOCUS
Integrated With Firm	Firms incorporate a CSR perspective within their culture and strategic planning process with the leadership, acceptance, and support of top management.
Business Relevant	The strategy should have a viable connection to a firm's core operations.
Stakeholder Interests	Firms seek to understand and respond to the needs of their stakeholders.
Strategic Plan	Objectives should be identified to meet goals through effective tactics.
Optimized Value	Firms aim to optimize the value that's created.
Evaluation	A specific plan should be in place to evaluate and analyze the program.
Not Short Term	Medium- to long-term CSR allows positive relationship management with stakeholders.

Sources: Chandler (2017, p. 248); Parnell, Strategic Public Relations (SPR) Master's Program

STRATEGIC BENEFITS OF SOCIAL RESPONSIBILITY

A firm and its stakeholders are synonymous in that a firm cannot exist independently of its stakeholders. A firm solves problems that have economic, social, moral, and ethical components and implications. This synergistic relationship between the firm and its stakeholders is why CSR is a key element of business strategy (Chandler, 2017, p. 246). "CSR is not about saving the whales or ending poverty or other worthwhile goals that are unrelated to a firm's operations and are better left to government or nonprofits," writes David Chandler, author of *Strategic Corporate Social Responsibility: Sustainable Value Creation*. "Instead, CSR is about the economic, legal, ethical, and discretionary issues that stakeholders view as directly related to the firm." He proposes seven pillars of strategic CSR (see Table 9.1).

Beyond *strategic CSR*, a company can "do good" by engaging in *responsive CSR* (Porter & Kramer, 2006, p. 89). These social or environmental efforts aren't tied to its business purpose or actions but rather to broader issues peripheral to the firm. Strategic CSR, however, engages in social or environmental efforts connected to issues that are central to the firm.

SIX PRACTICE AREAS OF CORPORATE SOCIAL RESPONSIBILITY

Breaking CSR programs down into different categories of activity helps explain strategic CSR and how it connects to the firm. There are six areas (Kotler & Lee, 2005) where CSR activities typically fall. Although there is no absolute rule to this, by identifying

TABLE 9.2

Six Types of Corporate Social Responsibility Engagement

TYPE	DEFINITION	EXAMPLE
Cause Promotions	Providing or donating money to support or increase awareness and concern for a cause or charity	Scotts Miracle-Gro matches customer donations for the Cleveland Clinic.
Cause-Related Marketing	Contributions to a cause or charity based on a percentage of sales revenues	Starbucks donates 10 cents for every handcrafted beverage sold to the Global Fund to Fight AIDS.
Corporate Social Marketing	Support for a behavior changing campaign to improve safety, health, or the environment	Allstate funds a campaign to stop teens from texting while driving.
Corporate Philanthropy	Direct contribution to a charity or cause	Google donates computers to school children to support computer science education.
Community Volunteering	Encouraging and facilitating employees to get involved in a cause via time off or sabbaticals	To serve its global community, Dow Corning sends employees to China to teach students scientific innovation.
Socially Responsible Business Practices	Adopting discretionary business practices to support causes or issues	Procter & Gamble has more than 80 "zero manufacturing waste" facilities around the world.

what type of CSR activity the company is practicing (or trying to practice), you can better evaluate its effectiveness in connecting to the business and communicating it to stakeholders. Knowing the six areas also is essential is making recommendations to your client or CEO about initiating CSR engagement (see Table 9.2).

Larger for-profit corporations, for example, Starbucks, may engage is all six areas of CSR. A good source for exploring firms' activities is the Reports page on csrwire. com. It features and links to recently published CSR and **sustainability** reports and press releases associated with them. Another avenue is to find links to detailed information and reports on individual corporate websites, usually located under a "social responsibility" or "sustainability" title.

Smaller to medium-sized firms may limit their engagement to philanthropy and volunteering. Other companies that are formed or structured with the priority of benefiting society often focus solely on socially responsible business practices. This chapter's special insights section, "The New Heroes: Social Entrepreneurs," talks about this growing sector.

SUCCESSFUL CORPORATE SOCIAL RESPONSIBILITY FLOWS FROM BUSINESS CULTURE AND BUILDS REPUTATION

>> **LO 9.2** **Examine how successful CSR activity is part of organizational culture and reputation management**

Successful, ongoing CSR activities have a few key building blocks in common, beginning with a connection to the organization's business and ending with a

The New Heroes: Social Entrepreneurs

The concept of **social entrepreneurship** started to gain serious attention in the mid-1990s with the Harvard Business School's 1993 launch of the Social Enterprise Initiative. The concept has since gained serious momentum in the 21st century (About History, n.d.). Many universities have developed research and training programs, and business incubators, offering undergraduate majors and minors, graduate programs, and shorter executive certificate programs to help social entrepreneurs succeed. Social entrepreneurs have been called the "new heroes" (Lauterer, 2005), pioneering breakthrough approaches to some of the world's most pressing problems (Elkington & Hartigan, 2008).

Social entrepreneurship differs from CSR in that its *priority* is to pursue a transformational benefit to society rather than generate substantial financial gain. This does not mean that social entrepreneurs do not make profits (they can be organized as for-profits or nonprofits), but social benefit characterizes their mission.

Social entrepreneurships tend to value relationships, taking a communal versus individualistic orientation, thus community building is a natural outcome. According to the Skoll Foundation, a promoter of social entrepreneurship worldwide, social entrepreneurs recognize social and environmental needs for change and then develop programs to address and solve the problems (Skoll Foundation, n.d.). For social entrepreneurships, supporting fund-raising is often a key objective requiring communication strategies. Some social entrepreneurships obtain the following legal status or certification:

Benefit corporation is a legal status, like a traditional corporation or a nonprofit corporation, that establishes the corporation must have a material positive benefit on society and the environment. In some states it specifically must consider its effects on all of its stakeholders. Each year it must publish a public report on its performance.

Companies as well-known as Patagonia, Kickstarter, and Eileen Fisher are benefit corporations, as are lesser known companies, for example, Global Cycling Adventures, Urban Space real estate, and Comet Skateboards.

B Corporation certification differs from a benefit corporation in that it is a certification, not a legal status. B Lab serves as an online hub for B corporation certification, measuring companies' rigorous adherence to SR and sustainability. B Lab partners with B the Change Media, which disseminates stories across print, digital, video, and live event platforms.

B Lab also annually reviews ratings of the more than 1,800 B corporation-certified companies worldwide to determine a list of the top 500 "Best For The World" companies (Be the Change Media, n.d.). In 2016, for example, Colorado's New Belgium Brewing Company was ranked one of the overall best companies with 250 or more employees. ●

---

thorough assessment of their results. Determining how the efforts are impacting the end recipients or cause is only one measurement; learning how various stakeholders interpret your CSR is critical, too. A desired outcome is enhanced reputation, sometimes spurred on by the visibility of an activist CEO.

KEY BUILDING BLOCKS OF CORPORATE SOCIAL RESPONSIBILITY

When it comes to *communicating* CSR, most research indicates that messages about CSR that are perceived as a "corporate fit" enjoy greater credibility and are therefore more effective than messages perceived as not a "fit." Consider Starbucks, whose mission is to "share great coffee with our friends and to help make the world a little better" (Starbucks, n.d.). Its CSR includes ethical and sustainable sourcing of coffee, tea, cocoa, and merchandise; environmental practices in its stores including waste and recycling and water and energy conservation; employee benefits like its "bean stock" stock option policy; and youth programs and community service projects. Starbucks's CSR initiatives have a few key things in common (see Table 9.3).

TABLE 9.3

Starbucks Corporate Social Responsibility: Ethical Sourcing

Fit	Tied to the business of the company	Coffee responsibly grown and ethically traded
Buy-In	Acceptance and support of top management	CSR led by long-time CEO Howard Schultz
Legs	Can and will continue beyond the year of its introduction.	2008 to 2015, increased ethically sourced coffee from 75% to 99%
Objectives	Strategy to meet overall goal through tactics	Inform and support coffee producers in the practices and benefits of meeting ethical standards
Measurement	Specific plan to evaluate and analyze program	Trained personnel third-party inspection and verification process

---

SOCIAL RESPONSIBILITY IN ACTION

Rumi Spice: Peace Through Trade

Rumi Spice works with Afghan farmers to grow saffron and make the crop profitable enough to discourage poppy cultivation. The founders appeared on the television show *Shark Tank* in 2016, seeking investment to grow the business.

Alamy Stock Photo

"Bomb-blasted roads, frequent blackouts, shortages of basic equipment and an untested consumer market are hardly conditions that make for natural entrepreneurial opportunities," begins a *New York Times* report (McConnon, 2016). Yet Rumi Spice proves they are.

Kimberly Jung Used to Search for Roadside Bombs in Afghanistan

But when her tour as an officer in the Army Corps of Engineers was over, she enrolled in Harvard Business School. This led to an amazing new venture: a small saffron processing plant in Herat, Afghanistan. Together with two other military veterans and a civilian, Jung returned to Afghanistan in 2014 to start Rumi Spice, a certified B corporation, providing high-quality, sustainably farmed saffron to international consumers—directly sourced from rural Afghan farmers.

Her Goal Now Is Replacing Opium With a Spice

Saffron, one of the most labor-intensive and expensive spices in the world, grows well in the hot, dry climate of Afghanistan. The cofounders envisioned helping the farmers sell their saffron to a global market, hopefully replacing the poppy crops used to make opium that helps fund the Taliban.

Empowering Farmers and Women

A major strategy cuts out the middleman, thus tripling the income for small-scale farmers. Beyond empowering farmers, it also employs 300 to 400 women in its processing plant during harvest season, paying them directly rather than following the Afghan practice of paying the male household head.

"Doing Food" Rewarded

Structured as a benefit corporation, it is required by law to report both societal impact and profit to shareholders. As the company grew through socially conscious investors, it sought messaging guidance from FamilyFarmed, a nonprofit incubator for food start-ups that connects new companies with retailers like Whole Foods.

Branding Shift

With this new guidance, it shifted its brand identity from "helping Afghan farmers to displace opium production" to the more simplified—and more strategic to high-end consumers—"ethical luxury brand" (McConnon, 2016), and it now partners with Michelin-rated restaurants and world-renowned chefs.

For communication strategies, the business uses Facebook, Twitter, Instagram, Pinterest, and an e-newsletter and has had feature coverage in *The New York Times*, the *Chicago Tribune*, NPR, PBS, and various online news sites (Rumi Spice, n.d.). ●

Being ethically sourced concerns the well-being of the producer, the farming and financial practices, SR, and environmental leadership, among other areas. Explore the questionnaire inspectors use to evaluate and verify that Starbucks's coffee is ethically sourced: https://www.scsglobalservices.com/files/cocoa_scr_v3.1_en_112015.pdf.

MORE CORPORATE SOCIAL RESPONSIBILITY BUILDING BLOCKS

Basic components of CSR include stakeholder engagement. Ideal initiatives should be participatory for customers, employees, and any volunteers involved, and the initiatives should adapt well to social media. There is significant PR potential in CSR, for example, announcing the launch, making progress reports, storytelling, and so on. However, the values of the intended audience should also be considered. Recent research (Villagra, Cardaba, & Ruiz San Ramon, 2015) shows that personal fit is also critical for positive perception. Thus adding a personal appeal by demonstrating relevance to the receiver may offset any chance of CSR messaging sending the wrong signal that it's done for promotional purposes.

Prime extensions of CSR are all the crossover applications, including internal communications to employees, advertising and merchandising tie-ins, attracting business partnerships, and providing shareholders with updates.

POSITIVE IMPACT ON REPUTATION

CSR can positively impact a company's perceived reputation. Cone Communications, a national leader in CSR and cause marketing, finds a majority of global consumers value social and environmental responsibility and look to companies as partners in progress (Cone, 2015a).

These findings reinforce Nielsen's 2015 Global Survey on CSR (Nielsen, 2015a) that reported 66% of consumers will pay more for sustainable brands. Millennials are even more engaged, with 73% willing to pay more. Millennials, while diverse, are found to be the most sustainability-conscious and CSR-engaged generation, with 91% willing to switch brands to one associated with a cause and two-thirds using social media to amplify a company's social responsible messages (Cone, 2015b).

Several sources measure and evaluate businesses' CSR engagement and reputation. The Global CSR RepTrak® 100, produced by the Reputation Institute, annually measures the reputation of the 100 most highly regarded companies across 15 countries. In 2016 these "top ten" companies ranked as "perceived to be the most socially responsible" (see Figure 9.2):

FIGURE 9.2

Top Ten Most Highly Regarded Companies

1. Google
2. Microsoft
3. Walt Disney
4. BMW
5. Lego
6. Daimler
7. Apple
8. Rolls-Royce
9. Rolex
10. Intel

Source: Reputation Institute (2016).

CORPORATE SOCIAL RESPONSIBILITY COMMUNICATION IS ESSENTIAL

The Global CSR RepTrak® 100 report notes, "Communication is required to capitalize on good reality and overcome poor perceptions" (Reputation Institute, 2016, p. 33). The report illustrates this by graphing the companies' actual CSR engagement with consumers' perceptions. In actual CSR, Unilever scores as high as BMW, but in reputation, BMW ranks fourth highest, yet Unilever ranks 88th. The report interprets this gap to a lack of consumer information about Unilever's CSR performance.

The RepTrak report recommends that for companies with a weak reputation, third-party communications have a strong impact on the CSR perception, primarily online and broadcast news sources and people's social media blogs, comments, and posts. For companies with a strong reputation, RepTrak recommends controlled communications have the strongest impact on CSR perception, primarily the company website, newsletters, e-mails from the company, ads, customer service, company events, and social media postings.

CEOs TAKE STANCES ON SOCIAL ISSUES

People want CEOs to speak up on issues linked to business. Corporate CEOs are increasingly speaking out about social and environmental issues such as climate change, income fairness, same-sex marriage, immigration, gun control, and discrimination—all issues that are not necessarily tied to the bottom line. And nearly 40% of American adults believe that CEOs have a responsibility to publicly address these hot-button issues, finds a 2016 survey by PR firm Weber Shandwick (KRC Research, n.d.).

However, when the issues are not directly linked to the company's business, one-third of Americans feel less favorable. For example, former Starbucks head Howard Schultz has publicly supported gun control and promoted race relations, despite risking offending employees, customers, or investors. PR should counsel management that making a closer link to business may help explain why CEOs are speaking up on societal issues.

CEO ACTIVISM INFLUENCES PURCHASE INTENT

A CEO's stance on controversial issues can also work for or against the company when it comes to sales. Along with approving CEO activism, 40% of Americans also say they are more likely to buy from a company when they agree with the CEO on an issue. However, slightly more (45%) say they are less likely to buy if they disagree with the CEO's position (KRC Research, n.d.). Since a CEO's external stance may affect behavior as basic as buying a product, companies need to have a firm understanding of the attitudes of key customers and other stakeholders before CEO activism goes public.

AMERICANS UNSURE OF MOTIVATIONS

When it comes to motive, CEOs' altruism is doubted. Americans feel the leading reason for CEO activism is to get media attention. Americans believe the second most-common reason is that CEOs are trying to build their own reputation. Just 14% thought CEOs are becoming more outspoken to "do what is right for society" (KRC Research, n.d.).

Most Socially Responsible Company in the World

Google has an excellent reputation for philanthropy and social responsibility.

iStock.com/tomch

Google's active philanthropy, socially responsible engagement, and environmental initiatives give new meaning to the phrase, "just Google it." In 2016 it topped the Global RepTrak® 100s ranking of best CSR reputation (Reputation Institute, 2016). Consider the wide range of activities that helped Google earn its exceptional reputation. While some are broad, many directly support the company's stated mission to organize the world's information and make it universally accessible and useful (Google, n.d.).

Helping Close the Education Gap

Google committed $50 million in 2016–2018 to support nonprofits that build tech-based learning solutions to tackle education challenges.

Hosts Annual "Geo for Good" User Summit

This is a free day workshop for nonprofit mapping and technology specialists.

Low Food Waste

In 2016 Google cafés in the Bay Area saved more than 1 million pounds of food from going to waste.

Carbon Neutral Since 2007, 100% Renewable Energy by 2017

This includes all global operations.

Racial and Social Justice

Google donated $11.5 million to nonprofits focused on racial and social justice and funded a first-of-its-kind 3-D interactive exhibit in the Smithsonian's National Museum of African American History and Culture.

Code for America

Google gives $3 million annually to help citizens develop technological solutions for local, county, and state governments.

Global Technology Initiatives

- Caring for China, Google's China Social Innovation Cup, is the country's first nationwide competition aimed at empowering China's college students to address pressing social issues through grassroots, innovative solutions.

- In Korea the Digital Media Campus educates both kids and parents.

- In France the Google Impact Challenge enables nonprofits to enhance their work through digital technologies.

- In Germany, Google funded educational programs using robots to teach children foundational technical concepts.

- In the U.K. and Japan it funded Raspberry Pi computers for 20,000 children to encourage their enthusiasm for computer science.

- Google supported the Clooney Foundation for Justice with a $1 million educational grant for refugee children in Lebanon. ●

MILLENNIALS MORE LIKELY TO GIVE THUMBS-UP

The largest generation in the workplace and the most coveted demographic for many marketers, those ages 18 to 35, are significantly more likely than others to be loyal to an employer if the CEO speaks out publicly on a controversial issue. More than one-third expressed loyalty compared to one-fifth of those ages 36 to 51. Even stronger, nearly half of Millennials say that they will buy from companies whose CEOs take a public position on an issue they agree with.

Top-level executives at major corporations are increasingly speaking out on social and environmental issues. Warren Buffett is well known for his philanthropic efforts and political views.

Alex Wong/Getty Images

Activist CEO Paul Polman of Unilever—one of the world's biggest consumer product companies encompassing Ben & Jerry's ice cream, Dove soap, Lipton tea, Hellmann's mayonnaise and other products—says, "We are finding out quite rapidly that to be successful long term we have to ask: What do we actually give to society to make it better? We've made it clear to the organization that it's our business model, starting from the top" (Browne & Nuttall, 2013, para. 15).

COMMUNICATING CORPORATE SOCIAL RESPONSIBILITY: OPPORTUNITIES AND CHALLENGES

>> **LO 9.3   Evaluate the opportunities and challenges in mounting an effective internal and external CSR campaign**

Increasingly CSR is a clear path for communications professionals to get that proverbial "seat at the table." The ideal executive to manage the CSR process is the communications professional—since this activity is truly a combination of issues management, stakeholder relations (internal and external), media relations, and event planning. Properly planned and executed, CSR touches all aspects of a company's operations and if done well can pay enormous dividends in terms of reputation, shareholder value, and desirability as an employer.

For the large, publicly traded, or multinational corporation, well-communicated CSR helps meet the goals of building corporate reputation, attracting investors, supporting recruitment and retention, and increasing profits. For the smaller socially conscious firm, communicating its mission and practice is essential in helping raise funds as well as build awareness, reputation, and often customers.

The Art of Being More in a World of Change

Mike Fernandez, U.S. Chief Executive Officer, Burson-Marsteller

The world we live in is more social and contentious than ever. It is also an era of scientific discovery, technological advancement, and global business and educational opportunity. Because of this, it is an extraordinary time to be a PR professional.

PR professionals are being asked to play bigger roles in their organizations. It is not enough to be a good communicator, writer, event organizer, or adept website and app designer. The complexities of the world require us to think deeply, ask questions, act with urgency, and be problem solvers.

Looking back, I believe I was prepared for this world by my humble beginnings. My mother was raised in an orphanage in South Carolina, and my father was one of nine children in Spanish Harlem (New York City). Growing up, I lived in four states and attended nine different schools—K through 12. Those moves, along with having a foot in both the American and Hispanic cultures, forced me to become adaptable, see change as positive, seize new opportunity, and become a student of people, cultures, and customs.

That orientation would serve me well as a young press secretary in the U.S. Senate, working for Senator Fritz Hollings (D, South Carolina) and also through my long career in PR—including 20 years as a chief communications officer (CCO) at Fortune 100 companies including Cargill and State Farm Insurance—and now in my role at B-M.

Working in politics early in my career, I learned two very important lessons. One, winning a highly contested campaign (in politics or business) requires talking to more than just your base. And two, it becomes harder to hate someone you have gotten to know and understand, even if you still disagree on the details or approach to an issue.

For example, my first meetings at Cargill with NGOs and community groups were not about establishing CSR initiatives. Instead they entailed meeting with skeptics and critics who took issue with our complex global supply chain and trying to find common ground.

None of this was easy. What we eventually agreed upon required changing our operations, incentivizing farmers and other suppliers, and working closely with stakeholders so we were clear about timelines and directions. As a result, Cargill not only advanced environmental and societal improvements but did so in a way that provided our customers with the competitively priced, sustainably grown, and responsibly processed food they and their consumers wanted.

Over time Cargill would receive many honors and recognitions from industry, environmental, and PR groups. For example, in 2014 the Cargill communications team won *PRWeek*'s Global Program of the Year Award, and in 2015 *Fortune* magazine listed Cargill among the top 50 "Change the World" companies making a positive global impact.

And it all started with asking good questions and working with—not always against—others who had different points of view. ●

Source: M. Fernandez (personal communication, 2017).

WHAT IS CORPORATE SOCIAL RESPONSIBILITY COMMUNICATIONS?

A formal definition offered by the Corporate and Marketing Communication Association reads, "The process of anticipating stakeholder expectations, articulation of corporate social responsible policy, and the managing of different communication tools designed to provide true and transparent information about a company or a brand's integration of its business operations, social and environmental concerns, and interactions with stakeholders" (CMCA, n.d.).

Yet the right way to talk about a firm's CSR has been somewhat problematical. It can be perceived as simply self-promotional, or even **greenwashing**, misleading consumers regarding the firm's environmental practices or the environmental

A company's CSR efforts must be handled carefully so as not to be seen as self-promoting or engaging in "greenwashing."

iStock.com/bodo23

benefits of a certain product. Fortunately, a lot of recent attention has been focused on the role of PR in effective CSR communications. Ethical awareness and performance characterize today's engaged PR professionals. Both company and professional codes of conduct shape their involvement with CSR planning, performance, and communication.

Today's PR professionals think and perform strategically, advising how CSR initiatives support a company's mission and formulating plans to communicate CSR to key stakeholders, both internal and external. This strategy also involves making logical choices of which communication channels to use. There are many choices, including packaging, events, interviews, websites, ads, newsletters, press releases, social media, and video storytelling. Basically it's important to talk about CSR— its successes, lessons learned, even trouble spots—and essential to develop strong relationships with media.

BEST PRACTICES IN CORPORATE SOCIAL RESPONSIBILITY COMMUNICATIONS

Most Americans can't go through a day without interacting with multiple brands. It's a fact of life, and in most cases preferred brands make life easier, more entertaining, more comfortable, and so on. The close relationship between people and the brands they live with helps explain why corporations that "do good" matter to them. People want to know the impact "their" brands have on social and environmental issues. Many people likely won't read a firm's annual report or CSR report—usually tucked away in a corner of a company website. There are, however, many communication options available.

A GOOD STARTING POINT

A successful CSR communications strategy begins with research. What are the values and principles the company has identified and structured past communications on? What do loyal customers know and believe about the firm or product? As CSR engagement should be tied to the firm's purpose and values, talking to customers with familiar language provides an authentic voice to CSR messaging. It rings true.

Also pay attention to the moment, the immediate environment, emerging societal issues, and concerns, and identify how the firm's CSR relates to or addresses them. Your audience is enmeshed in contemporary culture, so signaling the firm is actively addressing a current issue gives it credibility and immediacy.

Finally, remember that two-way dialogue is much better than one-way when it comes to CSR. Turn to social media platforms to know what key stakeholders are talking about, thinking, and feeling to influence how to craft compelling messages.

HOW TO TALK "CORPORATE SOCIAL RESPONSIBILITY"

In his book *Corporate Responsibility* (Argenti, 2016, pp. 293–296), business professor Paul Argenti shares wisdom gained from his distinguished career in corporate management, responsibility, and communication (see Figure 9.3).

FIGURE 9.3

Seven Tips for Effective CSR Communications

Avoid empty boasting.

- When talking about your CSR activities and outcomes, focus on authenticity by offering substance.

Match rhetoric with action.

- Differentiate your company from those that may be greenwashing by not making empty promises.

Be transparent.

- Tell the truth, good and bad. Being transparent with stakeholders about less-than-positive news allows companies to build trust. Avoid ambiguous or confusing language. Simple and direct is more authentic.

Know your audience.

- Identify the issues most relevant to select stakeholders, and know how to reach them with focused messaging.

Create an ongoing dialogue.

- Two-way dialogic communication is the ideal. Both reporting . . . and listening . . . create authentic communication and help you understand the expectations and concerns of your publics—and to adapt.

Listen . . . and collaborate.

- Beyond knowing who to talk to, know who's talking about you. Engage NGO or nonprofit partners as allies in your communication strategies.

Focus on employee engagement.

- Thoughtful internal communication about CSR can result in a more engaged workforce.

S-T-R-E-T-C-H THE ANNUAL
REPORT INTO MULTIMEDIA

One company took its sustainability report, typically just printed each year, to new heights with more engaging content and lively formats: video, infographics, blog posts, press releases, and other digital assets (Weiland, 2016).

Domtar Corporation, the largest producer of paper in the United States, is a leader in sustainable forestry practices. 3BL Media worked with Domtar to develop a communications strategy. The result was a traditional printed copy of the annual sustainability report but also a smaller brochure, a wallet card version, posters, and a multi-platform digital strategy that broke the report up into eight natural sections with 40 different stories. One or two of the stories were highlighted every week over a five-month period, and a "highlight" reel of the entire report was also created. Bite-size pieces of content were distributed over social media through this time. Analytics feedback helped evaluate which stories performed the best, helping inform future annual reports.

This case illustrates the utility in optimizing content, extending to different audiences, and increasing the life span of a story. With media consumption a 24-hour occupation, and fast-moving streams of content, creative messaging and channeling can secure interest and engagement from desired audiences (Weiland, 2016).

When Corporate Social Responsibility and News Reports Collide

Sometimes the best CSR reputations have blemishes, brought to light through investigative reporting. At Abbott Laboratories' "Citizenship" page on its http://www.abbott.com, a link to Citizenship Reporting reveals reports by country. The firm's 2015 India Citizenship Highlights Report covers various aspects of its business in India—its largest outside of the United States.

You learn Abbott has been "helping the people of India to live their best lives for more than 100 years" (Abbott in India, n.d.). It reports on the quality of its plants, its environmental sustainability efforts, its commitment to local sourcing, its products geared to the nutritional needs of local consumers, its efforts to empower women and girls, its support of local sanitation, its fight against diabetes, and its product donations to support disaster relief and humanitarian programs in India. Abbott Labs was named *Fortune* magazine's number one most admired company for SR in 2015 and has been a leading company in the Dow Jones Sustainability World Index regularly since 2004.

Yet a 2016 article in *The New York Times* carried the headline, "Driven to Suicide by an 'Inhuman and Unnatural' Pressure to Sell" (Anand & Joelving, 2016). The *Times* reported the stress that employees were under in Abbott Laboratories operations in India, telling the story of a young Abbott salesman—one of the company's top performers there—who had jumped in front of a train.

A six-month investigation by the *New York Times* found that in the "push to win customers in India's chaotic and highly competitive drug market, some Abbott managers instructed employees to pursue sales at virtually any cost—in violation of Indian law, professional medical standards, and the company's own ethics guidelines." The report cited sales agents fired or resigning due to immense pressure to conduct business in unethical ways. These included submitting fake invoices, giving kickbacks to wholesalers, and being persuaded to use their own money to buy expensive medicines to help meet sales targets.

Sales teams were also found to be running health camps that misdiagnosed patients for unnecessary treatment—with Abbott drugs. Abbott promotes its health camps as a core part of its CSR program. When CSR and negative news collide like in this case of Abbott Labs and its India operations, issues management (covered in Chapter 10) offers guidance on proper ways for a PR professional to counsel management's response. ●

COMMUNITY RELATIONS AND CORPORATE SOCIAL RESPONSIBILITY

>> LO 9.4 Understand the PR practice of community relations and its connection to CSR

It's essential for an organization to cultivate good relationships with the communities in which it operates. From local communities come employees and customers—and sometimes donors and investors. PR duties involve fostering and maintaining strategic relationships with community members. They can range from groups who may be impacted by building or relocating a business to diverse publics categorized by age, ethnicity, diversity, or special concerns. Practitioners of community relations must understand the structure, strengths, and weaknesses of a community before setting community outreach goals and objectives for the organization.

The PR professional who specializes in community relations is typically immersed in the community, humanizing the business by putting a visible and accessible face on it. She or he attends various functions and events and directly meets with community leaders—who may include public officials, educators, religious leaders, and heads of professional organizations and groups defined by special interests or ethnicities.

EARNING TRUST

COMMUNITY RELATIONS IN ACTION

When Comcast expanded its services into a new Illinois county, it hired a local PR practitioner to "open doors" between the utility and area leaders. Several days after hiring the practitioner, Comcast asked his help in boosting attendance at a meet and greet designed to introduce the company to the area and to showcase its new products.

Cultivating good relationships with the community in which an organization operates is essential for success, and many business leaders make a point of interacting with customers and stakeholders.

Paul Morigi/Getty Images

Over the years the PR practitioner had been involved in many community projects and had been a very visible fund-raiser for several local charities. He often gave his professional help pro bono for the pet projects of numerous local politicians and community influencers. These were the people he reached out to, and he simply asked them to join him and welcome his new client (Comcast) to the area.

The result was an overflow crowd, far exceeding the expectations of the Comcast executives on hand. The guests included a state senator, a state representative, three mayors, elected officials from several towns, and numerous community influencers. When the guests were asked what brought them to the event, the reason many gave for coming was simple: "Because Bill asked me to."

In other words, the practitioner, through his community involvement, had built up such a large reservoir of goodwill that just his asking was a good enough reason to attend for most.

BUSINESSES EARN TRUST AS GOOD CITIZENS

A business, as a citizen of its community, may benefit from tax breaks, favorable zoning, and a ready employee and consumer base. As a good citizen, at the bare minimum it should be respectful of the environment and society that hosts it as well as voluntarily support community projects.

Since 1995 the Boston College Center for Corporate Citizenship has studied how companies invest in communities and how these efforts connect to their businesses. Both corporate giving campaigns and employee volunteer programs benefitting the community work to strengthen the company's reputation and employee retention (Olphert, 2015). PR supports this engagement via social media, local mass media, event partnerships, outreach to charities, donations, and internal communications with employees, among other efforts.

PUBLIC RELATIONS WITH DIVERSE COMMUNITIES

LATINOS IN THE UNITED STATES: ONE IN FOUR BY 2050

Maria Cardona, principal at Dewey Square Group, explains to her clients why they should focus on the expanding Latino community. First she provides demographic facts: In 2015 Latinos were one in six of people living in the United States. By 2050, that statistic is projected at more than one in four (M. Cardona, personal communication, 2015). With that kind of growth, every single company and governmental entity or political campaign has to think about how they are going to reach this large and fast-growing demographic.

"From a public policy standpoint, this group is going to be impacted the most by whatever regulation or legislation that's passed. From a corporate standpoint, these are the consumers that businesses are going to want to reach to expand their bottom line (M. Cardona, personal communication, 2015).

"With this prospect in mind, clients get a real understanding of the potential impact of the Latino community. I then counsel them on the kinds of programmatic partnerships that are important to Hispanics for relationships to be authentic:

In light of the rapid growth of the Latino community, outreach tailored to that demographic can be crucial in politics (as seen here at a voter registration event), health, and business.

Thomas Cooper/Getty Images

partnering with different community organizations to help reduce the dropout rate, to live healthier, to get better healthcare, etc.

"When you look at community relations this way, it starts becoming something that is genuinely real. It is a mutually beneficial relationship and a friendship that is not just on a yearly basis, but it turns into something long term. That, for the bottom line from a corporate standpoint, is something I believe is invaluable."

ASIAN AMERICAN COMMUNITY: BREAKING THE SILENCE

Asian Americans, while only 6% of the U.S. population, surpassed Latinos in 2015 as the fastest-growing multicultural segment of the U.S. population (Nielsen, 2015b). They are also the highest-income and best-educated racial group in the United States (Patten, 2016). And they place a greater value on marriage, parenthood, hard work, and career success than does the general public. However, they uniquely have another not-so-positive characteristic: The Asian American community is disproportionately affected by chronic hepatitis B—one in 10.

The campaign, "Breaking the Silence on Hepatitis B in the Asian-American Community" aimed to start a discussion of hepatitis B. It won Weber Shandwick PR, together with APartnership and Gilead Sciences, the Best in Multicultural Marketing award from *PR News* in 2017.

Research showed older Asian Americans rely on their community for information, while younger cohorts serve as gatekeepers. So the team developed a 40-minute **unbranded** documentary, *Be About It*, which followed two families' struggles against this disease that's shrouded by stigma. Its primary subjects were Alan, a news journalist, and AJ, a radiology technician and triathlete, who had each lost loved ones to health complications related to hepatitis B. Their stories served as the campaign's centerpieces. Watch the trailer at https://www.youtube.com/watch?v=lMS1lcQX3A8.

The film engaged its target public on an emotional level by seeing the community as people, not just cases or numbers. It also leveraged storytelling as an antidote against the afflictions of silence and fear. The result was a campaign intimate enough to speak to each person individually yet with the scope to interact with a community on its own terms. The film was screened at seven film festivals, and media outreach was led at the local, in-language, and national levels.

Educational material was shared on an unbranded website, provided to influencers who could share resources and content, and disseminated at local market events with translations in Chinese, Korean, and Vietnamese. A community kit allowed local groups to host their own screenings. *Be About It* and its broader message generated more than 100 media placements in audience-targeted outlets.

YOUNG, BLACK, AND ONLINE

Nielsen (2015c) reports younger African Americans are more plugged in, tech savvy, and likely to interact with brands on social media. They are trendsetters and tastemakers for youth of all races, according to the Selig Center, a research institute at the University of Georgia. They define mainstream culture and wield immense influence over how Americans choose to engage in it. Any PR campaign targeting Millennials must include messages to reach African American youth, notes Nielsen.

"What social media does is it actually levels the playing field. It gives African Americans more voice in sharing how they react to brands and products and services," says Nielsen's Cheryl Pearson-McNeil, coauthor of the report (Boschma, 2016). She says it's a smart business move to take advantage of reaching people where it is convenient for them to engage and interact with a brand. Social media also serve the special health needs of the African American community: Thousands of African Americans suffer from sickle cell disease. Unfortunately, African Americans have the lowest odds of finding a match compared to any other racial and ethnic group.

PR agency Padilla won PRSA's prestigious Silver Anvil award (Padilla Wins, 2016) for its strategic campaign: "It's On You: Inspiring the African American Community to Step Up and Save Lives." The agency partnered with Be The Match®, a nonprofit matching patients with bone marrow donors, to create a powerful call to action within the African American community. The campaign staged during the month of July, which is African American Bone Marrow Awareness Month. Tactics included donor registry events nationwide and a dedicated landing page with facts dispelling myths and inspiring stories of real people who had donated.

In one month 400 African Americans stepped up to save lives by joining the Be The Match Registry®, a 40.7% increase from previous periods (Boschma, 2016).

The "It's on You" campaign was successful in increasing African American participation in the national bone marrow registry, which requires a simple cheek swab.

Kevin Clark/The Washington Post/Getty Images

PROFILES OF COMMUNITY CORPORATE SOCIAL RESPONSIBILITY SUCCESSES AND CHALLENGES

TARGET

The discount store retailer commits its efforts and assets toward supporting the local environment and communities in which it has stores. Over the past several years, the company's efforts, from promoting sustainable practices to educational grants, have amounted to 5% of its profit going to local communities—that's $4 million each week. In education alone, Target has donated $1 billion since 2010.

Thanks to Target, art museums for both adults and children across the United States offer free admission to all visitors on select days throughout the year. Its Meals for Minds program brings fresh and basic foods to K–12 elementary school students in 42 U.S. cities through a partnership with Feeding America and local food banks. Target also strengthens its global workers' communities in nearly 30 countries around the world through its International Giving Program supporting disaster relief and education programs for children and youth.

Target's corporate website, ABullseyeView.com, is a content-rich PR vehicle for anyone seeking information about the retailer. It carries news, features, interviews, photo slideshows, videos, and graphics. It stays fresh with up to three new editorial posts daily, five times a week. Target says, "We believe this unconventional approach to a corporate website and brand content offers an infinitely more engaging approach to company storytelling and better represents the Target brand" (A Bullseye View, n.d.).

H&M

The clothing retailer, whose brand makes the promise, "Look good, do good, feel good," stocks its stores with a community of suppliers in developing countries willing to sign H&M's extensive sustainability commitment. By doing so, it has created more

Over the past several years, Target's charitable efforts have amounted to 5 percent of its profit. It funds art museums, disaster relief, and education and enlists celebrities like Rocco DiSpirito in assembling meal boxes for foodbanks.

Jamie McCarthy/WireImage/Getty Images

than 1.6 million jobs for people employed by suppliers around the world, two-thirds of which have been taken by women—for many, their first job outside of the home and a first step to independence.

To ensure a close relationship with its suppliers, H&M staffs more than 2,600 employees worldwide to steer compliance with its sustainability commitment and influence positive change in the communities in which it does business. As the world's second-largest fashion retailer (after Inditex, owner of Zara), H&M's goal for 2018 is to have all its strategic suppliers pay fair living wages.

H&M has a long history of social consciousness. It was among the early adopters of the UN Guiding Principles on Human Rights and one of the first global fashion companies to make its supplier factory list public. Key suppliers are based in Bangladesh, Cambodia, India, China, and Turkey.

Yet it isn't always easy to achieve these goals, and H&M struggles to manage its supply chain. In 2013 the Rana Plaza building that housed garment factories collapsed in Bangladesh, killing more than 1,100 workers providing clothing for H&M, Walmart, and Gap, among others. While H&M had transparency and monitoring systems in place, they could not prevent the conditions that led to this disaster.

One way H&M communicates its sustainability story is through the media page on its corporate website. In 2017 the retailer received the Freedom House Corporate Award for its leadership in advancing global supply chain transparency. In 2017 H&M was also recognized by the Ethisphere Institute as one of the world's most ethical companies—for the seventh year in a row. The retailer has also been honored for excellence in caring for its community of employees—in Canada. And for the third consecutive year, in 2017 Canada's Great Place to Work Institute recognized H&M as one of its Best Workplaces in Canada (Great Place To Work, n.d.).

SCENARIO OUTCOME

To recap, nearly all the owners of eight small businesses in Illinois reported that their philanthropic giving, was "strategic," yet most of them had no communication strategy and little structure to measure the effectiveness of their giving.

Applying lessons from this chapter, you might answer the following questions in this manner:

What benefits are these local businesses missing from failing to communicate their good works?

Seeing this gap as an opportunity rather than a problem, the owners' passion and commitment to CSR engagement offers a pathway *to* strategic management of communication. Thinking only the giving or the event is enough does not consider the loss of impact on the businesses' stakeholders or community members who, by design or accident, were not involved or were less engaged. Without communication a business loses the potential for expanding awareness of its good works, engaging the larger community in dialogue and action, and nurturing the business while at the same time inspiring more people to do good deeds—a value deeply embedded in these small businesses.

Communicating CSR creates a healthy organization that is fluid and inclusive. It improves employee morale and reinforces positive reputation. A healthy organization communicating its CSR must use a dynamic process responsive to varying needs and conditions and its diverse stakeholders.

Why should the businesses communicate CSR with their publics?

▸ People want to know about and will support company efforts to be socially responsible.

▸ The language of SR resonates with people.

▸ People want to know *why* they should care.

▸ People value WOM information from trusted sources.

▸ People care more about *local* CSR.

▸ People don't actively seek CSR information.

▸ Telling your own CSR story lets you keep the message authentic.

How should businesses communicate CSR with their publics?

▸ Determine different stakeholders to reach and address each uniquely.

▸ Share your compassion and pride by focusing on CSR *results*.

▸ Place content visibly on the home page of your company website.

▸ Post photos and media articles in employee lounges.

▸ Announce CSR on your packaging.

▸ Use social media to allow quick and easy communication with broad involvement.

▸ Make your CSR noticeable in store to clients who visit your business.

▸ Communication that's authentic gives voice to your values and the values of your stakeholders, avoiding the perception that it's "marketing" or even "boasting."

WRAP UP

Five vital takeaways from this chapter are these:

1. CSR should be tied to an organization's core purpose and values.
2. CSR should be connected with and communicated to an organization's multiple stakeholders.
3. The ideal executive to manage the CSR process is the PR/communications professional.
4. CSR communication must be well researched, authentic, and carefully targeted to the personal interests of its receivers.
5. CSR is one of the most appropriate ways to build positive relationships with communities.

KEY TERMS

B Corporation: A certification awarded by B Lab, earned by a company's rigorous adherence to SR and sustainability, **221**

Benefit Corporation: A legal status that establishes a corporation must have a material positive benefit on society and the environment, **221**

Cause Promotions: When an organization provides or donates money to support or increase awareness and concern for a cause or charity, **216**

Cause-Related Marketing: Contributions to a cause or charity based on a percentage of sales revenues, **216**

Community Volunteering: Encouraging and facilitating employees to get involved in a cause via time off or sabbaticals, **216**

Corporate Philanthropy: Direct contribution to a charity or cause, **216**

Corporate Social Marketing: Support for a behavior changing campaign to improve safety, health, or the environment, **216**

Greenwashing: Misleading consumers regarding a firm's environmental practices or the environmental benefits of a certain product, **227**

Social Entrepreneurship: A type of business structure that prioritizes social, cultural,

and/or environmental benefits rather than substantial financial gain, **221**

Socially Responsible Business Practices: Adopting discretionary business practices to support causes or issues, **216**

Sustainability: In the CSR context, a business strategy that creates long-term stakeholder value by considering the ethical, social, environmental, cultural, and economic spheres, **220**

Triple Bottom Line: Framework with three parts: social, environmental, and financial; also referred to as the 3Ps: people, planet, and profit, **216**

Unbranded: Without evidence or identification of a specific associated brand, as in "unbranded content", **233**

THINK ABOUT IT

You read that a social enterprise's primary objective is social good, not profit. When Aaron Fishman found himself volunteering for an NGO in Bali, he learned the impoverished region shipped its cashew crops to India and Vietnam for processing. He envisioned an opportunity to provide jobs and training and produce uniquely local cashews—processed where they're grown. Read about his story in launching East Bali Cashews (EBC), and explore the website (http://eastbalicashews .com/) to get a better understanding of a successful social entrepreneurship. Look for evidence on how EBC communicates with its various stakeholders and assess whether or not you think it's doing a sufficient job.

WRITE LIKE A PRO

Imagine the hypothetical bicycle shop, Bikes and Trikes, is an established, locally owned business in your community, founded 30 years ago by its current owners, a husband and wife. While it has a full range of products for the novice and accomplished cyclist, including children's bikes, it also has a secondary stream of business (called Positive Spins) in adaptive bikes and trikes for riders with special needs. It was originally inspired by the needs of a family member. Bikes and Trikes relies on a website to communicate about both business streams and also hosts fund-raising events. Its social media presence consists of a Facebook page with frequent posts. It also regularly provides adaptive cycles to participants in the Wounded Warrior Project's Soldier Rides around the country. Drawing from lessons in this chapter, as their newly hired PR consultant, write a 200- to-300-word business memo to the owners of Bikes and Trikes outlining and justifying some recommendations for an improved communications program.

SOCIAL RESPONSIBILITY CASE STUDY

Comcast Cares Day Engages Employees, Their Families, Friends, and Community

Situation

For more than 15 years, Comcast NBCUniversal has harnessed the collective power of its employees and volunteers in an annual Comcast Cares Day. Known as the nation's largest single-day corporate service effort, it's when thousands of the cable giant's employees across the country go out and volunteer in their communities. It began with an impressive 6,100 volunteers in its first year, 2001.

Research and Strategy

Little things make a difference, for example, the Comcast Cares Day T-shirts. Only those who come out and volunteer get one, and it's become a source of pride with employees to continue wearing it to work or out in the community—thus the T-shirts create more engaged employees as well as get positive word out on Comcast. The company also raises visibility for Comcast Cares Day by changing e-mail signatures in advance of the event to be sure as many people as possible become aware of the event.

It's not a top-down program. Comcast's employees who live and work in the communities where the projects happen have a lot to do with the logistics of Cares Day, contributing to site selection and planning. They know firsthand where projects will have a long-term impact. Taking leadership helps employees get far more engaged and also motivates them to spread the word.

Execution

Social media is smartly leveraged. Beyond using Facebook and Twitter, Comcast Cares Day includes a special Flickr account that allows participants to upload images of themselves engaged in their communities in real time. Thus it starts up on the East Coast first and then sweeps across the country—thousands of pictures telling stories. It works to motivate more volunteers and is used for future promotion.

Evaluation

Comcast Cares Day in 2016 soared to a record-breaking 108,000 volunteers. Together they invested 5 million hours to improve more than 900 parks, schools, beaches, senior centers, and other vital community sites in the United States and 21 countries around the world. Projects included everything from installing computer labs to beautifying schools and planting trees. Volunteers included employees and their families (including children), friends, and community partners.

Beyond Cares Day, Comcast employees have invested more than 25,000 hours mentoring in the Big Brothers Big Sisters of America program. And its annual Toy Drive has collected toys valued at $430 million over its 22-year history. Perhaps most in line with its core business, the company has prioritized closing the digital divide. Its Internet Essentials program, which also engages employees, launched in 2011 and provides low-cost Internet service and digital literacy training to low-income families, seniors, and community college students. It also covers all children in schools where at least 50% of students are eligible for the National School Lunch Program.

ENGAGE

When the news source Consumerist, a subsidiary of *Consumer Reports*, labeled Comcast "the cable company America loves to hate," bloggers embraced the description—and the event that triggered it (Cox, 2016). Using Twitter to self-promote itself on Comcast Cares Day in 2016 turned out to be an invitation for a tweet-storm. "Comcast Cares Day is trending for entirely the wrong reasons and it's hilarious" headlined one online news site (Walsh, 2016). Comcast's reputation for bad service surfaced to haunt it when Twitter users hijacked the hashtag #ComcastCaresDay to complain about the cable company. Some of the tamer conversation included the following:

▸ Maybe @Comcast should extend #ComcastCaresDay so they actually care the other 364 days of the year?

▸ I can't tell if #ComcastCaresDay is a joke or an example of people in charge being embarrassingly out of touch with reality.

▸ So the month of April begins with April Fool's Day and ends with #ComcastCaresDay. Seems appropriate.

DISCUSS

▸ As the PR team for Comcast Cares Day, how do you handle this situation?

▸ How could Comcast turn its desire for reputation building and community engagement into a CSR initiative that addresses its dismal customer service identity?

▸ You identify that poor customer service stems from employee and workplace problems. How can improved communications take steps to solve them?

Source: Scott (2013).

SOCIAL RESPONSIBILITY CASE STUDY

Dollywood Foundation Launches "My People Fund" Relief Effort

Situation

In the fall of 2016 wildfires swept through the Smoky Mountains in western Tennessee, spreading over 18,000 acres and damaging or destroying more than 2,400 homes, vacation cabins, and buildings. Fourteen lives were lost. Brandon Reese, a freelance photographer, called it "an apocalyptic wasteland" (Sawyer, 2016).

The center of the destruction was Gatlinburg, Tennessee, home to the most-visited national park in the United States, Great Smokey Mountains National Park. It is also home to the famed Dollywood theme park and resort owned by country music celebrity Dolly Parton. In immediate response to the crisis, Parton created The Dollywood Foundation "My People Fund" to provide $1,000 each month, for up to six months, to area families with uninhabitable homes. Significant donors included Verizon, Tanger Outlets, and Miley Cyprus's Happy Hippie Foundation.

Research and Strategy

To publicize the fund and build engagement, the foundation issued a press release through Business Wire, a global news distribution service, secured a fund-raising radio-thon with the University of Tennessee's radio network and Cumulus Media/Knoxville, and created the hashtag #My PeopleFund and #someplacespecial for social media messaging. Dolly Parton also created an announcement video.

Execution

Within one month of its announcement, the fund raised nearly $9 million. At its six-month goal, the fund was able to fulfill its promise to all the area families who had lost their homes. The Mountain Tough Recovery Team, a partnership among Sevier County and the cities of Gatlinburg, Pigeon Forge, and Sevierville, Tennessee, continued to assist victims of the wildfire through its website mountaintough.org. It served as a resource center on housing, food, clothing, employment, and health and grief counseling.

A vital need for recovery affected the tourism sector. The city of Gatlinburg alone annually hosts 10 million visitors to Parton's theme park. Shortly after the devastating fire, rental cabins were fielding callers asking, "Why would we want to come there? Is everything gone?" (Solomon, 2017). While some cabins burned, most vacation rental properties were not affected by the fires. Yet tourism business declined by $19 million in the month following the fire—a 36% drop in revenue from the previous year (Ahillen, 2017). Many business owners in the area attributed the heavy media coverage of the fires to the prospective tourists' impressions that the town itself was gone.

Evaluation

The Smoky Mountain Tourism Development Authority (SMTDA) began a social media PR campaign to combat the negative impressions. Working with Mary Beth West Communications (MBWC) and Marshall Ramsey, a Pulitzer Prize-nominated editorial cartoonist, the SMTDA released a series of cartoons to support tourism in the two gateway counties to the Great Smokey Mountains National Park. The series won the public relations firm two ADDYs, awarded by the American Advertising Federation in 2017 (Mary Beth West, 2017). One spotlighted Dolly Parton's #MyPeopleFund relief effort, one paid tribute to aid workers, and one carried a humorous direct call-to-action message showing forest animals beckoning visitors to visit the Smoky Mountains.

ENGAGE

▸ Beyond Dolly Parton's efforts to help the wildfire victims, Dollywood supports its community in other ways. Explore them at http://www.dollywood.com/Community-Relations. Discover what the company's core values are and how they are addressed through its CSR engagement. Notice how it is discretionary, limiting who will benefit...and who won't.

▸ Cartoon messaging figured prominently in the response by the Smoky Mountain Tourism Development Authority, winning two ADDYs. Visit SMTDA's public relations firm, www .marybethwest.com, and browse the firm's work to see how cartooning—and visual messaging in general—effectively communicates in a variety of client and cause categories.

DISCUSS

After reaching its initial six-month goal, the My People Fund donated $3 million to www .mountaintough.org to help fund continued care for the community. An important step in the ROPES PR process is stewardship.

▸ Do you think Mountain Tough is a CSR program with longevity and legs? Does it go beyond making monetary contributions?

▸ Why do you think humor is often a response to tragedy? What purposes does it serve? Can it be used ethically?

Source. Business Wire (2016).

Valspar and Habitat for Humanity: CSR Partnerships

Valspar, a maker of home paints, is a longtime sponsor of Habitat for Humanity in the form of both cash and paint donations. In particular, Valspar has been a partner in Habitat's A Brush With Kindness program, which paints the exteriors of homes belonging to low-income, disabled, and senior homeowners. In 2015, Valspar pledged $36 million over 5 years to continue the program.

VIDEO

1. Discuss the benefits both Habitat for Humanity and Valspar reap from their partnership.

2. Which of the six types of CSR best describes Valspar's involvement with Habitat? If Valspar wanted to add another type to the partnership, which one would you advise and why?

3. How can Valspar's CSR efforts with Habitat also aid community relations efforts?

10 Employee Relations, Corporate Culture, and Social Responsibility

Learning Objectives

10.1 Describe the importance of employee relations in creating a healthy organization

10.2 Understand how PR supports employee engagement and solves problems during times of change

10.3 Examine the various needs, strategies, and tactics in employee communication

10.4 Identify the strategic connection between CSR and an organization's employees

How Do You Bring Together 100,000 Employees to Talk About Your Brand?

Intel, one of the early pioneers in the computer industry, conceived a bold vision in 2010: *This decade, we will create and extend computing technology to connect and enrich the life of every person on earth.*

A statement like that is no doubt powerful, but even Intel's leaders didn't realize the impact it would have on their employees.

Changing times. For years, Intel was admired as a technology darling boasting high stock prices, rapid growth, and big bonuses. Everything changed beginning in the early 2000s when the stock market's value plunged. Hundreds of thousands of technology professionals lost their jobs and any savings invested in stocks. By the mid-2000s, tech companies were restructured and operating with cost cuts and devalued stock options. Employee turnover was high.

In 2010, Intel realized it needed to address the fact that employees lacked an emotional connection to the company.

iStock.com/JasonDoiy

By 2010, however, a defining movement arrived for Intel. While the firm had recovered and transformed into a complex business with expanding product lines and markets, it realized its customary, top-down communication wasn't working.

Intel wasn't alone. Research revealed that trust in CEOs was low, while trust in employee peers was high—people were listening to each other more than their leaders. Power and titles were becoming a thing of the past as everyone was always "on." With information always accessible and narratives competing constantly, it was harder to engage people (Spreier, 2013). Yet it required a breakthrough because employee engagement is directly linked to positive business outcomes.

The problem. Intel was no longer its employees' first source of company information; instead people were turning to Twitter and other media channels to get news in real time. Company leaders knew they had to align with their employees' media needs if they wanted them to not just hear their words but to be motivated to act.

Intel also recognized it had to make an emotional connection, which is where the bold vision came in. Rather than saying, *"Let's go build the next product,"* the new Intel vision inspired people. It was a galvanizing force that showed where the company was going and how employees could help achieve that goal.

How to break through? Intel is a company of engineers who are not always the easiest to reach. The leaders knew they needed to be where their employees were instead of forcing them into channels they didn't want to use. Leaders also wanted to know what employees were thinking and why something may not be working so that the company could ask employees to be part of the solution.

The internal communications team knew its goal was to stimulate employee engagement using digital platforms and interactivity. It knew it needed to abandon the strategic language and bullet points used in the past. The team realized it needed to use many different and creative ways to get through to employees and to inspire the next great innovation.

After reading this chapter, you should be able to answer the following questions:

1. How can Intel connect employees together to encourage conversations with each other and with top management?

2. How can Intel show employees it values them?

3. Employees can be your best advocates. How can Intel inspire employees to explain to outsiders what they do?

At the end of the chapter, you'll learn what Intel did.

Note: This scenario is excerpted from McVicker (2013).

If all the people who make up an organization or company—from assembly line workers to designers to managers—aren't connecting positively to their work or aren't feeling valued, what's a company to do?

This chapter explains the importance of employee relations, also called internal relations, and how the employee's experience is deeply tied to a healthy corporate culture. PR's support includes counseling company leaders and listening to and communicating with all members of the workforce. The field of internal relations is now a major responsibility of PR practitioners. Another growing focus for PR is addressing corporate change. When companies are sold, downsized, or even shut down, PR must work with other departments and executive leadership to successfully facilitate and communicate what it means to employees. The chapter covers how companies have mishandled mergers and acquisitions, juxtaposing the worst practices with the best.

All of this requires communication tactics that are tailored to the corporate culture *and* the media practices of employees. The poster by the coffee machine may need to be replaced by an animated infographic. You'll find strategies for sending messages, inviting interactivity, and hosting employee-created content.

Finally the high value that a socially responsible company offers an employee—or a prospective one—is explained, proven by research, and illustrated with examples and case studies.

EMPLOYEE RELATIONS AND HEALTHY ORGANIZATIONS

>> **LO 10.1   Describe the importance of employee relations in creating a healthy organization**

The one thing that's certain about life is that things change. This couldn't be more true than with businesses and the workplace, whether it's merging personnel from another company, moving to a new location, shifting your brand identity, changing product priorities or strategy, adjusting to ever-changing channels of communication, closing a facility, terminating a product line or service, or encountering a crisis.

Master the content
edge.sagepub.com/page

Employee relations, or internal communication, is an important part of creating a corporate culture that will advance an organization's goals.

iStock.com/vm

At these times everyone involved needs to transform a little, too. The PR professional, working in an in-house or outside agency capacity, can help drive change for positive outcomes within an organization. People throughout a company often need to understand what's possible during times of challenge or change and what their role is in creating success and meeting business objectives.

More than three-quarters of senior-level PR/communication practitioners in the United States now report that internal communications is a major duty (GAP VII, n.d.). Their tasks are broad, including collaborating with and advising top management and facilitating understanding and motivation with varied employees.

INTERNAL COMMUNICATION

Employee relations. Sometimes referred to as "internal communication," employee relations focuses on all employees of an organization, from the head executives to the maintenance crew. It's a fast-growing field in PR due to several factors, including increasing competition for businesses, new avenues for communication, the economic uncertainty post 2008, a growing distrust of corporations, and the fact that the largest demographic, baby boomers, are leaving the workforce as Millennials enter it.

Depending on the size and structure of an organization, PR will often lead internal communication in partnership with chief executives and human resources. Internal communications' broad goal is to help create and sustain a healthy organizational culture. Its main responsibilities involve social media, employee engagement, counseling leadership, and facilitating change—especially in times of **mergers** and **acquisitions**—along with the accompanying communication challenges and opportunities.

CORPORATE CULTURE

The culture of an organization determines how it impacts workers' perceptions and behaviors. It's a filter, sometimes invisible and sometimes very evident, that guides how people interact and work. It affects communication styles and content, employee morale and initiative, and leadership behaviors.

Simply, a culture refers to the personality of an organization and how things are done. A more detailed definition identifies three dimensions to **corporate culture**: what's materially visible (e.g., the physical environment), people's behavior patterns (recurring and influential), and mind-sets (widely shared attitudes and beliefs; see Figure 10.1) (Katzenback, Oelschlegel, & Thomas, 2016). A healthy corporate culture has been identified as key to an innovative and successful company. Companies that use informal emotional approaches to influencing behavior are significantly more likely to experience change that lasts.

FIGURE 10.1

Three Dimensions to Corporate Culture

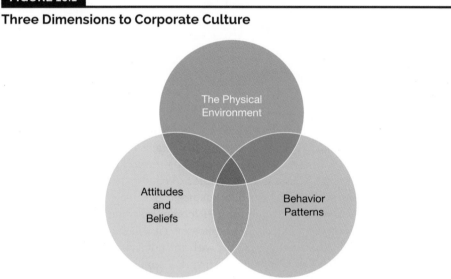

LEADERSHIP

Supportive leadership is a crucial element of a healthy organization. Employees should have personal and meaningful relationships with management that are based on trust. Managers should know how to get employees to function together, both in times of continuity and of change.

To support a healthy organizational culture, PR works to ensure that both the behavior and communication of management consistently adheres to company values. Company leaders set the tone for organizational culture, and PR advocates that a healthy culture in an organization begins with the example of its leaders.

SOCIAL RESPONSIBILITY A search of the websites of prominent corporations will likely find the agreed-upon corporate values and vision, often located on the "Our Company" or "About" pages. For example, Coca-Cola states, "Our values serve as a compass for our actions and describe how we behave in the world" (The Coca-Cola Company). According to Ahmet Bozer, past president of Coca-Cola International, "At Coca-Cola, supporting our friends, neighbors and communities has always been a vital part of who we are and how we operate" (Kerr, 2014). See how the company lives its values (see Table 10.1) by focusing on its core sustainability priorities of women, water, and community well-being.

TABLE 10.1

Coca-Cola Company Values

VALUES	SOCIAL RESPONSIBILITY ACTIONS
Leadership. The courage to shape a better future	Recognizing challenges faced by women, it launched the 5 × 20 initiative in 2010, a global commitment to empower 5 million women entrepreneurs by 2020.
Collaboration. Leveraging the collective genius of the company	Coca-Cola collaborates with 100s of organizations globally in "golden triangle" partnerships of businesses, governments, and civil society. One effort includes training malaria control agents and providing mosquito nets in Africa to save more than 100,000 children.
Integrity. Being real	Coca-Cola shares what it knows, using its supply chain expertise to help developing countries distribute medicines.
Accountability. If it is to be, it's up to me	The company replenishes all of the water it uses in its beverages through 248 local community water projects in 71 countries.
Passion. Committed in heart and mind	When Typhoon Yolanda devastated central Philippines, employees mobilized to deliver water and emergency supplies, and the company gave $2.5 million toward rebuilding efforts.
Diversity. As inclusive as our brands	For 11 consecutive years Coca-Cola has received a perfect score on the Human Rights Campaign's annual corporate equality index that measures the promotion of equality and inclusion in the workplace.
Quality. What we do, we do well	Coca-Cola produces independently verified sustainability reports documenting the breadth and success of its SR initiatives.

Sources: The Coca-Cola Company (n.d., 2017); Isidore (2016); Kerr (2014).

PUBLIC RELATIONS AND EMPLOYEE ENGAGEMENT

>> **LO 10.2** Understand how PR supports employee engagement and solves problems during times of change

Employee engagement with the goals of the organization is an essential component to the success of the organization's mission. To be blunt, if the employees don't support the mission, how can an organization convince the public to do so?

PR practices and theories, when applied to internal relations and employee communication, are focused on trust, transparency, and commitment, supporting multiple strategies for employee engagement. The foundation for all the strategies—the basis for everything to come—begins with defining the corporate culture for employees of all ranks.

Travis Kalanick, former CEO of Uber, was forced out of the company following accusations that he had helped create a toxic workplace culture.

Michael Kovac/Getty Images

Public Relations Supports Five Characteristics of a Healthy Organization

Good financial performance is not enough to make a company "healthy." To be successful, organizations need to create and maintain a workplace built on collaboration among its workers at all levels. Certain characteristics should be ingrained in the corporate culture for an organization to be healthy. As you read the following characteristics, you will see many communication and relationship-building tasks that call on the skills of the PR professional—to lead, nurture, or take corrective actions.

Effective Sharing of Goals

Using internal communication strategies with simple messaging, a healthy organization shares its business goals with employees at every level of the organization. Employees and managers understand the mission and vision of the organization and what is required to reach these shared goals, making every effort to achieve them. Short video messages from the CEO are one effective way to engage employees in these shared goals.

Teamwork

Healthy companies know how to develop teams that collaborate to achieve common goals. Relationship building is an important element. Employees and managers readily offer their assistance to each other to meet corporate objectives. To successfully encourage positive relationships, internal social networks help

flatten the corporate hierarchy, letting people collaborate more readily.

High Employee Morale

Employees know they are valued and in turn value their positions in the organizations and desire longevity and promotion. Productivity is high, and organizational events are enjoyable and successful. Morale can be raised through open lines of communication that allow employees across the organization to contribute ideas and opinions that are freely discussed.

Adapts to Risks, Opportunities, and Changes

Healthy organizations understand the risks they are open to and are proactive enough to take necessary steps to protect themselves. They also know how to recognize and seize good opportunities that allow them to grow, and they know how to adapt to technological or operational changes. The widespread growth of social media presents both threats and opportunities.

Defined Policies and Structure

Organizational policies and structure facilitate the positive function of the business but do not limit innovation and growth. Employees readily understand them and their benefits. ●

Sources: Johnson (n.d.); Raya and Panneerselvam (2013).

For employees to support the corporation, they must have a clear understanding of the values that are at its core. The company, in turn, must effectively communicate these values through internal PR to its employees before asking for their assistance as advocates.

TRAITS A CORPORATE CULTURE SHOULD EXHIBIT

CONSTRUCTIVE RELATIONSHIPS

It facilitates constructive relationships with fellow employees and management (see Figure 10.2). In its simplest terms, a corporation that has the best relationship with its employees is one that asks, "What do you think?"

EMPOWERMENT

It effectively sends the message that they encourage honest, open, and useful feedback from employees. When management openly respects the input of employees who make suggestions on how to solve workplace challenges and to improve productivity

---

FIGURE 10.2

Corporate Culture Traits

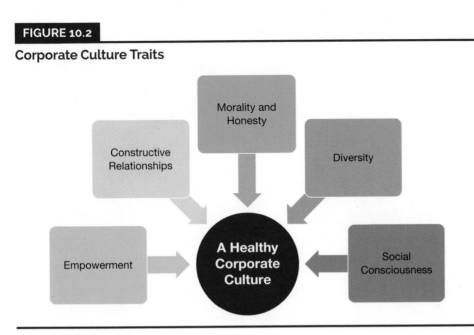

---

and performance, employees feel empowered to voice their ideas and concerns and feel those opinions will be fairly evaluated and acted upon. Encouraging participation in decision-making, and being supportive of creative and innovative approaches no matter where they come from, makes employees feel valued. And they will then more easily share their knowledge and experience within the corporate community.

MORALITY AND HONESTY

It is an organization seen as moral and honest in its business dealings, that its integrity is of the same high standards as its employees. People who work for a company want to be proud to say so; they want their friends and neighbors to know they're employed by an honest and ethical company.

DIVERSITY

It embraces diversity in its workforce and respects the different perspectives a diverse group of employees brings to the organization. By promoting inclusiveness and celebrating the various races, world cultures, genders, religions, sexual orientations, and so on of its workers, the corporation is saying it welcomes all of them on the same level.

SOCIAL CONSCIOUSNESS

Today, this trait is highly desirable by employees. It recognizes that social and environmental concerns are corporate responsibilities of interest to employees. The workforce now entering the job market is knowledgeable, and concerned, about their impact on the environment. That concern transfers to their choice of corporations where they would consider working. Is the company committed to sustainable practices? Does it do well by doing good? What does it take from the community versus what it brings to it? And clearly, does it support employees in volunteering during company time, working toward sustainability goals, matching donations to chosen charities, and in other ways that bring together the company and employee as good citizens?

> SOCIAL
> RESPONSIBILITY

Delta is considered a leader in corporate efforts to create a diverse workplace.

iStock.com/winhorse

Expressing the corporation's core culture and its commitment to the traits and positions listed here is the role of PR both in internal efforts, programs, and communications to employees and in external messaging to outside publics:

▸ **Company newsletters**, whether traditional or online, should reinforce the corporation's belief, for example, that the workplace honors diversity by spotlighting, among other things, the different religious or cultural holidays celebrated by its employees. Likewise, in support of the stated goal of accepting input from all levels, the newsletter should honor employees who have submitted suggestions for company improvements.

▸ **The corporate website** is the place for a bold statement of commitment to positive values. More than a mission statement, this should be a credo, a promise to follow certain guidelines. Putting this where all can see and read gives employees a place they can refer to—and refer their friends and family to also. It is an easy way for workers to say, "This is where I work; these are our values."

▸ **Internal and external communication** about the company's sustainability and SR programs addresses numerous audiences. Through internal methods, employees could be made aware of the organization's move toward sustainability by the promotion of, for instance, office and plant recycling efforts or, perhaps, the sustainable purchasing of raw goods. They could then be offered the opportunity to participate in more widespread efforts by joining employee groups to suggest other programs. Externally the greater public would be informed of the company's programs via traditional methods, such as press releases and video news releases, and through digital and social media avenues.

EMPLOYEE ADVOCACY

When employees share their support for their company or its products, it can generate both positive awareness and favorable impressions. **Employee advocacy** is an important activity for a company to cultivate to help advance its agenda.

GE, From Villain to Hero

Thanks to a corporate strategy it named "Ecomagination," GE became one of the world's top global green brands.

Adam Ferguson/Bloomberg/Getty Images

General Electric (GE) launched its Ecomagination strategy in 2005 to focus on cleaner technology innovation, with the commitment to reduce the company's footprint in greenhouse gas emissions. The inspiration for this step was its dismal environmental record and reputation as one of the worst polluters in the world. Thanks to Ecomagination, GE did a complete turnaround, and in 2014 was recognized by *Fortune* magazine as one of the world's top global green brands. How did GE change course so dramatically?

It Started With Top Management

From the beginning, CEO Jeff Immelt led the way, announcing the Ecomagination initiative in Washington, D.C., and making it a top priority in his communication throughout the years. The initiative generated support at all levels of the organization. GE embedded it throughout the entire organization, filtered into employee, supplier, and distributor goals.

Employees Participated in Personally Meaningful Ways

One powerful example is the Ecomagination Nation. One of its largest businesses, GE's Power & Water, created this program, which recognizes sites that take action to address environmental and social issues in their facilities and communities. During 2015 the total number of certified sites rose to 34. Over the first three years of the program, more than 8,000 employees worldwide engaged in community volunteer activities, such as cleaning up coastlines, tree plantings, and lighting upgrades in community schools. According to GE's 2015 sustainability report, the initiative reduced greenhouse gas (GHG) emissions by 31 percent and water use by 42 percent.

Excellence awarded. GE recognizes performance excellence for those operations that contribute most dramatically to reductions in energy use, GHG emissions, water use, and materials consumption through its annual EcoAwards. In 2015 GE opened nominations for the awards to teams across its value chain and recognized the team at its Greenville, South Carolina, site as overall winner for achieving significant reductions through conscientious practices. ●

Sources: Benson (2016); Haldemann (2015); Salim (2016).

Every employee is a billboard for his or her employer. Unhappy workers, those who feel ignored or unvalued are not positive spokespeople. The disengaged are likely to spread negativity to others. On the contrary, those who feel included, who are sure their voice is heard, who participate willingly in sustainable and socially responsible efforts, are likely a company's strongest proponents.

They also are the voices often most valued: Edelman PR's Trust Barometer Survey in 2016 reported that people are increasingly reliant on a "person like yourself" —a regular employee—for trustworthy information (Edelman, 2016a). In a nutshell, creating that proud and satisfied employee who authentically imparts that to others is the goal of PR through internal relations and employee communication.

MERGERS AND ACQUISITIONS

It is not unusual for one company to acquire another, or for two companies to come together under a single banner, or for a company to sell a business line or division it owns. Every year hundreds of businesses will be a part of a merger and acquisition (M&A) deal, to be sold by one corporation to another or be merged to create a single company out of two. PR plays a pivotal role in seeking corporate unity, both internally and externally.

A GROWING TREND

The year 2015 was a record-breaking one internationally for M&A, and in 2016 more than 13,300 deals were forecast for North America. M&A activity is predicted to accelerate in coming years. The major focus will be on companies shedding other businesses, with a secondary focus on companies merging (IMAA, n.d.; Deloitte, n.d.).

There are numerous reasons why a corporation will divest itself of one of the companies in its portfolio: markets have changed, it's no longer a good fit with the mission of the corporation, and so on. In the same vein, corporations will buy independent companies to strengthen their stake in the marketplace, usually to eliminate some of the competition and other times to acquire the technology the purchased company owns. Mergers are usually created to form a single, stronger company out of two like-minded businesses. A key concern for a successful M&A is corporate integration: the melding of the two company cultures.

YOGA ROOMS VERSUS BOARDROOMS

Workplace rules vary wildly from corporation to corporation; some offer casual dress, yoga rooms, and free lunches to their employees, while others demand business attire and offer no perks at all. If the traditional company acquires the one with the looser approach, and wishes to summarily impose its culture on that company's employees, the result will be unpredictable and likely negative.

While it may seem easier if the situation is reversed, with the corporation with the informal approach acquiring the one that is more traditional, the same sort of problems will arise. A worker cannot easily go from a workplace of coats and ties to one of flip-flops and flannel.

When a company is sold outright to a new owner, an important issue that must be considered is the emotional impact this will have on the employees of that

While some companies offer free food and on-site yoga classes, others are more straitlaced. Changes to an established corporate culture brought about by a merger or acquisition can be unsettling to employees.

iStock.com/FatCamera

M&As Can Often Disappoint

Any of these three events—acquisition, merger, or **divestiture**—will create business opportunities at the same time they create problems. The root of the problems lies in the fact that most corporations have their own way of doing business, a unique approach that it has purposely cultivated, and a corporate culture that has been inculcated in its workforce.

Swift PR response. When one such company acquires another, it gains more than the technology, factories, or storefronts of the other; part of the deal, so to speak, are the employees of the acquired company, along with its corporate culture and workplace habits. Meshing these two groups of strangers into a single workforce with a common corporate culture is an important task that must be accomplished as swiftly as possible. The demands on employee relations can be as challenging as those in crisis situations.

Culture integration is key. About 75% of M&A deals fail to achieve anticipated results, and the biggest impediment is their failure to effectively integrate the merging companies. One of the dominant barriers to effective integration is culture: the values, attitudes, and behaviors of the companies' people and how that culture is communicated. A large part of the M&A value relies on soft factors, such as strategic alignment, organizational integration, and low employee resistance.

"A $50 billion deal from hell." The 2008 acquisition of Merrill Lynch by Bank of America has been widely seen as a failure. Among the contributing factors for this failure were that the **due diligence** was rushed and incomplete and the actual financial picture was far direr than originally thought.

Other factors included that Bank of America headquarters were in Charlotte, North Carolina, whereas Merrill Lynch was based in New York City. The different cultures of the businesses were described as "Wall Street versus Main Street" and proved difficult to reconcile. The acquisition negatively affected many employees' statuses and compensation. Eventually thousands lost their jobs because of it. ●

Sources: Deloitte (n.d.); Moore (2009); Reeves (2013); Rothacker (2014); Seven Pillars Institute (n.d.).

organization. They may feel abandoned, betrayed, anxious, and fearful of the future. These emotions must be dealt with in an honest and open manner if the new owners hope to have a successful transition.

PUBLIC RELATIONS STRATEGY

In order for any of these business transfers or mergers to succeed, PR efforts must follow a communications plan that is open, consistent, and inclusive. The ideal situation is one where a longer planning time is an option as that will significantly improve the odds of success.

Who's in charge. The first decision that must be made is simple: Who's in charge? In a purchase situation, the obvious PR department to handle communication is from the buyer's side. This will guarantee a single, consistent message—one the new owners want to convey.

When to start. While sensitivity to employees of the purchased company must be observed, the simple truth is their company and its culture no longer exist. It is the role of the PR team to ease those workers, and all of the stakeholders of the former company, into their new reality. As noted, the sooner this process begins, the better—especially if there will be jarring changes to the workplace. Employees need time to adjust and can't be taken by surprise by significant differences that the new regime brings, such as start times, dress expectations, expense policies—every difference, right down to parking space allocation.

What's changed. Equally important to all concerned are the changes to hierarchal structure and departmental language. Who's my new boss? Am I being promoted or demoted? What's the name of my department now? These questions and others must be answered as soon as possible, so employees have time to adapt to the new policies and organizational chart.

How to frame it. At the same time, any message that can be perceived as negative or troubling must be balanced with one that is positive and uplifting. The acquired company's workers must be told of the good this change will bring to their lives, perhaps through new career opportunities or chances for advancement. Highlight the benefits: a better health plan, more liberal vacation or family leave policies, profit sharing—anything significantly better than what they have now.

In a merger of two entities, many compromises will have been made to achieve the merger, especially as it pertains to leadership and mission. These compromises are the ones that affect employees' lives the most and therefore become the core messages the PR team must communicate.

COMMUNICATION CHALLENGES AND OPPORTUNITIES

>> **LO 10.3**   **Examine the various needs, strategies, and tactics in employee communication**

With so many resources focused on the end user of an organization's services or products, it's understandable how the employee may be taken for granted or overlooked. Yet it can't be stressed enough: The workforce is essential to the health and success of a business. Look at it from the employees' perspective: This is a huge part of their lives. Our workplace helps confirm who we are and shapes our identity. Yet at times the workplace can confuse and alienate. Organizational clarity is needed, and various communication tactics are the means for providing that clarity. The PR professional is tasked with this important responsibility using both two-way and one-way communication strategies.

NEED FOR ORGANIZATIONAL CLARITY

In today's social reality, where there is more content than attention, employees are often overwhelmed with information. Thus organizations must communicate a clear vision and direction to employees. This need for **organizational clarity** prompted the Institute for Public Relations to conduct a global study of employees from various business sectors (Kochhar, 2016). Some of its key takeaways include the following:

▶ The understanding of employee interests and perceptions is the foundation for organizational clarity.

▶ Strategy and content must connect to employees.

▶ Listening and encouraging discussion help instill trust and confidence.

▶ The organizational "voice" should evolve from one of telling to one of facilitating, where employees learn, engage, and question.

PUBLIC RELATIONS COMMUNICATION TACTICS

The most common communication tools for employee relations are newsletters, e-mail, websites, and intranets or internal social media. Other responsibilities are writing executive speeches and developing frequently asked questions for management communication to employees. Relational strategies may involve organizing and managing employee meetings, retreats, workshops, celebrations, competitions, and the like.

According to Cision, the PR management company, employees are increasingly important voices due to their capability to interact with each other, customers, prospects, media, and the general public (Mireles, 2015). This ability increases with each technological advance, thus listening to employee insights can offer valuable perspective to both leadership and customers. Internal communications programs are being impacted by many of the same trends that impact PR as a whole (see the list that follows). In this chapter we will take a close-up look at three key tools: intranet, video storytelling, and employee programs.

Storytelling	Intranets
Real-time information sharing	Internal social networks
Mobile technology and platforms	Social software
Video	Analytics
Visuals including infographics	Employee influence measurement
Customization of messaging	Employee programs
Gamification	Print

INTRANET

Intranet is the Internet used specifically inside an organization, closed to the outside Internet community. It allows larger organizations the capacity to coordinate or communicate across departments and locations, centralizing information and interconnectivity. Intranets can carry a wealth of information for organization members, including employee newsletters, tutorials, press clips, project information, employee benefits information, and policies and includes conferencing functions and multimedia. For the PR professional, the Intranet provides for faster communication, wider distribution, and greater efficiency than many printed and electronic media. User interactivity is a growing trend in company Intranets. Here are some examples:

▶ *Personal Pages.* A winner of Ragan's Employee Communication award (Personal Pages, n.d.) is the PR firm Waggener Edstrom Worldwide, whose 800 employees around the globe use the company intranet for sharing, storytelling, and finding resources to help them in their jobs. It focuses on five topics—employee profiles, polls, personal pages, story comments, and a suggestion box—and it features videos, animation, text, and photos. A popular blog is "The Daily Buzz," which captures top stories and daily analysis of the agency and its competitors.

▶ *Tech-Savvy Appeal.* A winner of *PR News's* Digital PR Awards is the business software company Workiva, a fast-growing company with more than 1,200 employees in 16 offices (Seymour, 2016d). Unlike other corporate intranets

Canon: Living and Working for the Common Good

Canon is guided by a company culture called Kyosei, a Japanese word that means "living and working for the common good."

iStock.com/DaveAlan

Most people today know Canon from its business in cameras and printers. Founded in Japan in 1937, the Canon name has always been synonymous with photography and visual imagery—from medical to CCTV. The company culture, called Kyosei, a Japanese word that means "living and working for the common good," guides how it treats its employees and customers.

Miru Helps Employees Collaborate

A unique internal project, Miru, meaning "to see," was designed by the marketing and corporate communications team to bring employees in different countries, and different parts of the company, closer together via a new and engaging company intranet. Its intent was to encourage diverse teams across the company to work collaboratively instead of within their own offices. Canon employs 17,000 people throughout 116 countries—with obvious language barriers.

Cutting-Edge Digital and Social Platforms

The technology of Miru helped empower employees to truly experience Kyosei, to live and work together for the common good. It did this by bringing cutting-edge digital and social platforms like Yammer, Skype for Business, and OneDrive into the employees' daily lives—and facilitating the employees' digital dexterity. It's helped shift a culture of "knowledge is power" to one of "knowledge-sharing is power"—no longer rewarding heroes but celebrating collaboration.

Collaborating for the Environment

From product development, procurement, and manufacturing to logistics, usage, and recycling, Canon strives to reduce its environmental impact through every stage of the produce-use-recycle product life cycle.

Social Contribution

Guided by its corporate philosophy of *kyosei*, Canon contributes to enriching lifestyles for people around the world: Its Adopt a School project supports education in developing countries; Canon Wind employs persons with intellectual disabilities; and it served as official sponsor of the World Scout Jamboree, hosting more than 30,000 youth from 150 countries. ●

Sources: Canon (n.d.); MSLGROUP (2016).

that simply broadcast company information, Workiva's CONNECT creates a community where users collaborate and engage with each other through blogs, customizable profiles, and topic forums. While it integrates aspects of traditional intranets by providing the resources employees need to do their jobs, it has turned the company intranet into a social site that appeals to a younger, tech-savvy demographic—a large part of Workiva's employee base. And reporting company news is reaching new viewers through weekly videos.

VIDEO STORYTELLING

Video storytelling has the power to engage audiences more quickly and emotionally than text or static visuals. Studies show that 50% of PR practitioners use narrative storytelling techniques to engage internal audiences (GAP, n.d.). That's because people have a deeper affiliation with messages that tell a story as we tend to interpret them through our own experiences and understanding. Thus corporate stories

Patagonia attracts workers who are already committed to sustainable practices and, in some locations, those who like to surf on their lunchbreaks.

David Walter Banks/The Washington Post/Getty Images

that purposefully appeal to employees on a personal level can help bridge barriers, generate understanding, and encourage agreement or loyalty. Here's an example:

▶ *Animated Ideas.* A video award winner of the American Business Awards' Stevie Award is ICON Clinical Research, a global provider for the medical industries (Icon Clinical Research, n.d.). It was honored in the internal/ employee communications category for its launch video for SPARK—an internal online idea management and crowdsourcing platform. Its purpose is to encourage innovation by allowing ICON employees to submit ideas, collaborate on others' ideas, help with development, and interact with users at all ICON global sites. The video encouraged viewers to use, engage with, and share through the platform. Its high level of creativity accounted for its success: It told the story of the journey of an idea, illustrated through live action in various global ICON locations and animation of ideas forming, emerging, and developing—essentially the innovation process.

EMPLOYEE PROGRAMS

While seven in 10 American workplaces offer wellness programs, research suggests many employees don't know the programs exist, much less their benefits (Companies Need, 2015). Companies need to communicate much more persistently, clearly, and creatively, not only to inform but to address employees' doubts, privacy concerns, or lack of self-confidence. Here's an example of a successful communication campaign:

▶ *Who's Your Reason?* Blue Communications orchestrated an employee wellness campaign for AECOM, an engineering firm with 40,000 employees (Blue Communications, n.d.). The campaign, winner of the American Business Awards' Gold Stevie Award for Internal Communications, was conceived to drive engagement in a wellness program designed to ease cost increases for employee healthcare. Those who participated would pay less. The theme, "Be well" was illustrated with beautiful imagery asking the question, "Who's your reason?" The campaign helped employees recognize those in their lives who rely on them to stay healthy: spouses, children, friends, and even pets. Wellness ambassadors and a variety of media helped communicate the advantages of completing the program … and more than 75% of employees did.

EVALUATING EMPLOYEE COMMUNICATION

Measure and evaluate how communication reaches internal publics, as you would with any PR campaign. Consider your messaging outputs, outtakes, and outcomes.

▸ Was it well timed?

▸ Was the content truthful and accurate?

▸ Did it have relevance for the specific receivers?

▸ Was it accessed and read or viewed?

▸ Did it result in its objectives (inform, shape opinion, or encourage behavior)?

EMPLOYEE RELATIONS AND CORPORATE SOCIAL RESPONSIBILITY

>> **LO 10.4** **Identify the strategic connection between CSR and an organization's employees**

A strong commitment to SR is aligned with excellent company reputation. After quality products and services offered at a good value to meet customer needs, the strongest driver of a company's reputation is its positive influence on society (Reputation Institute, n.d.). Reputation is also an emotional bond that inspires employee engagement.

In companies that value sustainability and SR, employees are considered key stakeholders because their feedback can provide insight into issues and how to address them. For example, Starbucks initiated its College Achievement Plan and its FoodShare program out of listening to employee concerns. Employees offer a built-in sounding board for new ideas leading to social and environmental initiatives that everyone can be proud of.

SOCIAL
RESPONSIBILITY

CORPORATE SOCIAL RESPONSIBILITY ENGAGES EMPLOYEES

While sustainability and green practices are important to many in the workplace, it is in the area of SR where greatest opportunity for employee engagement lies. Many companies have programs that give back to the communities in which they are based; others support national or international issues and charities. The more successful of these corporate efforts are those in which the employees play a direct role in all aspects of the program, from selecting the charity or cause to raising money or to

Why Simplicity Is Beautiful in Employee Communication Strategy

Meg Wheaton, Gagen MacDonald

What Is a Strategy?

Strategy is the overarching path of how you're going to achieve your goals, and creating the strategy is only the first step. Activating a strategy and making it come to life inside an organization—that's what I'm really passionate about.

Anyone who has kids can attest to the fact that just because you tell them to pick up their socks doesn't mean they're going to. Whether you're at home or at work, simply telling people what to do isn't necessarily going to achieve the outcome that you are seeking. People need a compelling reason to do something or change their behavior, even if it's something as simple as picking up their socks.

How Do We Activate a Strategy?

Create a visual model of your strategy that's simple, impactful, and memorable. The model should include your strategy's pillars or key priorities that will get you the results you are seeking. Try to keep to four pillars as studies prove that people have a tough time remembering more than that. Use color coding, imagery, and iconography to make the visual model sing.

Understand your target audiences—all of them. Gagen specializes in internal communications, so our campaigns are addressed to employees. For the most part, we are asking them to do something differently or change their behavior. To do this, they need to know what we want them to do (tell them specifically what we need them to do differently) and why we want them to do it (tell them what benefits will come from changing). Holding focus groups, fielding surveys, and talking to people within an organization can help us get at the employee mind-set.

Create a compelling story that articulates the change and activates leaders as passionate storytellers. Storytelling is a fantastic way to help people connect the dots and see themselves inside a strategy shift or culture change. Leaders must connect to both the emotional and rational sides of the brain. Stories are memorable, tactile, and lasting. It's critical that leaders tell stories in their own words and that they "walk the talk." A story isn't a story until everyone can tell it.

Create communications that inspire others. People want to be part of something that is larger than themselves. Create communications that help employees understand the journey as well as the destination and the good that will come from it all. Because everyone consumes information in different ways, you need many different tactics—videos, animations, environmental signage, in-person meetings, digital communications, and so on—to reach all your audiences.

Create impactful experiences that allow employees to see themselves in the strategy. Bring workers together for collaborative, creative sessions where employees can roll up their sleeves and work together to map their own personal paths forward and how they'll contribute to the team effort. Make it fun, and make it exciting! ●

Meg Wheaton is a creative consultant and team lead at Gagen MacDonald, the leading strategy execution firm based in Chicago.

Source: M. Wheaton (personal communication, 2017).

---

donating time and physical effort. PR takes a vital role internally by promoting the cause and often recruiting employee volunteers. Externally the story of the good the company has done reflects on the employees and enhances their positive views of their employer.

The biggest, most enduring benefit to employees of company-wide CSR programs is the spirit of camaraderie they engender. Side by side as a group, managers and workers work toward a common goal that will benefit others and create a bond that benefits future workplace relationships. It also makes it easier to create support from within the company to advocate for the corporation's business goals.

CORPORATE SOCIAL RESPONSIBILITY AIDS EMPLOYEE RECRUITMENT AND RETENTION

CSR can be a mechanism for recruiting because it complements purpose-driven work, which often ties into professional fulfillment for workers. Susan Hunt Stevens, founder of WeSpire, says employees increasingly want jobs that have purpose and meaning. "They expect their employers to have sustainability programs, and they expect their company to make the world a better place" (Delisio, 2016). Research indicates that Millennials are the most socially conscious generation since the 1960s.

Companies' commitments toward social issues have become key drivers for recruiting employees, per Cone Communications (2016), a leading CSR public relations firm, in its Employee Engagement Study of 2016. Some of its significant findings:

▶ 58% consider a company's social and environmental commitments when deciding where to work.

▶ 55% would choose to work for a socially responsible company, even if the salary was less.

▶ 51% won't work for a company that doesn't have strong social or environmental commitments.

EXAMPLES OF EXCELLENCE

Patagonia. Patagonia's mission statement (build the best product, cause no unnecessary harm, and use business to inspire and implement solutions to the environmental crisis) attracts workers who are already committed to sustainable practices before they join the company, says Rick Ridgeway (Delisio, 2016), vice-president of public engagement.

Timberland. When Timberland is recruiting workers, applicants frequently ask about Timberland's Path of Service program, which allows employees to participate in a community project for up to 40 paid hours a year. It allows them to engage in whatever issues they feel most passionate about (Delisio, 2016).

Best Buy. Best Buy's Geek Squad offers an example of an employee CSR program that increases job satisfaction and retention. The Geek Squad Academy (GSA) is a two-day technology camp for girls and underserved teen populations. Employees from both the Geek Squad and the retail division are recruited as camp staff. Since the program's inception in 2007, the resulting impact on employees has been positive (Calderon, 2015):

▶ GSA employee participants were shown to be 2.9 times more likely to remain with Best Buy than a comparison group of nonparticipating employees.

▶ Managers of participating employees reported increases in employees' leadership and engagement following camps.

Girls who attend the Geek Squad Academy, a two-day technology camp, are taught by Best Buy employees.

AP Photo/Trent Nelson

- ▶ Employees indicated they had learned new knowledge or skills (90.8% favorable), felt more committed to Best Buy (96.2%), and felt more energized about their work (94.4%).

- ▶ GSA employee participants had longer tenure and higher performance appraisal scores than the comparison group on average.

SCENARIO OUTCOME

To recap, after the tech crash in the mid-2000s, Intel knew it had to transform, and thus it had to motivate its employees to be innovative. A key problem was how to best communicate with them. Intel's internal communications team developed communications in three broad categories in answer to these questions:

How can Intel connect employees together to encourage conversations with each other? With top management?

The solution was "Connect Me." Intel was serious about engaging its employees. All intranet articles allowed comments and dialogue. All full-time employees could have a company blog. It tapped the "wisdom of the crowd," through Intelpedia, Ask a Geek forums, and forums for asking peer advice during annual benefits enrollment. Employees could personalize their intranet home pages with the modules of their choice—and 40% did within the first few months. The Intel intranet also encouraged conversations with executives through leader profiles, blogs, one-to-a-few sessions, and quarterly webcasts.

How can Intel show employees it values them?

The solution was "Value Me." Intel used online platforms to show employees it cared in small and big ways. Intel started with fun recognition rewards like movie tickets and debit cards and soon added online tutoring and information about tuition assistance, health centers, and scholarships. It found that employees may not realize the benefits they're already getting, so it used social media to raise awareness of perks such as stock options using friendly, easy-to-understand language.

Employees can be your best advocates. How can Intel inspire employees to explain to outsiders what they do?

The solution was "Inspire Me." Intel is a very technical company where it's hard for employees to explain what they do, especially to outsiders. To make it easier, the communications team created an intranet platform where employees could share the Intel story then recruit ambassadors to start the conversations. It didn't take long before people were engaging before they were asked to. One example is the team who, on their own, turned a code of conduct training course into a fun, Bollywood-style presentation with much greater impact than the conventional version. Intel has learned that engaging 100,000 people starts with a good story.

It's working. Storytelling is enthralling and motivating. Since Intel started using digital platforms to engage employees, organizational health scores have gone up, dialogue is trending positive, turnover is less than 2%, and pride is at a record high. The company sees mobile as its next area of growth as it has 40,000 manufacturing employees without access to PCs. So far it has created an internal app that employees can put on their personal devices to receive news, benefits information, and other company updates.

WRAP UP

In this chapter you've learned employee relations is a growing and demanding area due to many factors, including a changing workforce, employee diversity, broader communication channels, the complexities of creating a healthy corporate culture, the increased frequency of change due to mergers and acquisitions, and employees' strong desire for a socially conscious workplace.

PR's role in supporting a healthy corporate culture includes counseling management's leadership style, encouraging teamwork, getting and valuing employee input, and supporting volunteer opportunities.

Facilitating employee engagement is a top priority, achieved by creating opportunities for dialogue and collaborative decision-making, encouraging creativity and new ideas, being truthful in your communication, welcoming diversity, and being socially conscious.

Corporate change happens often and can be done poorly or successfully; PR supports success with communication strategies as early as possible in the change cycle. Essential communication and engagement tactics include intranets, e-newsletters, video storytelling, and various employee programs. Throughout the chapter, you've explored the breadth of employee relations and PR's role in it.

Acquisitions: A corporate action in which a company buys most, if not all, of another firm's ownership stakes to assume control of it, **245**

Corporate Culture: Beliefs and behaviors that determine how a company's employees and management interact as well as handle outside business transactions, **246**

Divestiture: Corporate action of selling off subsidiary business units or interests, **253**

Due Diligence: Reasonable steps taken by a person or firm to satisfy a legal requirement or before entering into an agreement, **253**

Employee Advocacy: Promotion of an organization by its employees, **250**

Employee Relations: Strategic communication process that builds mutual relationships between an organization and its employees, **245**

Intranet: Private online network accessible only to an organization's employees, **255**

Mergers: Uniting of two existing companies into one new company, **245**

Organizational Clarity: When employees understand the organization's culture and brand identity, **254**

THINK ABOUT IT

Companies benefit from increased employee morale and loyalty. Timberland is a U.S. manufacturer and retailer of footwear, outdoor apparel, and accessories with worldwide operations. The company has a long history of social and environmental responsibility that is ingrained into its corporate culture. Visit Timberland's responsibility website at www.timberland.com/responsibility.html. Do you get the sense that Timberland is genuine in its commitment to CSR? Explore and note the many issues, programs, and opportunities that engage employees. See how Cone Communications reinforced Timberland's CSR brand positioning at www.conecom.com/case-studies/timberland.

WRITE LIKE A PRO

In this chapter you were challenged to solve Intel's internal communication problem. Now apply what you learned to this situation: Over the past three years, Hopkins College, a 120-year-old creative and media arts school in a Midwestern urban setting, has maintained excellent educational standards and placed graduates in top media positions. However, it has also lost some state funding, eliminated staff and faculty raises, and has experienced increased employee turnover. The leadership wants to reinvigorate a sense of community and motivate dedication in its employees (staff and faculty).

As Intel conceived of a new, bold vision statement—*This decade, we will create and extend computing technology to connect and enrich the life of every person on earth.* Now it's your turn. Brainstorm and draft a short vision statement that makes an emotional connection to Hopkins's employees and propose how it would be communicated to engage employees.

SOCIAL RESPONSIBILITY CASE STUDY

IBM's Corporate Service Corps Develops the Leaders of the Future

Situation

IBM has a long history of volunteerism involving employees, applying technology to innovative solutions for education, economic development, environmental sustainability, healthcare, and more.

Research and Strategy

IBM launched its Corporate Service Corps (CSC) in 2008 primarily as a vehicle for leadership development and CSR. Teams of eight to 15 members work pro bono with volunteers, government, business, and civic leaders in emerging markets to help address high-priority issues with societal significance. Key to success is their partnerships with NGOs who assist in providing strategic implementation for the programs.

IBM also has invited a number of its clients including FedEx, John Deere, and JPMorgan Chase to collaborate and join IBM CSC Teams. Among their goals was to foster a broader awareness of the value of integrating corporate citizenship with overall business strategy.

Execution

Inspired by the U.S. Peace Corps, the CSC program has sent more than 2,700 IBMers from nearly 60 countries to serve on more than 1,000 projects in 37 countries. The program is directly aligned with IBM's core value of innovation that matters by harnessing advanced technologies and problem-solving expertise in tackling some of the world's most pressing challenges.

First, teams of IBMers around the world work online for three months preparing for each project. Then the team takes up residency in the country for one month to work with a beneficiary organization to develop recommendations for both immediate and long-term impact. The feedback from the beneficiaries and partners served by CSC teams has been overwhelmingly positive and appreciative. "We're changing the way people see IBM," says Stanley Litow, IBM vice president of Corporate Citizenship and Corporate Affairs. "They now see us as a company that provides services and solves critical problems."

Evaluation

The CSC's corporate and non-profit partnership has produced many positive results (Table 10.2).

The corporation also realizes that engaged and committed employees are inspired to provide exceptional client experiences. Nine of every 10 IBM participants say their international corporate service experience provided them with excellent leadership opportunities while helping them better understand IBM's role in the developing world, increasing their cultural awareness, and making them more effective at their jobs. Most employees say that participation in the program boosted their desire to complete their careers at IBM.

TABLE 10.2

IBM Corporate Service Corps

COLLABORATIONS	SOCIAL RESPONSIBILITY ACTIONS
Ghanaian Health Service and the Yale School of Medicine	Together with CSC, they work to eliminate mother-to-child HIV transmission first in Ghana and then throughout sub-Saharan Africa.
NGO CerviCusco	Together they work to expand cervical cancer screening and treatment in Peru.
The Nature Conservancy	In a joint project, they develop strategies for conservation and commerce to coexist in Brazil's Amazon rain forest.
Global FoodBanking Network	Together they work to improve access to nutrition in Colombia, Ecuador, and Mexico.
SYSTEMS, PROGRAMS, APPS	**SOCIAL RESPONSIBILITY ACTIONS**
Knowledge Management	CSC developed web-based knowledge management systems to improve eye care in India.
Disaster Preparedness	CSC implemented a system for disaster preparedness integral to disaster relief and recovery in the Philippines.
Health-Care Programs	CSC developed policies and programs for healthcare for women and children in Nigeria.
Refugee Mobile App	CSC developed a free mobile app to better assist refugees and immigrants in need of medical care in Italy.

ENGAGE

- ▸ Go to the IBM website, and explore the breadth of the company's products, services, and industries served.

- ▸ After you've found a few areas that really interest you, go to "About IBM" and select "Corporate Responsibility" and then "Our Initiatives."

- ▸ Explore the four categories of initiatives: Education & Workforce Development, Citizen Diplomacy & Employee Engagement, Community Health & Wellness, and Environment & Disaster relief.

- ▸ Finally, at the bottom of the page, view the "Corporate Responsibility Report," and pay special attention to the "The IBMer" section.

DISCUSS

- ▸ Choose and discuss an IBM initiative that you think is particularly innovative.

- ▸ Assume you have the knowledge to participate in any of the initiatives. Which one would you choose, and why? What part of the experience might help strengthen your affinity with IBM?

- ▸ In the CSR report's "The IBMer" section, what did you learn about how IBM views and values employees? What surprised you or impressed you the most, and why?

Sources: IBM (n.d.a, b, c); PYXERA Global (n.d.).

SOCIAL RESPONSIBILITY CASE STUDY

Ben & Jerry's Ice Cream Gives Back to Vermont

Situation

More than 16 years after Unilever acquired it in 2000, Ben & Jerry's (B&J) has remained strongly mission driven, having a bigger impact than before because of its increased size (it nearly tripled). Unilever had agreed to a high level of autonomy for B&J, and to ensure middle managers did not contaminate the unique culture, Unilever established an "external board" charged with overseeing B&J's culture and social mission. Basically, B&J was given the freedom to pursue its own agenda if the ice cream kept flowing. In 2012 it became B Corp certified, the first wholly owned subsidiary in the world to do so.

Research and Strategy

One of its continuing responsibility efforts is Ben & Jerry's Foundation, established in 1985. Its philanthropy is led by employees who serve on committees that review grants. They focus on giving back to Vermont communities and supporting grassroots activism and community organizing for social and environmental justice around the country.

Execution

In 2015, 46 employees served on the committee, awarding about $2.5 million in grants. Its Grassroots Organizing for Social Change grant was made to approximately 65 organizations, including the Alliance for Appalachia, the Chicago Anti-Eviction Campaign, Committee for a Better New Orleans, the Garment Worker Center in Los Angeles, and the Student Immigrant Movement.

Each year the foundation member employees, staff, and trustees spend some time visiting with past grant recipients. In late October of 2013, they visited Tucson, Arizona, and Nogales, Mexico, to meet with grantees. The team spent three days visiting with organizers and service providers on both sides of the border to learn firsthand about the plight of migrants, U.S. immigration policies, Border Patrol practices, and Arizona laws that negatively impact immigrant and native-born communities.

Upon returning, the committee sent a letter to Patrick Senator Leahy, then chair of the Senate Judiciary Committee. It read, in part: "Dear Senator Leahy: We are a group of employees of Ben & Jerry's and the Ben & Jerry's Foundation who visited Tucson, Arizona and Nogales, Mexico in late October 2013 to observe firsthand the situation facing migrants and the impact of U.S. immigration policies and practices in the border region." It continued, "We quickly found . . . that there was much we did not know, much the American public does not know, about the persistent violations of human rights, the staggering cost and the too often cruel enforcement practices of U. S. government agencies." The letter went on to detail the culture of cruelty against migrants.

Evaluation

This is certainly putting B&J's values into action and encourages employee engagement, satisfaction, and ultimately retention. Along with giving employees the authority to act on important social justice issues like immigration, employees benefit in other ways. B&J employees are paid double the minimum wage. Young employees are encouraged to advance their education. They benefit from the B&J Core Academy, a partnership with Champlain College in Burlington, Vermont, offering an online program to help young retail and food service workers cultivate their passions and develop skills to advance their careers. Each year employee community service projects at B&J Vermont sites fix, clean, build, and improve quality of life for local communities.

ENGAGE

▸ Go to the B&J website (www.benjerry.com), and explore all the pages in the "Values" tab.

▸ On the dropdown menu for the "Values" tab, select the overview, and watch the *Our Social Mission* video.

▸ Back on the B&J home page, choose the "About Us" tab, and on the dropdown menu select "SEAR Reports." (SEAR stands for "Social & Environmental Assessment Report.") Take a quick look at some of the content from the company's 28th year of reporting.

DISCUSSION

▸ You met various employees in the *Our Social Mission* video. As a tactic to communicate its values, how authentic and believable do you think this video is? Why? What in the video worked or didn't?

▸ From what you've learned about communicating to stakeholders in this and past chapters, evaluate the effectiveness of this CSR report. Would you have produced it differently?

Sources: Ben & Jerry's (n.d.); Ben & Jerry's Foundation (n.d.); Gelles (2015)

VIDEO CASE

Blue Ballroom: Internal Communications

The Blue Ballroom is an internal communications agency. Like other PR firms, they are hired by outside companies, but to handle employee relations rather than external PR. This can include intranets, emails, newsletters, etc.

VIDEO

1. What strategies does Blue Ballroom use to promote employee engagement?

2. What is the role of empathy in crafting a message for a given audience? How might a message differ depending on the traits of the audience?

3. What channel would you choose to communicate a new company policy expanding the availability of flextime?

iStock.com/Jirsak

11 Corporate Communication and Reputation Management

Learning Objectives

11.1   Understand the context and environment surrounding the modern corporation

11.2   Describe the core competencies in corporate communications

11.3   Illustrate how SR enhances corporate communications

11.4   Explain the importance of financial communications, media relations, and investor relations in corporate communications

Scenario

Starbucks "Race Together"

Following the tragedies in Ferguson, Missouri, and New York City in 2014, Howard Schultz, CEO of Starbucks, was deeply saddened by the rising racial tensions in the United States. He felt his company needed to address the issue and refused to be a silent bystander. Schultz invited Starbucks employees to participate in internal discussion forums across the nation, where they could come together and discuss race issues in the United States.

Starbucks' attempts to encourage their employees to engage customers in conversations about race resulted in immediate mockery.

AP Photo/Ted S. Warren

As an outgrowth of these forums, on March 16, 2015, Starbucks released a memo to all retail employees encouraging them to engage customers in conversation about race in the company's stores by writing the words "Race Together" on their coffee cups.

Well intentioned, poorly received. The initiative was well intentioned, but when introduced to customers, it was poorly received. Most people did not want to discuss a topic as complex as race relations while they rushed to get their coffee. The public thought race was an inappropriate topic for a company to address with customers in a retail setting, and the idea was harshly mocked. Late-night talk show hosts ridiculed the initiative, including John Oliver (2015), host of *Last Week Tonight*, who suggested "a conversation about race relations in America is clearly important, but there is a time and a place." At the end of the piece he advised Starbucks to "just stay in your lane."

A fierce Twitter storm. The campaign was heavily criticized on social media to the extent that the vice president of corporate communications took down his Twitter account as he felt he was "being harshly attacked."

A sampling of negative tweets about "Race Together" follows:

Not sue what @Starbucks was thinking. I don't have time to sxplain 400 years of oppression to you & still make my train. #Race Together

> *@ReignOfApril*

yesterday: talk about Love at McDonalds
Today: talk about race at Starbucks
Tmrw: psychoanalysis from guy who makes blizzards at dairy queen

> *@MikeIsaac*

Would #Starbucks lower their prices in order to offset the emotional cost of discussing #Race Together with a clueless Barista?

> *@leviljkm*

269

The only folks about Starbucks baristas discussing race with customers are the suits who run it. Feel-good liberalism at its worst.

@JamilSmith

The Twitter storm was fierce but blew over quickly. The media response was equally critical, and the press labeled the initiative as poorly executed and gratuitous.

When the writing on the cups stopped a week later, most people thought the initiative had quietly shut down. Many believed the campaign had been cut short because of the negative reaction from the public and media.

Did Starbucks suffer lingering damage? Starbucks maintained that writing "Race Together" on cups lasted for its intended run date, March 16 to March 22, 2015, and only played a small role in the overall "Race Together" initiative (Ziv, 2015). The act of writing on cups was meant to serve as a jumping off point in the conversation, and Starbucks claimed it already had a larger plan in place to address the racial divide. At the end of the chapter, you will learn how this initiative played out.

As you read through the chapter, consider the following:

1. Should companies like Starbucks (or any other retail business) seek to engage customers in a discussion about race relations in the United States?

2. After the rocky start to the campaign, what would you advise them to do next?

3. What program options might have worked better and still be true to Starbucks's corporate culture?

4. Are there some topics or issues that corporations should avoid altogether? Why?

5. Was this an effective social responsibility initiative?

Source: Michael, Cauley, and Orengo (2016).

This chapter offers an overview on corporate communications and reputation management on a global basis in a digital society. It includes important lessons on building relationships between the corporation and its key stakeholders—including the internal audience. Through examples and case studies you will learn about the skills you need to succeed in a high-stakes environment. It will also focus on the role of corporate leaders and their expectations of the communications team and their outside advisors to protect and enhance corporate reputation.

Finally it includes short case studies throughout to illustrate the chapter's learning objectives and an opening scenario that puts you in the picture facing challenges that are part of the daily routine for corporate communications professionals.

THE MODERN CORPORATION— MEETING THE CHALLENGE

>> LO 11.1   Understand the context and environment surrounding the modern corporation

To understand the challenges faced daily by corporate communications professionals, whether they are on staff or serve as outside advisors, you must understand the

context and environment of today's corporations. Unless you have already worked in a corporate setting, your perceptions are likely driven by the popular media or corporate case studies you've read.

The images of corporate life and of business—as depicted in TV shows like *Mad Men* or *The Office* and movies like *Horrible Bosses* and *The Devil Wears Prada*—are dramatized for entertainment and effect. In the real world, life as a corporate communicator is no more like these stereotypes than working in crisis communications or politics is comparable to *Scandal* (ABC) or *House of Cards* (Netflix).

COMPANIES ARE MULTIFACETED

Companies are complex organizations with a variety of stakeholders who interact with them daily, both internally and externally. Companies are focused on operating profitably, providing quality goods and services to the marketplace, obeying the law, being a good place to work, and being regarded as a good corporate citizen.

In addition, companies—particularly the ones whose common stock is publicly traded on a **stock exchange**—like the NASDAQ or New York Stock Exchange (NYSE)—have set routines for reporting their financial results to the public, media, and shareholders. The schedule of financial communications—for example, quarterly and annual reports—must be adhered to by law and has its own set of rules and requirements. These will be addressed more in the section of this chapter on financial communications.

Communications in a corporate setting can be a high-stakes and challenging activity. You are tasked with representing the company, its products, and its employees to the external market. You may also be involved in communicating with employees—perhaps even globally—depending on the size and scope of the company. Often you are responsible for developing or promoting the company's SR initiatives as well. In some cases you may be involved in the company's communications with the financial community.

Finally, you must learn to interpret and convey trends in the marketplace *inward* to management and convey the character and reputation of the company *outward* to the public. This role—as an intermediary between the company and its external stakeholders—can be one of the most challenging.

THE ISSUE OF TRUST

The Edelman Trust Barometer examines this challenge and provides us with some guidance. In the years since it was first published in 2001, this study has become one of the definitive annual studies on how business, government, NGOs, and the media are perceived by the public and opinion leaders worldwide (Edelman, 2017).

The 2016 study noted a steadily increasing gap in trust in the four institutions (Figure 11.1), between the Mass Population and the "Informed" Public. The results starkly illustrate the growing divide and the sense of disenfranchisement which is impacting markets and elections worldwide.

The study also shows, among the general population, that business is most trusted to keep pace with the changing times compared to government and the media (Figure 11.2).

> SOCIAL
> RESPONSIBILITY

FIGURE 11.1

A Significant Divide

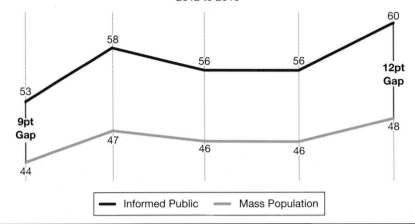

Percent trust in the four institutions of government, business, media, and NGOs, 2012 to 2016

Source: Edelman (2017).

FIGURE 11.2

Business Most Trusted to Keep Pace

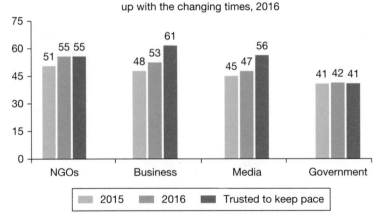

Percent trust, 2015 and 2016, and percent who trust each institution to keep up with the changing times, 2016

Source: Edelman (2017).

CRITICAL ROLE FOR CORPORATE PUBLIC RELATIONS

This is the challenge for corporate communications in today's global economy. A strong and effective corporate communications team must be able to accomplish the following:

▸ Identify and engage key stakeholders.

▸ Secure powerful and impactful media coverage.

▸ Develop **thought leadership** opportunities (research, speeches, and events) to promote and enhance executive visibility.

▸ Promote the corporate brand and enhance reputation by creating and leveraging CSR initiatives.

▸ Manage issues and crisis situations as needed.

The basic equation is: The more positive news the corporate PR team generates and the better it manages the negative stories (e.g., issues and crisis situations), the greater the chance the company can increase sales and revenue, engage stakeholders, and serve the market successfully. This may sound simple, but as any experienced corporate communicator can attest, it is far from simple. To "solve" this equation the corporate communicator must be skilled, ethical, honest, as transparent as possible, and accountable to both internal and external stakeholders.

Clearly this is a 360-degree role and requires your best efforts daily (see Figure 11.3). You will need to understand the company's business strategy, the financial markets, traditional and social media, government and political trends, and the needs and expectation of your fellow employees and external stakeholders.

Commenting on the importance of communicators helping companies to drive change and build trust, Gary Sheffer, retired vice president of corporate communications at General Electric, suggests, "Today, trust is crucial. Customers are more inclined to buy from a trusted company and advocate to others that they do the same. Costs decrease when a company has trusting relationships in its supply chain. Trusted companies retain employees and outperform their competitors. The role (of corporate communications) revolves around earning and preserving this valuable currency of trust" (Haran & Sheffer, 2015).

> "What do stakeholders expect of business today? Certainly, a solid and steady focus on financial returns, but even more [people] say [they expect] action around education, healthcare, income inequality and other [social] issues."
>
> —Kathryn Beiser, former global chair, corporate practice, Edelman (Edelman, 2016)

COMMUNICATIONS' PLACE IN THE COMPANY

All companies—regardless of their structure, size, and ownership (e.g., public or private)—have similar communications goals. They want to communicate their results; promote their products or services; be known as a good place to work and a reliable business partner; and earn a reputation as a good corporate citizen. Achieving these goals, as internal and external events unfold, and managing the challenges as they arise are the responsibility of the corporate communicator.

The organizational structure and reporting relationship of the corporate communications function differs from company to company. In some companies, the communications staff is part of the marketing function and reports to the senior executive responsible for marketing, PR, and advertising. These individuals, whose titles are usually **chief marketing officer (CMO)**, are responsible for overall marketing and the corporate brand.

In other companies the communications function is a separate discipline and reports directly to the chief executive officer (CEO) or president of the company. Communicators in this role are often referred to as the **chief communications officer (CCO)**. Still other companies have variations on these models, with the communications team reporting to another senior executive, such as human resources (personnel), general counsel (legal officer), or the chief financial officer (CFO)—although these are usually the exceptions.

FIGURE 11.3

Anatomy of the Corporate Communicator

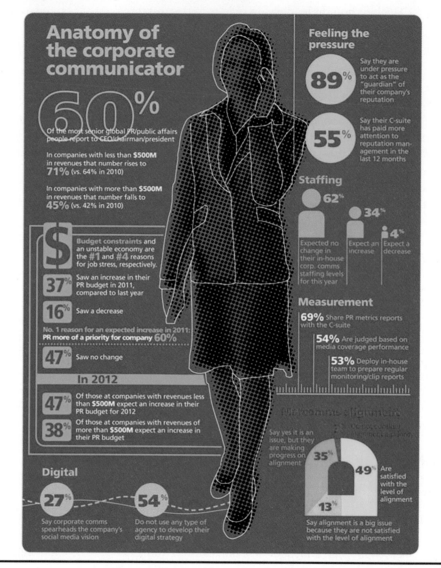

Source: PRWeek (2016).

The reporting relationship of the communications function has been debated over the years, and different models continue to be employed. Changes in reporting relationships are driven mostly by external market events (e.g., the trend toward integrated marketing communications in large consumer product companies) or management's changing view on how to structure the communications function.

Arthur W. Page Society President Roger Bolton says "there is a lot of ongoing discussion...about the CCO's role in relation to marketing and communications convergence, and there is a lot of substance behind that because those two areas are becoming so closely intertwined."

"I don't think we'll see a (consistent) trend toward one model or the other. CEOs want someone who 'gets it' and can run the two functions for them," Bolton adds.

"It is OK for each company to have its own approach as long as they understand that marketing and communications have two fundamentally different purposes" (Daniels, 2015).

Regardless of whether the communications team reports to the CEO or elsewhere, his or her direct involvement and support are critical to the success of the effort. A recent study states that "[t]he performance of corporate communications depends heavily on the perceptions, beliefs, and expectations that chief executive officers (CEOs), and other top executives, hold towards communication and its contribution to organizational goals" (Zerfass & Sherzada, 2014).

CORE COMPETENCIES OF CORPORATE COMMUNICATIONS

>> LO 11.2 Describe the core competencies in corporate communications

The specific duties of the corporate communications professional most often include: media relations (see also Chapter 7); branding, special events, and sponsorships (see also Chapter 13), internal or employee communications (see also Chapter 10); and community relations and sustainability communications (see also Chapter 9). These duties, along with **financial communications** for public companies, make up the overall function of corporate communications and are designed to help achieve the overall goals of the company or organization.

To meet their communications challenges, companies often engage outside PR and public affairs firms to assist them in work. According to the research firm IDC, companies spent 3.8% of their marketing budget on PR in 2014—5.7% on branding and content, 1.9% on social marketing, and 1.1% on industry analyst relations (see Table 11.1), all functions that are often handled by an outside PR agency (Comcowich, 2015).

As such, you do not need to be directly employed by a corporation to be engaged in corporate communications. You can work for a PR agency (like Edelman, Ketchum, Hill & Knowlton, or many others), a management consulting firm (like Booz Allen Hamilton), or as a sole practitioner and still be engaged in corporate communications.

CORPORATE MEDIA RELATIONS

Media relations, a topic covered in detail in Chapter 7, is a critical component of corporate communications for today's corporation. Not only is the corporate world a key focus of coverage by the traditional media, both local and national, but it is a hot

TABLE 11.1

Percent of Marketing Budget Spent on Corporate Communication Activities

ACTIVITIES	PERCENT OF BUDGET SPENT
Public Relations	3.8%
Branding	5.7%
Social Marketing	1.9%
Analyst Relations	1.1%

topic on social media as well. On any given day, you will find stories or conversations on the major social media platforms about corporate performance, issues, plans, and strategy. Media relations is challenging, dynamic, and ever changing. This is especially true for "big business" and for publicly traded companies. The explanation for this phenomenon is simple—the number of people and dollar amounts involved are bigger, the news is local *and* global, and the personalities and activities of the CEOs and senior management involved are compelling.

Looking at the target media for your company or client, you will find a vast array of options and outlets to consider. There are key national publications that track business performance, such as the *New York Times*, Bloomberg, and *The Wall Street Journal*, leading business magazines like *Fortune* and *Forbes*, as well as countless broadcast and cable outlets like CNN and MSNBC, to contend and interact daily. You also need to manage your company's relationship with the local media—both print and broadcast—where your company or client is based and/or has major operations, such as factories or regional offices – sometimes around the world. These publications have a vested interest in covering your company because you operate in their market area.

There are also numerous online outlets including Yahoo Finance, Google Finance, Business Insider, Market Watch, and The Huffington Post. Also, almost all the major traditional business media (e.g., *Fortune*, *Forbes*, *The Wall Street Journal*, etc.) maintain and update their own websites daily on a constant basis. These and other outlets, including trade media that cover your business or industry, are constantly looking for business news from companies—such as updates on corporate performance, management changes, product introductions, and other corporate news. That is the good news—especially if you have a good story to tell.

The bad news is that this constant attention cuts both ways. Should a crisis or major issue arise, the same content-hungry local and national media are there to pick up the story and run with it. Managing this two-edged sword and building— or defending—your company's reputation is a critical job for today's corporate communicators. While the stakes are high at this level, the media relations theory

United faced a media firestorm in 2017 when it summoned airport police to remove a passenger from an overbooked flight to make room for a United crewmember. The passenger suffered multiple injuries, and video of the incident circulated widely online.

Joshua Lott/AFP/Getty Images

and approach is the same as a smaller organization or nonprofit. The process is about building and maintaining relationships among the company, the media, and all its external stakeholders.

Supa and Zoch (2009) suggest that "media relations is the systematic, planned, purposeful and mutually beneficial relationship between a public relations practitioner and a mass media journalist." You can certainly extend that to the digital media as well. In a corporate setting, the process of media relations entails the PR professional being available and willing to meet with the media outlets and, selectively, to make senior management available to discuss a story idea or topic in detail. In turn the media representative is expected to provide a fair and accurate story on the issue or topic at hand as well as bring in other points of view to balance the story as they see fit. However, while this may sound simple, it is not. Some company executives will routinely expect their news coverage to always be positive or flattering. Further, some reporters are indeed out to promote themselves by putting corporate executives in difficult situations or by getting a scoop that creates follow-up stories, social media traffic, and a higher overall profile. Fortunately most reporters are professionals and looking to tell a balanced and interesting story.

Your goal as a communicator is to help produce an accurate, balanced story that represents the company's point of view and conveys your key messages to target audiences while meeting the reporter's needs. The independence of the media outlet and reporter must be respected, just as the company's point of view should be. That is the basis of the mutually beneficial working relationship of corporate media relations.

DIGITAL MEDIA RELATIONS

The most influential recent change in the practice of modern corporate media relations is the proliferation of social media. Social media allow PR practitioners to speak directly to target audiences, without interference or alteration by a media gatekeeper, as in traditional media relations. Internet-based technologies have become important direct distribution channels for company information. New media, however, offer a special set of challenges and opportunities as there is often no gatekeeper or control over what gets posted as "news" by these so-called citizen journalists.

The rise of social media platforms such as YouTube, Facebook, Instagram, and Twitter, among others, provides new PR opportunities as well as risks. You must think carefully about which option is the best option for communicating to your target publics. These stakeholders, in turn, have high expectations for how organizations should interact with them online.

Typically, stakeholders expect corporate communication that meets these criteria:

▶ Authentic

▶ Honest

▶ Candid

▶ Two-Way

Social media often blurs the line between the personal and the professional, so the key proficiency for PR practitioners is to master building and managing your organization's online identity and reputation.

A 24-HOUR-A-DAY JOB

The ability via social media to communicate directly and interactively has made media relations a 24-hour-a-day job with reporters expecting corporate websites to have up-to-the-second information available without them having to wait for a PR staffer. As a result online corporate content must be carefully screened, current, and well organized so that journalists will find the information they need from you quickly—instead of your competitors or, worse, your adversaries.

FUNDAMENTAL PRACTICES REMAIN

Despite these developments in digital media, the fundamental relationship between the PR practitioner and the journalist remains unchanged. Journalists still want access to accurate information so they can craft a fair and balanced story; PR practitioners still want, above all, coverage of client news—as positive and balanced as possible. Bloggers, Twitter users, and other commentators want interesting, factual, and truthful information as well.

SOCIAL RESPONSIBILITY

In the end the mutual dependence between the two camps nurtures a relationship that serves both parties well. Journalists and digital media outlets need PR practitioners to provide them information for stories, and the PR practitioners need journalists to provide voice and distribution for their messages. Jon Iwata, senior vice president of marketing, communications, and citizenship at IBM, summed up the challenge and opportunity of corporate communications in a 2009 Distinguished Lecture at the Institute of Public Relations (Iwata & Golin, 2009):

> As never before, people care about the corporation behind the soft drink, the bank account or the computer. They do not separate their opinions about the company from their opinions of that company's products and services … or its stock, for that matter. People care about the behavior and compensation of the company's executives … how the product was produced, and by whom … how the company treats its employees and suppliers … how it impacts the environment. Now, maybe people always cared about these things—but, really, how much could they know about what was happening inside our companies? Today they have an unprecedented view into the corporation's actual behavior and actual performance.

ON THE JOB IN MEDIA RELATIONS

Applying the core principles of corporate media relations—access to management, transparency, mutual benefit, accuracy, and fairness—is a challenging undertaking. As well, it is neither static nor totally predictable because the circumstances change often and your objectives and that of the media outlet will not always align. As a corporate communicator, you should assess each opportunity or challenge and determine the best course of action. This will depend on the nature of the opportunity or problem.

> Is it a positive story (new product, market trend, or management appointment) or a potentially negative one (issue, crisis, or a decline in sales and profits)?

INSIGHTS

How the Excellence Theory Is Helping Practitioners Manage Media Relations

James Grunig, a leading PR researcher, has developed a foundational communications theory that many corporate communicators interpret and apply in managing media relations in all its forms.

The Excellence Theory is a general theory of PR that resulted from a multiyear study of best practices in communication management funded by the International Association of Business Communicators (IABC) Research Foundation. Three books and multiple scholarly articles were published based on the study results (Dozier & Broom, 1995; Grunig, 1992; Grunig & Grunig, 2000, 2003, 2008).

The basis of the theory is the notion of symmetrical, or two-way, communication between an organization and its key publics, which almost always includes the mass media and social media (see Figure 11.4). Grunig theorizes that the building of these relationships, which ideally are mutually beneficial, leads to more effective communications.

In a recent blog post, Grunig discussed the role of the digital media, which has come into prominence since his theory was first published in 1992. He suggests the advent of digital media is an opportunity to increase and improve the two-way communications that is at the foundation of his model—if the platform is properly utilized.

FIGURE 11.4

Two-Way Symmetrical Model (Excellence Theory)

"I think that digital media, which includes social media but is a broader concept, are inherently interactive and therefore two-way. However, too many practitioners still use digital media as a way of dumping information on publics, the symbolic-interpretive approach, and therefore think of social media sites only as a means of disseminating messages. Instead, they should think of digital media as a way of identifying problems, publics, and issues that require the attention of strategic managers and as a way of engaging in dialogue with key publics" (James Grunig: Excellence Theory, blog post, 2013). ●

How will management react and comment if they are engaged? Will they listen to your advice?

Other factors to weigh include the following:

Does your company have a point of view on the issue?

Is your management team fully briefed and ready to respond to media questions on the topic?

What are the risks of participating in the discussion?

By answering these questions, and preparing accordingly, your corporate media relations efforts will likely be successful, and your company or client will benefit in an enhanced corporate reputation. Some recent campaigns illustrate how different companies responded to the challenge of implementing a corporate campaign with a strong media relations component.

A good example is an effort to publicize the role of the health insurance company Aflac during the implementation of the Affordable Care Act (ACA) in 2010. Many small businesses needed help in understanding and implementing the required

Responding to confusion regarding the requirements for small businesses created by ACA, Aflac launched a media campaign positioning itself as a source of expertise and assistance.

David Paul Morris/Bloomberg/ Getty Images

changes in their health insurance required by the ACA. Aflac is a leading insurance company that provides insurance and benefits-related services to the small business market and is well-known due to its commercials with the Aflac duck.

During the ACA rollout, the company had received feedback from its field agents about the confusion and designed a communications program with its agency (Hill & Knowlton) to create more awareness of the changes. Based on field research that showed only 17% of small business owners understood the ACA and how to comply, Aflac launched an integrated communications campaign with corporate media relations as a key element. The goal was to position Aflac as a source for information and guidance about the ACA for small businesspeople.

Media coverage created by the campaign was extensive, both in the national business press and in the specialized media serving the small business market. The campaign resulted in more than 700 placements in traditional media and 275 unique stories on social media as well as extensive coverage in the small business and insurance trade media (PRSA, 2014c).

Media relations can also play a key role in the launch of a new product, both to drive sales as well as enhance the reputation of the company behind a new product, such as the iPhone 6. During the launch of the iPhone 6 in 2014, Apple announced its intention to include a new proprietary payment platform (a "tap and go" feature) that would allow users to make purchases using only the new iPhone. The platform would use "the most advanced payment security technology" developed by MasterCard (MasterCard, 2015).

The use of the MasterCard-developed technology (now branded as Master Pay) offered the company, working with its agency (Ketchum), the opportunity to achieve three business goals: (1) capture market share from Visa and American Express; (2) position the company as the authority on payment safety and security; and (3) drive customer usage of the MasterCard network for payments with the iPhone 6. As noted the coverage would also support the reputation of MasterCard as a technology leader.

MasterCard and its spokespeople dominated media coverage of the new iPhone payment system and the online conversation about it as well. MasterCard's share of voice in the overall news coverage of the topic and related social media conversation was 37%, compared to Visa's 27% and American Express' 21%. Equally important, within 72 hours of the Apple Pay's launch, consumers had activated a million cards, creating the world's largest mobile payment system overnight (PRSA, 2015).

CRISIS MEDIA RELATIONS

On the other side of the equation, managing bad news or a crisis in a corporate setting also has media relations challenges. During the global banking and financial crisis in the early 2000s, many of the major banks and brokerage firms faced questions about their stability and, in some cases, their actual survival. The work of the major accounting firms advising these companies was also questioned, creating significant crisis and issues management challenges.

The corporate communicators inside those organizations, and their outside advisors, were front and center on those issues, managing an aggressive media, internal and external pressures, and management teams that were under fire for business practices that threatened the stability of the companies. The stakes were high for those communicators as they sought to balance the legitimate questions of the media and the public with the expectations of senior management.

So, you can see, protecting the corporate brand and reputation is a key challenge for corporate communicators in both good times and bad.

CORPORATE BRANDING AND REPUTATION

The practice of **corporate branding** is a relatively recent phenomenon and is an outgrowth of the trend toward reputation management as a key function of corporate communicators. More major companies and their leaders are seeing the value and benefits of building and maintaining a corporate brand as part of their reputation. Simply put a corporate brand is the attributes of a company that come to mind when you hear the name.

Apple has a strong corporate brand, reinforced by their innovative retail stores.

David Paul Morris/Bloomberg/Getty Images

For example, for a company like Apple you might think of innovation. The mention of Starbucks brings to mind SR. For a company like Tesla you might think of technology, design, or energy efficiency. Companies like these, and others such as General Motors, Google, and Under Armour, realize that successful corporate branding provides major benefits for their organizations and products. In addition a strong corporate brand can be a major asset in solidifying reputation when a major issue or a crisis impacts the company. Tom Martin (personal communication, 2016), who was responsible for corporate communications at two Fortune 500 companies (FedEx and ITT) notes:

> Having a strong organizational brand is particularly critical when a company faces a crisis. For example, General Motors faced numerous challenges in the last decade, including the ignition switch failures in 2014 that were blamed in several fatal crashes. The company accepted responsibility, focused on fixing the vehicles, doing right by its customers, and holding itself accountable. By doing the right thing, and by leveraging its strong global brand, sales rebounded within a year to pre-crisis levels and public opinion surveys overwhelmingly supported the company and its handling of the crisis.

Beyond crisis and issues management, creating a powerful brand enhances your business and reputation and paves the way for product launches, new corporate initiatives, and even mergers and acquisitions. Kevin Plank, CEO of Under Armour—the sports apparel and equipment company he founded in 1996 in a Washington, D.C., basement—believes in the power of building and living the corporate brand.

"Brand is not a product—that's for sure; it's not one item. It's an idea, it's a theory, it's a meaning, it's how you carry yourself and represent the company," Plank told CNBC (2015a).

For companies like Under Armour, the brand is paramount, and the corporate and marketing communications team focuses on it throughout all its communications activities. "We understand that our brand is our signature. It is how our customers, employees and investors see us and how we go to market," explains Diane Pelkey (personal communication, 2016), senior vice president, Global Communications and Entertainment. Under Armour has enjoyed a great reputation since its founding, but it has faced threats as well, especially recently. For example, when the U.S. speed skating team failed to meet expectations at the 2014 Winter Olympics in Sochi, Russia, it fell to the corporate communicators to manage these challenges.

A strong global corporate brand, such as Coca-Cola's, can have measurable financial value. The value of Coca-Cola's brand rose to $83.84 billion as of the end of 2014. This brand value is evident in the universal market acceptance and global consumer awareness of Coke products in nearly every corner of the world. Coke products are sold and enjoyed in every country in the world except two—North Korea and Cuba.

Clearly a lot of factors go into having a successful, dominant corporate brand. For Coca-Cola, the quality of its products, creative marketing, and a strong corporate reputation combine to boost its overall sales numbers. However, without question, the Coke brand creates a unique identity to distinguish its offerings from multiple global and local competitors. Coke's reputation is due in no small measure to the positive association most consumers have with its products and the company's global SR leadership and its commitment to diversity.

In general corporate branding employs the same methodology and tool box used in corporate PR and marketing communications. A strong and well-managed corporate branding strategy can add significant value to the company by helping the corporation implement a long-term vision, create a unique market position in the market place, and unlock the potential within the organization (Roll, 2009).

Most often the task of building and maintaining the corporate brand is the responsibility of the corporate communications team. This is the logical place for this responsibility because the PR function manages the relationships with most of a company's key stakeholders (e.g., employees, customers, investors, the local community, NGOs, issue activists, and the media).

SPECIAL EVENTS AND SPONSORSHIPS

Companies and organizations often take advantage of major corporate milestones, such as a historical anniversary, a name change, or other events to promote the organization and celebrate its contributions to the community or country where it is based. Leading companies will commit to major sponsorships (see Table 11.2) such as the 2018 FIFA World Cup of Soccer (e.g., Coca-Cola, Adidas, and Budweiser), the 2018 Winter Olympics (e.g., McDonald's, Proctor & Gamble, and Visa), or the 2016 Summer Olympics (e.g., Nissan, GE, and Nike).

Smaller, less expensive events such as arts and culture sponsorships, employee volunteer days, or local running events also create publicity opportunities for

---

INSIGHTS

Corporate Branding

What is the value of an organization's brand? Companies spend millions on market research to determine the value of product brands. Magazines publish lists of the world's most valuable brands, and those at the top are worth more than the gross domestic product (GDP) totals of some countries. But often the organizational brand, the value of the company *behind* the products, is underappreciated. In today's digital world, however, organizations are finding it necessary to focus not only on the way they brand the products and services they sell but also on the brand of the organization itself.

A few examples illustrate this:

▸ In the mid-1990s, Federal Express Corporation made the decision to re-brand itself as FedEx, the name its customers had begun to call the company years earlier. In part, FedEx did this because the name was shorter, easier to say, and already a part of the lexicon of business. But FedEx also recognized that its hundreds of planes and thousands of vehicles were huge, moving billboards. By designing a bold, distinctive corporate brand and prominently displaying it on all its aircraft and trucks—including the famous arrow between the letters—FedEx became a global icon and set itself apart from its primary competitor, UPS.

▸ An increasingly large number of global companies are embracing the notion that it is difficult to

support dozens, or hundreds, of product brands when they stand alone without a strong corporate brand. When these products are linked under a strong organizational brand, it builds employee pride, enhances customer loyalty, and heightens the overall prominence of both the company and its products.

▸ A few years ago, ITT Industries found itself in competition with strong global brands like GE and Siemens, yet it was still going to market in a fragmented way, with hundreds of individual product brands. By establishing a strong organizational brand and corporate identity, along with a new tagline—Engineered for Life—that resonated with its employees and customers, the company was in a better position to compete in the global marketplace.

With the increase in global competition and the pervasiveness of online commerce, organizational branding is more critical than ever before. Customers, employees, and investors are seeking authentic, trustworthy organizations to buy from, work for, and invest in. The corporate brand—properly positioned—provides the beacon by which all stakeholders can navigate. ●

Source: Provided by Thomas R. Martin, executive in residence, Department of Communication, The College of Charleston, and a former communications executive at FedEx and ITT.

Authenticity Is Key to Lesbian Gay Bisexual Transgender Public Relations

Bob Witeck, President and Founder of Witeck Communications

For early generations of Americans, gay men and lesbians understandably avoided and feared visibility, knowing that their lives and relationships, at best, were stigmatized by hostile majorities. Companies likewise feared risk and backlash when targeting gay customers or simply incorporating same-sex themes in their marketing mix. Today we see a dramatic sea change in the acceptance, visibility, and marketing presence of lesbian, gay, bisexual, and transgender (LGBT) people. What lessons do smart corporate communicators and marketers follow today to effectively communicate with LGBT audiences and households when considering LGBT-focused events or sponsorships?

Never Overlook the Rich Diversity Within the LGBT Community

Early PR and marketing strategies by companies often emphasized gay white men, leaving large segments of the community aside or simply in the shadows. Effective strategies today are mindful that there is a remarkable diversity of race, ethnicity, gender, and sexual orientation across the entire LGBT population. In fact as census data reveals, same-sex couples and households tend to be more racially diverse than traditional, opposite-sex couples. If a company wishes to reach the entire LGBT audience, they cannot really afford to overlook transgender and bisexual people too.

Millennials Make a Difference

Early on corporate communicators and marketers feared that reaching out to gay audiences risked losing their mainstream customers. Millennials, however, and other youthful consumers today are among the gay-friendliest generation ever—not merely accepting their LGBT friends, classmates, and family members but truly advocating for them. Marketers are smart to tap this "halo" effect in crafting inclusive, mainstream messaging that doesn't shy away or take risks.

Most of All, Authenticity Rules

LGBT consumers trust companies and brands most that acknowledge and embrace them fully. Before going to market, in brief, a company should demonstrate its values through a diverse workforce and nondiscriminatory employment policies. When a company practices family-friendly policies, do those families include same-sex couples and families too? Does the brand include LGBT spokespersons, and will the company sponsor significant LGBT causes and pride celebrations along with other causes meaningful to their workforce?

The opportunity for corporate leadership in the area is still not without risk, but companies and brands that are willing and able to *authentically* embrace the LGBT community will, no doubt, be rewarded with brand loyalty and purchase preference. Considering the LGBT market segment was estimated at $917 billion in 2016 by Bloomberg, this seems like smart business (Green, 2016). Some notable examples of successful engagement with the LGBT market are found in the hospitality/travel and tech markets: Hilton, Marriott, Alaska Airlines, and American Airlines; and Apple, Google and Intel. ●

Bob Witeck has consulted with corporations since 1993 on their LGBT business and market strategies. He is coauthor of Business Inside Out *(2006, Kaplan), considered the first business guide on effective LGBT marketing.*

Source: B. Witeck (personal communication, 2017).

sponsoring companies. These local events connect a company with the community, create goodwill, and enhance company reputation. In both cases, large and small events, it often falls to the corporate communications team to leverage these investments. This can involve designing strategic plans and PR tactics to create meaningful publicity and product promotions to create brand awareness consistent with the investment the company is making.

These special events also can serve as unique opportunities to remind employees and other key stakeholders about the mission, character, and contributions of the

TABLE 11.2

Examples of Major Global Sponsorships

SPORTING EVENT	SPONSOR
2018 FIFA World Cup of Soccer	Coca-Cola, Adidas, Budweiser
2018 Winter Olympics	McDonald's, P&G, Visa
2016 Summer Olympics	Nissan, GE, Nike

company and to maintain or expand its service to the communities where it operates. This was the case in the Hertz Corporation headquarters relocation that will be examined in Chapter 12, in which the company wanted to maintain ties to its old hometown in New Jersey while building new ones in Florida.

For Booz Allen Hamilton, the government consulting firm, the company sought to mark its 100th anniversary by recommitting to its home market of Washington, D.C., and providing a way for employees to give back through a company-wide volunteer community service effort, reflecting its historic SR focus. The corporate communications team was charged with leveraging the event to not only celebrate the company's long history but to look forward to a brighter future as well.

INTERNAL COMMUNICATIONS

One key aspect of corporate communications that is often overlooked is internal or employee communications. In some organizations, corporate communications reports to human resources. The tendency to overlook the importance of communicating with employees is widespread, but it is often a missed opportunity to create a unified corporate image and a solid reputation.

Red e APP, a mobile platform focused on internal communication and employee engagement suggests, "If you asked most public relations professionals to point out the hip and sexy practices in the field, internal communications would probably not come to mind. Nevertheless, the field is essential to keeping organizations gelled, providing valuable information inside the company and effectively communicating company goals and visions" externally (Kent, 2014).

For many companies, especially retailers where the employees interact directly with the public (known as business to consumer [B2C]), internal communication is essential to preparing employees to represent the company and corporate brand in their daily work. As they interact with customers, they represent the company more directly and with more impact than many other forms of communications.

For example, a well-placed news story in a high-profile publication or news broadcast will impress current and prospective customers. However, it can be quickly overshadowed or offset if the message is not reinforced by a knowledgeable and informed employee the customer encounters in a retail or online setting.

Because winning in the marketplace is the primary goal of most companies, it must be for the corporate communications function as well. It is imperative to devise a system of internal communications that allows the free flow of necessary and important information your fellow employees need to do their jobs. This communication goes way beyond rolling out a new employee benefits program or publishing a newsletter, especially when changes are underway at the company, such as will be pointed out in the Hertz headquarters relocation and Booz Allen Hamilton cases.

"To win in the marketplace you must first win in the workplace."

—Doug Conant, CEO of Campbell's Soup

Booz Allen Hamilton's 100th Anniversary Campaign: Celebrating a Tradition of Community Service and Market Leadership

To celebrate its 100th anniversary, Booz Allen pledged 100,000 hours of community service.

Jeffrey Greenberg/UIG/Getty Images

Booz Allen Hamilton, the Fortune 500 consulting firm, turned 100 during 2014. During its first century, Booz Allen's consultants had played key roles in advising clients on national defense, space exploration, new product development, corporate turnarounds, and even the NFL. Booz Allen's goal for its 100th anniversary celebration was to engage its stakeholders in the firm's vision for the future.

Focus on Service

Against this backdrop, Booz Allen chose a strategy of *partnership and service.* Externally the firm partnered with respected organizations such as the NYSE, National Gallery of Art, Aspen Institute, and USS Midway Museum.

Internally Booz Allen built on its history of CSR, challenging employees to volunteer 100,000 hours of community service during the anniversary year.

Coworkers challenged each other to do more, and top volunteers in the Centennial Community Challenge earned grants worth $25,000 for charities. At the end of 2014, Booz Allen employees had performed and documented 152,713 volunteer hours of service.

Key Media Took Notice

The 100th anniversary celebration resulted in two prominent positive stories in *The Washington Post*—a business feature in March 2014, "Company Constant" by Marjorie Censer, and a CSR-focused article in December, "Booz Allen Marks 100 Years with Emphasis on Giving" by Amrita Jayakumar.

To celebrate the company's historic support of arts and culture, Booz Allen sponsored a major exhibit at the National Gallery of Art in Washington, D.C., that drew more than 350,000 visitors.

Target Market Efforts

In San Diego, a key market for the company, Booz Allen sponsored patriotic events at the USS Midway Museum on Memorial Day, the Fourth of July, and Veterans Day 2014 and provided a grant to enable San Diego-area school children to attend onboard science lessons.

Social Responsibility Focus

Each element of the anniversary program emphasized the company's community service and SR tradition and recommitted it to more in the future. These efforts were gathered and catalogued in the company's annual report and in all its sustainability reporting as well. ●

Source: Marie Lerch, former executive vice president of marketing and communications at Booz Allen.

Gagen MacDonald, a consulting firm that specializes in internal communications and change management, found in a 2014 study that the failure rate of many corporate mergers to deliver on the results promised (e.g., cost savings, entering new markets, or other synergies and improvements) is greater than 50% (Gagen MacDonald, n.d.).

Their research notes the most common reason for coming up short was the failure to successfully combine the corporate cultures and create a sense of common purpose for the employees going forward. In short the job of communicating to internal stakeholders about the proposed transaction is often not done well—if at all.

Beyond managing high-profile mergers or supporting company-wide culture changes, the day-to-day task of communicating to employees is essential to building morale and implementing corporate strategy. The better informed your employees are, and the more they understand their jobs, the more successful the company will be in the long run.

Jack Welch, former CEO of GE and a leading commentator on business and management, notes, "There are three measurements that tell you nearly everything you need to know about your organization's overall performance: employee engagement, customer satisfaction, and cash flow.... It goes without saying that no company, small or large, can win over the long run without energized employees who believe in the mission and understand how to achieve it" (Brand!ntegrity, n.d.).

SOCIAL RESPONSIBILITY IN ACTION

Navistar Enlists Employees for Turnaround

After a major setback and revenue decline, Navistar launched a major employee communications campaign to rebuild confidence and win support for the company's turnaround efforts.

Kuni Takahashi/Bloomberg/Getty Images

Truck manufacturer Navistar had gone through a rough couple of years after making a big bet on exhaust gas recirculation engines that failed to pass Environmental Protection Agency (EPA) emissions standards. The scramble to replace these engines, along with strong industry headwinds, caused Navistar's revenue to decline by 23% between 2011 and 2013 (Trainer, 2014).

Technology Miss Has Ripple Effect

The failure of the strategy led to quality control problems, warranty claims and costs, loss of market share, depleted cash reserves, and a threat to its survival. The company's profile as an SR leader was also in jeopardy. In response the COO decided that immediate change was necessary to regain customer and investor confidence.

"Drive to Deliver" Launched

In response the company developed a turnaround plan ("Drive to Deliver"), which had four key priorities:

1. Launching new products quickly

2. Improving product quality

3. Cutting costs to meet the operating plan

4. Building sales momentum

Employee Confidence Was Key

Senior management of Navistar asked the communications team to develop an employee communications campaign to build employee confidence and convince staff of their ability to make a difference and contribute to the company's turnaround.

The campaign used innovative tactics such as a "Drive to Deliver" daily dashboard with information on the campaign; direct channels for employees to make suggestions to senior management; holding a series of informational meetings among employees and senior management; and conducting surveys pre- and post-campaign to gauge the success of "Drive to Deliver" at engaging employees and driving change. By all measures the campaign was a resounding success.

Results Exceed Expectations

The campaign delivered high levels of employee support and engagement in the turnaround plan. Employee confidence in the company and senior management steadily increased, and a sense of urgency led to the employees meeting all internal deadlines for the project. Navistar exceeded its financial goals, beat its goals for cost reduction, and reduced the outstanding debt due to warranty claims. Its traditional position as a CSR leader was reinforced as well.

Success Rewarded

The world's financial markets took note of the company's progress, and the stock price improved steadily, despite the short-term losses the company experienced as the turnaround was in process. Finally the interim CEO turned over leadership of the company to the executive who successfully led the turnaround effort. ●

Source: PRSA (2014b).

CORPORATE COMMUNICATIONS AND CORPORATE SOCIAL RESPONSIBILITY

>> LO 11.3   Illustrate how SR enhances corporate communications

CSR has become increasingly important in recent years to building and maintaining a solid corporate reputation. Research has shown that a profile as an environmentally and socially responsible company pays dividends in terms of product sales, employee recruitment, and retention and business growth and opportunities.

SOCIAL RESPONSIBILITY >

COMMUNICATING CORPORATE SOCIAL RESPONSIBILITY

In a corporate communications position, you may be given the task of publicizing the company's good works to target audiences. The key to success, as noted in Chapter 10, is to make sure that there is a clear business and strategic connection to the CSR activity and that your employees, business partners, and suppliers all understand and support the effort.

A disconnected CSR activity is no different than a business strategy that doesn't fit the company or connect with stakeholders or our fellow employees. History has shown that over time, these CSR programs will dissipate and/or fail because the idea does not "stick" to your brand or have relevance for your stakeholders and employees.

Messages should communicate the company's commitment to SR, its engagement with SR, and the results, benefits, and impacts of SR. Communicating SR enables new market penetration, profiles a product or organization, and converts stakeholders.

SR is a powerful driver for consumer demand.

EMPLOYEE VOLUNTEERING AND SOCIAL RESPONSIBILITY

Employees also represent a major asset in SR programs. Many leading companies, in addition to Navistar, support employee volunteering as a key aspect of their CSR activity. Hertz, as we learned in Chapter 12, and Booz Allen Hamilton, as noted earlier in this chapter, are good examples but there are many others.

The Points of Light Foundation produces a list of the companies who excel at employee volunteer programs (EVP). They define EVPs as "a planned, managed effort that seeks to motivate and enable employees to effectively volunteer under the leadership of the employer" (Points of Light, 2013).

Companies recognized recently by the foundation include the following:

Amway Corporation	IBM
Bank of America	JPMorgan Chase
BNY Mellon	Kraft Foods
Cisco	McKesson
Constellation Energy	PwC U.S.
Cummins Inc.	The Goldman Sachs Group

The foundation noted best practices in EVP by these companies in the report. They include making employee volunteering part of the corporate culture; time off to engage in EVP in the form of service days company-wide; providing grants to support the EVP efforts; in-kind contributions of materials and staff to the effort; and celebrating the EVP efforts of its employees with awards and celebrations (Points of Light, 2012).

It should be clear that this is an area of corporate communications that cannot be overlooked. Beyond that, by leveraging the internal audience you can improve your company's chances for success in the marketplace, while adding depth and dimension to the overall mission and purpose of the company, and reinforce your SR profile.

"Today, employee volunteerism is well on its way to becoming a 'norm in terms of one's professional identity. Employees, driven in part by the growing numbers of working millennials, expect their employer to provide ways for them to find purpose at work" (Garlinghouse & Dorsey, 2015).

FINANCIAL COMMUNICATIONS, MEDIA RELATIONS, AND INVESTOR RELATIONSHIPS

>> **LO 11.4** Explain the importance of financial communications, media relations, and investor relations in corporate communications

FINANCIAL COMMUNICATIONS

One of the principal differences between corporate communications and working in other settings is the added responsibility of telling the company's story to the financial community. As a public company you are required to provide accurate and timely information on a quarterly and yearly basis to your stockholders. These documents must adhere to a set format and provide in-depth information about the company and its financial health.

This enables the orderly trading of the company's stock on one of the major stock exchanges, such as the NYSE or the NASDAQ.

Often the corporate communications team is closely involved in this process, preparing the letter from senior management (called the shareholder letter) that puts the results into perspective and includes key corporate messages and management's views on the results. The detailed financial information in these documents is prepared by the company's finance and legal staff, usually with the help of outside advisors, including the company's external accounting firm and legal counsel.

It is important to note that companies *must* provide this information simultaneously to the public, media, and investment community. There can be no staging or phasing of information to improve the media response or soften the blow of an issue or crisis. This concept—known as disclosure of information—is a Securities and Exchange Commission (SEC) requirement that requires that everyone, regardless of stature or relationship to the company, gets the same information at the same time. Any deviation from this is considered a legal violation with serious consequences.

Quarterly and Annual Reports permit orderly trading of a company's stock on exchanges like NASDAQ or the NYSE.

Michael Nagle/Bloomberg/ Getty Images

GOING PUBLIC

So, you might wonder why companies bother to issue shares and sell them to the public if there are so many restrictions and legal requirements once they complete an **initial public offering (IPO)**, which is when a private company sells stock for the first time to the public. The short answer to this question is that by issuing shares and selling part of the company to investors, the company has access to a steady funding source to finance its future growth and expansion. In a sense, the company trades some of its independence for access to the financial resources necessary to implement its strategy and grow the business.

There are many advantages for a company going public. The financial benefit of raising working capital is the most distinct advantage. This capital can be used to fund research and development, support new initiatives, or to pay off existing loans from the banks and private investors that helped finance the start of the company.

Also, this is a major transaction and usually generates publicity in major media, making the company and its products known to a new group of customers and investors in the global markets. Subsequently this heightened awareness often leads to an increase in market share and revenue growth for the company (Balasubramaniam, n.d.).

BUSINESS, FINANCIAL, AND CONSUMER MEDIA

Beyond helping craft the message to the financial community, the corporate communicator is also active in working with the business and financial media who cover major public companies. This can include working with leading business magazines (e.g., *Fortune*, *Forbes*, and *Business Week*), top cable TV business shows (e.g., Bloomberg, CNBC, etc.), and finance-related newspapers such as *The Wall Street Journal* and *The Financial Times*.

Depending on the location of the company's headquarters and its major facilities, daily newspapers and broadcast media located nearby might also be interested in covering the company's financial performance—because many employees may live in the area as well.

Here the usual principles of media relations apply as discussed previously in this Chapter 7, which focuses on media relations. However, it is important to remember the concept of fair disclosure applies here as well, and you are *not* allowed to sequence the release of the news—everyone must get the same information simultaneously.

What most communications teams do in this case is distribute the information as required to all parties and then select which media outlets you provide with further access, such as interviews with senior management, in-depth briefings, or new product demonstrations. Again, no new information can be disclosed, but your target media gets access to and perspective from senior management that add to their coverage. These media strategy decisions should involve thoughtful internal discussion and consideration with your colleagues and advisors before being put into action.

INVESTOR RELATIONS

In most companies the people who are responsible for the ongoing interaction with the financial community are known as **investor relations** (**IR**) professionals. These people are highly trained and have finance backgrounds as well as an understanding of communications and the rules that govern contact with current and prospective investors. Their daily activities include meeting and talking with investors; setting up meetings with stock market analysts; monitoring the daily stock price and trading activity; and advising management on competitive and financial market developments.

As you can see, IR is a very specialized function with a demanding and expert audience, which includes major investors on Wall Street and around the world as well as individual shareholders who buy and trade shares on their own. It requires an understanding of corporate strategy, business conditions, the economy, securities law, and the investment community. The Rivel Research Group (2013), in a recent white paper on the value of investor relations, makes the point that IR professionals are "charged with marketing something equally as important as any of the company's individual products or services—the company's common stock."

IR best practices call for a close integration of corporate communications and IR to put out unified and consistent messages and leverage each other's efforts to advance their own (National Investor Relations Institute, n.d.). For example, if the PR team places a major story in a key business publication (like *Fortune*) or a leading Wall Street firm (such as Merrill Lynch or Goldman Sachs) issues a positive report about the company's financial performance or corporate strategy, both the PR and IR teams can build on that event and reach new stakeholders in their respective areas of focus. This synergy can pay off with a better stock price and an improved corporate reputation. "Research shows that IR and PR have an undeniable impact on a company's valuation or stock price—because these are the roads by which investors learn about a company's management, strategy and overall investment appeal" (Rivel Research Group, 2013). Conversely research has shown that companies that perform poorly at communicating with the financial community suffer as a result.

Rivel has quantified this differential through their ongoing research. They recently surveyed the U.S. investment community about the value of effective financial communications and found the difference between effective ("good") and ineffective ("bad") IR and financial communications was 30% in a typical company stock price (Rivel Research Group, 2013). This could be the difference between a company's common stock trading at $7 per share or $10 per share. When you are talking about millions of shares of stock, that is a significant difference in funds to support growth.

In financial communications the rules may be different, but the desired outcome is the same as for corporate communications. Companies want to maximize their value and reputation. They want to be well regarded in their key markets, in their communities, and by the government and elected officials who regulate and impact their businesses. They want to be viewed as good places to work and have motivated and empowered employees. And finally they want to be good corporate citizens.

SOCIALLY RESPONSIBLE INVESTING

SOCIAL RESPONSIBILITY

Companies that are successfully positioned as good corporate citizens have an additional opportunity to be recognized and rewarded—and that is by attracting the support and investment of institutions and individuals called **socially responsible investors (SRI)**. This is an investment style that considers investing only in companies with a demonstrated track record of meeting or exceeding environmental, social, and corporate governance (ESG) criteria and generating long-term competitive financial returns and positive societal impact (US SIF, n.d.).

According to the 2016 Report on Sustainable and Responsible Investing Trends in the United States, more than one out of every five dollars under professional management in the United States—which is equal to $8.72 trillion or more—was invested according to SRI strategies (US SIF, n.d.). Clearly this is a significant source of capital to support growth, and senior managements of many major companies have noticed and are actively positioning their companies as socially responsible to gain the support of this class of investors (US SIF, n.d.).

Attracting investment support from the SRI community is like developing a connection to target media or other external stakeholders. To begin with you must qualify as a socially responsible company, according to the fund's definition of that term, which can vary. For some it can be product related, for example, no tobacco,

Companies that are seen as socially responsible create new opportunities for themselves by attracting the interest of investors who value social good.

iStock.com/maxsattana

guns or weapons, or oil and gas. In others it is having corporate policies in place regarding employee benefits, areas of the world where you operate, or having signed corporate pledges on greenhouse gas emissions, energy efficiency, or human rights.

With that status in hand, you need to make sure to frequently communicate your progress and activity in the CSR space throughout your communications outreach, including media relations, financial communications, internal communications, CSR, and social media. With a demonstrable track record in hand, the investor relations staff can begin the process of reaching out to SRI funds and telling the SR story to attract new investors.

Some of the leading global companies have had success in reaching out to and attracting SRI to invest in their common stock. While there are hundreds that qualify, a recent list compiled by Kiplinger's Personal Finance (Kiplinger.com) provides some high-profile examples (*the company's stock trading symbol is indicated after each company name.*):

Apple (AAPL)

Gilead Sciences (GILD)

Google (GOOGL)

Johnson Controls (JCI)

Nestle (NSRGY)

Praxair (PX)

Qualcomm (QCOM)

T Rowe Price (TROW)

Xylem (XYL)

SCENARIO OUTCOME

At the beginning of the chapter, you were introduced to Starbuck's "Race Together" community relations initiative begun in 2014. However well intentioned it was, the concept was not well received at the retail level. Both the traditional and social media criticized the company for overstepping, at the least, and for not being authentic or realistic at the worst.

Commenting on the reaction to the "Race Together" program, CEO Schultz responded during a television interview: "Writing on the cup is a diminutive piece of this issue and it's not going to last long. It was a catalyst to start this. What's going to last is our company saying that we believe that there is a serious problem in America. We are in almost every community in America, and why not use our stores and our national footprint for good?" (CNBC, 2015b).

How did Starbucks respond? Faced with the poor initial reception, the company went into crisis mode to clarify its intentions and rebuild trust with its key stakeholders, including the employees who bore the brunt of the negative customer feedback. This included a media outreach program, employee communications activities, and monitoring and responding on social media once the initial storm ended.

The Starbucks's corporate media relations team had some limited success in turning the story around. The articles that resulted helped explain what the public did not realize, that writing on cups was the tip of the iceberg of a much larger initiative. *The Wall Street Journal* published an article title, "Why Starbucks Takes on Social Issues" that examined why Schultz would continue pushing the race discussion despite the backlash (Kesmodel & Brat, 2015).

Schultz also maintains that performing for his shareholders is top priority, "You have to understand, I spend 90% of my day on Starbucks business—I'm not spending my entire life on the issues of racial inequality, I have a company to run here" (Carr, 2015).

Lesson learned? Most observers feel that the lesson from this case is that the safest stance for a company when it comes to hot-button social issues, such as race, is to remain silent or to be prepared for the inevitable backlash that comes from taking a stand and (in this case) engaging retail customers in a cause or issue. However, consistent with the corporate culture of Starbucks, CEO Schultz seemed determined to continue to use Starbucks's global scale and market position for good. Even though Schultz is no longer CEO, Starbucks will continue to take on social causes and redefine the way for-profit public companies impact social issues, says new CEO Kevin Johnson (Taylor, 2017).

Source: Michael, Cauley, and Orengo (2016).

WRAP UP

This chapter examined the realm of corporate communications, financial communications, and IR. The chapter also detailed and discussed the makeup of today's large corporations and examined how corporate communications fits into the organization—which can differ depending on the industry and culture of the company.

You read about the multiple responsibilities of corporate communications professionals and discussed each one, including how they support or enhance corporate reputation and promote social responsibility. Finally the chapter reviewed the complex and important field of financial communications and provided an overview of IR and how it impacts the company's perception and valuation.

As you move ahead in your studies toward a career in PR and public affairs, understanding the complex areas of corporate communications and how they impact the perception of the company will be an important skill to develop. Due to the changing nature of the global marketplace and the media—both traditional and social—your commitment to continuous learning and PR skills development can set you apart from your peers as a leading corporate communications professional.

The rewards for succeeding in corporate and financial communications can be substantial over time, but the expectations of the role are significant.

KEY TERMS

Chief Marketing Officer (CMO)/Chief Communications Officer (CCO): Titles that denote the marketing or communications function at the most senior level of the company, **273**

Corporate Branding: The product of the combined perception of the company, its products, its people, and its overall reputation, **281**

Financial Communications: A category of communications that corporate communicators or IR professionals and their advisers engage in routinely for publicly traded companies, consisting of preparing the required reports, communicating with the financial community (current and prospective investors, stock market analysts, etc.), and the financial media, **275**

Initial Public Offering (IPO): The first time a company sells some of its shares (stock certificates representing partial ownership) to the financial community and the public, **290**

Investor Relations (IR): The practice area in which professionals interact with the financial community (investors, analysts, and government regulators) on behalf of a public company, **291**

Socially Responsible Investors (SRI): An investment style that focuses on companies with a demonstrated track record of meeting or exceeding environmental, social, and corporate governance (ESG) criteria and generating long-term competitive financial returns and positive societal impact, **292**

Stock Exchange: The major financial markets in the United States and the world, for example, NYSE and NASDAQ, **271**

Thought Leadership: A high-level communications tactic in which a company or organization produces a survey, in-depth research, or a detailed point of view on a major issue or trend in the marketplace or society, **273**

THINK ABOUT IT

In this chapter, you have learned about the challenge and opportunity of corporate communications in today's companies. Your ability to understand this dynamic environment, should your career take you in this direction, will be a major factor in your success.

Ultimately most corporate communications professionals seek a seat at the table and to be considered as communications strategists, not just tacticians.

Your task is to gather into groups and agree on a company you all admire and are interested in learning more about. Visit the company website and review their SR activities. Based on what you have read so far in the text, suggest a strategy to raise the company's profile with its key stakeholders. This can be a news conference, article in a key publication, or a community-based event for employees, for example. How would you implement the idea, and what results would you expect?

WRITE LIKE A PRO

Visit the website of a company based in your area that you are familiar with, and read about their SR program. If they are active, prepare a short plan to expand awareness of the company's activity on a cause that you are interested in and that relates to their business. If they are not very active, or if you feel there are missed opportunities, suggest a strategy and a few tactics to increase their involvement.

Be sure that the issue you suggest is relevant to the company's business and would appeal to the employees. For example, if they are a home improvement company, engaging them in a building project or in teaching home improvement skills to young people makes sense. Raising money for animal welfare programs, while important work, is not clearly connected to the company's core business and likely won't resonate with the management and employees.

SOCIAL RESPONSIBILITY CASE STUDY

Hertz Hits the Road—Being a Good Neighbor in Florida

Chapter 12 highlighted the issue management work done by the Hertz Corporation to minimize the disruption of its corporate headquarters relocation from New Jersey to Florida. Through careful planning, the company left New Jersey with its reputation as a good corporate citizen and employer there still intact.

After the move, as a new corporate member of the Tampa, Florida, area community, Hertz was anxious to get off to a good start. The company continued to work with Ketchum and relied on a CSR-based strategy to build its reputation in its new headquarters market.

Research and Strategy

In January 2016 Hertz officially opened its new headquarters in a suburb of Tampa. At the grand opening ceremony, which included more than 625 company staff members, the governor, and local and state dignitaries, the company announced significant contributions to the local community and plans for hundreds of hours of employee volunteer work. Hertz also declared its support for local nonprofits including The Immokalee Foundation, Junior Achievement, The Conservancy of Southwest Florida, Audubon's Corkscrew Swamp Sanctuary, and others.

Execution

The employee volunteer efforts were substantial. The company partnered with Habitat for Humanity of Lee, Hendry, and Collier counties in Florida to sponsor and build three homes. This required more than 400 hours of volunteer time and, in addition to physical labor, included hosting employee team-building days to raise the walls of the homes, finish cosmetic work, and hand the keys over to the new homeowners at a ceremony.

Other local volunteering efforts included a back-to-school backpack drive, including supplies for The Heights Foundation and The Immokalee Foundation and a new shoe collection to benefit Laces of Love, which provides new shoes to children in need. Two holiday initiatives were also driven by employee participation: a Thanksgiving food drive to benefit The Heights Foundation and a holiday gift project that benefited both The Shelter for Abused Women and Children and The Children's Advocacy Center of Tampa.

SR efforts continued after the headquarters launch as well. On Hertz's Make a Difference Day 2016, the company hosted several volunteer events, including Interfaith Charities of Southwest Florida and a beach cleanup in partnership with Keep Lee County Beautiful.

Evaluation

Due to these and other community-based activities, Hertz is now an integral part of the Tampa area community, and its employees feel engaged and welcome in their new home (Ketchum, 2016).

ENGAGE

▸ After forming into small work groups, visit the Hertz website (https://www.hertz.com/) to acquaint yourselves with the company, and review their ongoing sustainability activities.

▸ Follow that up with some basic research of the area (Tampa metropolitan area and Lee County) in Florida to identify the major issues facing the people and businesses in the area. What are the pressing social issues in the area? How is the government dealing with them?

DISCUSS

▸ Look for synergies and identify additional opportunities for local SR activity for Hertz—either in partnership with the city and county government, a nonprofit, or community-based organization.

▸ For example, should Hertz provide vehicles for driver training, safe driving clinics, or demonstrations of the dangers of impaired or distracted driving? Think of some other ideas that are related to their core business (transportation) that also provide an opportunity for employees and the community to get involved.

1. How would you organize these?

2. How might you publicize the events and results?

3. How would you know you were succeeding?

Source: PRSA (n.d.).

SOCIAL RESPONSIBILITY CASE STUDY

Snap Inc—From Dad's Garage to a $33 Billion Initial Public Offering

Starting as an application to send disappearing photos, Snap is now a camera company. Snap is the parent company of Snapchat, a mobile application to send disappearing photos and videos, as well as Spectacles, a product line of glasses to take photos and videos that are instantly added to the Snapchat application. Cofounders Evan Spiegel and Bobby Murphy were the first to capture a market of consumers who wanted to share photos of their daily lives without repercussions of that content being saved. Snapchat was the first successful start-up that allowed for temporary social media.

Snap created a new market for conversation through innovation in its products. Three differentiators include: (1) more intimate (focusing on closer friends), (2) for a younger generation (median age of 18), and (3) temporary (Colao, 2014). The company grew quickly in five years from an idea to seeking an IPO with a valuation of over $21 billion in 2017.

Research and Strategy

Evan Spiegel, a student at Stanford, and Bobby Murphy, a recent Harvard graduate, cofounded Picaboo in July 2009 at Spiegel's dad's house. When a mutual friend, Reggie Brown, complained about a photo he wished he had not posted, the pair began planning and developing an application to share disappearing photos. During the first summer Picaboo only achieved 127 users. Upon receiving a cease-and-desist order from Picaboo, a photo-book company, the name Snapchat was launched for the app. In the fall of 2011, Snapchat approached 1,000 users. Spiegel's niece introduced the app to her high school, and users surged in the surrounding high school population. By January 2012 Snapchat had 10,000 users and, by April 2012, 100,000 users.

Due to this exponential growth in year one, server bills became too much for the founders to cover on their own, with only Spiegel's grandfather and some of Murphy's paycheck funding the expenses (Colao, 2014). In April 2012, Jeremy Liew, a partner at the California investment firm Lightspeed Venture Partners, found Snapchat after another partner's daughter told him about this new app that was as popular as Angry Birds and Instagram. Lightspeed provided funding of $520,000 to support the company.

At this point Snapchat was still headquartered in Spiegel's dad's house in Stanford, however, with the inflow of capital and advice from Lightspeed, Snapchat moved to Los Angeles, California, and as of 2017 is headquartered in Venice Beach, California. This initial seed money helped fund monthly expenses, including high server bills, relocation, and continued code changes (Colao, 2014).

Execution

Snap makes money from the Snapchat app through various sources: (1) advertisements, that show up in between friends' "stories," (2) sponsored lenses, (3) on-demand geo-filters that anyone can create for a certain location, and (4) sales of Spectacles (Derrick, 2017).

From its original launch as Picaboo to growing from 1,000 daily active users to more than 150,000, introducing new features (from solely sharing photos to video, stories, snap filters, replay, geotags, memories, bitmoji, groupchat, etc.), selling a new product (Spectacles), and creating a new form of app revenue (ads, on-demand, geo-filters, etc.), Snap has gone through immense growth.

Evaluation

Snap completed its IPO on March 2, 2017, and is now publicly trading on the NYSE under the trading symbol of SNAP. The opening price of $24 per share on March 2, 2017, put the company's market capitalization at about $33 billion, about the size of Marriot and Target. Twitter's market cap is about $11 billion, while Facebook's is about $395 billion.

ENGAGE

- ▶ As a newly public company, Snap is still getting organized and ramping up to meet its obligations as a public company. In addition to quarterly and annual reports, the company will need to set up and conduct ongoing communications with the financial community.

- ▶ The company's founders and new management team will be faced with many challenges, one of which eventually will be to determine its SR policy and program.

- ▶ Imagine your group or class is assigned the task of developing this policy and identifying areas for the company to make its mark as a socially responsible company.

- ▶ Begin by doing some research into the company, including its business model, employee and customer base, and the needs and opportunities in the company's home market of Los Angeles.

DISCUSS

▸ Prepare an outline for an SR policy for Snap and suggest a few programs or sponsorship activities the company should consider. Also, how might you get the employees involved in volunteering? What issues or community needs are of interest and apply to the company's business?

▸ Suggest how the company might promote or publicize these activities and their progress to gain the interest and support of the SRI community. As you read in this chapter, there are thousands of investment companies in the United States and across the world who look for CSR leaders to invest in and support. How and when should Snap start on this effort?

Source: Taylor & Burton (2017). Adapted from Kayo Conference Series, March 2, 2017.

VIDEO CASE

Pepsi's Kendall Jenner Ad: Corporate Communication

In 2017, Pepsi premiered an advertisement featuring Kendall Jenner. The ad was posted online and was more than two and a half minutes long. Featuring hundreds of extras and multiple locations, it was seemingly expensive and long planned. The uproar in response was almost immediate, with commenters calling the ad insensitive and tone deaf by suggesting that Pepsi could solve the world's strife and bring about racial harmony. Pepsi eventually pulled the ad, but the company's reputation took a beating on social media and in the press.

VIDEO

The ad stars model and TV personality Kendall Jenner, who hands an officer a can of Pepsi at the ad's climax.

1. After the outcry that accompanied the launch of the video, what should Pepsi have done next? Was taking down the ad the right move?

2. What alternative avenues would you suggest Pepsi could have pursued to convey its stated "message of unity, peace, and understanding"?

3. Do you think corporations should engage in hot-button topics? Why or why not?

PRACTICE AND APPLY WHAT YOU'VE LEARNED

edge.sagepub.com/page

CHECK YOUR COMPREHENSION
ON THE STUDY SITE WITH:

- eFlashcards to strengthen your understanding of key terms

- Practice quizzes to test your comprehension of key concepts

- Videos and multimedia content to enhance your exploration of key topics

Andreas Rentz/Getty Images

12 Issues Management and Crisis Communication

Learning Objectives

12.1 Demonstrate how issues management can be a preemptive PR strategy

12.2 Differentiate among a crisis, disaster, and problems

12.3 Understand how to prepare for, manage, and communicate during a crisis

Wells Fargo's Cross-Selling Cross Up

September 20, 2016, was a beautiful day in Washington, D.C. Fall would officially begin the next day, and there was none of the heat and humidity so common in the area.

But for John Stumpf, chair and CEO of Wells Fargo, things were about to heat up. He was scheduled to testify before the Senate Banking Committee and face the wrath of its members in a hearing to examine the bank's controversial business practices that had come to public light less than two weeks earlier.

The reason for the high-profile hearing that day was reports of excessive cross-selling of bank services to existing customers. Reportedly the bank had put pressure on its branch employees to meet aggressive sales goals and quickly dismiss those who did not meet their quotas.

Wells Fargo's CEO John Stumpf testified before the Senate Banking Committee in September 2016 to answer questions about the company's aggressive cross-selling tactics.

Tom Williams/CQ Roll Call/Getty Images

Thousands of customers defrauded. This sales-driven culture led some bank employees, according to state and federal bank regulators, to defraud thousands of customers nationwide by opening 2 million accounts without customer permission, costing the customers a collective $2.5 million in fees in 2016 alone (Spross, 2016). Also note that the cross-selling strategy had been a key part of Wells Fargo's marketing strategy for more than five years (Wells Fargo, 2015).

By all accounts the CEO did not respond well to the panel during the Senate hearing. "This is a crisis-management 101 mistake," said an aide to Senator Warren, D–MA (Glazer, 2016b). By the end of the day, the reputation of Stumpf and the bank had suffered enormous damage.

A fallen star. Clearly the crisis was not over for Wells Fargo that afternoon, even if the hearings were. In this case Wells Fargo had a lot of work to do to rebuild its reputation.

Prior to this controversy Wells Fargo had been recognized for the critical and positive role it played during the 2008 banking crisis. In addition Wells Fargo had been highly regarded for its leadership in SR. Its track record was a model for the U.S. banking sector as well for other large companies. Social Responsible Investors (SRI) had historically held major ownership positions in the bank's common stock (NYSE: WFC) and supported its management.

As you read through this chapter, consider how you would have advised Wells Fargo management to respond—both to the Senate hearings described and in dealing with the early reports of cross-selling abuse by branch staff and managers.

Specific questions to consider include the following:

1. How well prepared was Wells Fargo for this crisis? Did they handle the fallout well?

2. What changes might have been put into place to monitor managers and staff stretching the rules to meet or exceed their sales goals?

3. Once the matter became apparent to senior management, how should they have responded versus what they did?

4. If you worked for a competitor of Wells Fargo, what advice would you give to your management team to prepare for media questions on cross-selling at your bank?

5. What role, if any, does Wells Fargo's track record of SR play in offsetting the reputation damage from this crisis? Could third-party groups who benefit from their community-based activities help?

What is a crisis? Is it natural disasters like earthquakes, volcanoes, or typhoons? Or product defects like Samsung's Galaxy 7 smartphone or Takata's automobile airbag? Is it cyberattacks or hacks like those at Target, Sony Entertainment, Yahoo, or the U.S. Office of Personnel Management (OPM)? Or is it bad business practices (like those at Wells Fargo), sexual harassment, discrimination, or insider trading?

The answer to these questions is, of course, yes. They are all legitimate crises for these companies and countless others like them. But could they also have first been *issues* that ultimately became a *crisis*? In most cases the answer to this question is also yes. Except for a natural disaster, most crises are not a complete surprise. Often you will find it could have been prevented, or at least minimized, if the companies were better prepared. This is where *issues management* comes in.

This chapter focuses on both issues management and crisis communications. It explores the key differences and details how one tactic—issues management—can prevent or minimize the need for the second—crisis communications. It also addresses how organizations respond to natural disasters and litigation, providing examples.

ISSUES MANAGEMENT

>> **LO 12.1   Demonstrate how issues management can be a preemptive PR strategy**

"An ounce of prevention is worth a pound of cure," said Benjamin Franklin. Although he made this statement in 1736 speaking about fire prevention, it is spot on when it comes to a discussion of crisis communications and issues management. Applying this to crisis and issues management today, one might say: While putting out a fire is a valuable skill, preventing one may be even more valuable. An all-too-common situation that PR practitioners face is the crisis. It's demanding and multifaceted, requiring proactive preparation for crisis scenarios, managing the cycles of a crisis

⑤SAGE edge™

Master the content
edge.sagepub.com/page

if and when it happens, and shepherding the necessary reputation recovery efforts. Thus we first turn to a PR practice that helps to avoid crises: **issues management**.

THE BENEFITS OF ISSUES MANAGEMENT

Issues management can be defined as an anticipatory, strategic management process that helps organizations detect and respond appropriately to emerging trends or changes in the sociopolitical environment (Dougall, 2008). Think of it as an early warning system or a risk management protocol designed to see things coming. It is a lot like forecasting the weather and preparing ahead of time instead of just trying to cope when the predicted storm happens.

Tracking emerging trends over time will allow you to see that many problems crystallize into an issue and, over time, erupt into a crisis for the organization, its key publics, and stakeholders. Consider the case of Wells Fargo, described in the opening scenario. The practice of pushing cross-selling by branch employees had been in place for years before it exploded into a crisis for the bank. Consider what might have happened if the bank had better controls in place to minimize abuse and improve customer communications or just eliminated the practice as soon as the problems began to surface through customer complaints to branch managers?

A good illustration of issue monitoring using customer feedback might be an automotive company tracking requests for warranty repairs and noticing a big increase in the number of brake problems in one of its newer models or a consumer products company monitoring customer service feedback online to identify posts complaining about one of its key products. In such cases a special group could be tasked to study the matter, determine if there was a problem, and then recommend corrective action before it leads to a product recall, litigation, or a decline in sales or employee morale. Last, you and your senior management should anticipate that a major corporate event—for example, a merger or acquisition or a relocation—might create concerns that are better addressed in advance versus after they have upset major stakeholders.

The key to understanding the value of issues management is that it is anticipatory and **proactive** as opposed to **crisis communications**, which is **reactive**. Issues management is a form of risk management with a specific focus on the company's reputation, products, and financial performance.

ISSUE LIFE CYCLE

Figure 12.1 depicts the flow of an issue from origination to a crisis if corrective action is not taken. If you were to track the Hertz corporate relocation story on this chart (see the case study in this chapter), you would see that the company's attention to the issues management process early on—in the potential and emerging stages—prevented it from becoming a crisis and damaging the company's reputation.

Conversely Wells Fargo management did not intervene in the early stages when cross-selling first surfaced as an issue, and the bank experienced a full-blown crisis as a result. As the crisis wound down and management and business practices were changed, the company entered the dormant stage, where it began to repair its image and move forward. In summary issues management is a planning and risk management process used to anticipate and address emerging issues. It allows organizations to clarify or correct a developing situation and avoid the issue becoming a crisis.

"Issues management encompasses the potential, emerging, and current stages of an issue's evolution before it reaches the crisis stage."

—Meng (2009)

FIGURE 12.1

Issue Life Cycle

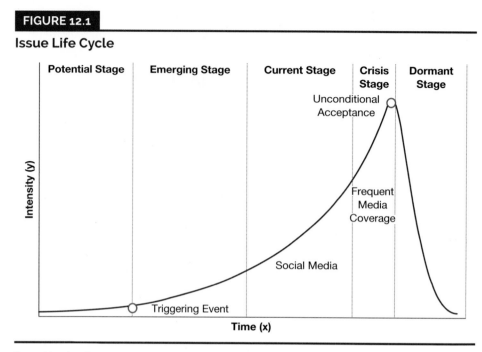

Source: Meng (2009).

CRISIS COMMUNICATIONS

>> **LO 12.2**   **Differentiate among a crisis, disaster, and problems**

The differences between a natural disaster or problem and an organizational crisis are important to clarify. "**Disasters** are events that are sudden, seriously disrupt routines of systems, require new courses of action to cope with the disruption, and pose a danger to values and social goals," suggests Coombs (2015). He adds that disasters often "are large in scale and require response from multiple government units."

THE ORGANIZATIONAL CRISIS

An organizational **crisis**, on the other hand, is defined by the Institute for Public Relations (IPR) as a significant threat to operations that can have long term, negative consequences to the company or organization involved (Coombs, n.d.). Some crises, the IPR suggests, such as major industrial accidents (like Union Carbide's Bhopal accidents in 1984) and product recalls (e.g., the famous Tylenol recall by Johnson & Johnson in the fall of 1982), result in injuries and even loss of life. A crisis can also cause financial loss by disrupting operations, creating a loss of market share, or spawning lawsuits related to the crisis, such as the banking crisis in 2008 or the Wells Fargo cross-selling fiasco in 2016.

In most cases involving a natural disaster, the company, organization, or government entity may not be at fault, *unless* their response is not well managed and the situation is made worse versus better by their actions. This is true also in the case of workplace violence, which is usually random, but all companies need to prepare for it. In such cases a disaster or accident could become a crisis.

FEMA's inadequate response to Hurricane Katrina turned the natural disaster into a crisis and led to a congressional investigation.

Chip Somodevilla/Getty Images

Recent history has provided several instances of disasters becoming crises, unfortunately. A well-known example was Hurricane Katrina, which struck New Orleans and the U.S. Gulf Coast in 2005. The U.S. government estimates that more than $80 billion in property damage was caused by the hurricane and flooding, and the total economic impact to the area was losses in excess of $150 billion (National Center for Environmental Information, 2016).

While the storm was anticipated due to forecasts and sophisticated storm tracking by the authorities, it was far worse than expected. Very quickly it overwhelmed the local government's ability to respond and assist area residents in recovering. At the end of the storm, it was estimated that 80% of New Orleans was underwater.

When New Orleans and the surrounding area were declared a federal disaster area, the Federal Emergency Management Authority (FEMA) was called in to assist. Here is where the situation became a crisis, most experts agree. According to a report prepared on Hurricane Katrina by the U.S. Congress titled "A Failure of Initiative," the Katrina relief effort was poorly handled, supplies were delayed or lost, the process of processing claims and coordinating federal assistance was botched, and the overall situation got worse instead of better once FEMA got involved (A Failure of Initiative, 2006). Eventually the mishandling of the Katrina disaster cost the Bush administration national credibility and political support. FEMA Director Michael Brown, appointed by President George W. Bush in January 2003, resigned in September 2005, one month after the crisis.

So, if a disaster is not necessarily a crisis, unless it is mishandled as it was in this case, what constitutes a real crisis, and how do we manage communications before, during, and after?

Jim Lukaszewski, a leading independent crisis counselor and author of 12 books on crisis communications, defines a crisis colorfully, suggesting, "A crisis is a show-stopping, people-stopping, product-stopping, reputation-defining, trust-busting event that creates *victims* and/or explosive visibility" (Lukaszewski, 2012). Notice that in his definition, Lukaszewski emphasizes the victim aspect (e.g., employees, customers, or the public) because he feels that is what creates the emotion and drama and is what the public and the media usually focus on in a crisis. "The principal ingredient of any crisis is the creation of victims," he maintains. "Avoiding responsibility and shifting blame can become significant barriers for the organization and its leadership to overcome," Lukaszewski (2013) notes. Eric Dezenhall (1999), a leading crisis counselor and author based in Washington D.C., agrees. He suggests that there are three key elements in any crisis: victim, villain, and vindicator. These categories answer the key questions for the media and the public in a crisis: What happened? Whose fault is it? Who is going to fix it so this does not happen again?

PROBLEM VERSUS A CRISIS

"All crises are problems, but not all problems are crises," Lukaszewski (2013) notes. One of the challenges of issues management and crisis communications is distinguishing a problem from an actual crisis. PR practitioners must guard against overreacting and going into crisis mode when confronted with a problem that may be solved without drama.

An example of a problem could be a slowdown in delivery of a key part, limited product availability caused by weather, or a shortage of perishable food or ingredients needed for a restaurant chain. Solving such problems, or better yet anticipating them—maybe by having backup suppliers or alternate shipping options—can prevent the problem from becoming an issue and eventually a crisis. Often the PR practitioner who solves a problem or issue before it escalates is more valued than the one who knows what to do when a crisis occurs.

You'll note our focus in this chapter is on **organizational crises**. These are situations that threaten an organization's stakeholders—shareholders, customers, employees, and so on—and can seriously impact performance and generate negative outcomes (Coombs, 2015). For public companies the common stock price—and therefore the company's access to the capital markets—can also be impacted. Most often these crises are man-made and are attributable to management or operational failures, criminal behavior, or a lack of oversight of people and process. The Wells Fargo cross-selling controversy is certainly one of these. Another recent example of a poorly handled operational problem is Samsung's Note 7 phone and the lithium ion battery crisis in 2016.

PRODUCT CRISIS

Beginning in the fall of 2016, the batteries in Samsung's very successful top-of-the-line smartphone started to spontaneously combust. For obvious reasons this created major problems for the company with customers, with regulators, and in the mobile tech marketplace. Soon government regulators became involved due to the safety issue, and the company was forced to issue a total recall of the product. Cost estimates of the impact of this decision for Samsung exceed $5 billion (Pandey, 2016), not to mention a major blow to the company's reputation as a technology leader.

Unfortunately the problems continued even after the initial recall when the new batteries and replacement phones provided to customers began to experience the same problems. This created more negative media coverage, which eventually led to a ban on the Samsung 7 phones on all commercial transportation in the United States.

Emotional Intelligence and Ethics— Keys to Crisis Management

Mike Paul, The Reputation Doctor®

My name is Mike Paul, and I am a global crisis communications and reputation management consultant known by the registered brand name The Reputation Doctor®. Since my teenage years, I've been known as a fixer, which ultimately transitioned into a career in crisis PR.

I started my career working as a political aide in the New York state legislature. I then went to Washington, D.C., and served as an aide to a U.S. senator. I have since learned that many leaders in PR also started their careers in politics. In hindsight this is not surprising as politics is a great training ground for crisis and issues management.

I returned to New York and earned a graduate degree from Columbia University. I was recruited into Burson-Marsteller's (B-M) management training program and spent time in their various practice areas, including crisis communications. It was there at B-M, working in the crisis communications division, that I realized this was something I loved.

After working for several other PR firms on crisis teams and on the client side as well, I started my own crisis communications and reputation management firm called MGP & Associates PR. After 20 years in business, I sold the assets of the firm. I also had a stint as SVP of corporate communications at Publicis Media (a global advertising and PR firm) after MGP & Associates.

The Reputation Doctor® trademark first started as a nickname from a client in 1994, and it later became a brand name. I had helped solve a major, global crisis for his corporation, and he attended a birthday party for me soon after. He gave me a nice gift and a memorable card. It was a Superman card. However, he crossed out "Superman" on the cover and wrote inside, "You are our Superman—but that name is already taken. Thanks for your hard work, wise counsel, and intestinal fortitude helping us survive the worst crisis of our corporate lives. You are our Reputation Doctor!" The guests at the party heard the nickname, and it stuck from that day forward.

My advice for anyone seeking to work in crisis communications is the following: In addition to developing a full PR tool belt, <u>you must have a strong moral and ethical compass to succeed</u>.

The most important tool in your crisis tool belt is your emotional intelligence (EQ). Lean on it and trust it—always. Also tell your clients and bosses the truth, with love, just like you would a family member. You may be the only one in the room with the courage and the expertise to do so, but they will need that if they are to survive and move forward. ●

Source: M. Paul (personal communication, 2017).

Research by International Data Corporation (IDC, 2016) offers hope to Samsung—and others in a similar situation—that the impact of the crisis may be short term depending on the success of its future product rollout. "The Note 7 recall along with all its repercussions, represents a significant event in the world of consumer electronics," commented Anthony Scarsella, research manager for mobile phones at IDC. "Moving forward, Samsung will need to put the Note 7 to rest as quickly as possible and focus all efforts on producing a stellar Galaxy 8. . . . If they are successful, consumers will quickly forget the Note 7 fiasco."

The lessons from this case are these (Bulldog Reporter, 2016):

1. Do a better job of responding and managing a crisis than Samsung.

2. Make sure to correct them in the next product rollout. In the technology field in particular the consumer will likely move on given the chance.

Samsung Employees Participate in a Nationwide Day of Service

Galaxy Note7 Press Conference

Samsung faced a crisis when the batteries in its Galaxy Note7 began bursting into flames. The company's response included press conferences to explain the issue and instituting a Service Day for employees to volunteer in their communities.

SeongJoon Cho/Bloomberg/Getty Images

Throughout most of 2016 and into 2017, Samsung suffered a product crisis with one of its top products—the Samsung 7 phone. These events often have a negative impact on the brand and company's reputation and can also negatively impact the employees who work for the company.

Rebuilding Trust After Samsung 7

As part of its ongoing CSR efforts, Samsung has staged a service day for its employees to volunteer in their local communities and show their pride in and commitment to the company. This allows company employees an opportunity to show a different side of the company and begin to rebuild trust and belief in the brand.

"Samsung Gives" Employees' Initiative

In May 2017 Samsung Electronics America held its biannual, company-wide Day of Service for employees in New Jersey, New York, Texas, California, Washington, D.C., and regional offices. The event, part of the company's overarching "Samsung Gives" initiative, creates service opportunities for Samsung employees to connect to meaningful causes within their own communities.

"Samsung believes in being an active corporate citizen and is committed to giving back to the communities where our employees live and work," said Gregory Lee, president and CEO, Samsung North America, "The Samsung Day of Service allows all employees to serve their communities, work in teams and offer help to causes in need—whether it be feeding the homeless, rebuilding communities or providing workplace training" (Samsung Newsroom, 2017).

One Day Benefits 50+ Nonprofits

Since its inception in 2014, the Day of Service has provided more than 80,000 hours of service to more than 60 local charities nationwide. In 2017 alone, nearly 4,000 Samsung employees joined in donating 16,000 hours of service to more than 50 nonprofit organizations within their communities, including the following:

▸ Local Boys & Girls Club of America

▸ Grow NYC in New York

▸ After-School All-Stars in New Jersey

▸ Special Olympics Texas

Samsung focuses its SR efforts in the United States in the following areas: environment, supply chain, contributions, compliance, and people (communities and employees). It states, "The Corporate Social Responsibility (CSR) vision is to build a society where people, the society and the environment coexist in harmony. As a part of our CSR efforts, we are committed to transparency and delivering important information to our shareholders to continuously build confidence and trust in us" (Samsung, 2016). ●

Could this recall and subsequent misstep have been prevented by earlier intervention or action by the company? While we will never know for sure, it certainly seems that more transparency, better communications, and more attention during the manufacturing process would have helped. The Samsung crisis was a **product crisis** initially, but became a corporate crisis, and the damage to the overall company brand was a serious side effect of the initial problem.

After it was accused of using filler rather than meat in its ground beef products, Taco Bell responded aggressively, refuting the claims across multiple platforms and in the media.

Patrick T. Fallon/Bloomberg/ Getty Images

Following a period of a product-based crisis, a company or organization, like Samsung, will look for opportunities to rebuild or repair their image in the marketplace. Often these companies will look to their ongoing SR efforts to rebuild their image and improve employee morale.

LITIGATION CRISIS

There are some issues that will become a crisis notwithstanding a company's best efforts. But even so the fact that a crisis was anticipated and preparations made should serve a company well. This is usually the case in a **litigation crisis** that's driven by a lawsuit and potential trial in the court of public opinion—as well as in the legal system. An example of a prompt and effective response to litigation was the "seasoned beef" ingredients lawsuit filed against Taco Bell in 2011. The company was prepared for such a situation via its ongoing monitoring of consumer comments and had a litigation response protocol already in place.

▸ *Taco Bell crisis*. Yum! Brands (Taco Bell's parent company) was sued over the contents of its signature menu item and the meat used in its tacos. The lawsuit, filed by a Taco Bell customer and California resident named Amanda Obney, alleged that the company's "seasoned beef" contained only 35% beef and that Taco Bell was lying in its advertising, which claimed the ingredients were all beef (NPR, 2011). The announcement of the lawsuit generated considerable initial coverage—mostly negative—and led to late-night talk show hosts and others ridiculing the company.

▸ *How Taco Bell responded*. Taco Bell responded aggressively. It explicitly declared the claims false and shared its percentages (88% beef, 12% secret recipe), along with the ingredients in the secret recipe itself, which included all natural products and spices. The company quickly fired up a multi-platform PR campaign to shoot down the allegations and get the word out about its not-so-secret recipe. It included traditional local market newspapers but also focused on online outreach with a YouTube channel, dedicated Facebook page, and more—online, in store, and in the traditional media. Fortunately for them, its quick response positively impacted news coverage and removed the story as fodder for comedians and social media commentators.

▶   *The result.* Taco Bell's existing consumer base responded overwhelmingly well to the campaign. The social media outreach was well received, with most comments online supporting the company's stance. Less than four months later, the lawsuit was dropped, and Taco Bell had completely averted a potential PR disaster (Business Insider, n.d.).

PREPARE FOR AND MANAGE A CRISIS

>> LO 12.3   **Understand how to prepare for, manage, and communicate during a crisis**

Having defined a crisis and provided examples of organizations that have struggled with this challenge, this chapter now turns to managing and communicating effectively during and after the crisis. It will also examine how to prepare your company or organization by developing a comprehensive plan to communicate during a crisis.

The three stages of crisis communications include three macro stages: precrisis, crisis impact, and crisis recovery (Coombs, 2015). Other scholars who have studied and written on crisis management include Fink (1986) and Mitroff (1994). Fink (1986) is widely quoted and recognized on the topic of crisis, and he proposes a four-stage model—prodromal, acute, chronic, and resolution—using medical terminology. Mitroff (1994) suggests a five-stage model—signal detection, probing and prevention, damage containment, recovery, and finally, learning. As these theories have much in common; for our purposes we will focus on the basic three-stage model (see Figure 12.2) in this text.

FIGURE 12.2

The Three Stages of Crisis Communications

Precrisis
- Warning signs appear, and the company moves to try to eliminate or reduce the risk.

Crisis Impact
- The actual crisis is underway, and your focus is on managing the situation and providing support to those impacted by the crisis.

Crisis Recovery
- The goal is to return to business as usual as fast as possible while making good on your promises and critically examining the company's response to see how it might be improved. Repairing damage to corporate reputation is also an important effort at this stage.

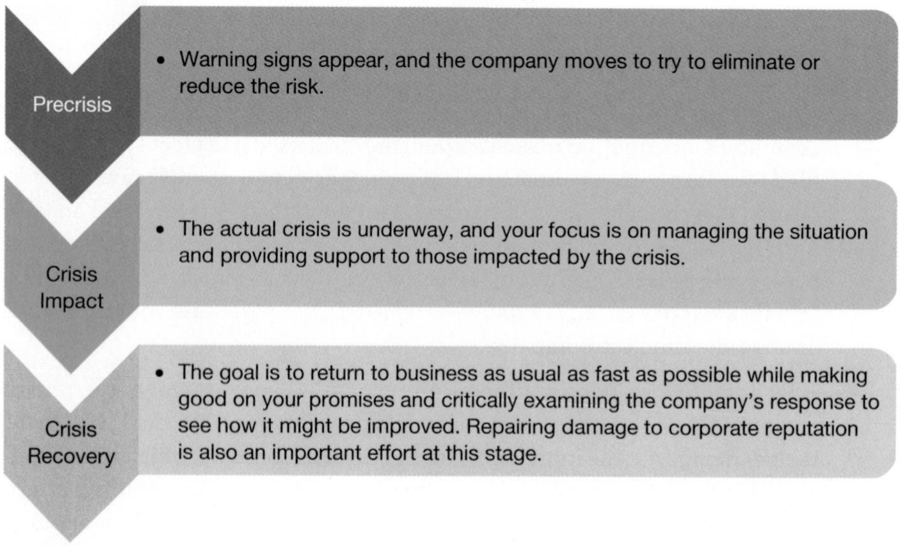

Restoring a Company's Image Using Benoit's Five Categories of Image Restoration

Any discussion of issues management and crisis communication would be incomplete without a look at the major communication theory that drives most responses by a company or organization when faced with a crisis. A frequently used guiding theory for assessing crisis communications is William Benoit's (1995) image restoration theory (see Table 12.1). Benoit's approach is most often cited in studies of crisis and issues management because it focuses on how companies monitor issues and manage crises once they occur.

Benoit's five categories of image restoration include denial, evasion of responsibility, reducing the offensive act, taking corrective action, and mortification.

His communications theory provides a "useful framework to understand and analyze how a company responds to stakeholders about issues that are indicators of a pre-crisis situation that could lead to fraudulent activity of severe business risks" (Cowden & Sellnow, 2002). Research shows that "[i]neffective management of these warning signs can result in a movement from the pre-crisis stage to the crisis stage" (Erickson, Weber, & Segovia, 2011).

In their research "Using Communication Theory to Analyze Corporate Reporting Strategies," Erickson, Weber, and Segovia (2011) apply Benoit's theory to corporate reporting of financial control issues or shortfalls and conclude that "[i]mage management is essential to corporations and other organizations." They suggest that if a company is perceived to be responsible for an event or problem (e.g., a crisis) and sought to deny it, dismiss its severity, shift blame, or otherwise evade responsibility versus apologize and take responsibility for corrective action, then "the firm's image will be tarnished and needs to be restored."

Often students and practitioners confuse the categories in Benoit's image restoration theory as a prescribed list that all companies go through in a crisis. This is not the intent of the list. It is more accurate to see this as predictive as quite often companies or individuals in trouble need to work through these stages before they get to admitting guilt and apologizing. Sometimes that is a period of hours and sometimes longer, depending on the situation and the company.

For example, think of a consumer product company with a recall or a government official who did something unethical or illegal, and then trace the steps of Benoit's typology to illustrate this point. First there is a denial and maybe an evasion of responsibility. Then the company or official might try to claim it was an "accident" or "one-time thing." Next some organizations blame somebody else or try to minimize the damage, and so on, right on through until, ultimately, they take responsibility and fix the problem. Some companies respond appropriately and go right to apologizing and fixing the problem, but many do not.

Thus Benoit's theory is most helpful in assessing where a company is in the image restoration process and then preparing your communications advice and plans accordingly to get to the corrective action stage. ●

TABLE 12.1

Benoit's Typology

Denial	1. Simple denial 2. Shifting the blame	1. Refuting outright that the organization had any part in the event 2. Asserting that someone else is responsible
Evasion of responsibility	3. Scapegoating 4. Defeasibility 5. Accident 6. Good intentions	3. Blaming the event on the provocation of another 4. Not knowing what to do; lacking knowledge to act properly 5. Claiming the event was "accidental" 6. Claiming the company had good intentions
Reducing the offensive act	7. Image bolstering 8. Minimization 9. Differentiation 10. Transcendence 11. Reducing the credibility 12. Compensation	7. Using puffery to build image 8. Stating the crisis is not bad 9. Indicating that this crisis is different from more offensive crises 10. Asserting good acts far outweigh the damage of this one crisis 11. Maintaining the accuser lacks credibility 12. Paying the victim; making restitution to set things to where they were before the event
Taking corrective action Mortification	13. Corrective action 14. Mortification	13. Taking measures to prevent event from reoccurring 14. Admitting guilt and apologizing

Source: Benoit (1995).

PRECRISIS PLAN DEVELOPMENT

A key step to minimize damage and shorten a crisis when it occurs is to proactively identify potential crises and plan accordingly. This activity usually occurs in the precrisis phase, where the planning and preparation take place. To be effective, a crisis communications plan must be current and accurate, with all the necessary information readily available. There is precious little time to refine and update the plan while a crisis is underway, to be sure. Some crisis experts have equated this with "[f]lying a plane while building it at the same time" (Phelps & Williams, n.d.).

The first step in creating the crisis communications plan is to gather a representative team of employees from throughout your organization—for example, senior managers from operations, human resources, sales and marketing, research and development, security, and so on—to brainstorm the potential things that could go wrong for your organization and then develop a response plan to address them. For example, you can plan to avoid or manage a product recall by streamlining your customer communications system to track trends in complaints and establishing a process to implement repairs in the field.

In the event of lawsuit against the company, you can pre-develop standard responses to lawsuits by topic, which note the following:

a)   You do not comment on the specifics of litigation in process.

b)   Assure the public and your employees that the company is investigating the matter or is confident in its case.

In a disaster or workplace accident, having protocols in place to manage employee and external communications and to monitor social media to put down rumors or clarify misstatements is critical. As well, an efficient system to get care to those injured and monitor their care to keep loved ones informed can be very beneficial.

Larry Smith, president of the Institute for Crisis Management (ICM), suggests that as many as two-thirds of crises that occur should never have been a crisis (Bonk, Tynes, Griggs, & Sparks 2008, p. 116), underscoring the need for issues management. However, he also counsels that companies should be vigilant for problems or issues that could escalate into a crisis and have three essential plans on hand that are current and ready for implementation. These include a crisis operation plan, a communications plan, and a business recovery plan (Bonk et al., 2008, p. 116). These suggestions are consistent with the three stages of crisis as outlined by Coombs.

PREPARE A CRISIS CHECKLIST

Most experts advocate that companies, nonprofits and even celebrities and elected officials have a current and up-to-date crisis plan in case one is needed. One, it provides you with a solid overview of the potential problems for your company, and two, once the trouble is identified, you can eliminate or minimize it. With a list of vulnerabilities in hand, you can develop your crisis plan. The key steps are as follows:

☐   *Identify your crisis response team (CRT)*. And designate a leader. This may—or may not—be your CEO. Either way, your team should include the necessary subject matter experts and advisers that participated in the brainstorming session.

- [ ] *Identify your spokespersons.* You will need articulate and expert managers and a system to respond to media inquiries. Depending on the nature of the crisis, the experts might include medical professionals, engineers, legal counsel, and/or bilingual staff if the situation requires it.

- [ ] *Train your spokespersons.* In addition to the subject matter expertise required by the crisis, managers must be able to answer media questions without overreacting and with a sense of the impact of what they say—or don't say.

- [ ] *Social media monitoring.* Personnel who know how to monitor social media and respond when necessary are essential as well.

- [ ] *Prepare customer-facing employees.* If your company has retail stores or locations, expect that customers will have questions. Preparing staff with materials to respond to customers and the public is critical.

- [ ] *Set up monitoring and notification systems.* This is a critical step before, during, and after the crisis. This should include online and traditional media and the customer feedback mechanisms as noted earlier.

- [ ] *Create a list of key audiences/stakeholders.* These are the people, both internal and external, that are impacted or who play roles in responding to the situation and the company's performance in addressing it. Understanding who they are and what concerns or motivates them is an important part of crisis preparation and management.

- [ ] *Develop holding or stand-by statements.* While you can't predict the specifics of a given crisis, you can predict the situations that *might* arise. Armed with this information, you can prepare templates of news releases, stand-by statements, background research on key areas of your business where a problem could occur, and questions and answers to be adapted and updated when needed.

CRISIS STAGE

The crisis phase usually begins with a trigger event that challenges the status quo and disrupts normal, daily operations of the company or organization. The crisis management phase ends when the crisis is resolved or under control. In the interval crisis stage, the company or organization is consumed with responding to all its stakeholders (government, media, customers, employees, and the public) as well as solving the underlying problem.

The foundation for coping with the active crisis stage should be in the crisis plan. The plan should include all the elements needed to respond—contact information for key executives, key media for outreach, a strong social media monitoring and outreach plan, available trained spokespeople and experts, and so on. However, do not assume that the existence of a plan by itself guarantees a smooth and effective response to the crisis. Crisis counselors like Lukaszewski, Smith, and Dezenhall agree the plan must be current and followed—not left behind on shelf—and adapted according to the situation and stakes.

Once a crisis is underway the CRT needs to be flexible. Inevitably the crisis will move and shift in ways not imagined or covered in the basic plan. Here is where the organization and the crisis team need to adapt to the matter at hand while staying true to its overall goals of transparency, accuracy, honesty, and timeliness in its response.

Habitat for Humanity and Wells Fargo Team Up With Veterans to Improve 100 Homes

To help counteract negative publicity from its "cross-selling" scandal, Wells Fargo partnered with Habitat for Humanity, donating money and employees' time to repair homes across the United States.

Tim Matsui/Getty Images

As part of it ongoing CSR programs in the community—and to help offset the reputation damage in the cross-selling scandal—Wells Fargo & Company launched a new initiative in 2017 with Habitat for Humanity to improve 100 homes with veterans in nearly 30 communities across the country from Seattle, Washington, to South Palm Beach, Florida.

Launched in May 2017 during Military Appreciation Month with the support of a $300,000 grant from the Wells Fargo Housing Foundation, Wells Fargo volunteers worked alongside veterans on projects such as painting, landscaping, and other improvements to support sustainable housing.

Affordable and Sustainable Housing

"Veterans have made extraordinary sacrifices for our country, and by teaming up with Habitat for Humanity we will work side-by-side with veterans to make important improvements to their homes that may otherwise be unattainable," said Martin Sundquist, executive director of the Wells Fargo Housing Foundation (Habitat for Humanity, 2017). "Our team members are active and engaged volunteers and support their local communities by applying their time and talents where they live and work, and this effort is one of several ways we work with Habitat to create affordable and sustainable housing."

Local Habitat organizations identified home improvement opportunities in their communities and led the work with veterans and Wells Fargo volunteers to beautify homes with landscaping, painting, and other improvements.

Positive Impact to Lives and Neighborhoods

"Access to safe and decent housing is a challenge for far too many households, including our country's veterans," said Colleen Finn Ridenhour, senior vice president of development, Habitat for Humanity International. "This most recent commitment by the Wells Fargo Housing Foundation will enable us to work with veterans to improve their homes and, we believe, make a positive impact to their lives and their neighborhoods" (Habitat for Humanity, 2017).

Wells Fargo team members have volunteered more than 315,000 hours to build and improve more than 2,100 Habitat homes with low-income homeowners, seniors, and veterans since 2010. Wells Fargo Housing Foundation donated more than $44 million from 2010 to 2016 to Habitat locally and nationally, of which $14 million has supported national programs with Habitat for Humanity International and its mission to create a world where everyone has a decent place to live. ●

CRISIS RECOVERY

Finally we have the recovery stage. In this stage both expert practitioners and scholars suggest the focus should be on two main points:

1. Following through on the promises made during the crisis to your stakeholders

2. Conducting a postcrisis review to assess the effectiveness of the plan and areas for improvement in your stand-by plan

For many PR practitioners and companies, there is a natural tendency to want to move away from the crisis as soon as possible. However, this can be a major mistake—or a missed opportunity. Instead, convening the CRT and other parties, conducting a thorough analysis of what happened, what worked and what did not from your plan, and cataloguing mistakes or surprises that were not anticipated are significant learning opportunities and will improve your ongoing crisis planning. In a way this is a form of advanced issues management. You can assess your plan's effectiveness, evaluate the response, and close out the outstanding issues that arose during the crisis to prevent or offset a future one.

Another important activity during the postcrisis stage is expanding your communications outreach and SR activity to get some positive messages and visibility in the community to offset the lingering effects of the crisis. However, these activities need to be consistent with the company's ongoing sustainability activities (see the Social Responsibility in Action box on Wells Fargo's work with Habitat for Humanity), or they risk being seen as not credible or a cover up.

SOCIAL RESPONSIBILITY

CRISIS AND SOCIAL MEDIA

Without question the dramatic increase in the public's reliance on social media for information and entertainment has had a major impact on the practice of issues management and crisis communications (Jin, Liu, & Austin, 2014). To get a sense of how widespread and integral social media has become, let's look at some recent statistics. According to a recent study by Pew Research (Perrin, 2015), nearly two-thirds of American adults (65%) use social networking sites daily (see Figure 12.3), up from 7% in 2005.

▸ Young adults most likely to use it—90%

▸ Women and men use at similar rates (68% of females and 62% of men)

▸ Higher education levels and income still most active, but 56% of lowest income levels now use social media

▸ No notable differences along racial lines—65% white, 65% Hispanic, and 56% African Americans

▸ Rural use at 58% versus 68% suburbs and 64% in urban areas

From an issues management and crisis communication perspective, social media can be both a positive and a negative force, as well as an early warning system, if it is monitored on a real-time basis. The positive side of social media is that

FIGURE 12.3

Social Networking Use Has Shot Up in the Past Decade

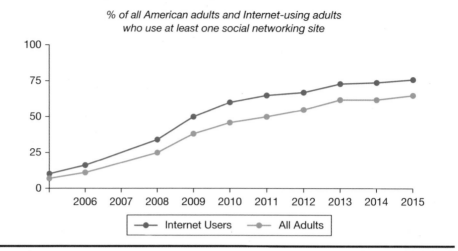

*% of all American adults and Internet-using adults
who use at least one social networking site*

Source: Perrin (2015).

it enables companies and organizations in precrisis, crisis, or recovery mode to have direct access to target audience(s) and deliver real-time updates without a time lag, bias, or filter by the media. Companies can post official statements, YouTube videos, situation updates, and instructions for recalls or a fix to the problem on a constant basis, 24/7 and 365 days a year. Social media provides direct access to push out news and updates on a given crisis as well as allows companies to post detailed statements or content to all interested parties on dedicated crisis websites (linked to the main site).

Conversely, on the negative side, the vast array of social media platforms and the public's reliance on them for news and information has a downside as well. A company in a crisis does not have control of the information that is being circulated online. As well, there is usually no gatekeeper who verifies the information that is being posted about the crisis or any comments on the way it is being handled. This requires a constant monitoring of key sites, the list of which is always shifting but must certainly include the major ones, for example, Facebook, Twitter, Snapchat, and Instagram. There is also the possibility that activist groups or "trolls," that is, people anxious to stir up a controversy or bring attention to their cause, might become active since open social platforms are ideal for that purpose.

INFAMOUS EXAMPLES

In the infamous Deepwater Horizon crisis in 2010, early on, a site popped up labeled #BPGlobalPR, which began to post "updates and comments," allegedly from the company's PR team, about the spill and its aftermath. After it became established, it began to post more and more outrageous comments on the disaster, causing the company to step in to correct it and thereby extend the fake site's impact and status in searches. The satirical account quickly surpassed BP America's official Twitter account in terms of followers, and it was able to succeed in part because of BP's limited social media presence when the crisis erupted (Schock, 2010).

In all phases of crisis management, companies must be vigilant for negative or satirical content that starts on social media. By monitoring this activity, the company can spot trends or issues that could erupt into a full-blown crisis and, hopefully, address them head-on before they gain traction and followers. You must also assess if your company should respond directly on the same site or indirectly on your own site—or other platforms.

BPGlobalPr
@britishpollute

Follow

Instant Updates on the BP Oilspill http://www.britishpolluting.com/updates/blo g.html #oilspill #bp #bpoilspill 17:30:01

3:30 PM - 24 Jul 2010

This was the case in the example detailed earlier in this chapter. The company was well prepared to respond to misinformation being circulated by its opponents in the "ingredients" lawsuit. The company used both traditional and social media platforms to respond aggressively without impacting the legal case that was in process. The result was that the crisis was short-lived and the case was ultimately abandoned as it did not gain much traction with the media or the public.

It is worth noting here that the traditional media, that is, print and broadcast journalists, often scan these social platforms for tips on stories or to identify a crisis in the making and thereby get a jump on a new story. Some news organizations will also cite a tweet or Facebook post and treat it as news or opinion that serves as the basis for a news story. "When consumers you've never met are rating your company's products in public forums on line with which you have no experience or influence, your company is vulnerable to a crisis or, at best, a threat to your reputation" (Li & Bernoff, 2011).

A Twitter account posing as an official BP source gained attention during the Deepwater Horizon spill in 2010. It posted increasingly outrageous comments as its follower count grew.

Twitter.com/britishpollute

VOLUME, VELOCITY, AND VARIETY

The need to be vigilant online to identify issues and respond aggressively to a crisis is underscored by some recent research by Zignal Labs (2016). This San Francisco-based media intelligence firm defines the current crisis environment in relation to a company's digital footprint. It suggests that in the current environment, every crisis needs to be managed with three key digital factors in mind—*volume, velocity,* and *variety*—as well as the conventional approaches to crisis communications (see Table 12.2).

The 2015 Volkswagen crisis that followed the disclosure that the company had engineered and installed a system for its diesel cars to cheat on U.S.-mandated emission tests is a case in point. VW has long been regarded as a leading socially responsible company and had marketed itself as the alternative for green-focused customers in the United States and around the world. Zignal reports that the fallout

TABLE 12.2

Key Digital Factors in Crisis Management

DIGITAL FACTOR	MEASUREMENT	EXAMPLES
Volume	The amount of data	Tweets, media mentions, shares, and posts on social media
Velocity	The speed at which the data is generated	Tweets per second or online news stories per hour
Variety	The types of data being generated and the various platforms it is being shared on	Images and hashtags on Twitter and Instagram, news stories posted and shared, Tweets, and videos on YouTube

Despite Volkswagen's reputation as a socially responsible and eco-conscious company, it installed software designed to cheat emissions tests in its clean diesel line of cars. When the software was discovered, VW faced immediate backlash.

Armando Arorizo/Bloomberg/ Getty Images

across the digital and social channels for VW was "swift and decisive"—the company went from being highly admired for its engineering expertise and fuel efficiency performance to "dead last" in The Harris Poll (2016), which asked Americans to rank "The 100 Most Visible Companies" by quality and reputation.

Gallup reported that due to the high awareness (71% among U.S. consumers surveyed) of the VW scandal, four in 10 people surveyed (41%) were less likely to purchase a car from VW. Gallup also found that 69% of the people they surveyed said the scandal would negatively impact the VW brand globally (O'Boyle & Adkins, 2015). Beyond the reputation damage to VW, there was a substantial financial penalty and management changes as well. Record-setting fines of $14.7 billion were levied against the company by the U.S. government (Isidore & Goldman, 2016), the US CEO was replaced (Beene, 2016), and the brand's reputation worldwide took a major hit (The Harris Poll, 2016). Hans-Gerd Bode, VW's communications chief executive at the time, described the company's experience on social media following the crisis as a "tsunami" in an interview with the *New York Times* (Hakim, 2016).

Since 2011 Zignal Labs has worked with hundreds of large enterprise brands, leading sports teams, and renowned political leaders. Zignal suggests that three trends ring true for every modern crisis:

1. *A modern crisis is fueled by data.* In today's modern marketplace, companies are inundated with massive amounts data. In fact major enterprises manage petabytes of big data every day. This influx of data grows exponentially due to the rapid proliferation of mobile devices and the digitization of consumers, generating an incredible 2.5 quintillion bytes of data every day.

While the nature of a crisis hasn't changed (e.g., an embarrassing public CEO flub or a global product recall), the digital channels through which a crisis will spread are fast and ferocious. For any crisis, both small and large, brands must be prepared for the massive volume, velocity, and variety of digital information that comes in its wake.

2. *Conventional approaches (alone) no longer work.* In a modern crisis, the volume, velocity, and variety of data will immediately overwhelm traditional tools and processes. Even the best laid plans can't adequately address the challenges associated with a crisis instantaneously unfolding and mutating across digital and mobile channels.

3. *Data provides the blueprint for a solution.* While the data deluge can pose an immediate challenge for any crisis communications team, data will also provide a path to a solution. Specifically, data will reveal critical trends, patterns, and insights in the wake of a crisis to empower communications, PR, public affairs, and marketing teams.

With an understanding that data can ultimately become a brand's biggest threat during a crisis and a path to a solution, cross-functional teams within the enterprise must modernize their crisis communications plans accordingly (Zignal Labs, 2016).

SCENARIO OUTCOME

In the Wells Fargo case, you read about the negative fallout due to the bank's poor handling of the cross-selling crisis in the fall of 2016 and how the company leaders were brought before Congress to explain unethical business practices.

You were asked: How well prepared was Wells Fargo for this crisis? Did they handle the fallout well? Here's what Wells Fargo did:

- No change in executive leadership happened until nearly three years after the misconduct was made public in a *New York Times* story; however, more than 5,000 employees had been fired during that time.

- Three weeks after the Senate hearing, John Stumpf announced he was stepping down from his position, "retiring" as chair and CEO effective immediately.

- Senate Banking Committee members and other critics were not impressed. "Unfortunately, Mr. Stumpf's retirement does nothing to answer the many questions that remain," said Senator Sherrod Brown, D–OH (Merle, 2016).

- The company announced Stumpf would relinquish $41 million in equity and would receive no severance pay (Glazer, 2016a).

- The board split apart the two roles previously held by Stumpf, appointing a longtime Wells Fargo executive as president and a Wells Fargo board member and former CEO of General Mills as CEO.

You were also asked: What role, if any, does Wells Fargo's track record of SR play in offsetting the reputation damage from this crisis? How has the bank responded to the crisis via CSR? With a little research, you may have learned:

In April 2017 Wells Fargo reported it had invested nearly $67 billion in its global CSR activities during the prior year (Wells Fargo, 2017a).

The Harris Poll (2017) revealed Wells Fargo at the bottom of a list of 100 U.S. companies regarding their corporate reputation and SR efforts—reflecting that a company's actions must be authentic and true to its professed values.

To address one final question, if you worked for a competitor of Wells Fargo, what advice would you give to the management team to prepare for media questions on cross-selling at the bank?

Here are some key considerations:

Complacency or relief that your company (or client) is not enmeshed in a crisis can be a serious oversight. As in any crisis, the damage or impact is not limited to just the company involved in the problem or issue. The wise move is to immediately conduct an in-depth issues audit to make sure that there are no hidden problems or business practices that could erupt into a crisis (like at Wells Fargo). This underscores the value and need for issues management as a preventative measure in your overall crisis planning and preparation.

Note: On July 9, 2017, a federal judge in San Francisco approved a $142-million class-action settlement to compensate possibly millions of customers who had unauthorized accounts opened in their names. Wells Fargo Chief Executive Tim Sloan said in a separate statement that the preliminary approval represents "a major milestone in our efforts to make things right for our customers" (Wells Fargo, 2017b).

WRAP UP

In this chapter, the focus has been on issues management and crisis communications and how they are related. Definitions of both terms were provided and examples cited to show how the proper implementation of one tactic—issues management—can offset the need for another—crisis communications.

Also we examined the predominant theory used by scholars to track how organizations deal with a crisis. Finally the chapter reviewed the impact of social media and provided guidance on how organizations can monitor and respond online to crisis situations.

Mastering issues management and crisis communications is essential for your growth and development as a PR professional. McKinsey (2009), a leading management consulting firm, said it well: "Now more than ever, it will be action—not spin—that builds strong reputations. Organizations need to enhance their listening skills so that they are sufficiently aware of emerging issues; to reinvigorate their understanding of, and relationships with, critical stakeholders; and to go beyond traditional PR by activating a network of supporters who can influence key constituencies."

KEY TERMS

Crisis: A significant threat to operations that can have long-term, negative consequences to the company or organization involved (Coombs, n.d.), **304**

Crisis Communications: The process by which organizations respond to and manage the situation to minimize damage to products, people, the public, and/or their reputation, **303**

Disasters: "[E]vents that are sudden, seriously disrupt routines of systems, require new course of action to cope with the disruption and pose a danger to values and social goals" (Coombs, 2015), **304**

Issues Management: An anticipatory, strategic management process that helps organizations detect and respond appropriately to emerging trends or changes in the sociopolitical environment (Dougall, 2008), **303**

Litigation Crisis: A crisis driven by a lawsuit (or the threat of one) and plays out in the court of public opinion as well as in the legal system, **309**

Organizational Crisis: A situation that threatens an organization and it stakeholders—for example, shareholders, customers, employees, and the public—and can seriously impact performance and generate negative outcomes (Coombs, 2015), **306**

Proactive: Monitoring and responding to situations as they are identified, before they erupt, **303**

Product Crisis: A case in which a problem in a major product—for example, brakes in a car, faulty batteries in a phone, bacteria in food, or unintended side effects of medicine—creates a public hazard and the company is held responsible, **308**

Reactive: When an organization does not act in advance and the situation escalates requiring an organizational, public response, **303**

Gather in small groups and identify a recent crisis in the news, preferably one involving a social issue or cause such as the impact of soft drinks on health and wellness of children or an increase in car accidents with teenage victims due to driver distraction.

As you review the coverage, ask yourselves a series of questions:

▸ What would you have done in that situation?

▸ What strategies or tactics would you employ?

▸ How would you measure your progress?

▸ Most important, assess the company's performance *after* the crisis ends. How did they rebuild trust or repair their reputation? What steps did they take to reassure customers, the public, and government that the situation will not be repeated?

Assessing another company's crisis is a way to test and improve your own plan and response strategies; you will be better off when the time comes. Your ability to see it coming, minimize the damage, and protect the company's reputation can enhance your career and make you a more complete PR professional.

In thinking about the Wells Fargo scenario that opened this chapter, consider how the bank's reputation for SR leadership might have been useful during the crisis in rebuilding the bank's reputation after the firestorm and investigations ended. Wells Fargo has been active for years in its communities, with a focus on diversity and inclusion, economic empowerment, environmental sustainability, and employee volunteerism. For more information see: https://www.wellsfargo .com/about/corporate-responsibility/:

▸ What should the company do to rebuild its brand?

▸ What role can CSR play?

▸ Was the company's profile as a CSR leader damaged?

▸ What can be done to rebuild the bank's image with its customers?

▸ Is there a risk of being accused of "greenwashing"?

▸ Can you think of any other company that has leveraged its SR activity after a crisis?

SOCIAL RESPONSIBILITY CASE STUDY

Hertz Moves Its Corporate Headquarters

In 2013 Hertz, a Fortune 500 company and a leader in the rental car industry, made the decision to relocate its corporate headquarters from Park Ridge, New Jersey, to Fort Myers, Florida (Hertz, 2013). Hertz had been in New Jersey since 1988 and had more than 1,000 working at its headquarters. The company had built up a strong reputation in its home market as a desirable employer and good corporate citizen.

Research and Strategy

The business case for the move to Florida was solid, including tax incentives, a workforce with experience in hospitality and tourism, and other economic considerations. Florida was also the state with the highest concentration of Hertz employees, more than New Jersey or metropolitan New York.

The company knew that this decision would have a major impact on its hometown, specifically its headquarters employees and the local and state economy. It also wanted to minimize the risk of being perceived as having deserted the communities near its corporate headquarters.

In anticipation of this, and consistent with sound issues management practice, the company engaged a PR firm (Ketchum) to manage the announcement process and help focus the media coverage on the business case for the decision.

This plan for public and media outreach required research on its impact on local economy and development of an economic case for the move. Ketchum would also need to prepare briefing materials for all the key stakeholders and have them ready before the announcement.

Its reputation for community involvement in New Jersey also had to be supported. Hertz's New Jersey headquarters building was LEED certified, so the company began the process to make sure its new Florida corporate headquarters building would be certified as well. (LEED certification, which stands for Leadership in Energy and Environmental Design, is a status awarded by the U.S. Green Buildings Council and certifies that the building is energy efficient and environmentally friendly. It signifies a commitment to sustainability and energy conservation and can provide tax incentives to the builder and owner for meeting the strict standards.)

Execution

The campaign strategy was to promote the business case for relocating its headquarters and provide details on how headquarters employees were being taken care of to balance the story. Seven hundred employees were to be relocated, and 2,000 head office employees would remain employed at the previous headquarters, thus maintaining a strong presence in its historic headquarters. To minimize the disruption, Hertz also pledged to maintain its community ties in northern New Jersey. These facts needed to be emphasized in the communications materials responding to stakeholder concerns.

The goal of the strategy was to manage the potential negative issue of relocating and balance news coverage of the move to include its key messages and business rationale. The tactics included briefings with headquarters employees, in addition to local officials in New Jersey and Florida, and working closely with key media outlets in both markets to get the story out in a measured and balanced way.

Evaluation

The news did not leak before it was to be announced, which had been a major concern of the executives. News coverage of the move was 93% positive to neutral, and more than 55% of the stories included quotes and key messages from Hertz spokespersons.

Anticipating issues and addressing them in advance led to a smoother announcement and move for Hertz. If the company had decided to simply issue a news release or just hold a press conference, the outcry from the media, politicians, and employees in New Jersey might have prevented or delayed the move.

That outcome would have cost the company money in lost tax incentives, negatively impacted employee morale, and diminished the company's reputation and relationships in both markets. In short the issue could have become a crisis for Hertz. Instead both the new location city in Florida and the host community in New Jersey felt their interests had been considered in a responsible way.

ENGAGE

‣ Break into small groups to do some initial research on Hertz and its SR activity.

‣ Visit the Hertz CSR site and review their annual report and current activity.

‣ Visit the sites of some of their main competitors to get a sense of what others in the industry are doing.

DISCUSS

‣ What are some of the CSR activities that Hertz should continue in the New Jersey location, and which ones ought to be adapted to Florida?

‣ Regarding Hertz's competitors (Avis, Enterprise, etc.), what are they doing in their CSR programs that might be of interest for Hertz?

‣ How can Hertz keep the New Jersey employees engaged in the company's CSR efforts?

SOCIAL RESPONSIBILITY CASE STUDY

Under Armour and the Sochi Winter Olympics: Protecting the Brand Against Unfair Criticism

Under Armour is the originator of performance apparel and sport gear engineered to keep athletes cool, dry, and light throughout the course of a game, practice, or workout. The 2014 Winter Olympics Games in Sochi, Russia, was Under Armour's opportunity to showcase its technology on the global stage. However, the brand soon faced a major crisis when its innovative long-track speed skating suit, the UA Mach39, came under scrutiny.

The U.S. Olympic speed skaters were performing below expectations, failing to reach the medal podium on any long track event. A 30-year speed skating medal streak for the United States had been broken, and what was described by the company as the "fastest speed skating suit ever made" was being blamed for the disappointing results.

While management knew the company was not at fault—and the team's coaching staff said as much to the media and public—this became a major problem for the company and required an immediate response. The world media, and others, assumed that because the team was mostly the same athletes who had competed successfully in previous Olympics, the new suits had to be at fault.

Research and Strategy

In responding to the crisis, Under Armour decided to focus on solving the problem and supporting the athletes instead of blaming them for the results. Direct involvement of CEO Kevin Plank and high-level executives were strategic in ensuring the messaging had credibility and trustworthiness. Also, its celebrity spokespeople would amplify its messaging on social media.

Execution

Under Armour arranged media interviews on site in Sochi for its CEO Kevin Plank and other executives to reinforce the company's core values and strong belief in its design and technology. Plank and key executives vigorously defended the suits *without* criticizing the athletes. In addition supportive statements from U.S. speed skating team officials that they didn't believe the suits were to blame were shared broadly, which helped balance the story.

The message from the company was clear: The brand stood by its product, but the athletes were top priority, and Under Armour wanted to ensure they were comfortable and confident. As the crisis wound down, to show its continued commitment, Under Armour doubled down on its partnership with U.S. Olympic speed skating and announced an eight-year partnership extension through the 2022 Olympics. This was deliberately done to reinforce the company's commitment to the skaters and the Olympics at a time when they were vulnerable.

Evaluation

Given the Olympic stage, the direct involvement of CEO Kevin Plank and high-level executives was imperative. Plank's interviews and sound bites resonated with key stakeholders. Twitter conversation related to the issue and the Olympics was overwhelmingly positive, with many individuals tweeting that the company and Plank "got it right." In addition, Under Armour's athlete spokespeople, like Lindsay Vonn and Michael Phelps (both successful Olympians), were active in social media and expressed their confidence in the company.

Under Armour stood by the athletes and refused to shift blame, generating goodwill with viewers worldwide. As Plank said in an interview with *USA Today*: "In no way, shape or form will we ever point fingers at the athletes.... There was no push back from us. We said, whatever will make the athletes more comfortable, we'll do" (Horovitz, 2014).

The company stayed true to its corporate mission to "Make all athletes better." SVP of Innovation Kevin Haley stated that the company was willing to "move heaven and Earth" to allay the concerns of the team. Under Armour's efforts were noted and appreciated—U.S. speed skater Brittany Bowe noted that "Under Armour has bent over backwards for us" (Gloster, 2014).

During the crisis, the company reaffirmed its commitment to quality products and responsible business practices to offset speculation about how or where the suits were made. In the middle of the controversy, Under Armour announced plans to renew its sponsorship of U.S. speed skating through 2022. In so doing, Under Armour demonstrated its resilience, and Plank noted that Under Armour will "get back up, bigger, better and stronger."

ENGAGE

▸ Do some research on the case and learn more about what happened and who might have been to blame for the poor performance—if it was in fact not due to the new uniforms.

▸ Is it fair to blame the equipment manufacturer for poor performance by an athlete? If the athletes had exceeded their prior performance, would the company have tried to share the credit?

DISCUSS

▸ How does a company defend its product integrity on the world stage without compromising its relationship with the athletes it relies on to use and endorse it?

▸ How might Under Armour's leadership position in sustainability in the industry have been of use in this situation?

▸ If not during the crisis, how about after? How might the company have stepped up or raised visibility of its CSR activity in a post-Olympics reputation enhancement effort?

▸ Should it have been the CEO taking the lead in as the principal spokesperson? What are the risks of this strategy? Who else might have served this role?

Source: Diane Pelkey, senior VP, Global Communications, Under Armour.

VIDEO CASE

GM Recalls: Campaign Development

In early 2014, GM announced a recall of about 800,000 vehicles due to a faulty ignition switch, which in rare cases resulted in vehicles turning off while in operation. The recall soon expanded, ultimately involving 30 million cars, as it became clear that GM had known about the problem since 2001 and that the defect had caused a number of deaths.

VIDEO

1. Discuss the differences between a problem, crisis, and disaster. How does the GM recall fit into this paradigm?

2. How could issues management have helped GM prepare for this?

3. If you were on GM's PR team, what strategies would you propose to help the company move past the recall and repair its reputation?

PRACTICE AND APPLY WHAT YOU'VE LEARNED

edge.sagepub.com/page

CHECK YOUR COMPREHENSION ON THE STUDY SITE WITH:

- eFlashcards to strengthen your understanding of key terms

- Practice quizzes to test your comprehension of key concepts

- Videos and multimedia content to enhance your exploration of key topics

Nardj Alberto/UIG/Getty Images

13 Sports, Tourism, and Entertainment

Learning Objectives

13.1 Identify the opportunities and challenges of sports PR and how CSR initiatives are a fit for both teams and fans

13.2 Explore the scope of the tourism industry and the essential role of PR, gaining insight on socially responsible and sustainability aspects that support organizational goals

13.3 Examine the breadth of PR and CSR engagement within the entertainment industry through the perspectives of talent, agencies, and entertainment companies

Being the Best While Doing Serious Good: Micato Safaris

Micato Safaris was started in 1966 by Felix Pinto, a well-known farmer in Kenya. The company has since been named by *Travel +Leisure* as the number one, world's best safari outfitter a record nine times.

Through its more than 50 years of hosting thousands of wealthy travelers, Micato has taken care to help protect the animals, their habitat, and Africa's cultural heritage through partnering with multiple wildlife and wilderness conservation foundations.

One long-term SR effort earned Micato Safaris the Legacy in Travel Philanthropy Award by Tourism Cares (n.d.), the charitable community of the travel and tourism industry that has the sponsorship support of American Express.

Micato Safaris works to preserve the animals and habitats its customers pay to see and also supports local communities in Kenya.

Wolfgang Kaehler/LightRocket/Getty Images

The cause. Micato Safaris identified a need to educate children, so it formed a U.S. nonprofit, AmericaShare, to focus solely on that effort. Micato and AmericaShare have enabled thousands of Nairobi youth to attend school and to graduate from high school at a rate approaching 100%—from a population where fewer than 50% of boys and 42% of girls graduate.

The recipients. Micato's two core educational programs address barriers to education faced by youth living in extreme poverty in Nairobi's Mukuru slum, home to 325,000 with low education, public health, and employment rates. It is also where AIDS has been epidemic, with a generation of AIDS orphans, which is one reason Micato was drawn to supporting the Mukuru community.

The programs. In 1986 it started a program that focuses on funding room and board for youths attending private boarding schools. And in 2010 it launched another program to help primary students stay in school through supplementing family finances. Local community, church, and tribal leaders guide selections of the recipients.

The extended focus. Although the same needy situations existed throughout Kenya, Micato held true to its focus on Mukuru to not dilute resources. Instead it amplified its impact right where it started, creating a community center equipped with a lending library, funding a learning center for students with disabilities, supporting a nursery school, and in partnership with Johnson & Johnson, providing girls with feminine products and HIV/AIDS prevention information.

PR for Micato Safaris has secured feature coverage in virtually every major news media outlet, including *Forbes*, *The New York Times*, *The Wall Street Journal*, *USA Today*, *Travel + Leisure*, *Condé Nast Traveler*, *Smart Money*, and many other publications, often reporting the local community benefits along with the travel experience. "Being the Best While Doing Serious Good: Micato Safaris" reads one *Forbes* headline.

Your challenge. After engaging with this chapter, draw from the information in this scenario and the chapter's section on ecotourism to prepare a best practices checklist for how an organization, operating in a developing country, can create a successful and sustainable SR program involving the local community. You'll find Micato Safaris's how-to lessons at the chapter's end.

The chapter covers three areas in PR that are linked by their popularity as lifestyle interests: the wide world of sports, the allure of travel, and the craving for entertainment. All of them have the pulse of SR and sustainability running through them.

You'll first read about the PR opportunities and challenges in sports. Athletes and teams are both doing good (foundations and fund-raisers) and being bad (crises and damaged reputations). You'll discover how Northwestern University engages its student athletes in SR. You'll also consider what a stadium's corporate name means to the team—and to fans—and learn when it becomes a PR problem.

Tourism is one of the fastest-growing economic sectors in the world. You'll read about PR's role in stimulating interest in a journey, destination, or event; the tasks of handling unexpected threats and crises; and the ever-expanding area of **ecotourism**.

Finally entertainment PR touches Hollywood films and actors, spreads across to New York stage plays, publishers, and authors, and reaches out anywhere that on-air and online visuals, voices, and tunes find audiences. Read publicity tales from a radio personality, and discover all the social and environmental good that entertainers and their industry support.

OPPORTUNITIES AND CHALLENGES OF SPORTS PUBLIC RELATIONS

>> LO 13.1   Identify the opportunities and challenges of sports PR and how CSR initiatives are a fit for both teams and fans

Sports are a big part of everyday life. A team's fans follow its ups and downs, cheer its wins, and suffer its losses. Whether high school, minor league, or professional, it becomes intertwined with the lives of its supporters and the question, "Did you see the game last night," launches thousands of conversations many mornings. A city's pride can swell with a team's good fortune, as Chicago's did when the Cubs won a World Series title after over a century of frustration, or plunge them into the depression like Atlanta felt when their Falcons lost a Super Bowl in overtime.

⑤SAGE edge™

Master the content
edge.sagepub.com/page

FIGURE 13.1

Sports in the Media

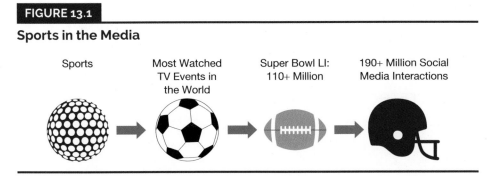

| Sports | Most Watched TV Events in the World | Super Bowl LI: 110+ Million | 190+ Million Social Media Interactions |

Source: (Nielsen, 2017).

PUBLIC RELATIONS PLAYS A STRATEGIC PART IN SPORTS

Sporting events and sports teams benefit from intense PR efforts. These efforts, on all levels, are designed to heighten public knowledge of teams and players—turn them into fans, in other words. It's fans, after all, who buy tickets and team apparel, purchase the products of corporate sponsors and advertisers, and follow the team's exploits in the media. Note the derivation of the word "fans" is from "fanatics," and certainly many fans are passionate devotees of "their" team.

Sports are also the most watched events on television around the world. In the United States, 19 of the top 20 most-watched television shows in Nielsen ratings history have been Super Bowl broadcasts (Nielsen, 2017). This includes 2017's Super Bowl LI with 111 million viewers (see Figure 13.1).

Publicists (sometimes called sports information directors) for teams employ numerous PR tactics, including developing and maintaining good relationships with sports writers and on-air personalities. They compile media kits and the accompanying mounds of statistics, write feature articles on players, handle interview requests from the media, provide website content, and occasionally handle player bookings and appearances.

SOCIAL MEDIA'S WINNING GAME

The use of social media, in all its forms and platforms, is a major function for any sports organization's PR department. The Chicago Cubs, for example, use Twitter, Snapchat, Instagram, and Facebook to interact with fans. The club's website carries Wrigley Field information, such as ticket prices and seating charts, upcoming game promotions, and includes help finding a parking space, too. The website also profiles players and team charities and even links to a fantasy league—an online game in which people manage rosters of league baseball players whose real-life statistics score points. All these channels and content are largely the responsibility of the Cubs' PR department.

The Cubs are not alone; the same social media tactics are used by most teams in Major League Baseball (MLB), the National Football League (NFL), the National Basketball Association (NBA), the Women's National Basketball Association

The Chicago Cubs have an active social media presence, sharing information, interacting with fans, and cracking jokes.

Twitter.com/cubs

(WNBA), Major League Soccer (MLS), the National Women's Soccer League (NWSL), and most college programs. That's a lot of opportunity *online* for PR professionals.

However, not every career in sports PR is with a professional team. In fact most are not. For the person who loves being associated with sports, the career choices are seemingly endless.

PUBLIC RELATIONS CAREERS FOR SPORTS LOVERS

The following list identifies some sports and sports-related jobs that may not be obvious and mentions a few of the duties.

▸ **Minor League teams:** MLB teams all have minor league affiliates on four levels, AAA, AA, A, and Rookie. Hockey follows a similar structure, and the NBA has a roster of minor league teams. All need PR professionals to do the same jobs as are done for the majors.

▸ **College athletic departments:** Ever wonder why an athlete is considered a Heisman candidate or why a gymnast is profiled as an Olympic hopeful? Thank their school's PR departments for creating the campaigns to raise their profiles. The same department is responsible for all the fan outreach done by the pro teams.

- ▸ **Sporting goods:** Wilson, Louisville Slugger, Coleman, Callaway, Bauer, Trek, and Dunlop didn't get to be sports household names without vigorous PR efforts with teams, pro and amateur athletes, and fans.

- ▸ **Sportswear:** The same is true of Under Armour, Nike, Adidas, Columbia, and Patagonia. Sportswear companies that enjoy instant name recognition and generally positive brand images have PR campaigns connected to celebrity athletes and professional and college athletic teams.

- ▸ **Sports food and drink:** This is an enormous field with many opportunities connecting PR pros to the sports world. It encompasses everything from working with the food manufacturer to retail placements and national awareness campaigns. The energy bar in some cyclist's seat pack didn't get there on its own.

- ▸ **Corporate sponsorships.** Sponsored sporting events, especially tournaments and championships, provide great opportunities for a company to put its name in front of the public—and even greater opportunities for PR practitioners. A complete list of sponsored sports events would run to hundreds of names and include college football bowl games, professional and amateur golf tournaments, NASCAR races, bicycle tours, tennis tourneys, and boxing matches, to name just a few.

Suffice to say that opportunities abound for the PR practitioner who wants to live and breathe sports.

PUBLICIZING THE GOOD, DEALING WITH THE BAD

PR professionals working for sports organizations of all sizes—professional and academic—deal with both news that benefits the team and news that casts a shadow on it. Rare is the year that no crisis rocks a sport or team, and dealing with those crises swiftly and honestly is key to keeping the public's support. On the opposite side of the same coin, teams and individual athletes, from pee wee to pro, are involved in good works year-round that benefit their communities. It is an equally important function of PR to highlight these positive activities.

THE RIGHT WAY TO HANDLE WRONGS

No matter the sport, there is an unfortunate certainty that some athletes will behave badly, and their misdeeds—minor or major—will reflect poorly on their teams, their schools, their own marketability, or even their communities. While it is the function of PR to cast a client in a positive light, it is not acceptable to issue false statements or to knowingly aid in the cover-up of an incident or issue that reflects poorly on them.

Unfortunately many PR wounds are self-inflicted, usually because of poor decisions made at the onset of the crisis and made worse by poor messaging later. Correcting an earlier PR misstep is much harder that being transparent and forthright from the start.

The NFL spent years denying even the existence of long-term brain injury in its former players, rejecting out of hand research that showed a direct link between concussions and Chronic Traumatic Encephalopathy (CTE). Although the league now has an aggressive program to protect players from concussions and their aftereffects,

The NFL's refusal to acknowledge the long-term impacts of repeated head injuries, known as CTE, harmed both its players and its reputation.

Jamie Squire/Getty Images

the damage to the league's credibility on any medical issue was substantial and still is not completely repaired.

The same can be said about how the various pro and college leagues have dealt with issues such as domestic abuse, sexual assault, and drug abuse. Even today those incidents continue to be mishandled by the PR staff of both the teams and the leagues. This can cause damage that will scar an organization for many years.

Penn State is still feeling the effects of the Jerry Sandusky child-abuse scandal that broke in late 2011. The Freeh report, commissioned by the university, alleged senior officials had credible knowledge of Sandusky's behavior as early as 1998. It was this revelation (cover-up) as much as Sandusky's acts that damaged Penn State's reputation.

However unsettling it may be for PR professionals to deal with such a situation, the accusations, and even the arrests, those must be acknowledged and dealt with openly and honestly. Covering up is no solution; it just makes the pain that much worse later on.

TALES OF THREE SPORTS STARS

The year 2016 was no different than previous ones when it came to scandals and PR crises. In no order of importance, a few of the more notable are listed here.

▸ Tennis star Maria Sharapova went public in March of 2016 that she had failed a drug test by testing positive for meldonium, a banned substance. Although Sharapova claimed that she had been taking the substance for many years for health issues, she was still handed a nine-month suspension. The failed drug test and suspension resulted in her losing lucrative endorsement deals, including one with Nike.

▸ When 49ers' quarterback Colin Kaepernick was spotted sitting during the national anthem, it became a national news story. Fans were split on the issue; some saw it as being disrespectful, others as patriotic. The act of not rising for the anthem spread to other teams, and so did the controversy. Whether

Being Good Sports: How Athletes and Teams Give Back to Their Community

The LeBron James Family Foundation has agreed to pay tuition at the University of Akron for thousands of qualifying students.

AP Photo/Karen Schiely

On all levels of athletics—and across all types of sports—good works are performed by individual athletes, teams, and entire leagues to benefit the community.

Big Names Have Big Impacts

Individual pro athletes, especially those with the highest profiles, often have foundations that support causes that have a direct connection to them or their families.

Started by the Chicago Cubs first baseman, Anthony Rizzo's Family Foundation has fighting cancer as its focus. Rizzo himself is a cancer survivor, having successfully battled Hodgkin's lymphoma.

Others raise money to aid the towns or states they came from. Eli Manning, quarterback for the New York Giants, raised nearly $3 million over a five year-period to build the Eli Manning Children's Clinic in Mississippi. The clinic reportedly provides outpatient care to more than 75,000 children each year (Powell, 2015).

Basketball superstar LeBron James's Wheels for Education program shepherds select Akron, Ohio, students from third grade through high school. Qualifying students will then enter the I Promise program with a guaranteed four-year college scholarship to the University of Akron. This act of generosity is expected to cost the James's foundation more than $41 million for 2021 graduates (LeBron James Family Foundation, n.d.).

Teams Dive Deep Into Charity, Too

Nearly every professional team's website, regardless of sport, lists the community outreach and charitable giving they support. From sponsoring youth leagues, to working with local after-school programs, to team members serving holiday meals to the needy, teams are visible in their support of their communities. It is important that the public is made aware of these stories of generosity and engagement. While the bad news will always get coverage, getting out the good news takes effort. The teams' PR departments must make sure that these good works are brought to the public's attention.

From Big Leagues to College Sports, All Do Their Part

MLB has as one of its official charities the Boys & Girls Clubs of America. The NFL foundation funds numerous youth-related programs, and MLS supports the Special Olympics. Colleges and university athletes are also active in lending a generous helping hand, such as those at Northwestern University, detailed in a separate section. ●

Kaepernick's marketability as a player has been affected remains to be seen as he heads toward free agency, but his personal brand may not have suffered as much as his critics may hope. In the weeks following his initial act, sales of his jersey were the top choice of fans.

▸ Scandal hit the U.S. Olympic team in Rio when swimmer Ryan Lochte became involved in a bizarre incident—or non-incident as it turned out. What began as a news report—that Lochte and several teammates had been held at gunpoint during a night out—quickly came apart. Instead of being victims, the story unfolded that Lochte and friends had been drunk and disorderly and damaged a gas station. Rather than staying in Rio to face the music, Lochte flew back to the states, leaving his teammates to meet with the police. After the Rio debacle, Ralph Lauren, Speedo, Gentle Hair Removal, and Airweave all parted ways with Lochte.

WHAT'S IN A NAME?

CORPORATIONS NAME STADIUMS

Over 700 athletic stadiums in the United States carry the name of a corporation (ESPN, 2017). This figure includes major and minor league baseball parks, soccer stadiums, basketball arenas, and professional and college football stadiums. In fact, on a professional level, it is more common for a team to play in a venue bearing a corporate name than not: 26 of 32 NFL teams (Long, 2016) and 21 of 30 MLB teams have a company name on the door (Barker, 2016).

HUGE INVESTMENTS OF MILLIONS EACH YEAR

Naming rights for NFL venues aren't cheap, but the fees vary widely. FedEx Field, home to Washington's NFL team, costs the corporation some $7.6 million a year. The San Francisco 49ers play in Levi's Stadium, for which the jeans company pays $11 million a year (Bien, 2013). And following the adage of everything being bigger in Texas, AT&T is reportedly paying around $19 million annually to have their name on the Dallas Cowboys' home turf (SportsDay, 2013).

Sponsors occasionally change, and with that switch can come some fan adjustments, as when the Chicago White Sox renamed their stadium. Called U.S. Cellular Park since its opening in 2003 (and quickly nicknamed "The Cell" by fans), the Sox will start play in 2017 in Guaranteed Rate Field. Time will tell how fans shorten that name into something less of a mouthful. American sports website SportingNews (Thomas, 2016) offers their opinion on the worst arena and stadium names in sports (see Table 13.1)—names that identify fast-food franchises, mortgage companies, and grocery stores.

PUBLIC RELATIONS VALUES AND RISKS

From a PR perspective, there can be real value in having your company's name associated with a city or college's team. On-site your name and logo is on everything from the front door and the roof to the ticket stubs and the concession cups. Off-site your name gets repeated mentions every time a story about the team refers to the stadium. While such exposure isn't necessarily free because of the naming fees, it most certainly is an efficient way of putting your company's name into the consumer's mind.

How One University's Athletes Give Back

Northwestern University, located in Evanston, Illinois, is noted for its overall excellence as an academic institution, ranking 12th in national universities (U.S. News & World Report, 2017). It's also highly respected as an athletic force in the Big Ten Conference; its women's lacrosse team has won seven National Collegiate Athletic Association (NCAA, n.d.) championships since 2005.

Beyond the competition, the participants on the 19 teams that Northwestern fields are involved in many acts that benefit the residents of the university's hometown.

According to Maureen Palchak, assistant athletic director for community relations, student athletes support efforts such as ROAR, an anti-bullying program designed in conjunction with the local school district for students in Grades 3 to 6.

"Our student athletes do it all. They run the 45-minute program and interact with the children. The younger kids love mixing with football players, swimmers, and field hockey stars."

Another outreach program involves student athletes who visit schools. The program, a partnership with the NFL and Dairy Management Inc.'s Fuel Up to Play 60 initiative, is aimed at getting schoolkids to eat healthy meals and to be active for at least an hour a day.

"Many other initiatives are created by the teams themselves," said Palchak. "It's my job to help facilitate their activities or even help partner them with a larger organization."

She points to the women's softball team's involvement in Toys for Tots, and the men's soccer team's annual Cycle for Survival. Over the years the latter event has raised hundreds of thousands of dollars for Sloan Kettering Cancer Center—chosen due to its dedication to fighting rare cancers. The annual event was started in 2007 by a former Northwestern soccer player's wife during her battle with cancer.

Over the course of the year, says Palchak, Northwestern student athletes will be involved in many local activities such as canned food drives, a Day of Service to help clean up Evanston neighborhoods and parks, and serving meals at local shelters. Although there are no community service hours required of student athletes, "it is an expectation," notes Palchak, but added, "We never have any shortage of volunteers."

Palchak places stories about Northwestern's student athletes' outreach and volunteerism with media outlets, ensuring their efforts are recognized. "We share these stories when appropriate," said Palchak, which includes inviting media coverage of events such as the Cycle for Survival. "It's important for the community to learn of these charitable activities and for the athletes to know their good works are appreciated" (M. Palchak, personal communication, 2017). ●

TABLE 13.1

Sporting News' Worst Arena and Stadium Names in Sports

NAME	LOCATION	SPORT TEAM	TYPE OF BUSINESS
Whataburger Field	Corpus Christi, TX	Hooks, MiLB	Fast food
Little Caesars Arena	Detroit	Red Wings, NHL	Fast food
Guaranteed Rate Field	Chicago	White Sox, MLB	Mortgages
Smoothie King Center	New Orleans	Pelicans, NBA	Beverages
Taco Bell Arena	Boise State Univ.	Basketball	Fast food
Papa John's Cardinal Stadium	Univ. of Louisville	Football	Fast food
InfoCision Stadium	Univ. of Akron	Football	Call centers
KFC Yum! Center	Univ. of Louisville	Basketball	Fast food

There are risks involved for teams and for corporations in the naming rights game; the Houston Astros played in Enron Stadium, named for a corporation that collapsed in scandal. The Astros quickly shed the name and now play in Minute Maid Park. FedEx finds itself in the uncomfortable position of being the stadium sponsor of Washington's NFL team whose nickname, the Redskins, is offensive to many. In 2013 Florida Atlantic University was set to earn $6 million for renaming its football stadium after the GEO Group, a prison corporation notorious for sexual abuse and mistreatment of prisoners. After university protests and online petitions, the decision was reversed.

TOURISM—MORE THAN SIGHTSEEING

>> **LO 13.2** **Explore the scope of the tourism industry and the essential role of PR, gaining insight on socially responsible and sustainability aspects that support organizational goals**

When you think of tourism, what picture comes to mind? Perhaps it's a cruise to the islands of the Caribbean, a bus tour of Italian cities, or maybe a hike among the ruins of Machu Picchu. You may also think of destinations within the United States where you might spend a few days, such as one of the theme parks in Florida, a campsite in Yosemite, or a ski resort in Colorado. Then again, you may associate tourism with sights and places you visit for a day—or even for just a few hours—such as a state fair, a local festival, or a roadside attraction that catches your eye.

You'd be right in any of those definitions of tourism, but you're probably not aware how much impact tourism has on our economy and on the economies of the world's nations. Whether riding a gondola in Venice or eating cotton candy at a county fair, tourists and tourism have an enormous economic impact.

According to the United Nations World Tourism Organization, tourism is one of the world's largest industries, ranking third behind fuels and chemicals but ahead of agricultural goods and automotive products (UNWTO, 2016). As one of the major segments in international commerce, tourism represents one of the most important sources of revenue for many developing nations.

The World Economic Forum (2015) reports that in 2015, travel and tourism accounted for 9 percent of the world's gross domestic product (GDP) and by 2022 will employ more than 10 percent of the world's workforce (World Economic Forum, 2015). In some countries travel and tourism's contribution to the GDP is higher: In the United States it's nearly 10 percent and in Spain, almost 15 percent. It is even as high as 24% in Greece (Smith, 2016).

For many years tourism has had steady growth and is now one of the *fastest-growing* economic sectors in the world. Today's tourism has close ties to economic development and includes a growing number of new destinations. Emerging nations are eager to attract travelers and tourists as the dynamics of tourism have turned it into a prime mover of economic progress.

THE ROLE OF PUBLIC RELATIONS

The tourism industry, whether it's a nation promoting its heritage or a small town promoting its annual festival, has a single goal: attract travelers and tourists. People want to go places, see things they've never seen, and do things they've never done, and the industry must turn that basic, but undirected, desire into action. PR is vital

Music festivals like Coachella, in California, can attract tens of thousands of people, but first people need to find out the event is taking place.

Christopher Polk/Getty Images

in this process. Beyond attracting visitors, communications help them get there and help shape their experience once they arrive.

Promoting the place or attraction is the first step and can include traditional tactics such as story placements in magazines and newspapers, advertising, brochures, and pre-produced video news releases for television and online. More and more, a strong online presence with social media content is becoming the preferred way to attract the interest of tourists.

PUBLIC RELATIONS PLAN FOR A MUSIC FESTIVAL

Imagine you're promoting a music festival hosted in your city. Let's run through your process, from beginning to end.

1. *First use the power of digital and social.* You want to use these and other online techniques to draw a crowd (see Table 13.2).

TABLE 13.2

How to Use the Power of Digital and Social Media

Colorful website	List performers, plus provide links to hotels, restaurants, and transportation options.
YouTube channel	Feature videos of past festivals.
Instagram account	Invite people to virtually explore all attractions.
Twitter feed	Update potential visitors on schedule additions and changes.
Facebook page	Duplicate information and also use it as an interactive questions-and-answer tool.

2. *Next, you'll want to promote* partnering airlines, tour operators, and car rental companies to offer special rates and cross-promote on their websites, as you do for them on yours.

3. *Once visitors arrive,* they need to feel welcome, comfortable, and appreciated. Work with local motels and restaurants to not only offer festival packages and discounts, but make them an integral part of the effort to welcome event guests with maps, schedules, and transportation.

4. *Finally, you'll want to have information kiosks* in key locations around the city to help visitors find their way around, get schedules, and obtain discounts—information duplicated on your online platforms.

5. *Once the festival begins,* turn your attention to promoting the events through television placements, news stories, live feeds online, and a festival blog that is written in real time. Also encourage attendees to post their own reviews and comments on social media. The reason you keep promoting is, first, to attract a crowd for the last day or two of the event—encouraging attendance by those people who did not anticipate coming but now want to be in on the fun. Second showing this year's festival to those who didn't come at all helps build interest for next year's show.

As you can see, there is no one job description that would suit all the tasks that need to be performed by PR professionals for a single event. What's also obvious are the numerous opportunities for employment in the field of PR represented in a single event. No matter your interest—travel, hospitality, social media, or event planning—there's a job for you in PR.

SOCIAL RESPONSIBILITY

SUSTAINABILITY AND SOCIAL RESPONSIBILITY PRACTICES

HOTELS

Sustainability goals have become increasingly important in guest attraction and loyalty. A study of business travelers revealed that 95% felt hotels should be investing in green initiatives (Deloitte, 2015). The hospitality industry has responded, placing itself in the forefront of sustainable practices, which extend from simple in-room cards encouraging guests to reuse their towels and linen to corporate-wide practices.

The Las Vegas Sands, Wyndham, MGM Resorts, Hilton, and Marriott are all high-ranking hospitality organizations in *Newsweek*'s 2016 Top Green Companies list (Newsweek, 2016). Marriott's Serve Our World initiative supports local communities and works to protect the environment. Its Ritz-Carlton properties encourage sustainable driving with electric charging stations at hotels around the world.

Starwood Hotels & Resorts was the first corporate partner of Clean the World, Soap Saves Lives. The Florida-based foundation collects and recycles soaps and bottled amenities. The soaps and cleaning products are sanitized, repackaged and distributed to children and families in the United States, Canada, and more than 40 countries (Lanz & Rackham, 2015).

Another Starwood worldwide focus is on energy and water: In partnership with Conservation International, the hotel chain is committed to reducing energy

Many hotels now encourage guests to reuse towels to conserve water, often appealing to their sense of environmental responsibility.

Jonathan Wiggs/The Boston Globe/Getty Images

consumption by 30% and water consumption by 20% by 2020, from a 2008 baseline (Starwood, n.d.). One way Starwood engages its publics is through video storytelling. Find "Starwood's Water Story: Thinking Beyond Conservation" on YouTube.

Indeed green practices and eco-friendly programs have become so widespread that many travelers not only willingly participate in them but are beginning to expect them. And the booming eco-friendly practices in the hospitality industry provide a plethora of material for PR practitioners using multiple communication platforms.

ECOTOURISM

A significant segment of today's tourists wants more from their travel than the familiar sites featured in glossy brochures and on panoramic websites. Not for them is a trip to the top of Paris' Eiffel Tower, a stein of beer at Munich's Octoberfest, or a shopping spree on Tokyo's glittering Ginza. Instead they're opting for ecotourism by taking a rugged trek to view gorillas in Rwanda, bundling up to see the penguin colonies in Antarctica, or boarding a boat to observe the wonders of the Galapagos Islands.

With the popularity of ecotourism on the rise, so too are concerns about the impact visitors have on areas that for centuries, were beyond the reach of all but the hardiest adventurers. Now these areas are playing host to thousands of tourists every year. Their trekking through often-fragile ecosystems can result in permanent and irreversible damage.

Ecotourism presents its own challenges for PR professionals. Promoting a destination such as Las Vegas would mainly focus on getting visitors to the city and describing the fun and excitement they will experience once there. It's hard to imagine a need to include talk of environmental impact.

Promoting ecotourism, however, includes the responsibility to not only attract visitors but the right kind of visitors. In other words there's a need to let the ecotourists know what is expected of them before they even book their trips. Imagine someone

Rising ecotourism in places like the Galapagos has led to concern about the impact of thousands of travelers on the ecosystems they are visiting.

In Pictures Ltd./Corbis/
Getty Images

arriving at a camp in Rwanda with false expectations of romping with the gorillas or being upset that riding giant Galapagos tortoises isn't on the agenda.

Good PR practices will present a thorough and accurate picture of the destination as well as an honest description of the responsibilities of the visitor. Because ecotourists come in contact with the local populace, their visits also affect the lives and well-being of their hosts. It is wise to share information from respected agencies in advance.

THREATS AND CRISES

Even in times when all seems well tourism is constantly affected by outside forces and events. PR professionals have to be ready at a moment's notice to cope with all manner of unexpected issues and crises that will seriously affect businesses that depend on tourists and travelers. These include, but aren't limited to, hotels, rental car companies, airlines, tour operators, cruise lines, airlines—even so far as damaging the entire tourism business of cities, states, and countries.

MOST UNFORESEEN, FEW PREVENTABLE

From 2008 into 2017, tourism has been affected by every possible crisis—most unforeseen and few preventable. The recession that began in earnest in 2008 reduced disposable income for many families and kept them from taking vacations. The BP Deepwater Horizon oil spill of 2010 blighted the pristine beaches of the southern states that border the Gulf of Mexico, an area just recovering from Hurricane Katrina five years earlier.

Travelers who planned to visit Mexico changed their minds in 2011, when drug war violence began reaching the resort towns of Acapulco and Puerto Vallarta. Greece was in the midst of a financial crisis that reached a boiling point in 2012 and saw tourism sharply decline as videos of riots and protests in Athens made potential visitors wary.

ECOTOURS and Outdoor Leadership

Ged Kaddick of Terra Incognita ECOTOURS leads trips to remote and exotic natural destinations around the world. With a website, a blog, and several social media platforms, the business communicates specific values and principles, helping potential clients understand what to expect on an ecotour. By doing so, guests self-select to adhere to them, and thus no one joins a tour only to be surprised at the destination.

> "Our company is committed to the idea that it's our responsibility to leave earth better than we found it, and we impart that belief to our guests."
>
> —Gerard "Ged" Kaddick, founder of Terra Incognita ECOTOURS

Kaddick's company takes additional steps to "instill in our tourists the concept of making a positive difference rather than a negative impact" (G. Kaddick, personal communication, 2017). For every person who joins one of their ecotours, the company makes a donation to one of the leading conservation organizations working in that area. Their tours are also joined by representative organizations (such as Gorilla Doctors) to explain their mission and provide insight to the tourists.

If the traveler is interested in a more rugged adventure, such as a trek into wilderness areas, it's very important the promotional efforts also educate potential participants about the hardships they will be facing and the impact their trips will have on the environment. Many tour companies and their leaders ascribe to guidelines created by environmental organizations.

Eric Boggs, expedition faculty for the National Outdoor Leadership School (NOLS), leads backpacking adventures around the world. "It is essential that anyone contemplating joining us understand what they'll be facing. There's no running water, toilets, or beds out here." He endorses the principles compiled by the organization Leave No Trace, which stress minimizing impact and respecting the environment, and uses those guidelines in his treks.

"I've been training my student leaders in *coincidental* socially responsible leadership," says Boggs. "The backpacking trips we've done have essential social and eco-responsible aspects to them; a quick synopsis is what Boy Scouts have always called the 'campsite rule:' leaving the place better than you find it—for ecological and social reasons" (E. Boggs, personal communication, 2017). ●

Fear for personal safety after terror attacks had a negative impact on tourism to major destination cities such as Paris, Brussels, Istanbul, and even London. Egypt, after years of political turmoil, has seen a drastic drop in tourists, especially to the well-known sites of Giza.

Each of these examples created enormous challenges for PR professionals, but most have been able to craft messages aimed to reassure and recapture tourists, although not all have been successful.

AGGRESSIVE PUBLIC RELATIONS RESPONSE TO BP OIL SPILL

> SOCIAL RESPONSIBILITY

The coastal states affected by the BP spill launched aggressive PR campaigns (largely funded by money from BP) to inform the public that the beaches were once again clean and the seafood safe to eat. Unrelated to the marketing money the company sent to coastal states, BP funded its own "Voices From the Gulf" television, radio and social media campaign. The result of these efforts helped the region rebound.

The pinched budgets that prevented families from vacation travel resulted in PR professionals in many major cities creating "staycations," or stay-at-home vacations aimed at their residents and suburbanites. Museum visits, free musical performances in public parks, day trips that targeted suburban visitors, and free guided city walking tours were promoted as ways to give families an inexpensive break.

SPOTLIGHT ON MEXICO AND GREECE

An example of good efforts derailed by unexpected events is what happened in Mexico. The Tourism Ministry's website, visitmexico.com, is aimed at English-speaking tourists, highlights most of the favored destinations, and as to be expected, avoids any negative references to safety. Instead the ministry released numerous reports showing a dramatic lessening of violence, and indeed tourists began to return. Tourism figures, last reported in 2015, show the industry contributes $17.5 billion in U.S. dollars to the Mexican economy, so reassuring visitors their trips will be safe and uneventful is crucial to their decision to come (McDonnell & Sanchez, 2016).

Unfortunately, in much of 2016, flare-ups of violence, including murders and kidnappings, led the U.S. Department of State to issue travel warnings to U.S. citizens contemplating travel to many of Mexico's states. The effect these warnings, and the renewed violence, will have on Mexico's budget won't be known for a few years.

For the Greek economy tourism is a vital element. The Greek Tourism Organization's PR efforts were initially designed to quell any fear that the demonstrations against the government would endanger tourists. Next it repositioned the financial crisis as a boon to visitors, making Greece a place where your money would go further. Tourists have responded in record numbers; in 2015 the country hosted some 23.5 million visitors, and their spending represented an astonishing 24% of Greece's GDP (Smith, 2016).

The recovery has extended well into 2016. "It's a miracle, what's been happening in Athens," said Greece's tourism chief, Andreas Andreadis, in an interview with the Guardian newspaper. "This year we expect around 4.5 million visitors in Athens alone" (Smith, 2016).

SMALL TOWN FESTIVALS DRAW BIG CROWDS

When discussing travel and tourism, it would be a huge mistake to omit those events that many of us will attend this year: small town festivals. Although not as dazzling as ones hosted by large cities, these fests and fairs draw thousands into small towns and villages and provide a real boost to the local economy.

MIDWESTERN TRADITIONS

The city of St. Charles, Illinois, for instance, will hold its 33rd annual Scarecrow Fest in October, 2018. More than 150,000 visitors will dwarf the normal population of 33,000 for the three days of the fest. According to Lula Cassidy, executive director of the city's Convention and Visitor's Bureau, those guests will add $6 million to the city's coffers (L. Cassidy, personal communication, 2017).

Further north, the town of Sauk Prairie, Wisconsin, population 3,900, will host up to 50,000 visitors for its 44th Wisconsin State Cow Chip Throw—which is exactly what you think it is. Director Marietta Reuter says the annual event, held on Labor Day weekend, is a "happy time for all" and a boon to the local economy (M. Reuter, personal communication, 2017). Reuter adds that if you're planning on tossing a chip to bear in mind, "No gloves, but licking your hand for a better grip is allowed." Other fun festivals include these:

▸ The Duct Tape Festival, Avon, Ohio

▸ Garlic Fest, Highwood, Illinois

Small-town festivals, like the Duct Tape Festival in Ohio, can draw large crowds and provide fertile training grounds for aspiring PR professionals.

AP Photo/Rachel Kasunicv

- ▸ The West Virginia Roadkill Cook-off, Marlinton, West Virginia
- ▸ National Hollerin' Contest, Spivey's Corner, North Carolina
- ▸ National Lentil Festival, Pullman, Washington
- ▸ Tarantula Awareness Festival, Coarsegold, California

GOOD TRAINING GROUNDS FOR PUBLIC RELATIONS

What all of these festivals, and the hundreds like them across the country, have in common is they attract visitors from well outside their city limits, and those visitors spend money. Although the crowds and dollars won't match those generated by an NFL championship game, they provide a nice boost to their hosts' economy. Also, even on their smaller scale, PR techniques are used to promote them. If you are new to the PR field, look no further than your community's festival to get started. These fairs and fests are great training grounds for aspiring PR professionals.

ENTERTAINMENT PUBLIC RELATIONS— PUBLICITY AND MUCH MORE

>> LO 13.3 Examine the breadth of PR and CSR engagement within the entertainment industry through the perspectives of talent, agencies, and entertainment companies

From the East to West Coast and in all corners of the world, the entertainment PR specialty flourishes along with the prominence of popular culture personalities, media, products, experiences, and trends. Entertainment PR encompasses a wide range of clients. And while you may think "publicist" when you think of entertainment—getting movie stars and other talent, plus their films, books, concerts,

Robin Baum (*right*) is considered one of the most powerful publicists in Hollywood, with clients such as Jared Leto.

Kevin Mazur/WireImage/ Getty Images

and so on into the "news"—actually entertainment PR practitioners provide a broad range of services.

PUBLICISTS AND CELEBRITIES

Let's first consider publicists. They promote the careers of celebrities by generating publicity through diverse methods, including issuing press releases; booking print, radio, and TV interviews; and arranging personal appearances. They look for opportunities to keep their clients in the public's eye and also are proactive in managing risk. Depending on the situation, a strategic communication campaign may be developed to raise, reposition, or rehabilitate a public profile.

Depending on your own tastes in music, media, and popular culture, you likely are more familiar with some types of celebrities than others. Yet "celebrity" touches a diverse population. Each year *Forbes* magazine releases a list of the top 100 highest-paid celebrities (Greenburg, 2016). In 2016 some of those ranking in the top 10 illustrate the wide range of "celebrity" personalities: singer Taylor Swift, British boyband One Direction, American author James Patterson, TV host Dr. Phil McGraw, comedian Kevin Hart, radio personality Howard Stern, and Argentine soccer player Lionel Messi.

THE BROADER FIELD

In the expansive field of entertainment PR, media relations in general is a high-activity task due to the need for constant communication with trade, mainstream, and business media outlets. PR tactics in entertainment differ for the type of client.

Let's look at some examples of *who* needs PR, separated into three categories: **talent**, **general entertainment**, and **content producers**. These lists are certainly not all-inclusive:

▸ **Talent:** actors, recording artists, musicians, DJs, designers, authors, and models

▸ **General Entertainment:** films, DVD/CD releases, TV and radio programs, video games, novels, magazines, online series, and concerts

▸ **Content Producers:** filmmakers, creative artists, film producers, broadcast and publishing companies; studios, film financiers, and distributors

The following news release headlines and leads illustrate the diverse stories that PR practitioners tell to publicize their clients:

▸ **Celebrity Fashion:** "Jessica Rey Swimwear Takes 'Going Green' to a New Level." Timeless style isn't the only forward-looking thing about Jessica Rey Swimwear. Designer Rey's latest silhouettes are helping preserve our planet's oceans too. Rey has partnered with Italian fabric company Aquafil to create designs that incorporate Econyl yarn, composed of 100% regenerated nylon waste, such as abandoned fishing nets, production scraps, and carpet fluff. Prior to launching her career as a designer, Rey was a Hollywood actress starring as Alyssa, the White Ranger on Disney's *Power Rangers Wild Force*. As a Power Ranger, saving the world was part of the routine, but for Rey, now it's for real (Business Wire, 2017c).

▸ **Movie Theaters:** "Dolby Cinema Showcases Strong Spring Lineup." Dolby Laboratories, Inc. today announced 13 new titles, adding to the growing slate of movies to be shown at more than 75 Dolby Cinema locations around the globe. Dolby Cinema enables richer and more action-packed storytelling through Dolby Vision and Dolby Atmos. The result is a dramatically different

TABLE 13.3

Public Relations Services in the Entertainment Industry

PR SERVICES RANGE FROM THE GENERAL . . .	. . . TO THE MORE SPECIFIC
▸ strategic communication counsel	▸ event & tour support
▸ corporate positioning	▸ product launches
▸ brand enhancement	▸ premieres
▸ image creation	▸ press junkets
▸ media relations	▸ film festival strategies
▸ reputation/issues management	▸ awards campaigns
▸ litigation support	▸ trade shows
▸ crisis management/communication	▸ red carpets
	▸ cause partnerships
	▸ sponsorships
	▸ product placement

viewing experience that presents strikingly vivid and realistic images, making viewers feel like they are inside the movie's world (Business Wire, 2017b).

▶ **Broadcast and Online Retailers:** "HSN Ignites Designers' Creativity With the Launch of Its Enchanting Disney 'Beauty and the Beast' Collection, Spanning Across Home, Apparel and Accessories." Leading entertainment and lifestyle retailer HSN is launching a marketing collaboration with Disney for the release of its all-new live-action adaptation of Disney's animated classic *Beauty and the Beast*, a stunning, cinematic event celebrating one of the most beloved tales ever told (HSN Inc., 2017).

▶ **Television Series:** "Cesar Millan Takes on Role as Rescuer and Rehabilitator in New Series." Follow world-famous dog behaviorist Cesar Millan (@cesarmillan) and his son Andre as they team up on a road trip across America to help organizations and people that are rescuing and rehabilitating dogs in the new series *Cesar Millan's Dog Nation* (Business Wire, 2017a).

ENTERTAINMENT PUBLIC RELATIONS AND SOCIAL CAUSES

SOCIAL RESPONSIBILITY

Just as with the sports and tourism industries, the entertainment industry is very visibly engaged in CSR. A brief review of initiatives undertaken by entertainment PR agencies, personalities themselves, and media companies and foundations offers a window into their world of giving (Mazzoni, 2015).

AGENCIES—A SHORT LIST

▶ Entertainment PR firms are guiding clients into CSR initiatives as well as investing in their own.

▶ The Creative Artists Agency (CAA) Foundation carries the tagline "Using pop culture to create social good." It counsels artists, athletes, and companies on philanthropic strategies, cause marketing, and social change campaigns, with a focus on supporting youth education.

▶ ICM Partners, a global talent and literary agency, enables employee volunteerism with more than 20 organizations, including the American Red Cross and the Assistance League.

▶ Havas, the multinational communications firm, offers a sports and entertainment network that specializes in sustainability PR.

▶ New York's 42West contributes a percentage of its annual profits to various philanthropic and advocacy groups.

PERSONALITIES—A SHORT LIST

▶ Actor Leonardo DiCaprio's long commitment to eco-activism began in 1998 when at age 25 he launched a foundation to protect biodiversity and combat climate change.

Celebrity Public Relations

Doug Dahlgren, Radio Personality

According to radio personality Doug Dahlgren, PR efforts have always been intertwined with his career and his role as a top celebrity. "While almost every promotion or event starts with the sales department coming up with a bright idea to generate ad dollars, the underlying goal is to generate positive publicity for the station and its on-air staff."

"Personality" Public Relations and Publicity Agents

Under what Dahlgren calls "personality public relations" are the efforts a station uses to promote its personalities. These include in-house spots and giant outdoor billboards profiling him. "The station would plaster my face on billboards near the expressways—which sounds cool until you actually see your 40-foot head grinning down as you drive to the station at 4 a.m."

Remotes

Part of a station's community promotions are remotes, a broadcast made from outside the studio, such as broadcasting from a parade route or a charity 5K. Others are a part of a sales package that includes a broadcast from the floor of an advertiser's business during business hours. "They're designed to drive business to the location, obviously, but they also serve as good PR opportunities," said Dahlgren. "The station's name and call letters are on banners all over the business and are a draw to bring folks in. Meeting your listeners is fun for them and great for me—and hopefully they buy something."

Celebrity Interviews

Dahlgren has interviewed many recording artists during his career, a task he says can be tricky.

"Everyone knows the real reason that so-and-so has 'stopped by' is because the artist has a concert or album to promote," said Dahlgren. "As the interviewer, you need to balance the guest's promotional needs with the station's. After the interview, the celebrity would tape a station promo, something like 'This is So-and-So, and I love the KKXX Morning Crew,' which the station would use to promote our show."

Community Engagement

Community engagement is always a focus for a station and its on-air talent. "It's important for a station and its personalities to be—and be seen as—friends and supporters of the community in which they work," said Dahlgren. "Sometimes it's as simple as a photo shoot with a local politician or citizen being honored for some achievement. Other times it means getting outside the studio and pitching in."

In his career, Dahlgren has been a part of many charity events. "I have loaded semitrailers during a station's canned food drives, ridden a motorcycle to collect Toys for Tots, emceed fund-raising concerts for cancer research, and even stood on a street corner selling giant cookies to benefit a charity." ●

Doug Dahlgren's first on-air job came when he was just 19 years old. Since then, his career has included long stints spinning rock and country music at major radio stations in the Midwest and West Coast.

Source: D. Dahlgren (personal communication, 2017).

▶ Actor Emma Watson, Harry Potter's Hermione, supports gender equality as a goodwill ambassador for UN Women.

▶ Recording artist and actor Alicia Keys cofounded both the Keep a Child Alive nonprofit to combat HIV and the We Are Here Movement for equality and social justice.

▶ Actor Mariska Hargitay's nonprofit, the Joyful Heart Foundation, works to address survivors of sexual assault, domestic violence, and child abuse.

▶ Actor and producer Adrian Grenier cofounded SHFT.com to promote sustainability through multimedia; clients have included Ford, Virgin America, and Estee Lauder.

NBC Keeps Edible Food Out of the Trash Can

After identifying food waste as a major problem, NBC launched #NoFoodWasted, a campaign aimed particularly at consumers who buy more of an item than they need for the meals they plan to make.

Alamy Stock Photo

Problem

Every year, about 40% of food in America is discarded—sometimes before it even reaches the market or the dinner table. This waste includes the perfectly healthy fruits and vegetables destroyed by farmers because they are "ugly" and not apt to be purchased by picky shoppers. Unsold, but edible, overstocked inventory at supermarkets is tossed in a dumpster on its way to the landfill. Consumers who purchase too many ingredients for the menus they're preparing are also major contributors to waste. It's this last situation that was targeted in a campaign led by a major media company.

Solution

Broadcast network NBC Universal launched a #NoFoodWasted campaign during Earth Week 2015 to address the increasing problem of food waste in America (see Figure 13.3). The campaign was developed by Havas, the multinational communications firm, and its Sports and Entertainment network that specializes in sustainability PR (Ignition, n.d.).

How It Played Out

In key media markets, NBC partnered with well-known food trucks and challenged the operators and chefs to develop a menu item that embodied the spirit of #NoFoodWasted from items they typically toss out. Once the cuisine was perfected and menus prepared, the food trucks hit the streets and offered samplings of delicious food while also sharing tips with consumers on reducing food waste at home. Through delivering food in reusable, eco-friendly containers and sharing "waste less" recipes, consumers were invited and equipped to take up the cause.

Results

The #NoFoodWasted campaign became a digital phenomenon. As popular channels in the NBCU family carried the message, stars like Meredith Vieira and Tom Colicchio promoted the #NoFoodWasted cause with interactive chats and digital video content. The hashtag allowed everyone to get in on the conversation as viewers and celebrities alike began sharing food waste tips, pictures of their waste-free meals, and menu planning ideas that emphasized buying only what was needed. The project is still having an impact, years after its launch, as hundreds of these tips can still be accessed at http://www.msnbc.com/take-the-nofoodwasted-challenge. ●

Sources: Ignition (n.d.); Sub-Zero (n.d.).

FOUNDATIONS AND CORPORATIONS

The Entertainment Industry Foundation (EIF, n.d.) is the industry's leading charitable organization. Since launching in 2008, its Stand Up To Cancer (SU2C) initiative has funded research through a biennial televised event featuring hundreds of celebrities. In collaboration with young filmmakers, it also creates celebrity PSAs to educate youths on the risks of smoking. Other programs include partnering with grocer Albertsons to provide breakfasts to hungry children and partnering with the Bill & Melinda Gates Foundation and ExxonMobil, among others, to coordinate funding for innovative classroom projects.

Major entertainment media companies have dedicated CSR programs (Variety, 2016). For example, 21st Century Fox is a founding partner of Ghetto Film School LA serving disadvantaged communities. Sony Picture Entertainment supports more than 45 organizations including community arts centers in L.A. Sony also uses its resources to fund and organize a global environmental campaign, Picture This. Disney's VoluntEARS supports hundreds of nonprofits.

SCENARIO OUTCOME

You read about Micato Safaris and their long-term community initiatives at the beginning of this chapter and then learned about eco-tourism. Your challenge was to brainstorm a best practices checklist for how an organization operating in a developing country can create a successful and sustainable SR program involving the local community. Lorna MacLeod (Tourism Cares, n.d.), founding executive director of Micato's nonprofit, America Share, offers these suggestions:

Invest appropriately in your effort and manage it professionally.

Social impact results, just like business results, take resources and execution. Micato Safaris recognized a problem in a local Nairobi community but had to develop a U.S.-based nonprofit to lead and manage the fund-raising. It formed AmericaShare as a nonprofit organization to give the charitable work sufficient separation and branding and to offer travelers and other donors tax deductibility for their contributions.

Don't be afraid to change tactics based on evidence.

While student sponsorship has always been a part of Micato, some earlier components of the program had to be discontinued. For instance, Micato used to encourage travelers to bring school supplies and books with them to donate, and they even shipped containers of donated goods from the United States to Kenya. This ended up being costly and time-consuming to manage; it also had the unintended effect of undermining local industries and businesses. Now Micato buys all clothing, books, food, and other items locally.

Be transparent and accountable to the community.

This is important in any operating context but especially one known for its corruption. Creating a culture of transparency and accountability requires investment. Students are selected by a range of third-party advisors, from school principals to community leaders, all of whom need engagement and oversight. On-the-ground AmericaShare social workers follow up on recipients and monitor their progress. They are also very diligent of financial transfers and controls.

Giving back matters to employees—on both sides of the business.

"When Micato-AmericaShare helps a child, they're also helping the (usually single) mother or parent, which in turn helps the community," notes MacLeod (Tourism Cares, n.d. p. 5). "Coming to work each day knowing that you'll be able to educate children and radically improve the lives of African families is a powerful motivator."

Let the community guide you.

"It's not about you. It's not about your company. It's about that community; it's about that family; it's about that child," urges McLeod (Tourism Cares, n.d. p. 5). In everything you do, be sensitive to the dynamics and potential community impacts, especially those that may be negative and unintended. It is for those reasons that Micato enlists community advisors in the selection process. It's also why they insist on being the intermediary between well-meaning travelers and local children. There are clear restrictions on the transfer of gifts and how resources are spread throughout the community.

Stay focused but stay opportunistic, too.

Resources should be concentrated where they can do the most good, meaning avoid expanding your mission unnecessarily. It's better to do the job that you've undertaken *really well* and look for areas of expansion that are logical extensions of it.

WRAP UP

After exploring the world of sports, tourism, and entertainment PR, it's likely you could see yourself in some role in these exciting fields, especially now that you know how "doing good" is both valued and acted on by athletes and leagues, destinations and agencies, and celebrities and entertainment institutions.

As you've learned, CSR is not viewed as an add-on by many of these athletes, actors, and high-profile personalities; they're seen as part of who they are and their public image. The same is true of adventure tours and ecotourism companies, whose core philosophies are rooted in sustainable tourism with a nature first approach. For sports teams on every level, performing good works that benefit the communities they represent are embedded activities, not afterthoughts.

KEY TERMS

Content Producers: In the entertainment field, those involved in content production and/or distribution, such as filmmakers and studios, **345**

Ecotourism: Environmentally responsible travel to natural areas that promote conservation and provide for beneficially active socioeconomic involvement of local peoples, **328**

General Entertainment: Broad category of entertainment products encompassing multiple media, such as TV programs, concerts, and online series, **345**

Talent: Entertainment performers, such as actors, DJs, and models, **345**

The lack of diversity in MLB leadership can be seen at the annual managers' lunch reception that brings together managers from both the American League and National League.

A visual snapshot of this group makes it clear baseball's power structure remains overwhelmingly white and male, despite the fact most teams' roster positions are evenly filled with Hispanic, Black, Asian, and White players. There are few non-White managers and fewer still in any part of team ownership.

This lack of diversity extends to the umpiring crews, too—an almost all white men's group.

With knowledge gained from this chapter, as well as previous chapters, what socially responsible steps do you think the MLB should take to address this problem?

You are the PR specialist for your city or town's tourism bureau, and you need to create an infographic for its Instagram page. It should feature an upcoming holiday or summer event to attract and engage out-of-area visitors. Once you select the holiday or event, gather facts to build your case—in a clean and visually exciting manner. A good infographic meets the following criteria:

- Address your target audience.
- Be simple.
- Stay focused.
- Show things visually.
- Be a manageable length and size.
- Incorporate "white" space (meaning any space void of content).

Use any of the free infographic generators, for example, canva, easel.ly, piktochart, infogr.am, or venngage.

SOCIAL RESPONSIBILITY CASE STUDY

#askMPLS Provides Virtual Concierges During Major League Baseball All-Star Week

Situation

The Meet Minneapolis Convention and Visitors Association had a mission to market, sell, and maximize the visitor experience of Minneapolis for the economic benefit of its community. When the 2014 MLB All-Star Game came to town, it was estimated the game would draw 160,000 visitors and have a $75 million economic impact. Meet Minneapolis wanted to speak to its visitors to showcase the city and assist with each visitor's unique needs to keep Minneapolis top of mind during any future travel decisions and encourage repeat visits.

Research and Strategy

Spong PR leveraged three insights to provide strategic direction for the basis of the campaign.

Insight 1: 85% of people bring their smartphones on vacation, and 61% use social media while traveling. Top reasons for use include looking for places to eat, looking for things to do, and to get overall recommendations (TripAdvisor, 2013).

Insight 2: Among U.S. leisure travelers with a household income of at least $50,000 who took a trip at least 75 miles from their home, 62% used smartphones, and 43% used tablets to search for things to do (Yarbrough, 2013).

Insight 3: People collect experiences along the way and share them during the trip. Social media and traveling go hand in hand (Weissmann, 2013).

Leading up to the event, the agency tested social media tools to manage live monitoring and tweeting, display the activity in a command center, and measure all conversations as well.

Spong recruited social media professionals from top employers around the Twin Cities to act as virtual concierges and help promote the center. Finally the agency developed response protocols, crisis plans, and a system to categorize incoming messages and assigned them to volunteers based on their areas of expertise.

Execution

Drawing on the research and insights about travelers, Spong and Meet Minneapolis teamed up to create the #askMPLS Social Media Command Center, the epicenter of information about Minneapolis during the MLB All-Star Game. It invited people to use #askMPLS to ask questions of Minneapolis experts and Twin Cities social media professionals. For nearly a week, the command center concierges welcomed visitors to the city, recommending nearby places to visit and things to do.

A social engagement team acted as traffic commanders, actively monitoring social posts using #askMPLS, and looking to help visitors in other ways, such as using geolocation to identify tweets from people in the downtown area looking for recommendations. Questions were all answered within minutes to maintain a steady stream of conversation.

The team worked with Minneapolis's network of Minneapolis Downtown Improvement District (DID) ambassadors. Hotel and restaurant employees handed out #askMPLS cards and wore T-shirts and buttons. Signage was abundant, encouraging people to "#askMPLS.

To garner more attention and engagement, guest tweeters answered visitors' questions as @MeetMinneapolis.

Evaluation

In one week #askMPLS generated more than 19 million social impressions thanks to nearly 3,000 mentions from almost 900 visitors. It saturated the Minneapolis media market, resulting in more than 4 million media impressions from several segments and live interviews.

The #askMPLS Command Center also created deeper understanding of what Meet Minneapolis does with key stakeholders. This all contributed to a record-setting year for Meet Minneapolis, with $16.6 million in revenue and record levels in four areas: the number of hotel room nights booked for future events, room nights booked for leisure, revenue from sponsorships, and revenue from the Minneapolis Convention Center.

#askMPLS continues to function as a local and visitor resource, with Meet Minneapolis maintaining the response service on an ongoing basis. These interactions can range from visitors just landing at the airport or in cabs asking for guidance on travel or residents looking for places to eat. Thanks to the success of the command center, Meet Minneapolis is also opening a social media command center within a new visitor center in downtown Minneapolis.

ENGAGE

Another type of visitor has come to stay in Minneapolis: immigrants and refugees—80% of whom live in counties surrounding the city. As of 2017 Minnesota's immigrant population is growing at a faster pace than the national average. It has the largest Somali population in the United States as well as the second-largest U.S. Hmong population.

- ▸ Conduct some Internet searches on the unique problems immigrants and refugees confront when moving to a U.S. urban area like Minneapolis.
- ▸ Discover which community groups are trying to make their city more welcoming and helpful to these new residents.

DISCUSS

- ▸ Drawing from the success of the #askMPLS tools and campaign, how would you craft a communication strategy—for a city or for an urban community group—to engage and assist these unique foreign visitors in finding their place in a new and puzzling environment?

Note: This case was awarded the PRSA 2015 Silver Anvil Award of Excellence Winner in Consumer Services, Travel and Tourism/Hospitality.

Sources: Exhibit City News (2014); Minnesota Compass (n.d.); Minnesota Legislative Reference Library (n.d.); Minnesota Meetings + Events (n.d.).

SOCIAL RESPONSIBILITY CASE STUDY

Stronger Than the Storm—Ribbon Cutting Marks Recovery From Superstorm Sandy

Situation

After Superstorm Sandy hit the coast of New Jersey in October 2012, vacationers and tourists were left with images of a devastated shore area. The New Jersey Economic Development Authority (NJEDA) hired the MWW Group to help tourists from in and out of state move beyond the pervasive imagery of storm-related destruction and get the word out that the shore was open for business and ready for summer.

Research and Strategy

The goal was straightforward: Correct public perception that the Jersey Shore had all but vanished, and replace that negative discernment with a call to action to return to the shore this summer.

Primary research in the form of a preseason poll of likely shore visitors showed this feedback:

- One-third believed the shore would be closed for the summer of 2013.
- 61% of past visitors said, "All I see or hear about the Jersey Shore these days are pictures of the devastation."

Based on additional research from tourism data and a social listening audit, officials were able to better construct a plan to reopen the shore in a big way. MWW created a comprehensive program with a rallying cry, "Stronger Than the Storm." It created the concept of a 130-mile ribbon cutting to serve as the grand reopening of the Jersey Shore, making it distinct and clear that the shore was indeed open for business.

The first step in determining how an event of this size and scale could be pulled off was to research how it could actually be executed. MWW started researching types of ribbon, other notable ribbon-cutting events, and the best possible way to execute the event in a way that would engage communities and the media. MWW worked with Guinness to identify the current holder of the Guinness World Record for the largest ribbon cutting. That ribbon measured 4.19 miles, and MWW wanted to beat the record by at least one mile.

Execution

Fourteen simultaneous ribbon cuttings were conducted down the 130 miles of shoreline, and "Stronger Than the Storm" signs were placed at the tollbooths along the Garden State Parkway, connecting the "We're Open" message to those visiting the shore. To create an environment that would best represent the full 130-mile coastline of the New Jersey Shore for a beachside ribbon-cutting ceremony, a stage was erected along the water. More than five miles of 14-inch-wide Tyvek ribbon was laid out, sewn together, branded, and staked onto the beach.

The Guinness Book of World Records qualifying event was held in Seaside, with a single ribbon stretching more than five miles along the coastline. Nearly 1,000 volunteers from neighboring shore communities dispersed along the ribbon to show their support and declare the shore open for business. NBC's broadcast of the entire event provided the scale and message distribution worthy of the cause. The event was held at the traditional "official" opening of the shore for the season, Memorial Day weekend, and prominent New Jersey citizens and officials were integrated into the events.

Evaluation

The event was a success on every level.

More than 12,000 people attended the Stronger Than the Storm Ribbon Cutting ceremonies in 14 shore communities. Results from an online survey fielded May 31–June 5, 2013, among 1,000 adults (18+) living in New Jersey, New York City, and Philadelphia, in regard to the ribbon-cutting ceremony showed nearly half of adult residents in these areas heard about events at the Jersey Shore over Memorial Day Weekend. Of those, 69% recalled the ribbon-cutting ceremony.

The conversation among an active social community showed more than 3,000 #STTS online mentions the morning of the event, more than 17 million Facebook and Twitter impressions, and more than 200 website visits per hour.

The goal to generate media placements to tell the real story about the state of the shore resulted in more than 420 million media impressions, including more than two dozen on-site broadcast outlets. The tonality generated from both traditional and social media was 98% positive.

ENGAGE

▸ This PR effort involved a stunt that generated significant community engagement and widespread traditional and social media attention. Search online for "Tourism Stunt—Call the Quietest Place in Switzerland" and read *AdWeek*'s article about another successful PR effort.

▸ Go to vimeo.com/120477308 and watch the Pomegranate Phone video.

DISCUSS

▸ How did the Swiss PR campaign engage people from around the world to visit a remote region of Switzerland? What's the connection between the Pomegranate phone and a tourism destination?

Note: The PRSA 2014 Silver Anvil in Events and Observances (Seven or Fewer Days)—Government, was awarded to the MWW Group and New Jersey Development Authority for this case.

Sources: Infosys (2013); Lofgren (2012); MyPRSA (n.d.); PhiladelphiaEagles.com (2013); Sullivan (2015).

VIDEO CASE

Outward Bound and Team Mascots: Professional Sports and CSR

Each year, Outward Bound's Philadelphia program runs a fundraiser called Building Adventure. Participants raise a minimum of $1,750 for the organization to secure a spot to rappel down the side of a skyscraper in downtown Philadelphia. For several years, the mascots of several Philly sports teams have rappelled, raising awareness and interest in the event.

VIDEO

1. How do the Philadelphia Phillies and 76ers benefit from having their mascots participate in events like this one?

2. If you worked for either team, what PR methods would you consider employing to promote the organization's involvement?

3. How would you evaluate whether you achieved your objectives?

PRACTICE AND APPLY WHAT YOU'VE LEARNED

edge.sagepub.com/page

CHECK YOUR COMPREHENSION
ON THE STUDY SITE WITH:

- eFlashcards to strengthen your understanding of key terms

- Practice quizzes to test your comprehension of key concepts

- Videos and multimedia content to enhance your exploration of key topics

Donna Ward/Getty Images

14 Nonprofit, Health, Education, and Grassroots Organizations

Learning Objectives

14.1 Examine the nonprofit industry and illustrate how to plan and manage nonprofit campaigns

14.2 Review the scope of health communication and its need for specialized content

14.3 Identify how PR supports the multiple needs of educational institutions

14.4 Discover and assess how community and special-interest organizations use PR strategies for advocacy

How Can We Keep Kids Safe in a World Filled With Risks?

Safe Kids Worldwide. This U.S. nonprofit, was honored in 2016 with a Golden Halo Award for nearly three decades of work protecting kids on the move, at home, and at play—achievements made possible by corporate sponsorships and partnerships with Johnson & Johnson, General Motors (GM), FedEx, Nationwide, and Bell Sports, just to name a few.

The Golden Halo was awarded by Engage for Good, a clearinghouse that supports alliances between businesses and nonprofits. Safe Kids Worldwide was recognized for these accomplishments from three corporate sponsors, among others:

Safe Kids Worldwide partners with companies around the world, including FedEx, to promote ways that kids can work, play, and live safely.

Tommaso Boddi/Safe Kids Worldwide/Getty Images

Johnson & Johnson. Since 1988, Johnson & Johnson and Safe Kids have collaborated to teach families about child injury prevention including water safety, fire safety, bike safety, medicine safety, home safety, and most recently, youth sports safety.

An alarming number of athletes are either hiding injuries to stay in the game, getting injured after a dirty play, or going back in the game right after they've had a concussion. Most sports injuries can be prevented with smart habits and good training for players, coaches, and parents. The partnership produced and distributed *Sports Safety 101* videos to teach skills to change the culture of youth sports and help young athletes stay in the game.

GM. Safe Kids teamed up with GM and the General Motors Foundation in 1997 to create the Buckle Up program. What started with a focus on child safety seat checks at GM dealerships has grown into a broad, multifaceted program that addresses child safety from heatstroke to teen drivers.

The partnership also includes activities that advocate for stronger state child passenger safety laws. The success of the Buckle Up program is measured by two things: lives saved and injuries prevented. When Buckle Up started, almost 1,800 kids died each year in car crashes. Another 331,000 were injured. By 2016 the number of deaths had been cut by a third, and the number of injuries had been cut in half.

FedEx. In 1999 FedEx and Safe Kids created the Safe Kids Walk This Way program to bring international, national, and local attention to pedestrian safety issues. What started as a pilot project in three U.S. cities has now grown to more than 225 cities in the United States and in nine additional countries around the world.

Since the beginning of the program, Safe Kids Walk This Way has enabled more than 18,100 FedEx volunteers to reach families in thousands of communities in the United States with life-saving pedestrian safety information through just one activity: International Walk to School Day. Leveraging online channels as well, the partners also recently developed an interactive infographic, How to Not Get Hit by a Car.

The challenge. Use the lessons in this chapter to brainstorm: What else should Fed Ex, GM and Johnson & Johnson do, not only in the United States but in their global markets, to further the cause of children's safety? How should they communicate it?

At the end of the chapter, you'll explore and discover the wider extent of these partnerships—and measure your own solutions against the pros.

Source: Engage for Good (n.d.).

This chapter first covers PR for nonprofits, an extremely broad and expansive category of organizations in the United States, more than 1 million strong and growing. With this robust outlook, PR practitioners can expect ample career opportunities. Especially at the beginning of a PR career, the nonprofit—whether through volunteer work or paid employment—is an excellent training ground, particularly for those with social media skills—a cost-efficient tactic for nonprofits.

Another growth area for PR practitioners is health communication. Americans are a more health-conscious population now than ever before and are seeking information and talking about it—online and in person. If your interest is in the field of science and health, opportunities abound with health-care organizations and PR firms with health specialties.

The chapter next covers higher education and K–12 schools, which both offer challenging and rewarding careers for strategic communicators—especially in a competitive environment for funding and enrollment. The functions for a PR professional are wide-ranging, including management counsel, internal PR, media relations, capital campaigns, issues management, crisis communication, research, branding, and community relations.

Finally you'll discover how grassroots community and special-interest organizations use PR strategies and tactics to pursue goals—for example, townspeople organizing to promote road safety or welcome refugees and larger social movements like the Rainbow PUSH Coalition for social change and United Students Against Sweatshops.

NONPROFITS: SIZE, IMPACT, AND OPPORTUNITY FOR PUBLIC RELATIONS PRACTITIONERS

Master the content
edge.sagepub.com/page

>> **LO 14.1**   **Examine the nonprofit industry and illustrate how to plan and manage nonprofit campaigns**

From neighborhood associations that meet a couple of times a year and have no assets to large universities and foundations with billions of dollars in assets—like the Bill and Melinda Gates Foundation—a wide variety of nonprofits operate in the United States.

THE WORLD OF NONPROFITS

According to the National Center for Charitable Statistics (NCCS), more than 1.5 million nonprofit organizations were registered in the United States in 2016. This number included more than 1 million public charities, approximately 100,000 private foundations, and other types of nonprofit organizations like chambers of commerce, fraternal organizations, and civic leagues.

Nonprofit organizations are tax exempt and usually have the common characteristics of serving the public interest, fostering goodwill, serving members, recruiting volunteers, and fund-raising (see Figure 14.1). Nonprofits include soup kitchens and traditional charities that serve the poor as well as local churches, the Sierra Club, the United Steel Workers Labor Union, and the Metropolitan Opera. The website www.NCCS.urban.org provides up-to-date information on the nonprofit sector in the United States.

FUND-RAISING, DEVELOPMENT, AND RECRUITING

Raising funds and recruiting volunteers are major challenges that face nonprofit organizations, driving the need to cultivate relationships with donors, volunteers, and the many organizations that help support a cause.

Fund-raising involves encouraging funds through donations, usually in a one-time instance. Development goes after big gifts made to universities or hospitals. Often in the seven-figure category, they come from relationships cultivated over time, often decades, thus the term *development*. This is how hospitals build buildings and universities endow faculty positions and establish new research institutes.

JOB GROWTH IN PUBLIC RELATIONS

More than half of nonprofits, 57%, anticipated creating new positions in 2016 (Nonprofit HR, n.d.), well ahead of the for-profit sector, where only 36% of companies planned to

FIGURE 14.1

Four Common Characteristics of Nonprofits

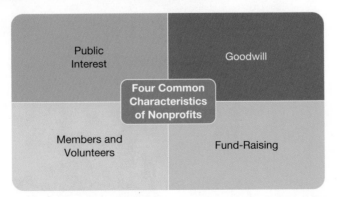

hire (Career Builder, n.d.). A survey of nonprofits across North America projected that the greatest job growth in 2016 was in fund-raising and development—44% projected an increase—and more than one-third, 37%, planned an employment increase in marketing communications and PR (Nonprofit HR, n.d.).

Or course changes in societal concerns, financial policies, and governing administrations will influence shifts in these projections. A case in point—upon the election of Donald Trump to the U.S. presidency, donations to some nonprofits surged to bolster and protect their operations; and tax reform portended more charitable giving. However, it will be up to PR practitioners to make sure that charities' missions continue to be communicated broadly for donors to remain aware and loyal.

Within nonprofits, PR duties may include supporting or directly soliciting corporate and foundation donations, managing structured capital campaigns, planning and running special events, branding, networking with partners and sponsors, and membership and volunteer support. PR duties may also include media contact with the mainstream press plus trade and special interest media as well as communicating with multiple publics through direct mail, online media, and social media.

NONGOVERNMENTAL ORGANIZATIONS

Non-governmental organizations, often referred to as simply NGOs, are a category of nonprofit organizations. They are not a part of a government, nor are they operated though a government; however, they often collaborate with governments as well as other groups as partners in addressing common concerns. While not completely voluntary, they are primarily run by volunteers and are funded by donations.

NGOs are organized to perform a variety of service, humanitarian, and investigative functions around environmental and social issues, economic development, healthcare, and human rights. Typically NGOs have a global presence; in fact, almost all NGOs based in the United States have some operations outside the United States—such as Human Rights Watch and the Committee to Protect Journalists.

In addition to typical media relations efforts, PR professionals at NGOs must consider fund-raising strategies and lobbying efforts to advance the organization's goals.

iStock.com/Steve Debenport

A Career in Service to Others

Aaron Sherinian, Former Chief Communications and Marketing Officer, United Nations Foundation

Is it possible to say where any career starts? As a high school student, I was incredibly inspired by hearing a U.S. diplomat speak during a trip to Washington. D.C. I will never forget what I felt when he talked about how you communicate what's going on in the world around you. He spoke about the complexities of a new world, and he predicted that in the future we would be using new technology to talk to each other—and boy, was he right. At that moment, I knew that I wanted to help bring peoples together and have my career be part international relations and part speaking to each other and the world.

I followed the path that I thought would get me closest to that intersection: diplomacy. I joined the foreign service, working with the U.S. State Department for 10 years in postings around the world. I loved every minute of it—being able to meet people from other places in their homelands and being able to represent a nation I love on issues that I care about.

That work carried me to the Millennium Challenge Corporation and then to the United Nations Foundation. Here, my job as chief communications and marketing officer is to lead, manage, and connect a team of communicators to make the most of our mission: helping the UN solve the world's problems. Our job is to communicate about our organization and the UN while also spotlighting the good work of groups that are working toward sustainable development and the global goals.

A key lesson I've learned along the way is that it's vitally important to remember that people want to tell their own stories, so the very best communicators are the ones who give individuals a voice. It's also important to remember that the quickest way to fail in a communications project is to have your pen be heavy. So, while we have to do our best to curate, edit, and tell stories, there's no replacement for direct storytelling.

Good PR is not about spin. Good PR is exactly what it says—good relations with your public. CSR is a basic part of the commitment that a brand or an organization has with the world in which it operates. Neither CSR nor PR can operate in a vacuum in any organization. It's got to be part of a brand's purpose. It's at the heart of what's going on—or it should be.

It's also at the heart of what I do. I love working in the sectors that straddle communications, philanthropy, development, and international policy because I know every day that I am working on something totally relevant to my present and totally relevant to my children's future. When I'm working on those two things at the same time, it's a good day. ●

After serving at UN Foundation, Aaron Sherinian moved to Paris to run the Aga Khan Foundation.

Source: A. Sherinian (personal communication, 2017).

Beyond the multiple outreach and engagement strategies PR practitioners employ in all types of organizations—social media, events, media relations—NGO tactics also include lobbying to influence policy debates and government legislation as well as fund-raising efforts. NGOs may also appoint well-known celebrities as spokespeople, helping attract attention and raise funds and conduct full-blown communications campaigns that include multimedia PSAs and media kits.

FACEBOOK "FRIENDS" NONPROFITS

Compared to advertising, promotions, and special events, Facebook has become an economical, accessible, and powerful communication tool for nonprofits. Because there is no fee to develop a Facebook page (other than paying personnel to post, listen, and interact), it's a smart way for many nonprofits with limited resources to get the word out and cultivate relationships.

In Chapter 4, you learned that relationship theory suggests that an ideal organization–public relationship should embody *mutuality* in trust, control, satisfaction, and commitment. Past research also reveals some best practices for nonprofit Facebook pages: organizations should use both one-way and two-way communication strategies and content characterized by openness, disclosure, access, positivity, and evidence of collaborations. This information guided Julie O'Neil's recent research into nonprofits' use of Facebook, and she found both good and bad practices.

THE GOOD

▸ Most nonprofits use content characterized by "openness and disclosure"— meaning information is available in the About, Founded, and Mission sections of Facebook and includes a website link.

▸ Nonprofits' Facebook pages shared an average of two photos and one video per 10 posts. Past research (Williams & Brunner, 2010) indicates that there's a link between this positivity—the use of engaging photos and videos—and relationships of trust and satisfaction.

THE BAD

▸ Less than half of nonprofits studied listed phone numbers and e-mail information. As 1.18 billion users worldwide were daily active users of Facebook in 2016 (Facebook, n.d.)—with a history of annually increasing by 17%—all organizations should be communicating this essential information that earlier would typically only be found on their websites.

▸ Nonprofits' use of assurance—meaning they responded to users' questions— was weak, with an average response rate of 45%. Nonprofits need to be more diligent in responding to user questions posted on Facebook walls. They were also not fully using interactive strategies of networking. Networking and sharing of tasks (both indicating collaborative efforts) were the least-used strategies. On average, nonprofits talked about collaborations with other groups in only two out of 10 posts, yet past research suggests that communication that clearly *demonstrates* the nonprofit's mission and work relates positively to donations (O'Neil, 2014).

HEALTH COMMUNICATION

>> **LO 14.2**   **Review the scope of health communication and its need for specialized content**

Thanks to a broad-based, increased focus on health, people have become more motivated to seek information and interact about their health, with each other, and with health-care providers. Conversely health-care organizations are reaching out more to their members and communities and are actively engaging in public health issues, policies, and crises. Technology has facilitated the growth of digital health-care networks and services, for example PatientsLikeMe and ZocDoc.

HEALTH COMMUNICATIONS IN ORGANIZATIONS

A health communications specialist is someone who works to help others understand more about medical treatment, healthy lifestyle choices, disease prevention, and

PR is growing in the health-care field, with new opportunities to work on community relations, fund-raising, and internal communications and to provide the public with key health and wellness information.

iStock.com/sturti

more, according to the Centers for Disease Control and Prevention (CDC, n.d.). They focus primarily on spreading information to the public that can have an overall impact on the health and well-being of the population.

The growth of health awareness and engagement, and the evolving health-care landscape, comes with new communication challenges and opportunities and is a key reason the field of health communications has become a strong growth area in PR. Career opportunities can include focusing on community relations, internal communications, publicity, and fund-raising.

PR practitioners working for health-care facilities generally handle both internal and external communication needs, programs, and campaigns. Internally communications are with doctors, nurses, aides, managers, administrators, and patients. Externally PR specialists disperse news as well as promote services and organize public events.

HEALTH COMMUNICATION PUBLIC RELATIONS AGENCIES

Many PR agencies specialize in health communications. Clients include pharmaceutical and medical technology companies, health-care startups, large hospitals, retail pharmacy chains, and nonprofit health organizations.

One respected ranking of North American PR agencies identifies the best "Healthcare Agencies of the Year" (The Holmes Report, n.d.a). In 2016 Washington, DC-based Spectrum ranked first, followed by four finalists. What qualified them for this recognition offers a lesson in best practices.

Health-Care Agencies of the Year

1. Spectrum is the founder of GLOBALHealthPR, the world's largest network of independent health and science communications firms that are passionate

Health-Care Public Relations: A Higher Calling

What person hasn't had a family member, or him- or herself, affected by heart disease? Or diabetes? Cancer? Alzheimer's? Or some rare disease? Obviously health-care matters to a lot of people, and it involves everyone. It is central to our lives. And communicating effectively to promote better health, through health-care PR, is more than just storytelling. It's the intersection of health, science, and communication and is the perfect career for a person who is interested in making a difference in the world. Health-care PR pros must understand how science works in medicine and must be able to communicate creatively and effectively to build awareness and change behavior. Assuming you own strong communications skills, excelling in health-care PR (see Figure 14.2) comes down to four points:

1. Do you appreciate the life sciences? Can you emulate the curiosity of a scientist and the scientific process?

2. Can you learn to recognize and interpret quality science for storytelling purposes?

3. Will you respect the magnitude of what you do in terms of affecting people's lives and health policy? Do you have a knack?

4. Can you accept the responsibility that health PR experts must maintain to act ethically and responsibly?

Everyone depends on good health to live another day, so health-care information must be accurate. If reporters or bloggers get it wrong, people can be harmed. If there's a new, lifesaving drug available, but the right people don't hear about it, patients may not survive their disease. If

FIGURE 14.2

Four Questions for Future Health-Care Public Relations Professionals

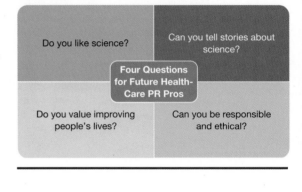

Do you like science?

Can you tell stories about science?

Four Questions for Future Health-Care PR Pros

Do you value improving people's lives?

Can you be responsible and ethical?

people don't ask better questions of their doctors, they may receive inferior care.

Our reach of influence far exceeds that of the average doctor with her or his patients. When a PR executive writes a press release or a fact sheet about health-care topics, it can be seen by tens of thousands, even millions, of people in a day, if not an hour.

Health-care PR work is rewarding and always interesting. If you like science and technology and develop a passion to make a difference in health-care, you will love this field. ●

Contributed by John J. Seng, founder & chair, Spectrum Science Communications and chair, GLOBALHealthPR

about scientific storytelling. One way to reach readers, viewers, or followers and generate WOM is to feature a known fact from a new perspective—but always with an evidenced-based approach. Spectrum favors making science and technology evidence understandable with visually appealing tactics: infographics, animations, and videos (Spectrum, n.d.).

2. Amendola Communications, in Scottsdale, Arizona, functions on the philosophy that PR is more science than art. It distinguishes itself with media relations and "thought leadership" content with cohesive, consistent, unified, and positive messages. For example, its specialized content helped position one client's leadership team as visionary resources on healthcare for journalists and, for another client, as the industry leader in population health management (The Holmes Report, n.d.).

Its successful PR programs all share three key ingredients: integrated communications, creative and proactive outreach with targeted pitching, and long-standing industry relationships (Amendola Communications, n.d.).

3. Chandler Chicco Agency (CCA), founded in New York City, was an "employer of choice" before the term became fashionable. It offers these employee initiatives: passion grants, a new sabbatical policy; an expanded interoffice exchange policy, and a program called Fresh IDEAS (Ideation Development, External Inspiration, Actively Sharing) to encourage greater creativity. CCA illustrates how employee relations is foundational to a *healthy* health communications agency (The Holmes Report, n.d.).

4. GCI Health focuses on where consumers actively look for health-care information: digital and social channels, for example, using bloggers to drive its clients' web traffic and employing grassroots efforts and culturally relevant spokespeople to help reach diverse publics and raise awareness of health issues (The Holmes Report, n.d.).

5. TogoRun focuses on corporate reputation, CSR, and executive leadership, as well as public affairs, through its Washington, DC, office. For example, the agency worked with the global beauty L'Oreal Paris and the Melanoma Research Alliance (MRA) on a melanoma awareness campaign. It implemented a crowd-speaking platform—the Thunderclap (which allows one message at a time to be distributed through all social channels of a participant in a movement, creating an online "flash mob"). The single message everyone was asked to accept was: "I'll stop melanoma by wearing sunscreen daily and using my voice to support MRA. A cure is near! #it'sTHATworthit." The results were reported as record breaking in the beauty category (TogoRun, n.d.).

HEALTH COMMUNICATION STRATEGIES

Ragan's Health Care Communication News (Ragan, n.d.) is a daily website with helpful information for professionals in health PR. Recommended strategies include the following:

▸ **Employee Advocacy**. Giving employees the freedom—with guidance—to talk about their organization on social media can be more effective than publishing a press release. Journalists increasingly seeking real stories on social media and employees are a valued source as authentic and trustworthy. According to the 2017 Edelman Trust Barometer, employee messaging is considered more credible than a CEO's or board of directors'—on multiple topics: customer relations, financial earnings, crises, innovation, industry issues, and programs addressing societal issues (Edelman, n.d.).

▸ **Consistent Communication Strategy.** Put health customers at the center at multiple touchpoints; for example, ensure staff members understand the company's brand values and deliver them to customers; provide customers with fast, easy access to information; and employ follow-up e-mails with personalized content.

▸ **Storytelling.** Share unique customer experiences and employee profiles in videos, newsletters, and on social media. Some of the most popular platforms like Facebook, Instagram, and Twitter offer easy avenues for storytelling. For example, create and share stories using the Twitter Moments feature, consisting of tweets and multimedia.

One Woman Makes Her Mark

The Make Your Mark contest was organized by Bayer Healthcare to promote Skyla, an IUD, and encouraged women pursuing something unique or brave to submit an entry describing how they are making their mark on the world.

iStock.com/Steve Debenport

The Skyla Make Your Mark contest was launched in 2014 to seek out women pursuing something unique or brave—inspiring others along the way. Skyla—the product that gives its name to the contest—is an IUD contraceptive introduced in 2013 by Bayer Healthcare. The contest call appealed to women engaged in artistic expressions, education or research endeavors, trailblazing entrepreneurship, daring physical feats, or noble philanthropy. Women submitted a brief essay and photo or video about how they are making their marks.

Spearheaded by Wendy Lund

CEO of the health-care communication agency GCI Health, Lund oversaw the women's health franchise for Bayer. She and her team created the Skyla Make Your

Mark contest for Bayer in partnership with *Glamour* magazine and its then columnist, actress Zosia Mamet of HBO's TV series *Girls*. The winning prize was a $5,000 grant and a trip to New York City to attend *Glamour's* Women of the Year Gala. The contest was covered by the Associated Press, AOL.com, MSN.com, and Yahoo.com as well as by more than 30 national print outlets.

Top Women in PR Honoree

In 2016 *PR News* honored Lund for her career achievements and *Medical Marketing & Media* magazine named her one of its Top 50 Health Influencers. She started her 30-year career in the nonprofit world, as marketing vice president for the National League of Nursing and then for Planned Parenthood. Shifting to the agency business, she worked for communications firms MS&L and Publicis Consultants before joining GCI in 2010. Under her leadership, GCI Health has tripled its size and expanded its geographic footprint in Europe.

High-Profile Products and Award-Winning Campaigns

Throughout her career, Lund has managed PR for many high-profile drugs and medical devices and has spearheaded award-winning programs in marketing, advocacy development, health and disease awareness and prevention outreach. She has counseled corporate leaders, executives for not-for-profits, and advocacy groups on reputation management, stakeholder relations, executive leadership, and corporate responsibility. With a great passion for women's health, Lund focuses on raising awareness for a wide array of women's contraceptive options, tackling sensitive matters, and understanding how women want to be activated to take charge of their health. ●

Sources: Multivu (n.d.); PRWeek (2016c); PMLive (n.d.); Renfree (2016).

Health-care publics are often defined by gender, race, age, location, and so on and combinations of those categories. This careful segmentation also affects choices of message delivery via mass media and interpersonal channels. Nearly 100% of U.S. teens in the United States now go online using a mobile device daily, and one-quarter of them are online "almost constantly" (Pew Research Center, 2015b), thus the Internet is likely an ideal source for adolescents seeking sensitive information—especially as it provides a one-way, confidential experience.

Northwestern University research (Deardorff, 2015) reports that 84% of U.S. teens ages 13 to 18 say they get health information online. The national survey of more than 1,000 teens also reported that nearly one-third say they changed their health behaviors based on Internet searches, with medical websites most visited, followed by YouTube. Research draws this conclusion: Online media should be harnessed

About a quarter of teens are online nearly all day, making the Internet the best way to reach them.

iStock.com/JackF

by communicators as important health information sources for adolescents, and multimedia content is essential.

PUBLIC RELATIONS SUPPORT OF EDUCATIONAL INSTITUTIONS

>> **LO 14.3** **Identify how PR supports the multiple needs of educational institutions**

Educational institutions serve the public as their primary function, thus an important focus of PR is on two-way communications. PR identifies people's interests and attitudes to enlighten and influence the institution as well as imparts information and engages publics to cultivate awareness, involvement, and support.

Contemporary conditions of dwindling financial resources, rapidly changing technologies, and an ever-competitive environment are all impacting educational institutions, increasing their communication needs with a wide range of audiences and stakeholders.

THE ROLE OF PUBLIC RELATIONS IN HIGHER EDUCATION

A problem between the general public and higher education is not that people are questioning what universities are actually doing or offering. Rather the disconnect lies more with how universities are *communicating* what they are doing (i.e., preparing graduates for real careers or advancing research that improves society).

Multicultural America, Multicultural Health-Care Public Relations

America of the 21st century will be the most pluralistic, multicultural nation on Earth with ethnic ties to every part of the globe, and by 2044, ethnic consumers will make up more than half of the U.S. population (U.S. Census, 2015). This emerging multicultural consumer segment will demand a new set of engagement touch points when it comes to building relationships with organizations and companies and connecting with their brand stories.

Another priority will be engaging the next-generation talent pool, which will be strongly multicultural. The entire U.S. millennial population in 2016 is already 44 percent multicultural (U.S. Census, 2015). Thus companies must define and market an employee experience that will resonate with a generation whose opinions are shaped by globalization, cultural preferences, social media, and a brand's corporate citizenship. Multicultural PR practitioners from all walks of life and diverse backgrounds should have a seat at the table.

Ascension, the largest nonprofit health system in the United States, identified a need to strengthen its outreach to African Americans and address their specific health-care needs. To reach the African-American community and increase understanding and trust of medical professionals, Ascension developed a program targeting key media outlets. It distributed columns about a wide range of nationally recognized health conditions and disparities overwhelmingly affecting African Americans. To ensure its messages reached the right public, Ascension partnered with America's largest association of minority-owned community newspapers, the National Newspaper Publishers Association (NNPA), to publish 10 op-eds on subjects from diabetes to pain management. The NNPA distribution reached an average of more than 20 million readers each week and evolved into a regular monthly column on African American health issues. Ascencion's efforts won a 2016 Diversity and Inclusion Award by *PRNews*. ●

Note: This case was drawn from Antonio Hernandez, chair of diversity initiatives for PRSA Chicago and founder and managing partner of Chicago-based Globovoz Communications LLC.

Sources: Ascension (2016); PRSA Chicago Chapter (2014).

This insight came out of the Edelman 2016 survey "University Reputations and the Public" (Edelman Insights, n.d.). Most important to the public is hearing education provides access to top job opportunities.

Therefore, to improve reputation, communications should assure the public that universities are impacting personal lives and society for the better, demonstrating this via media strategies like social networks, content sharing sites, and blogs. The places where the public discusses higher education is online, and while changing rapidly, that's where higher education communicators should be.

Education journalists say communications staff at educational institutions play a large role in their reporting, according to a 2016 report by the Education Writers Association (CASE, n.d.). Even though one-third of respondents admit they often find it difficult to get in-person access to schools and college campuses for reporting purposes, they emphasize that schools' PR efforts are an important part of education coverage. News releases, news conferences, or PR professionals themselves are the top sources of story ideas for 88% of the education journalists surveyed.

SOCIAL MEDIA STRATEGIES

As noted earlier, social and digital online content is a preferred avenue for connecting with education publics. *Inside Higher Ed* offers this advice (Read, 2017):

Colleges and universities must make clear the ways they improve society and individuals' lives.

Imeh Akpanudosen/ Getty Images

ALIGN SOCIAL MEDIA GOALS WITH INSTITUTIONAL GOALS

Social media enables institutions to be targeted with information sharing and facilitates two-way engagement among alumni, current students, prospects, and other priority audiences. Consider social media goals in the context of the institution's goals. What's most pressing? Retention? New enrollments? Alumni engagement? Then define social media success in support of those goals. This provides clear direction and a measurement for success.

MATCH PLATFORM(S) WITH AUDIENCE(S)

Decide what platforms connect with the appropriate audiences. Not all social platforms are created equal—some are better than others at reaching specific audiences. Do research to determine what platforms best reach your institution's target audiences based on their personas (their demographics, goals, preferences, motivators, etc.), and then focus your efforts on those platforms.

DEFINE YOUR INSTITUTION'S AUTHENTIC SOCIAL MEDIA VOICE

Before considering the actual content of what you'll be sharing on social media, think about your institution's social media voice—what's the tone? Personality? Point of view? Because in all communications consistency is key, your social media voice should be within an octave of your institution's tone and voice. A good way to determine voice is to identify the three or four most important adjectives you'd like your target audiences to use to describe your institution.

AUDIT THE INSTITUTION'S SOCIAL MEDIA PROFILES

The audit should include the institution's primary profiles as well as any profiles being managed at the school or department level, including athletics (see Figure 14.3). If you

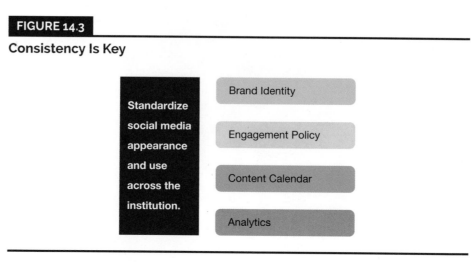

FIGURE 14.3

Consistency Is Key

uncover unauthorized accounts, duplicate accounts, and so on, action should be taken to disable, delete, or address those profiles. Then work closely with the individuals responsible for the remaining profiles across campus to make sure there is a common understanding about the purpose and goals of each. Also be sure to optimize all institution-affiliated social media profiles. Here's how:

▶ **Make sure the look and feel of each profile is consistent with the institution's brand identity.** This includes logos, images, color schemes, and "about" messaging.

▶ **Establish an engagement policy.** The policy should clearly articulate expectations for all posts or comments and consequences if the policy is violated.

▶ **Create a detailed social media editorial calendar that maps planned posts for the month—reflecting your target audiences and goals.** This may include posts related to upcoming announcements, events, and content packages, like video or other campaigns—everything you are aware of in advance. The calendar should also outline the time of day content and should be shared to increase engagement (drawn from analytics tools).

▶ **Leverage the full potential of available analytics tools.** Regularly review the data to see what posts are getting the greatest engagement, what times of day your audiences are most engaged, and so on. Pay special attention to the content topics and types performing the best, so you can use that intelligence to inform your planning.

K–12 EDUCATION

K–12 education has a long history of active debate and involvement by multiple publics. The National School Public Relations Association (NSPRA) says that a PR professional is essential to the 13,500 public school districts in the United States (Center for Education Reform, n.d.). To better understand the need for and function of PR in education today, the NSPRA identifies and defines 11 major functions provided by PR staff. As you can see by this list (see Table 14.1), working in PR for a school district is an all-encompassing role that demands versatility and offers challenges

TABLE 14.1

Ten Major Functions of Public Relations in K–12 School Districts

	FUNCTION	GOAL
1.	PR counsel	Takes a proactive stance, anticipating problems and providing solutions
2.	Communication with internal and external publics	Produces all district publications such as external newspaper and internal newsletter, etc.; publicizes student and staff achievement; develops staff and retirement recognition programs
3.	Media relations	Secures local media coverage of district news and serves as media liaison with district
4.	Budget and bond issue campaigns	Promotes community input to budget process and develops budget and bond issue campaigns and publications
5.	Communications planning	Develops communications plan for internal and external publics; develops crisis communications plan
6.	Research	Conducts surveys, polls, and informal research to determine public opinion as a basis for planning and action
7.	Imaging and marketing	Promotes district's brand, strengths, achievements, and its solutions to problems; plans for school district anniversary celebrations
8.	Community relations liaison	Liaises with grassroots organizations, civic associations, and service clubs and helps plan and publicize district's service programs
9.	Information station for the district	Answers public and new resident requests and keeps district's historical records
10.	PR trainer	Provides advocacy, media, and crisis communications training to staff and parent–teacher associations

Source: NSPRA (n.d.).

to communicate with diverse publics. It builds a wide range of PR proficiencies in a specialty that many choose to embrace for the benefits it provides the community.

PUBLIC RELATIONS IN GRASSROOTS ORGANIZATIONS

>> **LO 14.4** **Discover and assess how community and special-interest organizations use PR strategies for advocacy**

Community and special-interest organizations are groups of people who assemble with a like-minded purpose concerning community-level or special-interest issues. They are ordinary citizens from neighborhoods, school districts, cities, or broader boundaries, driven by a common interest or concern. They are not a part of government, nor are they a for-profit business, but are a grassroots effort that voluntarily forms a collaborative community, self-organized and without governmental support. While some may be incorporated as a nonprofit, others may be informally organized as an unincorporated nonprofit association.

PUBLIC RELATIONS TACTICS

Depending on the issues and the size of the groups, many traditional PR tactics can help advance the group's mission and produce desired results, including e-mail,

It Gets Better

Dan Savage and Terry Miller started the It Gets Better Project in 2010, posting messages of hope aimed at gay teens on YouTube. With the help of Blue State Digital, the pair turned the project into a lasting campaign of advocacy, outreach, and fund-raising.

Alamy Stock Photo

Digital Storytelling Advocates for Change

The connection between school bullying and suicides among gay teens prompted syndicated columnist Dan Savage and his partner Terry Miller to create the It Gets Better Project channel on YouTube. In 2010 they posted their first video sharing their stories of adolescent survival and the happiness they'd found as adults.

One Video Sparked a Movement

By the next week more than 200 videos had arrived, and soon they were deluged with e-mails from lesbian, gay, bisexual, and transgender (LGBT) adults, teens, and their parents. Realizing he'd touched on something bigger, Savage set out to turn the viral idea into a lasting movement and turned to Blue State Digital (BSD) for help.

An Online Community Is Born

BSD is a digital strategy and technology firm specializing in online advocacy. It's committed to bridge differences, defend civil and human rights, and help its clients put people first, according to its website (It Gets Better Project, n.d.a). Clients have ranged from Obama's 2008 and 2012 campaigns, the Sierra Club, and the NAACP to Google, the Green Bay Packers, and *Vogue* magazine.

Partnering with It Gets Better, BSD created the online infrastructure—a digital platform and clearinghouse to drive messaging, fund-raising and advocacy outcomes. More than a home for video content, the site was designed to get people involved by taking a pledge to speak out against anti-LGBT bullying and uploading their own inspiring stories.

Influencers, Celebrities, and Awards

In the years since the site went live, tens of thousands of people have signed on to say, "It gets better," thousands of videos have been uploaded to the It Gets Better channel, and ItGetsBetter.org and the YouTube channel have drawn viewership in the millions. Video contributors include President Obama and Hillary Clinton; employees at Google, Apple, Disney and EA; and celebrities like Lady Gaga, Kathy Griffin, Kesha, and the San Francisco Giants.

Its Twitter (@itgetsbetter) provides constant updates on stories of interest to the LGBTQ community and their supporters, friends, and families. The website, It Gets Better Project, states more than 625,000 people have taken a pledge of support for LGBTQ youth and to stand up against hate and intolerance (It Gets Better Project, n.d.b). In 2012 the project earned the Emmy's Governors Award from the Academy of Television Arts & Sciences Board of Governors. ●

Source: https://www.bluestatedigital.com/our-work/it-gets-better/
http://www.itgetsbetter.org/

letter-writing, and phone call campaigns; websites and social media; and events and public meetings to build community, share information, and get media attention. In situations needing immediate attention and action, they may adopt activist tactics, including unannounced visits to political offices, rallies, vigils, demonstrations, boycotts, and acts of civil disobedience. At the receiving end of activist engagement, best practices for targeted organizations are to personally meet with representatives to share information and perspectives leading to understanding, consensus, compromise, or some mutually agreed-upon resolution.

Communication strategies and tactics reflect the context of the issue. It may be a small group, perhaps townspeople advocating for slower speed limits on streets due to a pedestrian tragedy, to a much larger group like Mothers Against Drunk Driving, and still different yet, may be a large, loosely organized movement like Occupy Wall Street, which formed in response to the late-2000s financial crisis in the United States.

Women attending the grassroots Women's March on Washington and other cities around the world wore "pussy hats" to signal their unity and their protest of Donald J. Trump's treatment of women.

Credit: Johanna Page

TABLE 14.2

Headlines Tell Their Story

Beginning on November 12, with an early report by CNN, "Tens of Thousands Plan Women's March on Washington," headlines began to tell its evolving story of diversity and magnitude.

"200,000 Expected to Protest Trump the Day After Inauguration"	Town Hall	December 17
"Canadian Women to Join Washington March on Day After Trump's Inauguration"	Toronto Star	December 31
"How the Women's March on Washington Has Gone Global"	Huffington Post	January 5
"These Girls From Chicago's Toughest Area Raised $2,000 to Join the Women's March on Washington"	The Tab	January 17
"Latinas Are Playing a Major Role in the Women's March on Washington"	Latina	January 18
"Half a Million People Show Up for D.C. Women's March"	NY Daily News	January 21
"Women's March on Washington Yields Zero Arrests"	The Hill	January 22

The Women's March on Washington, on January 21, 2017, offers a good example of a fast-moving response to the surprise Trump victory in the 2016 presidential election.

DIGITAL ADDS MUSCLE: WOMEN'S MARCH ON WASHINGTON

With limited resources, grassroots community and special-interest groups can take giant steps toward meeting their goals with strategic online communication. The idea for a women's march in response to the 2016 presidential election is credited to Teresa Shook, a retired attorney and grandmother of four who lives in Hawaii.

The night after the election, she created a Facebook page suggesting a protest. By the time she went to bed, there were 40 RSVPs; when she woke up, there were more than 10,000. That same night, a fashion designer in Brooklyn named Bob Bland also proposed, on Facebook, a women's protest. (Bland had accrued a few thousand politically minded Facebook followers during the election, after she created T-shirts that said "Nasty Woman" and sold them to raise money for Planned Parenthood.) She and Shook combined their events; a few other women volunteered as organizers, and word spread.

The organizers wrote a diversity statement to ensure inclusivity and included veteran nonwhite activists into the leadership. They also clarified men should participate, writing that the Women's March invites "all defenders of human rights" to attend. The March experienced critical debate and infighting exhaustively on Facebook, acknowledged Jia Tolentino in *The New Yorker*, "Activism is internally contentious by nature. Organization is always tedious" (Tolintino, 2017). Yet it grew to one of the larger political demonstrations ever in Washington D.C. (see Table 14.2), with fund-raising for the event largely coming in chunks of $20 and $30 online donations. "It really remind(ed) me of the Sanders campaign," Linda Sarsour, a Palestinian-American Muslim activist from Brooklyn, told CNN. "A very grassroots, very grass-powered movement" (Krieg, 2017).

SCENARIO OUTCOME

At the beginning of this chapter, you read about a winner of the Golden Halo Award for nonprofits, Safe Kids Worldwide, and its corporate sponsors GM, FedEx, and Johnson & Johnson. You were asked to stretch your vision beyond the SR programs listed in this introduction and to recommend new outreach and initiatives.

To see if you're thinking like the CSR professionals at these three firms, explore their safety SR pages, and some specific initiatives, through visiting the sites that follow:

FedEx. First visit fedexcares.com, and select the "Road Safety" link. There you will find their Road Safety Report. Browse this 16-page booklet to discover the other partnerships and initiatives FedEx has engaged in to advance road safety. Who and what did you find? Did you imagine this breadth of partnerships? When you think about road safety, it invites a wide variety of public entities to invest time, money, and talent behind this critical cause. Did you brainstorm an opportunity that Fed Ex missed?

GM. Visit http://www.gmsustainability.com/, and navigate to their sustainability report. Then select the "Manage" link. Under "Community," you will find their story about community safety (or find it directly at http://www.gmsustainability.com/manage/community.html). Using your initial knowledge of GM's participation and drawing from lessons in this chapter, how did you imagine GM could extend its good work regarding road safety? How would you communicate it? Did you brainstorm an opportunity that GM missed?

Johnson & Johnson. Visit safekids.org/, and choose the "Videos" tab at the top. Then select "Sports Safety 101." View some of the Johnson & Johnson videos. What do you feel are the most effective parts of these videos? How could you promote more viewing of these videos? How would you extend some of the content of these videos into a WOM, interactive, or special event strategy?

WRAP UP

In this chapter, you explored the communication needs of nonprofit, health, education, and special-interest community organizations and role of PR. You discovered that these specialty areas offer strong career opportunities for the PR practitioner. No doubt you've observed personally the increased communication about health issues and the competitive environment educational institutions are in. And you probably participated in a special-interest community organization—or know someone who did—and realized the importance of strategic communication to advance issues and concerns. By engaging with this chapter's lessons and case studies, you had a trial run at handling the challenges and opportunities confronting a PR professional, from major campaigns like #GivingTuesday to the ad hoc effort of No Boston Olympics.

THINK ABOUT IT

You read in this chapter that organizations should use both one-way and two-way communication strategies and content characterized by openness, disclosure, access, positivity, and evidence of collaborations. Analyze a Facebook page of a nonprofit, based on the following criteria:

- **Openness and Disclosure**. Is information available in the About, Founded, and Mission sections?

- **Access**. Is a website link, along with phone numbers and e-mail information, listed?

- **Positivity.** Look at the organization's past 10 posts. How many photos and videos are included in them? Engaging visual communication helps build relationships of trust and satisfaction.

- **Assurance**. Are they actively responding to users' questions in a timely manner?

- **Collaborations**. Is there evidence of networking and sharing of tasks? Look for organization posts mentioning other groups and partnerships. This content demonstrates the organization's mission and has been shown to support fund-raising.

WRITE LIKE A PRO

Word clouds are an eye-catching visualization tool to communicate important information at a glance—whether on an organization's blog, social media platforms, or website. They're also a solution for adding visual interest when you have a lot of text without a ready image. Some free word cloud generators are wordclouds.com or worditout.com.

You will now create a word cloud for a nonprofit organization's blog. First identify a nonprofit in your local city or town, and find its mission or vision statement on its website. Then go to the word cloud generator of your choice, and create a word cloud by pasting the mission or vision statement into its "Word List" area. Try different colors and fonts to experiment with results. After you're satisfied with the word cloud, save it as a JPEG or PDF, or just take a screen shot.

SOCIAL RESPONSIBILITY CASE STUDY

GlobalGiving: Crowdfunding Gives to People and Companies Around the World

Situation

GlobalGiving is the first and largest global crowdfunding community for nonprofits. GlobalGiving makes it safe and easy for people and companies to give to local projects anywhere in the world. The organization also provides nonprofits with the tools, training, and support they need to become more effective.

Research and Strategy

Between 2002 and 2017 GlobalGiving has helped raise more than $261 million from 590,000 donors for more than 16,750 projects in 165 countries. Each of the nonprofits on GlobalGiving. org has been vetted and has committed to providing donors with regular updates about how donations are put to work.

New York Times columnist Nicholas Kristof offered a personal testimonial to GlobalGiving's unique outreach. "For Father's Day last year, I suggested that instead of giving Dad another necktie, people sponsor a 'HeroRat' through GlobalGiving. HeroRats are trained rats that sniff out landmines or cases of TB" (Kristof, 2010).

Beyond individual donors to causes, GlobalGiving involves many corporate partners in funding its nonprofit members—through programs in philanthropy, cause marketing, employee engagement, and disaster response. Examples of corporate partners who have worked with GlobalGiving on grassroots projects include Discovery Communications and Pepsi.

Discovery Communications, the global mass media and entertainment company (think Discovery Channel, Animal Planet, and Eurosport, among others) matches its employees' donations toward addressing famine in Ethiopia, South Sudan, and Somalia (Disaster Relief, n.d.). Pepsi redirected its entire 2010 Super Bowl budget of $20 million into the Pepsi Refresh Project that awarded grants to individuals with innovative ideas for improving local communities throughout the world.

Execution

Among the 1,000 community projects funded by GlobalGiving were those helping pregnant women get healthcare in Tanzania, fighting childhood malnutrition in Guatemala, and helping girls go to school in Afghanistan. Looking closer at one funded initiative launched by the Nike Foundation, the Girl Effect (n.d.) is an organization working for social norm change in various countries, including Rwanda, Nigeria, Ethiopia, Malawi, and Indonesia. It targets cultural barriers that hold girls and their communities back. One of its creations is a mobile network for girls, in partnership with Facebook's Free Basics initiative, that tailors content to each girl's geolocation.

In 2016 GlobalGiving's organizations had the advantage of using a wealth of communication tools provided by #GivingTuesday in a communications tool kit offering the following:

Mega Messages

Ideas to Get Involved

Social Media Tips

Sample Outreach E-Mail

Campaign Timeline

Press Release Template

Partner Case Studies

Ideas and Examples for Cities, Schools, Religious Organizations, and Families

Mayoral Proclamation Tool Kit

Evaluation

In 2016 GlobalGiving experienced its highest-volume fund-raising day in the nonprofit's 14-year history. Thanks to GlobalGiving's donors, partners, and nonprofits, the crowdfunding community helped raise more than $2.4 million for 1,477 nonprofit projects in 124 countries, GlobalGiving *nearly tripled* its previous one-day giving record from #GivingTuesday in 2013.

GlobalGiving's campaign featured a #MatchAMillion offer from the Bill & Melinda Gates Foundation, who gave $500,000 in matching funds (applied at a 50% match). Matching funds were available to all GlobalGiving's nonprofit partners, helping them motivate donors to give.

In another specific outcome, Hope Children's Ministries raised a total of $20,966 on #GivingTuesday 2016 for its youth empowerment project dedicated to orphaned and street children in Uganda. According to Founder and Executive Director Ruth Nambowa Bulyaba, "We are so grateful for GlobalGiving. I have never raised $10,000 in one day but you guys made it possible. You prepared me well to give the right messages at the right time."

ENGAGE

▶ Go to https://www.globalgiving.org/, and browse all its resources.

▶ After exploring the website, go to the "Learn" page, where it offers tips, tools, and resources for nonprofits, donors, and companies to help make the world a better place.

DISCUSSION

▶ Would you be attracted to an employer who partners with GlobalGiving to match employee donations to a worthy cause?

▶ If so, what types of causes would most motivate you?

▶ If your employer doesn't partner with GlobalGiving, how might you go about encouraging the organization to do so?

▶ What project or projects would you suggest to a company you work for, and why?

▶ What communication strategies and tools would you use to encourage fellow employees to participate?

Source: GlobalGiving (2016).

SOCIAL RESPONSIBILITY CASE STUDY

Two Bostonians Campaign to Stop the Olympics From Coming to Their Hometown

Situation

In 2013 and 2014 a plan was made to bring the 2024 Summer Olympics to Boston. The Olympic boosters promised political leaders, taxpayers, and the media that the games would produce enormous benefits—with little financial support from the taxpaying public.

However, these same boosters refused to divulge the details of their bid and, only when pressed, admitted their plan required billions of dollars in construction of venues. Winning the bid meant the public would guarantee taxpayer dollars to cover cost overruns—an issue that has dogged all modern Olympic Games.

In January 2015, the United States Olympic Committee (USOC) chose Boston 2024's bid over those of other U.S. cities. With the USOC's action, it appeared the stage was set for the International Olympic Committee (IOC) to award the Olympic Games to Boston 2024.

Research and Strategy

Activism can start small but mushroom when social media and a motivating cause meet. With little more than a Twitter account, a website, and a PowerPoint presentation that two Bostonians threw together in a couple of weeks, an organization was launched in 2013 whose name spoke for itself: No Boston Olympics. This grassroots effort was designed to battle the private nonprofit group formed to organize the city's Olympics bid: Boston 2024.

One of the founders of No Boston Olympics, Chris Dempsey, understood what Boston's Olympics boosters thought the city would get out of the deal, but it didn't make sense to him. He felt the years of focusing on the site and its plans would pull time and attention away from critical housing and education needs. So together with friend Liam Kerr, No Boston Olympics was born—with a giant task of defeating what's considered the "gold medal" for the world's brightest cities.

Execution

No Boston Olympics attempted to pull it off with a virtually nonexistent budget. Facts led the charge: Recent research was publicized revealing that the beneficiaries of Olympic cities were mainly big business, and the losers were the hospitality industry, public housing, and residents, due to congested public spaces, high prices, and security concerns.

The activist campaign, a David against a Goliath, also mustered community engagement and suspicion about the secretive pro-Olympics process. Upon discovering its plans to take over a treasured park, a local newspaper editor published a scathing editorial naming the effort a secret conspiracy of tycoons and special interests and calling on residents to organize to oppose it.

Within 12 hours they did, forming an ad hoc, grassroots ally to No Boston Olympics called No Boston 2024. Interestingly the effort was organized by young activists who had been involved in the Occupy movement, Black Lives Matter, and the American Civil Liberties Union (ACLU).

No Boston Olympics used focused messaging, identifying the opportunity costs—the damaging side effects of the games—including the excess costs the city and state would be obliged to pay through a taxpayer guarantee.

EVALUATION

After a protracted and very public fight that included contentious public meetings, Boston residents shocked city leaders and the Olympic Committee in 2015 by rejecting the proposal to host the Olympics. In retrospect the Boston 2024 organization conceded that immediately after Boston was announced as a bid city, it should have educated residents, gathered feedback, and incorporated public sentiment into the bid plans. Not long afterward, Dempsey and a No Boston 2024 colleague flew to Hamburg, Germany, to advise a group opposing an effort to bring the 2024 Games there. The following month Hamburg residents voted to withdraw the city's bid.

No Boston Olympics's success showed that an underfunded group of diverse and engaged citizens could join together to challenge a powerful group of boosters and ultimately derail Boston 2024 by demanding transparency and accountability and coordinating dissenting voices.

ENGAGE

- ▸ Go to http://www.nobostonolympics.org/10_myths_about_boston_2024, and read the post "10 Myths About Boston 2024."

DISCUSS

- ▸ No Boston Olympics took on powerful civic forces that wanted the event. If you had been part of that pro-games group, how would you have countered the statements on the "10 Myths" list?
- ▸ Consider any issue in your community that has triggered competing interests to organize advocacy groups. What is the issue, what are the positions of the opposing groups, and how well are they communicating those positions?

Sources: Dempsey (2017); New York Times Magazine (2016).

VIDEO CASE

CDC Anti-Smoking Campaign: Health Communications

In 2014, the CDC premiered a series of new advertisements highlighting some of the less well-known side effects of smoking and featuring actual smokers who had suffered those consequences.

VIDEO

1. How do the advertisements seen and described in the video target a particular audience?
2. How might the campaign be adjusted to reach a different audience—teenagers, for instance?
3. If you had been charged with designing this campaign, where would you have begun your research?

PRACTICE AND APPLY
WHAT YOU'VE LEARNED

edge.sagepub.com/page

CHECK YOUR COMPREHENSION
ON THE STUDY SITE WITH:

- eFlashcards to strengthen your
  understanding of key terms

- Practice quizzes to test your comprehension
  of key concepts

- Videos and multimedia content to
  enhance your exploration of key topics

15 Public Affairs, Government Relations, and Political Communications

Learning Objectives

15.1 Understand the similarities and differences between public affairs and PR

15.2 Understand the role of government relations and lobbying

15.3 Develop an understanding of political communications

Ebola on the Doorstep of America

In 2014 an outbreak of Ebola was detected in West Africa. As the disease progressed, it spread across borders in the region. Soon an international panic was imminent, and people grew concerned that an infected individual could transport the virus to other parts of the world, including the United States.

The federal government acted quickly, developing a rapid response to protect the health of its citizens and help individuals in Africa. The National Institutes of Health (NIH), which is part of the U.S. Department of Health and Human Services, played a vital role in this collaborative effort.

The Ebola outbreak posed both medical and communications challenges for the government agencies and hospitals involved.

iStock.com/zmeel

Two U.S. nurses infected. The growing fear surrounding the outbreak and its potential to spread to the United States reached a peak in the fall of 2014. This was when Thomas Eric Duncan, a Liberian visiting his family in Dallas, Texas, was diagnosed with Ebola and died following his hospital admission. Two nurses who treated him became infected with the virus while caring for Duncan, 26-year-old Nina Pham, and 29-year-old Amber Vinson.

Reports began to circulate in the national media suggesting flawed safety procedures at the hospital that treated Mr. Duncan. This had the effect of casting doubt on the ability of the medical infrastructure in the United States to prevent the Ebola outbreak that many feared was imminent. Once it was determined that the two American nurses required highly specialized treatment, the decision was made to fly them to hospital facilities with specially trained clinicians and special bio-containment capabilities to isolate and treat such highly infectious patients. As a result Ms. Vinson was sent to Emory University Hospital in Atlanta, Georgia, and Ms. Pham was sent to the Special Clinical Studies Unit at the NIH Clinical Center in Bethesda, Maryland.

Heightened communications concerns. In Bethesda the NIH staff, including communications personnel, had to quickly get ready for Ms. Pham's arrival. Working alongside the clinicians and scientists, the agency's communications staff had to prepare to address several important, but conflicting, concerns:

▸ How would the agency balance transparency with protecting the patient's privacy?

▸ How would the agency communicate that Ms. Pham was receiving excellent care while also acknowledging the riskiness of this disease?

▸ How would NIH balance its pride in having a facility capable of accommodating such a high-risk patient with the heightened public and employee fears about the risks involved?

A comprehensive, science-based communications plan was needed, and the stakes were high for the NIH, its employees, and the citizens living near the hospital. In addition media interest was at a fever pitch and would likely continue throughout the entire episode.

As you read this chapter, consider the following:

1. How did the government setting (public affairs) guide the practice of communications?

2. How are issues and crisis management both *similar* and *different* in this setting—as compared to the private sector?

3. How should the NIH communications team manage this unique, global challenge?

4. How might you apply best practices to a situation you may face in your current or future career?

In previous chapters, you have learned that PR can have many names, depending on the setting where the work is done and the audience you are targeting. In this chapter you will learn about the PR in a government setting, such as the NIH in the opening scenario, which is usually called **public affairs**. If your career path takes you into the U.S. military, public affairs is the common name for PR work there as well.

You will be introduced to **government relations**, which is a hybrid of PR and sometimes is referred to as lobbying. And you will also learn about **political communications**, which is usually deployed in election campaigns or by elected officials. The goal is to make you familiar with each area and understand the differences among them and traditional PR.

PUBLIC AFFAIRS, GOVERNMENT RELATIONS, AND POLITICAL COMMUNICATIONS

>> **LO 15.1**   **Understand the similarities and differences between public affairs and PR**

Let's begin with some definitions to help you understand how public affairs, government relations, and political communications are different from traditional PR (see Figure 15.1). Later in the chapter you will learn about each of these concepts and review examples of each. To be clear, in one form or another, a common thread to communications in a government setting is a focus on public service.

AN OVERVIEW OF PUBLIC AFFAIRS, GOVERNMENT RELATIONS, AND POLITICAL COMMUNICATION

PUBLIC AFFAIRS

Public affairs in a government setting combines media relations, crisis communications, issues management, social responsibility (SR), public

⑤SAGE edge™

Master the content
edge.sagepub.com/page

FIGURE 15.1

Categories of Government-Based Communications

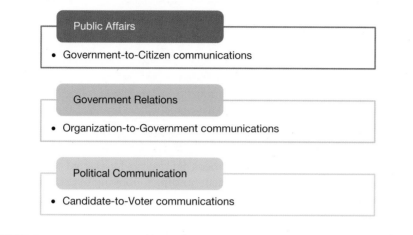

Public Affairs
- Government-to-Citizen communications

Government Relations
- Organization-to-Government communications

Political Communication
- Candidate-to-Voter communications

information, and strategic communications advice. **Public Information Officer (PIO)** is a related title and function to public affairs and is often used by government agencies. PIOs have a variety of job duties, but written and verbal communication and media relations are the basis for much of what they do. Speechwriting and preparing testimony for legislative and public hearings are often duties of a PIO as well.

▸ Both public affairs professionals and PIOs focus on *government-to-citizen communications*.

It is important to note that government communicators are restricted from promoting a candidate or elected official while working for the government by the Hatch Act. The Hatch Act was passed by Congress and signed by President Franklin Delano Roosevelt in 1939, and it was modernized by President Barack Obama in 2012. These activities fall into the political communications arena (see separate section in this chapter), and there are strict prohibitions against using public money for political purposes. Should a communicator desire to get involved in a campaign, the usual practice is for him or her to resign or take a leave of absence and be paid by the campaign instead of the government.

GOVERNMENT RELATIONS

Government relations is the branch of communications that helps organizations communicate with government agencies and elected officials. Most often a comprehensive government relations effort includes lobbying government officials directly. In lobbying the principal activity involves direct contact with politicians and government rule makers to express your company's point of view.

▸ Activities in this area focus on *organization-to-government communication*.

POLITICAL COMMUNICATION

Political communication is typically work done by a press secretary or campaign communications staff on behalf of an elected official or a candidate for office. It entails media relations, speechwriting, strategic messaging to key publics, and supporting get-out-the-vote and fund-raising efforts.

> ▶ The focus of these efforts is on *elected official (candidates)-to-public (voter) communications*.

David Payne (personal communication, 2017), founder and CEO of Codavate, a public affairs firm in Washington, D.C., distinguishes the terms in this way:

> Based on my experience, public affairs entails indirect communication aimed at policy and legislative outcomes. Political communication consists of the regulated speech that influences campaigns for elected office. And government relations is a euphemism for direct lobbying of policymakers to influence regulations or laws.

PUBLIC AFFAIRS IN RELATIONSHIP TO PUBLIC RELATIONS

In earlier chapters you learned that the job titles public affairs or public information became more commonly used to describe government communications early in the 20th century. There's a fascinating story behind this wording.

WHY DOES THE GOVERNMENT CALL IT PUBLIC AFFAIRS?

Following the success of publicity agents and publicists serving business clients in the 1800s and early 1900s, government agencies began to deploy these

The White House communications director manages the president's PR strategy and is usually a close adviser, like Dan Bartlett in the George W. Bush administration.

Carol T. Powers/Bloomberg/ Getty Images

professionals as well to help shape public opinion. Some big business interests were concerned about the impact of this trend on business. They pressured Congress to restrict the allocation of funds to government agencies for publicity purposes, which were often grouped under the function or title of PR. Additional pressure was put on Congress from politicians and activists concerned that government PR activity could be used to manipulate public opinion against the best interests of the public. As a result what became known as the Gillett Amendment was added to the Congressional legislation that created the Interstate Commerce Commission (ICC) in 1913 (Taylor & Kent, 2016).

Although it has come to be viewed as a ban or limit on government PR, the actual amendment didn't specifically prohibit "government communications." It simply said: "Appropriated funds may not be used to pay a 'publicity expert' unless specifically appropriated for that purpose" (Taylor & Kent, 2016). To address this concern, government officials dropped references to "public relations" and "publicity" (to avoid the pre-approval requirement) and began to refer to the function as public affairs or public information.

It is important to point out that the government did not stop practicing PR; it just gave these activities new labels—like "public affairs" and "public information"—and continued to communicate to its citizens (Taylor & Kent, 2016). This process continues today, where you will rarely find the term "public relations" used to describe public communications in a government setting.

Ironically the process of how this legislation came into being is a classic example of how government relations and lobbying impact public policy. Various stakeholders with competing agendas reach out to elected officials to change or impact public policy. In this case it was about restricting how the government practiced PR. Government then responds by passing legislation or issuing regulations to address the issue and thereby establishes a policy or law that others must follow.

COMMUNICATIONS SPENDING IS STILL AN ONGOING BATTLE

The effort to curb government spending on communications is an ongoing battle between the party in power and those seeking to limit their communications and promotional activity. In 2015 and 2016 the federal government was criticized about White House and federal agencies' spending on communications while President Obama was in office (2008–2016). In October 2015, *Business Insider* reported that U.S. Office of Management and Budget (OMB) research showed the Obama administration had spent more than $5 billion on "PR and advertising" since taking office (Pianin, 2015). Members of Congress, especially those from the other side (i.e., Republicans), criticized these expenditures as "excessive" and "self-promoting" and called for more oversight and controls on spending by the federal government on communications.

"Unnecessary media relations or PR spending is a cost that the nation simply cannot afford," Senate Budget Committee Chair Mike Enzi (R–WY) wrote in 2015. "With the administration asking Congress to raise the federal debt limit, it is essential that the Executive Branch avoid spending on such non-essential and inappropriate activities, and that Congress be made aware to the extent that such spending continues to occur" (Pianin, 2015).

The Obama White House, through Press Secretary Josh Earnest, defended the increase in expenditures, noting that the administration had made it a priority to

The White House press secretary is the public face of a presidential administration, delivering often daily briefings to the press.

Cheriss May/NurPhoto/Getty Images; Cheriss May/NurPhoto/Getty Images

interact with the public and keep them informed on essential government services and the president's policies.

"That is important work that requires dedicated professionals who are interested in furthering that goal and helping the American people understand exactly what the administration is doing, what we have prioritized and what our success has been in implementing the agenda laid out by President Obama," Earnest said (Boyer, 2016).

To be fair many government communications activities are essential to the well-being of the public. Government public affairs (or public information) teams focus their communications on key areas such as health and wellness, public safety, and information on how citizens can best utilize government services. For example, information is routinely provided to the public by federal, state, and local government communicators on how to register and vote, how to pay taxes, how to finance a home, or how to pay for college with the support of the government.

"Public affairs in a government agency setting has three unique aspects as compared to the private sector: First, your communications work is done in a 'glass house' since you are working for a government agency. Second, government public affairs teams are typically resource constrained and thus behind the private sector in terms of technology capability. Third in government, we must answer to many different clients simultaneously—including citizens, political officials, industry and the public," comments Aaron Lavalee (personal communication, 2017), deputy assistant administrator, USDA Food Safety and Inspection Service.

Summing up, Lavalee adds, "You have the opportunity to work every day to improve the lives of your fellow citizens by facilitating the delivery of government services and assistance to them when it is most needed."

CRISIS MANAGEMENT IN GOVERNMENTAL PUBLIC AFFAIRS

As you read in the earlier chapter on crisis communications and issues management, government communicators are also often called upon to manage crisis situations. These circumstances are usually in response to natural disasters like Hurricane Katrina, accidents like the BP Deepwater Horizon oil spill, or food safety and public health challenges.

Many of the elements of crisis communications are the same in both settings. Tactical strategies include media relations, social media management, speeches,

The U.S. Department of Agriculture Confronts "Pink Slime": A Case of Transparency, Safety, Nutrition, and Outrage

In 2012 the U.S. Department of Agriculture (USDA) was confronted with a crisis communications scenario on a national scale. The story of "Pink Slime," known officially as lean finely textured beef (LFTB), broke in a torrent of nightly news coverage, endless blogs, and online petitions and created havoc in the highly regulated agricultural field.

LFTB is beef that has been separated from the fat in beef trimmings. Historically these trimmings were discarded until a company, Beef Products Inc., invented a process to separate the remaining meat from those trimmings. Most importantly it was real beef—just beef harvested in a new, non-traditional method. The problem was that consumers did not know or understand the facts.

The crisis hit the USDA and the meat industry like a tsunami. It began with Diane Sawyer informing the American public on the ABC network news that we were all consuming "Pink Slime" and didn't even know it. This scenario had all the ingredients for a major crisis situation: a derogatory but memorable label, the all-American staple of ground beef, and widespread usage across the country (LFTB was in up to 70% of ground beef and kids were eating it as part of the National School Lunch Program [NSLP]).

From a public affairs perspective, the USDA had to navigate and communicate while overseeing three different agencies with three different roles and competing interests when it came to LFTB. The initial plan was to convince consumers that these beef products were safe and the product could be safely served to kids in our schools (see Figure 15.2). However, this plan was quickly derailed by the hysteria the news coverage caused.

The public outcry in this crisis was never just about product safety. It was driven by how LFTB was produced, inaccurate consumer perceptions, and the belief that consumers had been deceived. In the end nobody won. For Beef Products Inc. three of their four production plants closed. The USDA announced that it would give public schools a choice of beef products provided through their meal programs. Purchases for beef products without LFTB ultimately outpaced purchases with LFTB by about 20 to one. At the USDA, the agency settled on rebuilding public trust in its ability to provide safe and nutritious food to Americans. ●

Source: Aaron Lavalee (personal communication, 2017), deputy assistant administrator, USDA, Food Safety and Inspection Service.

press conferences, and providing the public with the information necessary to recover, respond, and rebuild. The main difference is that your primary audience is the public versus your customers or stockholders.

In the private sector during a crisis, communicators focus on multiple stakeholders—customers, employees, and shareholders—and on managing the media and briefing government regulators as well as the public. Depending on the situation, PR pros and the executive leaders in the private sector may need to take responsibility (if warranted) and address how they will prevent the problem from happening again.

MILITARY PUBLIC AFFAIRS

In the military, the **public affairs officer's (PAO)** primary responsibilities are to advise senior leaders on public affairs issues, assist them in making well-informed decisions, and translate those decisions into effective public affairs operations.

PAOs plan and execute communication strategies to achieve the unit's desired objectives and evaluate the effectiveness of the programs they undertake. The PAO also facilitates media relations with domestic and international news media on behalf of his or her unit or commanding officer. This is like the work of a nonmilitary PR professional, but the difference is in the primary audience and the organization doing the communicating.

PR professionals in the military and law enforcement are known as Public Affairs Officers.

Matthew Cavanaugh/Getty Images; Erich Schlegel/Getty Images

"Like civilian public relations practitioners, military PAOs focus on media relations, internal communications and community relations, while using the same communication tools that PR practitioners use. Unlike private companies, military units have a duty to inform their chain of command, fellow service members,

A Military Base Works to Repair Community Relations in Louisiana

In addition to providing information to the wider public, military PAOs monitor and foster relationships with key stakeholders. One of these key relationships is between a military base and its local community. If the relationship sours, it can lead to friction between the base and the community; in some cases, bad relationships have led to bases being shut down and their military missions transferred to other bases.

Barksdale Air Force Base is in Bossier City, Louisiana, and has been a military airfield since 1932, when it was built in the cotton fields outside of town. Over the years the community grew until the town eventually reached the edge of the base. Historically the aircraft landings had kept property values low near the runway, and this land was used for farming and pasture.

A real estate developer saw these low prices as an opportunity to build a high-end golf community. As the new homes were built and then bought, the base started receiving noise complaints from the residents. The homeowners became increasingly vocal, and the relationship between the community and the base was deteriorating, perhaps even threatening the future of the base.

In response the PAO staff invited the residents of the neighborhood to visit the base. They went out to the flight line to see the large bombers up close and meet the pilots who flew them. They were also allowed to climb into the aircraft and look around. This had the effect of personalizing the issue by creating a relationship between the pilots and homeowners.

Following this visit they were briefed by the commander, who noted that the Air Force had consistently recommended against using the land for residential use. City officials, who also participated in the briefing, told the homeowners the developer had been advised not to build homes on that property. As a result, during the event, the homeowners shifted from demanding the planes stop flying at night to asking why the developer hadn't warned them about the aircraft noise.

While not eliminating the issue, this effort enabled all parties to better understand each other, work together to improve the situation, and create a positive, ongoing dialog. In short the communications effort strengthened the relationship with the town and its citizens and enabled the base to continue its mission. ●

Source: Lt. Col. Mark Phillips (personal communication, 2017), USAF (Ret.).

and the public about their activities," explains Lt. Col. Mark Phillips (personal communication, 2017), U.S. Air Force (Ret.).

In addition to meeting the external communications needs of the unit or branch of the military they serve, many PAOs are also responsible for internal communications including newsletters, publications, digital media, and in-person communications when required. As well, PAOs are responsible for the base or service branch's efforts to address social issues that impact the military and society at large.

GOVERNMENT RELATIONS AND LOBBYING

>> LO 15.2   Understand the role of government relations and lobbying

Government relations and **lobbying** are forms of *organization-to-government communications*. The difference is the nature of the communication: indirect (government relations) or direct (lobbying). In most cases the overall goal is to advocate your company's or organization's point of view to the government and elected officials. The impetus for this outreach is often business related because new laws or regulatory requirements can add costs or complications to a product or service, and business leaders are focused on keeping costs down and profits up. Usually both approaches (government relations and lobbying) are pursued to increase the impact and influence on the process.

From the government side, however, there are other important considerations, for example, environmental issues, consumer protection, and preserving competition, that must also be weighed by elected officials in their policy making. The decision-making and legislative process is complex, and the role of the communicators is to represent the company's interest to the government while decisions are being made or the law is being debated. This usually involves conversations and meetings with regulators and/or elected officials and their staff.

> "*Lobbying* and *government relations* have come to mean targeted outreach to elected officials by representatives of companies, governments, non-profits and professional associations as well as regular citizens with the goal of impacting legislation or regulations."
>
> —Popik (2010)

WHEN GOVERNMENT RELATIONS IS CALLED PUBLIC AFFAIRS

In some cases advocacy can also include indirect communications activity to raise awareness and bring public pressure on government officials through media coverage, petitions, online campaigns, and so on. Government relations departments and agencies use the term "public affairs" to signal this indirect activity.

"Public affairs teams often work in lock step with their government relations colleagues—the distinguishing factor is that public affairs efforts by companies aim to shape policy without stepping foot on Capitol Hill to lobby," explains Lindsay Murphy (personal communication, 2017) of Racepoint Global, a prominent Washington, DC public affairs firm.

"Knowing your audience is vital to both approaches, particularly in identifying which elected officials are most likely to be for or against your position" she adds. "That information drives outreach efforts aimed at influencing key government decision makers—including which publications and congressional districts are prioritized for media placements and in deploying your social media outreach. Together with the lobbying efforts, this process places your message front and center with decision makers and positions you for success," Murphy concludes.

"Keep What You've Earned"

After recognizing binge drinking by off-duty personnel was an increasingly serious issue, the U.S. Navy launched their "Keep What You've Earned" campaign.

Roberto Schmidt/AFP/Getty Images

This U.S. Navy communications program was developed to address a challenging social issue. The plan was developed by the public affairs staff following a DOD Survey of health-related behaviors among active duty personnel. The study revealed that there had been an alarming increase in binge drinking among off-duty sailors between 2005 and 2008.

Binge Drinking Impacted Communities

Around the world where the bases were located, this problem was significant. The potential for vehicle accidents, incidents involving the sailors and civilians, and property damage clearly would increase if alcohol abuse was left unchecked. Further, the relationship between the neighboring community and the base would suffer as well. Something needed to be done.

Social Media Campaign

The U.S. Navy developed and mounted a social media-based internal communications campaign to change this dangerous and harmful behavior. Community leaders, sailors, and their family members were interviewed to discover the triggers for this behavior and to determine if there were patterns that could be identified. The research showed this increase was largely attributable to the stresses of the modern military life—constant travel, periodic relocation, and deployment in hostile surroundings—that can lead to substance abuse.

Key Motivators: Docked Pay and Demotion

The campaign, which was designed with the assistance of Booz Allen, focused on promoting responsible drinking among active duty sailors. It encouraged them to use better judgment when on leave and off duty in the community. Sailors were encouraged to be proactive and prevent alcohol-related incidents—their own or of fellow sailors—and preserve their pay and status by avoiding disciplinary action. Under military rules sailors who engaged in this behavior were subject to having their pay docked, being demoted, or losing privileges.

Results Overwhelmingly Positive

In a follow-up survey, conducted in April 2014, which included family members as well as active duty sailors, a dramatic change in perception and behaviors was identified. An overwhelming 80% of the respondents described the campaign as *very effective* or *effective*, and 38% were motivated to take one of the recommended actions (decrease consumption, seek help, or assist another sailor) of the campaign. In September 2014 the U.S. Navy announced a 51% decrease in alcohol-related incidents during the summer months (Memorial Day to Labor Day) and the "Keep What You've Earned" campaign was credited as a major factor in that decline (PRSA, 2015a). ●

WHY DO THEY CALL IT LOBBYING?

The British Broadcasting Company (BBC) suggests that the term "lobbying" comes from the informal meetings of members of parliament and citizens in the hallways (or "lobbies") of the Houses of Parliament before and after debates, which began in the early 18th century. In the United States, many believe that the term originated in the 19th century at the Willard Hotel in Washington, D.C. It was reportedly used by Ulysses S. Grant to describe the political wheelers and dealers frequenting hotel lobbies near the White House to access him and members of his inner circle who were often found there, enjoying a cigar and some brandy in the evenings. The "lobbyists" would seek him out to discuss issues and politics while he was there.

Lobbyists from organizations and industries, in this case the National Association of Music Merchants, regularly meet with U.S. senators.

Kris Connor/Getty Images

POLITICAL COMMUNICATION: APPLYING PUBLIC RELATIONS STRATEGY TO CAMPAIGNS AND ELECTIONS

>> LO 15.3   Develop an understanding of political communications

Political communication is a dynamic, interactive process for the transmission of information among politicians, the news media, and the public. The process (see Figure 15.2) operates downward from governing institutions toward citizens, horizontally in linkages among political actors (e.g., candidates, advisors, and party officials), and upward from public opinion toward authorities (Norris, 2004).

FIGURE 15.2

Transmission of Information in Political Communications Process

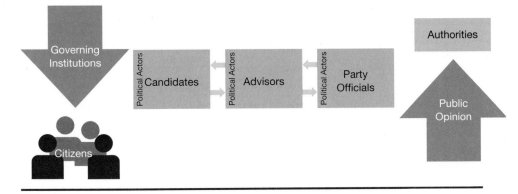

Humana's Campaign for a Healthy Mississippi

In the lead-up to the Obamacare rollout in early 2014, Humana positioned itself as a source of information about the new requirements, as well as a provider of insurance coverage.

iStock.com/SelectStock

Humana (n.d.) is a $27 billion health and well-being company based in Louisville, Kentucky, that offers health insurance and managed care in most of the United States. An excellent example of a combined corporate public affairs and government relations effort was the award-winning work done in Mississippi by Humana and its PR firm Coyne Public Relations.

Focus: Access to Healthcare

In the fall of 2013, the Affordable Care Act (ACA, or "Obamacare" as it became known) was set to launch. Independent research by Gallup showed that one in

five people in Mississippi were uninsured and needed to take advantage of the affordable insurance coverage the law provided. However, awareness of the plan and how to enroll was low, and the marketplace for insurance coverage was limited in the state. Clearly there was a need for an information-based, community outreach effort to increase the number of citizens with healthcare in the state. Access to healthcare is a critical issue, and Humana—as a provider of health-care insurance—decided to respond with a comprehensive program that leveraged its core competency into an SR outreach program to address the issue.

Challenge: Position Humana Ahead of Competitors

Humana was one of several companies providing health coverage in the state, and it decided to launch a communications campaign to "position itself as a source of knowledge and provide a solution by significantly expanding its coverage" (Humana, n.d.) to serve more Mississippians. Working with elected officials at the national, state, and local levels, Humana launched a comprehensive campaign. The campaign featured a dedicated campaign website, RVs equipped with Humana-certified health insurance experts, and a social and traditional media outreach effort to generate awareness of the issue and was highly successful.

When the enrollment period ended in March 2014, nearly 50,000 Mississippians were enrolled from the target areas of the state, and the media coverage of Humana's efforts had exceeded expectations. This campaign illustrates how an **integrated public affairs campaign**—with SR elements—can help position a company as responsive to the community and enhance the company's overall reputation. Further, by working closely with national, state, and local politicians and officials, Humana created strong governmental connections at each level, which may prove useful in the future. ●

Source: PRSA (n.d.a).

FUNDAMENTAL TO POLITICS

In some way, shape, or form, communications has always been an integral part of politics. Experts have observed that communicating with voters to influencing their behavior is an age-old practice. For as long as there have been elections, candidates have worked to persuade the public to favor them" (Foster, 2010).

In recent times political communication represents the best and the worst of communications—especially at the presidential campaign level. In 2008 and 2012 the candidates (Obama and McCain in 2008 and Obama and Romney in 2012) used cutting-edge social media strategies and tactics to convey patriotic messages of hope and change, and the tone was generally civil—with some exceptions. Obama is widely credited with pioneering the use of social media and big data in a major campaign in 2008, and expanding it in 2012, to increase campaign donations, create supporters, and drive voter turnout. These tactics have become staples of the modern political campaign as a result.

GAME OF LEAPFROG

Michael Cornfield, Ph.D., has studied and taught online politics since its inception in the mid-1990s. He suggests, "Since the start of the new millennium, Republicans and Democrats have played a game of technological leapfrog, with the out-of-power party generally taking greater advantage of the latest innovations in digital communications" (M. Cornfield, personal communication, 2017).

"In the final general-election phase of the 2016 race, the Trump campaign combined the candidate's use of Twitter and Facebook with a data operation developed by the Republican National Committee, out-performing a Hillary Clinton team stacked with many Obama veterans," he concludes.

During the 2016 campaign overall spending on campaign communications, including social media, advertising, and PR and staff, was at record levels. The Center for Responsive Politics (CRP) estimated that campaign spending during the 2016 election cycle reached $6.6 billion, a record (OpenSecrets.org, 2016).

NEGATIVE VERSUS POSITIVE

One unintended impact of the "attack" style strategy used by both candidates was a sharp decrease in attention paid by voters to the social media posts from political figures. In a special study on social media and the 2016 election, a Pew Research

The Internet and social media are now essential parts of a successful political campaign.

Frederic J. Brown/AFP/Getty Images

Center report found that many users described their online political encounter as "stressful and frustrating," and (as a result) nearly four in 10 took steps to block or minimize the political content (Duggan & Smith, 2016).

Most experts agree that while traditional media will have to adjust to keep up in political communications, there is no doubt it remains highly relevant. Steven Foster (2010), writing in *Political Communications* suggests that "it is quite *impossible* to conceive of political communications outside of the nexus linking politician to journalist."

Commenting on the 2016 election's aftermath and its impact on political communications, Dr. Lara M. Brown (personal communication, 2017), executive director of the Graduate School of Political Management at The George Washington University, suggests:

> Although candidates challenging the incumbent party's hold on the White House have long campaigned by touting their "outsider" credentials and promising to change what's "wrong with Washington," the volume and ferocity of the appeals during the 2016 electoral cycle reached a new low. Moving forward, political communicators will need to place a sustained focus on crafting positive messages and brand associations. Whatever their basis for inspiration, they would benefit from thinking about how to use their skills to create rather than destroy.

SOCIAL MEDIA: 2016 AND BEYOND

One of the most important changes to political and governmental communication in recent years has been the rise of the Internet as a tool for politicians, particularly in countries at the forefront of the information movement—such as the United States. As a result more voters and prospects sought news online versus in the traditional media. The Pew Research Center in a study called "Political Engagement on Social Media" reports that in January 2016, 44% of U.S. adults reported having learned about the 2016 presidential election "in the past week" from social media, far outpacing the numbers for both local and national print newspapers (Gottfried, Barthel, Shearer, & Mitchell, 2016; see Table 15.1).

TABLE 15.1

One-Week Political Snapshot, January 2016,
U.S. Adult Users of Social Media

Obtained information on 2016 campaign	44%
Via Facebook	37%
Via YouTube	11%
Via Twitter	9%
Shared election information on a social media site	36%

Source: Gottfried, Barthel, Shearer, and Mitchell (2016).

An Interview With Former White House Press Secretaries

**Mike McCurry and Dana Perino, former
White House Press Secretaries**

"The best way to understand the job of White House Press Secretary is to think about the geography of the West Wing itself," explains Mike McCurry. "If you go out the back door of the press secretary's office you can turn right and 50 steps away you're in the Oval Office. You turn left and you're 50 steps away in that briefing room."

As the link between the president and members of the press, the press secretary has a daunting responsibility. "You're equally distanced between these two actors in this adversarial relationship." And as the voice of the president, McCurry reveals, "By evaluating how the press was likely going to react to a certain statement or a development or a decision, you began to impact the decision itself."

He observes some differences between a Democratic and a Republican White House. "Democrats tend to believe that the press is going to be on your side, because they're all about comforting the afflicted and afflicting the comfortable and speaking truth to power, so they're going to be with the little guy." On the other hand, he says, "Republicans never have that supposition in mind. They're more adept at what we might call corporate communications, and they always kind of view the press very skeptically."

McCurry expressed some frustration with the media's obsession with the Lewinsky scandal. "You can practically stand up there and say, 'Doesn't anybody want to talk about the things that actually might put young people at risk?' And the reporters shrug their shoulders and say, 'The only thing our editors want us to ask about today is the scandal involving the intern.' I kept thinking to myself, 'This is what I worked hard to train myself to do? To be able to stand here and talk about the hijinks in the White House? '"

He admits, "I was once asked, 'Is there any circumstance under which the press secretary can ever lie to the American public?' And I said, 'By and large, no.' Sometimes the art of the job is learning how to tell the truth slowly."

Dana Perino states, "One of the things that people see every single day at the podium is the press secretary defending the president to the press. But as important as that is, what people don't see is the press secretary defending the press to the president or members of his senior staff."

She reveals a particularly tough role: "I got a lot of experience delivering bad news. I was very loyal to President Bush. He was quite unpopular as a president, and I remember listening to all of the attacks coming against us, from our friends as well. When asked about it in the press briefing, instead of turning the other cheek, I popped back. Within an hour, there was a fundraising appeal by the Democrats showing how they had gotten under our skin." ●

Sources: M. McCurry (personal communication, 2017); D. Perino (personal communication, 2017).

Moreover, as of July of 2016, 24% of survey respondents say they followed the social media posts of Donald Trump or Hillary Clinton for news and information about the election—more than either of the candidates' websites or e-mails combined (Duggan & Smith, 2016).

Pew also reported that direct communication by candidates to voters (e.g., Twitter) increased substantially above the level of the prior two presidential campaigns, 2008 and 2012, in which social media emerged onto the political communications stage. In 2012 candidates Barack Obama and Mitt Romney updated their Facebook statuses twice a day on average—less than half as often as the 2016 candidates, Trump and Clinton, did throughout the 2016 campaign cycle (Duggan & Smith, 2016).

"We've come a long way in the field of political communications since simple black and white TV ads or cozy radio broadcasts," comments Dennis W. Johnson (personal communication, 2017), Ph.D., an author and expert on political communications. "Today, the world of political communication is robust, multifaceted, and wide open. Politicians must continually figure out the most effective way to connect directly with the voters. For now, it looks like Twitter is dominant—thanks in part to President Trump—a decade from now, who knows?"

SCENARIO OUTCOME

At the beginning of this chapter, you read about the challenge the NIH public affairs team faced in 2014 preparing for the arrival of Ebola patient Nina Pham at their Bethesda hospital for care and diagnosis.

The NIH public affairs team was challenged to handle a daily international media presence, respect the patient's privacy, and manage the fears of its employees and the neighbors near its Bethesda, Maryland, hospital and headquarters. While Ms. Pham was being prepared to travel to NIH, via a chartered, medically equipped airplane, media inquiries poured in. The NIH communications team anticipated that media would have questions about the care that Ms. Pham was receiving, what this mysterious, ultra-safe clinical unit looked like, and if there was any threat to the community.

How did they respond?

- ▶ To provide transparency about the facility's capabilities and what Ms. Pham's care would be like, the team prepared media materials that could be shared proactively with reporters and included the images (e.g., photos and video) that are critical for broadcast media.

- ▶ NIH communicators also realized the value of keeping employees and the community informed. The NIH director sent an e-mail to all employees alerting them to the patient's arrival and noted the measures being taken to protect her and the staff as well as the surrounding area. Staff scientists created informational materials for the NIH website explaining the disease and spoke at town hall meetings for all staff to allay concerns.

- ▶ Ahead of Ms. Pham's arrival, broadcast outlets and media from national outlets, local Texas stations following Ms. Pham's case, and foreign press from around the globe converged on the NIH campus. Communications staff arrived before dawn to greet satellite trucks at security and direct them to the front of the hospital, where teams of staff from communications offices across the agency worked shifts to assist reporters and supply information, help stage camera shots and stand-ups, and escort them inside the hospital for food and restrooms.

- ▶ To ensure that her medical privacy was protected, NIH spokespeople adhered to the American Hospital Association guidelines on describing a patient's condition to the media, which use one-word descriptions like "good," "fair," or "serious." While the NIH most often distributes news in written press releases, in this case, in-person press conferences were set up to provide updates for national, local, and cable news channels to ensure that all media present had access to the same information simultaneously. The spokespeople also helped put a face on the scientists and medical staff who were caring for Ms. Pham.

On October 24, NIH held a final news conference to announce that Ms. Pham was Ebola free. She appeared at the news conference with her family, smiling and recovered. To help remove the stigma of disease, NIH leaders greeted her with warm hugs at the news conference. Later that day she received another warm embrace from President Barack Obama in the Oval Office.

Source: Anne Rancourt (personal communication, 2017), section chief, Office of Communications and Government Relations. National Institute of Allergy and Infectious Diseases. National Institutes of Health.

WRAP UP

In this chapter, you have read about three exciting and unique areas of strategic communications—*public affairs*, *government relations* and *lobbying*, and *political communications*. You also explored *military public affairs*, which is a unique audience and function unto itself.

While one of these may not be the career path you choose, it is important to know the many options a career in communications has for young professionals.

One career option is government-to-citizen communications in public affairs, usually practiced in a government or nonprofit setting. Another is the field of government relations and lobbying that focuses on organization-to-government communications. You also examined political communications, a PR field that manages elected official (or candidate)-to-voter communication. Finally if you are in, or will enter, the military and are interested in strategic communication, military public affairs offers a career path as a PAO.

KEY TERMS

Government Relations: Organization-to-government communications in which organizations communicate with government agencies and elected officials, **382**

Integrated Public Affairs Campaign: A comprehensive communications campaign (usually directed at influencing public policy or legislation) that combines the disciplines and activities of government relations, lobbying, public affairs, and traditional public relations, **392**

Lobbying: Organization-to-government communications involving direct contact with politicians and government rule makers to provide a point of view, **389**

Political Communications: Candidate-to-voter communications; dynamic, interactive campaign-based process among politicians, the news media, and the public, **382**

Public Affairs: Communications activity engaged in by companies directed at impacting government policy or legislation, **382**

Public Affairs Officer (PAO): Communicators working in a military setting whose responsibilities are to advise senior officers and leaders on communications issues, assist them in making well-informed decisions, and translate those decisions into effective military operations, **387**

Public Information Officer (PIO): Related to public affairs and often used by government agencies involving written and verbal communication and media relations including speechwriting and preparing testimony for legislative hearings, **383**

THINK ABOUT IT

To help reinforce the key lessons of this chapter, what follows are a series of questions for you to discuss in small groups and then share with the class:

1. What are the principal differences between government-based public affairs work and traditional PR?

2. What is lobbying, and why is it called that?

3. What made the 2016 presidential election different from previous ones? Research and discuss the role of social media and its impact on campaign messages and voter sentiment.

4. How has the role of traditional media impacted the efforts of government and nonprofit PR to deliver key messages, and how is the media responding?

5. Is SR practiced by government agencies and nonprofits? Research and identify a few examples (Note: csrwire.com is a good, searchable source).

| **WRITE LIKE A PRO** |

In this chapter, you read about two crisis situations faced by government public affairs professionals. Pick one and answer the questions that follow in a short essay (250 words). You may want to do a media search or visit the website of the agency to get information.

Ebola/NIH Case

What suggestions do you have to improve the crisis management approach used?

What Best practices can you identify that other government agencies and companies should consider?

Put yourself in the role of the public affairs team, and recommend next steps for the NIH to improve its image and reputation in the community.

USDA "Pink Slime" Case

What is your assessment of how the "Pink Slime" crisis was managed?

What could have been done differently or better to improve the outcome?

What are the unique challenges a government public affairs office faces in a crisis, and how can these be offset?

SOCIAL RESPONSIBILITY CASE STUDY

CCPHA Serves Up the Bitter Truth About Sugary Drinks

There is substantial scientific evidence that sugar plays a major role in driving the country's rising diabetes rate. Further, sugary drinks—including soda, energy drinks, and sports drinks—are seen by experts as the largest contributors to the obesity epidemic. Public health advocates have begun focusing on promoting, establishing, and strengthening policies to reduce sugary drink consumption by American consumers.

In 2014 the California Center for Public Health Advocacy (CCPHA) sought to increase public understanding of these and create a favorable environment for legislative action to stem their use among residents.

Research and Strategy

Research provided independent, essential proof linking sugary drinks to health concerns. The research also became the vehicle for motivating the media, policy makers, and the public through a strategic public affairs program implemented by CCPHA and Brown-Miller Communications.

Primary research included a statewide poll to assess voter attitudes toward test messages and two new studies to determine sugary drink consumption rates and develop a reliable estimate of sugary drink-related diabetes cases in California.

Existing research on the health impacts of consumption was studied, and a media content analysis of influential California media was conducted to identify attitudes and editorial positions on the issue.

To meet its overall goal of advancing public understanding of the dangers of sugary drink consumption, the campaign's objectives sought to accomplish the following:

▸ Collaborate with key influencers, including ethnic health organizations, medical organizations, and politicians to disseminate campaign messages.

▸ Collect and disseminate research on the negative impacts of sugary drinks.

▸ Convene a panel of health experts to review research showing the negative health impact of sugary drinks.

▸ Introduce the nation's first warning label bill, and maintain constant media exposure on the issue. Educate editorial boards, and suggest they take a position on overconsumption of sugary drinks.

▸ Provide the media with fresh stories and new research reports to sustain coverage of the issue.

▸ Create a positive media environment for legislators to take a leadership role in educating and protecting consumers.

Execution

Major media stories were distributed, noting the high consumption rates of sugary drinks, the link to diabetes and obesity, and the high personal and public costs of these diseases. Poll results in California were promoted, showing public support for consumer protections and education on the subject. A press conference at the state capitol was held, pressing lawmakers to introduce legislation calling for soda warning labels. And media stories, op-eds, and editorials with legislators were shared on social media to create a positive environment for legislative action.

A statewide network of health advocates was also activated to echo the campaign messages with letters to the editor, public forums, and calls for legislation to limit the promotion, sale, and consumption of sugary drinks.

Evaluation

The campaign elevated understanding of the danger of sugary drinks and significantly increased public support for policies to educate and protect consumers.

Statewide media coverage was captured, with 95% of the stories echoing the campaign's key messages and research. The campaign won the support of 41 media outlets, including 27 editorials endorsing the soda warning label bill and another 14 outlets calling out the dangers of sugary drinks. Op-eds were successfully placed in 12 media outlets.

Legislation calling for the nation's first sugary drink warning label was introduced, and Berkeley, California, became the first city in the country to adopt a soda tax in 2014.

ENGAGE

▸ Search for research on the impact of sugary drinks on obesity and diabetes, and review the highlights (abstracts or executive summaries).

▸ Collect the highlights of the research, and assess the tone of the media coverage—positive, negative, or neutral—to get an overview of popular sentiment on the issue.

DISCUSS

▸ Based on your initial research, how would you approach the issue? Would you encourage citizens to voluntarily cut down on consuming the beverages, support a tax to make it more expensive to buy or drink them, or suggest warning labels (i.e., similar to alcohol and tobacco package warnings) on the bottles and cans?

▸ Anticipate how the soft drink industry might respond to your efforts to cut down on or make consumption of sugary drinks more expensive. What strategies might they pursue, and how would you recommend your client respond?

▸ How will you measure success: labels on containers, legislation passed to restrict sales, or declines in consumption?

Source: PRSA (n.d.a).

Note: This case involves a 2015 Silver Anvil Award Winner, Public Service, Nonprofit Organizations

SOCIAL RESPONSIBILITY CASE STUDY

The First Ladies Health Initiative: Walgreens Supports HIV/AIDS Screenings in Urban Churches

This CSR initiative funded primarily by Walgreens involves a partnership that includes more than 100 "first ladies"—pastors' wives working with health organizations and volunteers to improve the health of African Americans. The program began in Chicago (Walgreens's headquarters city) in 2008 with more than 200 pastors' wives and dozens of medical experts convening to learn why HIV/AIDS was disproportionately high among African Americans.

Research and Strategy

The HIV/AIDS epidemic is a particularly serious problem in Chicago and Los Angeles, which is why these were the pilot cities for this project. Since the discovery of the disease more than 30 years ago, more than 32,000 Chicagoans had been diagnosed with HIV infection and/or AIDS, according to the Chicago Department of Public Health. Of equal concern, it is estimated that at the time of the program's launch, more than 5,000 Chicagoans were HIV positive but not yet aware of their infection. The numbers in Los Angeles are also striking. According to the Los Angeles County Department of Public Health, African Americans accounted for 41% of all new HIV infections in LA.

The Centers for Disease Control and Prevention reported in 2010 that African Americans accounted for an estimated 44% of all new HIV infections among adults and adolescents, despite representing only 12% of the United States population. The AIDS case rate for African Americans was more than nine times that of Whites, and the HIV rate was seven times greater among Blacks than Whites.

Several years prior, Walgreens Corporation made a commitment to become more involved in the overall health of the African American community, particularly regarding the HIV/AIDS epidemic. The company and its local PR agency (the Danielle Ashley Group) recognized the important role churches play in the African American community, and it was decided to involve the wives of the head pastors.

Execution

The goals of the inaugural First Ladies Health Day were to furnish about a dozen Chicago churches with Walgreens pharmacists, medical supplies, and volunteer medical technicians from associated organizations to provide free health screenings on site at the churches all in one day. About 20 churches signed on that first year in Chicago. In 2013 the number had grown to more than 45 participating churches. When Walgreens expanded the initiative to Los Angeles in 2011, nearly 100,000 free health tests were performed during the six combined Chicago/Los Angeles health days.

Evaluation

Between 2008 and 2013 the Chicago and Los Angeles programs completed 96,500 screenings (see Table 15.2). This successful program was a natural fit, underlining Walgreen's commitment to healthcare, its hometown (Chicago) as well as an important segment of its national customer base —African Americans in major cities.

ENGAGE

- ▸ Visit Walgreens' website and read about its many CSR initiatives around the world.
- ▸ Research current statistics about the incidence of HIV/AIDS. Pay particular attention on how it impacts minorities.

TABLE 15.2

Statistical Information From Chicago and Los Angeles Health Days to Date, Provided by Medical Partners via Patient-by-Patient Surveys

	2008	2010	2011	2012	2013
Chicago Luncheon	75 First Ladies	200 First Ladies	225 First Ladies	220+ First Ladies	250+ First Ladies
Chicago Health Day	___	9,500+ Screenings	15,000+ Screenings	20,000+ Screenings	20,000+ Screenings
No. of Participating Churches on Health Day	___	35	40	42	46
Los Angeles Luncheon	___	___	100 First Ladies	125 First Ladies	185 First Ladies
Los Angeles Health Day	___	___	___	17,000+ Screenings	15,000+ Screenings
No. of Participating Churches on Health Day	___	___	___	30	37

Source: PRSA (n.d.a).

▸ Scan media coverage of CSR initiatives both for Walgreens and its major competitors (e.g., CVS, Rite Aid, etc.).

▸ Identify what themes or topics tend to get more coverage than others. Determine if having a nonprofit partner impacts success and coverage, and gather your data.

DISCUSS

▸ This case involves a program launched in 2008 and continuing to 2013. What would you recommend that Walgreens do going forward to sustain the momentum?

▸ Should they broaden the focus beyond HIV/AIDS to the other diseases identified as having a disproportionate impact on the African American community?

▸ Is there any potential for negative reaction to Walgreens getting involved in a controversial disease like HIV/AIDS? How might they have prepared for this possibility?

▸ Is there a risk of a program that is focused more on one ethnic group versus all in a city or area? Should they expand this to include free health screenings for everyone?

▸ How might Walgreens' competitors respond with similar SR ideas and programs? Does that matter to Walgreens?

Source: PRSA (n.d.a).

Note: This case involves 2014 Silver Anvil winners.

BP Oil Spill: Crisis Management, PR Misfires

On April 20, 2010, a BP Deepwater Horizon oil rig exploded, causing what has been called the worst environmental disaster in U.S. history. For 87 straight days, oil and methane gas spewed from an uncapped wellhead 1 mile below the surface of the ocean. The long duration of the event and the intense media coverage created multiple opportunities for both the company and our government to comment on the event.

The following two clips illustrate how BP executives and President Barack Obama responded to public opinion.

VIDEO

VIDEO

1. What strategies did BP and President Obama use in dealing with the Deepwater Horizon explosion and oil spill?

2. Evaluate the effectiveness of both responses. Do you think the CEO's response was informed by the company's crisis management strategy? Did BP's efforts to contain the story over the last few weeks affect President Obama's address?

3. Did either of these parties address the public's main concern? From this perspective, what else could have been done or said to improve this situation?

iStock.com/TommL

16 International Public Relations and Public Diplomacy

Learning Objectives

16.1   Understand the globalization of PR

16.2   Examine global PR and SR in different settings

16.3   Demonstrate how public diplomacy applies to communications, economic development, and SR

"Like a Girl"—Positive and Confident

Inside the Cincinnati headquarters of the global company Procter & Gamble, brand managers for the feminine hygiene category recognized that one of its top products, Always, was being challenged as the market leader. Always was still the global leader in the product category, but its biggest competitor was gaining, primarily by connecting with Millennial girls on social platforms like Facebook and Instagram.

Research reveals issues and steers strategy. Based on research that revealed most women experience a decline in self-confidence during puberty, the "Like a Girl" campaign was created to empower young girls. By linking the brand with a positive message about self-confidence, the goal was to provide an emotional connection with the target market. This connection would solidify the brand's market position and a "powerful, relevant and purposeful role in this empowerment" (PRSA, n.d.a).

Always' "Like a Girl" campaign was created to empower young girls and, in consumers' minds, link that empowerment to the brand.

iStock.com/diego_cervo

The company engaged its ad agency, Leo Burnett, and its PR firm, MSL, to work together on a new campaign communicating that "Like a Girl" was not an insult but a compliment and a source of pride. The goal was to demonstrate that the Always brand "understands the issues that young girls face."

To begin its work the agency conducted primary and secondary research to track the issues that impact girls' confidence before, during, and after puberty.

From the research it became clear:

▸ More than half of the girls surveyed experienced a decline in confidence at puberty.

▸ The lowest point was at the beginning of puberty and can last into adulthood.

▸ The majority (89%) of females ages 16 to 24 agreed that words impact self-confidence—in some cases for a lifetime.

Linking a product and social message. The agencies reviewed other global campaigns linking a product and a social message to determine the keys to a successful cause-related campaign. Several insights were identified:

▸ Clear articulation of the idea and proposed response was required.

▸ Authenticity is critical, especially for this demographic.

▸ Insights needed to be validated with data points.

▸ Celebrity influencers were important to create visibility.

With the campaign strategy set—i.e., making "Like a Girl" a positive message—the agencies set out to connect the Always brand to this critical moment in the lives of young women and build brand loyalty.

Your challenge. As you read through this chapter, imagine you are on the agency account team charged with creating this campaign. Key questions to consider include the following:

1. What media platforms would you leverage?

2. Which organizations or causes might you reach out to and engage?

3. How will you know if the campaign is working and reaching the target audience?

4. Which celebrities and influencers would you engage to support "Like a Girl"?

5. How can you engage or enlist males in supporting the campaign's message?

At the end of the chapter, you will learn how "Like a Girl" was built into a highly successful, global marketing communication campaign and why it has received multiple awards for creativity and impact since its launch.

In this chapter the focus shifts to another area of growth for the PR profession, global PR. Following a review of this dynamic field, you will explore the opportunities for communications professionals, particularly those who work in government or for NGOs. The area is called public diplomacy, and it focuses on how communications theory and PR practices are being applied to support nation branding and building so-called soft power (Nye, 1990) for countries around the world. We will also examine career paths and the integration of SR into global PR. This is an important discussion because all organizations, national or multinational, must be prepared to interact with global and local stakeholders in a process that researchers suggest "parallels the evolution of public relations as a profession, practice and field of study in every corner of the planet" (Bates, 2006). Through a discussion of current practices, research, and an exploration of the applicable theories and strategies, this chapter will provide guidance and suggestions to help you understand these trends and the career opportunities they represent.

AN OVERVIEW OF GLOBAL COMMUNICATIONS

>> LO 16.1   Understand the globalization of PR

The area of **global communications** is one of dynamic growth and challenge for the PR profession. The Institute of Public Relations (IPR) reported that there were approximately 2.3 to 4.5 million active PR professionals globally in 2006 (Muzi Falconi, 2006). This number has undoubtedly increased since then as the profession has grown in reach and influence across the globe considerably since this study was completed.

The shift to a global market place for communications raises key questions for PR professionals. Some of the more pressing ones include the following:

Master the content
edge.sagepub.com/page

▸ How do you go about communicating globally?

▸ What are the guidelines for success and the pitfalls to avoid?

▸ How do you gain experience in the field?

As **globalization** takes hold, the demand for skilled communicators with a worldview increases. Access to the Internet has spread fast across the globe, and thus the stakes and the opportunities for global communications have increased. By all accounts we are well past the point where any significant news or business or political development is exclusively "local" anymore (Sriramesh & Vercic, 2009).

What is meant by global PR or communications? The IPR defines it as "strategic communications and actions carried out by private, government or nonprofit organizations to build and maintain relationships in socioeconomic and political environments outside their home location" (Molleda, 2009). According to Wakefield (2007), global or international PR "boils down to where the entity is located and to which publics it must build relationships" (Molleda, 2009).

In unpacking these definitions and guidelines, you can see the inherent challenges. To be effective a global communicator must know the company's business and understand the needs and preferences of key stakeholders, for example, media, government, activists, and customers, in each of the markets where an organization operates. Further, you must develop an understanding of each market's unique dynamics and characteristics, both economic and social.

To do that some basic questions must be addressed (Culbertson, Jeffers, Stone, & Terrell, 2012):

▸ Is the media free and unrestricted, or is there government control or censorship?

▸ Is the media active or passive? Does that impact setting agendas and building brands?

With the rise of globalization, the potential reach of PR is now worldwide.

John Moore/Getty Images

▸ What is the political ideology represented by the government in power?

▸ What is the development stage and reach of broadband technology, and how do citizens access it (mobile, laptop, or desktop)?

▸ What are the rates of poverty and literacy, which impact who can purchase and comprehend news coverage and social media material?

▸ What is the history of activism and major social movements?

▸ What are the laws and regulations that govern advertising and PR practices?

As with any PR challenge, the key is to know the audience you want to reach. Once you have this information, you can develop new strategies, refine existing communications plans, and create your "story" with key messages to share locally in each market. This focus on local PR has always been a hallmark of PR as far back as its origins in the United States and in Western Europe (see Chapter 1). What has changed now is the need to engage on a global basis for most large companies and enterprises. With the advent of social media and the access it provides citizens and consumers to information, corporations, governments, and nonprofits do not have a choice about engaging in global communications.

"I wonder whether one should talk any longer about 'international public relations' or 'global public relations' as a specialty because even 'domestic' publics now are multinational and multicultural due to globalization. So, understanding the needs, expectations and values of a diverse set of publics is becoming more important even as it is growing more complex, requiring great skills and thereby becoming more and more strategic and less technical" (Sriramesh & Vercic, 2009, p. xxxv).

STORYTELLING AND GLOBAL PUBLIC RELATIONS

Tom Mattia has managed communications for four Fortune 500 companies, including Coca-Cola, as well as at Yale University. He's also worked in China for five years with two global PR firms. Mattia suggests that developing the corporate "story" is the key. That, along with understanding the local culture and market environment, is essential.

"The focus for international communications campaigns is to define and build the organization's narrative or story. Once the narrative has been constructed, one that reflects the DNA of the organization, PR practitioners can mold the narrative to the culture, climate and technical capabilities of the target audience," Mattia (personal communication, 2017) suggests. Now retired, Mattia is a senior lecturer at Rutgers University's School of Communications and Information (his alma mater).

"For example, I might use a different platform to tell the Mars candy story in China than I would to tell the Coca-Cola story in Spain, but in either case I would begin with the company's basic story. In North America, short, illustrated bursts via Instagram or Twitter can be effective in moving a narrative. In India and Asia, longer-form YouTube videos are very popular. In Europe, there is more opportunity for biting, satirical commentary. The key is never losing sight of the story being told or the market you are trying to impact."

Let's look more closely at the cultural adaptation required in China. If your company plans to enter or increase market share there, you need to have your corporate narrative set and adapt it to the way "stories" get told in China. To do that all parties should be aware that the media is government controlled and social media is monitored and censored.

Based on his experience, Mattia says several global companies he has worked with in China have managed this "storytelling" process quite well, including Starbucks, Mars, Audi, Samsung, and Apple. Mattia reports that Starbucks and Mars have treated China like a second home and worked hard to develop their own local management talent since entering the market. Now, a few years later, these managers can play major roles in the company's growth in China.

Elsewhere in Asia the challenge is different—reflecting less government control and a freer media. For example, Oh and Ramaprasad (2003) report that for companies seeking to build awareness and market share in the Republic of South Korea, the halo theory best explains the relationship between foreign multinational companies (MNC), key Korean stakeholders, and the public.

THE HALO EFFECT

The **halo effect** is a term used to explain the positive bias shown by customers toward certain products because of a favorable experience with other products made by the same manufacturer (Leuthesser, Kohli, & Harich, 1995). In this example the country of origin is the source of the "halo" that extends to products from that country. You will learn more about strategies to build or enhance the perception of the United States in our discussion of **public diplomacy** later in this chapter.

In Korea the research of Oh and Ramaprasad (2003) indicates that the perception of an MNC's home country (e.g., the United States) and its current relationship with

Though a company's story is important across markets, it must be tailored to be delivered in a way that appeals to the audience. Apple is still Apple in China, but the story must be told in a different, culturally appropriate way.

VCG/Getty Images

Korea "plays a relevant role in determining the public perception of the MNC with the host nation." Conversely, a South Korean company seeking to build brand equity in the U.S. market is often welcome in the United States due to the historically good relationship between the two countries. Companies like Samsung, Hyundai, and Kia have had success in building shares in the U.S. market. Korean-based airlines such as Korean Air and Asiana have done well also.

CRISIS CONSIDERATIONS

Asian companies and their communications styles need to adapt to U.S. market expectations for accountability and transparency, especially in a crisis, as we learned in the discussion of Samsung's Note 7 in Chapter 12. Another example of how cultural expectations impact a crisis occurred on July 6, 2013, when Asiana Airlines's Flight 214 crashed while attempting to land at the San Francisco International Airport. Out of 291 passengers, there were three fatalities and over 180 injured.

The crisis communication efforts that Asiana undertook following the crash were viewed as insufficient by most U.S. observers. Notable among these was the failure of the senior management of the company to be on site in San Francisco soon after the crash to personally address the concerns of the passengers and the public.

The company was also criticized for its slow response to the media and federal and local U.S. officials who were investigating the crash. Instead of senior management being on site immediately after the accident (as the "playbook" for crisis management suggests—see Chapter 12), senior management remained in Korea, issuing a series of sympathetic, and sometimes conflicting, statements. The task of managing the aftermath of the crash was left to locally based company officials. This created the unfortunate impression that senior management was not sufficiently engaged or responding appropriately to the tragedy.

The crash and the crisis management efforts of Asiana demonstrate the need for corporate communication professionals in MNCs to have cross-cultural competence and training to respond in the way that is expected in a host country.

Asiana Airlines Flight 214— International crises have driven home the need for cultural intelligence.

Justin Sullivan/Getty Images

Coca-Cola Creates Brand Loyalty Through Sustainability Efforts in India

Coca-Cola successfully re-entered the market in India after buying a local soft drink company and tailoring its message to the diversity of the local market.

Manoli Weber/ullstein bild/Getty Images

As one of the world's largest countries, India is a prized market for MNCs, especially in the consumer product space. Coca-Cola had been in India for many years when it was presented with a challenge that led the company to leave the market in 1977. The government passed legislation requiring all foreign companies doing business in India to disclose the ingredients in their products to be allowed to operate there. Since Coca-Cola was unwilling to disclose its secret formula, it decided to leave India to protect its business secrets. When the rule was eased years later, Coca-Cola sought to reenter the market, but its key competitor, Pepsi, had already entered the market in the 1980s through a joint venture with a local company.

Coca-Cola Goes Native

Coca-Cola's response was to acquire the leading soft drink company in India, maintain their native brands, and offer Coke as well. To regain market share, Coca-Cola customized its marketing communications to address the diversity of the Indian market with specially tailored messages.

Enter Corporate Social Responsibility

Recognizing the importance of CSR in creating brand loyalty in India, Coca-Cola revised and refocused its sustainability strategy as well. The company enhanced its existing CSR efforts to emphasize education, water conservation, and health—all areas that their research indicated were the greatest needs in India and where Coca-Cola had global experience and resources.

The Water Battle

The build-out of its CSR platform to support the different communities and regions of India became a valuable resource when the company faced a crisis in 2003. Coca-Cola and Pepsi were both subjected to a ban of sales in India following claims by a local activist group that their products were not safe to drink because of pesticides in the product, allegedly due to poor water purification processes. Coca-Cola overcame the ban and got its products reinstated after a prolonged battle with the activists and the provincial government where the opposition was centered. Coca-Cola proved their product was safe via independent scientific research. They also improved their water management and conservation technology in response to the concerns raised by the activists. These steps were effective in alleviating customer concerns.

Sharing Technology

Later, in another strategic move, Coca-Cola shared the technology it had developed to improve water management with local Indian companies. This enabled them to improve their manufacturing processes and reduce waste. This move further enhanced Coca-Cola's reputation in India as a leading company committed to sustainability and water management (Kaye, 2005). ●

CULTURAL INTELLIGENCE

The Asiana case pointedly illustrates the theory of **cultural intelligence**, which is defined as the ability to recognize and comprehend different beliefs, practices, attitudes, and behaviors of a group and then apply that cultural knowledge to attain your goals—whether those goals are political, business, or otherwise.

The case is valuable as a cautionary tale to global companies seeking to build cross-cultural acumen. Fundamentally this case demonstrates that global companies have to adapt to the cultural norms and expectations of the countries where they operate, especially in a crisis situation, if they are to be viewed as authentic (Gomez & Reed, n.d.).

Elsewhere around the world, the challenge is the same. PR professionals need to understand the market and the forces that drive behavior before seeking to impact in a new country or manage their company's reputation there. In India, scholars (e.g., Bardhan and Patwardhan, 2004) suggest that MNCs must overcome a history of resistance to entry by foreign businesses into the country. This can be accomplished by understanding the country's expectations for CSR and by developing an affiliation with a locally based company or enterprise to pave the way to market entry. The experience of Coca-Cola in India in the late 1990s and early 2000s illustrates these points quite well (see "Social Responsibility in Action: Coca-Cola Creates Brand Loyalty"). In South America, research suggests that MNCs will have a smoother road if they "stress the social role of the organization and ... emphasize an active but intelligent involvement in changing and improving societal conditions" (de Brooks & Waymer, 2009).

CEO ACTIVISM AND GLOBAL PUBLIC RELATIONS/ CORPORATE SOCIAL RESPONSIBILITY

Activism and taking public positions on political and social issues by CEOs and company leaders is a relatively new phenomenon, yet it is increasing, research indicates. The Edelman (2017) Trust Barometer reports that the world's population increasingly looks to business to lead because the other institutions they track— government, media, and the nonprofit community—have seen declines in their trust levels compared to prior years. In the area of SR, three out of four respondents agreed a company can take actions to both increase profits and improve economic and social conditions in the community where it operates.

"Business is the last retaining wall for trust," said Kathryn Beiser, global chair of Edelman's Corporate Practice (Edelman, 2017). The report suggests that trust is built through specific attributes: integrity, engagement, products and services, purpose, and operations. Of these sectors the agency's research indicates that integrity and engagement are tied as most important (see Figure 16.1). Integrity encompasses ethical business practices, issues management, and transparency. Engagement encompasses employee well-being, customer concern, and frequent communication (Edelman, 2017).

Aaron Chatterji, a professor at the Fuqua School of Business at Duke University, has studied the phenomenon of **CEO activism** and stakeholder expectations. He suggests in an interview with the *Washington Post* that social media has played a major role. "Silence used to be the default posture for CEOs," but social media has changed that significantly, he notes. "It's a choose-a-side mentality. The middle is harder to occupy. And, with the proliferation of social media, it's kind of like a microphone that is always on. If you're not speaking out it's more conspicuous" (McGregor, 2017).

SOCIAL RESPONSIBILITY The *Washington Post* article (McGregor, 2017) cited research by Chatterji and by Michael Toffel at Harvard Business School that found that CEO activism—especially as it relates to SR—can help shape public opinion on controversial social issues and increase interest in buying by consumers who favor the company's point of view.

FIGURE 16.1

Engagement and Integrity

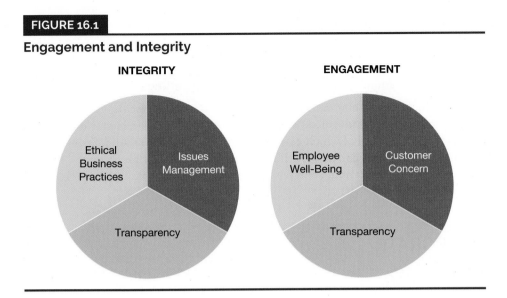

Clearly this is an area where communications professionals will be called upon in the future to advise their clients and senior management teams. Weber Shandwick, the global PR firm, has been actively researching CEO activism as well for the past few years.

WORKING INTERNATIONALLY TO DEVELOP GLOBAL PUBLIC RELATIONS SKILLS

For many communications professionals the chance to work internationally can be a significant opportunity for career development and learning. Many senior communications professionals working for (or advising) large, global companies have, at one point in their careers, taken advantage of the chance to learn how business and communications is conducted in different markets. Leading academic institutions are enhancing their communications and business curricula with international residencies to provide this learning opportunity as well. This is because international experience and training can broaden your horizons and prepare you to be a more effective strategic advisor for your clients and/or senior managers. From a career development perspective, a global posting or training is an attribute that companies and organizations look for in making middle or senior level promotions or hires.

Bill Heyman, principal of Heyman & Associates, an executive search firm, suggests: "International PR roles present a high degree of difficulty and show that a candidate can navigate different cultures, manage across distances and time zones—even overcome language barriers. It is a good indication that you are a well-rounded, intelligent person who isn't afraid of a challenge" B. Heyman (personal communication, 2017).

Richard Marshall, global managing director of corporate affairs for the executive search firm Korn Ferry, agrees adding, "International experience sets candidates apart and puts them in a better position to succeed, in our view" R. Marshall (personal communication, 2017).

GLOBAL PUBLIC RELATIONS IN DIFFERENT SETTINGS

>> **LO 16.2**   **Examine global PR and SR in different settings**

While there are many commonalities in working on a global scale, there are many differences as well. These include managing different languages, media formats, and cultural traditions—all of which can vary depending on the setting. Specifically a staff or consulting role can be very different in a corporate, nonprofit, or government global setting. Understanding and preparing for these will enhance your chances for success.

CORPORATE

As you will read in Michael Fanning's profile on the challenges of working internationally (on page 413), companies with operations across multiple countries and continents have numerous (and sometime simultaneous) communications challenges to manage and different styles of decision-making.

It might be a local event or issue, for example, getting permission to build a new plant or introducing new products and services. Or it may be a company-wide challenge that must be managed globally with a sensitivity to local customs and practice. It may also be a company transition, following an acquisition or major strategy shift, to be implemented in multiple countries simultaneously.

In 2002 when Ernst &Young LLP (E&Y) took over the assets of the Arthur Andersen accounting firm, following the shutdown of the Andersen firm's U.S. operations due to the Enron scandal, the E&Y communications team had to implement a global communications plan to support the acquisition in a little over a month. Fittingly, the global communications team and the firm were recognized by *PRWeek* for their work the following year.

Understanding the company's business, strategy, and the markets and countries where the organization operates is critical for success. Further, a working knowledge of which communications tactics work best where—for example, social media in one market, mainstream media in another—is needed. If it is a culture or strategy shift— you must also consider the employee communications aspects of the problem. A case involving IBM (see "Insights: Changing Perceptions of a Global Brand" on page 414) undertaking a global identity change serves as a good example.

NONPROFITS

Another sector where successful global campaigns are occurring is the nonprofit (NGO) segment. However, as with the global efforts discussed elsewhere in this chapter, PR professionals working for nonprofits need to understand and adapt to the unique aspects of each target market as well as understand the media mix—social and traditional—that serves it.

Further, nonprofit PR professionals must contend with fewer resources—staff, budget, and technology—than their corporate or agency counterparts have for their global campaigns.

A Manager's Journal: Working Internationally for a Global Corporation

Michael Fanning, President, Business Partnership Foundation, Darla Moore School of Business, University of South Carolina

I was fortunate to work in communications for several global companies during my career: IBM, The Reader's Digest Association, and finally Michelin beginning in 2000. After 10 years as vice president of corporate affairs at Michelin North America, headquartered in Greenville, South Carolina, I had an opportunity to move to the company's global headquarters in France.

Headquartered in Clermont-Ferrand, France, Michelin operates in more than 170 countries, has 112,300 employees, and operates 68 production plants in 17 different countries (Michelin, n.d.).

As Michelin Group's worldwide director of sustainable development from 2011 through 2015, I led the Michelin performance and responsibility process, which charted the company's response to global sustainability challenges. I was also the delegate from my company to the World Business Council for Sustainable Development, headquartered in Geneva.

While director of sustainable development for Michelin, I led the creation of Michelin's six sustainable development goals for the year 2020 and the company's receipt of the top ranking in its sector on the Dow-Jones Sustainability Index.

In considering a global posting, I loved the thought of cross-cultural assimilation, learning new skills, developing a second-language capability, exploring new countries, and making new international friends.

The experience did not disappoint. I came away with a few observations about the value of such a posting:

First it's easy while living in the United States to get lulled into thinking that our country is at the center of the world. Living abroad opens one up to a diverse way of thinking and different attitudes.

Next, decision-making in a global context can be frustrating for some Americans. At Michelin in France, for instance, meetings were not always designed as conduits for action; sometimes they were opportunities to let everyone make their point, and meetings often ended without clear direction. Decisions would eventually be made by our top executives after taking multiple viewpoints into account.

Finally the value of developing personal relationships to strengthen business relationships cannot be underestimated. The business lunches and invitations to Sunday meals with families and office celebrations—all these interactions—served to align the personal relationship with the business relationship.

Through this experience I discovered that the ability to transact business and be an effective strategic advisor was much improved after my time living and working in France. I developed personal relationships with my international colleagues and better understood the global marketplace through first-person work experience outside the United States. Take advantage of the opportunity if you get it; that's my advice! ●

Michael Fanning is a former global director of sustainability at Michelin Group.

Source: M. Fanning (personal communication, 2017).

Changing Perceptions of a Global Brand

The IBM "Building a Smarter Planet" initiative began in 2008 and was designed to solve two key challenges:

> First, IBM had changed its business focus from being a producer of technology equipment (e.g., typewriters) to services (consulting, data management, and analysis).

> Second, the company's brand and identity had changed to match its new strategy. However, the perception of the company remained stuck in the past.

The new strategic direction of the company was "making the world better in our day," with a focus on creating a "smarter planet." This overarching theme, which had marketing, PR, and CSR components, was to be achieved through implementing the new vision and focus on improving both business and society.

The transformation impacted the internal communications team structure at IBM as well: Marketing, communications and citizenship (CSR) were integrated into one new department. This restructuring ignited "compelling conversations associating the IBM brand with solving clients' toughest problems and positioning IBM as a thought leader in its target industries," said Jon Iwata, senior vice president of marketing, communications, and citizenship.

At the outset, the company set three overarching goals:

> Clarify the identity and brand of IBM to all its key stakeholders.

> Motivate IBM employees to become communications agents to represent the new brand identity.

> Drive a behavior change for the company, merging civic engagement, marketing, and traditional communications into a dominant message to be delivered consistently by employees to customers and stakeholders.

The campaign exceeded the company's expectations by its completion. It spanned more than 170 countries and included input from more than 150,000 IBM employees. It was well received by the market and clients, producing double-digit growth in new and existing client assignments and yielding dramatic revenue growth for the company. Finally it redefined the company—both to employees internally and externally to clients and prospects—as a firm well positioned for business success and focused on meeting its obligations to its key stakeholders.

"The 'Smarter Planet' initiative proved that a major global corporation could credibly pursue an authentic, positive message of hope and progress even in a cynical world," Iwata noted. ●

Source: Stacks, Wright, and Bowen (2014).

This is against a backdrop of declining support, both financial and personal, of nonprofits globally by the public, according to recent research on the topic. The 2017 research showed that **nongovernmental organizations (NGOs)** are increasingly viewed as focused on serving the most vulnerable people and are therefore ineffective advocates for the global middle class (Edelman, 2017). Thus the middle class, often a key source of financial support for these charities, is becoming less generous.

This new reality places a heavier emphasis for the NGO to be creative and resourceful to tie into a trend or a cause that has impact and generates support and enthusiasm among the target audience—not an easy task in a crowded digital world.

The "Ice Bucket Challenge," which started locally and grew globally via social media, is a great example of what works well in the current environment. The "Ice Bucket Challenge" began quietly during the summer of 2014, and its subsequent explosive growth was driven by media interest, celebrity participation, social media posts, shares, and re-tweets. According to the *Boston Globe* (August 14, 2014), Facebook reported 1.2 million videos were posted about the "Ice Bucket Challenge"

The Ice Bucket Challenge, which was started by two Boston College athletes to raise money for a former teammate, raised $115 million in eight weeks.

John Blanding/The Boston Globe/Getty Images

and more than 15 million people commented or "liked" the videos in less than two months. It became a true overnight sensation (Cloutier, 2014).

The campaign started out as a dare between two Boston College athletes to raise money for their former teammate (Pete Frates) and took off globally almost overnight. The challenge raised $115 million in eight weeks and generated unprecedented levels of awareness for the disease and the need for a cure (see Figure 16.2).

As the campaign grew the ALS Foundation became the source for information and updates about the disease. The ALS Foundation received support from the government and private sources and a huge increase in donations and awareness. "We have never seen anything like this in the history of the disease," Barbara Newhouse, president and CEO of the ALS Association, said in a statement (ALS Association, 2014).

Not every global campaign for a charity—or any organization—will have the spontaneous, worldwide success of the "Ice Bucket Challenge," although many hope for that when they launch a new awareness and fund-raising effort. Avinash Murthy (personal communication, August 2014), suggests four key takeaways from this campaign:

▸ **Relate the campaign.** Link it to a cause people can commit to, in this case a debilitating disease impacting all ages.

▸ **Keep it simple.** The "Ice Bucket Challenge" only required a mobile device and a social media account to participate (along with a willing participant and a donation).

▸ **Make it fun.** The "challenge" was entertaining, visual, timely (e.g., summertime), and easy to share, post, or tweet.

▸ **Celebrity endorsers (influential) are key**. In this case, they were critical to increase views and generate interest in the cause and activity.

FIGURE 16.2

ALS Ice Bucket Challenge

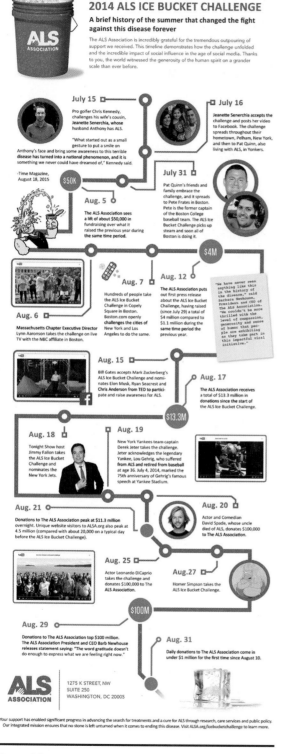

Source: ALS Association.

Since the campaign ended, the foundation has worked to extend awareness and fund-raising and developed a new slogan—"Every Drop Counts." They have garnered extensive media coverage, raised more money, and made progress in treating this devastating disease. And they have continued to communicate their progress to sustain the interest and support. The "Ice Bucket Challenge" may have been a spontaneous, organic campaign, but the ALS Foundation leveraged it to build awareness of its work worldwide.

GOVERNMENT

SR initiatives launched by national and local governments is a recent trend that many experts see as one that will grow in the future. The ability of government officials and agencies to implement specific SR efforts beyond their own agency or government offices is limited because they are public and not private enterprises. However, in the United States and other major countries, elected and appointed government officials are implementing sustainable business practices such as LEED-certified buildings, agency-wide recycling, and improved resource and power management. In addition the public sector is developing outreach programs to assist and support their employees and communities in areas where they have large government complexes or military bases.

The *Sustainability Measures* newsletter (Hartford, CT) published a list in 2010 of government-sponsored sustainability initiatives, and it is quite impressive. The projects listed a range of activities involving small groups of volunteers, city and county agencies, large partnerships of nonprofits, businesses, and government agencies themselves. The projects range in scale from local neighborhoods and individual towns and cities to metropolitan regions and even multinational efforts.

Providing communications support for these programs inevitably becomes the responsibility of the government public affairs and public information offices you read about in Chapter 15. By all accounts, this activity is expected to increase for many of the same reasons it grew to prominence in the private sector. Sustainable business initiatives save taxpayer money, support the community, and motivate employees in government roles—just as they do in the private sector. In addition, given the increased expectation on business and nonprofits to initiate new and support existing SR efforts worldwide (Edelman, 2017), governments have a role to play here as well.

Governments worldwide have a role to play in fostering and assisting companies to succeed in their SR activity, suggests Jane Nelson (2008), a senior fellow and director of the CSR Initiative at the John F. Kennedy School of Government at Harvard. This is particularly true in areas when the host country or region lacks the infrastructure or political will to solve their most pressing problems alone.

"The ability to identify and prioritize those public goods and issues, and then determine the best strategies for addressing them...will be an increasingly important mark of good business (CSR) leadership in the years ahead," Nelson suggests. The role of the government, both in the host country and the home country, is to lend support where possible and recognize and encourage the efforts by companies to help overcome these issues.

PUBLIC DIPLOMACY, STRATEGIC PUBLIC RELATIONS, AND SOCIAL RESPONSIBILITY

>> LO 16.3 Demonstrate how public diplomacy applies to communications, economic development, and SR

An excellent example of government supporting and recognizing SR by companies is the U.S. Secretary of State's Awards for Corporate Excellence (ACE), which was launched in 1999. Secretary of State Madeline Albright launched the ACE awards to recognize "the important role U.S. businesses play abroad as good corporate citizens" (U.S. Department of State, n.d.). The award sends a strong signal of the State Department's commitment to further CSR, innovation, exemplary practices, and democratic values worldwide.

The ACE awards are presented to U.S.-based companies in two categories—multinational and small-to-medium enterprises. The award recognizes good works undertaken by these businesses in six categories:

1. Environmental Stewardship and Sustainability

2. Education and Entrepreneurship

3. Advocacy of Human and Workers' Rights

4. Engagement in Humanitarian and Health-Care Assistance

5. Job Growth and Economic Development

6. Technology

Companies as large and well-known as Procter & Gamble, Intel, and Coca-Cola have been recognized in the MNC category. Smaller companies such as Taylor Guitars, Salman Seafood, and Denimatrix have received awards in the small-to-medium category. A full list of the winners of the ACE awards can be found at http://www.state.gov/e/eb/ace/.

Research on the characteristics and impact of these companies has suggested a link between the SR activities of these enterprises and the image and reputation of the United States in the host countries. Page and Parnell (2016) have proposed that through this program, U.S. firms function as third-party mediators for U.S. public diplomacy efforts through their global CSR. Commenting on this connection in

Creating Business Opportunities Through Sustainability

Community outreach was key in Barrick Gold Corporation's efforts to secure rights to a new gold mine in Peru.

Sebastian Castañeda/Anadolu Agency/Getty Images

Barrick Gold Corporation, one of the largest gold-mining companies in the world, has had success in South America and elsewhere since its global expansion began in 2001, with the acquisition of San Francisco-based Homestake Mining. Through this transaction, the company inherited mining operations in several new continents, well beyond its traditional base in North America.

In the early 2000s, Barrick was seeking a license to build a second mine in Peru following the success of its Pierina mine in southern Peru. The company designed a clever strategy to leverage its community involvement in one market in Peru to boost its chances of getting the mining rights in another.

Competitive Strategy

At the same time, other gold-mining companies were competing for the rights to the proposed new mine,

and the provincial government was closely considering each one. Aware of the importance of a track record of community involvement in the decision, Barrick leveraged its CSR accomplishments in Pierina to indicate what the government and community could expect in Alto Chicama (the site of the proposed new mine) if they were given the rights.

Community Focus

The company launched an effort to bring local officials and community leaders from the Alto Chicama district to meet with local leaders in Pierina to hear firsthand about Barrick's record as a corporate citizen there. Later in the day these officials were brought to the company's offices for a presentation on the company's plans for the project.

Mining Rights Awarded

The combination of an informal "meet and greet" with the community and a formal briefing to demonstrate the company's expertise won the day. Barrick was awarded the mining rights in 2003 and began working right away. The first gold pour, using gold mined at the new site, was in 2005. True to its word, Barrick has been a good neighbor and member of the community in the Alto Chicama district and enjoys a good relationship in the area still.

Commenting on his company's approach to global communications and SR, Barrick's President Kelvin Dushnisky (personal communication, 2017) said: "Our goal is to be a welcome and trusted partner of our host governments and communities, the most sought-after employer, and the natural choice for long-term investors. Sustainability and community relations, therefore, are woven into everything we do around the world, from exploration to mine closure. It is who we are." ●

2012, former Secretary of State Hillary Rodham Clinton stated, "The core tenets of corporate social responsibility complement both our diplomatic and development efforts" (U.S. Department of State, n.d.), "[F]or many people around the world, the most direct contact they will ever have with the United States is through American businesses.... That's how they learn what we stand for and who we are and what aspirations we share."

These initiatives require the active support and involvement of both the PR and SR teams at these companies to raise awareness and stimulate the participation needed to make the local programs work to maximum effect. The PR practices used vary due to type of CSR initiative, size and organization of the company, and in-country situations. Yet through their corporation-to-government and corporation-to-citizen good deeds, select U.S. firms fulfill the function of public diplomacy, both relational and mediated, in their global CSR.

PUBLIC DIPLOMACY AND PUBLIC RELATIONS

The practice of public diplomacy is when governments communicate and build relationships with foreign publics to achieve political objectives (Fitzpatrick, Fullerton, & Kendrick, 2013). Practitioners in public diplomacy may be called public affairs officers (PAOs) or public information officers (PIOs) and are usually government employees. Practicing public diplomacy involves mediated communication, image building, and soft power, a concept developed by Joseph Nye (1990) that highlights a two-way relational approach versus coercion or payment.

Public diplomacy can now be considered a specialization in PR. Due to the tragic events of 9/11, it was recognized by government agencies for its emphasis on dialogue and relationship building. It was abundantly clear that the United States needed to more effectively engage with foreign publics, connect with them, exchange ideas and cultures, and foster two-way, horizontal communication. Refocused communications sought to remove or offset misperceptions of the United States and to enhance trade and understanding between the United States and the developing world.

The public diplomacy shift from a persuasion strategy to an engagement strategy involves the following:

▶ **Focus on mediated communication.** Work with the global news media to emphasize shared core values and framing content to improve public opinion and ideally influence key members of a foreign audience.

▶ **Focus on branding efforts for country image and reputation.** Once conducted and received successfully, nation-branding campaigns (e.g., tourism promotion, communicating shared values, promotion of technology and innovation, etc.) may provide a strong foundation for better relations (Golan, Yang, & Kinsey, 2015).

▶ **Focus on a relational soft power approach.** Soft power is built through educational programs, cultural exchanges, language training, and development tools and also through how a country "lives" its political values and its legitimately held and morally driven foreign policies. PR knowledge and skills are regarded as "most important" and "most effective" for public diplomacy, according to a study of former officers in the U.S. Information Agency (Golan, 2013, p. 1251). The similarities between PR and PD are these:

  ○ Interactive approaches that involve engagement with publics

  ○ Rejection of propaganda use and disinformation

  ○ Efforts to influence political opinion formation or policy-making processes

  ○ The need for understanding and command of global media

As current and future communications professionals, it is up to you to apply your strategic skills to encourage corporate and nonprofit participation in SR globally and thereby in public diplomacy. Properly, this work can make a major difference in the world and improve a company's reputation at the same time—a true win-win situation.

How Is International Public Opinion Shaped?

We tend to think of a superpower as a very strong nation like the United States or the former USSR during the Cold War, but one international strategist believes that global public opinion—what the world *thinks* about your country—is the only remaining super power (Anholt, 2014). International public opinion is very important to governments, businesses, and citizens as it influences national security, the economy, and cultural opportunities for citizens.

Fullerton and Kendrick (2017, p. 1) developed the Model of Country Concept (see Figure 16.3) to describe how international public opinion is shaped, and it has been used to illustrate recent developments in relationships between the United States and other countries.

▸ According to the model, Country Concept is a product of both a country's reputation (long-term) and image (more recent or top of mind) among global citizens.

▸ Government representatives, corporate managers, hospitality executives, tourism agents, or arts and entertainment managers or performers can impact a country's concept by influencing certain components in the model.

▸ These individuals typically have little to no control over the components that appear on the outer ring of the model, such as international politics, natural and man-made disasters (including war), historical relationships among countries, and foreign media.

▸ They are more likely, however, to impact diplomatic and nation-branding components in the upper half of the inner ring, including public diplomacy, citizen diplomacy, exported products both manufactured and cultural, investment, tourism marketing and advertising, and news coverage.

FIGURE 16.3

Model of the Country Concept

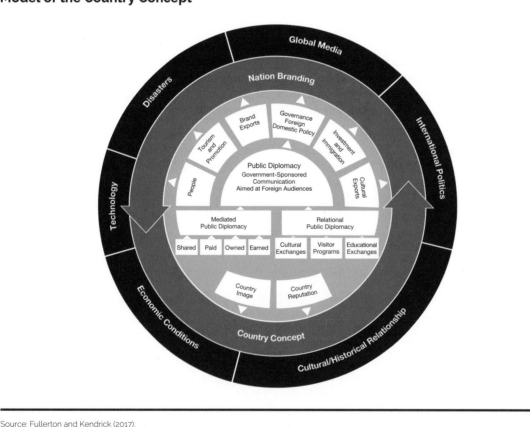

Source: Fullerton and Kendrick (2017).

> ▸ As the arrows indicate, when country concept changes, nation-branding activities could be adjusted as well, representing a dynamic relationship among components and outcomes.

Illustrating the model. Cuba has been a "forbidden" destination for U.S. citizens for more than 50 years. Fullerton, Kendrick, and Broyles (2016) conducted surveys among U.S. adults before and after the December 2014 announcement about improved U.S.-Cuba relations.

After the announcement (widely covered on national and international media), U.S. citizens' concepts of Cuba improved significantly. Respondents knew more about Cuba, were more favorable toward the Cuban people and government, and had a better impression of Cuban leadership and culture. This improved country concept portended economic benefits for Cuba through future tourism and trade with the United States under the Obama administration. ●

SCENARIO OUTCOME

Because Always is a global brand, Procter & Gamble set out to develop a global campaign and connect the brand's identity to young women worldwide. The messaging of "Like a Girl" had to resonate across national and cultural boundaries in the United States and adapt to different segments of the global target market. By the end of the initial launch phase, the campaign had been expanded to 20 major markets worldwide.

Independent research has shown that the "Like a Girl" campaign has positively impacted the self-confidence of young women worldwide—76% of girls today have a positive association with the formerly insulting phrase "like a girl," versus only 19% at the start. The campaign has opened the eyes of many others to the damage that bullying and insults can do to a young person's confidence and success later in life.

Which organizations or causes might you reach out to and engage?

The strategy was to take an insult and make it a rallying cry—changing "like a girl" into a phrase that empowered and inspired young women. The centerpiece of the launch campaign was a short video directed by an award-winning documentary filmmaker. It showed how people (especially young women) had interpreted the phrase "like a girl" historically to mean weakness or vanity and revealed the impact this was having on young women worldwide.

The film then revealed how the phrase could be made into a positive statement, that young girls should be proud of doing things "like a girl," and showcased the achievements of young girls worldwide.

What media platforms would you leverage?

The video was launched through an exclusive with *Advertising Age* (a major trade paper covering marketing and advertising), and soon after, it was previewed on the Always YouTube site. Copies of the video were made available to key influencers and prominent bloggers, asking them to share it on their sites. This had the effect of generating WOM awareness and global visibility for the video and the campaign. Soon after the hashtag #LikeAGirl and video went viral across the Internet.

In addition to the social media initiatives, the agency reached out to the online and traditional media to generate coverage about #LikeAGirl and female empowerment. This widespread coverage added to the excitement and buzz about the campaign and stimulated extensive online conversations.

Which celebrities and influencers would you engage to support "Like a Girl"?

To extend the launch's impact, the Always account team reached out to celebrities to post and tweet about the campaign. The effort started with Vanessa Hudgens and Bella Thorne, but soon many other well-known female celebrities and opinion leaders joined in. Sarah Silverman, Tyler Oakley, Maria Shriver, Cher, Kristen Bell, Chelsea Clinton, and Melinda Gates all participated with tweets and posts on Facebook and Instagram.

Finally the agency and its client created a 24-hour, real-time news desk that monitored the conversations online and engaged where appropriate to further amplify the #LikeAGirl campaign.

What began as a social experiment and campaign to bolster the self-image of young girls blossomed into a global movement that changed the conversation online, in the media, and impacted young women all over the world.

How will you know if the campaign is working and reaching the target audience?

The program goals were quickly achieved. Postlaunch research showed that it had succeeded beyond the team's hopes or expectations:

▸ 81% of women 16 to 24 surveyed supported Always for creating a movement to reclaim "like a girl" as a positive and inspiring statement.

▸ The "Like a Girl" launch video was viewed 76 million times on YouTube in more than 150 countries (90% from the United States and the 20 target countries) during the target time period.

▸ The program earned almost 2,000 media placements around the world on network morning news shows, broadcast networks, print media, and online.

▸ The program created 290 million social media impressions and 133,000 mentions on Twitter, Facebook, and other major platforms.

By the end of the initial launch period, "Like a Girl" had become a worldwide phenomenon and was a core part of the Always brand message.

How can you engage or enlist males in supporting the campaign's message?

At this point it was decided that the campaign would participate in Super Bowl XLIX (49) in February 2015, with a commercial that asked boys, women, and men to join the #LikeAGirl movement. The new campaign featured a teenage girl who played quarterback on her local tackle football team. It led to 19 onsite interviews at the Super Bowl and four more videos being produced. The Always campaign was a major story in the post-Super Bowl news cycle with more than 1,600 media placements, and it trended nationally on Twitter and Facebook. In turn, these placements, tweets, and posts were echoed online by influential leaders, celebrities, activists, and bloggers—extending the impact of the campaign.

Source: PRSA (n.d.a).

Note: This case involves a 2015 PRSA Silver Anvil Award-winning entry.

WRAP UP

In this chapter you learned about *global public relations*, which was defined as the strategic communications of organizations in social and political environments outside their home location (Molleda, 2009). You also learned about the concept of *cultural intelligence*, that is, understanding the behavior expected of foreign companies by local stakeholders in global markets. Note: this may be different than the expectations for corporate conduct in your home market.

Later you were introduced to a new concept in international communications—*public diplomacy*—which has a lot in common with sustainability and marketing communications. But it is concerned more with the reputation of countries than companies. The goal is to generate a halo effect for other U.S.-based businesses and improve the perception of the United States as a diplomatic and business partner. These fields represent great opportunities for expanding and building your career in PR.

KEY TERMS

CEO Activism: CEOs and company leaders taking public positions on political and social issues on a local, national, or global basis, **410**

Cultural Intelligence: The need for company leaders to recognize and comprehend different beliefs, practices, attitudes, and behaviors of a group or market area and then apply that cultural knowledge to attain goals, **409**

Global Communications: Strategic communications and actions carried out by private, government, or nonprofit organizations to build and maintain relationships in social and political environments *outside* their home location (Molleda, 2009), **404**

Globalization: The worldwide movement toward economic, financial, trade, and communications integration, **405**

Halo Effect: The positive bias shown by customers toward certain products because of a favorable experience with other products made by the same manufacturer (Leuthesser, Kohli, & Harich, 1995), **407**

Nongovernmental Organizations (NGOs): Private sector and voluntary (and usually nonprofit) organizations that contribute to, or participate in, projects, education, training or other humanitarian, progressive, or watchdog activities, **414**

Public Diplomacy: A process wherein governments communicate and build relationships with foreign publics to achieve their political and diplomatic objectives, **407**

THINK ABOUT IT

As a group activity look up the ACE awards on the State Department website (http://www.state.gov/e/eb/ace/), and pick one example of each of the two categories (multinational and small to medium) of winners that are of interest to you and your fellow students.

Summarize the two examples, and then propose some next steps for the company to take to expand the program, gain recognition in the United States for its global SR efforts, or launch new, similar activities elsewhere in the operation. Present your findings and views to your classmates.

In addition to visiting the ACE awards site, you should review the individual company websites, SR reports, and any SR news coverage they have received to get a full picture of what they are already doing as part of their outreach efforts.

WRITE LIKE A PRO

On your own, watch the short video *Public Diplomacy & the Role of a Public Affairs Officer (PAO)* from the USC Center on Public Diplomacy (https://www.youtube.com/watch?v=3DFtBAcF60Y). It illustrates the critical importance of soft power in public diplomacy. Consider how it might apply as a PR specialty or career internationally.

Prepare a short essay (250 words) on how the U.S. government should or could proceed in promoting the U.S. reputation in developing countries around the world using SR as the focus.

Questions to consider include the following:

▸ How does the change in the U.S. administration from Obama to Trump impact this activity?

▸ What role does SR and community development by U.S.-based companies play in building America's reputation in the world?

▸ What PR strategy and tactics lend themselves to supporting this activity?

▸ Are there countries or topic areas that companies should avoid?

▸ Is this a career path that might interest you?

SOCIAL RESPONSIBILITY CASE STUDY

Dell Women's Entrepreneurial Network Creates Opportunities for Women

Dell has a long history of SR since its founding in 1984. As the company grew and developed into an international corporation with operations in more than 50 countries and employing more than 110,000 people worldwide in 2013, it has made major commitments to SR throughout its operations. One major goal was to expand opportunities for women entrepreneurs.

Research and Strategy

To define how Dell could make a significant impact with women entrepreneurs, the company conducted qualitative and quantitative research. Dell assembled an advisory board of entrepreneurs, including leading technologists and global ambassadors for entrepreneurship. This group identified several areas for Dell to focus on to accelerate growth for women entrepreneurs: enhanced access to networks, new markets, capital, and technology.

To drive the conversation the team partnered with the Global Entrepreneurship Development Institute (GEDI) to commission creation of the GEDI Index, a unique tool to measure the rate of female entrepreneurship across 30 developed and developing economies spanning multiple global regions. The goal of the research was to develop the information to be communicated to academics, business leaders, and government policy makers to create more favorable conditions for women entrepreneurs to thrive. In addition, both the qualitative and quantitative research was used to develop a multifaceted, global communications plan.

The program's strategy was to develop personal connections and ongoing dialogues with global women entrepreneurs, influencers, and policy makers, showcasing that Dell is more than an information technology vendor but a trusted business advisor and partner advocating for the success of women entrepreneurs and the jobs they create globally.

Dell was to be positioned as a trusted advisor and advocate for women entrepreneurs, and a global network of women entrepreneurs was to be created to serve as Dell's brand evangelists in media coverage, at events, online, and in sales. In addition, global economic stability was to be promoted by supporting women, innovation, and job creation.

Execution

The Dell Women's Entrepreneurial Network (DWEN) program was launched by the company in 2010. By spotlighting entrepreneurial success and creating a supportive atmosphere for women entrepreneurs, DWEN helped a group of new businesswomen share best practices, build opportunities, explore international expansion, and access the resources—like capital and technology—that support economic growth and job creation. Networking events were sponsored to bring entrepreneurs and potential funding sources together.

An annual global conference of female business founders, CEOs, and other leaders was created to discuss business issues, networking, and technology. More than 200 women leaders representing 15 countries attended. In addition, 40 reporters representing 75 publications and 12 countries covered the conference.

Traditional and social media outreach resulted in 224 articles in key media and 6,522 tweets, reaching 50,000 visitors. This resulted in building an active online community to help company start-ups meet peers and mentors. And an e-book was commissioned and promoted, profiling 10 women entrepreneurs who overcame major challenges identified to be successful.

The company also partnered with the UN Foundation to promote entrepreneurship and job creation globally. This connection led to the appointment of Dell CEO (Michael Dell) as the UN Foundation's global advocate for entrepreneurship.

Evaluation

The success of this program led to hundreds of women of all ages and backgrounds launching companies all over the world. Further, it created business opportunities and jobs for related companies and individuals and connected Dell to the growing market of women entrepreneurs. In that sense it was an ideal recipient of the PRSA Silver Anvil award that year as it connected an SR program to a business opportunity for Dell and enhanced the company's reputation and business at the same time.

ENGAGE

Gather into small groups for an activity to examine this case in the context of Dell's overall CSR efforts and to get a sense of the scope of the problem/opportunity this initiative was designed to address, that is, empowering women globally to start and sustain small businesses.

> ▸ Visit the Dell Social Responsibility page (http://www.dell.com/learn/us/en/uscorp1/cr), and learn more about the company's activities in this area. You will note that they have set areas of interest and priority for their outreach effort.

> ▸ Conduct some brief research on the issues facing women in the United States and elsewhere to start and maintain a small business.

DISCUSS

> ▸ Review and discuss your findings within the group. Prepare a series of two or three recommendations to evaluate the program's success (why did it work?) and to make two or three specific recommendations that would improve the program going forward to bring more positive recognition to the company.

Source: PRSA (n.d.).

SOCIAL RESPONSIBILITY CASE STUDY

"Blue Corridor" Natural Gas Vehicle Rally

Natural gas vehicles (NGVs) can reduce greenhouse gas emissions 20% to 30% compared to petrol and diesel while costing at least 30% less than conventional fuels. So it's no surprise that demand for NGVs has grown rapidly, especially in Europe, where traditional fuel (e.g., gasoline) is expensive. However, until 2008, relatively few NGVs were on the road in Europe.

Some experts believe it's the limited number of natural gas fueling stations in Europe that have discouraged potential NGV producers and buyers. The small number of NGVs on the road, in turn, has discouraged energy companies from constructing more fueling stations. Breaking this cycle was essential to expanding NGV use.

Research and Strategy

This was the idea behind the annual "Blue Corridor" NGV Rally, created by Gazprom, the world's largest natural gas producer. With its PR team, Gazprom put together a strategic communications plan, with an environmental sustainability theme, to deliver its key messages to the energy and natural gas industry, transportation partners, and governmental policy makers, as well as potential NGV consumers, in multiple countries across Europe.

The plan, once implemented, would deliver the "Blue Corridor" campaign messages to thousands of stakeholders worldwide and led to greater NGV use across the critical European markets for Gazprom. The primary objectives were to raise awareness of what "Blue Corridor" supporters were doing to encourage the use of natural gas in transport and ultimately increase use of NGVs.

The separate communications objectives were to attract target audiences to "Blue Corridor" events and to increase coverage in target media globally and the local target markets: Russia, Finland, Sweden, Denmark, Germany, Poland, Lithuania, Latvia, and Estonia.

In addition key audiences globally would be reached through "Blue Corridor's" social media properties.

Execution

Each year starting in 2008, a caravan of NGVs drive across Europe in an auto rally event to demonstrate the benefits and ease of traveling by NGVs. Gazprom worked with communications advisers from Europe (g+ Europe) and the United States (Ketchum), expanding staff on the ground and remotely to promote the rally 24/7. This was crucial to faster turnaround times on stories, roundtables, interviews, and more as well as frequent, live updates on social media. The group ran a comprehensive media outreach campaign, creating media opportunities for company executives to discuss its vision for the NGV market and responding to journalists' requests.

Evaluation

As a result of their efforts, use of NGV filling stations grew 40% in Europe and 110% worldwide. The 2013 "Blue Corridor" NGV Rally was the most successful in the event's five-year history. "Blue Corridor's" messages reached hundreds of key stakeholders directly via on-the-ground events and millions more via media coverage and online views.

Media coverage of the rally spanned 17 countries. The outcome included three interviews with Gazprom executives, nine background articles on the rally and Gazprom's activities in the NGV market, an op-ed from the CEO of Gazprom Export placed in 19 outlets, and nine press releases on the rally picked up in 71 articles. Governments and regulators around the world took notice and specific action to encourage the use and support of NGVs for personal and business transportation.

ENGAGE

▸ After reading the case and visiting the Gazprom website, gather into small groups and brainstorm to determine the key steps and tactics that led to the campaign being so successful.

▸ Was it the on-the-ground teams traveling with the rally and promoting it or the expanded social media presence to extend the delivery of the company's key messages about NGV use?

▸ What role did the direct and indirect outreach to government officials and other stakeholders play in the impact the campaign had on increasing the number of NGV filling stations?

DISCUSS

▸ Prepare your answers to these questions, and develop a consensus to share with the class.

▸ On an individual basis give some thought to what you would recommend to the company to extend and improve the impact of the "Blue Corridor" rally.

▸ Would you recommend duplicating it in other major markets for NGVs? How about the United States? Would this idea work here?

VIDEO CASE

Olympic Games: Public Diplomacy

After several failed attempts, Los Angeles was awarded the 2028 Summer Olympic Games by the IOC. The mayor and others involved in the bid held a press conference to announce the news and begin the process of promoting the city and the Games, which will draw athletes from around 200 countries.

VIDEO

1. Discuss the ways the Olympic Games can serve as a vehicle for public diplomacy.

2. What would be your strategy in advancing the U.S.'s message through the Games?

3. What challenges do you anticipate in this mission?

GLOSSARY

Absolutism: A deontological theory (also called nonconsequentialism) that emphasizes duties or rules; what's morally right applies to everyone

Acquisitions: A corporate action in which a company buys most, if not all, of another firm's ownership stakes to assume control of it

Active Publics: PR term for people who do something about their beliefs, problems, or opportunities

Advertising Value Equivalency (AVE): A practice, now largely discredited and abandoned, whereby the impact or value of an article in a publication or a news segment is measured by the relative cost of purchasing that same amount of space or airtime

Agenda-Setting Theory: Explains that media have a large influence on audiences by choosing which stories to make prominent

App: Short for application—software designed to run on a smartphone or other mobile devices

Appropriation: Involves using some aspect of a person's identity that causes mental or physical distress

Assessment or Evaluation Phase: The element in a strategic plan (usually at the end) that allows you to measure progress toward the stated goals and objectives

Aware Publics: PR term for people who recognize a problem or opportunity

B Corporation: A certification awarded by B Lab, earned by a company's rigorous adherence to SR and sustainability

Backgrounder: A written document, usually part of a media kit, that provides additional information on an organization and its situation to help a media worker craft a story

Benefit Corporation: A legal status that establishes a corporation must have a material positive benefit on society and the environment

Benoit's Image Restoration Theory: Explains how to evaluate, or recommend, a response to a harmful situation

Blogger: An individual who writes and posts his or her thoughts about news, issues, or trends on a blog that is then shared, liked, or re-posted by others on social media

Boilerplate: A paragraph appearing at the bottom of a news release, summarizing information about the sending organization

Business Ethics: A process or theory in which companies are expected to conduct their business in an open and honest and way to gain market acceptance and build a solid reputation

Business-to-Business (B-to-B): Communications efforts focused on a business audience or customer

Business-to-Consumer (B-to-C): Traditional PR focused on promoting a product or service to consumers

Business-to-Government Communications (B-to-G): Outreach designed to support the purchase of goods and services by government agencies

Cause Promotions: When an organization provides or donates money to support or increase awareness and concern for a cause or charity

Cause-Related Marketing: Contributions to a cause or charity based on a percentage of sales revenues

CEO Activism: CEOs and company leaders taking public positions on political and social issues on a local, national or global basis

Channel: The medium of communication, such as television, radio, e-mail, and so on

Chatbots: Computer programs designed to answer questions that mimic conversation with people using artificial intelligence

Chief Marketing Officer (CMO)/Chief Communications Officer (CCO): Titles that denote the marketing or communications function at the most senior level of the company

Cialdini's Influence Principles: Six different cues that trigger mental shortcuts

Click-Through Rate: A ratio showing how often people who see an online ad end up clicking it

Commonsense Theory: Using anecdotal information to guide understanding

Community Volunteering: Encouraging and facilitating employees to get involved in a cause via time off or sabbaticals

Consequentialist Theory: Utilitarianism

Content Analysis: Research method of examining and categorizing existing communication

Content Producers: In the entertainment field, those involved in content production and/or distribution, such as filmmakers and studios

Copyright: Legal protection for any creative work that is published, broadcast, presented, or displayed publicly, including video, audio, imagery, or written work on the Web

Corporate Branding: The product of the combined perception of the company, its products, its people, and its overall reputation

Corporate Culture: Beliefs and behaviors that determine how a company's employees and management interact as well as handle outside business transactions

Corporate Philanthropy: Direct contribution to a charity or cause

Corporate Reputation: How a company (or organization) is perceived by its key stakeholders

Corporate Social Marketing: Support for a behavior changing campaign to improve safety, health, or the environment

Crisis: A significant threat to operations that can have long-term, negative consequences to the company or organization involved

Crisis Communications: The process by which organizations respond to and manage the situation to minimize damage to products, people, the public, and/or their reputation

Crowdsourcing: Obtaining information or input from a large number of people, typically via the Internet

Cultural Intelligence: The need for company leaders to recognize and comprehend different beliefs, practices, attitudes, and behaviors of a group or market area and then apply that cultural knowledge to attain goals

Cybernetics: A theory of message transmission

Defamation: The act of making a statement that can be proven to be false, with the intention of causing harm to another's reputation or livelihood (see definitions for libel and slander)

Demographics: A term used to categorize or analyze the audience for a media outlet or, more broadly, a segment of the population

Deontological Ethics: Ethics that are rules based

Depth Interview: Research method that searches to answer how and why through a one-on-one conversation

Diffusion of Innovations Theory: Theory explaining that a new idea or a product must pass through a sequential process with a public to ultimately be adopted

Digital Analytics: Tools that allow collection, organization, and analysis of online data

Disasters: "[E]vents that are sudden, seriously disrupt routines of systems, require new courses of action to cope with the disruption and pose a danger to values and social goals" (Coombs, 2015)

Disclosure: (1) The process by which publicly traded companies share significant news and information to all its key publics, stockholders, and the financial markets simultaneously (2) Release of information, for example, the FTC mandates that bloggers or celebrities who make endorsements must disclose the material connections they

share with the seller of the product/service; disclosure also establishes that publishing information already publicly disclosed is not an invasion of privacy

Divestiture: Corporate action of selling off subsidiary business units or interests

Due Diligence: Reasonable steps taken by a person or firm to satisfy a legal requirement or before entering into an agreement

Ecotourism: Environmentally responsible travel to natural areas that promote conservation and provide for beneficially active socioeconomic involvement of local peoples

Elaboration Likelihood Model (ELM): A major persuasion theory explaining that persuasive messages are received by people through two different routes: central and peripheral

Employee Advocacy: Promotion of an organization by its employees

Employee Relations: Strategic communication process that builds mutual relationships between an organization and its employees

Encoded: The way meaning is produced in a message to ensure comprehension by the receiver

Engagement: A state of attention, comprehension, interest, attitude formation, and/or participation; in social media, interactions people have with content, for example, likes, comments, shares, and re-tweets

Excellence Theory: General theory of PR that explains characteristics of excellent communications

Exposure: Frequency and timeframe of content's appearance on a media platform

Fair Use: In some situations, under this rule limited use of another's copyrighted work may be allowed without asking permission or infringing on the original copyright

Fake News: The proposed practice of publishing news stories online (initially) or in the traditional media that are not based on acts or proven research

False Light: Refers to information either untrue or suggestive of false impressions that is widely publicized

Financial Communications: A category of communications that corporate communicators or IR professionals and their advisers engage in routinely for publicly traded companies, consisting of preparing the required reports, communicating with the financial community (current and prospective investors, stock market analysts, etc.), and the financial media

Focus Group: Research method that involves a collective depth interview

Framing Theory: Suggests that how something is presented to the audience (called "the frame") influences the choices people make about how to process that information

Free Speech: Legally protected right to public speech defined by the U.S. Constitution's First Amendment

Gamification: Process of incorporating game-playing elements into marketing or communication campaigns

Gatekeeper: A person who controls access to the media and decides if a story or news item will be published, posted, or put on the air at a TV or radio station, for example, an editor, producer, or reporter

General Entertainment: Broad category of entertainment products encompassing multiple media, such as TV programs, concerts, and online series

Global Communications: Strategic communications and actions carried out by private, government, or nonprofit organizations to build and maintain relationships in social and political environments *outside* their home location (Molleda, 2009)

Globalization: The worldwide movement toward economic, financial, trade, and communications integration

Government Relations: Organization-to-government communications in which organizations communicate with government agencies and elected officials

Greenwashing: Misleading consumers regarding a firm's environmental practices or the environmental benefits of a certain product

Halo Effect: The positive bias shown by customers toward certain products because of a favorable experience with other products made by the same manufacturer (Leuthesser, Kohli, & Harich, 1995)

Hashtags: Words or phrases, with hash or pound sign appearing before them, for use on social media sites

Immediacy: The quality or experience of something happening now or "being in the moment"

Impressions: A tactic designed to measure the impact of news coverage that assumes that the number of subscribers to a publication or viewers/listeners to a broadcast is equal to the audience reached with a news item or story they placed

Influencer: An individual who develops a following and becomes a trendsetter or opinion leader and can influence the success or failure of a communications campaign

Informational Objectives: Objectives focused on creating awareness of a product, company, or issue by sharing information and attributes

Initial Public Offering (IPO): The first time a company sells some of its shares (stock certificates representing partial ownership) to the financial community and the public

Inoculation Theory: Explains that inoculation (giving audiences a small dose of an opposing argument and then refuting it) builds their resistance to future opposing messages

Integrated Marketing Communications (IMC): A strategic communications activity combining the activities of advertising, promotion, and PR to plan, develop, and implement brand-focused communications programs to generate sales or attract customers to a product or service

Integrated Public Affairs Campaign: A comprehensive communications campaign (usually directed at influencing public policy or legislation) that combines the disciplines and activities of government relations, lobbying, public affairs, and traditional public relations

Intranet: Private online network accessible only to an organization's employees

Intrusion: The intentional disturbance, physically or otherwise, upon the solitude or seclusion of another that causes offense, mental anguish, or suffering

Inverted Pyramid: The traditional structure of news writing and the writing of news releases

Investor Relations (IR): The practice area in which professionals interact with the financial community (investors, analysts, and government regulators) on behalf of a public company

Issues Management: An anticipatory, strategic management process that helps organizations detect and respond appropriately to emerging trends or changes in the sociopolitical environment (Dougall, 2008)

Key Message: Theme or idea in a strategic plan that is specially designed to communicate an essential point or view that is critical to accomplishing an overall objective

Latent Publics: People who are not aware of a problem or opportunity

Lead: The first paragraph of a news story or news release

Libel: A written or published statement of defamation

Litigation Crisis: A crisis driven by a lawsuit (or the threat of one) that plays out in the court of public opinion as well as in the legal system

Lobbying: Organization-to-government communications involving direct contact with politicians and government rule makers to provide a point of view

Mainstream Media: Media that consists of newspapers, magazines, television (network and local), and radio that have existed in one form or another throughout history (also known as traditional media)

Material Events: News or developments that the Securities and Exchange Commission views as potentially having an impact on the stock price of a public company, including a new product or a product recall, a change in senior management, the announcement of a merger or major transaction, a major news or economic event, or annual and quarterly earnings announcements

Media Tour: A media relations tactic that involves a multi-city tour, usually with a celebrity or other spokesperson, to promote a new product or service

Memes: Virally transmitted cultural symbols, often a photograph and often captioned

Mentions: Direct reference or quotes of an entity by a media outlet

Mergers: Uniting of two existing companies into one new company

Modern Era of PR: The time period beginning in the early 1900s when PR moved beyond the era of the publicists and promoters to the current era of applying the strategies and tactics advanced by Edward Bernays and others to corporations and organizations

Moral Impulse: The human instinct to behave morally

Motivational Objectives: Designed to share information, change attitudes, and influence behavior

Noise: Unplanned factors that affect the communication process

Nonconsequentialist Theory: Utilitarianism

Nongovernmental Organizations (NGOs): Private sector and voluntary (and usually nonprofit) organizations that contribute to, or participate in, projects, education, training, or other humanitarian, progressive, or watchdog activities

Normative Ethics: Ethical frameworks or theories that present moral standards guiding right or wrong conduct

Op-Eds: Opinion pieces that usually concern current issues

Organizational Clarity: When employees understand the organization's culture and brand identity

Organizational Crisis: A situation that threatens an organization and its stakeholders—for example, shareholders, customers, employees, and the public—and can seriously impact performance and generate negative outcomes (Coombs, 2015)

Participant Observation: Research method in which the researcher participates in an activity to observe and better understand the people involved and their perspectives

Pitch: Outreach from a PR professional to reporters to get them to consider a story idea they are proposing to seek news coverage

Political Communications: Candidate-to-voter communications; dynamic, interactive campaign-based process among politicians, the news media, and the public

Press Event/Publicity Stunt: An event or activity specifically designed to draw attention to a product, service, or celebrity that creates lots of news coverage or publicity

Primary Research: New research activity undertaken to prepare a communications plan or activity (e.g., a survey, focus group, or other form of research)

Privacy: A right that protects citizens from harm caused by the public dissemination of truthful but private information about them; it is divided into four legal actions: intrusion, disclosure, false light, and appropriation

Pro Bono Work: Professional work undertaken voluntarily and without expectation of payment

Proactive: Monitoring and responding to situations as they are identified, before they erupt

Product Crisis: A case in which a problem in a major product—for example, brakes in a car, faulty batteries in a phone, bacteria in food, or unintended side effects of medicine—creates a public hazard and the company is held responsible

Public Affairs: (1) Communications activity engaged in by companies directed at impacting government policy or legislation (2) Communications outreach and public information activities by government employees to the public in place of the term PR

Public Affairs Officer (PAO): Communicators working in a military setting whose responsibilities are to advise senior officers and leaders on communications issues, assist them in making well-informed decisions, and translate those decisions into effective military operations

Public Company (Publicly Traded Company): A company that sells stock (shares) to the public to raise money (capital) to fund its growth and expansion

Public Diplomacy: A process wherein governments communicate and build relationships with foreign publics to achieve their political and diplomatic objectives

Public Information Officer (PIO): Related to public affairs and often used by government agencies involving written and verbal communication and media relations including speechwriting and preparing testimony for legislative hearings

Publicist: Most common in the entertainment, fashion, and celebrity arenas, this professional focuses on keeping the client visible and in the news to boost popularity and promote projects (e.g., movies and television shows)

Qualitative Methods: Types of research useful to explore attitudes, perceptions, values, and opinions

Quantitative Methods: Types of research to observe effects, test relationships, and generate numerical data that is considered objective

Reactive: When an organization does not act in advance and the situation escalates requiring an organizational, public response

Reach: Measurement of audience size; the number of people who are exposed to content

Reputational Objectives: Designed to change perceptions and rebuild reputations or trust after a crisis

Right of Publicity: Most states allow a citizen to control the commercial use of his or her identity

ROI: Return on investment

ROPES: Acronym for the PR process, standing for research, objectives, programming, evaluation, and stewardship

Scholarly Theory: Widely tested explanations of human behavior and events generated through systematic research

Secondary Research: Reviewing existing research for new insights or trends, including reviewing a recent public opinion survey; scanning news coverage on a topic, issue, or individual; or reading scholarly research for insights on communications theory and its application to a current issue or opportunity

SEM: Search engine marketing; promotion of websites by increasing their visibility in search engine results pages primarily through paid advertising

Sentiment: The analysis of sentiment, also known as opinion mining; identifies the feelings (attitudes, emotions, etc.) expressed through social media communication

SEO: Search engine optimization; affecting the visibility of a website or a Web page in a search engine's unpaid results—often referred to as "natural," "organic," or "earned" results

Serifs: On some typefaces, short lines attached to ends of letter strokes

Slander: Defamation that is spoken

Snapchat Stories: Compilation of Snaps posted over a 24-hour period that become a "story" lasting for 24 hours

Social Entrepreneurship: A type of business structure that prioritizes social, cultural, and/or environmental benefits rather than substantial financial gain

Social Network Theory (SNT): Examines and explains the web of interrelationships among people and organizations

Socially Responsible Business Practices: Adopting discretionary business practices to support causes or issues

Socially Responsible Investors (SRI): An investment style that focuses on companies with a demonstrated track record of meeting or exceeding environmental, social, and corporate governance criteria and generating long-term competitive financial returns and positive societal impact

Spiral of Silence Theory: Explains that ideas and opinions expressed in mass media can discourage expressions by people who hold dissenting opinions due to a sensitivity of feeling isolated or rejected

Spokespersons: People or experts associated with a company, organization, or government entity who are authorized to speak to the media

Stakeholders: People or organizations who have a "stake" in a company/organization, including employees, voters, government agencies and elected officials, customers, prospective employees, as well as customers and other similar individuals

Stewardship: Tactics to maintain relationships with publics after a communication campaign has been executed

Stock Exchange: The major financial markets in the United States and the world, for example, NYSE and NASDAQ

Strategic Philanthropy: When the materials donated or the recipient organization has a connection to the core business of the company making the donation

Surveys: Research method that asks both closed questions (multiple choice, yes or no, true or false) and open-ended questions

Sustainability: In the CSR context, a business strategy that creates long-term stakeholder value by considering the ethical, social, environmental, cultural, and economic spheres

Sustainable Business Practices (Sustainability Communications): Activities that improve an organization's reputation that can also have positive economic and social aspects

Tagged: The act of a social media user identifying someone in a post, photo, tweet, or update; the "tag" is a clickable name that notifies the person that they have been identified

Talent: Entertainment performers, such as actors, DJs, and models

Teleological Ethics: Ethics that are value based

Thought Leadership: A high-level communications tactic in which a company or organization produces a survey, in-depth research, or a detailed point of view on a major issue or trend in the marketplace or society

Triple Bottom Line: Framework with three parts: social, environmental, and financial; also referred to as the 3Ps: people, planet, and profit

Two-Step Flow Theory: Explains that media can also influence early adopters of new ideas (called "opinion leaders") who filter the content through their own interpretations and then pass it on to influence certain groups of publics

Unbranded: Without evidence or identification of a specific associated brand, as in "unbranded content"

Upward Flow Theory: Explains how grassroots or general public opinions can influence an organization or political leaders

Uses and Gratifications Theory: Explains that users of media take an active role by choosing and using certain media to meet various needs

Utilitarianism: A teleological theory (also called consequentialism) that emphasizes consequences of actions, weighing the greatest good for the greatest number of people

Viral: Describes a piece of information, that is, a story, image or video, that is circulated rapidly and widely from one Internet user to another

Virtue Ethics: Ethics that emphasize individual moral character, guided by one's virtue and practical wisdom

Vloggers: People who produce video blogs (a form of Web television)

WOM: Word of mouth

Working Theory: Agreed-upon ways of doing things; a hypothesis that has not been tested or proven through structured research

REFERENCES

Abbott in India. (n.d.). Retrieved from http://dam.abbott.com/en-us/documents/pdfs/abbott-citizenship/India_Highlights.pdf

About History. (n.d.). Social enterprise. Harvard Business School. Retrieved from http://www.hbs.edu/socialenterprise/about/Pages/history.aspx

Acohido, B. and Swartz, J. (2011). Google deflects PR firm's attack of Gmail privacy. USA Today. Retrieved from https://usatoday30.usatoday.com/money/media/2011-05-06-google_n.htm

AFSP Annual Report. (2015). National Suicide Prevention Week 2015. Retrieved from https://afsp.org/about-afsp/annual-reports/#section1

Agozzino, A. (2015). Dialogic communication through "Pinning": An analysis of top 10 most-followed organizations' Pinterest profiles. *Public Relations Journal, 9*(3). Retrieved from http://www.prsa.org/Intelligence/PRJournal/Vol9/No3/

Ahillen, S. (March 1, 2017). Gatlinburg took $19 million tourism hit after November wildfire. *Knoxville News Sentinel.* Retrieved from http://www.knoxnews.com/story/news/local/tennessee/gatlinburg/2017/03/01/gatlinburg-took-19-million-tourism-hit-after-november-wildfire/98586418/

Alaimo, K. (2016a). *Pitch, tweet, or engage on the street: How to practice global public relations and strategic communication.* New York, NY: Routledge.

Alaimo, K. (2016b). Engagement ring: Takeways from the mobile marketing leadership forum. *Public Relations Tactics* (July), 15.

Alaimo, K. (2016c). Updating the generic/specific theory of international public relations: More Factors to consider when practicing in new markets. Institute for Public Relations. Retrieved from http://www.instituteforpr.org/updating-genericspecific-theory-international-public-relations-factors-consider-practicing-new-markets/

ALS Association. (2014). Ice Bucket Challenge takes U.S. by storm. Retrieved from http://web.alsa.org/site/PageNavigator/als_ice_bucket_challenge.html

Amendola Communications. (n.d.). Public relations. Retrieved from http://www.acmarketingpr.com/our-services/#pr

America's Charities. (2017, April 3). Facts & statistics on workplace giving, matching gifts, and volunteer programs. Retrieved from https://www.charities.org/facts-statistics-workplace-giving-matching-gifts-and-volunteer-programs

American Academy of Pediatric Dentistry. (2014). America's pediatric dentists bite into problem of rampant tooth decay in little teeth and encourage parents to join the monster-free mouths movement. Retrieved from JDG_Chapter 5 – Implementing your Strategic PR.docx

Anand, G., & Joelving, F. (August 11, 2016). Driven to suicide by an "inhuman and unnatural" pressure to sell. *New York Times.* http://www.nytimes.com/2016/08/11/business/international/abbott-india-suicide-inhuman-drug-sales-tactics.html?_r=0

Anderson, F. (2014). Measurable objective is critical to successful evaluation. [Blog]. Measurement Week/IPR. Retrieved from http://www.instituteforpr.org/measurable-objective-critical-successful-evaluation/

Anholt, S. (2014). Which country does the most good for the world? TED. Retrieved from https://www.ted.com/talks/simon_anholt_which_country_does_the_most_good_for_the_world

Arenstein, S. (2016, November 17). How a Small Brand Used Google Analytics and a Blog to Grow. *PR News.* Retrieved from http://www.prnewsonline.com/google-analytics-menaker

Argenti, P. A. (2016). *Corporate responsibility.* Thousand Oaks, CA: Sage.

Arthur W. Page Center. (1932, March). Talk on public relations. Retrieved from http://comm.psu.edu/page-center/speech/talk-on-public-relations

Arthur W. Page Society. (2017). The CEO view: Communications at the center of the enterprise. Retrieved from http://awpagesociety.com/thought-leadership/the-ceo-view-communications-at-the-center-of-the-enterprise

Ascension. (2016, December 7). Ascension honored for diversity & inclusion campaign. Retrieved from https://ascension.org/news/news-articles/2016/12/07/16/40/ascension-honored-for-diversity-inclusion-campaign

Balasubramaniam, K. (n.d.). What are the advantages and disadvantages for a company going public? Investopedia. Retrieved from http://www.investopedia.com/ask/answers/06/ipoadvantagedisadvantage.asp

Ballotpedia. (n.d.). State sunshine laws. Retrieved from https://ballotpedia.org/State_sunshine_laws

Banjo, S. (2014). Inside Nike's struggle to balance cost and worker safety in Bangladesh. *Wall Street Journal.* Retrieved from http://www.wsj.com/articles/SB10001424052702303873604579493502231397942

Barcelona Principals 2.0. (n.d.) AMEC. Retrieved from https://amecorg.com/barcelona-principles-2-0-infographic/

Bardhan, N., & Patwardhan, P. (2004). Multinational corporations and public relations in a historically resistant host culture. *Journal of Communication Management, 8*(3), 246–263.

Barker, J. (2016, April 24). As teams seek stadium deals, Camden Yards' name not for sale. Retrieved from http://www.baltimoresun.com/business/bs-bz-baseball-naming-rights-20160424-story.html

Bates, D. (2006). "Mini-Me" history—Public relations from the dawn of civilization. Institute for Public Relations. Retrieved from http://www.instituteforpr.org/wp-content/uploads/MiniMe_HistoryOfPR.pdf

Baus, H. M. (1942). *Publicity, how to plan, produce and place it.* New York, NY: Harper.

Be the Change Media. (n.d.). The 2016 Best for the World honorees. Retrieved from http://bftw.bthechange.com/wp-content/uploads/2016/09/BFoverall-list.pdf

Beene, R. (2016). Michael Horn out as CEO at Volkswagen Group of America. Automotive News. Retrieved from http://www.autonews.com/article/20160309/OEM02/160309848/michael-horn-out-as-ceo-at-volkswagen-group-of-america

Ben & Jerry's. (n.d.). 2015 Social & environmental assessment report. Retrieved from http://www.benjerry.com/about-us/sear-reports/2015-sear-report

Ben & Jerry's Foundation. (n.d.). Retrieved from http://benandjerrysfoundation.org/files/new%20pdfs/Sen.%20Leahy%20Immigration%20Report.pdf

Benady, A. (2014). The godfather of modern PR Harold Burson on moral responsibilities and controversial clients. *PRWeek.* Retrieved from http://www.prweek.com/article/1281156/godfather-modern-pr-harold-burson-moral-responsibilities-controversial-clients

Bendeler, G. (2017). The art of modern sustainability communications: How to embrace an audience-first approach. Sustainable Brands. Retrieved from http://www.sustainablebrands.com/news_and_views/marketing_comms/guusje_bendeler/art_modern_sustainability_communications_how_embrace_

Benoit, W. L. (1995). *Accounts, excuses, and apologies: A theory of image restoration strategies*. Albany, NY: State University of New York Press.

Benson, T. (2016, February 11). Motivating Millennials takes more than flexible work policies. *Harvard Business Review*. Retrieved from https://hbr.org/2016/02/motivating-millennials-takes-more-than-flexible-work-policies

Bernays, E. L. (2015a). *Biography of an idea: The founding principles of public relations*. New York, NY: Open Road Media.

Bernays, E. L. (2015b). *Crystallizing public opinion*. New York, NY: Open Road Media.

Bialik, C. (2011). Publicists pump up value of buzz; don't believe the hype. *Wall Street Journal*. Retrieved from http://www.wsj.com/articles/SB10001424052702303339904576405683745990342

Bien, L. (2013, May 8). 49ers' Levi's Stadium the 3rd-biggest naming rights deal in American sports. Retrieved from http://www.sbnation.com/nfl/2013/5/8/4313344/49ers-levis-stadium-biggest-naming-rights-contracts

Block, E. M. (n.d.). The legacy of public relations excellence behind the name. Arthur W. Page Society. Retrieved from http://www.awpagesociety.com/site/historical-perspective

Blue Communications. (n.d.). Wellness at AECOM. The American Business Awards. Retrieved from https://stevieawards.com/aba/blue-communications-wellness-aecom

Blythe, J. (n.d.). The Schramm model of communication. Retrieved from http://sk.sagepub.com/books/key-concepts-in-marketing/n46.xml

Bonk, K., Tynes, E., Griggs, H., & Sparks, P. (2008). Strategic communications for nonprofits: A step-by-step guide to working with the media (2nd ed.). San Francisco, CA: Jossey-Bass.

Bortree, D. (2016). Building legitimacy through video sustainability reports: Trends from 2010 to 2015. Conference paper. pp. 23-30. Proceedings, *19th International Public Relations Research Conference*. Coral Gables, FL. Retrieved from http://media.wix.com/ugd/27a53c_f9e0941a0ccb4ad09d89254b8e56bb54.pdf

Boschma, J. (2016). Black consumers have "unprecedented impact" in 2015. *The Atlantic*. Retrieved from https://www.theatlantic.com/politics/archive/2016/02/black-consumers-have-unprecedented-impact-in-2015/433725/

Bowen, S. A. (2013). Ethics of public relations. In R. L. Heath (Ed.), *Encyclopedia of public relations* (Vol. 1, 2nd ed.). Thousand Oaks, CA: Sage. Retrieved from http://go.galegroup.com/ps/i.do?id=GALE%7CCCX3719500175&v=2.1&u=trlst298&it=r&p=GVRL&sw=w&asid=12c92cebbd03c1251bb7baf50021307d

Bowler, T. (2015). Volkswagen: From the Third Reich to emissions scandal. BBC. Retrieved from http://www.bbc.com/news/business-34358783

Broom, G. M., & Dozier, D. M. (1990). *Using research in public relations: Applications to program management*. Englewood Cliffs, NJ: Prentice-Hall.

A Bullseye View. (n.d.). Shorty Award entry in "Branded Content" category. Retrieved at http://shortyawards.com/9th/a-bullseye-view-behind-the-scenes-at-target

Bureau of Labor Statistics. (2014a). Public relations and fundraising managers. United States Department of Labor. Retrieved from http://www.bls.gov/ooh/management/public-relations-managers.htm

Bureau of Labor Statistics. (2014b). Public relations specialists. United States Department of Labor. Retrieved from http://www.bls.gov/ooh/media-and-communication/public-relations-specialists.htm

Business Insider. (n.d.). 9 PR fiascos that were handled brilliantly by management. Retrieved from http://www.businessinsider.com/pr-disasters-crisis-management-2011-5-taco-bells-seasoned-beef-meat-filling-lawsuit-2011-9

Boyer, D. (2016). White House defends $500 million yearly public-relations budget used to spread Obama's message. *Washington Times*. Retrieved from http://www.washingtontimes.com/news/2016/oct/6/white-house-defends-500-million-yearly-public-rela/

Brand!ntegrity (n.d.). The only three measurements that matter [Web log post]. Retrieved from http://www.brandintegrity.com/blog/three-measurements-matter/

Branson, R. (2013). *Virgin rebel: Richard Branson in his own words*. Chicago, IL: Agate Publishing.

Broom, G. M., Center, A. H., & Cutlip, S. M. (1994). *Effective public relations*. Upper Saddle River, NJ: Prentice Hall.

Browne, J., & Nuttall, R. (2013). Beyond corporate social responsibility: Integrated external engagement. McKinsey & Company. Retrieved from http://www.mckinsey.com/business-functions/strategy-and-corporate-finance/our-insights/beyond-corporate-social-responsibility-integrated-external-engagement

Bullas, J. (2016). 10 top social media marketing trends to look out for in 2017. Retrieved from http://www.jeffbullas.com/2016/09/19/0-top-social-media-marketing-trends-to-look-out-for-in-2017/

Bulldog Reporter. (2016, October 31). Assessing the Crisis Collateral Damage: How Did Samsung's Brand Weather the Note 7 Storm?. Retrieved from https://www.bulldogreporter.com/assessing-the-crisis-collateral-damage-how-did-samsungs-brand-weather-the-note-7-storm/

Bureau of Labor Statistics. (n.d.). Advertising, public relations, and related services. Retrieved from https://www.bls.gov/oes/current/naics4_541800.htm

Burton, C. (2014). Exclusive: Meet Judy Smith, the real-life Olivia Pope. Retrieved from http://abc7chicago.com/entertainment/exclusive-meet-judy-smith-the-real-life-olivia-pope/324838/

Burton, L., & Taylor, C. (2017, March 2). Case study: From venture to IPO exit (Snap Inc.) [Web log post]. Retrieved from http://www.kayoconferenceseries.com/single-post/2017/02/21/Case-Study-The-Path-to-an-IPO-Snap-Inc

Business Wire. (2015). Business Wire 2015 media survey. Retrieved from http://go.businesswire.com/2015-business-wire-media-survey-results

Business Wire. (2016, December 2). Dollywood foundation announces details for My People Fund. Retrieved from http://www.businesswire.com/news/home/20161202005776/en/

Business Wire. (2017a, February 9). Cesar Millan takes on role as rescuer and rehabilitator in new series *Cesar Millan's Dog Nation*. Retrieved from http://www.businesswire.com/news/home/20170209005948/en/

Business Wire. (2017b, February 9). Dolby Cinema showcases strong spring lineup http://www.businesswire.com/news/home/20170209005564/en/

Business Wire. (2017c, February 9). Jessica Ray swimwear. Retrieved from http://www.businesswire.com/news/home/20170209006179/en/

Calderon, T. (February 20, 2015). Inter-departmental collaboration: Strengthen your brand and employee retention through working together. CSRwire Talkback. Retrieved from http://www.csrwire

.com/blog/posts/1523-inter-departmental-collaboration-strengthen-your-brand-and-employee-retention-through-working-together

Canon. (n.d.). Retrieved from http://downloads.canon.com/nw/about/corporate-pub/canon-story-2016-2017-e.pdf

Capital One. (n.d.). Financial education. Retrieved from https://www.capitalone.com/about/corporate-citizenship/financial-education/

Career Builder. (n.d.). 2016 U.S. job forecast. Retrieved from http://s3.amazonaws.com/cb-talent-development-cortex-prod/media/attachments/000/001/651/original/BRO-0165_Q1JobForcastFA.pdf?1452109082

Carr, A. (2015). The inside story of Starbucks's race together campaign, no foam. Fast Company. Retrieved from https://www.fastcompany.com/3046890/the-inside-story-of-starbuckss-race-together-campaign-no-foam

Carroll, A. B. (2008). A history of corporate social responsibility: Concepts and practices. In A. Crane, A. McWilliams, D. Matten, J. Moon, & D. Siegel (Eds.), The Oxford handbook of corporate social responsibility (pp. 19–46). Oxford University Press.

Carroll, A. B., & Buchholtz, A. K. (2014). Business and society: Ethics, sustainability, and stakeholder management. Nelson Education.

Carroll, C. (2011). Media relations and corporate social responsibility. In O. Ilhen, J. L. Bartless & S. May (Eds.), Handbook of communication and corporate social responsibility (pp. 432–444). Hoboken, NJ: Wiley.

Carufel, R. (2017, April 7). Deep research and expert media targeting earn Duffy & Shanley huge coverage for client Deepwater Wind's offshore wind farm campaign—and a Gold Bulldog award. Bulldog Reporter. Retrieved September 17, 2017, from https://www.bulldogreporter.com/deep-research-and-expert-media-targeting-earn-duffy-shanley-huge-coverage-for-client-deepwater-winds-offshore-wind-farm-campaign-and-a-gold-bulldog-award/

Carvell, T., Gurewitch, D., & Oliver, J. (Writers). (2015, March 22). Municipal violations [Television series episode]. In Carvell, T., & Oliver, J. (Producers), Last Week Tonight with John Oliver. New York, NY: Avalon Productions.

CASE. (n.d.). Research and news of note: Public relations efforts top source for education journalists. Retrieved from http://www.case.org/Publications_and_Products/September_2016_BriefCASE/Research_and_News_of_Note_September_2016/Public_Relations_Efforts_Top_Source_for_Education_Journalists.html

Cayce, M. (2015). Public relations confidentiality: An analysis of PR practitioner–client privilege in high profile litigation. Public Relations Review, 41(1), 14–21.

Center for Education Reform. (n.d.). K–12 facts. Retrieved from https://www.edreform.com/2012/04/k-12-facts/#schools

Centers for Disease Control and Prevention. (n.d.). What is health communications? Retrieved from https://www.cdc.gov/healthcommunication/healthbasics/whatishc.html

Chadwick, P. (2017). Defining fake news will help us expose it. The Guardian (U.S. edition). Retrieved from https://www.theguardian.com/media/commentisfree/2017/may/12/defining-fake-news-will-help-us-expose-it

Chandler, D. (2017). Strategic corporate social responsibility (4th ed.). Thousand Oakes, CA: Sage.

Chandler, D., & Werther, Jr., W. B. (2014). Strategic corporate social responsibility. Thousand Oaks, CA: Sage.

Children's Specialized Hospital. (2006). Children's Specialized Hospital's #FightFace social media campaign wins national public relations award. Retrieved from https://www.childrens-specialized.org/news/childrens-specialized-hospitals-fightface-social-media-campaign-wins-national-public-relations-award

Christensen, L. J., Peirce, E., Hartman, L. P., Hoffman, W. M., & Carrier, J. (2007). Ethics, CSR, and sustainability education in the Financial Times top 50 global business schools: Baseline data and future research directions. Journal of Business Ethics, 73(4): 347–368.

Citizens United v. FEC, 130 S. Ct. 876 (2010).

Cision. (2016). State of the media report. Retrieved from http://www.cision.com/us/resources/white-papers/state-of-the-media-2016-report/?clid=whitepaper-ty

Cision. (2017, April 13). How your news release can help the media do their job. Cision's 2017 State of the Media Report. Retrieved from http://www.cision.com/us/2017/04/how-your-news-release-can-help-the-media-do-their-job/ and http://www.cision.com/us/resources/white-papers/the-cision-2017-state-of-the-media-report/?clid=whitepaper-ty

Cision Bloggers. (2012). How social media is changing PR. Beyond PR. Retrieved from http://www.prnewswire.com/blog/how-social-media-is-changing-pr-4406.html

Clinton, H. (2012). Clinton's remarks at corporate excellence awards ceremony. Retrieved from https://geneva.usmission.gov/2012/01/19/clinton's-remarks-at-corporate-excellence-awards-ceremony/

Cloutier, C. (2014). Facebook: 1.2 million #IceBucketChallenge videos posted. Boston Globe. Retrieved from https://www.bostonglobe.com/business/2014/08/15/facebook-million-icebucketchallenge-videos-posted/24D8bnxFlrMce5BRTixAEM/story.html

CMCA. (n.d.). CSR communication. Retrieved from http://csr-com.org/csr_comunication

CNBC. (2015a). I am American business. Retrieved from https://www.cnbc.com/id/100000662

CNBC. (2015b, March 18). Starbucks CEO Howard Schultz: "Race Together" campaign [Television series segment]. In Mad Money. Englewood Cliffs, NJ: Author.

Cobb, J. G. (1999). This just in: Model T gets award. New York Times. Retrieved from https://www.nytimes.com/1999/12/24/automobiles/this-just-in-model-t-gets-award.html

The Coca-Cola Company. (n.d.). Mission, vision, and values. Retrieved from http://www.coca-colacompany.com/out-company/mission-vision-values

The Coca-Cola Company. (2017, August 18). 2016 Sustainability report: Assuring the accuracy of our disclosures. Retrieved from http://www.coca-colacompany.com/stories/sustainability-report-assuring-the-accuracy-of-our-disclosures

Colao, J. J. (2014). The inside story of Snapchat: The world's hottest app or a $3 billion disappearing act? Forbes. Retrieved from https://www.forbes.com/sites/jjcolao/2014/01/06/the-inside-story-of-snapchat-the-worlds-hottest-app-or-a-3-billion-disappearing-act/#6cf6a2fc67d2

Collins, D. (2005). More heat over Bush-pundit payoff. AP/CBS News. Retrieved from http://www.cbsnews.com/news/more-heat-over-bush-pundit-payoff/

Comcowich, W. (2015). How much should companies spend on marketing & PR? CyberAlert. Retrieved from http://www.cyberalert.com/blog/how-much-should-companies-spend-on-marketing-pr/?replytocom=89418

Companies need to communication workplace wellness programs. (August 9, 2015). The Holmes Report. Retrieved from http://www.holmesreport.com/research/article/companies-need-to-communicate-workplace-wellness-programs

Cone. (2015a). Cone communications/ebiquity global CSR study. Retrieved from http://www.conecomm.com/news-blog/2015-cone-ebiquity-csr-study-press-release

Cone. (2015b). Cone communications millennial CSR study, 2015. Retrieved from http://www.conecomm.com/research-blog/2015-cone-communications-millennial-csr-study

Cone, C. (2012, April 15). Introducing: goodpurpose 2012. [Web log post]. Retrieved September 15, 2017, from https://www.edelman.com/post/introducing-goodpurpose-2012/

Cone Communications. (2014, June 19). Cone Communications and Johnson & Johnson awarded PRSA's 2014 Silver Anvil Award of Excellence. [Press Release]. Retrieved from http://www.conecomm.com/news-blog/cone-communications-and-johnson-johnson-awarded-prsas-2014-silver-anvil-award-of-excellence

Cone Communications. (2016). Employee engagement study. Retrieved from http://www.conecomm.com/research-blog/2016-employee-engagement-study

Conway, D. (2012). Copyright and the PR professional in the digital age. *Bulldog Reporter*. Retrieved from https://www.bulldogreporter.com/copyright-and-pr-professional-digital-age/

Coombs, W. T. (n.d.). State of crisis communication: Evidence and the bleeding edge. Institute for Public Relations. Retrieved from http://www.instituteforpr.org/wp-content/uploads/CoombsFinalWES.pdf

Coombs, W. T. (2014). Crisis management and communications. Institute for Public Relations. Retrieved from http://www.instituteforpr.org/crisis-management-communications/

Coombs, W. T. (2015). Ongoing crisis communication: *Planning, managing, and responding* (4th ed.). Thousand Oaks, CA: Sage Publications.

Cowden, K., & Sellnow, T. L. (2002). Issues advertising as crisis communication: Northwest Airlines' use of image restoration strategies during the 1998 pilots' strike. *Journal of Business Communication, 39*(2), 193–219.

Cox, K. (2016, May 2). Comcastic: Comcast "cares" on Twitter. What could possibly go wrong? Consumerist. Retrieved from https://consumerist.com/2016/05/02/comcast-cares-on-twitter-what-could-possibly-go-wrong/

Creel, G. (1920). How we advertised America: The first telling of the amazing story of the Committee on Public Information that carried the gospel of Americanism to every corner of the globe. New York, NY: Harper & Brothers.

Crisis Communications Strategies. (n.d.). DoD Joint Course in Communications, University of Oklahoma. Retrieved from http://www.ou.edu.deptcomm/dodjss/groups/O2C2

CSRlive Commentary. (2011, May 25). Gap year leads to global stage for NGOs. CSRWire. Retrieved from http://www.csrwire.com/csrlive/commentary_detail/4576-Gap-Year-Leads-to-Global-Stage-for-NGOs

Culbertson, H. M., Jeffers, D. W., Stone, D. B., & Terrell, M. (2012). *Social, political, and economic contexts in public relations: Theory and cases*. Abingdon, United Kingdom: Routledge.

Curtin, P. A., & Boynton, L.A. (2000). Ethics in public relations: Theory and practice. In R. L. Heath (Ed.), *Handbook of public relations* (pp. 411–421). Thousand Oaks: Sage.

Cutlip, S. M. (2013a). *Public relations history: From the 17th to the 20th century: The antecedents*. New York, NY: Routledge.

Cutlip, S. M. (2013b). *The unseen power: Public relations: A history*. New York, NY: Routledge.

Cutlip, S. M., Center, A. H., & Broom, G. M. (2000). *Effective public relations*. New Jersey: Prentice Hall.

Daniels, C. (2015). How the CCO role is changing—it's complicated. PRWeek. Retrieved from http://www.prweek.com/article/1342255/cco-role-changing-its-complicated

de Brooks, K. P., & Waymer, D. (2009). Public relations and strategic issues management challenges in Venezuela: A discourse analysis of Crystallex International Corporation in Las Cristinas. *Public Relations Review, 35*(1), 31–39.

Deardorff, J. (2015). Teens turn to Internet to cope with health challenges. Northwestern Now. Retrieved from https://news.northwestern.edu/stories/2015/06/teens-turn-to-internet-to-cope-with-health-challenges/

Delisio, E. R. (July, 2017). How companies can engage employees to support the core sustainability missions. Green Edge. Retrieved from https://greenedge.co.za/2017/06/29/companies-can-engage-employees-support-core-sustainability-missions/

Deloitte. (n.d.). M&A trends report 2016, year-end edition. Key findings. Retrieved from https://www2.deloitte.com/us/en/pages/mergers-and-acquisitions/articles/ma-trends-report.html#

Deloitte. (2015). Sustainability a key driver for hospitality in 2015. Retrieved from https://www2.deloitte.com/mt/en/pages/about-deloitte/articles/mt-pr2014-2.html

Dempsey, C. (2017, May 2). No Boston Olympics: How and why smart cities are passing on the torch. No Boston Olympics. Retrieved from http://www.nobostonolympics.org/

Derrick, J. (2017, February 27). Snap Inc's revenue model, explained. *Benzinga*. Retrieved from https://www.benzinga.com/media/cnbc/17/02/9100736/snap-incs-revenue-model-explained

Desens, L. C., & Hughes, L. (2013). Entertainment-education and strategic communication: A case study of Sesame Workshop's "Talk, Listen, Connect" initiative for military families. *International Journal of Strategic Communication, 7*, 292–309.

Dezenhall, E. (1999). *Nail 'em!: Confronting high-profile attacks on celebrities & businesses*. Amherst, NY: Prometheus Books.

Disaster Relief. (n.d.). Discover Communications. Retrieved from https://www.globalgiving.org/discovery/

Dorfman, J. (2017). Super Bowl ads are a bargain at $5 million. Retrieved from https://www.forbes.com/sites/jeffreydorfman/2017/02/04/super-bowl-ads-are-a-bargain-at-5-million/#2b24c7912bce

Dougall, E. (2008). Issues management. Institute for Public Relations. Retrieved from http://www.instituteforpr.org/issues-management/

Dozier, D. M. (1985). Planning and evaluation in PR practice. *Public Relations Review, 11*(2), 17–25.

Dozier, D. M., & Broom, G. M. (1995). Evolution of the manager role in public relations practice. *Journal of Public Relations Research, 7*(1), 3–26.

Dozier, D., & Grunig. L. A. (1992). Organization of public relations function. In J. E. Grunig (Ed.), *Excellence in public relations and communication management* (pp. 395–418). New York, NY: Routledge.

Duggan, M., & Smith, A. (2016). The political environment on social media. Pew Research Center. Retrieved from http://www.pewinternet.org/2016/10/25/the-political-environment-on-social-media/

ebizMBA. (n.d.) The 15 most popular social media sites. Retrieved from http://www.ebizmba.com/articles/social-networking-websites

Eckels, L. (2012, October 8). IBM's largest corporate volunteer event. Prezi. Retrieved from https://prezi.com/evzeuizwewgb/ibms-largest-corporate-volunteer-event/

Economy, P. (2017, May). A 5-step social-responsibility action plan. Inc. Retrieved from https://www.inc.com/peter-economy/a-social-responsibility-action-plan-for-2014.html

Edelman. (n.d.). 2017 Edelman Trust Barometer. Executive summary. Retrieved from http://www.edelman.com/executive-summary/

Edelman. (2010). Citizens Engage! Edelman goodpurpose study 2010—fourth annual global consumer survey. Retrieved from http://ppqty.com/GoodPurpose2010globalPPT_WEBversion (1).pdf

Edelman. (2015). Edelman's position on climate change. Retrieved from http://www.edelman.com/who-we-are/values-and-mission/edelmans-position-climate-change/

Edelman. (2016, January 17). 2016 Edelman trust barometer finds global trust inequality is growing. [Press Release]. Retrieved from http://www.edelman.com/news/2016-edelman-trust-barometer-release/

Edelman. (2017). Edelman trust barometer annual global study. Retrieved from http://www.edelman.com/global-results/

Edelman Insights. (n.d.). University reputations and the public. Retrieved from http://www.slideshare.net/EdelmanInsights/university-reputations-and-the-public

Edelman, R. (2014). The rise of communications marketing. Retrieved from http://www.edelman.com/insights/intellectual-property/the-rise-of-communications-marketing/

edie.net. (2016a). Rap battle: Sustainability's latest Millennial marketing trend. Retrieved from https://www.edie.net/library/Business-sustainability-and-CSR-marketing-rap-music-2016/6702

edie.net. (2016b). Virgin Media and Heineken USA revolutionise CSR reporting with gamification and 360-degree video. Retrieved from https://www.edie.net/news/7/Virgin-and-Heineken-turn-to-technology-and-gamification-to-level-up-CSR/

edie.net. (2017). Captivating CSR: How to produce an engaging sustainability report. edie.net. Retrieved from https://www.edie.net/library/Captivating-CSR--How-to-produce-an-engaging-sustainability-report/6748

Editorial Board. (2016, April 24). Long road to trust for the car industry. Christian Science Monitor. Retrieved from http://www.csmonitor.com/Commentary/the-monitors-view/2016/0424/Long-road-to-trust-for-the-car-industry

Ehrlich, S. (March 21, 2016). Multimedia press releases and other visual news trends. Tempo Blog. Retrieved from https://services.businesswire.com/blog/-/blogs/the-national-press-club-presents-multimedia-press-releases-and-other-visual-news-trends

EIF. (n.d.). Retrieved from http://www.eifoundation.org/

Eilbirt, H., & Parket, I. R. (1973). The practice of business: The current status of corporate social responsibility. Business Horizons, 16(4), 5–14.

Elliott, S. (2011). Redefining public relations in the age of social media. New York Times. Retrieved from http://www.nytimes.com/2011/11/21/business/media/redefining-public-relations-in-the-age-of-social-media.html?_r=0

Elkington, J., & Hartigan, P. (2008). The power of unreasonable people: How social entrepreneurs create markets that change the world. Boston, MA: Harvard Business Press.

Ember, S. (2016). New York Times Co. reports loss as digital subscriptions grow. New York Times. Retrieved from http://www.nytimes.com/2016/05/04/business/media/new-york-times-co-q1-earnings.html

Engage for Good. (n.d.). Safe Kids Worldwide. Retrieved from http://engageforgood.com/halo-award/2016-golden-halo-award-nonprofit/

Entman, R. M. (1993). Framing: Toward clarification of a fractured paradigm. Journal of Communication, 43(4), 51–58.

Erickson, S. L., Weber, M., & Segovia, J. (2011). Using communication theory to analyze corporate reporting strategies. Journal of Business Communication, 48(2), 207–223.

Eriksson, G., & Eriksson, M. (2012). Managing political crisis: An interactional approach to "image repair." Journal of Communication Management, 16(3), 264–279.

ESPN. (2017, January 14). Sports business: Stadium naming rights. Retrieved from http://www.espn.com/sportsbusiness/s/stadiumnames.html

Esty, D., & Winston, A. (2006). The green to gold: How smart companies use environmental strategy to innovate, create value, and build competitive advantage. Hoboken, NJ: Wiley.

Exhibit City News. (2014, August 1). Minneapolis charities benefit from MPI convention. Retrieved from http://www.exhibitcitynews.com/minneapolis-charities-benefit-mpi-convention/

Facebook. (n.d.). Stats. Retrieved from http://newsroom.fb.com/company-info/

A Failure of Initiative. (2006). Final report of the Select Bipartisan Committee to Investigate the Preparation for and Response to Hurricane Katrina. U.S. House of Representatives. Retrieved from https://www.uscg.mil/history/katrina/docs/USHouseOfRepKatrina2006MainR1eport.pdf

FDIC. (2013). Addendum to the 2011 FDIC national survey of unbanked and underbanked Households. Retrieved from https://www.fdic.gov/householdsurvey/2013_afsaddendum_web.pdf

Feldman, E. (2015). How to handle copyright's 50 shades of gray. Cision. Retrieved from http://www.cision.com/us/2015/12/how-to-handle-copyrights-50-shades-of-gray/

Fink, S. (1986). Crisis management: Planning for the inevitable. New York, NY: American Management Association.

Fiske, R. M. (2011). PR pros: Haven't we learned anything about disclosure? Retrieved from https://prsay.prsa.org/2011/05/11/pr-and-communications-pros-havent-we-learned-anything-about-disclosure/

Fitzpatrick, K., Fullerton, J., & Kendrick, A. (2013). Public relations and public diplomacy: Conceptual and practical connections. Public Relations Journal, 7(4), 1–21.

FOIA. (n.d.). Freedom of Information Act. Retrieved from https://www.foia.gov/

Fontein, D. (2016). The best time to post on Facebook, Twitter, and Instagram. Hootsuite Blog. Retrieved from https://blog.hootsuite.com/best-time-to-post-on-facebook-twitter-instagram/

Forbes. (Mary 29, 2017). Warren Buffett. Retrieved from https://www.forbes.com/profile/warren-buffett/

Fortune. (2017). World's most admired companies. Retrieved from http://fortune.com/worlds-most-admired-companies/

Foster, S. (2010). Political communication. Edinburgh, Scotland: Edinburgh University Press.

Freeman, C. P. (2009). A greater means to the greater good: Ethical guidelines to meet social movement organization advocacy challenges. Journal of Mass Media Ethics, 24, 269–288.

FTC. (2009). FTC publishes final guides governing endorsements, testimonials. Retrieved from https://www.ftc.gov/news-events/press-releases/2009/10/ftc-publishes-final-guides-governing-endorsements-testimonials

Fullerton, J., & Kendrick, A. (2017). Shaping international public opinion: A model for nation branding and public diplomacy. New York, NY: Peter Lang Publishing.

Fullerton, J., Kendrick, A., & Broyles, S. J. (2016). Attitude change among US adults after the Castro-Obama announcement: The role of *agenda-setting.* Paper presented at the Association for Education in Journalism and Mass Communication, Minneapolis, MN.

Gagen MacDonald. (n.d.). The soft stuff may be the hard stuff in a successful M&A. Retrieved from https://www.gagenmacdonald .com/2015/the-hard-stuff-in-a-successful-ma/

GAP VII. (n.d.) Eighth communication and public relations generally accepted practices study (Q4 2013 data). USC Annenberg, Strategic Communication and Public Relations Center. Retrieved from http://ascjweb.org/gapstudy/wp-content/uploads/2014/06/ GAP-VIII-Presentation-Final-6.12.2014.pdf

Garcia, T. (2011). R-M pitch on behalf of unnamed client raises ethical questions. Adweek/PR Newser. Retrieved from http://www .adweek.com/digital/b-m-pitch-on-behalf-of-unnamed-client- raises-ethical-questions/?red=pr

Garfield, B. (1999). Ad Age advertising century: The top 100 campaigns. *Ad Age.* Retrieved from http://adage.com/article/ special-report-the-advertising-century/ad-age-advertising- century-top-100-campaigns/140918/

Garlinghouse, M., & Dorsey, A. (2015). The power and unrealized promise of skilled volunteering. In *Volunteer engagement 2.0: Ideas and insights changing the world* (pp. 197–209). Hoboken, NJ: John Wiley & Sons.

Gebbia, B. (2015). National Suicide Prevention Week. Wink. Retrieved from https://www.looktowink.com/2015/09/national- suicide-prevention-week/

Gelles, D. (2015, August 21). How the social mission of Ben & Jerry's survived being gobbled up. *New York Times.* Retrieved from http:// www.nytimes.com/2015/08/23/business/how-ben-jerrys-social- mission-survived-being-gobbled-up.html

Gibson, W. (2014). How organizations should handle false, defamatory Reddit posts. PR Daily. Retrieved from http://www .prdaily.com/Main/Articles/17649.aspx

Girion, L. (2003). Nike settles lawsuit over labor claims. *LA Times.* Retrieved from http://articles.latimes.com/2003/sep/13/ business/fi-nike13

Gitlin, T. (2003). *The whole world is watching: Mass media in the making and unmaking of the new left.* Berkeley, CA: University of California Press.

Glazer, E. (2016a, October 12). Wells Fargo CEO John Stumpf steps down. *The Wall Street Journal.* Retrieved from https://www.wsj .com/articles/wells-fargo-ceo-stumpf-to-retire-1476306019

Glazer, E. (2016b, October 13). Wells Fargo's textbook case of botched crisis management. *The Wall Street Journal.* Retrieved from https://www.wsj.com/articles/wells-fargos-textbook-case- of-how-not-to-handle-a-crisis-1476380576

Global Alliance PR. (2016). Global communications report 2016. Retrieved from http://www.globalalliancepr.org/ news/2016/5/29/global-communications-report?rq=globalreport

GlobalGiving. (2016, December 2). GlobalGiving breaks donation records on #GivingTuesday. CSRWire. Retrieved from http:// www.csrwire.com/press_releases/39505-GlobalGiving-Breaks- Donation-Records-on-GivingTuesday

Globalization. (n.d.). In Business Dictionary. Retrieved from http:// www.businessdictionary.com/definition/globalization.html

Gloster, R. (2014, February 19). Under Armour goes to damage control instead of gold in Sochi. Bloomberg Technology. Retrieved from https://www.bloomberg.com/news/articles/2014-02-17/ under-armour-goes-for-damage-control-instead-of-gold-at- olympics

Goffman, E. (1974). *Frame analysis: An essay on the organization of experience.* Cambridge, MA: Harvard University Press.

Golan, G. J. (2013). *An integrated approach to public diplomacy.* Los Angeles, CA. Sage Publications Sage.

Golan, G. J., Yang, S.-U., & Kinsey, D. F. (2015). *International public relations and public diplomacy.* New York, NY: Peter Lang.

Goldenberg, S. (2015). Edelman ends work with coal producers and climate change deniers. *The Guardian.* Retrieved from https:// www.theguardian.com/environment/2015/sep/15/edelman- ends-work-with-coal-and-climate-change-deniers

Gomez, D., & Reed, E. (n.d.). The need for cultural intelligence. Arthur W. Page Society. Retrieved from http://www.awpagesociety.com/attachments/ c41877da2bcd2e784530e629e003dec046743055/ store/15fb6cb1e84b2c4e026b43edf0efbf4fb46dde3 d0beb4feb7a5b2b8fc006/AsianaAirlinesCaseStudy.pdf

Google. (n.d.). Corporate social responsibility. Retrieved from http://www.google.cn/intl/en/about/company/responsibility/

Gordon, R. (2009). Penn defends firm post-Maddow show. *PRWeek.* Retrieved from http://www.prweek.com/article/1272801/penn- defends-firm-post-maddow-show

Gottfried, J., Barthel, M., Shearer, E., & Mitchell, A. (2016). The 2016 presidential campaign—a news event that's hard to miss. Pew Research Center. Retrieved from http://www.journalism .org/2016/02/04/the-2016-presidential-campaign-a-news-event- thats-hard-to-miss/

Gottfried, J., & Shearer, E. (2016). News use across social media platforms 2016. Pew Research Center. Retrieved from http://www .journalism.org/files/2016/05/PJ_2016.05.26_social-media-and- news_FINAL-1.pdf

Granovetter, M. S. (1973). The strength of weak ties. *American Journal of Sociology, 78*(6), 1360–1380.

Great Place To Work. (n.d.) The best workplaces in Canada/large and multinational organizations. Retrieved from https://www .greatplacetowork.ca/en/best-workplaces/best-workplaces-in- canada-large-and-international

Green, J. (2016). LGBT purchasing power near $1 Trillion rivals other minorities. Bloomberg. Retrieved from https://www.bloomberg .com/news/articles/2016-07-20/lgbt-purchasing-power-near-1- trillion-rivals-other-minorities

Greenburg, Z. O. (2016, July 13). Full list: The world's highest paid celebrities of 2016. Retrieved from https://www.forbes.com/sites/ zackomalleygreenburg/2016/07/13/full-list-the-worlds-highest- paid-celebrities-of-2016/#3ea03c5dd9c2

Gregory, D., & Kirschenbaum, J. (2012). Chester Burger. Retrieved from https://jmc492pr.wordpress.com/2012/02/page/7/

Griffin, E. (2017). Theories covered in 9th edition. Retrieved from http://www.afirstlook.com/edition_9/theory_list

Grunig, J. E. (1992). *Excellence in public relations and communication management.* Mahwah, NJ: Lawrence Erlbaum Associates.

Grunig, J. E., & Grunig, L. A. (2000). Public relations in strategic management and strategic management of public relations: Theory and evidence from the IABC Excellence project. *Journalism Studies, 1*(2), 303–321.

Grunig, J. E., & Grunig, L. A. (2003). Implications of the IABC excellence study for PR education. *Journal of Communication Management, 7*(1), 34–42.

Grunig, J. E., & Grunig, L. A. (2008). Excellence theory in public relations: Past, present, and future. In Zerfass, A., van Ruler, B., & Sriramesh, K. (Eds.) *Public relations research* (pp. 327–347). Wiesbaden, Germany: VS Verlag für Sozialwissenschaften.

Grunig, J. E., & Hunt, T. (1984). *Managing public relations.* New York: Holt, Rinehart and Winston.

Grunig, L. A., Grunig, J. E., & Verčič, D. (1998). Are the IABC's excellence principles generic? Comparing Slovenia and the United States, the United Kingdom and Canada. *Journal of Communication Management, 2*(4): 335–356.

Habitat for Humanity. (2017, May 25). Habitat for Humanity and Wells Fargo team up with veterans to improve 100 homes [Press release]. Retrieved from https://www.habitat.org/newsroom/2017/habitat-humanity-and-wells-fargo-team-veterans-improve-100-homes

Hakim, D. (2016, February 26). VW's crisis strategy: Forward, reverse, u-turn. *New York Times*. Retrieved from http://www.nytimes.com/2016/02/28/business/international/vws-crisis-strategy-forward-reverse-u-turn.html?_r=0

Haldemann, A. (2016, September 16). GE's Ecomagination Turns 10: How a Brand Can Be a Driver for Change. The Huffington Post. Retrieved from http://www.huffingtonpost.com/dr-alexander-haldemann/startup-slideshow-test_b_7181672.html

Hamilton, J. T. (2003). Media coverage of corporate social responsibility. Shorenstein Center on Media, Politics and Public Policy. Retrieved from https://shorensteincenter.org/media-coverage-of-corporate-social-responsibility/

Haran, L., & Sheffer, G. (2015). Is the chief communications officer position going the way of the dodo? PRWeek. Retrieved from http://www.prweek.com/article/1339638/chief-communications-officer-position-going-dodo

The Harris Poll. (2016). The Harris Poll releases annual reputation rankings for the 100 most visible companies in the U.S. Retrieved from http://www.theharrispoll.com/business/Reputation-Rankings-Most-Visible-Companies.html

The Harris Poll. (2017, June 7). Wegmans, Publix Super Markets, Amazon, Tesla and USAA draw top social responsibility scores in Harris Poll. Retrieved from http://www.theharrispoll.com/business/Top-Social-Responsibility-Scores.html

Heath, D., & Heath, C. (2007). *Make to stick: Why some ideas survive and others die*. New York, NY: Random House.

Heath, R. L. (Ed.). (2001). *Handbook of public relations*. Thousand Oaks, CA: Sage.

Hector, M. (2015). Starbucks uses gamification to enhance end-user loyalty. appmakr. Retrieved from https://www.appmakr.com/blog/starbucks-app/

Hellmich, N. (2013). Critics pounce on Coca-Cola obesity campaign. *USA Today*. Retrieved from https://usatoday30.usatoday.com/LIFE/usaedition/2013-01-15-Critics-attack-Cokes-antiobesity-ad_ST_U.htm

Hertz. (2013). Hertz announces corporate headquarters relocation. Retrieved from http://newsroom.hertz.com/2013-05-07-Hertz-Announces-Corporate-Headquarters-Relocation

Hewitt, J. L. (2016). Graze—now available at Walgreens! Subscription box ramblings. Retrieved from http://subscriptionboxramblings.com/2016/11/graze-now-available-walgreens/

Ho Lee, T. (2017). The status of corporate social responsibility research in public relations: A content analysis of published articles in eleven scholarly journals from 1980 to 2015. Public Relations Review, 43(1), 211–218.

Holmes, P. (2017a, March 30). 2017 Global communications report predicts convergence of marketing and PR. The Holmes Report. Retrieved from https://www.holmesreport.com/latest/article/2017-global-communications-report-predicts-convergence-of-marketing-and-pr

Holmes, P. (2017b, May 1). "Public relations": Now more than ever. The Holmes Report. Retrieved from https://www.holmesreport.com/long-reads/article/%27public-relations%27-now-more-than-ever

Holmes, S. L. (1976). Executive perceptions of corporate social responsibility. *Business Horizons, 19*(3), 34–40.

The Holmes Report. (n.d.a). 2016 North America agencies of the year. Retrieved from http://www.holmesreport.com/events-awards/agencies-of-the-year/2016-agencies-of-the-year/north-america/healthcare-agencies-of-the-year

The Holmes Report. (n.d.b). Research: Growth & opportunities. Retrieved from http://www.holmesreport.com/ranking-and-data/world-pr-report/research/growth-opportunities

The Holmes Report. (2015a). Global PR industry up 7% to more than $13bn in 2015. Retrieved from https://www.holmesreport.com/ranking-and-data/world-pr-report/analysis/executive-summary

The Holmes Report. (2015b). USC Annenberg Center for Public Relations. Retrieved from http://annenberg.usc.edu/sites/default/files/USC_REPORT_New.pdf

Holtzhausen, D. R. (2015). The unethical consequences of professional communication codes of ethics: A postmodern analysis of ethical decision-making in communication practice. *Public Relations Review, 41*, 769–776.

Horovitz, B. (2013). Coca-Cola ad to defend artificial sweeteners. USA Today. Retrieved from https://www.usatoday.com/story/money/business/2013/08/13/coca-cola-aspartame-diet-soft-drinks/2650755/

Horovitz, B. (2014, February 21). Under Armour surges on Olympic renewal news. *USA Today*. Retrieved from https://www.usatoday.com/story/money/business/2014/02/21/under-armour-olympic-games-winter-olympics-sochi-games-mach-39/5645977/

HSN Inc. (2017, February 19). HSN ignites designers' creativity with the launch of its enchanting Disney "Beauty and the Beast" collection. Retrieved from https://globenewswire.com/news-release/2017/02/09/915638/0/en/HSN-Ignites-Designers-Creativity-With-the-Launch-of-Its-Enchanting-Disney-Beauty-and-the-Beast-Collection.html

Humana. (n.d.). Humana believes everyone should have access to affordable, quality healthcare coverage. Retrieved from https://closethegap.humana.com/how-we-are-closing-the-gap/mississipi-story-health-insurance-access/

Hyundai Motor America with Ketchum. (2015). Driving on hydrogen—Launching Hyundai's Tucson fuel cell vehicle. Retrieved from http://apps.prsa.org/SearchResults/Download/6BE-1502AG1553/0/Driving_on_Hydrogen_Launching_Hyundai_s_Tucson_Fue

IBM. (n.d.a). Education & workforce development. Retrieved from http://www.ibm.com/ibm/responsibility/initiatives.html#cce

IBM. (n.d.b). IBM Corporate Service Corps. Retrieved from http://www.ibm.com/ibm/responsibility/corporateservicecorps/pdf/CSC-Benefits_Infographic.pdf

IBM. (n.d.c). IBM's Corporate Service Corps and the Global FoodBanking Network. Retrieved from http://www.ibm.com/ibm/responsibility/corporateservicecorps/pdf/GFN_case_study.pdf

Icon Clinical Research—Launch Video for Spark. (n.d.). The American Business Awards. Retrieved from https://stevieawards.com/aba/icon-clinical-research-launch-video-spark

Ignition. (n.d.). NBC Universal. Shavrick and Partners. Retrieved from http://www.shavrick.com/#/nbc/

IHME. (2014). The vast majority of American adults are overweight or obese, and weight is a growing problem among US children. Institute for Health Metrics and Evaluation. Retrieved from http://www.healthdata.org/news-release/vast-majority-american-adults-are-overweight-or-obese-and-weight-growing-problem-among

Infosys. (2013, July 9). Infosys employees donate more than $30,000 to Hurricane Sandy New Jersey Relief Fund. CSRWire. Retrieved from http://www.csrwire.com/press_releases/35879-Infosys-Employees-Donate-More-Than-30-000-to-Hurricane-Sandy-New-Jersey-Relief-Fund

Inglespc. (n.d.). A brief history of social media (1969–2015). Retrieved from http://inglespc.com/a-brief-history-of-social-media-1969-2012/

Institute for Mergers, Acquisitions & Alliances (IMAA). (n.d.). M&A statistics. Retrieved from https://imaa-institute.org/mergers-and-acquisitions-statistics/

International Data Corporation (IDC). (2016, October 28). IDC survey looks to assess damage to Samsung brand after Note 7 recall [Press release]. Retrieved from https://www.idc.com/getdoc.jsp?containerId=prUS41886616

Isidore, C. (2016, August 29). Coca-Cola: We're replenishing all of the water we use. CNN Money. Retrieved from http://money.cnn.com/2016/08/29/news/companies/coca-cola-water/

Isidore, C., & Goldman, D. (2016). Volkswagen agrees to record $14.7 billion settlement over emissions cheating. CNN Money. Retrieved from http://money.cnn.com/2016/06/28/news/companies/volkswagen-fine/

It Gets Better Project. (n.d.a). How do you turn momentum into a movement? Retrieved from https://www.bluestatedigital.com/our-work/it-gets-better/

It Gets Better Project. (n.d.b). Retrieved from http://www.itgetsbetter.org/

Iwata, J., & Golin, A. (2009). Toward a new profession: Brand, constituency and eminence on the global commons. Institute for Public Relations. Retrieved from http://www.instituteforpr.org/global-brand-constituency-eminence/

James Grunig: Excellence Theory. (2013). Retrieved from https://excellencetheory.wordpress.com/2013/09/27/pr-professional-3-qa/

Jin, Y., Liu, B. F., & Austin, L. L. (2014). Examining the role of social media in effective crisis management: The effects of crisis origin, information form, and source on publics' crisis responses. Communication Research, 41(1), pp. 74–94. Originally published 2011.doi: 10.1177/0093650211423918

Johnson, R. (n.d.). The top 10 characteristics of a healthy organization. Chron. Retrieved from http://smallbusiness.chron.com/top-10-characteristics-healthy-organization-20452.html

Jones-Christensen, L., Peirce, E., Hartman, L. P., Hoffman, W. M., Carrier, J. (2007). Ethics, CSR, and sustainability education in the Financial Times top 50 global business schools: Baseline data and future research directions. Journal of Business Ethics, 73(4), 347–368.

Jurnecka, R. (2015). Volkswagen Golf is the 2015 Motor Trend car of the year. Retrieved from http://www.motortrend.com/news/2015-volkswagen-golf-is-the-motor-trend-car-of-the-year/

Kaplan, T. (2005). The Tylenol crisis: How effective public relations saved Johnson & Johnson. Retrieved from http://www.aerobiologicalengineering.com/wxk116/TylenolMurders/crisis.html

Katz, A. J. (2016). Led by Lester Holt, NBC Nightly News is now no. 1 for 20 consecutive seasons. Adweek. Retrieved from http://www.adweek.com/tvnewser/led-by-lester-holt-nbc-nightly-news-is-now-no-1-for-20-consecutive-seasons/305030

Katzenback, J., Oelschlegel, C., & Thomas, J. (2016). Ten principles of organizational culture. Strategy+Business, 82. Retrieved from http://www.strategy-business.com/article/10-Principles-of-Organizational-Culture?gko=71d2f

Kaye, J. (2005). Coca-Cola India. Artur W. Page Society. Retrieved from http://www.awpagesociety.com/study_competitions/2005-case-study-competition

Kaye. L. (2013, August 8). The business case for strategic philanthropy. Retrieved from http://www.triplepundit.com/2013/08/business-case-strategic-philanthropy/

Kelly, K. S. (2001). Stewardship. In R. Heath (Ed.), Handbook of public relations (pp. 279–289). Thousand Oaks, CA: Sage.

Kent, A. (2014). 10 internal communications thought leaders you should follow. Red e APP. Retrieved from https://redeapp.com/2014/12/22/10-internal-communications-thought-leaders-you-should-follow/

Kerr, O. (2014, December 15).   Coca-Cola recognized by state department for Typhoon Haiyan relief. Retrieved from http://www.coca-colacompany.com/coca-cola-unbottled/coca-cola-recognized-by-state-department-for-typhoon-haiyan-relief

Kesmodel, D., & Brat, I. (2015). Why Starbucks takes on social issues. Wall Street Journal. Retrieved from http://www.wsj.com/articles/why-starbucks-takes-on-social-issues-1427155129

Ketchum. (2016). Retrieved from http://www.kethum.com

Kim, C. M., & Brown, W. J. (2015, Winter). Conceptualizing credibility in social media spaces of public relations. Public Relations Journal, 9(4). Retrieved from http://www.prsa.org/Intelligence/PRJournal/Vol9/No4/

Kochhar, S. (2016, Summer). Organizational clarity: The new engagement for internal communications. The Public Relations Strategist, 22(2). Retrieved from http://apps.prsa.org/Intelligence/TheStrategist/Articles/view/11587/1129/Organizational_Clarity_The_New_Engagement_for_Inte#.WaN2DCh95PY

Kotler, P., & Gertner, D. (2002). Country as brand, product, and beyond: A place marketing and brand management perspective. Journal of Brand Management, 9(4), 249–261.

Kotler, P., & Lee, K. (2005). Corporate social responsibility: Doing the most good for your company and your cause. Hoboken, NJ: Wiley.

KRC Research. (n.d.). The dawn of CEO activism. Retrieved from http://www.webershandwick.com/uploads/news/files/the-dawn-of-ceo-activism.pdf

Krieg, G. (2017, January 17). Police injured, more than 200 arrested at Trump inauguration protests in DC. CNN Politics. Retrieved from http://www.cnn.com//2017/01/19/politics/trump-inauguration-protests-womens-march/index.html

Kristof, N. (October 20, 2010). How to change the world. The New York Times. Retrieved from https://kristof.blogs.nytimes.com/2010/10/20/how-to-change-the-world/

Lahav, T., & Zimand-Sheiner, D. (2016). Public relations and the practice of paid content: Practical, theoretical propositions and ethical implications. Public Relations Review, 42(3), 395–401.

Lanz, L., & Rackham, B. (2015). Hotel CSR: Social causes and "doing good" will remain integral in hospitality. HospitalityNet. Retrieved from http://www.hospitalitynet.org/news/4070395.html

Lauterer, S. (2005). Oregon Public Broadcasting: Calvert underwrites PBS documentary celebrating social entrepreneurship. Retrieved from http://www.businesswire.com/news/home/20050606005339/en/Oregon-Public-Broadcasting-Calvert-Underwrites-PBS-Documentary

LeBron James Family Foundation. (n.d.). Retrieved from http://lebronjamesfamilyfoundation.org/

Lee, H., Oshita, T., Oh, H. J., & Hove, T. (2014). When do people speak out? Integrating the spiral of silence and the situational theory of problem solving. Journal of Public Relations Research, 26(3), 185–199.

Leuthesser, L., Kohli, C. S., & Harich, K. R. (1995). Brand equity: The halo effect measure. *European Journal of Marketing, 29*(4), 57–66.

Leveille, D. (2015). VW scandal threatens "Made in Germany" image. PRI. Retrieved from https://www.pri.org/stories/2015-09-23/vw-scandal-threatens-made-germany-image

Li, C., & Bernoff, J. (2011). *Groundswell: Winning in a world transformed by social technologies.* Boston, MA: Harvard Business Review Press.

Lofgren, K. (2012, November 7). Architecture for Humanity teams up with MTV's Jersey Shore to 'Restore the Shore' after Hurricane Sandy. Inhabitat. Retrieved from http://inhabitat.com/architecture-for-humanity-teams-up-with-mtvs-jersey-shore-to-restore-the-shore-after-hurricane-sandy/

Long, M. (2016, August 19). Names and numbers: Your handy NFL stadium naming rights guide. Sports Pro Media. Retrieved from http://www.sportspromedia.com/notes_and_insights/your_handy_nfl_naming_rights_guide

Lukaszewski, J. E. (2012). Managing the victim dimension of large-scale disasters. *Leadership and Management in Engineering, 12*(4), 210–221.

Lukaszewski, J. (2013). *Crisis communications: What your CEO needs to know about reputation risk and crisis management.* Brookfield, CT: Rothstein Associates.

Lyons, D. (2011). Facebook busted in clumsy smear attempt on Google. Daily Beast. Retrieved from http://www.thedailybeast.com/articles/2011/05/12/facebook-busted-in-clumsy-smear-attempt-on-google

Marklein, T. (2016). Impressions are a sham: The path to better media metrics. Institute for Public Relations. Retrieved from http://www.instituteforpr.org/impressions-are-a-sham-and-the-path-to-better-media-metrics/

Martin, D., & Wright, D. (2015). *Public relations: How to practice PR without losing your soul.* New York, NY: Business Expert Press.

Mary Beth West. (2017, February 25). Mary Beth West Communications garners Addys for post-wild-fire cartoon series. Retrieved from http://www.marybethwest.com/mary-beth-west-communications-garners-addys-for-post-wildfire-cartoon-series/

Marzilli, T. (2014). Carnival Cruise Lines—In perspective. YouGov BrandIndex. Retrieved from http://www.brandindex.com/article/carnival-cruise-lines-perspective

MasterCard. (2015). MasterCard works with Apple to integrate Apple Pay. Retrieved from http://newsroom.mastercard.com/digital-press-kits/mastercard-powers-mobile-payments-safe-and-simple/

Mazzoni, M. (2015, October 30). 3p weekend: 12 celebrities who use their fame for good. Triple Pundit. Retrieved from http://www.triplepundit.com/2015/10/12-celebrities-using-their-fame-for-good/

McCombs, M. E., & Shaw, D. L. (1972). The agenda-setting function of mass media. *Public Opinion Quarterly, 36*(2), 176–187.

McConnon, A. (2016, August 10). A start-up turns to saffron to help Afghanistan regrow. *The New York Times.* Retrieved at http://www.nytimes.com/2016/08/11/business/smallbusiness/a-start-up-turns-to-saffron-to-help-afghanistan-regrow.html

McDonnell, P. J., & Sanchez, C. (2016, August 15). Wary of losing tourists, Mexico says mass abduction in Puerto Vallarta was likely a gang-on-gang crime. *LA Times.* Retrieved from http://www.latimes.com/world/la-fg-puerto-vallarta-abduction-20160815-snap-story.html

McElhaney, K. A. (2008). *Just good business: The strategic guide to aligning corporate responsibility and brand.* San Francisco, CA: Berrett-Koehler.

McGregor, J. (2017). What Millennials want from their CEOs: Activism. *Washington Post.* Retrieved from https://www.washingtonpost.com/news/on-leadership/wp/2017/07/24/what-millennials-want-from-their-ceos-activism/?utm_term=.084323cd83d8

McKinsey. (2009). Rebuilding corporate reputations. Retrieved from http://www.mckinsey.com/global-themes/leadership/rebuilding-corporate-reputations

McQuail, D., & Windahl, S. (1993). *Communication models for the study of mass communications.* New York, NY: Routledge.

McVicker, M. (2013, July 16). Engaging the social workforce. Digital, Employee Engagement. Retrieved from http://blog.mslgroup.com/aligning-and-inspiring-employees/

Meng, M. (2009, February 5). Issue life cycle clarifies difference between "issues management" and "crisis management." [Web log post]. Retrieved from http://www.alexanderps.com/Index/BLOG/CC888933-80F7-4617-A3BC-1B63C45C6776.html

Merle, R. (2016, October 12). Wells Fargo CEO steps down in wake of sham accounts scandal. *The Washington Post.* Retrieved from https://www.washingtonpost.com/news/business/wp/2016/10/12/wells-fargo-ceo-to-retire-in-wake-of-sham-accounts-scandal

Michael, C., Cauley, M., & Orengo, L. (2016). The third place on a third rail issue: An analysis of Starbucks' Race Together initiative. Arthur W. Page Society. Retrieved from http://www.awpagesociety.com/attachments/7615245b5d1bb6a740d82c0b099b31d30dc2cf20/store/1b2a6ddf451cf14676f0415b54d8ac628451de30ff38edafbaa06041f0df/Starbucks+Case+Study+3.25_FINAL.pdf

Michaelson, D., & Stacks, D. W. (2011). Standardization in public relations measurement and evaluation. *Public Relations Journal, 5*(2), 1–22.

Michaelson, D., & Wright, D. (n.d.). A practitioner's guide to public relations research, measurement and evaluation Retrieved from http://amecorg.com/wp-content/uploads/2012/10/16JuneDavidMichaelsonandDonaldK-APractitionersGuide.pdf

Michelin. (n.d.). Michelin. Retrieved from http://www.michelin.com/eng

Miller, K. S. (1999). Public relations in film and fiction: 1930 to 1995. *Journal of Public Relations Research, 11*(1), 3-28.

Minnesota Compass. (n.d.). Overview. Retrieved from http://www.mncompass.org/immigration/overview

Minnesota Legislative Reference Library. (n.d.) Immigrants in Minnesota. Retrieved from https://www.leg.state.mn.us/lrl/guides/guides?issue=immigration

Minnesota Meetings + Events. (n.d.). How to give attendees more with give-back events. Retrieved from http://mn.meetingsmags.com/how-give-attendees-more-give-back-events

Mireles, A. (2014). PR is facing challenges, but they're NOT insurmountable! Cision. Retrieved from http://www.cision.com/us/2014/11/pr-is-facing-challenges-but-theyre-not-insurmountable/

Mireles, A. (2015, January 15). PR and internal communications: Changing with the times? Cision. Retrieved from http://www.cision.com/us/2015/01/pr-and-internal-communications-changing-with-the-times/

Mitroff, I. I. (1994). Crisis management and environmentalism: A natural fit. *California Management Review, 36*(2), 101–113.

Molleda, J.-C. (2009). Global public relations. Institute for Public Relations. Retrieved from http://www.instituteforpr.org/global-public-relations/

Moore, H. N. (2009, January 22). Bank of America-Merrill Lynch: A $50 billion deal from hell. *Wall Street Journal*. Retrieved from http://blogs.wsj.com/deals/2009/01/22/bank-of-america-merrill-lynch-a-50-billion-deal-from-hell/

MSLGROUP. (2016, February 19). Behind the scenes at Canon. Retrieved from http://blog.mslgroup.com/behind-the-scenes-at-canon/

MSNBC. (2009). The Rachel Maddow Show transcript 03/05/09. Retrieved from http://www.msnbc.com/transcripts/rachel-maddow-show/2009-03-05

MSNBC. (2014, March 30). FBI Agent Watts on Russia: They believe in criminality. *Hardball With Chris Matthews*. Retrieved from http://www.msnbc.com/hardball/watch/fbi-agent-watts-on-russia-they-believe-in-criminality-910592067916

Multivu. (n.d.). Make your mark. Retrieved from http://www.multivu.com/players/English/7123753-bayer-skyla-glamour-make-your-mark-contest/

The Museum of Public Relations. (n.d.a). 1923—Soap and art. Retrieved from http://prvisionaries.com/bernays/bernays_1923.html

The Museum of Public Relations. (n.d.b). 1929—Torches of freedom. Retrieved from http://prvisionaries.com/bernays/bernays_1929.html

The Museum of Public Relations. (n.d.c). Moss Kendrix. Retrieved from http://prvisionaries.com/kendrix/moss1.html

The Museum of Public Relations. (2016). Inez Kaiser—A woman of many "firsts." Retrieved from. http://www.prmuseum.org/blog/2016/3/10/pngkebu59urr39l5bj6ynbxh3q6tkz?rq=inez kaiser

Muzi Falconi, T. (2006). How big is public relations, and why does it matter?: The economic impact of our profession. Retrieved from http://www.instituteforpr.org/toni-muzi-falconi-from-personal-to-organizational-influence/

Myers, C. (2013). Free speech v. social media: Is your policy legal? Institute for Public Relations. Retrieved from http://www.instituteforpr.org/free-speech-v-social-media-is-your-policy-legal/

MyPRSA. (n.d.). Stronger than the storm—ribbon cutting. Retrieved from http://apps.prsa.org/SearchResults/View/6BW-1406D01/0/Stronger_Than_The_Storm_Ribbon_Cutting#.Wab5T2xK02x

National Center for Environmental Information. (2016). Billion-Dollar weather and climate disasters: Table of events. Retrieved from https://www.ncdc.noaa.gov/billions/events

National Investor Relations Institute. (n.d.). Global IR considerations. Retrieved from https://www.niri.org/resources/resource-libraries/free-resources/wp-global-ir-considerations

National Park Service. (n.d.). John Muir. Retrieved from https://www.nps.gov/yose/learn/historyculture/muir.htm

NCAA. (n.d.). Women's lacrosse championship history. Retrieved from http://www.ncaa.com/history/lacrosse-women/d1

Nelson, C. (2015, September 11). WVU launches "Ask WVU" Snapchat campaign for #WVU19. West Virginia University Social. Retrieved from http://social.wvu.edu/blog/2015/09/11/wvu-launches-ask-wvu-snapchat-campaign-for-wvu19

Nelson, J. (2008). CSR and public policy: New forms of engagement between business and government. Corporate Social Responsibility Initiative Working Paper No 45. John F. Kennedy School of Government. Cambridge, MA: Harvard University. Retrieved from https://www.hks.harvard.edu/m-rcbg/CSRI/publications/workingpaper_45_nelson.pdf

New York Times Magazine. (2016, July 31). The Olympics issue. Retrieved from https://www.nytimes.com/interactive/2016/07/31/magazine/rio-olympics-issue.html?_r=0#/olympics-issue-the-olympics-issue

Newell, A. (2015). How Nike embraced CSR and went from villain to hero. TriplePundit. Retrieved from http://www.triplepundit.com/special/roi-of-sustainability/how-nike-embraced-csr-and-went-from-villain-to-hero/

Newsweek. (2016). Top green companies in the world. Retrieved from http://www.newsweek.com/green-2016/top-green-companies-world-2016

Nielsen. (2015a). Consumer-goods' brands that demonstrate commitment to sustainability outperform those that don't. Retrieved from http://www.nielsen.com/us/en/press-room/2015/consumer-goods-brands-that-demonstrate-commitment-to-sustainability-outperform.html

Nielsen. (2015b). Meet the fastest-growing multicultural segment in the U.S.: Asian-Americans. Retrieved from http://www.nielsen.com/us/en/insights/news/2015/meet-the-fastest-growing-multicultural-segment-in-the-us-asian-americans.html

Nielsen. (2015c). Increasingly affluent, educated and diverse: African-American consumers. Retrieved from http://www.nielsen.com/us/en/insights/reports/2015/increasingly-affluent-educated-and-diverse—african-american-consumers.html

Nielsen. (2017, February 6). Super Bowl LI 50 draws 111.3 million TV viewers, 190.8 million social media interactions. Retrieved from http://www.nielsen.com/us/en/insights/news/2017/super-bowl-li-draws-111-3-million-tv-viewers-190-8-million-social-media-interactions.html

Nike. (2006). Nike named top 10 for social responsibility reporting. Nike News. Retrieved from http://news.nike.com/news/nike-named-top-10-for-social-responsibility-reporting

NOLO. (n.d.a). Defamation, slander and libel. Retrieved from http://www.nolo.com/legal-encyclopedia/defamation-slander-libel

NOLO. (n.d.b). The "fair use" rule: When use of copyrighted material is acceptable. Retrieved from http://www.nolo.com/legal-encyclopedia/fair-use-rule-copyright-material-30100.html

Nonprofit HR. (n.d.). 2016 nonprofit employment practices survey results. Retrieved from http://www.nonprofithr.com/2016-survey/

Norris, P. (2004). Global political communication In F. Esser & B. Pfetch (Eds.), *Comparing political* communication: Theories, cases and challenges (pp. 115–150). Cambridge, United Kingdom: Cambridge University Press.

NPR. (2011). Taco Bell faces lawsuit over "seasoned beef." Retrieved from http://www.npr.org/2011/01/25/133218485/Taco-Bell-Faces-Lawsuit-Over-Seasoned-Beef

NSPRA (n.d.). Getting started. Retrieved from https://www.nspra.org/getting_started

Nye, J. S. (1990). Soft power. *Foreign Policy, 80*, 153–171.

O'Boyle, E., & Adkins, A. (2015). Can Volkswagen salvage its damaged brand? Gallup. Retrieved from http://www.gallup.com/businessjournal/187472/volkswagen-salvage-damaged-brand.aspx

O'Neil, J. (2014). An examination of *Fortune* 500 companies' and *Philanthropy* 200 nonprofit organizations' relationship cultivation strategies on Facebook. *Public Relations Journal, 8*(1). Retrieved from http://www.prsa.org/Intelligence/PRJournal/Vol8/No1/

Oh, M.-Y., & Ramaprasad, J. (2003). Halo effect: Conceptual definition and empirical exploration with regard to South Korean subsidiaries of US and Japanese multinational corporations. *Journal of Communication Management, 7*(4), 317–332.

Oliver, J. (2015). *Last Week Tonight*. HBO.

Olphert, C. (2015, November 16). How does community involvement benefit the business? Corporate Citizenship Blog. Boston College Center for Corporate Citizenship. Retrieved from http://corporatecitizenship.bc.edu/how-does-community-involvement-benefit-the-business

OpenSecrets.org. (2016). Total cost of 2016 election could reach $6.6 billion, CRP predicts. Retrieved from https://www.opensecrets.org/news/2016/10/total-cost-of-2016-election-could-reach-6-6-billion-crp-predicts/

Padilla Wins. (2016, June 17). Padilla wins at PRSA awards. Retrieved from http://www.padillaco.com/the-news/news-items/padilla-wins-at-prsa-awards

Page, J. T., & Page, W. S. (2013). The state of micro CSR: Small businesses in a sample of U.S. firms. Presented to the 2nd International CSR Communication Conference, Aarhus, Denmark.

Page, J. T., & Page, W. S. (in press). Taylor Guitars: Guardians of the forest. In B. Brunner & C. Hickerson (Eds.), *Cases in public relations: Translating ethics into action*. New York, NY: Oxford University Press.

Page, J., & Parnell, L. (2016). U.S. Secretary of State's Award for Corporate Excellence. In J. Fullerton & A. Kendrick (Eds.), *Shaping international public opinion: A model for nation branding and public diplomacy* (pp. 221–239). New York, NY: Peter Lang.

Pandey, A. (2016). Samsung Galaxy Note 7 debacle to cost company over $5 Billion. IBT. Retrieved from http://www.ibtimes.com/samsung-galaxy-note-7-debacle-cost-company-over-5-billion-2431578

Patten, E. (2016). Racial, gender wage gaps persist in U.S. despite some progress. Pew Research Center. Retrieved from http://www.pewresearch.org/fact-tank/2016/07/01/racial-gender-wage-gaps-persist-in-u-s-despite-some-progress

Pendrous, R. (2016, March 21). Graze has global expansion snack plans. Retrieved from http://www.foodmanufacture.co.uk/Supply-Chain/Graze-to-start-selling-in-US-stores-this-summer?utm_source=copyright&utm_medium=OnSite&utm_campaign=copyright

Penning, T. (2011). The value of public relations in investor relations: Individual investors' preferred information types, qualities, and sources. *Journalism & Mass Communication Quarterly, 88*(3), 615–631.

Perrin, A. (2015). Social media usage: 2005–2015. Pew Research Center. Retrieved from http://www.pewinternet.org/files/2015/10/PI_2015-10-08_Social-Networking-Usage-2005-2015_FINAL.pdf

Personal pages on PR firm's intranet connect employees worldwide. (n.d.). Ragan.com. Retrieved from http://www.ragan.com/Awards/SpecialEdition/43.aspx

Pew Research Center. (2015a, October 8). Social Media Usage: 2005–2015. Retrieved from http://www.pewinternet.org/2015/10/08/social-networking-usage-2005-2015/

Pew Research Center. (2015b, April 9). Teens, social media & technology overview 2015. Retrieved from http://www.pewinternet.org/2015/04/09/teens-social-media-technology-2015/

Pew Research Center. (2016a, November 10). Facebook remains the most popular social media platform. Retrieved from http://www.pewinternet.org/2016/11/11/social-media-update-2016/pi_2016-11-11_social-media-update_0-01/

Pew Research Center. (2016b). State of the news media 2016. Retrieved from https://assets.pewresearch.org/wp-content/uploads/sites/13/2016/06/30143308/state-of-the-news-media-report-2016-final.pdf

Phelps, R., & Williams, K. D. (n.d.). From routine to crisis: Handling an escalating IT incident. Everbridge. Retrieved from http://ems-solutionsinc.com/wp-content/uploads/2015/11/From-Routine-to-Crisis-Handling-an-Escalating-IT-Incident.pdf

PhiladelphiaEagles.com. (2013, May 1). 2013 calendar shoot down the shore. Retrieved from http://www.philadelphiaeagles.com/news/article-1/2013-Calendar-Shoot-Down-The-Shore/17b3d58a-c60b-499b-8477-9496899b8bc5

Pianin, E. (2015). The Obama administration spent some $5.3 billion on PR to improve the government's image. Business Insider. Retrieved from http://www.businessinsider.com/obama-spent-billion-on-government-image-2015-10

Piasecki, A. (2000). Blowing the railroad trumpet: Public relations on the American frontier. *Public Relations Review, 26*(1), 53–65.

Plato, L. (2017, May 11). How to start a corporate giving program. Causecast. Retrieved from https://www.causecast.com/blog/how-to-start-a-corporate-giving-program

PMLive. (n.d.). Bayer partners with *Glamour* on female empowerment. Retrieved from http://www.pmlive.com/pharma_news/bayer_partners_with_glamour_on_female_empowerment_598152?SQ_ACTION=clear_design_name&full=true

Points of Light. (2012). News flash: Just released: Trends in excellence—Innovations in employee volunteering. Retrieved from http://www.pointsoflight.org/blog/2012/03/28/news-flash-just-released-trends-excellence---innovations-employee-volunteering

Points of Light. (2013). Nominations open for 2013 corporate engagement awards of excellence from Points of Light. Retrieved from http://www.pointsoflight.org/press-releases/nominations-open-2013-corporate-engagement-awards-excellence-points-light

Popik, B. (2010). Origin, myth of the "lobbyist"; Glenn Beck uses another fake Thomas Jefferson quote. RedState. Retrieved from http://www.redstate.com/diary/barrypopik/2010/01/31/origin-myth-of-the-lobbyist-glenn-beck-uses-another-fake-thomas-jefferson-quote/

Porter, M. E., & Kramer, M. R. (2006, December). *Harvard Business Review, 84*(12), 78–92.

Poushter, J. (2016). Smartphone ownership and Internet usage continues to climb in emerging economies. Pew Research Center. Retrieved from http://www.pewglobal.org/files/2016/02/pew_research_center_global_technology_report_final_february_22__2016.pdf

Powell, N. (2015, April 11). Giants' Eli Manning named one of the top philanthropists under 40. Retrieved from http://www.nj.com/giants/index.ssf/2015/04/giants_eli_manning_named_one_of_the_top_philanthro.html

PR Daily. (n.d.a). Apparel company takes multi-faceted approach to deepening customer connections via Instagram. Retrieved from http://www.prdaily.com/awards/specialedition/535.aspx

PR Daily. (n.d.b). Email security company gets attention by making LinkedIn the focus of its campaign. Retrieved from https://www.prdaily.com/Awards/SpecialEdition/536.aspx

PR Daily. (n.d.c). McDonald's New York Tri-State jazzes its website with local color, local stories, neighborhood look and feel. Retrieved from http://www.prdaily.com/awards/specialedition/528.aspx

PR Daily. (n.d.d). Videos help launch new low-calorie brown sugar blend, Retrieved from http://www.prdaily.com/awards/specialedition/530.aspx

PR Daily. (n.d.e). World Wildlife Fund scores big media coverage in its fight for endangered animals. Retrieved from https://www.prdaily.com/Awards/SpecialEdition/405.aspx

PR Daily. (2015a). Metrolink marries timely updates with compelling content to boost off-peak ridership. Retrieved from http://www.prdaily.com/awards/specialedition/534.aspx

PR Daily. (2015b). Transamerica turns a simple idea about a bland, "boring" industry into a trending topic on Twitter. Retrieved from https://www.prdaily.com/Awards/SpecialEdition/533.aspx

PR Measurement Standards. (n.d.). Institute for Public Relations. Retrieved from http://www.instituteforpr.org/wp-content/uploads/Standards-dos-and-donts-09302014.pdf

PR News. (2016). PR News 2016 CSR Awards: Annual report. Retrieved from http://www.prnewsonline.com/awards/csr-2016/annual-report

Praccreditation.org. (n.d.). Laws for PR professionals. Retrieved from http://www.praccreditation.org/resources/documents/APRSG-Law-Ethics.pdf

Project ROI. (n.d.). Retrieved from http://projectroi.com/

PRSA. (n.d.a) Awards. Retrieved from www.prsa.org/awards

PRSA. (n.d.b). Code provisions of conduct. Retrieved from http://apps.prsa.org/AboutPRSA/Ethics/CodeEnglish#Provisions

PRSA (n.d.c). Member code of ethics. Retrieved from http://apps.prsa.org/AboutPRSA/Ethics/CodeEnglish

PRSA. (2012). Toms One Day Without Shoes: Engaging one million people in a meaningful movement. 2012 Silver Anvil Award of Excellence Winner. Retrieved from https://apps.prsa.org/Awards/SilverAnvil/Search?sakeyword=one%20day%20without%20shoes&pg=1&sayear=All&sacategory=&saoutcome=&saindustry=

PRSA. (2014a). 2014 Silver Anvil results. Retrieved from http://www.prsa.org/Awards/SilverAnvil/SilverAnvilResults/PreviousResults/2014SilverAnvilResults.pdf

PRSA. (2014b). Drive to deliver: Building employee support for Navistar's turnaround strategy. Retrieved from http://www.prsa.org/searchresults/view/6be-1410c03/0/drive_to_deliver_building_employee_support_for_nav.WFLCUrGZPvE

PRSA. (2014c). Health care reform essentials: Aflac supports small business owners in the new health care reality. Retrieved from http://www.prsa.org/searchresults/view/6be-1404a04/0/health_care_reform_essentials_aflac_supports_small.WFLL77GZPvE

PRSA. (2015a). Keep what you've earned: A social marketing approach to responsible drinking in the U.S. Navy. Retrieved from https://test.prsa.org/Conferences/InternationalConference/program/data/display/6795/Keep_What_You_ve_Earned_A_Social_Marketing_Approac

PRSA. (2015b). MasterCard bites into Apple Pay, gets to the core of safe & secure contactless payments. Retrieved from http://www.prsa.org/searchresults/view/6be-1504bb2185/0/mastercard_bites_into_apple_pay_gets_to_the_core_o.WFLMTLGZPvE

PRSA Chicago Chapter. (2014, September 23). Why diversity in public relations is a business necessity. Retrieved from http://www.prsachicago.com/insights-blog/why-diversity-in-public-relations-is-a-business-necessity/

PRSA New York. (2016). John W. Hill award. Retrieved from http://c.ymcdn.com/sites/www.prsany.org/resource/resmgr/Docs/Press_Releases/2016_Big_Apple_Chapter_Winne.pdf?hhSearchTerms=%22John+and+W+and+Hill+and+Award%22

PRWeek. (2016a). Anatomy of the corporate communicator. Ragan.com. Retrieved from https://www.ragan.com/Main/Articles/Infographic_Anatomy_of_the_corporate_communicator_43749.aspx

PRWeek. (2016b). Harold Burson turns 95. Retrieved from http://www.prweek.com/article/1383080/harold-burson-turns-95

PRWeek. (2016c, October 28). Health influencer 50: 30–21. Retrieved from http://www.prweek.com/article/1412218/health-influencer-50-30-21

PRWeek. (2016d). Rankings tables: PRWeek global agency business report 2016. PR Week. Retrieved from http://www.prweek.com/article/1391811/rankings-tables-prweek-global-agency-business-report-2016

PRWeek. (2017, March17). Best for a cause 2017. Retrieved from http://www.prweek.com/article/1427590/best-cause-2017

Public Relations Society of America. (n.d.). About public relations. Retrieved from https://www.prsa.org/aboutprsa/publicrelationsdefined/-.V51c4WXcRpo

PYXERA Global. (n.d.). The PYXERA Global Engagement Forum. Retrieved from https://newglobalcitizen.com/global-pro-bono/collaboration-community-impact?cm_mc_uid=79784914602814787315344&cm_mc_sid_50200000=1481562906

Ragan. (n.d.). Health care communication news. Retrieved from https://www.healthcarecommunication.com

Ranking The Brands. (2016). Brand rankings. Global CSR RepTrak 100/2016. Retrieved from https://www.rankingthebrands.com/The-Brand-ankings.aspx?rankingID=331&nav=category

Raya, R. B., & Panneerselvam, S. (2013). The healthy organization construct: A review and research agenda. *Indian Journal of Occupational and Environmental Medicine*, *17*(3). doi: 10.4103/0019-5278.130835

Read, L. (2017, January 5). #HigherEd: Making social strategic. *Inside Higher Ed*. Retrieved from https://www.insidehighered.com/blogs/call-action-marketing-and-communications-higher-education/highered-making-social-strategic

Reeves, J. (2013, September 14). 3 Troubling questions about Bank of America's epic acquisition of Merrill Lynch. The Motley Fool. Retrieved from http://www.fool.com/investing/general/2013/09/14/3-troubling-questions-about-bank-of-americas-epic.aspx

Regester, M., & Larkin, J. (2008). *Risk issues and crisis management in public relations: A casebook of best practice*. London, UK: Kogan Page Publishers.

Renfree, M. (2016, January 26). Top women in PR: Wendy Lund. *PRNews*. Retrieved from http://www.prnewsonline.com/awards/topwomen2016_lund

Reputation Institute. (n.d.). 2017 Global RepTrak 100. Retrieved from https://www.reputationinstitute.com/research/Global-RepTrak-100.aspx

Reputation Institute. (2016). 2016 global CSR rep trak. Retrieved from https://www.reputationinstitute.com/thought-leadership/csr-reptrak-100

Ries, A., & Ries, L. (2002). *The fall of advertising and the rise of PR*. New York: Harper Collins.

Rivel Research Group. (2013). Harnessing IR's power to impact a company's valuation. Retrieved from http://www.rivel.com/PDFs/power.pdf

Rockland, D. (2010). Ketchum. Retrieved from https://www.ketchum.com/

Roll, M. (2009). Benefits of the corporate brand. Branding Strategy Insider. Retrieved from http://www.brandingstrategyinsider.com/2009/07/benefits-of-the-corporate-brand.html.WFCOj3eZOIY

Rothacker, J. (2014, August 16). The deal that cost Bank of America $50 billion—and counting. *The Charlotte Observer*. Retrieved from http://www.charlotteobserver.com/news/business/banking/article9151889.html

Ruddick, G. (2016). Graze aims for healthy bit of U.S. snack market with bricks and mortar. *The Guardian*. Retrieved from https://www.theguardian.com/business/2016/oct/17/graze-aims-for-healthy-bite-of-us-snack-market-with-bricks-and-mortar

Ruggieri, M. (2016, January 28). Five successful Periscope campaigns to watch and learn from. Growthweaver. Retrieved from http://www.growthweaver.com/five-successful-periscope-campaigns-to-watch-and-learn-from/

Rumi Spice. (n.d.). Retrieved from http://www.rumispice.com

Sacks, M. A., & Graves, N. (2012). How many "friends" do you need? Teaching students how to network using social media. *Business Communication Quarterly* (75)1, 80–88.

Salim, A. (2016, November 21). General Electric: "We overcame our sceptics with Ecomagination." *The Drum News*. Retrieved from http://www.thedrum.com/news/2016/11/21/general-electric-we-overcame-our-sceptics-with-ecomagination

Saltzman, J. (2005). Analyzing the images of the journalist in popular culture: A unique method of studying the public's perception of its journalists and the news media. *Association for Education in Journalism & Communication*. Retrieved from http://www.ijpc.org/uploads/files/AEJMC%20Paper%20San%20Antonio%20Saltzman%202005.pdf

Samsung. (2016). Corporate social responsibility. Retrieved from https://secureus.samsung.com/us/aboutsamsung/investor_relations/corporate_governance/corporatesocialresponsibility/

Samsung Newsroom (2017, May 19). Samsung employees nationwide swap the office for Day of Service [Press release]. Retrieved from https://news.samsung.com/us/samsung-employees-nationwide-swap-the-office-for-day-of-service-samsunggives/

Savage, D. G. (2002). Nike takes ad liability case to high court. *Los Angeles Times*. Retrieved from http://articles.latimes.com/2002/oct/15/local/me-nike15

Sawyer, A. (2016, December 1). First person account of Gatlinburg: City like "apocalyptic wasteland." *The Tennessean*. Retrieved from http://www.tennessean.com/story/news/environment/2016/11/30/first-person-account-gatlinburg-city-like-apocalyptic-wasteland/94698970/

SBE. (n.d.). Facts & data on small business and entrepreneurship. Retrieved from http://sbecouncil.org/about-us/facts-and-data/

Schock, N. (2010). Handling a fake Twitter account: @BPGlobalPR leaves lasting impression on crisis communications. PRSA. Retrieved from http://www.prsa.org/Intelligence/TheStrategist/Articles/view/8757/1019/Handling_a_Fake_Twitter_Account_BPGlobalPR_Leaves.WDsNB3eZPfA

Schofield, J. (2006). What's a flog—a fake blog? The Guardian. Retrieved from https://www.theguardian.com/technology/blog/2006/oct/16/whatsafloga

Scott, R. (2013, October 3). 3 ways to fire up your company's community impact. Causecast. Retrieved from https://www.causecast.com/blog/3-ways-to-fire-up-your-companys-community-impact

Seitel, F. P. (2013). *The practice of public relations*. New York, NY: Pearson.

Seven Pillars Institute. (n.d.). Bank of America's takeover of Merrill Lynch. http://sevenpillarsinstitute.org/case-studies/bank-of-americas-takeover-of-merrill-lynch

Seymour, C. (2015, November 9). PR News. 2015 digital PR awards: Contest/game. Retrieved from http://www.prnewsonline.com/awards/digital-pr-2015/contest

Seymour, C. (2016a, March 17). 2016 CSR awards: Social media campaign. *PR News*. Retrieved from http://www.prnewsonline.com/awards/csr-2016/social-media

Seymour, C. (2016b, June 2). 2016 Social media awards: Facebook | Use of video. *PR News*. Retrieved from http://www.prnewsonline.com/thelists/social-media-2016/facebook-video

Seymour, C. (2016c, June 6). 2016 Social media awards: Periscope campaign. *PR Daily*. Retrieved from http://www.prnewsonline.com/thelists/social-media-2016/periscope

Seymour, C. (2016d, November 16). 2016 Digital PR Awards: Intranet. Winner: Workiva. Retrieved from http://www.prnewsonline.com/awards/2016-digital-PR-winners/intranet

Shir-Raz, Y., & Avraham, E. (2017). "Under the regulation radar": PR strategies of pharmaceutical companies in countries where direct advertising of prescription drugs is banned—The Israeli case. *Public Relations Review, 43*, 382–391.

Shorty Social Good Awards. (n.d.). M&M'S Red Nose Day campaign. Retrieved from http://shortyawards.com/8th/mms-red-nose-day-campaign

Skin Cancer Foundation. (n.d.). Bob Marley shouldn't have died from melanoma. Retrieved from http://www.skincancer.org/news/melanoma/marley

Skin Cancer Foundation. (2016). The dangers of skin cancer in skin of color. Retrieved from http://www.skincancer.org/prevention/skin-cancer-and-skin-of-color

Skoll Foundation. (n.d.). About the forum. Retrieved from http://skoll.org/skoll-world-forum/about/

Sleek, S. (2015). The curse of knowledge: Pinker describes a key cause of bad writing. Association for Psychological Science. Retrieved from http://www.psychologicalscience.org/index.php/convention/the-curse-of-knowledge-pinker-describes-a-key-cause-of-bad-writing.html

Smith, H. (2016, May 28). Miracle in Athens as Greek tourism numbers keep growing. *The Guardian*. Retrieved from https://www.theguardian.com/business/2016/may/28/greece-tourism-boom-athens-jobs-growth

Smith, R. (2011). Agenda-Setting, priming & framing. Retrieved from http://faculty.buffalostate.edu/smithrd/PR/Framing.htm

Smith, R. (2013). *Strategic planning for public relations*. New York, NY: Routledge.

Solomon, A. (2017, January 10). After devastating wildfires, Gatlinburg, Tenn. welcomes back tourists. *Chicago Tribune*. Retrieved from http://www.chicagotribune.com/lifestyles/travel/sc-gatlinburg-tennessee-after-the-fires-travel-0117-20170109-story.html

Spectrum. (n.d.). Who we are. Retrieved from http://www.spectrumscience.com/we-are-spectrum

SportsDay (2013, July). Report: AT&T naming rights for Dallas Cowboys' stadium $17–19M a year. Retrieved from http://sportsday.dallasnews.com/dallas-cowboys/cowboysheadlines/2013/07/25/report-att-naming-rights-for-dallas-cowboys-stadium-17-19m-a-year

Spreier, S. (2013, July 4). How global trends affect employee communication and engagement. Retrieved from http://blog.mslgroup.com/how-global-trends-affect-employee-communication-and-engagement/

Spross, J. (2016). What on Earth does Wells Fargo's CEO do all day? The Week. Retrieved from http://theweek.com/articles/649900/what-earth-does-wells-fargos-all-day

Sriramesh, K., & Vercic, D. (2009). *The global public relations handbook: Theory, research, and practice* (rev. ed.). New York, NY: Routledge.

St. John, B. (2006). The case for ethical propaganda within a democracy: Ivy Lee's successful 1913–1914 railroad rate campaign." *Public Relations Review, 32*(3), 221–228.

Stacks, D. W. (2010). *Primer of public relations research*. New York, NY: Guilford Press.

Stacks, D., & Michaelson, D. (2010). *A Practitioner's Guide to Public Relations Research, Measurement and Evaluation.* New York, NY: Business Expert Press.

Stacks, D. W., Wright, D. K., & Bowen, S. A. (2014). IBM's smarter planet initiative: Building a more intelligent world. In J. V. Turk, J. Paluszek, & J. Valin (Eds.), *Public relations case studies from around the world* (pp. 3–20). New York: Peter Lang Publishing.

Starbucks. (n.d.). Company information. Retrieved from https://www.starbucks.com/about-us/company-information

Starwood. (n.d.). Global citizenship environmental initiatives. Starwood Hotels and Resorts. Retrieved from http://www.starwoodhotels.com/corporate/about/citizenship/environment.html?language=en_US

Stimson, S. (2013). Why the PR industry lacks diversity. Retrieved from https://www.theguardian.com/careers/pr-industry-lack-diversity

Stuart, E. (2015, September 25). Volkswagen's big scandal—social media shows how big a blow emissions scandal is. The Street. Retrieved from https://www.thestreet.com/story/13301990/1/volkswagen-s-big-scandal-social-media-shows-how-big-a-blow-emissions-scandal-is.html

Sub-Zero. (n.d.). Solving the problem of food waste. *Washington Post.* Retrieved from http://www.washingtonpost.com/sf/brand-connect/sub-zero/solving-the-problem-of-food-waste/

Sudhaman, A. (2016). Global PR industry hits $14bn in 2016 as growth slows to 5%. The Holmes Report. Retrieved from https://www.holmesreport.com/research/article/global-pr-industry-hits-$14bn-in-2016-as-growth-slows-to-5

Sullivan, P. (2015, October 15). Jon Bon Jovi, the Jersey Shore and the Impact Investing Strategy. *New York Times.* Retrieved from https://www.nytimes.com/2015/10/31/your-money/jon-bon-jovi-the-jersey-shore-and-the-impact-investing-strategy.html

Supa, D. W. (2014). The academic inquiry of media relations as both a tactical and strategic function of public relations. *Research Journal of the Institute for Public Relations, 1*(1), 1–15.

Supa, D. W., & Zoch, L. M. (2009). Maximizing media relations through a better understanding of the public relations-journalist relationship: A quantitative analysis of changes over the past 23 years. *Public Relations Journal, 3*(4), 1–28.

Sutter, K. (2012). The growing importance of more sustainable products in the global health care industry. Johnson & Johnson. Retrieved from https://www.jnj.com/_document?id=00000159-6a81-dba3-afdb-7aeba25f0000

Tamraz, C. B. (2015). The future of news is here—and it's visual, social, mobile and global. HuffPost, The Blog. Retrieved from http://www.huffingtonpost.com/communications-week/the-future-of-news-is-her_b_8337158.html

Taylor, K. (2017). Starbucks' new CEO tells us he'll never be Howard Schultz—and that's great news for the brand. *Business Insider.* Retrieved from http://www.businessinsider.com/interview-with-starbucks-new-ceo-kevin-johnson-2017-4

Taylor, M., & Kent, M. L. (2016). Towards legitimacy and professionalism: A call to repeal the Gillett Amendment. *Public Relations Review, 42*(1), 1–8.

Taylor, M., Vasquez, G. M., & Doorley, J. (2003). Merck and AIDS activists: Engagement as a framework for extending issues management. *Public Relations Review, 29*(3), 257–270.

Ten Berge, D. (1990). *The first 24 hours: A comprehensive guide to successful crisis communications.* Hoboken, NJ: Blackwell.

Terilli, S. A., Splichal, S. L., & Driscol, P. J. (2007). Lowering the bar: Privileged court filings as substitutes for press releases in the court of public opinion. *Communication Law & Policy, 12*(2), 143–175.

Thomas, C. (2016, August 24). The worst arena and stadium names in sports. SportingNews. Retrieved from http://www.sportingnews.com/other-sports/list/worst-arena-stadium-names-guaranteed-rate-field-little-caesars-kfc-yum-center-oco-coliseum-taco-bell-arena/1hujyc2ubxqvp1i0b994h9phqv

TogoRun. (n.d.). Retrieved from http://togorun.com/case-studies/its-that-worth-it

Tolintino, J. (2017, January 18). The somehow controversial Women's March on Washington. *New Yorker.* Retrieved from http://www.newyorker.com/culture/jia-tolentino/the-somehow-controversial-womens-march-on-washington

Tourism Cares. (n.d.). Retrieved from https://static1.squarespace.com/static/54de6549e4b054179782b0eb/t/555f803ce4b097314db898b0/1432322108313/micatocasestudy.pdf

Trainer, D. (2014). Navistar has a tough road ahead. *Forbes.* Retrieved from http://www.forbes.com/sites/greatspeculations/2014/01/13/navistar-has-a-tough-road-ahead/-4624e0d73e08

TripAdvisor. (2013). TripBarometer Mobile & Social Survey find 85% of US travelers bring their smartphones on vacation & 61% report using social media while traveling. Retrieved from https://www.tripadvisor.com/TripAdvisorInsights/n2006/tripbarometer-mobile-social-survey-finds-85-us-travelers-bring-their-smartphones-vacation-61-report

Tsetsura, K. (2011). Cultural and historical aspects of media transparency in Russia. In *Ethical Issues in International Communication* (pp. 172–182). London, England: Palgrave Macmillan.

Tugby, L. (2016). Graze ties up with Walgreens for launch into US stores. *Retail Week.* Retrieved from https://www.retail-week.com/sectors/grocery/graze-ties-up-with-walgreens-for-launch-into-us-stores/7013023.article

Turney, M. (n.d.). Government public relations. Northern Kentucky University. Retrieved from http://www.nku.edu/~turney/prclass/readings/government.html

Tye, L. (2002). *The father of spin: Edward L. Bernays and the birth of public relations.* Basingstoke, United Kingdom: Macmillan.

United Nations. (n.d.). Global compact. Retrieved from https://www.unglobalcompact.org/what-is-gc

UNWTO. (2016). Tourism highlights. Retrieved from http://www.e-unwto.org/doi/pdf/10.18111/9789284418145

U.S. Census. (2015, March 3). New Census Bureau report analyzes U.S. population projections. Retrieved from http://www.census.gov/newsroom/press-releases/2015/cb15-tps16.html

U.S. Census Bureau. (2011). 2010 census shows America's diversity. Retrieved from https://www.census.gov/newsroom/releases/archives/2010_census/cb11-cn125.html

U.S. Department of State. (n.d.). Secretary of state's award for corporate excellence. Retrieved from https://2001-2009.state.gov/e/eeb/ace/

U.S. News & World Report. (2017). Northwestern University. Retrieved from http://colleges.usnews.rankingsandreviews.com/best-colleges/northwestern-1739

US SIF. (n.d.). SRI basics. Retrieved from http://www.ussif.org/sribasics

Variety. (2016, August 2). Corporate citizenship programs seize the chance to give back. Retrieved from http://variety.com/2016/biz/spotlight/10-entertainment-corporate-philanthropy-wme-caa-1201828893/

Vaughn, J. R., Colley, C., Pound, P., Carlson, V. R., Davila, R. R., Hill, G., ... Williams, T. (2009). *Invisible wounds: Serving service members and veterans with PTSD and TBI.* Retrieved from https://archive.org/stream/ERIC_ED507750/ERIC_ED507750_djvu.txt

Veil, S. R., & Kent, M. (2008). Issues management and inoculation: Tylenol's responsible dosing advertising. *Public Relations Review, 34*(4), 399–402.

Verčič, D., Grunig, L. A., & Grunig, J. E. (1996). Global and specific principles of public relations: Evidence from Slovenia. In H. Culbertson & N. Chen (Eds.), *International public relations: A comparative analysis*, (pp. 31–65). New York, NY: Routledge.

Villagra, N., Cardaba, M. A. M., & Ruiz San Ramon, J. A. (2015). Communicating corporate social responsibility: Re-assessment of classical theories about fit between CSR actions and corporate activities. *Communication & Society, 29*(2), 122–146.

Wakefield, R. I. (2007). Theory of international public relations, the Internet, and activism: A personal reflection. *Journal of Public Relations Research, 20*(1), 138–157.

Walden, J., Bortree, D., & DiStaso, M. (2014). This blog brought to you by . . . exploring blogger perceptions of a product endorsement policy and reviews. *Journal of Communication Management, 19* (3), 254–269.

Walsh, D. (2016, April 30). Comcast Cares Day is trending for entirely the wrong reasons and it's hilarious. UPROXX. Retrieved from http://uproxx.com/webculture/comcast-cares-day-backlash/

Waters, R. (2009). Measuring stewardship in public relations: A test exploring impact on the fundraising relationship. *Public Relations Review, 35*(2), 113–119.

Weikamp, E., & Torill, E. (2014). Agenda building in media coverage of food research. *Journalism Practice, 8*(6), 871–886.

Weiland, G. (2016, October 21). CSR perspectives: Getting your company's sustainability efforts recognized. *Bulldog Reporter.* Retrieved from https://www.bulldogreporter.com/csr-perspectives-getting-your-companys-sustainability-efforts-recognized/

Weissmann, E. (2013). Consumer Trends 2013: Photos key to social media experience. Travel Weekly. Retrieved from http://www.travelweekly.com/Travel-News/Online-Travel/Photos-key-to-travelers-social-media-experience

Wells Fargo. (2015). Wells Fargo annual report: Earning lifelong relationships. Retrieved from https://www08.wellsfargomedia.com/assets/pdf/about/investor-relations/annual-reports/2015-annual-report.pdf

Wells Fargo. (2017a). Wells Fargo invested $67 billion in 2016 to advance CSR goals. Retrieved from https://newsroom.wf.com/press-release/community-banking-and-small-business/wells-fargo-invested-67-billion-2016-advance-csr

Wells Fargo. (2017b, July 9). Wells Fargo: Proposed class-action settlement for retail sales practices receives preliminary court approval. [Press release]. Retrieved from https://newsroom.wf.com/press-release/corporate-and-financial/wells-fargo-proposed-class-action-settlement-retail-sales

Whirlpool Corporation. (2016, August 2). Care Counts™ school laundry program exposes link between clean clothes and attendance. Retrieved from http://www.whirlpoolcorp.com/care-counts-school-laundry-program-exposes-link-between-clean-clothes-and-attendance/

White, D. M. (1950). The "gate keeper": A case study in the selection of news. *Journalism Quarterly, 27*(4), 383–390.

Whiteley, M. (2013, August 27). Strategic public relations planning—Positioning for success. [Web log post]. *PRSay.* Retrieved from https://prsay.prsa.org/2013/08/27/strategic-public-relations-planning-positioning-for-success/

Whytas, K. J. (2016). Impact of a brand crisis on nation branding: An analysis of tweets about VW's emissions crisis (Unpublished master's thesis). University of South Florida, Tampa, FL.

Wiener, N. (1988). *The human use of human beings: Cybernetics and society.* Cambridge, MA: Da Capo Press.

Williams, K. D., & Brunner, B. R. (2010). Using cultivation strategies to manage public relationships: A content analysis of non-profit organizations' websites. *Prism, 7*(2). Retrieved from http://www.prismjournal.org/fileadmin/Praxis/Files/Journal_Files/Williams_Brunner.pdf

Wise, K. (2003). Linking public relations processes and organizational effectiveness at a state health department. *Journal of Health & Human Services Administration, 25*(4), 497–525.

Wisner, F. (2012). *Edelman and the rise of public relations.* New York, NY: Eight Communications.

Wright, D. K., & Hinson, M. D. (2014). An updated examination of social and emerging media use in public relations practice: A longitudinal analysis between 2006 and 2014. Public Relations Journal (8)2. Retrieved from http://apps.prsa.org/Intelligence/PRJournal/Documents/2014WrightHinson.pdf

World Economic Forum. (2015). Travel and tourism competitiveness report 2015. Retrieved from https://reports.weforum.org/travel-and-tourism-competitiveness-report-2015/

WWF. (n.d.). Fighting ilicit wildlife trafficking: A consultation with governments. World Wildlife Fund Global. Retrieved from http://wwf.panda.org/about_our_earth/species/problems/illegal_trade/wildlife_trade_campaign/wildlife_trafficking_report/

Wynne, R. (2014). The real difference between PR and advertising. *Forbes.* Retrieved from http://www.forbes.com/sites/robertwynne/2014/07/08/the-real-difference-between-pr-and-advertising-credibility/-c5e46a322700

Yarbrough, B. (2013). Are you part of the new "digital elite" travel class. *The Mercury News.* Retrieved from http://www.mercurynews.com/2013/08/15/are-you-part-of-the-new-digital-elite-travel-class/

Yu, L., Asur, S., & Huberman, B. A. (2011). What trends in Chinese social media. *arXiv.* Retrieved from https://arxiv.org/pdf/1107.3522.pdf

Yum! Brands Recognized as a 2016 Healthiest 100 Workplace in America. (2016, September 7). Yum! Retrieved from http://www.yum.com/press-releases/yum-brands-recognized-as-a-2016-healthiest-100-workplace-in-america/

Zerfass, A., & Sherzada, M. (2014). *Corporate communications from the CEO's perspective: How top executives conceptualize and value strategic communication.* Paper presented at the 17th International Public Relations Research Conference, Coral Gables, FL.

Zheng, L. (2013). A case study of Audi's brand repositioning in China. *China Media Research 9*(3), 64–73.

Zignal Labs. (2016). *10 ways big data will modernize your crisis communications plan.* Retrieved from http://go.zignallabs.com/crisis-communications-ebook

Ziv, S. (2015). Starbucks ends phase one of race together initiative after grande fail. *Newsweek.* Retrieved from http://www.newsweek.com/starbucks-ends-phase-one-race-together-initiative-after-grande-fail-316043

INDEX